E-deployment

About MC Professional Books

Developed by Merrikay Lee, the MC Press line of professional books emphasizes practical solutions, application-based examples, tips, and techniques for the IBM midrange community of IT professionals.

Merrikay Lee is series editor for the MC Press line of professional books, which comprises more than 75 titles. She has spent more than 20 years as a technical professional in the IBM midrange industry and 15 years in the publishing field. She is the author of four books and has worked with numerous IT technical professionals to develop titles for the IBM midrange community of IT professionals. She is president of Lee Publishing Services Inc. in Dallas, Texas, and can be reached at mlee@leepublishing.com.

E-deployment
The Fastest Path to the Web

Joe Pluta

MIDRANGE COMPUTING
IIR PUBLICATIONS INC.

First Edition
First Printing—October 2000

Every attempt has been made to provide correct information. However, the publisher and the author do not guarantee the accuracy of the book and do not assume responsibility for information included in or omitted from it.

The following terms are trademarks of International Business Machines Corporation in the United States, other countries, or both: IBM, AS/400, OS/400, and 400. Other trademarked company names and product names mentioned herein are the property of their respective owners.

Printed in Canada. All rights reserved. No part of this publication may be reproduced in any form without prior permission of the copyright owner.

© 2000 Midrange Computing
ISBN: 1-58347-021-2

**Midrange Computing
5650 El Camino Real, Suite 225
Carlsbad, CA 92008–7147 USA
www.midrangecomputing.com**

For information on translations or book distribution outside the United States or to arrange bulk-purchase discounts for sales promotions, premiums, or fund-raisers, please contact Midrange Computing at the above address.

V4R3

*To my son Jon, who has always looked up to me,
and my Dad, who will always look over me:
love you both very much.*

ACKNOWLEDGMENTS

When I started this book, I had already written dozens of articles for *Midrange Computing* magazine, for internal publications, for newsletters, and the like. I'd gotten quite used to the fact that I could write three or four thousand words at a sitting. I just thought the book would be twenty or thirty extended sittings and BAM! I'd be done.

I have been mightily disabused of that notion.

So, I'd like to first acknowledge my publisher/agent/mentor, Merrikay Lee, without whose help, faith, and guidance this book would have never gotten past the stage of being a series of slightly coherent, semi-related articles.

I'd also like to acknowledge the folks at Midrange Computing who gave me this opportunity, in particular Victoria Mack, my friend and coconspirator in this craziness, who decided to keep looking for me even after I'd decided to get lost, and Ted Holt, who spurred me on in the first place. I'd also like to acknowledge the many people, past and present, who have worked behind the scenes to make my writing look a lot better than when I'm done with it.

I have to recognize the folks who helped me along as I struggled through the trials and tribulations of learning Java for the AS/400, particularly Don Denoncourt and Alex Garrison.

Acknowledgments

These two guys are shining examples of what we in the software community should aspire to be: brilliantly creative and willing to share that brilliance with the rest of us.

And finally, I couldn't possibly end this section without acknowledging the people in Rochester who developed IBM's Java Toolbox for the AS/400. I've said before that the toolbox is probably one of the single greatest pieces of *software* I've ever seen, not to mention that it's *freeware*. It's even more awesome now that the JTOpen group has made it open-source. Thank you IBM, and thank you all.

CONTENTS

	INTRODUCTION xv	
~ *Part 1:*	REDEPLOYMENT AND REVITALIZATION 1	
Chapter 1:	OVERVIEW 5	
	WHERE WE ARE TODAY 5	
	THE GOALS OF DISTRIBUTED PROGRAMMING 9	
	Graphical Interfaces 9	
	Platform Independence 10	
	Desktop Integration 10	
	Object Architecture 10	
	End-User Information Tools 11	
	THE GOALS OF OPEN SYSTEMS 11	
Chapter 2:	EXISTING TECHNOLOGIES 15	
	REPLACING 15	
	REFACING 16	
	REWRITING 17	
	THUS THE NEED FOR DISTRIBUTED PROGRAMMING 18	
	Offline Processing 18	
	Client/Server Processing 19	

Contents

     Structured Query Language 19
     Browser-Based Applications 20
    The Progression of the Browser Model 21
    The Advent of Server/Client Programming 24

Chapter 3: **Redeployment: The New Strategy** **25**
    The Big Picture 27
    The Process 27
     Revitalization 28
     Restructuring 29
     Re-engineering 31
    The Results 32

Chapter 4: **Revitalization** **35**
    The Display File's Role
    in 5250 Communications 35
     The Output Operation 36
     The Input Operation 37
     The Whole Picture 37
    The Goals of Revitalization 37
    Implementing Revitalization 38

Part 2:   **Implementing Revitalization** **41**

Chapter 5: **The Starting Point** **45**
    The Screens 46
    The Database 48
    The Display File 49
    The RPG Program 51
    The Issues   56
     Display Attributes 57
     Subfiles 57
     Message Subfiles 57
     Help Support 58
     General 58

Chapter 6: **Breaking Apart the Monolith** **59**
    The Application Client 62
    The Green-Screen UI Server 65
    The JSPAPI Library: Client APIs 69
     DQMBAPIC 72
     DQMBAPI 73

	DQMBAPI1.	75
	DQMBAPI2.	75
	DQMBAPI3.	81
	THE JSPAPI LIBRARY: I/O PROXY APIs.	81
Chapter 7:	**CONVERTING THE DATA.**	**93**
	DEFINING A DC400STRUCTURE	94
	THE DC400 CLASSES.	97
	THE FUTURE OF DC400	108
Chapter 8:	**BUILDING THE DISPLAY FILE OBJECT**	**111**
	DEFINING A JDSPFDISPLAYFILE: ITMMNT1D_DISPLAYFILE.	112
	Record UI Objects.	117
	THE JDSPF CLASSES.	117
	THE FUTURE OF JDSPF	124
	Subfiles.	124
	Display Attributes.	126
	Related Record Formats.	127
	Many Miles to Go.	130
Chapter 9:	**IMPLEMENTING THE SERVER/CLIENT ARCHITECTURE.**	**131**
	SC400CLIENT AND ITS SUBCLASS, ITMMNT1_CLIENT.	132
	AS/400 Definitions.	135
	Server/Client Definitions.	135
	Making ITMMNT1_Client.	135
	INHERITANCE: SC400MESSAGE AND SC400API.	137
	COMPOSITION: SCJDSPFUISERVER.	144
Chapter 10:	**DESIGNING A SWING INTERFACE.**	**149**
	FINISHING THE APPLICATION: ITMMNT1_JBUIDISPLAY.	150
	Application Client Interface Definition.	151
	UI Server Definition.	151
	Making ITMMNT1_JbuiDisplay.	152
	THE SC400 JBUI CLASSES: SPECIALIZATION THROUGH SUBCLASSING	158
	Making a JbuiDisplay Object.	158
	SC400 JBUI.	160
	ScJdspfJbuiDisplay.	161
	THE FUTURE OF SC400 JBUI:	
	BIGGER AND BETTER JBUI EXTENSIONS	166
	Subfiles.	166
	The Future Looks Bright.	168

CONTENTS

Chapter 11: DESIGNING THE BROWSER INTERFACE 169
    FINISHING THE APPLICATION: ITMMNT1_SERVLET AND ITS JSPS . . 171
        The Application-Client-Interface Definition 172
        The UI Server Definition 172
        Making the JavaServer Pages 173
        Defining the Servlet 177
    RUNNING THE APPLICATION: ITMMNT1_SERVLET 183
        The HTTP Configuration File, QUSRSYS/QATMHTTPC 183
        The Properties Files 183
        The JavaServer Pages 184
        The Servlet 185
        The Support Classes 185
    MODELING AN OBJECT: THE JSP PACKAGE 188
    MORE EXTENSIONS: THE SC400 JSP PACKAGE 194
        SC400 JSP 194
        Defining a JavaServer Page 195
        Defining an SC400 JSP Servlet 199
    THE FUTURE OF SC400 JSP:
    BIGGER AND BETTER EXTENSIONS   209
        Subfiles. 210

Part 3:   RUNNING THE APPLICATION 215

Chapter 12: THE GREEN SCREEN 217
    DOWNLOADING THE SOFTWARE 217
    INSTALLING THE GREEN-SCREEN SOFTWARE 219
        Create the Transfer Library and Save Files 220
        FTP the Save Files to the AS/400 221
        Restore the Libraries. 222
    TESTING THE GREEN-SCREEN SOFTWARE 224
        Run ITMMNT1 224
        Run ITMMNT1UI 229

Chapter 13: THE JBUI (THICK CLIENT) UI SERVER 235
    CHECK YOUR JAVA ENVIRONMENT 235
        My Environment 236
    TEST THE JBUI UI SERVER 237
        Run the JBUI UI Server 237
        Errors. 238

***Chapter 14:* THE SERVLET** **243**
    INSTALL THE SERVLET SOFTWARE 244
        WebSphere. 244
        Copy the Files 244
        Modify the CLASSPATH 247
        Modify the Configuration File. 249
        Create *JVAPGM for the Support Jar 254
    CUSTOMIZE ITMMNT1_CLIENT 255
        Copy the Jar Files 255
        Customize ITMMNT1_Client.java 256
        Create *JVAPGM Objects for the Client and Display File 257
    TEST THE SERVLET 259
        Restart the HTTP Server. 259
        Run the Servlet. 262
        Errors. 265

***Appendix A:* WEB UPDATES** **267**

***Appendix B:* ABOUT THE CD-ROM** **269**

***Appendix C:* JAVADOC** **273**

    GLOSSARY 481

    INDEX. 507

INTRODUCTION

Welcome to revitalization! This is a different kind of book. Some programming books are extensive reference materials designed to show you every facet of the programming language. Other books are more example-oriented (sometimes with examples that are simple to the point of being abstract). Both of these types of books are good for general learning, but they don't provide the overall strategy necessary to develop real applications.

This book has two purposes:

1. To provide you with a guide to the various technologies available today for Web-enabling your legacy applications, and to show you how I designed the redeployment strategy and implemented the revitalization architecture.

2. To provide a step-by-step guide on how to use revitalization as the fastest way to get your legacy systems on the Internet without sacrificing your investment in programs or programmers.

Anyone who has taken one of my classes or visited the Java installation page on my Web site (originally on *www.zappie.net*, and now on *www.java400.net*) knows that I stress practical, hands-on techniques. I like to start with a real goal and move towards it. I learn best when I'm doing something applicable to my day-to-day problems. Nearly two years ago, I set a goal for myself to provide a graphical interface for existing AS/400 applications. During these past two years, I have learned that there is no single resource that ties together the many interlocking technologies required to reach that goal.

This book is designed to be that resource. It guides you through the process of putting your AS/400 applications on the Web, on a local network, or, probably, on both. It shows you a step-by-step technique to move gradually and with a minimum of disruption, leveraging your current investment in not only programs, but also programmers.

Most of you have gone through (or are still going through!) the expensive process of Y2K-enabling your software. Having invested so much time and money, it just doesn't make sense to toss out all that code in a mass rewrite. However, it also doesn't make sense to invest in a technological dead end. Redeployment is the vehicle by which you can make the transition in as practical a fashion as possible. Redeployment keeps the core of your legacy systems intact, while providing a definite path to the future.

Redeployment is not a single technical solution. Rather, it incorporates the best of all of today's available technologies and provides specific ways to use those technologies to move your applications into the graphical network environment. It builds upon your existing systems and takes advantages of the skills and business knowledge of your current RPG programmers, while opening your system to the newest technologies (including those that haven't been designed yet). This book provides specific instructions for the first step on that path: revitalization.

Part 1 of this book starts with a review of where we are today and where we need to go. You'll learn:

- The benefits of going to a graphical network-capable architecture.
- The technologies that are available today, including the following:
  - Client/server architecture.
  - SQL, ODBC, and JDBC.
  - Browser-based technologies.
- The conflicts among the various solutions.
- The implementation strategies available today.

Part 1 also introduces the concept of redeployment. You'll see how redeployment uses the strengths of each of today's existing solutions and combines them into a flexible, staged conversion process. Applications can be modified one at a time, and different interfaces (green screen, client/server, or browser-based) can be used for each. Development can proceed in parallel, and different teams can work simultaneously. You can effectively make use of your existing staff, hire new talent, and even outsource portions of the work.

You'll discover the basic design of the message-based client/server architecture that underlies the redeployment solution and see how it enables the different deployment goals. The focus is on the first stage of redeployment, which is revitalization. Simply put, revitalization is the fastest way to put a legacy system on the Web or any other network.

Part 2 focuses on the technical aspects of the revitalization stage of redeployment. It reviews every piece of code required to implement revitalization, explains the design decisions, and outlines future enhancements. In Part 2, you'll take a real, working monolithic AS/400 green-screen application through carefully detailed steps that apply this first stage of redeployment. Upon completing this step, you will have revitalized the application into a fully network-enabled application. You'll see how to implement each of the three user interface techniques, and you can then decide which ones are appropriate for each of your applications.

You'll also find out how to use the PBD (Pluta Brothers Design) packages that are included with this book. You'll discover why they were designed the way they were, so that you can create your own packages specific to your environment.

Pluta Brothers Design (*www.plutabrothers.com*) manages the Java/400 Website, *www.java400.net*, which is the Web's original open-source Java/400 site, and the home for current and future releases of the open-source versions of the PBD software. The PBD packages included with this book are designed to help AS/400 programmers move from green screens to graphical interfaces. However, I know that even with Javadoc and README files, it's not easy to make the leap from RPG or COBOL to Java. That's why I decided to write this book. It distills over two years of my Java/400 research into a straightforward, by-the-numbers tutorial for moving a real, functional AS/400 program to the Web.

I know from experience that trying to learn everything about Java at one time is a daunting task. Therefore, Part 2 has a special fast-path feature. Certain parts of each chapter are marked with lightning bolt icons (✒) as fast-path sections, so that you quickly can review the basic steps of the procedures, and apply them in your own environment to see how they work. Once that's done, you can return to the book for a more in-depth look at each of the chapters as necessary.

Part 3 addresses the actual implementation details of a distributed application. Unlike a simple reference book, this book is designed to answer some of the practical questions you'll have when actually running your application. Here you'll see the actual details of not only the target application, but the supporting software as well. This section of the book takes nothing for granted; it walks you through the process of using FTP to transfer software to your AS/400, helps you install the Java Development Kit, and even guides you through the configuration of IBM's WebSphere application server.

The final, and perhaps most valuable, part of this book is on the CD-ROM that is included. This CD-ROM contains all of the workstation, host, and middleware software required to use the revitalization architecture. The full PBD packages, including source and Javadoc (in browser-friendly HTML format) are included, as are the thick- and thin-client example programs. The AS/400 support library JSPAPI is included, with full source, as is the JSPPROTO library, which contains the example program used in this book.

So there it is—book plus software to help you through a successful redeployment of your legacy systems. Oh, and one more thing: there is also a Website specifically for the readers of this book at *www.java400.net/edeployment*. This Website is updated regularly with tips and techniques, enhancements to the software, and a forum for ongoing discussion of the redeployment process.

Part 1

REDEPLOYMENT AND REVITALIZATION

The buzzwords abound: e-commerce, e-business, business-to-business, Web-enabled, object technology, distributed systems, application modernization. Everything sounds so good, but it's hard to get a grasp on what these things really mean. And lost in the clutter is the idea that technology for technology's sake isn't necessarily a good thing.

That might seem like an unlikely reminder coming from me, since I'm probably one of the most vocal proponents of Java in the business world, and especially of Java on the AS/400. Why else would I give away over 10,000 lines of Java/400 code in this book? The truth is that, while technological evolution is a good thing—even a necessary thing—it needs to be managed. This sudden explosion of new technology in and around the AS/400 often makes it difficult to decide what is really necessary and what is just so much hype.

A fact often lost in the mad rush to the Web is that most of today's enabling technologies are designed for new applications. Event-driven programming, object brokers, and

Enterprise JavaBeans are all technologies that must be incorporated into the original design of an application, not just tacked on as an afterthought. Putting an existing system on the Web, therefore, is more than just a quick fix, but that doesn't mean you have to throw away all your investment.

There are dozens of vendors willing to sell you a shiny new system, or a flashy paint job for your old system. This book takes a different approach. It shows you how to rebuild your tried-and-true legacy system so that it runs like new—or better—on the information superhighway.

The chapters that make up this first part of the book introduce the technologies available for Web-enabling your legacy applications, and show you why redeployment, and specifically revitalization, is the best answer for turning your legacy systems into powerful distributed applications:

- Chapter 1 starts off with a detailed look at the real, practical goals of moving to a distributed architecture. Rather than simply assuming that everything about the Web is good, this chapter instead looks at the actual business benefits of moving to open, distributed systems.

- Chapter 2 takes a concise but comprehensive look at the benefits and drawbacks of today's existing technologies. While reviewing every option, even total replacement, chapter 2 introduces you to the idea of server/client programming—the distributed twist on perhaps the most productive user interface in history.

- Chapter 3 introduces redeployment, the only gradual, staged implementation of a network enabling strategy. With redeployment, you not only leverage your existing programs and programmers, but at the same time you create a "region of change" as a buffer zone that allows you to decide which applications need to move to the next stage (client/server or even full object technology).

- Chapter 4 explains revitalization, the focus of this book. Revitalization is the first, most important step in the redeployment process. By applying the revitalization architecture to your existing legacy applications, you can quickly give network access to your legacy systems. Within weeks, your programs will run simultaneously on green screens, on networks, and even on the Web. With a little breathing room, you can begin the real business decisions of determining which applications need to be re-engineered into the next generation of application design. You can do this at your pace because revitalization stems the flood of user requirements for graphical network access.

This book is designed to help you dictate the evolution of your information systems. The constant, ever-quickening pace of technological advancement can place you in a position where you are reactive rather than proactive: putting out fires rather than heading off problems. The rush to the Web can feel like one more thing spinning out of your control. Revitalization puts that control back where it belongs—in your hands.

1

OVERVIEW

The IBM midrange platform has been a wonderfully stable environment for a long time. As far as the user interface goes, it's been sort of the "land where time stood still." In the past two decades, the major changes to the interface have included subfiles, windows, and UIM help text—hardly revolutionary, but sufficient to meet the needs of the end users, at least until recently. In fact, the very resilience of the 24-by-80 green screen is actually a good indicator that business applications don't need fancy graphics; they only require a good, solid data-entry display.

WHERE WE ARE TODAY

Typical green-screen business applications run on two types of data: *master files* and *transaction files*. Master files are normally maintained with a relatively simple interface; many packages adhere to the AS/400's PDM interface. A typical maintenance program for a master file is shown in Figure 1.1.

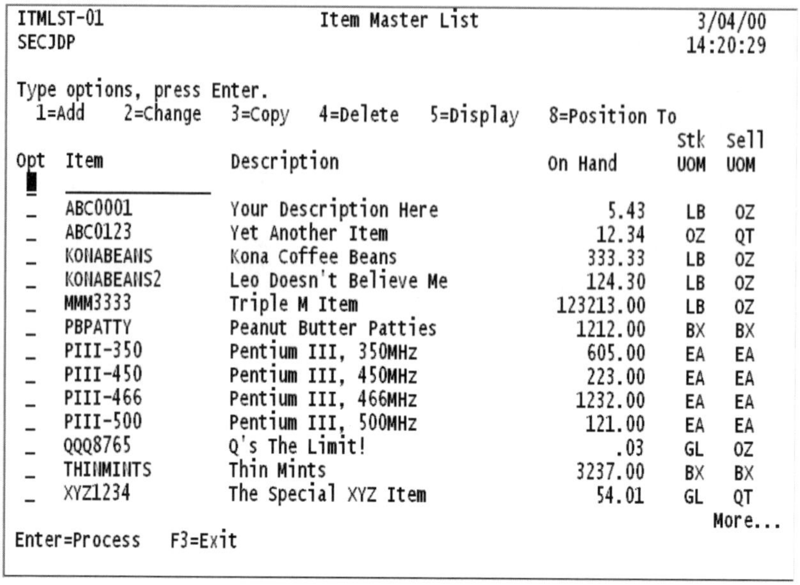

PART 1: REDEPLOYMENT AND REVITALIZATION

```
ITMLST-01                 Item Master List                 3/04/00
SECJDP                                                    14:20:29

Type options, press Enter.
  1=Add     2=Change    3=Copy    4=Delete    5=Display   8=Position To
                                                         Stk    Sell
Opt  Item            Description                On Hand  UOM    UOM

  _  ABC0001         Your Description Here         5.43   LB    OZ
  _  ABC0123         Yet Another Item             12.34   OZ    QT
  _  KONABEANS       Kona Coffee Beans           333.33   LB    OZ
  _  KONABEANS2      Leo Doesn't Believe Me      124.30   LB    OZ
  _  MMM3333         Triple M Item            123213.00   LB    OZ
  _  PBPATTY         Peanut Butter Patties      1212.00   BX    BX
  _  PIII-350        Pentium III, 350MHz         605.00   EA    EA
  _  PIII-450        Pentium III, 450MHz         223.00   EA    EA
  _  PIII-466        Pentium III, 466MHz        1232.00   EA    EA
  _  PIII-500        Pentium III, 500MHz         121.00   EA    EA
  _  QQQ8765         Q's The Limit!                 .03   GL    OZ
  _  THINMINTS       Thin Mints                 3237.00   BX    BX
  _  XYZ1234         The Special XYZ Item         54.01   GL    QT
                                                                More...
Enter=Process   F3=Exit
```

Figure 1.1: A typical green-screen maintenance panel.

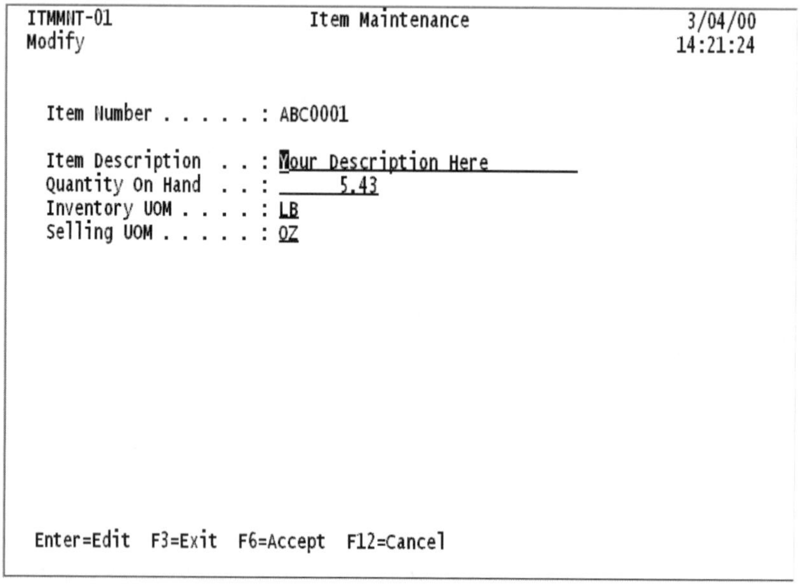

```
ITMMNT-01                  Item Maintenance                3/04/00
Modify                                                    14:21:24


   Item Number . . . . . : ABC0001

   Item Description  . . : Your Description Here
   Quantity On Hand  . . :      5.43
   Inventory UOM . . . . : LB
   Selling UOM . . . . . : OZ












Enter=Edit   F3=Exit   F6=Accept   F12=Cancel
```

Figure 1.2: The green-screen maintenance detail panel.

This panel usually allows scrolling and positioning within the list. Advanced options might include changing the sort sequence or allowing some filtering criteria. Selecting an option from the list brings up the maintenance screen. For example, selecting option 2 in Figure 1.1 to edit an item brings up an edit panel, shown in Figure 1.2. Here, the user enters data, changing whatever fields are necessary, and then presses either Enter or a function key to update the data.

The maintenance program edits the data, and either accepts the transaction, or rejects it by highlighting the field in error and positioning the cursor appropriately. Error messages are often displayed at the bottom of the screen in an error message subfile. Figure 1.3 shows a typical example of this kind of interface.

```
ITMMNT-01                    Item Maintenance                  3/04/00
Modify                                                        14:23:49


    Item Number . . . . . : ABC0001

     Item Description . . : _____
     Quantity On Hand . . :         5.43
     Inventory UOM . . . . : LB
     Selling UOM . . . . . : OZ










    Enter=Edit   F3=Exit   F6=Accept   F12=Cancel
    Description cannot be blank.
```

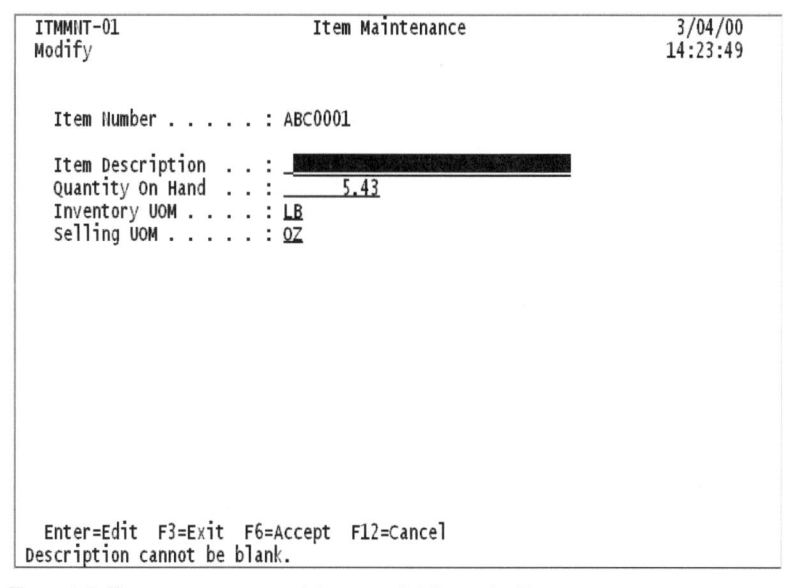

Figure 1.3: The green-screen maintenance detail panel with an error.

Promptable fields and help text round out the list of features for this sort of program. Occasionally, you might see some more sophisticated features, such as hidden fields and full-screen data entry allowing multiple records to be entered or maintained at the same time. For the most part, however, this is the extent of the typical master-file maintenance interface. This is partly because the 24-by-80 interface is somewhat limited, but mainly because there really is no need for anything more sophisticated. Files can only be maintained so many ways, and end users are accustomed to this sort of interface.

The other sort of data entry usually involves some form of transaction data. It might be something semi-static like a customer order, or something completely dynamic, like an inventory adjustment. In either case, the interface usually involves an optional header screen followed by a full-screen detail data-entry panel. (Older applications or more complex transactions might require one-at-a-time entry panels.) Figures 1.4 and 1.5 show the header and line-item screens for a typical order-entry program.

```
ORDENT-01                      Order Entry                        4/08/00
Create                                                            22:58:40


   Order/Customer Number: 0001232 / 209764        Ship To: _____

   Name . . . . . . . . : Pluta Brothers Design
   Attention  . . . . . : 35 S. Wilmette Ave.
   Address Line 1 . . . : Westmont
   Address Line 2 . . . :
   Address Line 3 . . . :
   Ste/Post/Country . . : IL  60559       USA


   Request Date . . . . : 4/01/00     Salesperson  . . . . : 2411
   Scheduled Date . . . : 4/15/00     Terms Code . . . . . : NET30


   Customer PO  . . . . : PBD-040100-0001




   Enter=Edit  F3=Exit  F6=Accept  F12=Cancel
```

Figure 1.4: A green-screen order-entry header panel.

```
ORDENT-02                 Order Entry Detail Panel                4/08/00
SECJDP                                                           23:45:11

   Type options, press Enter.
     A=(Move)After  B=(Move)Before  C=Copy  D=Delete  M=Move
     AL=Allocate  EN=Edit Notes  PR=Pricing  SH=Sales History

   Act Line Item/Desc        Quantity        Price   U/M  Extended Amount
    _  001  PBPATTY             12.00        2.950   BX            35.40
    _  002  PIII450            150.00       59.000   EA          8850.00
    _  003  _____      _____   _____   _       _____
    _  004  _____      _____   _____   _       _____
    _  005  _____      _____   _____   _       _____
    _  006  _____      _____   _____   _       _____
    _  007  _____      _____   _____   _       _____
    _  008  _____      _____   _____   _       _____
    _  009  _____      _____   _____   _       _____
    _  010  _____      _____   _____   _       _____
    _  011  _____      _____   _____   _       _____
    _  012  _____      _____   _____   _       _____
                                                                 More...

   F3=Exit   F6=Accept   F14=Customer Notes   F15=Order Notes   F16=Header
```

Figure 1.5: A green-screen order-entry detail panel.

A third category of interactive business programs is the *inquiry* category. Usually, inquiry programs display the raw data from master and/or transaction files in a way that is meaningful to the end user. They might sort, filter, and summarize data; allow drilldown into underlying information; or allow the user to call a maintenance program for specific data. In addition, the inquiry application might have batch-processing programs and printed reports that are run through simple prompt screens, such as the one in Figure 1.6.

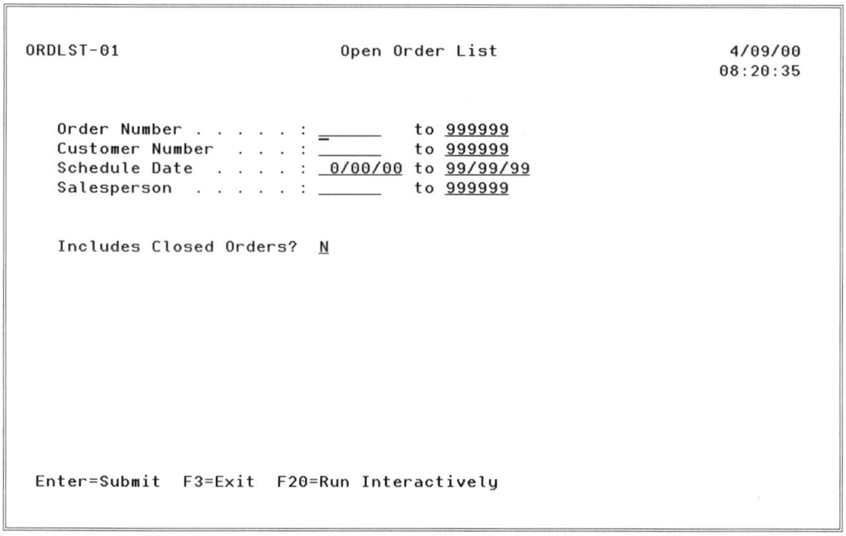

```
ORDLST-01                    Open Order List                      4/09/00
                                                                  08:20:35


     Order Number  . . . . . :  _____   to  999999
     Customer Number  . . . :  _____   to  999999
     Schedule Date  . . . . :  0/00/00  to  99/99/99
     Salesperson  . . . . . :  _____   to  999999


     Includes Closed Orders?  N










     Enter=Submit   F3=Exit   F20=Run Interactively
```

Figure 1.6: A report-prompt green screen.

While there are other types of programs, most fit reasonably well within this list. Those that don't might require some additional design effort, but you'll see that the redeployment model fits well with any type of interface.

THE GOALS OF DISTRIBUTED PROGRAMMING

Having taken a brief look at the green-screen user interface, it's time to identify the goals you want to achieve during your move to distributed programming.

Graphical Interfaces

The first goal, and the one that will be most appreciated by your end users, is to create a graphical interface. This means more than simply creating a graphical representation of a 5250 display screen. In order to be an integral part of the desktop, your user interface must present the same "look and feel" as other programs. For browser-based applications, this means a consistent HTML interface. For applications that require a more sophisticated graphical interface, a Java client becomes the best choice.

Platform Independence

The next issue, at least from an end-user standpoint, is that of platform independence. With redeployment, platform independence is phased in. An AS/400-only green-screen interface is supported for backward compatibility, but the goal is to implement either a thick-client or browser-based interface. By their nature, browsers are platform-independent, especially if you use HTML as the interface. Thick clients can be written using a platform-independent language. At this time, the strongest contender is Java.

While the UI is being redeployed, the business logic remains in its original high-level language, so you can have RPG programmers and graphical designers working simultaneously. Once the UI is rewritten, you can redeploy the corresponding business-logic server without any changes for the end user. The redeployment of servers can be done as time and conditions warrant: you might redeploy the whole system at once, an application at a time, or even a program at a time. Conceivably, some applications could become entirely platform-independent, while others could remain AS/400-specific. This should be a business decision, not a technical decision; redeployment supports a mix of server languages.

Desktop Integration

Another benefit of network programming is integration with existing desktop applications. By their nature, browser-based solutions have a predetermined level of desktop integration, supporting cut-and-paste operations and hyperlinks to other documents. More sophisticated features require a thick-client interface. In fact, those features are the primary reason to use a thick client as opposed to a browser-based solution.

For example, with a thick client, you can provide true drag-and-drop capabilities, allowing a user to click on an entry in, say, a customer list and drag it onto a telephone icon. This would autodial the customer and create a call log. Dragging the call log onto an order-entry icon would start the order-entry program, preloading the information for that customer. With this capability, it is just that easy to design a component-based telemarketing application.

Object Architecture

The most far-reaching goal for redesign is to implement object architecture. Unfortunately, this goal is probably the most difficult to implement and justify, especially from a short-term economic standpoint. While both object and procedural solutions can generate the same short-term benefits, object architecture is far more important in its long-term benefits, especially in the reduction of hidden and ongoing costs.

True object-oriented programming takes full advantage of inheritance, encapsulation, and polymorphism. This increases productivity by both reducing debugging costs and reducing the cost and time-to-market of enhancements. Sadly, neither of these benefits makes a big impact when you're estimating the time for the conversion of existing systems.

End-User Information Tools

A final benefit of network programming is the ability for end users to gather their own information directly from the central database. This level of access is probably the most misunderstood and potentially most troublesome aspect of distributed architectures. Since few end-user tools are object-oriented, but instead directly access the database, they create a binding point between the user application and the structure of the database. If you want to change the database schema for any reason, you potentially disrupt the user applications—and that's just for inquiry applications.

Any environment that gives end users unregulated update access to the database is, by definition, unsecured and unstable. Object Query Language (OQL) and stored procedures that intercept user queries can alleviate these problems, but they need to be designed into the system from the start.

THE GOALS OF OPEN SYSTEMS

Just as important as the end-user goals are the architectural goals of any distributed programming approach. These goals fall under a somewhat different umbrella, that of *open systems*. Some of the goals are similar, while others are different.

When designing a system from the ground up, the open systems strategy has very clear-cut goals:

- Separation of the user interface from the business logic.
- Consistent, extensible object interfaces.
- Reusable software components.
- Platform independence.

Strict adherence to interface standards makes it easy for application programs to interact, and more importantly for programs outside the system to communicate with your applications. Extensibility guarantees that enhancements can coexist with older software as long as necessary for your particular environment.

Reusable software components ensure not only that no development time is wasted on code duplication, but that internal inconsistencies due to code divergence don't creep in. No doubt you have your own horror stories of supposedly "cloned" programs that get out of sync, requiring all kinds of extra effort to modify. Components avoid that particular pitfall. Finally, platform independence guards against hardware obsolescence. By developing code that can move from platform to platform, you can make advances in hardware transparent to your actual development effort.

These are wonderful goals. If I were to design a system from scratch today, I'd probably use JavaServer Pages/servlet architecture for Web-based interfaces and RMI (Remote Method Invocation) for locally attached graphics-intensive interfaces. I'd also take a long look at EJB (Enterprise JavaBeans) as the persistence engine. All code would be object-oriented and in fact would be written using JavaBeans, with the elegant simplicity of the property and event architecture. Applications would have four tiers: interface, application flow, business logic, and database. Only the database server would be eligible for native programming, and even then I would probably build in an SQL contingency option. (That is, any native database server would have a corresponding SQL implementation, to provide portability.)

In the real world, however, you probably already have an existing base of application code that has been tweaked and tuned for your particular business environment. You've probably undergone a rather expensive Y2K conversion process. Because of that, your systems might actually be in the best shape they've ever been—source code matches object code, unit and system tests have been run, and so on. It simply isn't reasonable to consider rewriting your application in a new language with new tools and new programmers.

At the same time, you need to move into the world of electronic business, if for no other reason than because your competitors undoubtedly will be doing so. However, you don't want to spend a lot of time and effort implementing a technological dead-end that will need to be rewritten again.

The goal of open systems in this environment is to somehow integrate the existing business knowledge of your legacy programs (and programmers) into a new application framework. This framework must allow you to quickly implement network-enabled applications, while at the same time position you for growth into the evolving component architecture. This framework is what I call *redeployment* or, more precisely, *e-deployment*.

Like open systems, e-deployment must attain several objectives, which have a slightly different focus than those mentioned earlier in this chapter:

- Separation of user interface and business logic.

- Consistent, extensible messages that allow migration to object interfaces.

- Reusable software wrappers that allow migration to components.

- Staged platform independence.

As you can see, the objectives of e-deployment mirror those of open systems. However, they are designed to allow the maximum reuse of legacy software, rather than requiring you to immediately rewrite your applications. E-deployment does this by providing "regions of change," which allow you to determine the speed at which existing software is migrated to object languages.

For example, the first step is to separate your monolithic applications into user-interface and business-logic components. These two entities then communicate with one another using messages. This creates two regions of change bounded by the messaging API; changes can occur in either region without affecting the other. You can apply object technology to either side or both.

This decision-making process can be applied individually to each of your business applications. As you read this book, you'll see how powerful this concept is when applied throughout the system.

13

2

EXISTING TECHNOLOGIES

Taking green-screen business applications into a graphical, distributed, open-systems environment is quite a challenge. It's been a challenge for many years, and a wide range of alternatives are available for distributing legacy systems. Traditionally, they can be broken down into three broad categories:

- Replacing.
- Refacing.
- Rewriting.

REPLACING

On the surface, the simplest idea seems to be simply replacing your existing applications with an off-the-shelf solution designed from the start to be object-oriented and Web-enabled. If such a system were available that exactly matched your business needs, it would indeed be the most cost-effective way to proceed. However, if your application-development procedures are like those of most companies, even if you started with a third-party solution, you have long since modified the applications to fit your particular business requirements. Therefore, you're going to need modifications—perhaps extensive ones—to get the new system to run.

Since the modifications will probably require a new language and maybe even a new platform, you're going to have to hire new staff—and possibly lay off the old staff. Of course, the new programmers won't have the in-depth knowledge of your business that is in the heads of the old staff, whom you've let go (or, who, having read the writing on the wall, have quit). After the modifications, you'll have to go through a comprehensive test suite, which you just did for the Y2K problem. Now, though, you'll do it with programmers who are unfamiliar with your business.

As you can see, unless your current software no longer meets the functional needs of your business, replacing it has far too many ongoing costs.

REFACING

Refacing is the next solution. This is a non-intrusive technique in which the old system is left in place. The simplest method by far is terminal emulation. Figure 2.1 shows a traditional monolithic application, and Figure 2.2 shows the corresponding terminal emulation. The 5250 display is directly emulated on the workstation, although the emulation package usually adds bells and whistles such as macros and hotkey support.

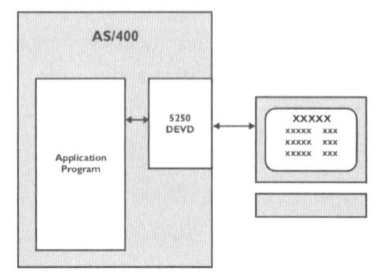

Figure 2.1: A traditional 5250-based application.

Figure 2.2: The application from Figure 2.1 using terminal emulation.

The other form of non-intrusive deployment is to graft a graphical front-end onto the 5250 stream. This grafting is done through emulation tools (sometimes called *screen scrapers*). Middleware programs actually simulate entering data via the 5250 data stream, and the results are read and presented to the user via a graphical user interface.

The primary advantage of such an approach is that virtually no changes need to be made to the existing legacy systems, as Figure 2.3 shows. However, in practice, the implementation problems can range from moderate to severe.

A relatively minor problem is that some green-screen panels simply do not lend themselves to a GUI. For example, there is no real GUI component that corresponds exactly to a green-screen subfile. Although list boxes and tables are similar, and work reasonably well for small lists of data, they become very difficult to use with large lists, such as master files or (especially) transaction files. You can deal with this by writing code to add additional features to a standard table, such as reading data a block at a time and automatically extending the table. These extended features, however, aren't part of the base GUI.

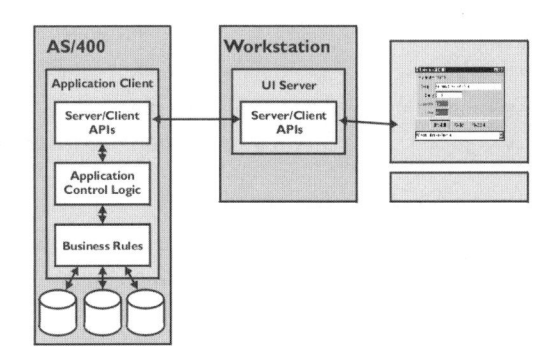

Figure 2.3: How a screen scraper is implemented.

This brings up the more difficult issue of additional code development. Emulation tools usually have their own language for defining the interaction between the GUI and the legacy application screens. Most have some sort of automatic generation to directly map legacy screens to graphical panels, but the generated panels are often just as ugly as the green screens they've replaced. If you directly map one of the cluttered, highly abbreviated screens sometimes seen in simple 24-by-80 applications onto a GUI panel, you end up with a cluttered GUI panel.

Clutter might be acceptable in the green-screen world, but people who are used to the functional, aesthetically pleasing screens of everyday GUI applications expect better. Therefore, you have to manually adjust the screens in order to make them acceptable, which means developing code for each panel. You'll probably have to do some of the same things for each panel, which means you'll need to duplicate code—and in another language, at that, since most screen scrapers aren't designed to be object-oriented. Also, since these tools usually rely on hard-coded comparisons to screen literals and field positions, any change to your base system will require modifications to the GUI emulation as well. Rather than simplifying your development environment, you'll be making it far more complex.

REWRITING

This leaves the third option, rewriting. If this were 1997 or early 1998, I'd probably suggest this as a serious alternative. At that time, it would have made sense to at least explore the idea of rewriting your system using an object-oriented approach. You would have been able to enable your system for the Web while at the same time eliminating the Y2K problem. You might have been able to afford delaying additional functional enhancements because the move to an object architecture would have resulted in a quicker development cycle once the conversion was complete.

This is not 1997, however, and you've probably already delayed enhancements during your Y2K conversion. Your users aren't going to allow you the time to completely redesign and rewrite your system. Therefore, you need a strategy that lets you move your applications to the Web while continuing to add the new features and functions your users demand. This is the goal of redeployment.

THUS THE NEED FOR DISTRIBUTED PROGRAMMING

Since none of the options discussed so far provide a solution that can quickly get a legacy program onto the Web and provide a starting point for conversion to object technology, a different approach is needed. You'll obviously need to put some of the workload on each machine, so it makes sense to start out by assessing the various distributed programming technologies available.

As programming techniques have progressed, several varieties of network programming have developed. The first distributed architectures involving workstations were usually remote PCs that emulated standard, locally attached dumb terminals. Next came workstations that dialed into a central host to exchange data in batch mode. This evolved into client/server processing, with online transaction processing. Then, ODBC connectivity provided standard SQL access for the workstation to directly access the host database. Finally, the newest entrant uses browser-based applications, where the Internet provides the connectivity between the workstation and the host.

Offline Processing

One of the earliest forms of distributed or network computing was offline processing, also known as detached processing. In this architecture, a connection is made with the host, and chunks of data are downloaded into the workstation. The workstation can then be disconnected (detached) from the host, and the user can perform all kinds of local processing, ranging from simple data entry to sophisticated modeling and forecasting. Once the user is satisfied with the modified data, it is uploaded back to the host.

Coordinating modifications made by many users is the most difficult aspect of this architecture, requiring busy flags and data collision detection. Although most offline processing has been replaced by online transaction processing, there are still cases where it makes sense; simulations and graphic modeling come to mind. The growth of mobile computing has also triggered a resurgence of detached processing models.

Client/Server Processing

With client/server processing, the workstation is connected to the host during the entire session. The original client/server implementations for the midrange grew out of the early 5250 emulators. In fact, some of the early applications did little more than talk to the 5250 data stream. This technique is still used extensively today in many screen-scraper products.

Later, APPC, and then TCP/IP, began to be used to provide the connection between the client and the server, allowing a more robust message-based conversation. With these connections, messages are no longer constrained by the limitations of the 5250 protocol; instead, they can contain any sort of data and can be used to transmit large amounts of information in realtime. This immediate access avoids the conflicts associated with data collisions because database records can actually be locked while the session is connected.

A wide variety of client/server models are available. Figure 2.4 shows a typical architecture, in which portions of the database are entirely encapsulated in server programs, and the client/server application running on the workstation simply makes calls as necessary.

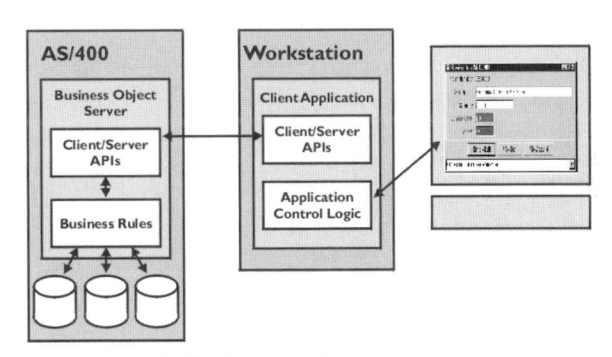

Figure 2.4: A client/server environment.

The problem with this approach has historically been that it requires separation of the application-control logic and the business rules. This usually can only be done with a major rewrite of any existing legacy code, and so it cannot be used to get systems to the market quickly.

Structured Query Language

Originally designed in the 1970s, SQL has long been a standard database-access technique for midrange and mainframe computers. Its simple, English-like syntax makes it easy for even nonprogrammers to access data. However, using SQL requires an intimate knowledge of the layout of the database and binds the SQL application to the names of tables and columns (roughly equivalent to files and fields in a traditional AS/400 DDS environment). If the database changes, the SQL applications must be rewritten as well. Not only that, but SQL can also be used to update the database, sometimes with disastrous results. You have to be very careful in who can use SQL and how much they can do with it if you want to maintain the integrity of your data.

The biggest problem with the SQL approach, as shown in Figure 2.5, is that all the logic must reside on the workstation. The ODBC-based application that runs on the workstation has not only the simple application-control logic of which screens to display, and when, but more importantly, all of the business logic as well. If two workstations have conflicting business rules, your database integrity will suffer.

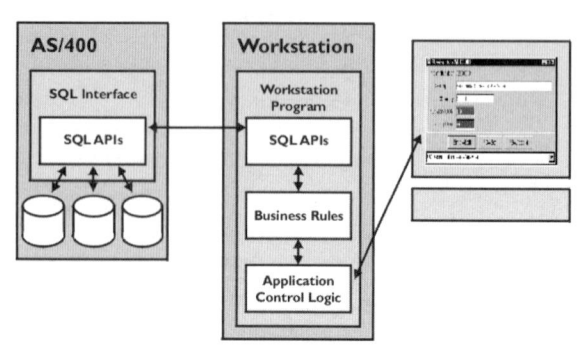

Figure 2.5: The SQL approach.

Browser-Based Applications

Finally, browser-based applications have brought the entire development environment full-circle. By using the browser as the user interface, the software designer once again is in control of the appearance of the user's screen. The user sees only what the designer wants to show. In this way, the browser is simply a graphical version of the old 5250 interface (except that there are millions of potential end users). Figure 2.6 shows a graphical representation of this type of approach.

Unfortunately, the first take on browser-based applications has been to design them in a client/server architecture, using

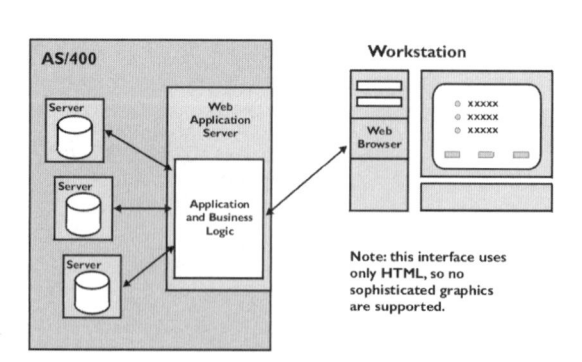

Figure 2.6: A browser-based client/server approach.

HTML as the user interface. With this technique, you indeed have a clean, platform-independent application, but at the cost of rewriting much of your legacy systems, and still without any sophisticated graphics. In some ways, this is the worst of all worlds.

Nevertheless, the browser model held out the most hope for putting legacy systems on the Web. HTML seemed to be a good replacement for the 5250 data stream, and the lack of any special software requirements on the workstation was a definite plus from the point of view of platform independence. It took several (very fast) evolutionary steps in the browser model, however, to make it a viable substitute for the old 5250 display.

THE PROGRESSION OF THE BROWSER MODEL

The advent of the browser and the World Wide Web has ushered in a new model of user interface. While at first simply a way to show simple, unchanging information, the browser has quickly become a vehicle to display dynamic content to a large audience. This model has evolved rapidly, through several stages:

1. Static Web pages. A browser requests a page from a server using a URL (Uniform Resource Locator). A URL is a combination of the Internet address of the server and the path and file name of the Web page. The Web page is simply a text file containing HTML statements.

2. Common Gateway Interface, or CGI, programs. In this technique, the URL actually points to a program on the host. This program is called, and is responsible for formatting and sending HTML to the user. CGI programs were first written in Perl on UNIX machines. On AS/400s, most CGI programs are written in RPG.

3. Servlets. These are similar to CGI programs. The primary difference is that servlets are written in Java. There are also some performance and persistence differences, but the idea is fundamentally the same: the program formats and sends HTML to the end user.

4. JavaServer Pages (JSP). These are similar to Web pages, but JavaServer Pages use a special superset of HTML that allows access to *JavaBeans*, special Java classes passed to the JSP. The JSP can call the methods of the JavaBean, which can, in turn, call other programs to dynamically retrieve

PART 1: REDEPLOYMENT AND REVITALIZATION

data. This technique is rarely used, however, because it is much more effective to combine JSP and servlets, as discussed in stage 5.

5. JSP and servlets. Used together, JSP and servlets provide the separation of business logic and user interface that is so necessary in creating today's sophisticated applications. The servlet controls the application and collects data, but does not actually generate any HTML. Instead, it passes the data to the JSP in JavaBeans, and the JSP formats the data for display to the user.

Browsers started out displaying static Web pages, as shown in Figure 2.7. These pages are HTML-formatted documents, stored in a database, and served up in direct response to a user request. While they can show images and support hyperlinking from one document to another, the data can't be changed in response to user input. This model is good only for the types of Web content we call "brochureware."

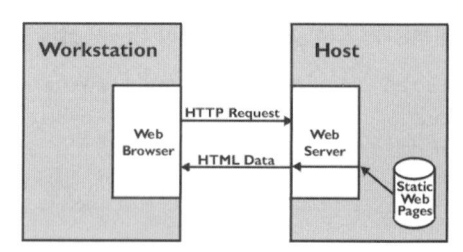

Figure 2.7: The initial browser model, using static Web pages.

In the next phase of the development of Web content, CGI programs enable the Web to serve up data in response to a user's input. The CGI can read data entered in a form, and then output HTML combined with database data to create complex, interactive applications. The biggest problem is that the application programmer not only has to understand the legacy business-system rules, but must also be an expert at HTML.

This technique, shown in Figure 2.8, is still widely used. However, the binding between user interface and application programming makes it very difficult to change the look of a Web site without a massive rewriting of the CGI.

Servlets began the move to Java. With servlets, you can write the interface HTML using Java, which is far better suited to the required string manipulation than RPG or other HLLs (high-level languages). However, Java is not very well suited for business programming, so you still have to modify your legacy application to communi-

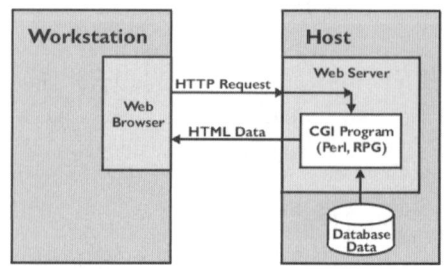

Figure 2.8: The first phase of dynamic pages, the Common Gateway Interface.

22

cate with the servlets. At the same time, any changes to the Web site require you to modify existing code—code which was difficult to debug in the first place. Figure 2.9 shows the components of servlet-based interfaces.

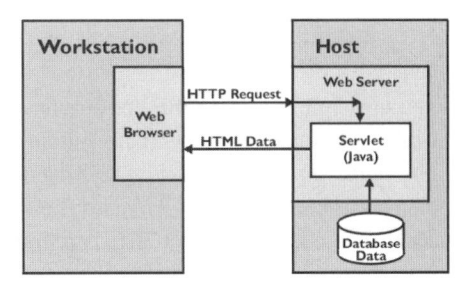

Figure 2.9: The architecture behind servlets.

JavaServer Pages (JSP), shown in Figure 2.10, provided the next move forward. JSP is essentially an extension of the HTML specification allowing easy access to JavaBeans. JavaBeans are self-contained *smart parameters*, entities containing not only data but also the methods to retrieve and manipulate that data. In this way, the JSP developer can concentrate primarily on Web site design, and let the JavaBean programmer worry about the data. The only problem with this approach is that it is difficult to include complex application-control logic within the HTML hyperlinks.

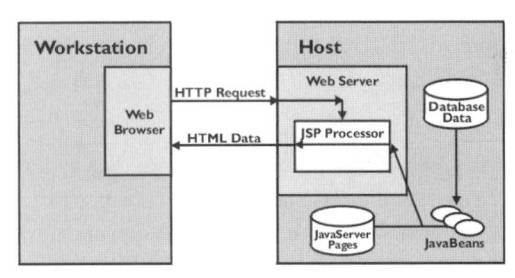

Figure 2.10: The JavaServer Page interface.

The culmination of the browser model is the ability of servlets to create JavaBeans and pass them directly to the JSP, as shown in Figure 2.11. This way, the servlet can perform all the necessary application-control logic to determine the next JSP and generate the appropriate JavaBean, while the JSP designer only needs to be concerned with the appearance of the actual user interface. This provides true separation of function, which had been lacking in browser models up to this point.

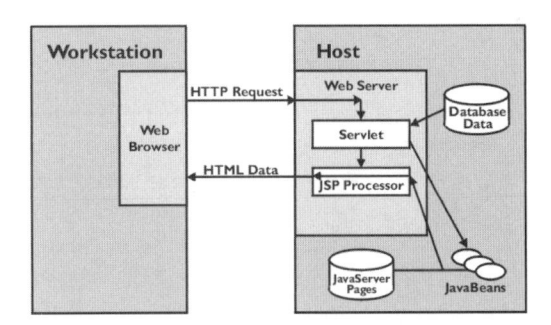

Figure 2.11: The combination of servlets and JSP.

THE ADVENT OF SERVER/CLIENT PROGRAMMING

Even the combination of JSP and servlets did not solve the immediate problem, however. Still lacking was the ability to easily graft this interface onto an existing legacy application. Legacy applications know nothing about Java, servlets, and JavaBeans. A new technology was needed, to be a mediator between the old programming model and the new user interface model. Server/client programming is that technology, and revitalization is the strategy to implement it.

Server/client programming has been around for a long time. In fact, the first programmable workstations (the 3270- and 5250-type display terminals) were crude forms of server/client processing. In this architecture, the display interface is entirely slaved to the computer, responding only to requests to display data to the user and accept input.

In the AS/400, the primary device for displaying data and accepting input is the display file. The display file accepts I/O requests from an HLL program and translates them into a 5250 data stream. With revitalization, the display-file I/O requests are replaced with API calls. The data is sent to a data queue, which is read by a servlet. The servlet sends the data to a display-file-emulation JavaBean, and when input is needed, sends it the JavaBean to the appropriate JavaServer Page. The resulting architecture is shown in Figure 2.12.

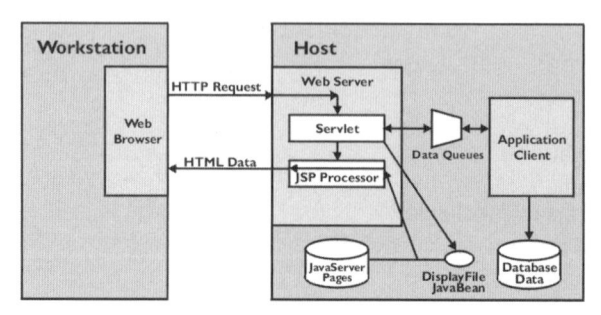

Figure 2.12: The browser implementation of the server/client revitalization architecture.

The real breakthrough of this architecture is that while it supports the browser model very well, the separation of user interface and application programming is so complete that the same strategy can also be used to support green screens and thick client interfaces. You'll see that as you implement the example in this book.

3

REDEPLOYMENT: THE NEW STRATEGY

Before addressing the mechanics of redeployment and, specifically, revitalization, a short review of the events that led to this juncture is worthwhile. Until recently, progress in midrange computing, especially on the AS/400, has been a fairly steady, uneventful process. Changes have occurred gradually, with a heavy emphasis on backward compatibility and preservation of existing assets. This is part of what makes the AS/400 such a superior platform for business application development. Unlike more volatile fields, such as games programming or artificial intelligence, much of what we do today in business application programming is very similar to what was done five, ten, and 20 years ago. In fact, it's often very similar to what was done before computers were used. That's why the proprietary nature of the AS/400 and its operating system didn't cause much worry when it came time to select a computer system. However, today's computing environment is very different.

Not too long ago, about the only user interface decision I had to make when designing an AS/400 application was whether to load my subfiles all at once, or one page at a time. Since then, the widespread reliance on the World Wide Web has made graphical network connectivity a requirement—and graphics is the one area where my trusty AS/400 can't help me. So, I learned about CGI, Java, servlets, applets, Active Server Pages, and all the other buzzwords. It seemed that every day another new technique came along. At the same time, old familiar techniques like SQL and screen-scraping popped up in everyday conversations. Every option seemed to have its proponents and detractors.

Through all of this, I noticed two disturbing trends:

1. Every solution was touted as the one and only solution.

2. Except for CGI and screen-scraping, none of the solutions had room for RPG programmers.

The first situation was predictable, if only because of the nature of our industry. Until recently, the idea in software development was to garner as much market share as possible using proprietary techniques, shutting out the competition. Given that atmosphere, we became used to the notion that you had to choose the single best product for your needs, and it became the core of your business. Add-on products for niche markets were sold, but it was extremely difficult to get competing products from major vendors to work together.

As a case in point, in my industry, ERP (enterprise resource planning), the major products were BPCS and PRMS. MAPICS had some market share, as did J.D. Edwards and a few others, and there were vague rumblings about some UNIX upstart named SAP making inroads into the AS/400 market. About the only time you would see more than one of these packages in any shop was through mergers. In fact, a fairly lucrative consulting business developed around simply getting these packages to communicate.

Today, in contrast, BPCS heralds itself as a completely "open" system, with its Semantic Message Gateways providing the ability for any other software package to interact with the core BPCS functions. This trend toward interoperability is notably missing from the various network enabling solutions being proposed today.

Even more troublesome than lack of interoperability, however, is the notion that it's time to replace RPG. There seems to be an attitude that RPG is some sort of second-rate kludge that must be removed from our systems, and that only platform-independent, object-oriented programming can be tolerated.

I absolutely agree that reusable software components are the next necessary step in the evolution of software development; systems continue to grow more complex and prone to errors, creating backlogs of bug fixes, and draining resources that could be better used to build enhancements. However, there is currently a huge investment in RPG, not only in business logic, but also in the people who understand how that logic works. Any business "solution" that involves making those human assets obsolete is really no solution at all.

THE BIG PICTURE

Redeployment is a network enabling strategy based on two fundamental principles: a gradual, staged implementation, and a maximum reuse of all your assets, the most important of which are your current programmers. With redeployment, you start with architectural modifications that create small, manageable regions of change without affecting how your end users operate. User interface code is separated from business logic, and then the user interface is redeployed according to your business needs. The business logic is encapsulated into servers written in your current high-level language. (This book is devoted to redeploying existing legacy systems. Since the bulk of existing applications are written in RPG III, this book focuses on RPG III as the server language. If your code is written in RPG IV, the redeployment process will be the same.)

Small, efficient green-screen user interfaces are the first stage; users can continue to use these screens just as they did before the modification. The important point is that your entire business is still in the hands of your RPG programmers. They can makes changes to both the green-screen clients and the business-logic servers, enhancing the applications just as easily as before. Remember, your current RPG programmers know your particular business practices, and redeployment allows them to use their knowledge to the benefit of your company.

Meanwhile, a completely different team can begin to reengineer your user interfaces, using the technologies best suited for your needs. Each application can have a different solution. In fact, you can continue to use a green-screen interface where that makes sense. One of the biggest complaints I've had against the move to an entirely graphical user interface is that there are some environments, such as the shop floor, where it just doesn't make sense to replace a cheap, sturdy dumb terminal with a costly and perhaps less reliable PC. With redeployment, you can choose the applications or even the programs to redeploy, and how. You can have a mix of green-screen, local intranet, and Internet applications, while still leveraging your existing programs—and programmers.

THE PROCESS

Redeployment is a three-stage process designed to move traditional green-screen applications to a graphical, distributed architecture. The first stage, *revitalization*, replaces the existing display-file operations with a simple API that communicates via data queues with a user-interface server. The user interface can be a green screen, thick client, thin client or any combination of the three. The second stage, *restructuring*, moves the application logic out of the legacy programs and into a platform-independent server (typically a Java servlet). The final stage, *re-engineering*, rewrites the legacy business logic as true objects, setting the stage for platform independence.

Revitalization

Revitalization is the first and most highly visible stage in the redeployment process, and is the focus of this book. The goal of this stage is to give your existing legacy applications a flexible user interface—whether green screen, thick client, or thin client—with a minimum of disruption. If you complete this step successfully, your application will support a graphical interface, yet will still be maintainable by your original legacy programmers. In fact, you can still support the original green-screen interface, allowing your end users to migrate to the graphical interface at a pace that is appropriate for them.

Figure 3.1 shows the basic structure of a typical monolithic program. Programming is done in a high-level language, and the user interface is a display file. Although this book focuses on RPG as the HLL, there are very few changes to the application program, so any other HLL can be revitalized just as easily.

Chapter 4 covers the details of the modifications, but the concept is quite simple: replace all I/O operations to the display with calls to an API, which sends the data normally sent to the display file to a data queue instead. The data queue is monitored by a user interface server that sends the data to the user via the appropriate user interface.

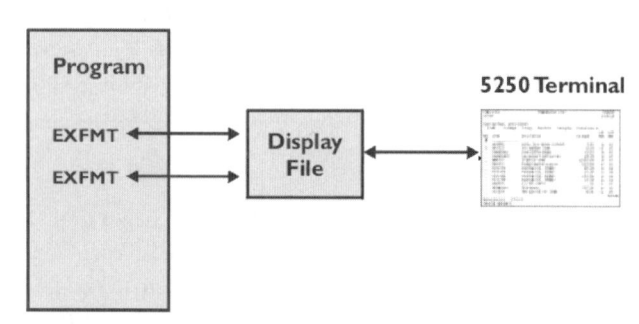

Figure 3.1: A typical monolithic program, using a display file to communicate with the green screen.

Figure 3.2 shows how various configurations can provide green-screen, thick-client, or thin-client user interfaces. A vital characteristic of this technique is its flexibility. The same revitalized application program can be used to communicate with any of the user interface servers, so your users are not required to switch to any specific user interface. They can choose the interface that best suits their particular business needs.

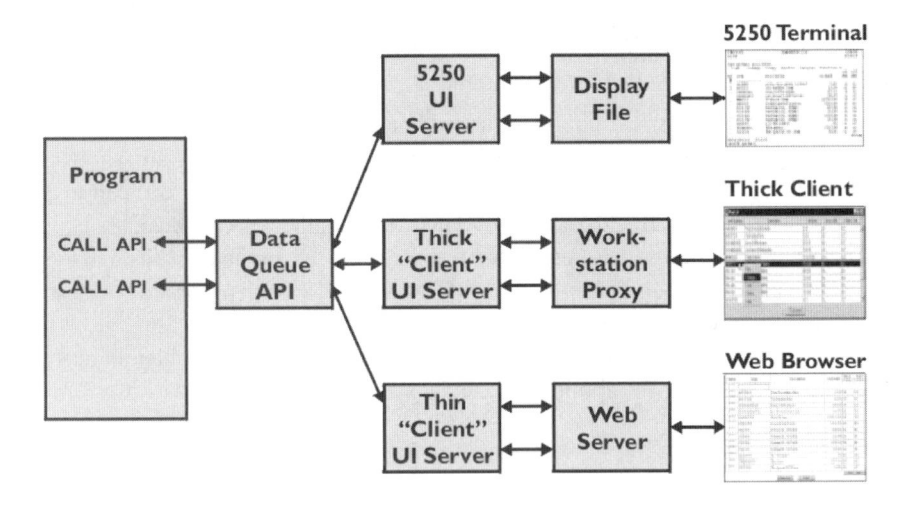

Figure 3.2: The revitalized application, using any combination of user interface servers to provide the appropriate interface to the end user.

Restructuring

Revitalization alone might be sufficient for a large percentage of existing legacy systems. By providing either thick-client or browser-based access to legacy applications, revitalization provides a low-cost graphical interface. You'll see in subsequent chapters just how easy it is to implement the revitalization technique.

Low cost and ease of implementation are not the only reasons to use the redeployment model. Other techniques exist to provide a simple user interface upgrade. For example, many applet-based solutions simply repackage the 5250 data stream. These are collectively called *screen scrapers*, although some of them have become quite a bit more sophisticated than that name might suggest. However, no matter how sophisticated a technique is used, if it doesn't modify the underlying program, it doesn't provide a basis for the next step of redeployment: restructuring.

In restructuring, the existing application program undergoes fundamental modifications to separate the business logic from the application-control logic. Business logic is encapsulated into true servers, which process messages. The business-logic servers remain in the original HLL, while the application-control logic is moved up a level. Restructuring and the subsequent stage, re-engineering, are not the focus of this book. However, it's important to understand how they work in order to get a feeling for how the entire redeployment process can be implemented.

Figure 3.3 shows how restructuring is achieved in a thin-client (browser-based) environment. This figure represents a hypothetical "average" maintenance program, showing how the application-control logic works in the application client. The initial call to **get** is used to populate the screen with the appropriate data from the selected business entity. Then, until a program flag indicates the program is done, the application sits in a loop: it sends data to a panel, receives user input, and forwards it to the appropriate business-rules server. Upon return, the **done** flag is set to **on** if the transaction is complete, at which point the program sends an end-of-program message to the UI server, which in turn invokes the index panel for the application.

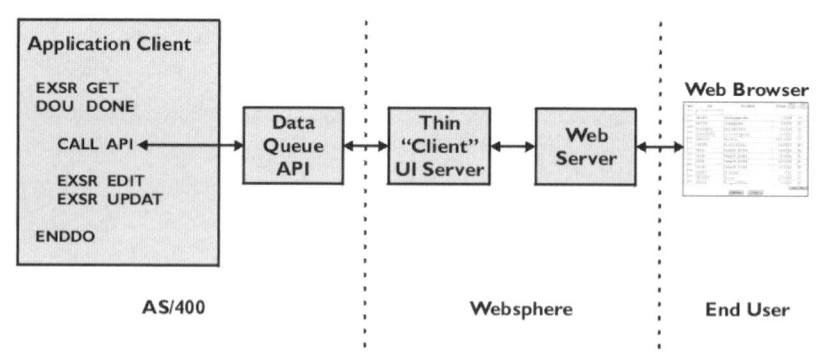

Figure 3.3: Business and application-control logic residing in the same program prior to restructuring.

Figure 3.4 shows the same program as Figure 3.3, after restructuring. As you can see, there is no longer any application-control logic on the AS/400. Rather than defining a loop based on whether or not a business function succeeds or fails, the business-rules server handles a single request at a time and returns the result to the application controller. This is the essence of a business entity (or *object*). An object does not perform a looping function. Instead, it performs only a specific function on a specific instance of the business entity class. As an intermediate step to true object technology, business servers also are limited to processing a function on a single entity. If looping is needed, an application controller performs it.

The important thing to notice in Figures 3.3 and 3.4 is that the Web server portion of the interface doesn't change at all. The thin-client application controller shows the same panels that the thin-client UI server does in the revitalized application. In practical terms, this means that your end users won't even notice that you're rewriting the architecture underneath them.

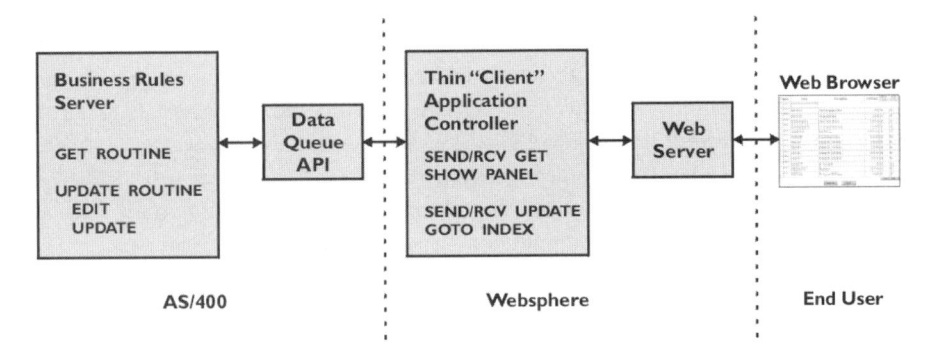

Figure 3.4: The business rules and application-control logic separated after restructuring.

You might be wondering exactly what benefits are gained from restructuring. First, you can offload the application control to another platform. Everything that runs on WebSphere can be ported to AIX, Linux, Novell NetWare, or even Windows NT. In fact, you don't have to use WebSphere; you could use any other Web server that supports servlets and JavaServer Pages. The AS/400 can be dedicated to processing your database transactions, which is what it is designed to do.

Second, you can now write true thick clients that use business-logic servers without having to go through a thick-client UI server. For example, once you have written the business-rules server to handle item-maintenance messages, you can easily write a thick-client item master-maintenance program taking advantage of all the capabilities of a true event-driven interface. As you write more business-rules servers, your thick-client applications can become more and more sophisticated. Imagine an order status screen that allows you to drag a customer icon from an order directly onto your dialer to allow you to call the customer. A thick-client interface combined with the appropriate customer server could do just that.

Re-engineering

The most important goal of restructuring from a redeployment perspective, however, is the ability to rewrite your business-logic servers. This is the third stage of redeployment, known as re-engineering. With re-engineering, business servers are redesigned as Java classes. The methods of a class should match the messages used by the server. This is why it is so important to think the redeployment strategy through completely before beginning the design—if the original messages don't mesh nicely into an object-oriented design, it will be much more difficult to progress to this stage.

Figure 3.5 shows a re-engineered, platform-independent application. The server objects can start out wrapped in message wrappers, which support the original message design. Once the servers are in place, the wrappers can be removed and replaced with a more appropriate distributed-programming architecture, such as Common Object Request Broker Architecture (CORBA) or Enterprise JavaBeans (EJB). Once this is done, the servers can be distributed anywhere in the network. This can become especially important when attempting to combine applications running on different databases.

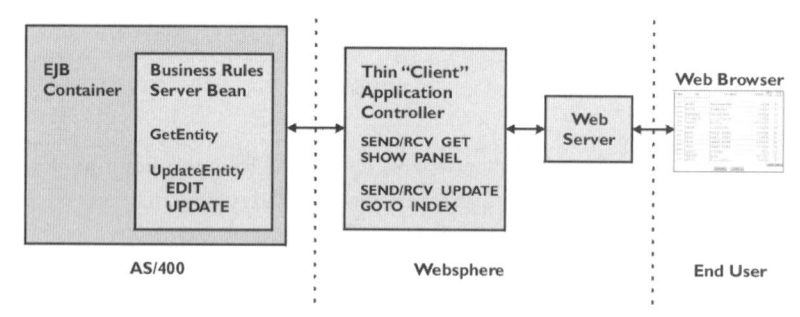

Figure 3.5: One completely platform-independent configuration, using Enterprise JavaBeans as the object distribution method.

Once again, however, the strategy has been designed to allow gradual implementation. If some applications still require the message-based strategy, you can easily leave the message wrappers in place. This will not affect the ability to distribute the objects as needed. The wrappers will communicate with the Java server objects using the correct distributed object architecture, while providing a more platform-dependent interface for applications with short lifespans, or those that will be converted later.

THE RESULTS

You can use the redeployment strategy to give each of your applications the appropriate technology. Your shop floor data-entry application can remain on a green screen, your order entry can have an e-commerce front end, your executive information system can be an intranet applet, and your customer service department can be an entirely integrated workflow environment.

With redeployment, your existing legacy programs are reused for as long as possible. The application clients developed for stage 1 (revitalization) can be maintained as if they were monolithic green-screen applications, while at the same time you begin to see where the business servers need to be written. As your end users begin to see a graphical user interface, your legacy programmers can continue fixing and enhancing the base code.

Stage 2 (restructuring) distills the business rules from your existing applications. In most cases, this will actually result in a decrease in the total lines of code in the system, as redundant code is eliminated. You will begin to develop your own standards for Java development at this stage. Since the code for the application controllers is very simple, you don't need to spend a lot of time training your programmers in all the intricacies of object-oriented programming techniques. This is a good place for legacy programmers with no OO experience to begin to make the transition.

Even if your ultimate goal is to re-engineer all of your legacy systems to Java (stage 3), redeployment enables you to do it gradually. Your legacy programmers remain productive all the way to stage 3, which gives them plenty of time to either learn Java technologies or mentor other programmers in the company. During stage 3, programmers who have decided not to pursue the new technology can still provide valuable assistance in the final design of the business server objects.

The gradual approach of redeployment allows you achieve true platform independence with the highest possible return on your programming investments, both in systems and people. Let's move on to stage 1, then, and see just how easy it is to revitalize an existing legacy application!

4

REVITALIZATION

The theory behind revitalization, the first stage of redeployment, is very simple. Normally, a monolithic application communicates with a display file using buffers of data. The buffers contain a combination of fields and indicators. Revitalization intercepts the outgoing buffers and sends them to a UI server instead, which emulates the display file. The UI server sends the user's response back to the program, which continues just as if it had been working with a display file.

THE DISPLAY FILE'S ROLE IN 5250 COMMUNICATIONS

To fully understand the revitalization strategy, you need to examine the interaction between a typical monolithic program and a display file. For example, let's review a very simple screen with two output fields and two input/output fields, and follow that screen through a typical output and input cycle.

Typically, an RPG programmer uses an EXFMT op code to write data to the display file and read back the user response. For this discussion, however, a WRITE op code is processed, followed by a READ op code. This is functionally equivalent to the EXFMT, but allows the two phases to be examined individually.

The Output Operation

Figure 4.1 shows the operational flow for a simple WRITE operation. In the figure, the display file defines the constants, such as "User ID" or "Enter=Update," their positions, and their attributes (including color). The display file also defines *fields*, areas on the screen used to display data to the user and/or receive data from the user. In this example, there are four such fields. The data buffer contains the actual data to be inserted into those fields. For example, the first field, labeled "User ID," will display the value "PLUTA." Each of the other fields will display data the same way.[1]

There are two other important points. First, the date field comes in without slashes separating the month, day, and year. It is the responsibility of the display file to edit the data from the buffer to insert the slashes appropriately. Second, two *indicators* are passed in the buffer to determine one or more characteristics of fields in the file. In this case, indicator 01 is used to protect the Item field; if indicator 01 is on, data cannot be entered in the fields. Indicator 02 is used the same way to protect the Description field. Because indicator 01 is on, the Item field is protected. Since indicator 02 is off, the Description field is not protected; the field is underlined in the user display to show that it is input-capable.

The final outcome of the whole operation is that the constant data of the display file, the variable data of the buffer, and the display attributes as specified by the conditioning indicators are all combined into a single, cohesive display for the user. At this point, the user is able to perform whatever actions are necessary, and then hit a function key, at which point the input operation begins.

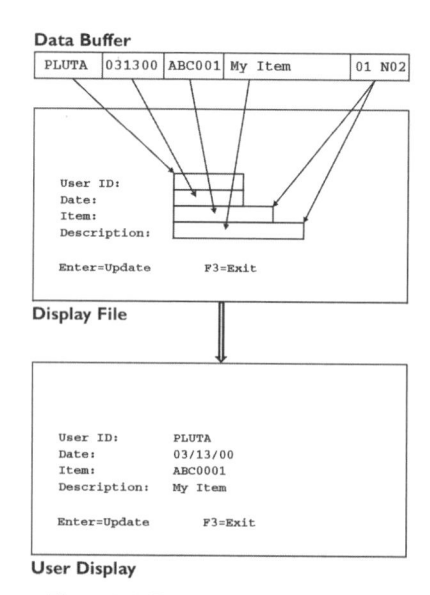

Figure 4.1: The output flow of a simple WRITE operation.

---

1   It is rare for a field to be input-only; most fields are either output or input/output fields.

The Input Operation

Figure 4.2 shows the operational flow for the READ operation shown in Figure 4.1. As you can see, the data input by the user is placed into the data buffer to be returned to the program.

Of course, the proceedings in these figures are simplifications. For example, some fields might be input-only, and so would not appear in the input data stream. Also, the indicator bucket is replaced with the word *Enter* because a flag identifying which function key the user pressed is passed back to the user. Other indicators might be returned as well, but none are in this very simple example.

Data Buffer

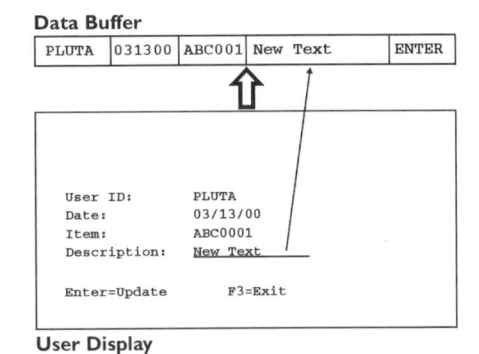

| PLUTA | 031300 | ABC001 | New Text | ENTER |

```
User ID:      PLUTA
Date:         03/13/00
Item:         ABC0001
Description:  New Text

Enter=Update       F3=Exit
```
User Display

Figure 4.2: Input flow of the corresponding READ operation.

The Whole Picture

The display file, then, performs three basic functions: defining the constant data displayed on the screen, defining the variable fields on the screen, and defining the behavior of the screen based on conditioning indicators received from the calling program. With this knowledge, you can begin to design the emulation packages necessary to enable the revitalization process.

THE GOALS OF REVITALIZATION

While distributed programming has some rather far-reaching objectives, the aims of revitalization are much less ambitious. Since the primary purpose of revitalization is to be the first step in the entire redeployment process, it needs a certain limited scope. These are the goals of revitalization:

- Ease of implementation.
- Minimum disruption of the current business.
- Maximum reuse of existing programs and programmers.
- Quick time to implementation.
- Flexible user interface.
- Support for later stages of redeployment.

With those goals in mind, six requirements can be identified:

1. Changes to the existing code must be kept to a minimum. If at all possible, these changes should be performed programmatically.

2. The original green screen must still be supported, and no major rework should be required anywhere in the job streams.

3. Any new technology must be completely isolated from existing technology. Current programmers should not need to learn new skills in order to implement the strategy.

4. The architecture must support a staged approach, in which some applications are converted while others are not.

5. The interface must support a wide range of platforms and interconnectivity approaches. Internet support is crucial.

6. Each revitalized application should be in a position to potentially move to the next level of redeployment, namely client/server programming.

As you can see, this is a rather strict set of goals. In fact, some seem diametrically opposed. For example, how do you make a program ready for the move to client/server while at the same time making minimal changes to it? Well, let's take a look at how revitalization is implemented.

IMPLEMENTING REVITALIZATION

The primary idea behind the revitalization process is that it will not materially affect the existing high-level language (HLL) program. That's easy to say, but not so easy to do. Traditionally, this has been done by intercepting the 5250 data stream after it has been sent to the user (the screen-scraper concept). However, there are significant drawbacks to this approach, primarily that not all the necessary information is actually being sent.

Remember that the display file acts as an intermediary between the HLL program and the user display, merging constant data, variable data, and conditioning information. The 5250 data stream is only the final product of that process. Lots of data that the user does not see is actually kept in the display file, and the screen-scraping approach can get at that information only by performing additional, "hidden" I/O operations.

For example, if a number of errors are received in an error-message subfile, the only way that information can be gathered by a screen-scraper is to simulate placing the cursor on the message subfile and pressing the scroll key until all the messages have been read. This is a simple but effective example of why intercepting the information after it has been converted to 5250 data is simply not sufficient.

Instead, revitalization intercepts the data *before* it is sent to the display file. In chapter 6, you will see a simple but powerful API that I developed for this purpose. To use it, the application program is modified so that wherever it originally performed an I/O operation to the display file (such as WRITE or EXFMT), the API is called instead. The only information passed to the API is the information contained within the program itself, such as the name of the format and the operation to perform. This information is combined into a message that is sent to the display-file emulation object. A buffer is sent to the API containing only those fields that were originally sent to the display file. If this is an output-only operation, the program proceeds as if it had written to the display file.

If, on the other hand, a response is required, the API returns data into the same fields that the display file would have. In addition, a means of determining the function key pressed is included to make it easy for a programmer to write the API call. More to the point, the API call can be generated quite easily by another program. Therefore, the API meets the design criteria of requirements 1 and 2 introduced in the previous section.

The next point is that the design centers on the display-file emulation object. This is truly an object; in fact, it is a Java object. Creating the display-file emulation object is quite simple. It is designed to be a JavaBean, which can be used by simply setting its attributes. No other Java programming is required. This emulation object can then be used to support both thick and thin clients.

For Internet access, the servlet/JSP architecture introduced in chapter 2 provides a fast, HTML-based browser interface. For more sophisticated graphical applications, such as those requiring integration with other desktop applications, the platform-independent graphical interface of Java, called Swing,[2] could be used instead. In either case, the display-file emulation object isolates the user interface from the HLL program. Any programming done on the user interface is completely independent of application programming done on the host, which satisfies the third design requirement.

---

2 For more information on Swing, visit The Swing Connection on the Javasoft Web site, at *http://java.sun.com/products/jfc/tsc/index.html*.

The fact that the existing programs stay almost untouched meets requirement 4. In fact, requirement 4 eliminates any approach that uses rewriting as an option.

By using Java solutions for new technology, the design is sure to have the most flexibility available today. JavaServer Pages are a completely thin-client approach, using pure HTML as the communication medium, while the Swing GUI runs on any platform that supports a Java Virtual Machine, including UNIX, Linux, Macintosh, Windows, NextStep, and nearly any other workstation you can name. This far surpasses any other solution, and since it is non-proprietary (the code that comes with this book is free for your use), you are not tied to a strategy based on what a third-party vendor deems important—something no screen-scraping approach can guarantee.

Finally, the use of the display-file emulation object as an intermediate object means that the design truly separates the user interface and the business logic. Because of this, when you decide to later detach the application logic from the business logic (as you would if you chose to go to a client/server architecture), you can do so without changing your user interface at all. Your new application logic needs to talk to the display-file emulation object, which is perfectly serviceable until you have completely redesigned your application. If you then decide to redesign your user interface without using a display-file emulation object, you can do so without having to debug your application logic at the same time.

I hope I've shown you why revitalization is an excellent strategy for moving legacy systems into a distributed programming environment. The following chapters show you just how easy it is to do.

Part 2

IMPLEMENTING REVITALIZATION

If you've read this far, you're probably more than ready to get started with the actual implementation process—and if you've skipped directly here, that speaks for itself. So, let's begin. First, take a look at the diagram in Figure P2.1. This is an important diagram, and you'll be referring to it throughout this part of the book. As you can see, there are three distinct layers: the AS/400 RPG portion, the server/client classes, and the UI severs. The diagram is drawn that way for a reason: each level in the diagram has its own chapters. Chapters 5 and 6 outline the top layer, the green-screen interface. No Java is needed here, just a strong understanding of RPG and how display-file programs work, along with a working knowledge of data queues. Chapters 7 through 9 detail the Java server/client middleware that emulates an AS/400 display file. Finally, chapters 10 and 11 show how to build a Swing user interface and a browser user interface, respectively.

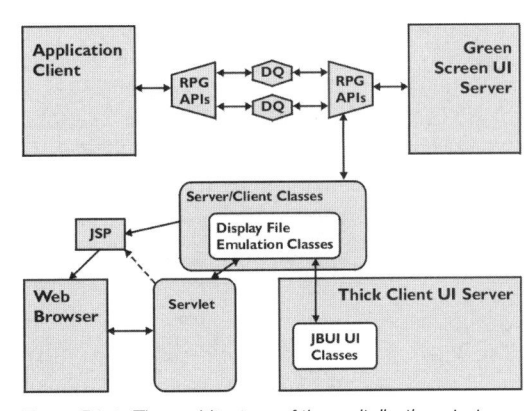

Figure P2.1: The architecture of the revitalization strategy.

PART 2: IMPLEMENTING REVITALIZATION

The chapters in this part of the book are designed to allow a fast path to implementation. Each section in these chapters is marked by an icon:

- The lightning bolt (𝒩) denotes a topic on the fast path to that particular destination. You can apply the fast-path topics in chapters 6, 7, 8, and 11 in order to quickly put a browser interface on your programs.

- The plus sign (✦) identifies a topic about an additional feature not required for the browser client.

- The magnifying glass (⚲) indicates a topic that gives detailed information about the revitalization architecture.

- The rocket ship (🚀) denotes a topic that discusses future enhancements to the revitalization strategy.

Part 2 covers the following topics:

- Chapter 5 introduces ITMMNT1, a simple two-screen program that maintains an item master file. It has a prompt screen and a maintenance screen with a little bit of field validation logic. While ITMMNT1 is a very simple program, read through this chapter to make sure you have a good sense of how it works, since it is the basis for the other chapters in part 2.

- Chapter 6 coincides with the top layer of the diagram in Figure P2.1. In it, you'll convert the existing ITMMNT1 program into an application client. If you choose, you can also create a green-screen UI server, or you can go immediately to chapter 8 to create the display file object, which is used by the graphical UI servers. This chapter requires no knowledge of Java; all code is written in RPG, RPGLE, and CL.

- Chapter 7 is a small but very important chapter. The Data Conversion 400 package, com.pbd.pub.dc400, is the core of the rest of the system. Whenever data is sent between RPG and Java, it needs to move from EBCDIC to ASCII, and vice versa. While there are already routines written in the IBM Java Toolbox to support these conversions, they don't provide all the features that I want, so instead you'll examine my package to see how I've managed to encapsulate IBM's classes, simplifying them and at the same time making them more powerful.

- Chapter 8 discusses in detail how to create a display-file object. The display-file object is the critical common link between the RPG world of the application client and the Java world of the graphical UI servers. You only need to read the first section of this chapter to fast-path through to the UI servers, but if you want to understand the architectural underpinning of the entire revitalization strategy, you might want to take the time to read the rest.

- In chapter 9, you'll combine the classes in the previous two chapters, together with some additional IBM Toolbox classes, to create a generic server/client architecture that will act as a bridge between any application client and any UI server, using the display-file classes as the data model. You'll see how to first emulate the I/O proxy API architecture from chapter 6, and then encapsulate that into a simpler but still flexible interface.

- The Swing UI server discussed in chapter 10 takes advantage of packages I wrote. These packages make it easy to quickly build a simple, clean Swing user interface without requiring much Java knowledge beyond the basic syntax.

- Chapter 11 is probably the reason you bought this book. (Well, this chapter and the chapter on actually running servlets in part 3.) It briefly introduces JSP, servlets, and WebSphere,[1] and shows how they work together to provide an excellent vehicle for replacing the 5250 interface.

The first section is a review of the simple maintenance program that is the focus of this book. ITMMNT1 treads the fine line between being a barebones example of a useful program and being trivial (and it some places it crosses it), but by the time you're finished, I hope you'll see that the revitalization architecture has been designed in such a way that it will scale up to programs of any arbitrary length or complexity.

---

[1] This book attempts to be as nonspecific as possible when it comes to the Web server platform, but where forced to be specific, it uses IBM's WebSphere Application Server.

5

THE STARTING POINT

The beginning of your journey to e-deployment starts with a humble little maintenance application. It's pretty trivial, but adequate for our purposes. The program maintains a master file record, and uses a few other files for field validation. If you do something wrong when using the program, you get an error message. This chapter is broken down into the following sections (see "Building a Browser Interface" in part 2's introduction for an explanation of the symbols):

- "The Screens" introduces the ITMMNT1 application, reviewing the screens and how they are used.

- "The Database" examines the database in detail.

- "The Display File" examines the display file.

- "The RPG Program" reviews the RPG program.

- "The Issues" lists features that are not supported in the version of the revitalization API included with this book.

This chapter is short and to the point because it reflects ITMMNT1, which is meant to be a very concise example. In particular, this example doesn't handle subfiles or even display attributes. However, these topics are covered in later chapters.

THE SCREENS

This book is designed to provide real-world examples, not just a theoretical discussion. You'll be implementing a real program, ITMMNT1, which is a very simple two-screen maintenance program. You might recognize the screens from chapter 1.

ITMMNT1 maintains a file called ITEM. ITEM is a very simplified item master file, with only a few simple attributes: item number, item description, quantity onhand, inventory unit of measure, and sales unit of measure. The unit-of-measure (UOM) fields are edited against two files: a UOM master and a UOM cross-reference.

Figure 5.1 shows the first screen of the program. The first screen simply prompts for an item number. You can press F3 to end the program, or enter an item number and press Enter. If you enter a bad item number, an error message is displayed. If you enter a good item number, the next screen, shown in Figure 5.2, is displayed.

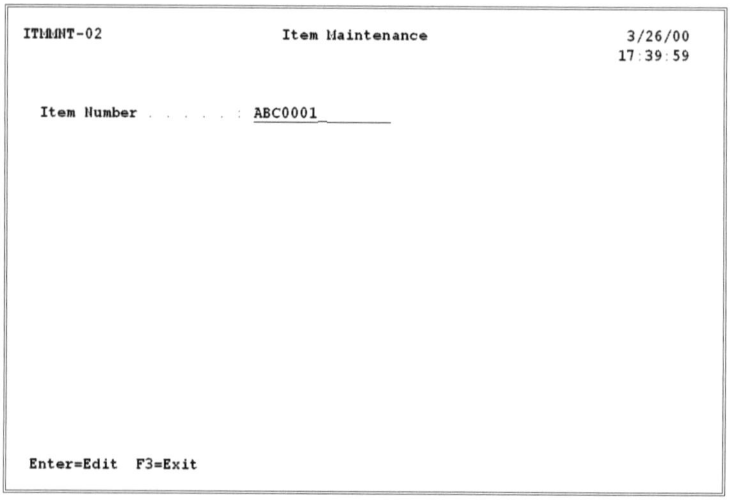

```
ITMMNT-02              Item Maintenance              3/26/00
                                                    17:39:59


      Item Number . . . . . : ABC0001












Enter=Edit   F3=Exit
```

Figure 5.1: The prompt screen for the ITMMNT1 program.

Panel 2 shows the item number of the item you are maintaining, and presents the various item master fields for maintenance. Pressing F3 exits the program, pressing F12 takes you back to the first panel, and pressing Enter edits the fields.

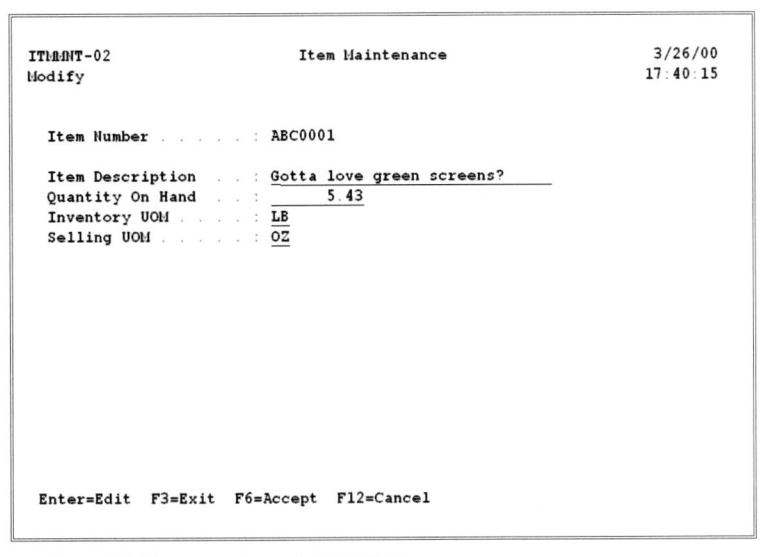

```
ITMMNT-02               Item Maintenance                    3/26/00
Modify                                                     17:40:15

   Item Number . . . . . : ABC0001
   Item Description  . . : Gotta love green screens?
   Quantity On Hand  . . :      5.43
   Inventory UOM . . . . : LB
   Selling UOM . . . . . : OZ




   Enter=Edit   F3=Exit   F6=Accept   F12=Cancel
```

Figure 5.2: The second panel of ITMMNT1.

If a field is in error, a message is displayed, as shown in Figure 5.3. If you press F6 and no errors are found, the record is updated and you are returned to the first panel. (If an error is found, you'll see the display shown in Figure 5.3, and the record will not be edited.)

```
ITMMNT-02               Item Maintenance                    3/26/00
Modify                                                     17:40:28

   Item Number . . . . . : ABC0001
   Item Description  . . : _____
   Quantity On Hand  . . :      5.43
   Inventory UOM . . . . : LB
   Selling UOM . . . . . : OZ



   ERROR: Description cannot be blank.



   Enter=Edit   F3=Exit   F6=Accept   F12=Cancel
```

Figure 5.3: The second screen, with an error message.

PART 2: IMPLEMENTING REVITALIZATION

ITMMNT1 is quite primitive to limit the number of design issues that must be dealt with. For example, this program uses no subfiles; the issues there are almost enough for a book by themselves. A slightly more archaic design decision is the lack of display attributes. Again, this is to limit the design issues.

This is not to imply that the revitalization architecture will not support subfiles or display attributes. In fact, in the **JdspfDisplayFile** display-file object in chapter 10, you'll see that the infrastructure is in place to support both subfiles and display attributes.

THE DATABASE

The entity relationships for the database used in the ITMMNT1 application are shown in Figure 5.4.

Listings 5.1, 5.2, and 5.3 show the item master file, the unit-of-measure master file, and the unit-of-measure cross-reference file, respectively. Listing 5.4 shows the contents of the UXRF file.

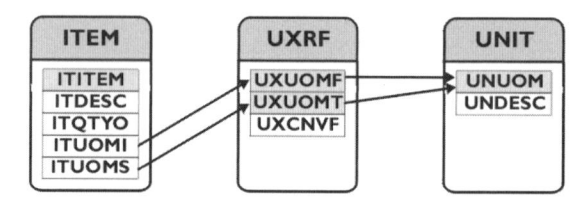

Figure 5.4: The entity relationships for the files in the ITMMNT1 example.

```
Physical File ITEM
A            R ITEMR
A              ITITEM     15           TEXT('Item Number')
A              ITDESC     30           TEXT('Item Description')
A              ITQTYO     9S 2         TEXT('Quantity Onhand')
A              ITUOMI     2            TEXT('Inventory UOM')
A              ITUOMS     2            TEXT('Selling UOM')
Logical File ITEML1
A            R ITEMR                   PFILE(ITEM)
A            K ITITEM
```

Listing 5.1: The item master file ITEM and its logical, ITEML1.

```
Physical File UNIT
A            R UNITR
A              UNUOM      2            TEXT('Unit of Measure')
A              UNDESC     30           TEXT('Description')
Logical File UNITL1
A            R UNITR                   PFILE(UNIT)
A            K UNUOM
```

Listing 5.2: The unit of measure master file UNIT and its logical, UNITL1.

```
Physical File ITEM
    A           R UXRFR
    A             UXUOMF      2           TEXT('From UOM')
    A             UXUOMT      2           TEXT('To UOM')
    A             UXCNVF     15P 5        TEXT('Conversion Factor')

Logical File ITEML1
    A           R UXRFR                   PFILE(UXRF)
    A           K UXUOMF
    A           K UXUOMT
```

Listing 5.3: *The unit of measure cross-reference file UXRF and its logical, UXRFL1.*

UXUOMF	UXUOMT	UXCNVF
GL	OZ	128.00000
GL	QT	4.00000
LB	OZ	16.00000
QT	OZ	32.00000
TN	LB	2,000.00000

Listing 5.4: *The contents of the UXRF file, as shipped.*

As you can see from the source listings, I prefer nonkeyed physical files. This is a habit from long days of debugging. It's much easier to copy a file off for save purposes if you don't have to keep the access path. The listings should give you a good feel for the contents of the files. The only exception might be the unit-of-measure cross-reference filE, UXRF. Listing 5.4 shows an SQL display of the contents of UXRF, as shipped. Only one record is used for each relationship, so there is a record to convert from gallons to ounces, but not vice versa. It's not a big deal, but it will explain the editing in the ITMMNT1 program later in this chapter.

THE DISPLAY FILE

The display file, ITMMNT1D, is quite simple. The section shown in Listing 5.5 simply defines the display file to be the typical 24-by-80 green screen.

```
    A                                     DSPSIZ(24 80 *DS3)
```

Listing 5.5: *The file-level definitions.*

The PROMPT record, shown in Listing 5.6, displays the first screen. It defines the function key F3, puts some heading information on the screen, and defines the input file X1ITEM. There is also an output field, X1ERR, where error messages are returned. To keep this example simple, the program does not use a message subfile.

```
A          R PROMPT
A                                          CA03
A                                       1  3'ITMMNT1-01'
A                                          COLOR(BLU)
A                                       1 32'Item Maintenance'
A                                          COLOR(WHT)
A                                       1 69DATE
A                                          EDTCDE(Y)
A                                          COLOR(BLU)
A                                       2 69TIME
A                                          COLOR(BLU)
A                                       5  5'Item Number . . . . . :'
A            X1ITEM      15A  B  5 29
A            X1ERR       70   0 16  5COLOR(RED)
A                                      23  4'Enter=Edit   F3=Exit'
A                                          COLOR(BLU)
```

Listing 5.6: Defining the first record, PROMPT.

The second screen, MAINT, is shown in Listing 5.7. It is used for the actual maintenance. It, too, uses an error field, in this case X2ERR, to return error messages to the user. It also has two other output fields: X2MODE and X2ITEM. X2MODE currently only displays the value *Modify* because that's the only mode supported by ITMMNT1. X2ITEM is the item number keyed on the previous screen. ITMMNT1 does not allow changing the key of an item master record.

```
A          R MAINT
A                                          CA03
A                                          CF06
A                                          CA12
A                                       1  3'ITMMNT1-02'
A                                          COLOR(BLU)
A                                       1 32'Item Maintenance'
A                                          COLOR(WHT)
A                                       1 69DATE
A                                          EDTCDE(Y)
A                                          COLOR(BLU)
A            X2MODE      10A   0  2  3COLOR(WHT)
A                                       2 69TIME
A                                          COLOR(BLU)
```

Listing 5.7: Defining the second record, MAINT (part 1 of 2).

CHAPTER 5: THE STARTING POINT

```
A                                 5  5'Item Number . . . . . :'
A              X2ITEM     15A  O  5 29
A                                 7  5'Item Description . . :'
A              X2DESC     30A  B  7 29
A                                 8  5'Quantity On Hand . . :'
A              X2QTYO      9Y 2B  8 29EDTWRD('        . ')
A                                 9  5'Inventory UOM . . . . :'
A              X2UOMI      2A  B  9 29
A                                10  5'Selling UOM . . . . . :'
A              X2UOMS      2A  B 10 29
A              X2ERR       70  O 16  5COLOR(RED)
A                                23  4'Enter=Edit   F3=Exit   F6=Accept
A    F1-
A                                    2=Cancel'
A                                    COLOR(BLU)
```

Listing 5.7: *Defining the second record, MAINT (part 2 of 2).*

Note that the fields are named differently from one screen to the next. This will be important later, when the screen are redefined as data structures. If the screens in your own application do use the same field names from one screen to the next, they will require a little additional work. You'll learn more about this in chapter 7.

THE RPG PROGRAM

ITMMNT1 is not meant to be a paragon of programming excellence. In order to make it fairly easy to code and understand, I took a basic architecture that I helped develop in the early 1990s, pared it down ruthlessly, and used it to create the barest minimum of a maintenance program. Since it's pretty straightforward, let's move right to it.

The file definitions, shown in Listing 5.8, are as follows:

- The display file, ITMMNT1D, as a combined full-procedural file.
- The maintained file, ITEML1, as an update full-procedural file.
- The two validation files as input full-procedural files.

```
FITMMNT1DCF  E                    WORKSTN
FITEML1   UF E             K      DISK
FUNITL1   IF E             K      DISK
FUXRFL1   IF E             K      DISK
     *
```

Listing 5.8: *The file definitions for ITMMNT1.*

51

Listing 5.9 shows the error messages. Thanks to the simplicity of the program, the compile-time array defining an array message is followed directly by the constants used to access it. For example, XCEDB is the constant for the "description blank" error message. I'm a firm believer in using named constants as often as possible rather than literals because it's a lot easier to maintain a list of named constants than it is to search through a program and fix all the instances of a literal.

```
E                              XEERRM   1   6 30
*
I           1                     C           XCENF
I           2                     C           XCEDB
I           3                     C           XCEQN
I           4                     C           XCEUIN
I           5                     C           XCEUSN
I           6                     C           XCEUNX
*
```

Listing 5.9: Defining a compile-time array of error messages, and the constants to access the array.

The primary processing loop is shown in Listing 5.10. As I mentioned earlier, this architecture was originally developed a decade or so ago. Back then, I worked for System Software Associates, where I had the good fortune to work with a couple of really talented programmers, Barry Hartman and Gary Drake. This was a time of tremendous growth at SSA, both in personnel and in the size of the product line, and we were the keepers of the architecture. While musing over the numerous programming styles that had proliferated throughout BPCS, we decided to develop a standard methodology for developing screen programs. Basically, we controlled the flow of the program with two state variables, one that identified which screen we were on and one that determined the function to perform for that screen, such as edit or load (for a subfile).

```
C                          MOVEL'Modify'   X2MODE
*
C                          MOVE 'SCR1'     XWSCR   4
C           XWSCR          DOUEQ'*END'
C           XWSCR          CASEQ'SCR1'     SCR1
C           XWSCR          CASEQ'SCR2'     SCR2
C                          ENDCS
C                          ENDDO
C*
C                          MOVE *ON        *INLR
C                          RETRN
C*
```

Listing 5.10: The primary processing loop of the program.

ITMMNT1 is very simple, so I didn't need to incorporate the entire architecture. Instead, a simple field called XWSCR is used to move from screen to screen. The indicated screen is displayed, and if a user action requires the program to display a different screen, the processing routine changes the XWSCR variables. Putting *END in XWSCR ends the program. There's nothing fancy here, but it works quite well. You can add any number of screens by simply expanding the CASE construct.

One very significant point to remember here is that the architecture of the program is not important. The revitalization architecture is designed to allow a program to be modified down at the op code level; that is, there are very simple rules for replacing an op code in the program with a different op code. The rest of the processing logic has absolutely no bearing on how the program is modified. So, while I am partial to the way this program is coded, that by no means implies that revitalization only works on programs coded exactly this way. Revitalization works on *any* program!

The processing loop for the first screen, shown in Listing 5.11, is very simple. If the user presses F3, the program ends by setting XWSCR to *END. Otherwise, the program chains to the item master file to see if the record exists. If the item is not found, the program outputs an error message, and since it doesn't change XWSCR, the prompt screen is redisplayed. If the record is found, the data fields are moved into the I/O fields for screen 2, and XWSCR is updated to process screen 2. As you can see, there's no logic for help text, prompting, or any other "advanced" features. It's a very simple display.

```
C           SCR1      BEGSR
C                     EXFMTPROMPT
C           *INKC     IFEQ *ON
C                     MOVE '*END'    XWSCR
C                     ELSE
C                     EXSR GETITM
C                     ENDIF
C                     ENDSR
C*
C           GETITM    BEGSR
C           X1ITEM    CHAINITEML1             90
C           *IN90     IFEQ *ON
C                     MOVELXEERRM,1  X1ERR
C                     ELSE
C                     MOVE *BLANKS   X1ERR
C                     MOVE ITITEM    X2ITEM
C                     MOVE ITDESC    X2DESC
C                     MOVE ITQTYO    X2QTYO
C                     MOVE ITUOMI    X2UOMI
```

Listing 5.11: The processing routines for the PROMPT panel (part 1 of 2).

```
C                         MOVE  ITUOMS     X2UOMS
C                         MOVE  'SCR2'     XWSCR
C                         ENDIF
C                         ENDSR
C*
```

Listing 5.11: The processing routines for the PROMPT panel (part 2 of 2).

The maintenance panel shown in Listing 5.12 has enough logic in it to make it non-trivial. Several edits are made, including validation against other files. While this is not a very substantial program, this architecture could conceivably handle a number of real-world maintenance tasks. The same XWSCR field is used to determine the next screen, and if the user presses F3 or F12, the field is set appropriately. Otherwise, indicator *IN60 is used to indicate whether an error has occurred. If there is no error and the user presses F6, the UPDATE routine is called, and the program returns to the first panel.

```
C           SCR2      BEGSR
C                     EXFMTMAINT
C           *INKC     IFEQ  *ON
C                     MOVE  '*END'     XWSCR
C                     ELSE
C           *INKL     IFEQ  *ON
C                     MOVE  'SCR1'     XWSCR
C                     ELSE
C                     EXSR  PROCES
C                     ENDIF
C                     ENDIF
C                     ENDSR
C*
C           PROCES    BEGSR
C                     EXSR  EDIT
C           *IN60     IFEQ  *OFF
C           *INKF     ANDEQ *ON
C                     EXSR  UPDATE
C                     MOVE  'SCR1'     XWSCR
C                     ENDIF
C                     ENDSR
C*
C           EDIT      BEGSR
C                     MOVE  *OFF       *IN60
C                     MOVE  *BLANKS    X2ERR
C*
C           X2DESC    IFEQ  *BLANKS
C                     Z-ADDXCEDB       XWERR    30
C                     EXSR  ERROR
C                     GOTO  $EDIT
C                     ENDIF
```

Listing 5.12: All the processing for the maintenance panel (part 1 of 2).

```
C*
C           X2QTY0    IFLT *ZERO
C                     Z-ADDXCEQN     XWERR
C                     EXSR ERROR
C                     GOTO $EDIT
C                     ENDIF
C*
C           X2UOMI    SETLLUNITL1                   90
C           *IN90     IFEQ *OFF
C                     Z-ADDXCEUIN    XWERR
C                     EXSR ERROR
C                     GOTO $EDIT
C                     ENDIF
C*
C           X2UOMS    SETLLUNITL1                   90
C           *IN90     IFEQ *OFF
C                     Z-ADDXCEUSN    XWERR
C                     EXSR ERROR
C                     GOTO $EDIT
C                     ENDIF
C*
C           XKUX1     KLIST
C                     KFLD           X2UOMI
C                     KFLD           X2UOMS
C*
C           XKUX2     KLIST
C                     KFLD           X2UOMS
C                     KFLD           X2UOMI
C*
C           XKUX1     SETLLUXRFL1                   90
C   N90     XKUX2     SETLLUXRFL1                   90
C           *IN90     IFEQ *OFF
C                     Z-ADDXCEUNX    XWERR
C                     EXSR ERROR
C                     GOTO $EDIT
C                     ENDIF
C*
C           $EDIT     ENDSR
C*
C           ERROR     BEGSR
C                     MOVE *ON       *IN60
C                     Z-ADDXWERR     X         20
C           'ERROR: ' CAT  XEERRM,X  X2ERR
C                     ENDSR
C*
C           UPDATE    BEGSR
C                     MOVE X2ITEM    ITITEM
C                     MOVE X2DESC    ITDESC
C                     MOVE X2QTY0    ITQTY0
C                     MOVE X2UOMI    ITUOMI
C                     MOVE X2UOMS    ITUOMS
C                     UPDATITEMR
C                     ENDSR
```

Listing 5.12: All the processing for the maintenance panel (part 2 of 2).

You might notice a slightly strange bit of code (which even uses a left-handed indicator) near the end of the edit routine in Listing 5.12. Earlier in the chapter, I mentioned that there is only one record for each conversion factor. So, if you stock in pounds and sell in ounces, you'll find a record that converts from pounds to ounces with a conversion factor of 16. However, if you also stock in ounces and sell in pounds, you wouldn't find that record.

The code gets around this by first checking for a record with the stocking unit of measure in the FROM field and the selling UOM in the TO field. If there is no record, it reverses the order of the UOM fields and checks again. (Maybe I got a little carried away when I was writing this part of the program, but I didn't want it to be entirely trivial.)

Finally, Listing 5.13 shows the error messages contained in the array in Listing 5.2. Looking at the complete program, you can probably find a number of glaring omissions. For example, if the user presses F12 from the maintenance panel, the record is not released.

Feel free to add code as you see fit; this is simply meant to be an example program. In chapter 6, you'll see that no matter how complex the program is, breaking it apart is still very easy.

```
**
Item does not exist.
Description cannot be blank.
Quantity is negative.
Bad inventory UOM.
Bad selling UOM.
UOMs do not cross-reference.
```

Listing 5.13: The compile-time array containing the error messages.

THE ISSUES

As mentioned at the beginning of this chapter, ITMMNT1 is not meant to win any programming achievement awards. It's about two steps away from a "Hello World" program, but it is sufficient to show how the concept works. However, after reviewing the code, you might have some concerns that the code is too basic, and that while revitalization might work for this particular program, it might not be robust enough for a "real" application. The following sections review some of the apparent deficiencies in the program.

Display Attributes

There are no display attributes. I wish I could just wander off into a diatribe about "back when I started programming, we didn't *have* any display attributes! Nope, all we had was green screens! With green letters on 'em! You couldn't even see the letters, cuz they were green on a green screen!"

The truth is, though, that while display attributes aren't included in this code, the infrastructure is there. In order to support attributes, you would need to pass the indicators, and in reviewing the JSPAPI interface in chapter 6, you'll see that there is already an area set aside for the indicators. I am continuing to develop the software, and new versions will be available on the Web site for this book, *http://www.java400.net/edeployment*.

Subfiles

Similarly, subfiles are not included in this version of the software, but the infrastructure is in place to support them. In early design tests, a subfile mechanism was created for HTML that used a table and required only a few lines of JavaScript, so subfiles work conceptually in the browser interface. For the Swing interface, the **JbuiList** object is already designed to support multiple rows of data. Finally, the **JdspfDisplayFile** object is already designed to support a subfile record and a subfile control record, so it would not be much of a stretch to provide subfile capabilities. However, the code required to support subfiles would have made this book much too large. Look for an implementation of subfiles on the Web site.

Message Subfiles

The same issue of size applies to message subfiles, except that they can be handled a little more creatively, especially in the Swing interface. Figure 5.5 shows how the JBUI package is already set up to handle errors and error messages. JBUI supports both a PROTECT attribute and an ERROR attribute, and the dropdown list at the bottom

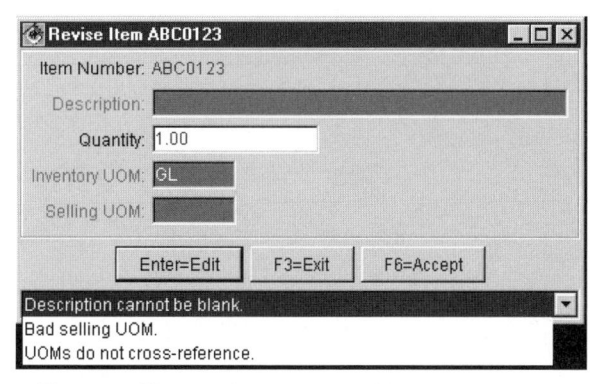

Figure 5.5: The error-handling capabilities already present in the JBUI package.

of the panel is an integral part of the **JbuiDisplay** object. Adding these attributes to the browser interface would be no problem.

Help Support

I feel at this point that AS/400 help text is not sufficient for the desktop or for the browser because users have come to expect hypertext documentation. I'm simply staying out of the help issue for now, but I'm carefully reviewing JavaHelp to see if it might be incorporated into future versions of the JBUI model.

General

Generally, the architecture of the software included in the book should be flexible and extensible enough to support most of what you'll need for the first pass of revitalization. Of course, the source code is included, so if you have some Java skills, you can add additional features yourself. Throughout this book, I have included insights into where those changes should be made. Otherwise, you can wait until new features are available on the Web site.

6

BREAKING APART THE MONOLITH

This chapter details the AS/400 side of the revitalization process. In it, you'll find a simple, step-by-step procedure for splitting apart the user interface and the application and business logic. You'll learn how to create an application client and a user interface server, and then examine in detail how each one works.

First, let's take another look at the revitalization diagram, this time concentrating on just the portion that has to do with the AS/400. Figure 6.1 shows the pieces used to split the green-screen user interface from the application and business logic.

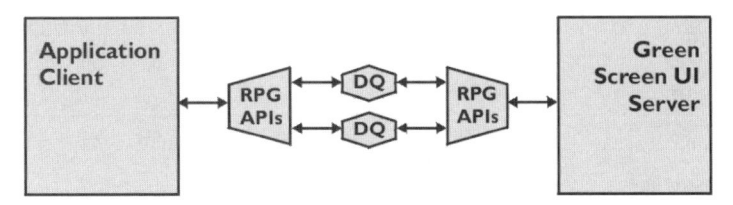

Figure 6.1: The AS/400 components of the revitalization process.

The left side of the figure shows the application client, which is basically the original application program with a few modifications to remove the screen I/O. The right side of the diagram is the green-screen UI server, which is a simple program whose sole function

59

is to execute the I/O requests from the application client. The central section consists of APIs that use data queues to provide the bridge between the two components. Figure 6.2 shows this in much greater detail.

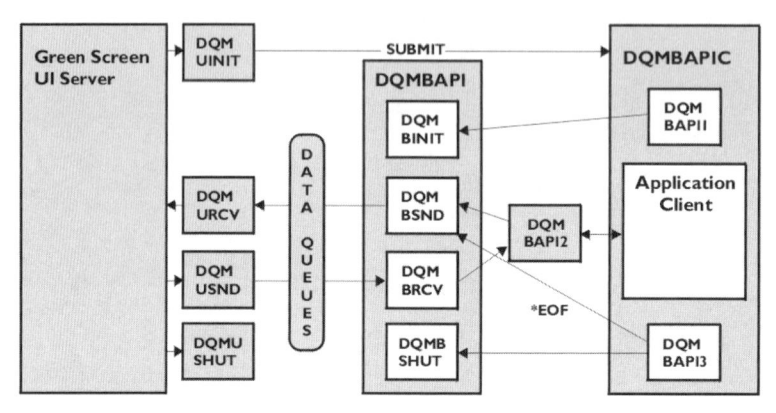

Figure 6.2: The interaction of the I/O proxy APIs and client APIs.

The APIs can be broken down into two categories: the I/O proxy APIs and the client APIs. The I/O proxy APIs emulate the I/O flow to and from the display file. There are basically two identical sets of APIs, one on the UI server side and the other on the application client side. However, in order to make it as easy as possible to transform a monolithic program into an application client, the client-side APIs are further wrapped into a set of client APIs. The contents of the individual APIs are described in Tables 6.1, 6.2, and 6.3.

Table 6.1: The Five UI-Server-Side I/O Proxy APIs and Their Uses

API Name	Description
DQMUINITC	Sets up the environment for distributed requests.
DQMUINIT	Creates the request data queue.
DQMURCV	Receives a request from the application client.
DQMUSND	Sends a response back to the application client.
DQMUSHUT	Deletes the request data queue.

Table 6.2: The Four Application-Client-Side I/O Proxy APIs and Their Uses

API Name	Description
DQMBINIT	Creates the response data queue.
DQMBRCV	Receives a response back from the UI server.
DQMBSND	Sends a request to the UI server.
DQMBSHUT	Deletes the response data queue.

Table 6.3: The Five Client APIs and Their Uses

API Name	Description
DQMBAPIC	Encapsulates the application client.
DQMBAPI	Encapsulates the client APIs.
DQMBAPI1	Performs application client initialization.
DQMBAPI2	Sends requests and receives responses.
DQMBAPI3	Shuts down the application client.

The remainder of this chapter is broken down as follows:

- "The Application Client" is a quick overview of how to convert a traditional monolithic program into an application client. This section is all you need if you won't be supporting a green-screen interface.

- "The Green-Screen UI Server" demonstrates the steps necessary to build a green-screen UI server. You need this section if you want to provide green-screen support, so your users can move gradually to a graphical user interface.

- "The JSPAPI Library: Client APIs" takes a close look at the APIs that are called by the application client.

- "The JSPAPI Library: I/O Proxy APIs" examines the I/O proxy APIs that perform the actual data movement between the two programs.

THE APPLICATION CLIENT

This section shows you the steps necessary to convert your existing application. You'll see how to change ITMMNT1 from a traditional monolithic application into an application client—by simply removing three lines of code and adding about a dozen!

Before starting the conversion, the display file must be processed. The fundamental architecture of the revitalization strategy requires that each record format in a display file be treated as a separate message. The easiest way to do this is to create an external data structure for each message. You'll need to keep track of the names of each data structure, and preferably associate them somehow with the original display file. In this book, I assume that the RPG program and the display file both have eight-character (or shorter) names. This makes it easy to name the revitalization components by appending a simple suffix on each name, as shown in Table 6.4.

Table 6.4: Naming Convention for Programs and Data Structures in the Revitalization Process

Original Display File	dddddddd
Record 1 Data Structure:	ddddddddR1
Record 2 Data Structure:	ddddddddR2
(...)	(...)
Original RPG program:	rrrrrrrr
Application Client:	rrrrrrrrAC
Green Screen UI Server:	rrrrrrrrUI

Refer to "The RPG Program" in chapter 5 to see the original listing being converted. In this case, you simply copy the program from ITMMNT1 to ITMMNT1AC, following the naming conventions outlined in Table 6.4, then make the changes shown in Listings 6.1 through 6.5.

```
External Data Structure ITMMNT1DR1
     A          R PROMPT
     A            X1ITEM        15
     A            X1ERR         70
```

Listing 6.1: The data structure that replaces the PROMPT record.

Chapter 6: Breaking Apart the Monolith

```
External Data Structure ITMMNT1DR2
     A          R MAINT
     A            X2MODE      10
     A            X2ITEM      15
     A            X2DESC      30
     A            X2QTYO       9S 2
     A            X2UOMI       2
     A            X2UOMS       2
     A            X2ERR       70
```

Listing 6.2: The data structure that replaces the MAINT record.

```
RV01dF**ITMMNT1DCF   E                    WORKSTN
     FITEML1   UF  E            K         DISK
     FUNITL1   IF  E            K         DISK
     FUXRFL1   IF  E            K         DISK
     *
     E                    XEERRM  1     6 30
     *
RV01aIRECDS1       E DSITMMNT1DR1             2000
RV01aIRECDS2       E DSITMMNT1DR2             2000
     I               1                   C    XCENF
     I               2                   C    XCEDB
     I               3                   C    XCEQN
     I               4                   C    XCEUIN
     I               5                   C    XCEUSN
     I               6                   C    XCEUNX
```

Listing 6.3: How the display file is replaced with data structures.

```
     C          SCR1       BEGSR
RV01dC*                    EXFMTPROMPT
RV01aC                     CALL 'DQMBAPI2'
RV01aC                     PARM 'PROMPT'    'DQMSCR  8
RV01aC                     PARM 'EXFMT'      DQMOPC  5
RV01aC                     PARM              RECDS1
RV01aC     *INKC           PARM 'C'          DQMI01  1
     C     *INKC           IFEQ *ON
     C                     MOVE '*END'       XWSCR
     C                     ELSE
     C                     EXSR GETITM
     C                     ENDIF
     C                     ENDSR
```

Listing 6.4: How to replace the first EXFMT op code with a call to the DQMAPI2 client API.

63

```
C             SCR2      BEGSR
RV01dC*                 EXFMTMAINT
RV01aC                  CALL 'DQMBAPI2'
RV01aC                  PARM 'MAINT'    'DQMSCR 8
RV01aC                  PARM 'EXFMT'    DQMOPC  5
RV01aC                  PARM            RECDS2
RV01aC        *INKC     PARM 'C'        DQMI01  1
RV01aC        *INKF     PARM 'F'        DQMI02  1
RV01aC        *INKL     PARM 'L'        DQMI03  1
C             *INKC     IFEQ *ON
C                       MOVE '*END'     XWSCR
C                       ELSE
C             *INKL     IFEQ *ON
C                       MOVE 'SCR1'     XWSCR
C                       ELSE
C                       EXSR PROCES
C                       ENDIF
C                       ENDIF
C                       ENDSR
```

Listing 6.5: How to replace the other EXFMT.

In keeping with the fast-path nature of this section, here are the three steps required to convert a monolithic RPG program into an application client:

1. Create the data structure for each record format. This is very straightforward. For each record, create a physical file with fields having the same names and sizes as the fields in the corresponding record. Listings 6.1 and 6.2 show the DDS source for the two data structures used to define the messages for the ITMMNT1D display file.

2. Delete the line defining the display file and add a line for each of the record-format data structures. If the same name exists in more than one record, you'll have to have rename specifications here. In my example, I changed the name of the data structure to RECDSX, where *x* matches the last character in the data structure name. Listing 6.3 shows the changes required in ITMMNT1AC.

3. Replace each I/O operation with a call to DQMAPI2, as shown in Listings 6.4 and 6.5. This is a relatively straightforward replacement, with the exception of the command keys. Take a closer look at the last three lines added in Listing 6.5:

```
                RV01aC          *INKC       PARM 'C'        DQMI01  1
                RV01aC          *INKF       PARM 'F'        DQMI02  1
                RV01aC          *INKL       PARM 'L'        DQMI03  1
```

You must specify one line for each command key defined for the record format in the original display file. You can specify up to 24 different command keys. Factor 1 contains the indicator to turn on, while factor 2 identifies the key to test for. Factor 2 uses the same naming convention as the *INK*x* command keys; for example, 'A' is F1, 'J' is F10, and 'Y' is F24. If your display file sets on a regular indicator instead of a command-key indicator, put that indicator in factor 1 instead.

Also, note that if you had to rename a field in this data structure in step 2, you must move the original field into the renamed field prior to the call, and then move the renamed field back into the original field immediately after the call.

That's it! With those three simple steps, your monolithic program is now an application client, ready to talk to any type of UI server. For a green-screen user interface, continue with the next section. Otherwise, you can move straight on to chapter 7 and create the display file object required to support the graphical UI servers.

The Green-Screen UI Server

A green-screen UI server is used in conjunction with the application client to present the "old" interface to the user. It acts exactly like the original screen, so your users won't need any retraining. Listings 6.6 through 6.10 show how to create a green-screen interface. If you understand how this program works, you will be able to use it as a skeleton to support any other program. You only need to insert the appropriate file specification and data structures, and then change the UIPROC subroutine to support the I/O commands used in the application client.

```
          FITMMNT1DCF  E                        WORKSTN
          E                     DQMDTA     10200
          IREC1DS      E DSITMMNT1DR1
          IREC2DS      E DSITMMNT1DR2
          IDQMMSG      E DS
          I                 'ITMMNT1AC '           C         XCACPN
```

Listing 6.6: File and data structure statements for the program, and a constant that identifies the application client.

```
C                   EXSR UIINIT
C                   EXSR UIPROC
C                   EXSR UISHUT
C                   MOVE *ON       *INLR
C*
```

Listing 6.7: The primary processing loop. This doesn't change.

```
C         UIINIT    BEGSR
C                   MOVE XCACPN    DQMBNM
C                   CALL 'DQMUINIT'
C                   PARM           DQMMSG
C                   ENDSR
C*
```

Listing 6.8: The initialization routine. This doesn't change, either.

```
C         UIPROC    BEGSR
C                   CALL 'DQMURCV'
C                   PARM           DQMMSG
C         DQMOPC    DOWNE'*EOF '
C                   EXSR UIIO
C         RSPREQ    IFEQ *ON
C                   CALL 'DQMUSND'
C                   PARM           DQMMSG
C                   ENDIF
C                   CALL 'DQMURCV'
C                   PARM           DQMMSG
C                   ENDDO
C                   ENDSR
C*
```

Listing 6.9: The message processing routine, which also doesn't change.

```
C         UIIO      BEGSR
C                   MOVE *OFF      RSPREQ 1
C                   SELEC
C*
C         DQMSCR    WHEQ 'PROMPT'
C         DQMOPC    ANDEQ'EXFMT'
C                   MOVEADQMDTA    REC1DS
C                   EXFMTPROMPT
C                   MOVEAREC1DS    DQMDTA
```

Listing 6.10: The I/O processing routine, which is the only other thing that changes (part 1 of 2).

```
C                         MOVE '00'       DQMRTC
C         KC              MOVE '03'       DQMRTC
C                         MOVE *ON        RSPREQ
C*
C         DQMSCR          WHEQ 'MAINT'
C         DQMOPC          ANDEQ'EXFMT'
C                         MOVEADQMDTA     REC2DS
C                         EXFMTMAINT
C                         MOVEAREC2DS     DQMDTA
C                         MOVE '00'       DQMRTC
C         KC              MOVE '03'       DQMRTC
C         KF              MOVE '06'       DQMRTC
C         KL              MOVE '12'       DQMRTC
C                         MOVE *ON        RSPREQ
C*
C                         ENDSL
C                         ENDSR
C*
```

Listing 6.10: The I/O processing routine, which is the only other thing that changes (part 2 of 2).

```
C         UISHUT          BEGSR
C                         CALL 'DQMUSHUT'
C                         PARM            DQMMSG
C                         ENDSR
```

Listing 6.11: The shutdown routine. This doesn't change.

A quick review of the listings shows six basic parts:

1. Listing 6.6 contains definitions. Here, you insert the file specification for the display file from the original monolithic program. Next, you add the data structures for each of the record formats that were built when you created the application client. You also need to add the DQMMSG structure, which is used to communicate with the I/O proxy APIs. Finally, add a line defining the name of the application client. This is the binding between the UI server and the application client.

2. Listing 6.7 is the main processing loop. It performs initialization, processing, and shutdown, then turns on *INLR and ends the program.

3. Listing 6.8 is the initialization. Here, you call DQMUINIT, which in the current software submits the application client and establishes a connection with it.

4. Listing 6.9 shows the message-processing loop. Messages are received via DQMURCV until the end-of-file *EOF message is received. The requested operation is performed by UIIO and, if required, a response is sent back via DQMUSND.

5. Listing 6.10 is the bulk of the program, and is the part that changes for each different application. The concept is to process each I/O request individually. This is best done via a SELEC/WH*xx* construct. You'll need to create one section of code for each operation, but the code is essentially the same. Here's the pseudocode:

```
Move message data to record data structure
Execute I/O operation
Move data from record data structure to message
Set appropriate response code based on function key
Set "response required" flag on
```

The last three steps are necessary only for operations that require a response. These are input or combined operations such as EXFMT, READC, or CHAIN. This is an important binding point between the application client and the UI server; if a response is expected, it is mandatory, while if it is not expected, it is prohibited. Breaking this protocol will cause the application client to fail.

DQMSCR contains the name of the record to use, and DQMOPC contains the operation to perform. The response code is based on the two-digit number of the function key pressed. For example, *INKC indicates function key 3, so 03 is sent back. If no function key is pressed, 00 is sent back to denote Enter.

6. In Listing 6.11, the shutdown routine simply calls DQMUSHUT to close the connection. This shuts down the application client.

That's all there is to the green-screen UI server. Since it directly mirrors the original monolithic program's I/O instructions, the green-screen UI server can use the I/O proxy APIs, which communicate at the I/O operation level. Since there is no application logic in the UI server, it would be very simple to develop a program generator. By reading a file containing the data structures, operations, and function keys for each record format, a program could easily build the green-screen UI server. I'll leave that as an exercise for you.

THE JSPAPI LIBRARY: CLIENT APIs

The concept behind the JSPAPI client APIs is taken directly from the techniques for designing object-oriented APIs in Java. The idea is to create as simple an interface for the application client as possible by encapsulating the I/O proxy APIs. You can do this by taking advantage of as many of the features of the AS/400 operating system and languages as you can.

Let's examine the goals of the interface:

- To be able to support any sort of I/O operations.
- To be as transparent to the application client as possible.

The I/O proxy APIs provide the solution for the first goal. They allow one program to act as a complete I/O proxy for another program. The problem is that they are very low-level, so embedding them in the application client takes quite a bit of coding. After converting a few programs using the I/O proxy APIs, I decided that they weren't sufficient to support the second goal. (To see how to use the I/O proxy APIs in an application environment, look at the code for the green-screen UI server in the previous section.)

The primary problem with using the I/O proxy APIs is that there are a lot of different programs to call to support the protocol. The single parameter for the APIs, the message block defined by the external data structure DQMMSG, must be stored in the application client because it keeps data from one call to the next. This single parameter requires data to be moved into and out of it prior to a call to an API. Finally, both initialization and shutdown code must be added. All in all, the modifications become very intrusive.

So, it's time sit back and decide the bare minimum of information that needs to be passed from the application to the interface and back. This, by the way, is the underlying philosophy used to develop a good object-oriented interface; I learned it only through months of trial and error, building the Java support classes. To be honest, my RPG programming skills wouldn't have gotten me past the I/O proxy APIs. It was the work in Java that gave me the insights necessary to build the client APIs. Here's a summary of my thought processes:

1. The only changes required to convert a monolithic program to an application client should be to replace the display file and I/O statements.

2. Removing the display file means losing the field definitions. They'll need to be replaced, and the best way to do that is through externally described data structures. So, the display file is replaced by externally described data structures.

3. The only data that should pass from the application client to the interface is the same data that would pass to the display file. So, each I/O statement should be replaced by a call to a program that receives only the record format name, the operation, and the data buffer. This same program should return data and the function key that was pressed.

4. Returning the function-key information requires setting the command-key indicators. This turned out to be the most difficult piece of the architecture, but I worked around it by taking advantage of RPG's ability to pass a variable number of parameters.

5. The message structure should not be part of the application client, for two reasons: first, it's another intrusion into the application code, and second, it's another point of binding. By making the underlying mechanics of the protocol as transparent as possible, you can make changes and add features much more easily. But to do that, you have to store the information somewhere. I accomplished this by taking advantage of OS/400's version of "terminate and stay resident," calling a program that doesn't set on *INLR. The message data is encapsulated in the program DQMBAPI, as you'll see a little later in this chapter.

6. Finally, initialization and shutdown code should not be added to the application client. I've spent the better part of the last ten years designing code that modified other code, and I've found that the hardest thing to do is to find the right place to put those routines. With RPG, it can be especially difficult. While the addition of the *INZSR routine has made it a little easier to add initialization code, it's still very difficult to unobtrusively add shutdown code. As far as I know, the only way is to find every RETRN op code, and then you still have the issue of locating the last C-spec in the mainline and checking whether *INLR (or *INRT) is on. In order to avoid that, I've encapsulated the call to the application client inside another API, whose purpose is to wrapper the application-client call between calls to the initialization and shutdown APIs.

The final design involves two wrapper APIs: DQMBAPI and DQMBAPIC. The first encapsulates all the complexity of the I/O proxy APIs within a simple op-code-driven interface, while the second encapsulates the application client within the message protocol. Figure 6.3 highlights the client APIs.

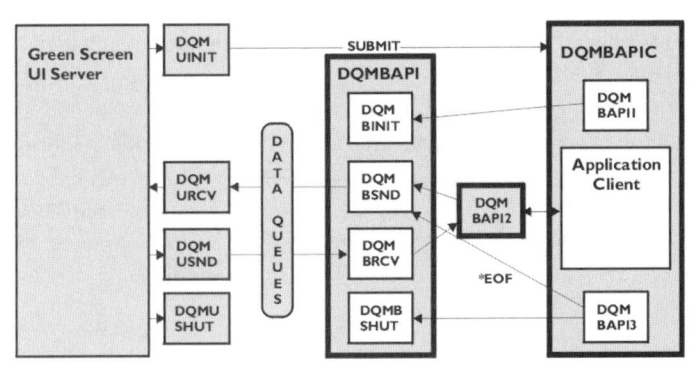

Figure 6.3: The client APIs in relation to the rest of the revitalization protocol.

From the figure, you can see how the application client is completely encapsulated inside the client APIs. As far as the application client is concerned, its only contact with the interface is through the DQMAPI2 program, which, as you'll see, is designed to emulate a standard RPG I/O operation. The life cycle of the application client is as follows:

1. The UI server calls I/O proxy API DQMUINIT, which establishes the session (identified by the session ID[1]) and creates the request data queue. DQMUNIT then submits the client API DQMAPIC, passing it the application client name and the session ID.

2. DQMBAPIC calls DQMBAPI1, which in turn calls DQMBAPI with an op code of 'I' for initialization. This creates a copy of DQMBAPI that will be resident for the rest of the session. DQMBAPI calls DQMBINIT, which creates the response data queue. This information is stored in the DQMMSG data structure.

3. DQMBAPIC next calls the application client. From this point on, the application is under the control of the application client, until the application client exits and returns control to DQMBAPIC.

4. Whenever the application client needs I/O services, it calls DQMBAPI2. If the operation originally did not expect a response (because it was an output-only operation, such as a write), DQMBAPI2 is called with only the record format name, the op code, and the data buffer. If a response is expected, such as for

---

1 For more on session IDs, refer to the section on I/O proxy APIs later in this chapter.

an EXFMT operation, one or more additional parameters are attached to check for function keys.

5. If the application client expects a response, DQMBAPI2 calls DQMBAPI with a 'G' (put-get) op code. DQMBAPI calls DQMBSND, which sends the data to the UI server. DQMBAPI then receives the response by calling DQMURCV (discussed later in this chapter). If no response is required, DQMBAPI2 calls DQMBAPI with a 'P' (put) op code, and DQMBAPI simply calls DQMBSND, then returns.

6. Once the user ends the program (say, by pressing F3 on a panel), the application program ends as normal. DQMBAPIC then calls DQMBAPI3, which sends a final *EOF message to the request data queue. This shuts down the UI server. DQMBAPI3 then calls DQMBAPI with an 'S' op code. DQMBAPI calls DQMBSHUT to close the session and then returns with *INLR on.

The following sections quickly run through each of the client APIs and show how they are used.

DQMBAPIC

DQMBAPIC is not called by application programs. A call to DQMBAPIC is submitted by DQMUINIT, the UI-server-initialization I/O proxy API. The call passes the application name and the session ID. These parameters are used to call DQMAPI1, which performs the initialization portion of the protocol. Next, the application client is called. Finally, DQMAPI3 is called, which performs the shutdown procedures. The code for DQMBAPIC is shown in Listing 6.12.

```
DQMBAPIC:   PGM        PARM(&DQMBNM &DQMSID)
            DCL        VAR(&DQMBNM) TYPE(*CHAR) LEN(10)
            DCL        VAR(&DQMSID) TYPE(*CHAR) LEN(10)

    /*      CALL       BREAKPOINT */
            CALL       PGM(DQMBAPI1) PARM(&DQMBNM &DQMSID)
            CALL       PGM(&DQMBNM)
            CALL       PGM(DQMBAPI3)

            ENDPGM
```

Listing 6.12: The code for DQMBAPIC.

DQMBAPI

DQMBAPI encapsulates the I/O proxy APIs. Each of the other DQMBAPIN programs eventually calls DQMBAPI, which in turn calls the DQMB*xxxx* programs of the I/O proxy APIs. DQMBAPI must be called in a specific sequence:

- Initialize.
- One or more Put and Put-then-Get commands.
- Shutdown.

Table 6.5 shows the parameters passed to DQMBAPI. The design for DQMBAPI, as shown in Listing 6.13, is to have all client APIs converge into a single program. This program encapsulates the session information in the DQMMSG data structure. To do that, it needs a single parameter list. While the program name and session ID are only used for the initial call, they stay on the list for the I/O calls. (I briefly toyed with the idea of overlapping the program name and session ID with the screen name and I/O operation, but ultimately decided that was inviting confusion.)

Table 6.5: The Parameters Passed to DQMBAPI. Only Non-blank Entries Are Passed

	Initialize	Put Only	Put, Then Get	Shutdown
Op Code	'I'	'P'	'G'	'S'
Program Name	Y	(n/u)	(n/u)	
Session ID	Y	(n/u)	(n/u)	
Screen Name		Y	Y	
I/O Operation		Y	Y	
Data Buffer		Y	Y	
Return Code			Y	

An important point of the design is that the return code from DQMBAPI for Put-then-Get operations is a two-character function-key identification. DQMBAPI2 is responsible for mapping that to RPG's unique concept of command-key indicators. The code for DQMBAPI is shown in Listing 6.13.

```
DDQMMSG          E DS
C*
C        *ENTRY      PLIST
C                    PARM                    XIOPCD         1
C                    PARM                    XIPGM         10
C                    PARM                    XISID         10
C                    PARM                    XISCR          8
C                    PARM                    XICMD          5
C                    PARM                    XIBUF       2000
C                    PARM                    XIRC           2
C*
C        XPMSG       PLIST
C                    PARM                    DQMMSG
C*
C        XIOPCD      CASEQ    'I'            INIT
C        XIOPCD      CASEQ    'P'            PUT
C        XIOPCD      CASEQ    'G'            PUTGET
C        XIOPCD      CASEQ    'S'            SHUT
C                    ENDCS
C*
C                    RETURN
C*
C        INIT        BEGSR
C                    MOVEL    XIPGM          DQMBNM
C                    MOVEL    XISID          DQMSID
C                    CALL     'DQMBINIT'     XPMSG
C                    ENDSR
C*
C        PUT         BEGSR
C                    MOVE     XISCR          DQMSCR
C                    MOVE     XICMD          DQMOPC
C                    MOVEL    XIBUF          DQMDTA
C                    CALL     'DQMBSND'      XPMSG
C                    ENDSR
C*
C        PUTGET      BEGSR
C                    EXSR     PUT
C                    CALL     'DQMBRCV'      XPMSG
C                    MOVEL    DQMDTA         XIBUF
C                    MOVE     DQMRTC         XIRC
C                    ENDSR
C*
C        SHUT        BEGSR
C                    MOVE     '*EOF '        DQMOPC
C                    CALL     'DQMBSND'      XPMSG
C                    CALL     'DQMBSHUT'     XPMSG
C                    MOVE     *ON            *INLR
C                    ENDSR
```

Listing 6.13: The code for DQMBAPI.

DQMBAPI1

DQMBAPI1 initializes the application client interface. It passes the session information (session ID and application client name) to DQMBAPI via the initialization op code, then returns. The code for DQMBAPI1 is shown in Listing 6.14.

```
 C           *ENTRY        PLIST
 C                         PARM                    XIPGM            10
 C                         PARM                    XISID            10
 C*
 C                         CALL      'DQMBAPI'
 C                         PARM      'I'           XOOPCD            1
 C                         PARM                    XIPGM
 C                         PARM                    XISID
 C*
 C                         MOVE      *ON           *INLR
```

Listing 6.14: The code for DQMBAPI1.

DQMBAPI2

DQMBAPI2 is the primary interface API for application clients. When a monolithic program is converted to an application client, the display file I/O operations are replaced with calls to DQMAPI2. For output-only operations such as WRITE, the parameter list is very simple, consisting of the record format name, the I/O operation to perform, and the data buffer. For operations that receive input, such as EXFMT, the design is a little more complex.

Let's take a look at one of the calls added earlier in this chapter. Listing 6.15 shows the code fragment that replaces the EXFMT op code to record format MAINT. As you can see, the original display file supports command keys 3, 6, and 12. Since there are no special indicators associated with these command keys, they will be returned as *INKC, *INKF, and *INKL, respectively.

```
From Display File ITMMNT1D

 A          R MAINT
 A*%%TS  SD  19991225  224656  SECJDP        REL-V4R2M0  5769-PW1
 A                                     CA03
 A                                     CF06
 A                                     CA12
```

Listing 6.15: A comparison of the original display-file command-key definitions and the modification made to the application client (part 1 of 2).

```
From Application Client ITMMNT1AC

RV01dC*                    EXFMTMAINT
RV01aC                     CALL  'DQMBAPI2'
RV01aC                     PARM  'MAINT'    'DQMSCR  8
RV01aC                     PARM  'EXFMT'    DQMOPC   5
RV01aC                     PARM             RECDS2
RV01aC           *INKC     PARM  'C'        DQMI01   1
RV01aC           *INKF     PARM  'F'        DQMI02   1
RV01aC           *INKL     PARM  'L'        DQMI03   1
```

Listing 6.15: A comparison of the original display-file command-key definitions and the modification made to the application client (part 2 of 2).

DQMAPI2 is designed to support this by allowing the addition of up to 24 different parameters for the various command keys. The program takes advantage of RPG's ability to support a variable number of parameters, as well as the PARM operation's ability to perform data movement both before and after a program call. For DQMBAPI2 command-key parameters (anything after the buffer), factor 2 is the "function key ID," and factor 1 is the indicator to be set on if the associated function key is pressed. The function key ID mirrors the RPG command definitions shown in Table 6.6 (for example, F10 is *INKJ).

Table 6.6: Function Key IDs and Their Associated Function Key Numbers

A	01	F	06	K	11	Q	16	V	21
B	02	G	07	L	12	R	17	W	22
C	03	H	08	M	13	S	18	X	23
D	04	I	09	N	14	T	19	Y	24
E	05	J	10	P	15	U	20		

By adding a parameter to the DQMBAPI2 call for each function key, the application client can test the resulting indicators just like in the original program. The code for DQMBAPI2 is shown in Listing 6.16.

```
D CFKEY            S              1    DIM(25) CTDATA PERRCD(24)
*
D                  SDS
D  XSPARM            *PARMS
*
C      *ENTRY      PLIST
C                  PARM                 XISCR          8
C                  PARM                 XICMD          5
C                  PARM                 XIBUF       2000
C                  PARM                 XIIN01         1
C                  PARM                 XIIN02         1
C                  PARM                 XIIN03         1
C                  PARM                 XIIN04         1
C                  PARM                 XIIN05         1
C                  PARM                 XIIN06         1
C                  PARM                 XIIN07         1
C                  PARM                 XIIN08         1
C                  PARM                 XIIN09         1
C                  PARM                 XIIN10         1
C                  PARM                 XIIN11         1
C                  PARM                 XIIN12         1
C                  PARM                 XIIN13         1
C                  PARM                 XIIN14         1
C                  PARM                 XIIN15         1
C                  PARM                 XIIN16         1
C                  PARM                 XIIN17         1
C                  PARM                 XIIN18         1
C                  PARM                 XIIN19         1
C                  PARM                 XIIN20         1
C                  PARM                 XIIN21         1
C                  PARM                 XIIN22         1
C                  PARM                 XIIN23         1
C                  PARM                 XIIN24         1
C*
C      XSPARM      IFEQ         3
C                  CALL         'DQMBAPI'
C                  PARM         'P'     XOOPCD         1
C                  PARM                 XOPGM         10
C                  PARM                 XOSID         10
C                  PARM                 XISCR          8
C                  PARM                 XICMD          5
C                  PARM                 XIBUF       2000
C*
C                  ELSE
C                  CALL         'DQMBAPI'
C                  PARM         'G'     XOOPCD         1
C                  PARM                 XOPGM         10
C                  PARM                 XOSID         10
C                  PARM                 XISCR          8
C                  PARM                 XICMD          5
C                  PARM                 XIBUF       2000
C                  PARM                 XORC           2
C                  EXSR         CheckRC
```

Listing 6.16: The code for DQMBAPI2 (part 1 of 5).

PART 2: IMPLEMENTING REVITALIZATION

```
C                       ENDIF
C*
C                       MOVE      *ON            *INLR
C*
C       CheckRC         BEGSR
C                       MOVE      XORC           XWRC          2 0
C                       ADD       1              XWRC
C                       MOVE      CFKEY(XWRC)    XWKEY         1
C       XIIN01          IFEQ      XWKEY
C                       MOVE      *ON            XIIN01
C                       ELSE
C                       MOVE      *OFF           XIIN01
C                       ENDIF
C       XSPARM          IFGT      04
C       XIIN02          IFEQ      XWKEY
C                       MOVE      *ON            XIIN02
C                       ELSE
C                       MOVE      *OFF           XIIN02
C                       ENDIF
C       XSPARM          IFGT      05
C       XIIN03          IFEQ      XWKEY
C                       MOVE      *ON            XIIN03
C                       ELSE
C                       MOVE      *OFF           XIIN03
C                       ENDIF
C       XSPARM          IFGT      06
C       XIIN04          IFEQ      XWKEY
C                       MOVE      *ON            XIIN04
C                       ELSE
C                       MOVE      *OFF           XIIN04
C                       ENDIF
C       XSPARM          IFGT      07
C       XIIN05          IFEQ      XWKEY
C                       MOVE      *ON            XIIN05
C                       ELSE
C                       MOVE      *OFF           XIIN05
C                       ENDIF
C       XSPARM          IFGT      08
C       XIIN06          IFEQ      XWKEY
C                       MOVE      *ON            XIIN06
C                       ELSE
C                       MOVE      *OFF           XIIN06
C                       ENDIF
C       XSPARM          IFGT      09
C       XIIN07          IFEQ      XWKEY
C                       MOVE      *ON            XIIN07
C                       ELSE
C                       MOVE      *OFF           XIIN07
C                       ENDIF
C       XSPARM          IFGT      10
C       XIIN08          IFEQ      XWKEY
C                       MOVE      *ON            XIIN08
C                       ELSE
```

Listing 6.16: The code for DQMBAPI2 (part 2 of 5).

```
C                       MOVE      *OFF      XIIN08
C                       ENDIF
C           XSPARM      IFGT      11
C           XIIN09      IFEQ      XWKEY
C                       MOVE      *ON       XIIN09
C                       ELSE
C                       MOVE      *OFF      XIIN09
C                       ENDIF
C           XSPARM      IFGT      12
C           XIIN10      IFEQ      XWKEY
C                       MOVE      *ON       XIIN10
C                       ELSE
C                       MOVE      *OFF      XIIN10
C                       ENDIF
C           XSPARM      IFGT      13
C           XIIN11      IFEQ      XWKEY
C                       MOVE      *ON       XIIN11
C                       ELSE
C                       MOVE      *OFF      XIIN11
C                       ENDIF
C           XSPARM      IFGT      14
C           XIIN12      IFEQ      XWKEY
C                       MOVE      *ON       XIIN12
C                       ELSE
C                       MOVE      *OFF      XIIN12
C                       ENDIF
C           XSPARM      IFGT      15
C           XIIN13      IFEQ      XWKEY
C                       MOVE      *ON       XIIN13
C                       ELSE
C                       MOVE      *OFF      XIIN13
C                       ENDIF
C           XSPARM      IFGT      16
C           XIIN14      IFEQ      XWKEY
C                       MOVE      *ON       XIIN14
C                       ELSE
C                       MOVE      *OFF      XIIN14
C                       ENDIF
C           XSPARM      IFGT      17
C           XIIN15      IFEQ      XWKEY
C                       MOVE      *ON       XIIN15
C                       ELSE
C                       MOVE      *OFF      XIIN15
C                       ENDIF
C           XSPARM      IFGT      18
C           XIIN16      IFEQ      XWKEY
C                       MOVE      *ON       XIIN16
C                       ELSE
C                       MOVE      *OFF      XIIN16
C                       ENDIF
C           XSPARM      IFGT      19
C           XIIN17      IFEQ      XWKEY
C                       MOVE      *ON       XIIN17
```

Listing 6.16: The code for DQMBAPI2 (part 3 of 5).

```
C                   ELSE
C                   MOVE      *OFF            XIIN17
C                   ENDIF
C         XSPARM    IFGT      20
C         XIIN18    IFEQ      XWKEY
C                   MOVE      *ON             XIIN18
C                   ELSE
C                   MOVE      *OFF            XIIN18
C                   ENDIF
C         XSPARM    IFGT      21
C         XIIN19    IFEQ      XWKEY
C                   MOVE      *ON             XIIN19
C                   ELSE
C                   MOVE      *OFF            XIIN19
C                   ENDIF
C         XSPARM    IFGT      22
C         XIIN20    IFEQ      XWKEY
C                   MOVE      *ON             XIIN20
C                   ELSE
C                   MOVE      *OFF            XIIN20
C                   ENDIF
C         XSPARM    IFGT      23
C         XIIN21    IFEQ      XWKEY
C                   MOVE      *ON             XIIN21
C                   ELSE
C                   MOVE      *OFF            XIIN21
C                   ENDIF
C         XSPARM    IFGT      24
C         XIIN22    IFEQ      XWKEY
C                   MOVE      *ON             XIIN22
C                   ELSE
C                   MOVE      *OFF            XIIN22
C                   ENDIF
C         XSPARM    IFGT      25
C         XIIN23    IFEQ      XWKEY
C                   MOVE      *ON             XIIN23
C                   ELSE
C                   MOVE      *OFF            XIIN23
C                   ENDIF
C         XSPARM    IFGT      26
C         XIIN24    IFEQ      XWKEY
C                   MOVE      *ON             XIIN24
C                   ELSE
C                   MOVE      *OFF            XIIN24
C                   ENDIF
C                   ENDIF
C                   ENDIF
C                   ENDIF
C                   ENDIF
C                   ENDIF
C                   ENDIF
C                   ENDIF
```

Listing 6.16: The code for DQMBAPI2 (part 4 of 5).

```
C                   ENDIF
C                   ENDIF
C                   ENDIF
C                   ENDIF
C                   ENDIF
C                   ENDIF
C                   ENDIF
C                   ENDIF
C                   ENDIF
C                   ENDIF
C                   ENDIF
C                   ENDIF
C                   ENDIF
C                   ENDIF
C                   ENDIF
C                   ENDSR
 **
ABCDEFGHIJKLMNPQRSTUVWXY
```

Listing 6.16: The code for DQMBAPI2 (part 5 of 5).

DQMBAPI3

The last API, DQMBAPI3, is the simplest. It calls DQMBAPI with the shutdown op code, and then exits. The code for DQMBAPI3 is shown in Listing 6.17.

```
C                   CALL      'DQMBAPI'
C                   PARM      'S'           XOOPCD            1
C*
C                   MOVE      *ON           *INLR
```

Listing 6.17: The code for DQMBAPI3.

THE JSPAPI LIBRARY: I/O PROXY APIs

The previous section mentions that the JSPAPI I/O proxy APIs were designed to allow one program to act as an I/O proxy server for another. There are certainly quite a few ways to do this, but over the years I've come to believe that data queues work quite well, and APIs interfaces should be as simple as possible. Using those guidelines, the structure of the I/O proxy APIs becomes very simple. Figure 6.4 shows the I/O proxy APIs as they relate to the rest of the revitalization architecture.

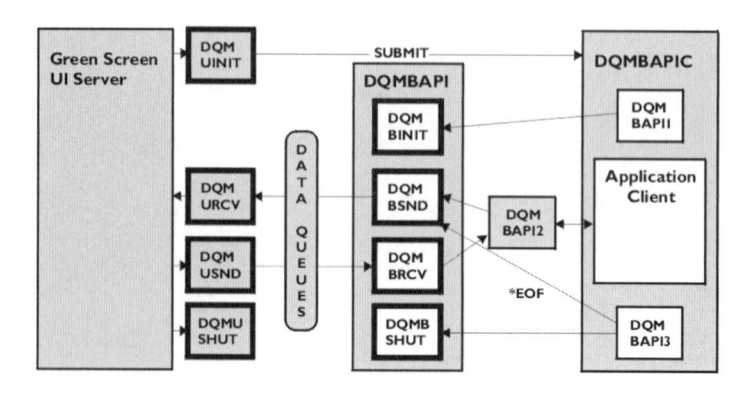

Figure 6.4: The I/O proxy APIs in relation to the rest of the revitalization architecture.

The I/O proxy APIs provide a simple, symmetrical set of APIs bound together through data queues. A program on either side of the data queues goes through roughly the same protocol: initialization, one or more I/O operations, and shutdown. The primary difference is based on which side is the requester and which the responder. In the revitalization architecture, the application client is the requester, and the UI server is the responder. Interestingly, since the UI server is the program that actually communicates with the end user, the UI server initiates the application client, but from that point on, the UI server assumes a passive role, responding to requests from the application client.

The I/O proxy APIs, and the client APIs as well, all share a common three-letter prefix, *DQM*. This prefix stems from the underlying transport architecture, and stands for "data queue messaging." I prefer to leave this naming convention because the DQM architecture is actually viable for a wide range of communications between any two programs, and is not limited to the rather narrow use it is put to here (that of a single client communicating with a dedicated server). I point this out because, as you delve into the implementation details of the I/O proxy APIs, you might wonder why there are two data queues rather than the single one that would be sufficient for our purposes. The reason is that the DQM architecture will support other protocols, regardless of the structure and content of the actual messages. While this book doesn't go into the other uses of the architecture, having a queue in each direction is vital when moving from dedicated servers to general-purpose servers.

Let's now take a close look at the APIs. As it turns out, the I/O proxy APIs actually require less code than the client APIs. They are very lean, stripped-down programs designed for a particular purpose. At the same time, they are comprehensive, except that they are not designed for robust error handling.[2] They are in charge of assigning session IDs and the creation and deletion of the supporting data queues. After a successful session, there are no leftover objects in the system. Figure 6.5 shows the lifecycle and data flow of the I/O proxy APIs.

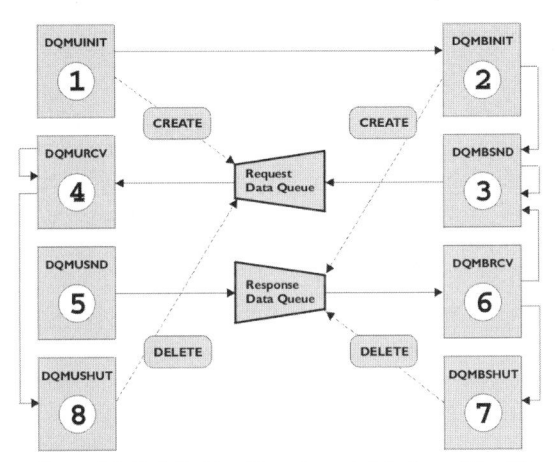

Figure 6.5: Detail of the lifecycle and data flow of the I/O proxy APIs.

There are eight I/O proxy APIs and a few supporting programs. All of the APIs share the same parameter structure: a single parameter containing the DQMMSG data structure. Listing 6.18 shows the source for the DQMMSG externally described data structure.

```
     A          R DQMMSGR
     A            DQMBNM        10      TEXT('Business Logic Name')
     A            DQMSID        10      TEXT('Session ID')
     A            DQMBID        10      TEXT('Business Logic ID')
     A            DQMSCR         8      TEXT('Screen ID')
     A            DQMOPC         5      TEXT('Operation Code')
     A            DQMRTC         2      TEXT('Return Code')
     A            DQMRTS         2      TEXT('Return SubCode')
     A            DQMIND        99      TEXT('Indicators')
     A            DQMDTA      2000      TEXT('Data Buffer')
```

Listing 6.18: The source for the DQMMSG data structure.

---

2 Error handling is an issue outside the scope of this chapter.

There are some slight quirks in the naming conventions of this API. For example, the B in DQMB stands for "business logic," a term I occasionally use instead of "application client." In some ways, "business logic" better describes the function of that component: it contains the application control and business rules from the original program. The UI server is nothing more than a skeleton that performs display-file I/O. The term "application client" helps to identify that component as the one that is really making requests, and the UI server as the one servicing those requests. So, DQMBNM is the name of the application client, or business logic.

DQMSID is the data queue for the request session (the UI server session), while DQMBID is the data queue for the response session (the application client session). DQMSCR and DQMOPC are the record format and I/O operation, respectively, while DQMRTC is the two-character function-key code discussed in the previous section. DQMDTA is the buffer that holds the data structure containing the fields for the specified record format. A few of the fields are not implemented in this chapter. DQMRTS will be used to indicate a specific error condition when one occurs, while DQMIND will be used to transport the numeric (non-command-key) indicators back and forth between the application client and the UI server.

Having examined DQMMSG, let's walk through the cycle, one step at a time. To start, the UI server calls DQMUINITC, passing it the name of the application client to which it wants to connect in the DQMMSG structure.[3] DQMUNITC is not shown in Figure 6.5; it's a special interface program that resides in the application (or production) library rather than the API library. Its purpose is to set the library list appropriately for the application client because when the application client is submitted, it will assume the current library list. Once that's done, DQMUNITC calls the DQMUNIT API, and then the sequence is as follows:

1. The first phase is to initialize the UI-server side of the connection. Listing 6.19 shows DQMUINIT and its support programs, DQMUSBM and DQMUCRT. DQMUINIT accesses the DQMSNO (session number) data area to get the next session ID, adds the prefix DQU, and calls DQMUCRT to create the request data queue. This session ID is stored in field DQMSID in the DQMMSG data structure for future calls. Next, DQMUSBM is called to submit the application client. Since this book uses the revitalization-architecture client APIs, DQMUSBM submits a call to DQMBAPIC, the main client API, passing it the

---

[3] Remember that all eight I/O proxy APIs share a single DQMMSG data structure.

application name and UI server session ID.[4] At this point, the UI server goes into a wait by calling DQMURCV. We'll return to the UI server at step 4.

```
DQMUINIT
     D DQMMSG         E DS
     I*
     C     *ENTRY     PLIST
     C                PARM                  DQMMSG
     C*
     C     *DTAARA    DEFINE                DQMSNO           7 0
     C     *LOCK      IN         DQMSNO
     C                ADD        1          DQMSNO
     C                OUT        DQMSNO
     C                MOVEL      'DQU'      DQMSID
     C                MOVE       DQMSNO     DQMSID
     C*
     C                CALL       'DQMUCRT'
     C                PARM                  DQMSID
     C*
     C                CALL       'DQMUSBM'
     C                PARM                  DQMBNM
     C                PARM                  DQMSID
     C*
     C                MOVE       '00'       DQMRTC
     C                MOVE       *ON        *INLR

DQMUCRT
     DQMUCRT:   PGM       PARM(&DQMSID)
                DCL       VAR(&DQMSID) TYPE(*CHAR) LEN(10)
                CRTDTAQ   DTAQ(JSPAPI/&DQMSID) MAXLEN(2146) TEXT('DQM +
                            Data Queue for UI' *BCAT &DQMSID)
                ENDPGM

DQMUSBM
     DQMUSBM:   PGM       PARM(&DQMBNM &DQMSID)
                DCL       VAR(&DQMBNM) TYPE(*CHAR) LEN(10)
                DCL       VAR(&DQMSID) TYPE(*CHAR) LEN(10)
                SBMJOB    CMD(CALL PGM(DQMBAPIC) PARM(&DQMBNM +
                            &DQMSID)) JOB(&DQMBNM)
                ENDPGM
```

Listing 6.19: *DQMUINIT and its support programs, DQMUCRT and DQMUSBM.*

---

4 You don't have to call DQMBAPIC or the client APIs. Conceivably, you could submit a call to some other program, provided it used the I/O proxy APIs to communicate.

2. The submitted program calls DQMBINIT. If you're using the client APIs, DQMBAPIC calls DQMBAPI1, which in turn calls DQMBINIT. Listing 6.20 shows DQMBINIT and its support program, DQMBCRT. DQMBINIT is nearly a mirror of DQMUINIT. It accesses the DQMSNO (session number) data area to get the next session ID, adds the prefix DQL, and calls DQMBCRT to create the response data queue. This session ID is stored in the field DQMBID in the DQMMSG data structure for future calls. At this point, DQMBAPIC calls the application client. If you're not using the client APIs, your application client will have to do these calls itself.

```
DQMBINIT

     D DQMMSG          E DS
     I*
     C     *ENTRY       PLIST
     C                  PARM                    DQMMSG
     C*
     C     *DTAARA      DEFINE                  DQMSNO           7 0
     C     *LOCK        IN         DQMSNO
     C                  ADD        1            DQMSNO
     C                  OUT        DQMSNO
     C                  MOVEL      'DQL'        DQMBID
     C                  MOVE       DQMSNO       DQMBID
     C*
     C                  CALL       'DQMBCRT'
     C                  PARM                    DQMBID
     C*
     C                  MOVE       '00'         DQMRTC
     C                  MOVE       *ON          *INLR

DQMBCRT

     DQMBCRT:   PGM      PARM(&DQMBID)
                DCL      VAR(&DQMBID) TYPE(*CHAR) LEN(10)
                CRTDTAQ  DTAQ(JSPAPI/&DQMBID) MAXLEN(2146) TEXT('DQM +
                         Data Queue for Logic' *BCAT &DQMBID)
                ENDPGM
```

Listing 6.20: DQMBINIT and its support program, DQMBUCRT.

3. When the application client needs I/O, it moves the record-format name into the field DQMSCR in the DQMMSG data structure, the operation (for example, EXFMT) into DQMOPC, and the data from the appropriate record-format data structure into DQMDTA. It then calls DQMUSND, as shown in Listing 6.21.

DQMUSND sends the DQMMSG data structure to the request data queue identified in the DQMSID field. In the client APIs, this is all done by DQMBAPI2. If no response is required, the application continues processing until the next I/O statement, at which point it returns here. If it does require a response, it goes into a wait state by calling DQMBRCV. Let's assume that's the case, and switch back to the UI-server side for steps 4 and 5.

```
DQMBSND

      D DQMMSG          E DS
      I*
      C     *ENTRY      PLIST
      C                 PARM                    DQMMSG
      C*
      C                 CALL     'QSNDDTAQ'
      C                 PARM                    DQMSID
      C                 PARM     'JSPAPI'       XWQLIB        10
      C                 PARM     2146           XWMLEN         5 0
      C                 PARM                    DQMMSG
      C*
      C                 MOVE     *ON            *INLR
      C*
      C                 RETURN
```

Listing 6.21: DQMBSND, used by application clients to send requests.

4. The UI server is patiently waiting on a response from DQMURCV, shown in Listing 6.22. Unfortunately, this program is a good (or bad) example of the incompleteness of the implementation. In this version of the software, the timeout is set to 60 seconds, at which point the program will simply return an empty buffer. This is not a very effective means of handling errors. A more robust implementation would have a configurable timeout and a soft error message. The revitalization architecture supports this: the DQMMSG data structure has a field for errors. In fact it has two, DQMRTC and DQMRTS, which are available to indicate error conditions.

Throughout this implementation, the code assumes that everything will run smoothly—not a very good assumption in distributed programming, but I've found that on the UI server side, this is rarely an issue, since the response time from the application client is the same as the original monolithic program. Unless you've got really long-running programs, this timeout is sufficient. On the other hand, if you do have long-running interactive programs (and there are some out there), you might want to raise the timeout to a very high value.

If the request is a shutdown request (signaled by *EOF in the operation code), the UI server skips to step 8 without performing any I/O. Otherwise, the UI server performs the requested I/O operation based on the values in DQMSCR and DQMOPC, using the data from DQMDTA. After the I/O is complete, if this is an operation such as WRITE or UPDAT that doesn't expect a response, the UI server returns to this step to wait for the next request. Otherwise, it continues to step 5.

```
D DQMMSG          E DS
I*
C      *ENTRY       PLIST
C                   PARM                    DQMMSG
C*
C                   CALL    'QRCVDTAQ'
C                   PARM                    DQMSID
C                   PARM    'JSPAPI'  XWQLIB       10
C                   PARM    2146      XWMLEN        5 0
C                   PARM              DQMMSG
C                   PARM    60        XQWAIT        5 0
C*
C                   MOVE    *ON       *INLR
C*
C                   RETURN
```

Listing 6.22: DQMURCV, the UI server API used to receive requests.

5. The UI server now sends the response back to the application client, as shown in Listing 6.23. In a mirror of step 3, the returned data is loaded into the DQMDTA field. However, the UI server needs an additional response field. The DQMRTC field is used to return the function key pressed—01 through 24, for the various command keys, or 00 to indicate that no command key was pressed. Although it's not implemented in this example, an invalid request would return error information in DQMRTC and DQMRTS. The UI server then returns to step 4, and the application flow moves back to the application client.

```
D DQMMSG         E DS
I*
C     *ENTRY      PLIST
C                 PARM                    DQMMSG
C*
C                 CALL      'QSNDDTAQ'
C                 PARM                    DQMBID
C                 PARM      'JSPAPI'      XWQLIB       10
C                 PARM      2146          XWMLEN        5 0
C                 PARM                    DQMMSG
C*
C                 MOVE      *ON           *INLR
C*
C                 RETURN
```

Listing 6.23: DQMUSND, used by the UI server to send responses.

6. At this point, the application client expects a response, and so calls DQMBRCV. If you're using the client APIs, this call is done inside of DQMBAPI2 as part of the Put-then-Get command. As you can see in Listing 6.24, DQMBRCV isn't particularly robust when it comes to error handling, either. This shortcoming is more of a problem here because the delay is based on a user's think time, and could easily become quite lengthy. You need to carefully consider how you handle this, since it will depend on the implementation: green-screen interfaces often have very high, or even infinite, timeouts because the screen is dedicated to the application. On the other hand, a browser interface might need to set some maximum timeout value to guard against loss of connection or even the user moving to another Web page. Since this is a complicated issue, I chose to take the easy route and time out after an hour.

Moving past this bit of "dirty laundry," the application client receives the data from DQMBRCV and moves it back into the record-format data structure. The application client also has to decode the function-key information from DQMRTC and use it to set on the appropriate command-key indicators, as originally defined in the display file. Once this is done, it can continue with the application logic. If more I/O is required, the application client returns to step 3. If, however, the program is ready to end, it continues to step 7.

```
D DQMMSG         E DS
I*
C      *ENTRY    PLIST
C                PARM                    DQMMSG
C*
C                CALL      'QRCVDTAQ'
C                PARM                    DQMBID
C                PARM      'JSPAPI'      XWQLIB        10
C                PARM      2146          XWMLEN         5 0
C                PARM                    DQMMSG
C                PARM      3600          XQWAIT         5 0
C*
C                MOVE      *ON           *INLR
C*
C                RETURN
```

Listing 6.24: DQMBRCV, used by the application client to receive responses.

7. In this step, the program calls DQMBSHUT to clean up (that is, delete) the request data queue. Listing 6.25 shows DQMBSHUT and its support program, DQMBDLT. Not shown, though, is one crucial step: the application client must send a shutdown request to the UI server. (You might want to refer back to step 4 to see how a shutdown is handled.) A simple call to DQMBSND with *EOF in the DQMOPC operation code field is all that is needed. In the client APIs, this is handled automatically by DQMBAPIC; the application client program simply ends as normal, and DQMBAPIC calls DQMBAPI3, which in turn calls DQMBSND to send the shutdown request to the UI server and then calls DQMUSHUT to shutdown the application client. If you're not using the client APIs, you'll have to do these calls yourself prior to ending the application client.

```
DQMBSHUT

       D DQMMSG         E DS
       I*
       C      *ENTRY    PLIST
       C                PARM                    DQMMSG
       C*
       C                CALL      'DQMBDLT'
       C                PARM                    DQMBID
       C*
       C                MOVE      '00'          DQMRTC
       C                MOVE      *ON           *INLR
DQMBDLT

       DQMBDLT:  PGM     PARM(&DQMBID)
                 DCL     VAR(&DQMBID) TYPE(*CHAR) LEN(10)
                 DLTDTAQ DTAQ(JSPAPI/&DQMBID)
                 ENDPGM
```

Listing 6.25: DQMBSHUT and its support program, DQMBDLT.

8. Returning to the UI server, the shutdown request has finally been received. At this point, the program simply calls DQMUSHUT, shown in Listing 6.26, which calls DQMUDLT to delete the request data queue. The program ends and returns to the caller.

That sums up the I/O proxy APIs. Using this technique, you can split your original monolithic program into an application client and a UI server, while users are completely unaware that most of the code they've been executing has actually been running in batch. Of course, seeing the same old green screen, you might wonder what all the fuss is about. As you continue through this book, though, you'll see exactly what benefits this process brings.

I realize that the UI server code is not nearly as clean as the application client. The application client uses the client APIs, which completely encapsulate all the client-side I/O proxy APIs into a very simple interface. However, since it's important to see how the individual I/O proxy APIs work, I left all the low-level calls in the green-screen UI server. Your implementation could just as easily encapsulate the server-side APIs. In fact, in chapter 7, you'll use Java classes to encapsulate the I/O proxy APIs for the Swing and browser clients.

```
DQMUSHUT

     D DQMMSG         E DS
     I*
     C      *ENTRY    PLIST
     C                PARM                    DQMMSG
     C*
     C                CALL      'DQMBDLT'
     C                PARM                    DQMBID
     C*
     C                MOVE      '00'          DQMRTC
     C                MOVE      *ON           *INLR

DQMUDLT

     DQMUDLT:  PGM       PARM(&DQMSID)
               DCL       VAR(&DQMSID) TYPE(*CHAR) LEN(10)
               DLTDTAQ   DTAQ(JSPAPI/&DQMSID)
               ENDPGM
```

Listing 6.26: DQMUSHUT and its support program, DQMUDLT.

7

CONVERTING THE DATA

This chapter describes the **com.pub.pbd.dc400** package, which is used to convert data from EBCDIC to ASCII and back. This package relies heavily on, and is closely related to, the **AS400Field** classes in IBM's Java Toolbox for the AS/400. In fact, I might have been able to just use the JT400 data types, but while designing the architecture, I decided there were some features needed in the basic classes that just weren't present in the JT400 package.

This chapter is broken down as follows:

- "Defining a Dc400Structure" quickly explains how to use the **com.pub.pbd.dc400** package to define a conversion object for an AS/400 data structure. This information is all you need to use these classes as input to the other classes in the subsequent chapters.

- "The Dc400 Classes" shows how the classes work, and why they were created. This section explains why I decided to create my own hierarchy that contained the IBM JT400 classes, rather than subclass them.

- "The Future of Dc400" takes a look at the future of the **Dc400** package. It discusses field types and takes a close look at the concept of field attributes.

Defining a Dc400Structure

A **Dc400Structure** is meant to represent a data structure on the AS/400. In chapter 6, you saw data structures used throughout the design. They were used in the application code to define the data in the individual record formats of the display file, and in the APIs to define the message that was passed between the client APIs and the I/O proxy APIs.

Data structures are an easy way to transport a whole set of related fields from one place to another, and are used quite often in RPG. However, there is no related concept in Java, for a good reason. In RPG, each subfield in a data structure is just a contiguous string of data bytes, and so you can simply lay them end-to-end in a data structure. In Java, each subfield is an object in its own right. You really don't know how big the object is, so in order to treat the subfields as contiguous data, you have to emulate the idea of a data structure. The **Dc400Structure** object is designed to do that.

A **Dc400Structure** is created from an array of **Dc400Field** objects. **Dc400Field** is an abstract class from which all the other Dc400 field types are subclassed. At the time this book was written, only three basic types have been defined: **Character, Numeric,** and **Raw.** **Character** fields are used to convert to AS/400 alpha fields. **Numeric** fields are used to convert zoned numeric fields.[1] **Raw** fields are placeholders for data that either doesn't need to be converted (filler fields) or data that will be converted later, such as a data structure within a data structure. For example, the DQMDTA field in the DQMMSG data structure defined in chapter 6 contains another data structure; the layout of that structure depends on the record format identified in the DQMSCR field. A **Raw** field can be used to extract the EBCDIC data without the cost of translation. It can then be converted later as needed.

Listing 7.1 identifies the classes and constructors for the parent class, **Dc400Field,** and the three subclasses, **Dc400CharacterField, Dc400NumericField,** and **Dc400RawField.** The constructors for the subclasses are quite simple: define the name and the length, and in the case of the **Numeric** type, the number of decimal positions. The name is important because unlike the IBM idea of a structure, you don't access the fields by position within the structure, but instead by name.

---

[1] Currently, there is no data type for packed fields, but you can easily add one by subclassing the **Dc400Field** class and overriding the **getAS400DataType** method appropriately.

Dc400Field
public Dc400Field()

Abstract superclass for fields in a Dc400Structure.

Dc400CharacterField
public Dc400CharacterField(String name, int length)

Creates a Dc400CharacterField with the specified name and length.

Parameters:
name—The field name.
length—The length of the field.

Dc400NumericField
public Dc400NumericField(String name, int length, int decimals)

Creates a Dc400NumericField with the specified name, length and decimal positions.

Parameters:
name—The field name.
length—The length of the field.
decimals—The number of decimals positions.

Dc400RawField
public Dc400RawField(String name, int length)

Creates a Dc400RawField with the specified name and length.

Parameters:
name—The field name.
length—The length of the field.

*Listing 7.1: The classes and constructors for the various **Dc400Field** types.*

Let's define a field:

```
Dc400CharacterField programName = new Dc400CharacterField("PGMNAM", 10);
```

This is actually a fairly rare line of code. Normally, you wouldn't create a **Dc400Field** by itself because the whole purpose of a **Dc400Field** is to define a structure. In this case, however, a single **Dc400CharacterField** is defined and stored in a variable called **programName**. The field name is PGMNAM, and it's ten positions long.

Here's another field:

```
Dc400NumericField standardCost = new Dc400NumericField("STDCST", 9, 2);
```

Again, it would be rare to see a line like this. It defines a zoned decimal field named STDCST that is nine digits total, with two decimal positions. The **Dc400NumericField** is stored in the variable **standardCost**.

Let's do something a little more realistic. In fact, let's define the data structure that would be used to define the PROMPT record format for the ITMMNT1D display file. First, let's see how a **Dc400Structure** is defined. Listing 7.2 shows the class definition for the **Dc400Structure**. It's quite simple—you merely pass an array of **Dc400Field** objects.

Dc400Structure
 public Dc400Structure(Dc400Field fields[])

Creates a Dc400Structure containing the specified fields.

Parameter:
 fields—The Dc400Field objects defining the data in the structure.

Listing 7.2: The class and constructor for the **Dc400Structure** class.

Of course, you can't instantiate **Dc400Field** objects directly because **Dc400Field** is an abstract class, but you can pass an array containing the subclasses **Dc400CharacterField**, **Dc400NumericField**, or **Dc400RawField**. Knowing that, you're ready to create the "real" **Dc400Structure**. Listing 7.3 shows the DDS for the externally described data structure and the corresponding **Dc400Structure**.

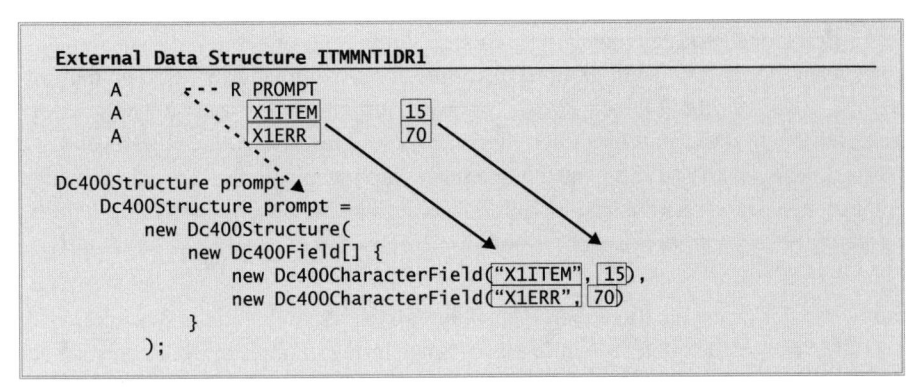

```
External Data Structure ITMMNT1DR1
A         ┌── R PROMPT
A         │   X1ITEM        15
A         │   X1ERR         70

Dc400Structure prompt
    Dc400Structure prompt =
        new Dc400Structure(
            new Dc400Field[] {
                new Dc400CharacterField("X1ITEM", 15),
                new Dc400CharacterField("X1ERR", 70)
            }
        );
```

Listing 7.3: How to define a **Dc400Structure** to emulate an externally described data structure.

As you can see, it's a one-to-one correspondence between the fields in the data structure and the **Dc400Field** objects in the array in the **Dc400Structure** constructor. Although there are a lot of uses of the **new** keyword in the constructor, it's perfectly acceptable because of the way the classes are designed. The only changes that need to be made from one structure to another are the name of the variable and the **Dc400xxxField** entries, as you'll see in chapter 8.

To continue on the fast path through this book, you can skip straight to chapter 8 to learn how to create a **JdspfDisplayFile** object. Otherwise, continue with the next section of this chapter to learn more about the **Dc400** classes and the reasons behind their design.

THE DC400 CLASSES

The **Dc400** classes begin to show how Java allows you to create uniquely flexible models of the real world. The classes in the package **com.pbd.pub.dc400** are deceptively simple—there are only about 500 lines, of which more than half are comments, and another third are variable definitions, method definitions, and closing braces. These classes, however, are designed to make it easy to work with a very non-Java concept, that of a data structure, in a way that's familiar to AS/400 programmers. While they're fairly small, that doesn't mean that they didn't require some careful thought. This section not only takes a close look at the classes as they finally were designed, but explains, for better or worse, some of my decisions as I designed them.

When I first looked at data conversion, I thought I might be able to use the standard classes from IBM's Java Toolbox for the AS/400. They're already written, and they're designed to do everything I need, so why not use them, right? There are a whole set of classes for the various data types (including data types I never use, like BLOBs and CLOBs), and even a class called **AS400Structure**, which seemed to be the toolbox's implementation of a data structure. The more I looked at them, however, the more I realized they weren't exactly what I needed.

I had two major concerns. First, there's no way to name the fields in the structure. With the toolbox classes, a structure is little more than an array of objects, which must be accessed by an integer index. I could do some tricks, like defining final constants with the field names, but that didn't allow really assigning a name. As you'll see later in this chapter, field names become very important. Second, the toolbox classes are closely tied to the AS/400. In fact, the recommended constructors require an AS/400 object. While I know this is to support the intricacies of CCSIDs, it still complicates things.

The next option was to subclass the toolbox classes. I could use the **Record** class, but that required a **RecordFormat**, which had no immediate constructor; I had to create it by adding **FieldDescriptions** to an empty **RecordFormat**. I've found that it's a bad idea to not have an immediate constructor (that is, a constructor that just takes an array of objects) because it becomes difficult to create such objects on the fly.

On the other hand, the **AS400Structure** object did have a constructor that accepted an array. Perhaps I could just add a name attribute to the data types and some new "getter" methods to the structure class. Again, though, I've found that it's rarely a good idea to subclass somebody else's classes. Unless you are specifically making a new version of something such as taking a text field and making a special text field with a colored background, you shouldn't use inheritance. You should instead use composition.[2]

Which is the case here? Well, one of the biggest problems with inheritance is that you inherit all the public methods and variables of the superclass. This makes sense when you have a situation such as the text field just mentioned. In the **Dc400** package, however, the IBM classes have many methods that just aren't needed, and would simply tend to clutter up the interface. Composition is a good way to encapsulate the working of a member class.

---

[2] This took me some time to learn. Some of my earlier packages are going to need to be reworked because I was a little bit overzealous in my use of inheritance.

So, now I was stuck creating my own classes. This meant designing a class that could be easily created on the fly (with a new operation), but just as easily subclassed to something more specific. I usually create classes that can be used as JavaBeans, though I rarely "beanify" them. My perfect low-level classes have a set of private attributes, accessed only through setters and getters (some of which may also be private or protected). Constructors only call the setters. No real work is done until an "action" method is called. The Dc400 classes became a perfect example of this philosophy. First, let's take a look at the Dc400Field abstract class.

I'm actually kind of fond of Dc400Field. It is as close to trivial as you'll probably see outside of "HelloWorld," yet it serves as the base for some very powerful classes. When I say trivial, I'm referring to the fact that there is no code in Dc400Field outside of constructors, setters, and getters. All the real work is done by its subclasses and by the class that encapsulates it, Dc400Structure.

The idea behind Dc400Field was to define a field with the minimum possible parameters, and use it to create a data structure that can convert data types between RPG and Java. More importantly, the class had to be very flexible, to allow easy addition of new data types as time went on. As I thought about the class, I realized that what I wanted was the ability to define the class as easily as I would define a field in a data structure. Since my ultimate goal was to allow these classes to be generated programmatically, I wanted the definition of a Dc400Structure to mirror the definition of an RPG data structure. So, I distilled the minimum parameters needed to define a field: name, type, and length.

At this point, I still had to make a design decision. Did I want to create a concrete class Dc400Field that had a type attribute, or separate specific concrete classes, such as Dc400CharacterField and Dc400NumericField, with an abstract superclass Dc400Field? I chose the latter to start, but I think that initial decision had more to do with the fact that IBM's toolbox has separate types than any conscious decision on my part.

The beauty of Java is that much of the mechanics of what the programmer does is hidden; you don't need to worry about the implementation details because the user never sees them. When I'm writing prototyping code, I rarely worry about what's between the open and close braces of my methods.[3] In fact, as you go through some of my code, you can

---

[3] I will be the first to admit that occasionally I get distracted and forget about some particularly quirky code, and eventually it bites me. I still believe, though, that what's between the braces is not as important as what's outside of them.

see where I learned new techniques. For example, some of my early classes have an array of objects with a getName() method. To find a particular object, I do a loop through the array, doing if (object[i].getName().equals(key)). By checking the release dates on my code, you can pretty much figure out when I learned what a hashtable was.

The decision of how to construct Dc400Field, though, was one I had to try to make correctly the first time because it involved the class hierarchy. Changes to the class hierarchy or method signatures, especially constructors, are always painful and never backwards compatible, so they should be avoided whenever possible.

So, I started to fall into a little bit of "analysis paralysis." I don't like the feeling of not knowing why I'm doing something; there's a chance that I'll come to my senses later and have to change it. I looked at the two options—one class or many classes—over and over, trying to decide which was correct. I thought that going with a single class was perhaps safest, since adding classes to the hierarchy is more backwards compatible than removing them, and backwards compatibility is a good goal.

That was almost enough to sway me, but as I started implementing this design decision, I had a thought: What are the essential goals of object orientation, and in this specific case, of inheritance and polymorphism? Well, one of the key goals is to reduce errors. It's pretty widely agreed that the largest single source of errors in programming, the one thing most likely to topple the most powerful algorithm, is conditional code—the lowly "if" statement. Lumping all the different field types into a single class would require conditional code somewhere down the line. I needed to include one of the JT400 AS/400 classes as a member variable, and right off the bat, it was obvious that I would have to create an object of a different class for each field type: character data needed AS400Text, numeric data needed AS400ZonedDecimal, and raw data needed AS400ByteArray. The only way to do that in a single class would be with a conditional statement, one of the key things I was trying to avoid. That finally swayed me toward the final hierarchy of Dc400Field as an abstract class with concrete subclasses for the different data types.

With that decision made, I could finally design my classes. Listing 7.4 shows class DC400Field. As I said, this class is almost trivial. It has several private fields that can be accessed via setter and getter routines. Four of the fields—name, type, length, and decimals—are set by the constructor, while the structure and offset are set when the field is added to a structure. The only exception is the display attributes field, which is in place for future expansion.

com.pub.pbd.dc400.Dc400Field

public abstract class Dc400Field

Dc400Field defines a field in a Dc400Structure. Its primary characteristics are type and length (and decimals for numeric fields). Currently, only CHARACTER and NUMERIC fields are supported. I expect to have some more sophisticated field types in later versions. There is also a type RAW, which converts to a byte array. These are used for filler fields or structures within structures. A Dc400Field can be attached to a Dc400Structure; in fact, that's the idea. Once fields are attached to a Dc400Structure, they can be used to automatically generate the objects required to convert data between the EBCDIC buffer and Java objects. Finally, a JdspfFieldAttributes structure can be attached to a field. This allows the definition of display attributes such as color and field-protect, and optionally associates those attributes with an indicator.

Fields

RAW
public static final int RAW

CHARACTER
public static final int CHARACTER

NUMERIC
public static final int NUMERIC

Constructors

Dc400Field
public Dc400Field()

Creates an undefined Dc400Field.

Dc400Field
public Dc400Field(String name,
        int type,
        int length,
        int decimals)

Creates a Dc400Field with the specified name, type, length, and decimal positions.

Parameters:
name—The field name.
type—The field type.
length—The field length.
decimals—The number of decimals.

Listing 7.4: The variables, constructors, and methods of the Dc400Field class (part 1 of 3).

Methods

getAS400DataType
public abstract AS400DataType getAS400DataType()

getAttributes
public JdspfFieldAttributes getAttributes()

getDecimals
public int getDecimals()

getLength
public int getLength()

getName
public String getName()

getOffset
public int getOffset()

getStructure
public Dc400Structure getStructure()

getType
public int getType()

setAttributes
public void setAttributes(JdspfFieldAttributes newValue)

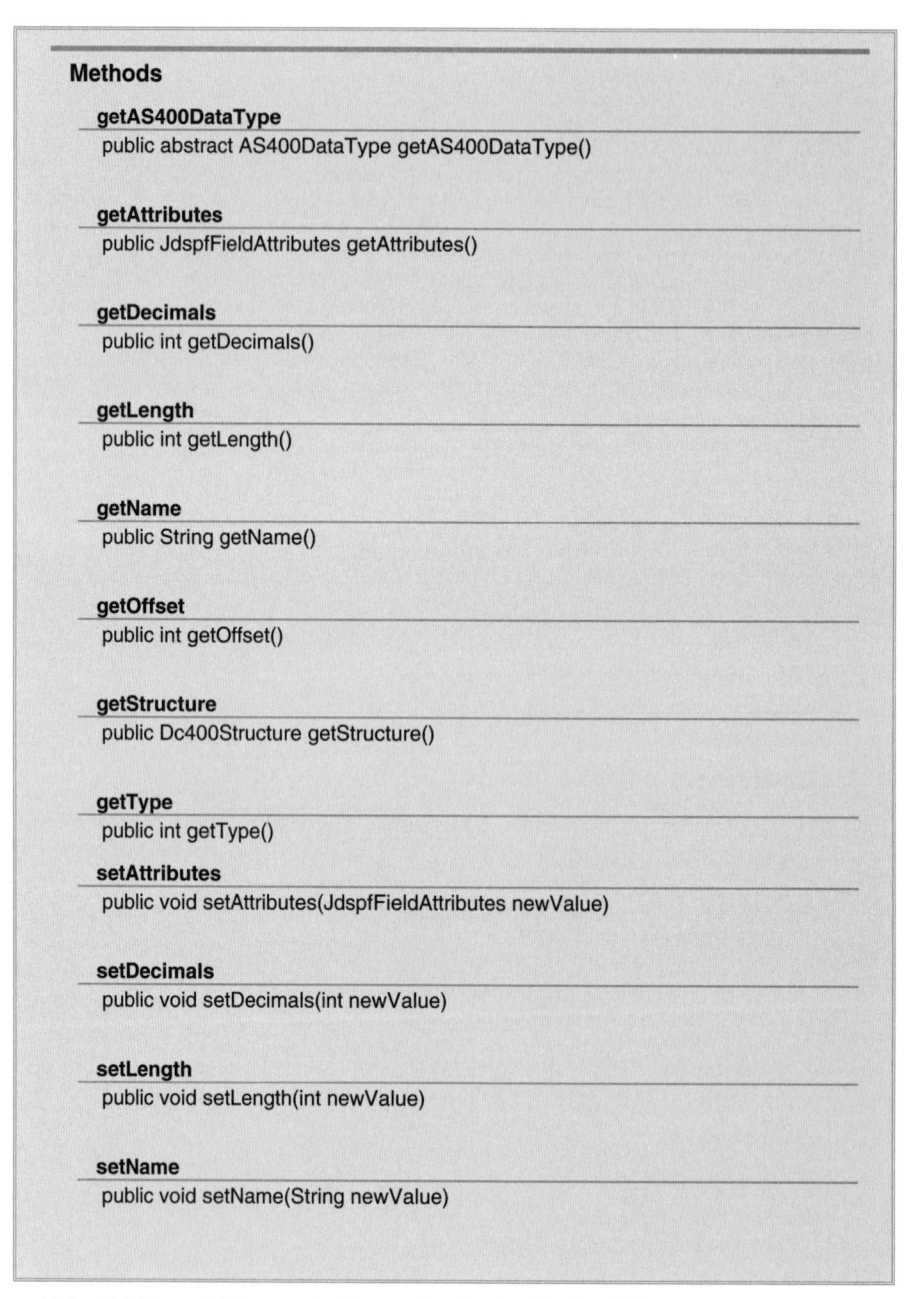

setDecimals
public void setDecimals(int newValue)

setLength
public void setLength(int newValue)

setName
public void setName(String newValue)

Listing 7.4: The variables, constructors, and methods of the **Dc400Field** class (part 2 of 3).

> **setOffset**
> public void setOffset(int newValue)
>
> **setStructure**
> public void setStructure(Dc400Structure newValue)
>
> **setType**
> public void setType(int newValue)

*Listing 7.4: The variables, constructors, and methods of the **Dc400Field** class (part 3 of 3).*

Two things in Listing 7.4 are not trivial: the **getAS400DataType** method and the attributes field. The **getAS400DataType** method addresses the concern about conditional code. The primary difference between the various data types is the JT400 class that is used to convert them, and **getAS400DataType** is the method that returns the appropriate object. So, instead of a big conditional statement, each subclass overrides the method with a single line consistent with the subclass. Listing 7.5 compares the **getAS400DataType** methods from the three concrete subclasses of **Dc400Field**.

> **Dc400CharacterField**
> ```
> public AS400DataType getAS400DataType() {
>     return new AS400Text(getLength());
> }
> ```
>
> **Dc400NumericField**
> ```
> public AS400DataType getAS400DataType() {
>     return new AS400ZonedDecimal(getLength(), getDecimals());
> }
> ```
>
> **Dc400RawField**
> ```
> public AS400DataType getAS400DataType() {
>     return new AS400ByteArray(getLength());
> }
> ```

*Listing 7.5: The **getAS400DataType** method from **Dc400RawField**.*

Simply overriding the method in each subclass avoids all the conditional code that would be necessary. Listing 7.6 shows how the **getAS400DataType** method would look if it were implemented in the **Dc400Field** class. You'd have to add conditional statements every time you wanted to implement a new class. Instead, by creating concrete subclasses that override the **getAS400DataType** method, you can add new types without changing any other code. This is polymorphism at its most succinct.

```
public AS400DataType getAS400DataType() {
    AS400DataType as400type = null;

    if (getType() == CHARACTER)
        as400type = new AS400Text(getLength());
    else if (getType() == NUMERIC)
        as400type = new AS400ZonedDecimal(getLength(), getDecimals());
    else if (getType() == RAW)
        as400type = new AS400ByteArray(getLength());

    return type;
}
```

Listing 7.6: How the **getAS400DataType** method would look in **Dc400Field**.

The second issue is the display-attributes concept. I have trouble with this because the display attributes class belongs to a different package, the JDSPF package, as it should. Display attributes such as PROTECT are definitely specific to the AS/400 display-file concept, especially when they're conditioned by indicators. However, I don't much like the idea of including a field in the **Dc400Field** class that isn't in the **Dc400** package (other than the JT400 classes, which are the classes that **Dc400** was written to encapsulate). I sometimes think I need to further subclass the **Dc400Field** classes to become **JdspfField** classes, but that becomes impractical because of the concrete subclasses; I'd have to subclass each of those in the JDSPF package. (Perhaps you can see why I kept bouncing back and forth with the "one class versus many classes" argument.) As of this writing, there is a special field with a public getter and setter for associating a **JdspfAttributes** object with a **Dc400Field**.

Okay, on to the other classes in the package, starting with the three concrete subclasses currently defined, **Dc400CharacterField**, **Dc400NumericField**, and **Dc400RawField**. Each class defines a specific type of field. Let's take another look at translating an external data structure DDS to a **Dc400Structure**. In chapter 6, you saw how to convert the PROMPT record format. Listing 7.7 translates the MAINT format. This design achieves the goal of a one-to-one relationship between the **Dc400Structure** and the external data structure. The alphanumeric fields are represented as **Dc400CharacterField** objects, while the lone numeric field is defined as a **Dc400NumericField**.

```
External Data Structure ITMMNT1DR2
     A          R MAINT
     A            X2MODE        10
     A            X2ITEM        15
     A            X2DESC        30
     A            X2QTY0         9S 2
     A            X2UOMI         2
     A            X2UOMS         2
     A            X2ERR         70
```

```
Dc400Structure maint
    Dc400Structure maint =
        new Dc400Structure(
            new Dc400Field[] {
                new Dc400CharacterField("X2MODE", 10),
                new Dc400CharacterField("X2ITEM", 15),
                new Dc400CharacterField("X2DESC", 30),
                new Dc400NumericField("X2QTY0", 9, 2),
                new Dc400CharacterField("X2UOMI", 2),
                new Dc400CharacterField("X2UOMS", 2),
                new Dc400CharacterField("X2ERR", 70)
            }
        );
```

Listing 7.7: The **Dc400Structure** for the MAINT record format.

At the time of this writing, the code only supports zoned decimal fields, but it would be very easy to create a new field of type **Dc400PackedField** if you were so inclined. Here's a brief synopsis of how that would be done:

1. Add a new constant, such as PACKED, to the constants in **Dc400Field**.

2. Add a new type called **Dc400PackedField**, which extends **Dc400Field**.

3. Pattern the constructor after the one in **Dc400NumericField**, only passing PACKED instead of NUMERIC to the superclass constructor.

4. Modify the **getAS400DataType** method to return an **AS400PackedDecimal** object with the appropriate length and decimals.

That's it. You could, in fact, create other types that supported other AS/400 data types, or even develop your own (although creating your own types would mean you'd have to create your own class to mimic the behavior of an **AS400DataType**).

You might notice that the `Dc400RawField` hasn't been used yet. That's because we haven't yet run into a situation with *nested data structures*, that is, a field in a data structure that really contains another data structure. Chapter 9 examines the `Sc400Message` class, which subclasses `Dc400Structure` and makes use of the `Dc400RawField` object.

Speaking of `Dc400Structure`, it's time to look at that class in detail. Listing 7.8 shows part of the `Dc400Structure` definition.

---

com.pbd.pub.dc400.Dc400Structure
public class Dc400Structure

Dc400Structure is used to allow data conversion into and out of an AS/400 data structure. The Dc400Structure is constructed from an array of Dc400Fields. The Java object for a corresponding Dc400Field can be retrieved or updated by name or by index. The EBCDIC buffer can also be retrieved or updated. A Dc400Structure is created with no actual data; it must be populated by setBuffer or setObjects (or multiple calls to setObject). Attempting to perform a getObject without a setBuffer, or vice versa, will result in an exception.

Constructors

Dc400Structure
public Dc400Structure()

Dc400Structure
public Dc400Structure(Dc400Field fields[])

Dc400Structure
public Dc400Structure(Dc400Structure initStructure)

Methods

getBigDecimal
public BigDecimal getByteArray(String name)

getBuffer
public byte[] getBuffer()

getBufferLength

---

*Listing 7.8: The constructors and selected methods of the **Dc400Structure** class (part 1 of 2).*

```
            public int getBufferLength()

       getByteArray
            public byte[] getByteArray(String name)

       getObject
            public Object getObject(String name)

       getString
            public String getString(String name)

       setBuffer
            public void setBuffer(byte newValue[])

       setObject
            public void setObject(String name,
                      Object newValue)
       setObjects
            public void setObjects(Vector newValue)
```

*Listing 7.8: The constructors and selected methods of the **Dc400Structure** class (part 1 of 2).*

The design of Listing 7.8 is simple: create a structure from an array of field definitions, then use it to convert back and forth between an EBCDIC buffer and Java objects. The primary methods are shown; you can get or set an object by name, and you can get and set the EBCDIC buffer. There are also convenience methods for retrieving more specific Java objects such as a **String** or a **BigDecimal**, although you will get an exception if you use the wrong method. A number of methods not shown here allow getting and setting fields by index and converting directly between an array of EBCDIC bytes and an array of Java objects without storing them in the structure. However, RPG programmers will probably be more comfortable with the concept of data being actually stored in the structure, and accessing the data by field name.

Actually, the **Dc400Structure** is not used often in the UI server programs. It is usually just a storage area inside a larger structure. In the next chapter, you'll see the JDSPF classes, which are the primary means of moving data from an application client to a UI server, and which rely heavily on the **Dc400Structure** classes.

107

THE FUTURE OF Dc400

There are three primary areas to expand the capabilities Dc400 classes: formatting, editing, and display attributes. I expect to address each of these in a later release, but if you can't wait, this section outlines how you should go about extending the Dc400 package.

Formatting is the easiest addition, probably by stealing a page from the AS/400 and adding an edit-code/edit-word parameter. Editing is a little more complex, involving the use of a new class, Dc400Exception (time for error checking!). Display attributes are the most complex. Although I have a good model for how they should work, I'm still troubled by the idea of including the display attributes as part of the Dc400 package.

Formatting, as I mentioned, is pretty straightforward. Add an edit-mask parameter, either an integer defining a special Dc400-specific editing type (such as PHONENUMBER or SOCIALSECURITY), a single character to echo the AS/400 edit codes (such as 'Z' for zero suppress), or a string containing an edit word such as "mmm-DD-yyyy" for a date or "9X 999 999 99 9999 999 9" for a UPS tracking number. Add a toString( ) method to Dc400Field, which will use the mask, if any, to format the output field.

For editing, the value typed by the user needs to be edited against the mask. Microsoft Outlook is a good example of an application that uses *field exit editing*: you type a phone number, and after you exit the field, Outlook displays a formatted version. This allows the user to enter either a full ten-digit phone number, or just a seven-digit phone number. Outlook prefixes a seven-digit number with the local area code. You couldn't easily do that with a character-by-character edit. A failed edit will generate an exception.

Display attributes are a very important addition to the package. The Swing UI server easily mimics most display attributes (with the exception of handling X,Y cursor positioning), but it's going to be a bit more complicated for the browser UI server. Since the browser interface uses HTML, the classes have to become HTML-aware when returning data.

Consider the different HTML required for different scenarios of an item field. Suppose you have a 15-character field named X1ITEM, which has the value ITEM001:

1. Presenting the value as an output-only field is simple:

   ITEM001

2. Displaying it in green requires the following:

```
<font color=green>ITEM001</font>
```

3. Presenting it as an input-capable field is much more complex:

```
<input type="text" name="X1ITEM" value="ITEM001"
       maxlength=15 size="15"></p>
```

4. Finally, to show it as an input-capable field, but with a red background to indicate an error, you would need this:

```
<input type="text" name="X1ITEM" value="ITEM001"
       style="background-color: red" maxlength=15
    size="15"></p>
```

The best answer might be to create an adapter class that attaches to the method that gets a field from the display-file proxy object. Such an adapter class would be defined at the JDSPF level.

8

BUILDING THE DISPLAY FILE OBJECT

This chapter begins the study of the **com.pbd.pub.jdspf** package. Of necessity, this package is considerably larger, more complex, and less complete than the others discussed so far. The limits of this book don't allow me to delve any deeper into the architecture than the simplest of operations: the EXFMT. If you take a look at the code, though, you'll see that the foundation is in place to add any of the other features needed to create a fully functioning display-file emulator. In this chapter, you'll learn to create your first actual revitalization object, the **ITMMNT1D_DisplayFile** object. This chapter is broken down into the following sections:

- "Defining a **JdspfDisplayFile**: **ITMMNT1D_DisplayFile**" is part of the fast path (as defined in the introduction to part 2 of this book). It is designed to allow you to quickly define a **JdspfDisplayFile** object to emulate the **ITMMNT1D** display file. You'll see how easy it is to define the display file object without having to be a Java expert.

- "The JDSPF Classes" goes into the JDSPF package in much more detail. You'll see how it is designed to be a bridge between the old procedural model and the brave new world of events and listeners, and how that idea is implemented in the **JdspfDisplayFile** object. This bridge is what you'll exploit when you use JDSPF as a common conduit to both the Swing client and the browser client in later sections.

* "The Future of JDSPF" examines some of the considerable possibilities that still exist. At this writing, the JDSPF package only supports EXFMT and no display attributes, although the infrastructure exists for much more. This section takes a look at what needs to be added, and how it can be done.

Defining a JdspfDisplayFile: ITMMNT1D_DisplayFile

In order to define the **ITMMNT1D_DisplayFile** object, you need to learn about two sets of classes: the **JdspfAbstractRecord** class and its subclasses, and the **JdspfDisplayFile** class. **JdspfAbstractRecord** is an abstract class that defines the basic workings of a display-file record format. Since all program I/O on the AS/400 is performed at the record-format level, the **JdspfAbstractRecord** is designed to support the various I/O operations.

At the same time, the actual user interface may display multiple records at one time. A perfect example is a subfile and its subfile control record. Both are displayed at the same time; in fact, in many cases, both have input-capable fields. At some point, these records need to be combined into a single entity accessible by the UI server. The **JdspfDisplayFile** class performs this function.

It's time to create a **JdspfDisplayFile**, specifically the **ITMMNT1_DisplayFile**. First, take a look at Listings 8.1 and 8.2: the **JdspfAbstractRecord** and the only currently supported concrete subclass, the **JdspfRecord**.

```
Class com.pbd.pub.jdspf.JdspfAbstractRecord
   public abstract class JdspfAbstractRecord

   This is the abstract superclass for all JDSPF record classes.

Constructors
   JdspfAbstractRecord
   public JdspfAbstractRecord(String name,
              Dc400Structure structure)
```

Listing 8.1: The constructor for the *JdspfAbstractRecord* class.

JdspfAbstractRecord is the base class for all other record classes. It is reviewed in detail later in this chapter; for now, it's enough to know that the class requires a record name and a **Dc400Structure**. The **Dc400Structure** must describe the data in the externally described data structure assigned to this record. For example, for the PROMPT record format, you need a structure that describes the ITMMNT1DR1 data structure.[1] All record types descend from this basic type. In fact, the **JdspfRecord** shown in Listing 8.2, which emulates the AS/400 display-file record-format type RECORD, has exactly the same constructor.

Class com.pbd.pub.jdspf.JdspfRecord

public class JdspfRecord
extends JdspfAbstractRecord

This class corresponds to DDS type RECORD.

Constructor
JdspfRecord
   public JdspfRecord(String name,
             Dc400Structure structure)

Listing 8.2: The constructor for the *JdspfRecord* class.

Creating a record is very simple once you're comfortable with creating a **Dc400Structure**. Listing 8.3 shows two slightly different ways to create the prompt record. The first uses the structure variable created in chapter 7 as an intermediate variable, while the second creates all the needed objects in one declaration. All records are created the same basic way, with slight differences; a subfile control record needs to point to its corresponding subfile record. The general idea of a record having a name and a structure is consistent throughout the revitalization architecture.

```
Creating the JdspfRecord, Style 1
    Dc400Structure prompt =
        new Dc400Structure(
            new Dc400Field[] {
                new Dc400CharacterField("X1ITEM", 15),
                new Dc400CharacterField("X1ERR", 70)
```

Listing 8.3: Two alternate styles for creating a *JdspfRecord* object (part 1 of 2).

---

[1] At this writing, there's really no way to create a record format with no data fields, only command keys. However, that's a fairly trivial change, and is left to you as an exercise.

```
            }
        );

    JdspfRecord promptRecord = new JdspfRecord("PROMPT   ", prompt);
```

Creating the JdspfRecord, Style 2
```
    JdspfRecord promptRecord =
        new JdspfRecord(
            "PROMPT   ",
            new Dc400Structure(
                new Dc400Field[] {
                    new Dc400CharacterField("X1ITEM", 15),
                    new Dc400CharacterField("X1ERR", 70)
                }
            )
        );
```

Listing 8.3: Two alternate styles for creating a *JdspfRecord* object (part 2 of 2).

Up to this point, whenever a specific version of a more generalized object was needed, you created a variable. For the first time, in creating the **JdspfDisplayFile** object, you're going to use inheritance to make something more specific. When you're done, you'll have your first "working" class definition, the ITMMNT1D_DisplayFile class, with everything needed to emulate the ITMMNT1D display file on the AS/400. To begin, examine the **JdspfDisplayFile** class and its constructors in Listing 8.4.

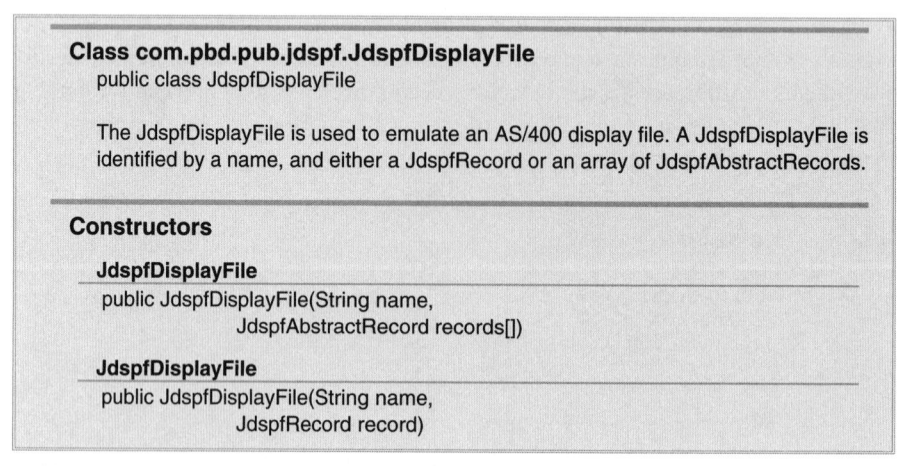

Class com.pbd.pub.jdspf.JdspfDisplayFile
public class JdspfDisplayFile

The JdspfDisplayFile is used to emulate an AS/400 display file. A JdspfDisplayFile is identified by a name, and either a JdspfRecord or an array of JdspfAbstractRecords.

Constructors

JdspfDisplayFile
public JdspfDisplayFile(String name,
         JdspfAbstractRecord records[])

JdspfDisplayFile
public JdspfDisplayFile(String name,
         JdspfRecord record)

Listing 8.4: The *JdspfDisplayFile* class and its constructors.

A **JdspfDisplayFile** is actually a relatively simple construct. It's simply a name and one or more **JdspfAbstractRecord** objects. There are two constructors: one accepts an array of

JdspfAbstractRecords, and one accepts a single **JdspfRecord**. You might wonder why the second constructor only accepts a **JdspfRecord** object rather than a **JdspfAbstractRecord**. It's because you'll need to have at least one record that supports the EXFMT method, and only **JdspfRecord** and its descendants support EXFMT.

Therefore, to create a **JdspfDisplayFile**, you can predefine some variables containing descendants of **JdspfAbstractRecord**, or you can create them on the fly with a nested constructor similar to the ones used to create the **JdspfRecord** prompt earlier in the chapter. Listing 8.5 shows how to create a display file that only supports the single-prompt-record format, using intermediate variables.

```
Dc400Structure prompt =
    new Dc400Structure(
        new Dc400Field[] {
            new Dc400CharacterField("X1ITEM", 15),
            new Dc400CharacterField("X1ERR", 70)
        }
    );

JdspfRecord promptRecord = new JdspfRecord("PROMPT   ", prompt);

JdspfDisplayFile promptOnlyDisplayFile =
    new JdspfDisplayFile("PROMPTER", promptRecord);
```

Listing 8.5: How to use intermediate variables to create a single-record display file.

Since all the classes required to build a **JdspfDisplayFile** allow immediate constructors (constructors that accept arrays of objects), it's quite easy to define the entire display file as a single call to the superclass constructor. This can get somewhat complex, but when you take a close look, you can see how well it mirrors the original display file DDS. Any actual fields (as opposed to constants) are defined as **Dc400Fields** within a record, and each record is defined as a **JdspfRecord**. The array of records is passed, along with the display-file name, to the superclass constructor, resulting in a concrete subclass specific to the ITMMNT1D display file. Listing 8.6 shows how this is done.

```
import com.pbd.pub.dc400.*;
import com.pbd.pub.jdspf.*;

/**
 * This is the emulation object for the ITMMNT1D display file.
 * This object supports the PROMPT and MAINT records.
```

Listing 8.6: How to subclass the **JdspfDisplayFile** class to make a specific display file by using a call to the superclass constructor with a nested constructor (part 1 of 2).

PART 2: IMPLEMENTING REVITALIZATION

```java
*/
public class ITMMNT1D_DisplayFile extends JdspfDisplayFile {
/**
 * ITMMNT1D_DisplayFile constructor comment.
 * @param name java.lang.String
 * @param records com.pbd.pub.jdspf.JdspfAbstractRecord[]
 */
public ITMMNT1D_DisplayFile() {

    // Call superclass constructor
    super(

        // Display file name ITMMNT1D
        "ITMMNT1D",

        // Array of record formats
        new JdspfAbstractRecord[] {

            // PROMPT record format
            new JdspfRecord(
                "PROMPT    ",
                new Dc400Structure(
                    new Dc400Field[] {
                        new Dc400CharacterField("X1ITEM", 15),
                        new Dc400CharacterField("X1ERR", 70)
                    }
                )
            ),

            // MAINT record format
            new JdspfRecord(
                "MAINT     ",
                new Dc400Structure(
                    new Dc400Field[] {
                        new Dc400CharacterField("X2MODE", 10),
                        new Dc400CharacterField("X2ITEM", 15),
                        new Dc400CharacterField("X2DESC", 30),
                        new Dc400NumericField("X2QTYO", 9, 2),
                        new Dc400CharacterField("X2UOMI", 2),
                        new Dc400CharacterField("X2UOMS", 2),
                        new Dc400CharacterField("X2ERR", 70)
                    }
                )
            )
        }
    );
}
}
```

*Listing 8.6: How to subclass the **JdspfDisplayFile** class to make a specific display file by using a call to the superclass constructor with a nested constructor (part 2 of 2).*

Record UI Objects

The final piece of the puzzle is the **JdspfRecordUI** class, an array of which is passed to the display file using the **setRecordUIObjects** method. This is another area where I've had a little difficulty placing a particular bit of code. Up to this point, the definition of the display file has been completely independent of the type of user interface that will be used. However, throughout the design, the assumption has been that at some point an actual UI object of some kind would have to be associated with each record format, or perhaps with each group of related record formats.

Because I haven't nailed that part of the architecture down entirely, I haven't included the record UI objects as part of the constructor. However I decide to approach it, the very simple **JdspfRecordUI** class will be used to communicate between the display file and the UI server. The **JdspfRecordUI** class simply specifies a record-format name and an object of any class. The type of object is known to the UI server, but not to the display file. The **setRecordUIObjects** method associates the objects with their particular record formats. It stores the UI object in the record-format object. The UI server gets the record-format object either from the **JdspfDisplayFileAction** event or by querying the **JdspfDisplayFile**. Either way, the UI server can then retrieve the record UI object and perform the necessary steps to display the data to the user.

Record UI objects are reviewed in more detail in chapters 10 and 11, which discuss actually creating UI servers. I wanted to touch on the concept here because the record UI objects might be part of a **JdspfDisplayFile** constructor in later releases of the software.

THE JDSPF CLASSES

The primary concept behind the JDSPF classes is to emulate the AS/400 display file as directly as possible, which seems pretty straightforward. At first, I thought I'd just have to define record formats and combine them into a display file, then allow access through methods that mimicked the various I/O operations, such as WRITE and EXFMT. As I started looking into the design a little more, however, a few discrepancies popped up. You'll see how some of those were addressed here, and more in chapter 10.

The first design point involved the various DDS record types. While I wasn't terribly worried about the difference between a popup window and a regular display panel, I did have a concern when it came to the subfile record. While a regular record contains a single buffer of data, the subfile record actually contains a whole array of buffers. I realized that this would require two different classes, one that supported a single buffer and one that supported multiple buffers. Also, in looking at the UPDAT operation for the subfile, it became obvious that there was even the concept of a "current" buffer within the subfile. (In the case of the UPDAT operation, this is the last record retrieved via CHAIN, READ, or READC.)

At the same time, I had to think of how the UI servers would get the data out of the record. While I had a lot of control over the Swing UI server, and I could easily imagine an adapter class that could convert a vector of data buffers into a table model, it wasn't so easy to determine how the browser UI server would handle it.[2] An important goal was to keep the interface as clean as possible. I soon realized that I'd already run across the concept earlier: the "current" buffer.

This buffer class, shown in Listing 8.7, is the first one in this book that extends another of class. When I first looked at it, I thought I might just use the **Dc400Structure** class directly. But it became obvious that **JdspfBuffer** needed a little bit more. Like the display-attributes field in the **Dc400Field** class, the indicators field is not used in this release, but is there as the hook for the next release. I left the indicators field in place as a reminder that the **JdspfBuffer** eventually will need a little more intelligence than the simple **Dc400Structure**.

Class com.pbd.pub.jdspf.JdspfBuffer
   public class JdspfBuffer
   extends Dc400Structure

   The JdspfBuffer class extends the Dc400Structure to include indicators and a "changed" flag.

Constructors

   JdspfBuffer
     public JdspfBuffer()

   JdspfBuffer
     public JdspfBuffer(Dc400Structure structure)

Listing 8.7: The constructors and methods specific to the **JdspfBuffer** class, which extends the **Dc400Structure** class (part 1 of 2).

---

2 You haven't seen the JSP definitions required to create the browser interface at this point. If you'd like to take quick look, glance through chapter 11 to see the ITMMNT1 implementation.

> **JdspfBuffer**
> public JdspfBuffer(Dc400Structure structure,
>   byte buffer[],
>   byte indicators[])
>
> **JdspfBuffer**
> public JdspfBuffer(JdspfAbstractRecord record,
>   byte buffer[],
>   byte indicators[])
>
> **Methods**
>
> **getIndicators**
> public JdspfIndicatorArray getIndicators()
>
> **isChanged**
> public boolean isChanged()
>
> **setIndicators**
> public void setIndicators(byte indicators[])
>
> **setIndicators**
> public void setIndicators(JdspfIndicatorArray newValue)

Listing 8.7: *The constructors and methods specific to the* **JdspfBuffer** *class, which extends the* **Dc400Structure** *class (part 2 of 2).*

JdspfBuffer extends the **Dc400Structure** class. This is another area where a difficult design decision had to be made, between making the **JdspfBuffer** an aggregate that simply contained a **Dc400Structure** as a variable, and having it directly subclass **Dc400Structure**. In the end, I decided on the subclass option because I needed to get fields in and out of a **JdspfBuffer** as efficiently as I needed to get them out of a **Dc400Structure**. Since those methods already existed for the **Dc400Structure**, it made sense to inherit them, rather than have to delegate them, which basically requires copying the signature of every method and then passing it through to the contained class. Since **Dc400Structure** has a pretty hefty API, I decided to inherit it.

The additional features of the **JdspfBuffer** aren't being used here, so you can think of it as a **Dc400Structure**: basically a buffer containing a bunch of different fields that you can access by name. Keeping this in mind, let's continue with the other classes, starting with the **JdspfAbstractRecord** and its descendants, shown in Listing 8.8.

119

Class com.pbd.pub.jdspf.JdspfAbstractRecord
public abstract class JdspfAbstractRecord

This is the abstract superclass for all JdspfDisplayFile records.

Constructors

JdspfAbstractRecord
public JdspfAbstractRecord(String name,
            Dc400Structure structure)

Methods

CHAIN
public boolean CHAIN(JdspfBuffer buffer) throws JdspfInvalidOperationException

EXFMT
public boolean EXFMT(JdspfBuffer buffer) throws JdspfInvalidOperationException

getCurrentBuffer
protected abstract JdspfBuffer getCurrentBuffer()

getString
public String getString(String name)

getUIObject
public Object getUIObject()

READ
public boolean READ(JdspfBuffer buffer) throws JdspfInvalidOperationException

READC
public boolean READC(JdspfBuffer buffer) throws JdspfInvalidOperationException

setObject
public void setObject(String name,
            Object newValue)

Listing 8.8: The constructor and selected methods of the **JdspfAbstractRecord** class (part 1 of 2).

> **UPDAT**
> public boolean UPDAT(JdspfBuffer buffer) throws JdspfInvalidOperationException
>
> **WRITE**
> public boolean WRITE(JdspfBuffer buffer) throws JdspfInvalidOperationException

*Listing 8.8: The constructor and selected methods of the **JdspfAbstractRecord** class (part 1 of 2).*

The current function of the JDSPF package is quite limited because I haven't decided on some of the specifics of handling multiple related records. The rest of this section shows you how the package currently works, which is sufficient for the simple fast-path example. The remaining sections of this chapter go into much more detail about how this area will work in more complex display files.

Today, the **JdspfAbstractRecord** has nearly every feature required to support record I/O operations. There is only one abstract method in the entire class, which is the method **getCurrentBuffer**. The method **getString** in **JdspfAbstractRecord** gets the string representation of a field from the current buffer, but it's up to the subclass to tell **JdspfAbstractRecord** which buffer is the current buffer. That's done by overriding the abstract **getCurrentBuffer** method. This way, a single buffer class like the **JdspfRecord**, shown in Listing 8.9, can simply return its one and only buffer, while the subfile emulation classes can keep track of the "current" buffer, and return it instead.

> **Class com.pbd.pub.jdspf.JdspfRecord**
>
> public class JdspfRecord
> extends JdspfAbstractRecord
>
> This class corresponds to DDS type RECORD.
>
> **Constructor**
> JdspfRecord
> public JdspfRecord(String name,
>   Dc400Structure structure)
>
> **Methods**

*Listing 8.9: The constructor and methods for the **JdspfRecord** class (part 1 of 2).*

PART 2: IMPLEMENTING REVITALIZATION

> **READ**
> public boolean READ(JdspfBuffer ioBuffer)
>
> **WRITE**
> public boolean WRITE(JdspfBuffer buffer)

*Listing 8.9: The constructor and methods for the **JdspfRecord** class (part 2 of 2).*

More importantly for the ITMMNT1 implementation, the **JdspfAbstractRecord**, while it does implement all I/O operations, implements them as a stub method that does nothing except throw a **JdspfInvalidOperationException** message. It's up to the subclasses to implement the appropriate methods. For example, **JdspfRecord** implements the READ and WRITE methods; a subfile emulation class would also implement CHAIN, READC, and UPDAT.

Finally, there's the issue of actually interfacing to the UI server. For the most part, the **ScJdspfJbuiDisplay** object is a holding area, not particularly concerned with the actual mechanics of the display process. At some point, though, the data has to get to the user. That's where the **UIObject** concept comes in. Each record is meant to have a **UIObject** associated with it. The kind of **UIObject** and what it does depends on the UI server. In the case of the Swing UI server, the **UIObject** is a version of **ScJdspfJbuiDisplay**, which is a class that allows the display of fields in a manner similar to a 5250 display, only with the nice graphical input fields and buttons users have come to expect. With the browser UI server, the **UIObject** is an **ScJspfJsp** object, which represents a JavaServer Page (JSP). The JSP is invoked when user interaction is required.

There is one further refinement within the **JdspfDisplayFile** object, having to do with user interaction. The issue surrounds the sequence of events. With a 5250 display, the screen is presented to the user, and the program is suspended until the user presses a command key. This can be emulated nicely with a **JbuiDisplay**. In fact, it is one of the fundamental design concepts behind the class. However, it's not as easy to do with a browser interface. The data is sent to the user, and then the servlet basically stops execution. It doesn't start again until the user clicks a button on a form, which is then sent to the servlet through a call to the **doPost** method. (In fact, the form could go to a completely different servlet, although that's not how **ITMMNT1_Servlet** is designed.)

I had a number of long nights trying to work my way out of this nasty little paradox. I finally hit on a solution that, while not exactly elegant, is functional. To understand it, start by reviewing one of the internal methods of the **JdspfDisplayFile**, **putGetUI**, shown in Listing 8.10.

```
public boolean putGetUI(JdspfBuffer buffer)
    throws JdspfInvalidOperationException
{
    currentRecord.WRITE(buffer);

    boolean breakRequired = true;

    if (listener != null) {
        JdspfDisplayFileAction action =
            new JdspfDisplayFileAction(
                this,
                JdspfDisplayFileAction.JDSPF_EXFMT,
                currentRecord);
        breakRequired = listener.actionPerformed(action);
    }

    if (!breakRequired)
        currentRecord.READ(buffer);

    return breakRequired;
}
```

Listing 8.10: The **putGetUI** method from **JdspfDisplayFile**.

The **putGetUI** method is invoked when an EXFMT is received. At the record level, it will be doing a WRITE and then a READ, but somehow the actual **UIObject** needs to be invoked. You can do this by making use of the concept of a *listener* object. The listener is invoked when interaction with the user is required. Here's what happens:

1. The WRITE method is called for the record object. This sets the record format to the current buffer from the UI server (which, in turn, received it from the application client).

2. The **breakRequired** flag is set to default to true.

3. If there is no listener, exit with true, in effect telling the UI server that it needs to make sure the user interaction happens. This is how the browser UI server works. It then sets a flag, shows the JSP, and waits for its **doPost** method to be called.

4. Otherwise, execute the listener's **actionPerformed** method, passing it the current record. Currently, this is how the Swing UI server works. It gets the appropriate **JbuiDisplay** object from the **getUIObject** method of the record, updates it with the buffer data, and then executes its EXFMT method. Once the user enters data and clicks a button, the UI server moves the data from the **ScJdspfJbuiDisplay** back into the buffer and returns false, which tells the **JdspfDisplayFile** to retrieve the data from the record. The **JdspfDisplayFile**, in turn, tells the UI server to send the data back to the application client.

You'll see this architecture in a little more detail in the implementation sections of the Swing and browser client classes in chapters 10 and 11, respectively, and in the implementation section of the **ScJdspfUIServer** class in chapter 12.

THE FUTURE OF JDSPF

As mentioned earlier, this release of the software does not support display attributes or subfiles, but the hooks are in place to give you an idea of how they will be implemented. This section provides a little direction if you decide to try your hand at adding these features yourself. That way, you'll have a reasonable chance of being compatible with the next release when it appears.

Subfiles

Let's take a look at what should be accomplished by adding subfile processing to the packages. Listing 8.11 shows a small excerpt from the JSP that would be used to emulate a subfile. Although the **setRecord** and **getNextRow** methods are not used in the fast-path example earlier in this chapter, it's appropriate to touch on them briefly here. Hopefully, even without a strong background in JSP, you can get a sense for what this code fragment does.[3] First, it sets the record to use in the **JdspfDisplayFile** (in variable **jdspf**) to **SFLRCD01**, which is the subfile record format. Next, it cycles through the subfile using the **getNextRow** method. Like the **next** method in an SQL result set, **getNextRow** returns true if there is another row, and false if there is not. Then, for each field in the subfile record, it calls the **getString** method to get each field and store it in an HTML table. Figure 8.1 shows what the resulting browser screen might look like.

```
<%
jdspf.setRecord("SFLRCD01");
while (jdspf.getNextRow()) {
%>

   <tr>
     <td width="25%" align="right"><%= jdspf.getString("XXCNUM") %></td>
     <td width="50%">            <%= jdspf.getString("XXCNAM") %></td>
     <td width="25%" align="right"><%= jdspf.getString("XXCBAL") %></td>
   </tr>

<%
}
%>
```

Listing 8.11: An excerpt of the code from a JSP that emulates a subfile.

---

[3] If you're not familiar with the HTML or JSP syntax, I apologize; either topic is far too large for the scope of this chapter. I'll address them a little more in part 3.

00000123	Lillian Johnston	142,314.25
00000134	Jon Nave	317,321.34
00000192	Joe Pluta	1.23

Figure 8.1: The browser output that might result from the JSP in Listing 8.11.

Did you notice that the **getString** method in this JSP accepts only a field name? That means that the **JdspfDisplayFile** not only knows which of its record formats to look at, but in the case of a subfile, which buffer to look for within that record format. You'll need to implement that logic as you create the subfile support classes.

In order to implement subfiles, you'll have to create a few new classes. I recommend creating four new descendants of the **JdspfAbstractRecord**: **JdspfSubfile**, **JdspfSubfileControl**, **JdspfMessageSubfile**, and **JdspfMessageSubfileControl**. Figure 8.2 shows the proposed hierarchy.

```
JdspfAbstractRecord
    |
JdspfOutputRecord
    |
    +----------------------------+
    |                            |
JdspfRecord                      |
    |                            |
    |                            |
JdspfSubfileControl <----------> JdspfSubfile
    |                            |
    |                            |
JdspfMessageSubfileControl <----> JdspfMessageSubfile
```

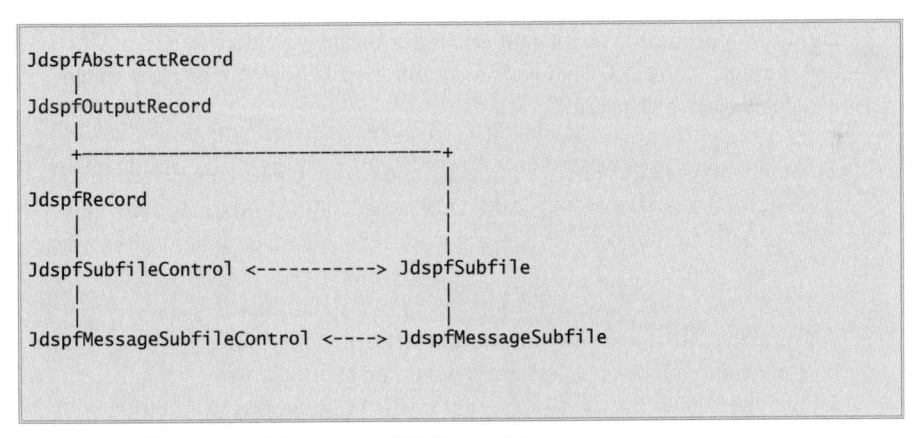

Figure 8.2: The intended hierarchy of JDSPF record classes

Take a look at the existing, nonfunctional **JdspfSubfile** class to get an idea of how the more advanced classes will look. You'll see how multiple buffers will be handled: performing a READ, READC, or CHAIN will set an internal "cursor," which will indicate the current buffer. That way, an UPDAT will set the contents of the appropriate buffer. The **getNextRow** method will allow the UI server to iterate through the buffers one at a time, changing the cursor position. Subsequent calls to **getCurrentBuffer** will then return the buffer at the cursor position, so the **getString** operation will return the field from the appropriate buffer.

Display Attributes

Display attributes are a more complicated issue. They are part of a larger concept, the use of indicators in general. Indicators are a unique RPG feature, but one that is so heavily used that it needs to be dealt with in any attempt at emulating a display file. Just about every facet of the display file, from the attribute of the fields to the relationships between the records, is controlled with indicators. Since they're so prevalent, I've added an indicator area to the **JdspfBuffer** class. In fact, this indicator area is in place all the way up in the green-screen interface. Although not used by the current release of the software, this indicator area can easily be accommodated, and will be in the next release of the software. It's part of the DQMMSG data structure used to communicate between the application client and the UI server.

The first step to implement indicators would be to add a parameter to the DQMBAPI2 program that would allow the indicators to be passed from the application client and returned. To finish implementing the design, you'd need to add the following classes and relationships:

1. Define an indicator to be the numeric index of the indicator, from 1 to 99, and the state, on or off. That way, a condition of N99 would be represented by **JdspfIndicator(99, false)**.

2. Combine multiple indicators with ANDs and ORs to create complex conditions like **((61 and N99) or N73)**. Add constructors or methods designed to allow the definition of not only the conditions, but also their relationships (the ANDs and ORs).

3. Allow a combination of a condition and an attribute—such as PROTECT—to be assigned to a field. The attributes would be queried prior to actually presenting the data to the user. In the case of the browser, this would trigger special HTML, while in the case of the Swing interface, it would require calls to some of the field methods.

You will need to be able to assign conditions to the other keywords used in a display file. For example, you might have a condition for the SFLCLR keyword in the subfile control record. Whenever a WRITE is performed on that record and the corresponding condition is met, the **JdspfDisplayFile** object must clear the corresponding subfile. If the SFLNXTCHG keyword is on during a WRITE or UPDAT to a subfile, it will force the **changed** flag to be set for that buffer. More indicators can be implemented within the **JdspfDisplayFile** object as time goes on.

Related Record Formats

This section does not discuss a functional enhancement, but instead a purely architectural issue. It revolves around the way display files and record formats are related in the real world. This is a rather tricky issue because, unlike a feature such as display attributes, there are no DDS keywords or file attributes that define these relationships.

For example, most of my subfiles have four sections, as shown in Figure 8.3. The top section is the subfile control record, the second section is the subfile, the third section is a simple record format (usually containing just the function key assignments), and the last section is the message subfile. This involves five different record formats: the subfile, the subfile control, the simple record, the message subfile, and the message subfile control record.

The only relationships among these records that can be discovered from the display file itself is that the subfile record and subfile control record go together, as do the message subfile record and the message subfile control record. There is no indication anywhere that these three sets of records are actually combined on a single display. Instead, you will know which record formats go together, and will design the UI object accordingly. You should create a class that's sort of a "meta-record." You'll create the subfile and the subfile control, and they'll be related by necessity. (There will, indeed, be a field in the subfile control constructor that points to the associated subfile.) The message subfile and message subfile control will be similarly related. You'll also create the simple record for the function key record. That being done, you'll join those three into a single meta-record. At this level in the structure, you'll define the UI object.

```
SRVMNT-01                      Server Maintenance                  3/26/00
SPUD                                                              17:26:35

Type options, press Enter.
   1=Add    2=Change    3=Copy    4=Delete   5=Display   8=Position To

Opt  Type        Server      Start  Description                 Attr Cmd

     *HOST       *CENTRAL      Y    Central Services
  9  *HOST       *DATABASE     Y    Upload/Download
     *HOST       *DTAQ         Y    Data Queue Processing
     *HOST       *FILE         N    File (allows browser access)
     *HOST       *NETPRT       Y    Network Printing
     *HOST       *RMTCMD       Y    Remote Commands
     *HOST       *SIGNON       Y    TCP/IP Signon Support
     *HOST       *SRVMAP       Y    Server Port Mapping
     *TCP        *BOOTP        N    Bootstrap Protocol           CHGBPA
     *TCP        *DCE          N    Distributed Computing Environ.
     *TCP        *DDM          N    Distributed Data Manager     CHGDDMTCPA
     *TCP        *DHCP         N    Dynamic Host Configuration   CHGDHCPA
     *TCP        *DIRSRV       N    Directory Services (LDAP)
                                                                  Bottom
Enter=Process    F3=Exit
Invalid option 9.
```

Figure 8.3: A typical subfile display, with the output of four different records indicated.

Let's take a look at a typical subfile DDS and the objects you might create for it. Listing 8.12 shows the listing for the subfile in Figure 8.3. The record formats are reordered slightly, placing CTL01 before SFL01 to keep the vertical positioning on the screen consistent. (This file would not compile as shown, since a subfile record must appear in the DDS before its associated subfile control record.) As you can see, there are five record formats; MSGCTL does not actually appear on the screen anywhere.

```
     A                                         DSPSIZ(24 80 *DS3)
     A*
     A          R CTL01                        SFLCTL(SFL01)
     A                                         OVERLAY
     A                                         CA03
     A N51                                     SFLDSP
     A N50                                     SFLDSPCTL
     A  50                                     SFLCLR
     A N52                                     SFLEND(*MORE)
     A                                         SFLSIZ(0014)
     A                                         SFLPAG(0013)
     A                                       1  2'SRVMNT-01'
     A                                         COLOR(BLU)
     A                                       1 32'Server Maintenance'
     A                                         DSPATR(HI)
     A                                       1 70DATE
     A                                         EDTCDE(Y)
     A                                         COLOR(BLU)
     A                                       2  2USER
     A                                         COLOR(BLU)
     A                                       2 70TIME
     A                                         COLOR(BLU)
     A                                       4  2'Type options, press Enter.'
     A                                         COLOR(BLU)
     A                                       5  2'   1=Add    2=Change    3=Copy    4=D-
     A                                         elete   5=Display   8=Position To'
     A                                         COLOR(BLU)
     A                                       7  2'Opt'
     A                                         COLOR(WHT)
     A                                       7  7'Type'
     A                                         COLOR(WHT)
     A                                       7 19'Server'
     A                                         COLOR(WHT)
     A                                       7 30'Start'
     A                                         COLOR(WHT)
     A                                       7 37'Description'
     A                                         COLOR(WHT)
     A                                       7 69'Attr Cmd'
     A                                         COLOR(WHT)
     A            X1OPT          1   B   8  3
     A            X1TYPE        10   B   8  7
     A            X1SVR         10   B   8 19
```

Listing 8.12: The DDS for the display in Figure 8.3 (part 1 of 2).

```
A*
A              R SFL01                           SFL
A                X2OPT         1   B  9   3
A                X2TYPE       10   0  9   7
A                X2SVR        10   0  9  19
A                X2STR         1   0  9  32
A                X2DESC       30   0  9  37
A                X2CHGA       10   0  9  69
A*
A              R RCD01
A                                    23  2'Enter=Process    F3=Exit'
A                                        COLOR(BLU)
A*
A              R MSGSFL                         SFL
A                                               SFLMSGRCD(24)
A                MSGKEY                         SFLMSGKEY
A                PGMSGQ                         SFLPGMQ(10)
A*
A              R MSGCTL                         SFLCTL(MSGSFL)
A                                               OVERLAY
A                                               SFLDSP
A                                               SFLDSPCTL
A                                               SFLINZ
A  N01                                          SFLEND
A                                               SFLSIZ(0002)
A                                               SFLPAG(0001)
A                PGMSGQ                         SFLPGMQ(10)
```

Listing 8.12: The DDS for the display in Figure 8.3 (part 2 of 2).

Listing 8.13 shows how the constructor might look for a **JdspfDisplayFile** object meant to emulate the display file. It introduces a new class, the **JdspfRecordGroup**, which is an array of related record formats. It also introduces the **JdspfOutputRecord** and the **Jdspf MessageSubfile**, both of which are special-purpose versions of the **JdspfAbstractRecord**. The **JdspfOutputRecord** doesn't support the EXFMT operation, while the **JdspfMessage Subfile** supports all the operations necessary to hold the data for a message subfile.

```
/**
 * SVRMNT1D_DisplayFile constructor comment.
 */
public SVRMNT1D_DisplayFile() {
  super(
    "SVRMNT1D",
    new JdspfRecordGroup(
      new JdspfRecord[] {
```

*Listing 8.13: What the constructor might look like for a **JdspfDisplayFile** that emulates SVRMNT1D (part 1 of 2).*

```
            new JdspfSubfileControl(
               "CTL01    ",
               new Dc400Structure(
                  new Dc400Field[] {
                     new Dc400CharacterField("X1OPT",    1),
                     new Dc400CharacterField("X1TYPE",  10),
                     new Dc400CharacterField("X1SVR",   10)
                  }
               ),
               new JdspfSubfile(
                  "SFL01    ",
                  new Dc400Structure(
                     new Dc400Field[] {
                        new Dc400CharacterField("X2OPT",    1),
                        new Dc400CharacterField("X2TYPE",  10),
                        new Dc400CharacterField("X2SVR",   10),
                        new Dc400CharacterField("X2STR",    1),
                        new Dc400CharacterField("X2DESC",  30),
                        new Dc400CharacterField("X2CHGA", 10)
                     }
                  )
               )
            ),

            new JdspfOutputRecord("RCD01    "),

            new JdspfMessageSubfile("MSGCTL   ", "MSGSFL   ")
         }
      )
   );
}
```

*Listing 8.13: What the constructor might look like for a **JdspfDisplayFile** that emulates SVRMNT1D (part 2 of 2).*

The only record format in the record group that supports the EXFMT operation is the subfile control record. When an EXFMT is received, the UI server will invoke the associated UI object, which should be built to display the data from all of the record formats within the record group.

Many Miles to Go

As you can see, there is still considerable work to be done to fully realize the capabilities of this interface. On the other hand, the groundwork has been laid so that these additional features can be added without comprising the original design.

9

IMPLEMENTING THE SERVER/CLIENT ARCHITECTURE

In chapter 7, you learned how to create classes that are primarily used as building blocks for other classes. This chapter discusses much the same kind of thing, except that most of these classes are completely hidden from the application programmer. Other than the **Sc400Client** class and its exception, **Sc400Exception**, you don't really need to know the workings of any of these classes.

On the other hand, if you want to learn how Java and object-oriented programming techniques can be used to make your programming much more productive, this is an important chapter for you. It shows you how to use inheritance, polymorphism, and composition to create new classes from more basic classes, including ones you've already seen in this package and ones from IBM's Java Toolbox for the AS/400.

Remember how the client's I/O proxy APIs used by the application client were encapsulated into the client APIs? Well, this chapter discusses something very similar for the I/O proxy APIs used by the UI server. When you're done with this chapter, you will have a generic UI server that uses a display-file emulation object and supports either a Swing interface or a browser interface. More importantly, this UI server could be subclassed to support any other interface. For example, you might want to create an XML interface to your legacy program—the generic **ScJdspfUIServer** interface could easily be subclassed to do just that.

To get an idea about how subclassing and composition can encapsulate logic once, to be used over and over by application programs, take the time to read through the following sections carefully:

- "Encapsulation: Sc400Client and Its Subclass, ITMMNT1_Client" shows how **Sc400Client** manages to encapsulate the four server-side I/O proxy APIs into a single class. **Sc400Client** is, in effect, a proxy for the entire application client. The UI server classes communicates with the AS/400 application client using the **Sc400Client** class. The **Sc400Client** is used as the base class for the second application object, **ITMMNT1_Client**.

- "Inheritance: Sc400Message and Sc400Api" provides examples of how to turn a generic class into a specific one through subclassing. In **Sc400Message**, the generic **Dc400Structure** class is subclassed to be specific to the server/client interface. This new message class is then used as one of the base classes for the **Sc400Api** class. **Sc400Api** is a specialized version of the **ProgramCall** class in IBM's Java Toolbox for the AS/400. With these two classes, you can communicate with the I/O proxy APIs in library JSPAPI on the AS/400.

- "Composition: ScJdspfUIServer" uses the other specialization technique, composition. **ScJdspfUIServer** is a composite of the **Sc400Client** and the **JdspfDisplayFile**. **ScJdspfUIServer** takes the four interfaces of the **Sc400Client** (init, receive, send, and shutdown), customizes them with logic specific to emulating a display file, and distills them down to a single method, run.

Sc400Client
and Its Subclass, ITMMNT1_Client

In chapter 8, you created your first application object, the **ITMMNT1D_DisplayFile**. That object emulates the ITMMNT1D display file on the AS/400. Now, you need an object that emulates the ITMMNT1AC application client program. This object is **ITMMNT1_Client**. Since **ITMMNT1_Client** subclasses the **Sc400Client** class, both need to be reviewed here.

Chapter 6 outlined the I/O proxy APIs, and even gave them names. The UI server APIs are of particular interest now. They're reviewed in Table 9.1.

Table 9.1: The Four I/O Proxy APIs and Their Uses

API Name	Description
DQMUINIT	Creates the request data queue.
DQMURCV	Receives a request from the application client.
DQMUSND	Sends a response back to the application client.
DQMUSHUT	Deletes the request data queue.

These four simple APIs are fairly easy to use in the closed environment of the AS/400—you just add a library or two to your library list, and away you go. However, they're a little less straightforward in the more complex world of a distributed application, where programs run on different machines. Not only do you need to know the names of the individual API programs, you've got to identify the host machine and how to connect to it, as well as the libraries those programs reside in, and you need to do all that at execution time. In the SC400 package, this information is all encapsulated within the **Sc400Client**.

The **Sc400Client** serves as a proxy for the application client program on the AS/400. In addition to performing the login procedure for the AS/400, it identifies the individual API program names and their libraries, and allows them to be called via meaningful method names: **init**, **receive**, **send**, and **shutdown**. This way, if the program or library names should change for some reason, the UI server won't change. Encapsulation is a good way of creating *regions of change*, allowing different aspects of the architecture to evolve while limiting the effect on existing programs.

So, the **Sc400Client** is basically a set of attributes that controls the communication between the UI server and the application client. Let's review those attributes, starting with a look at the **Sc400Client** in Listing 9.1.

> **Class com.pbd.pub.sc400.Sc400Client**
> public class **Sc400Client**
> This is the application client proxy for an AS/400 application client in the server/client architecture. It provides a single place to define all parameters for communication with an AS/400 application client, and also provides methods to support the UI server-side I/O proxy APIs.

Listing 9.1: Identifying the constructors and public methods for the **Sc400Client** *class (part 1 of 3).*

Fields

LOGON
public static final String LOGON

Constructors

Sc400Client
public Sc400Client()

Sc400Client
public Sc400Client(String clientName)

Methods

getMessage
public Sc400Message getMessage()

init
public Sc400Message init() throws Sc400Exception

receive
public boolean receive() throws Sc400Exception

send
public void send() throws Sc400Exception

setApiLibrary
public void setApiLibrary(String newValue)

setClientName
public void setClientName(String newValue)

setPassword
public void setPassword(String newValue)

setProductionLibrary
public void setProductionLibrary(String newValue)

*Listing 9.1: Identifying the constructors and public methods for the **Sc400Client** class (part 2 of 3).*

CHAPTER 9: IMPLEMENTING THE SERVER/CLIENT ARCHITECTURE

setSystemName
public void setSystemName(String newValue)

setUserID
public void setUserID(String newValue)

shutdown
public void shutdown() throws Sc400Exception

Listing 9.1: Identifying the constructors and public methods for the **Sc400Client** class (part 3 of 3).

As you can see in Listing 9.1, there is only a single getter for the Sc400Client class, along with four methods corresponding to the I/O proxy APIs: **init**, **receive**, **send**, and **shutdown**. The rest of the methods are setters, which set the various attributes. You'll learn more about those later in this chapter.

AS/400 Definitions

The system name is the host name of the AS/400, as you would enter it to connect via TCP/IP. The user ID and password are the ones you want to run the application client under. Note that this information is only required for the browser UI server; the servlet must have that information in order to connect to the AS/400, since there is no opportunity to prompt for it. The Swing API can use the special system name Sc400Client.LOGON, which will cause the JT400 toolbox to prompt for the system, user ID, and password. In this case, you don't need to set the user ID and password.

Server/Client Definitions

There are two library definitions and a client name. In most cases, the API library will probably stay JSPAPI, which is how the software is shipped. The production library is wherever you put your application client and the version of DQMUNITC that sets your library list accordingly, JSPPROTO as the package is shipped. (Refer to chapter 6 for more on DQMUNITC.) Finally, the client name is the name of the application client program—in the case of this example, ITMMNT1AC.

Making ITMMNT1_Client

Earlier in this chapter, you saw the attributes that need to be set in order to make the Sc400Client communicate with a specific application client on a specific machine. Once these attributes are set, you can use the other four methods to begin the actual communication with the application client. Listing 9.2 shows that done in the **ITMMNT1_Client** class, which is the concrete application version of the generic **Sc400Client** class.

At this point, you could write a UI server using only the **ITMMNT1_Client** class and perform all the appropriate user-interface emulation yourself. However, that's not the way the classes were designed. There is one more class that further encapsulates the server/client protocol specifically to help implement the revitalization strategy. That's the **ScJdspfUIServer** class, which is covered in chapter 12.

```java
import com.pbd.pub.sc400.*;

/**
 * ITMMNT1_Client is the application client proxy for ITMMNT1AC.
 */
public class ITMMNT1_Client extends Sc400Client {
/**
 * ITMMNT1_Client constructor comment.
 */
public ITMMNT1_Client()
    throws Sc400Exception
{
    this(false);
}
/**
 * ITMMNT1_Client constructor comment.
 */
public ITMMNT1_Client(boolean mustLogon)
    throws Sc400Exception
{
    super();

    setClientName("ITMMNT1AC");
    setProductionLibrary("JSPPROTO");

    if (mustLogon)
        setSystemName(Sc400Client.LOGON);
    else {
        setSystemName("MYAS400");
        setUserID("MYUSERID");
        setPassword("MYPASSWORD");
    }
}
}
```

Listing 9.2: The complete listing of the **ITMMNT1_Client** class.

There are two points to note about the **ITMMNT1_Client** class. The first is that the client name and production library are the name and library of the application-client program,

CHAPTER 9: IMPLEMENTING THE SERVER/CLIENT ARCHITECTURE

JSPPROTO/ITMMNT1AC. This is the same library and program used by the green-screen UI server in chapter 6. I can't overemphasize that the production library is where the modified version of DQMUNITC *must* reside, and that version of DQMUNITIC must set the library list appropriately.

The second point is a design quibble about the **mustLogon** parameter. Some people won't like how I've done this, but I don't have a better way today. When accessed from a Swing interface, you can allow the AS400 class from IBM's Java Toolbox for the AS/400 to prompt the user for a logon. (The AS400 variable is firmly buried inside **Sc400Client**.) To do that, the Boolean value TRUE is passed to the constructor. However, for the servlet, there's no good way to do that without a special HTML logon page. To avoid cluttering the design with a lot of specifics about HTML and nested Web pages, there is a place in the application client where you can hard-code the system name, user ID, and password. This isn't very secure, so if you'd like to do something a little better here, feel free to do so. That's the very reason I did not encapsulate the logon parameters—I felt it was up to each individual installation to decide how to handle its security.

If you're taking the fast path, now that you have a client and a display file, it's time to create the user interface. You can jump directly to chapter 11 to create the browser interface and see how well you did. Or, if you'd like something a little more AS/400-like, go to chapter 10 and create the Swing interface. Either way, you're almost ready to get graphical!

INHERITANCE: Sc400Message AND Sc400Api

Chapter 6 took a close look at the I/O proxy APIs on the AS/400. All these programs had a very important common trait: they each had a single parameter, and that parameter was defined to be a structure of type DQMMSG. That is, the DQMMSG external data structure was used to define that single parameter.

This might have seemed sort of arbitrary. For example, the shutdown program certainly didn't need all the data in the DQMMSG structure. It just needed one field, the UI server session ID. However, now that the API needs to be defined in Java terms, I hope you'll see that there is some method to this madness. Keeping the interface as consistent as possible helps quite a bit when you're actually implementing the API in a cross-platform, cross-language environment.

Consider the **Sc400Message**. It is designed to exactly emulate the DQMMSG data structure on the AS/400. As mentioned earlier, **Sc400Message** is an example of specialization through subclassing, which takes a general class, encapsulates the details in the constructor, and provides some subclass-specific methods. For example, the **Dc400Structure** class, which is **Sc400Message's** direct superclass, has no idea what data it contains. All that information is passed in the constructor. For data structures that are application-specific, like the contents of a record format for a specific display file, you can create that information dynamically within the application. For something as pervasive and consistent as the **Sc400Message**, though, something a little more concrete is in order. The best way to really see how this works is to study the **Sc400Message** class in detail, as shown in Listing 9.3.

```
package com.pbd.pub.sc400;

import com.pbd.pub.common.*;
import com.pbd.pub.dc400.*;

/**
 * Sc400Message is the Java equivalent of the DQMMSG data structure
 * on the AS/400.
 */
public class Sc400Message extends Dc400Structure {

    private static Dc400Field[] messageFields =    {
        // Header Fields
        new Dc400CharacterField("DQMBNM", 10),
        new Dc400CharacterField("DQMSID", 10),
        new Dc400CharacterField("DQMBID", 10),
        new Dc400CharacterField("DQMSCR", 8),
        new Dc400CharacterField("DQMOPC", 5),
        new Dc400CharacterField("DQMRTC", 2),
        new Dc400CharacterField("DQMRTS", 2),
        // Data fields
        new Dc400RawField("DQMIND", 99),
        new Dc400RawField("DQMBUF", 2000)
    };

    private static final int DQMBNM = 0;
    private static final int DQMSID = 1;
    private static final int DQMBID = 2;
    private static final int DQMSCR = 3;
    private static final int DQMOPC = 4;
    private static final int DQMRTC = 5;
    private static final int DQMRTS = 6;
    private static final int DQMIND = 7;
    private static final int DQMBUF = 8;

    // Operation codes
    private static final String SC400_EOF   = "*EOF ";
```

*Listing 9.3: The source for the **Sc400Message** class (part 1 of 4).*

```java
    private static final String SC400_CHAIN = "CHAIN";
    private static final String SC400_EXFMT = "EXFMT";
    private static final String SC400_READ  = "READ ";
    private static final String SC400_READC = "READC";

/**
 * Creates a non-client-specific Sc400Message.
 */
public Sc400Message() {
    this("");
}

/**
 * Creates an Sc400Message for the specified client
 * @param applicationClientName Client name
 */
public Sc400Message(String applicationClientName) {
    super(messageFields);
    setObjects(Pbd.makeVector(
        new Object[] { "", "", "", "", "", "", "", new byte[0], new byte[0]
}));
    setApplicationClientName(applicationClientName);
}

/**
 * Returns the application client session ID
 * @return the application client session ID
 */
public String getApplicationClientID() {
    return getString(DQMBID);
}

/**
 * Returns the application client name
 * @return the application client name
 */
public String getApplicationClientName() {
    return getString(DQMBID);
}

/**
 * Returns the data buffer (in EBCDIC)
 * @return the data buffer (in EBCDIC)
 */
public byte[] getDataBuffer() {
    return getByteArray(DQMBUF);
}

/**
 * Returns the indicator array (in EBCDIC)
 * @return the indicator array (in EBCDIC)
 */
```

Listing 9.3: The source for the **Sc400Message** class (part 2 of 4).

```java
public byte[] getIndicators() {
    return getByteArray(DQMIND);
}

/**
 * Returns the operation code
 * @return the operation code
 */
public String getOperationCode() {
    return getString(DQMOPC);
}

/**
 * Returns the record name
 * @return the record name
 */
public String getRecordName() {
    return getString(DQMSCR);
}

/**
 * Returns the UI server session ID
 * @return the UI server session ID
 */
public String getSessionID() {
    return getString(DQMSID);
}

/**
 * Returns true if this is a shutdown request
 * @return true if this is a shutdown request
 */
public boolean isEof() {
    return getOperationCode().equals(SC400_EOF);
}

/**
 * Returns true if the application client should receive data
 * @return true if the application client should receive data
 */
public boolean requiresResponse() {
    String op = getOperationCode();
    return (op.equals(SC400_CHAIN) ||
            op.equals(SC400_EXFMT) ||
            op.equals(SC400_READ)  ||
            op.equals(SC400_READC));
}

/**
 * Set the application client name
 * @param newValue new client name
 */
```

Listing 9.3: The source for the **Sc400Message** class (part 3 of 4).

```
    public void setApplicationClientName(String newValue) {
        setObject(DQMBNM, newValue);
    }

/**
 * Set the data buffer (in EBCDIC)
 * @param newValue data buffer (in EBCDIC)
 */
    public void setDataBuffer(byte[] newValue) {
        setObject(DQMBUF, newValue);
    }

/**
 * Set the indicator array (in EBCDIC)
 * @param newValue indicator array (in EBCDIC)
 */
    public void setIndicators(byte[] newValue) {
        setObject(DQMIND, newValue);
    }

/**
 * Set the return code (the key pressed)
 * @param newValue return code (the key pressed)
 */
    public void setReturnCode(String newValue) {
        setObject(DQMRTC, newValue);
    }
}
```

*Listing 9.3: The source for the **Sc400Message** class (part 4 of 4).*

At the very beginning of the class, there is an array of **Dc400Field** objects. This is the definition of the **Sc400Message**, and directly matches the DQMMSG data structure (listed in chapter 8). This includes the seven header fields of the standard server/client architecture and the two-byte arrays that pass the data back and forth. Next are a set of static integers, representing the index positions within the structure. While I like application programmers to be able to use field names, here in the **Sc400Message** structure itself it makes sense to use the actual indices. This eliminates the overhead of looking up field names. Of course, if the field names were to change or the fields were to be moved, you'd have to modify the **Sc400Message** class accordingly, but if the data structure changed, far more serious changes would occur, and you'd probably have to modify **Sc400Message** anyway.

Specialization via subclassing involves two facets: a subclass-specific constructor and subclass-specific methods. (A third, optional part of specialization is adding one or more additional subclass-specific attributes; **Sc400Message** does not use this technique.) Let's take a look at the two ways **Sc400Message** specializes the **Dc400Structure** class. First, the constructor uses the predefined array of **Dc400Fields** laid out in the class header. Second, a number of very specific methods are added. Rather than getting a field by name, subfields of the structure are accessed through dedicated methods such as **getOperationCode** and **setReturnCode**. Additionally, there are some protocol specific methods: **isEof**, for instance, very specifically tests the operation code to determine whether this is a shutdown request.

By using a predefined constructor and wrapping some of the more generic methods inside some protocol-specific methods, the **Sc400Message** subclass integrates the **Dc400Structure** directly into the server/client architecture. The same can be said for the **Sc400Api** class, shown in Listing 9.4.

```java
package com.pbd.pub.sc400;

import com.ibm.as400.access.*;

/**
 * Sc400Api is used to call one of the I/O proxy APIs on the AS/400.
 * It uses the ProgramCall class, along with a single parameter of type
 * Sc400Message.
 */
public class Sc400Api extends ProgramCall {
    private String name;
    private ProgramParameter[] parm = new ProgramParameter[1];

/**
 * Sc400Api requires a target AS/400, a library and a program name.
 */
public Sc400Api(AS400 as400, String apiLib, String apiProgram) {
    super(as400);
    name = apiProgram;
    String programPath = new QSYSObjectPathName(apiLib, name, "PGM");
    parm[0] = new ProgramParameter(new Sc400Message().getBufferLength());
    try {
        setProgram(programPath, parm);
    } catch (Exception e) {}
}

/**
 * Calls the method.  If getData is true, the method will copy the data
 * from the AS/400 back to the structure.
 * @param message Sc400Message structure to pass to the program
 * @param getData if true, the return value is copied back to the message
 */
public void call(Sc400Message message, boolean getData)
    throws Sc400Exception
{
    try {
        parm[0].setInputData(message.getBuffer());
```

*Listing 9.4: The source for the **Sc400Api** class (part 1 of 2).*

```
            if (run() == false) {
                throw new Sc400Exception(name + " failed.");
            } else {
                if (getData)
                    message.setBuffer(parm[0].getOutputData());
            }
        } catch (Exception e) {
            throw new Sc400Exception(name + " exception: " + e);
        }
    }
}
```

*Listing 9.4: The source for the **Sc400Api** class (part 2 of 2).*

The **ProgramCall** feature of IBM's Java Toolbox for the AS/400 is actually a rather sophisticated and relatively tricky interface. As always, IBM prepares for every possible combination of circumstances, so the interface will work no matter what your requirements might be. Unfortunately, in order to support the more powerful features, the standard interface is often more complex than the average program needs.

In RPG, this often results in seriously complex programs—take a look at the D-specs required to access some of the OS/400 APIs for a good example. However, in Java, this goes from a coding and maintenance headache to an opportunity to take advantage of creative subclassing. This example subclasses IBM's **ProgramCall** class to the point where it's almost trivial. You can only do this, however, because good architectural choices were made at the beginning of the design.

Suppose you've decided that all I/O proxy APIs have the exact same signature: a single parameter of type DQMMSG. This sort of consistency lends itself very well to subclassing. Let's see how, starting with a quick recap of the technique for calling an AS/400 program:

1. Create an AS400 object for the appropriate AS/400.

2. Create a string containing the qsys path name for the program.

3. Create a parameter array for the parameters.

4. Create a parameter for each element of the parameter array.

5. Create a program call object for the AS400, path, and parameters.

6. Set the parameters with the input data.

7. Call the **run** method to execute the program.

8. Retrieve the return data from the parameters.

This is quite a bit of work, especially since the first five steps could be done once for each program. The **Sc400Api** encapsulates almost all of these steps. At construction, the calling class passes in the AS400 object, the library name, and the program name. The constructor creates itself as a new **ProgramCall** by passing the AS400 object to the superclass constructor, then creates the path name and parameter list, and assigns them to itself. Since all I/O proxy APIs share the same signature, the same parameter list can be used for all programs and can be assumed to be an **Sc400Message**. This merely leaves creating a call interface, which will take an **Sc400Message** structure and use it to populate the parameter, call the program, and if required, copy the return value back into the message.

If you review the requirements of this class, you might begin to wonder whether it should perhaps contain, rather than subclass, the **ProgramCall** class. Unlike **Sc400Message**, which needs to have some of the methods of the superclass visible, none of the **ProgramCall** methods need to be visible for the **Sc400Api**. This is a classic argument for containing rather than subclassing. While currently implemented as a subclass, a later version may use composition.

COMPOSITION: ScJdspfUIServer

As mentioned in chapter 8, the **ScJdspfUIServer** class is designed to provide all the support necessary to create a UI server. The problem is that the I/O proxy APIs by themselves provide a very low level of interaction with the application client, and would require in-depth knowledge of how a display file works in order to create a UI server. Instead, the **JdspfDisplayFile** object is designed to act as a data model in the *MVC* (*model-view-controller*) architecture that is becoming widely used in the graphical programming world. All the I/O operations from the host application client are sent to the **JdspfDisplayFile** until actual user interaction is required—primarily when an EXFMT operation is requested. At that point, the current data is presented to the user, the user's response is recorded, and the information is returned to the application program for processing.

This is no small amount of work. However, because of the nature of the classes created earlier in this book, the **ScJdspfUIServer** class isn't all that difficult to develop. The trick is to make sure that it will support both the Swing interface and the browser interface without serious compromise.

At first glance, this looks rather easy. Both UI servers seem to do essentially the same thing: receive data from the application client, interact with the user, and send the response back to the application client. While this is true, the actual mechanics become very different as you begin to implement the two solutions, because the browser interface is fixed in its cycle. In addition, this fixed cycle has a predefined break in it: when a page of HTML is sent to the user, the servlet basically stops processing. It's up to the user to press the right button and return to that servlet—or perhaps another! This is due to the fact that the user really doesn't have control over the browser window. (I'm looking into ways around that problem.)

Regardless of the mechanics, the servlet isn't suspended on an I/O operation waiting for a user response. Instead, if the user does finally press the right button, a post operation is sent to the servlet with the appropriate data. This means the **doPost** method of the servlet is called.

So in effect, there are two cycles, **doGet** and **doPost**. The **doGet** cycle involves the following steps:

1. Initialize the application client.
2. Receive a request.
3. Send it to the user via the browser UI.

The **doPost** involves these steps:

1. Receive a user response from POST data.
2. Send it back to the client.
3. Receive a request.
4. Send it to the user via browser UI.

The steps of the Swing interface adhere much more closely to the original 5250 model:

1. Initialize the application client.
2. Receive a request.
3. Display data with the Swing UI and receive a response.
4. Send it back to the client.
5. Go to step 2.

These seem like very different cycles at first, primarily because of the two entry points in the servlet interface, and the fact that the servlet pretty much ends after sending the data to the user, while the Swing interface has a call to an interactive UI object right in the middle of its cycle. How could these two entirely different processes be reconciled?

The more I looked at the processes, the more I saw the similarities. I decided to take a look at them from the application-client point of view, not the UI server, and see what I could come up with. From that standpoint, it became clear that there really was only one cycle, but that the entry points were different for the two techniques.

Mulling over Figure 9.1, it became obvious that I could design a single generic UI server that simply had a break in it at the "wait for UI" point. The break would allow either the Swing UI to perform an EXFMT (something already designed into the JBUI classes) or the servlet to send a JSP to the user and wait for the input. In either case, the UI server object would preserve the connection to the application and wait for a "continue" method to be called, which would, in effect, be the signal to send data received from the user back to the application client.

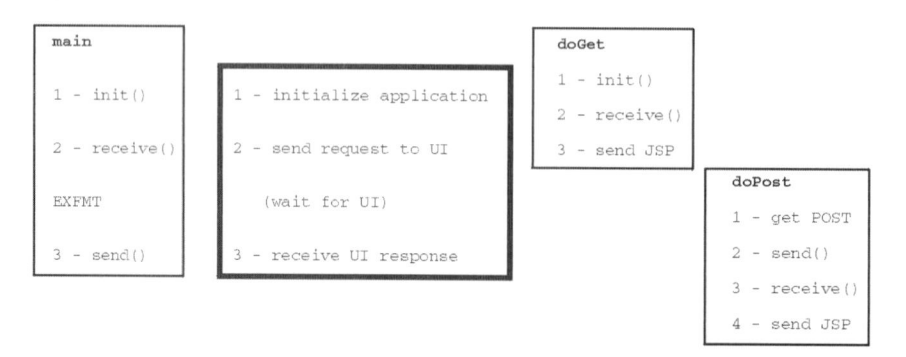

```
main                                                      doGet
1 - init()                1 - initialize application      1 - init()
                                                          2 - receive()
2 - receive()             2 - send request to UI          3 - send JSP

EXFMT                       (wait for UI)                 doPost
                                                          1 - get POST
3 - send()                3 - receive UI response         2 - send()
                                                          3 - receive()
                                                          4 - send JSP
```

Figure 9.1: Comparing the Swing UI cycle on the left to the browser UI cycle on the right.

At this point, it makes sense to take a look at the main processing method for the **ScJdspfUIServer** class. The **run** method is shown in Listing 9.5. One thing glossed over during the discussion is the fact that the application client might issue a shutdown request, but that's taken care of in the **run** method. The idea is that the UI server receives requests until one requires user interaction. The call to **client.receive** will return true only if a shutdown request is received. At that point, it returns true back to the caller, indicating that it's time to exit this application.

```
/**
 * This method was created in VisualAge.
 * @return boolean finished processing flag
 */
public boolean run() throws Sc400Exception {

    boolean shutdown = false;

    if (!isInit) init();

    if (saveBuffer != null) send();

    while (true) {
        if (client.receive()) {
            client.shutdown();
            shutdown = true;
            break;
        } else {
            if (processMessage())
                break;
        }
    }

    return shutdown;
}
```

*Listing 9.5: The main processing method of the **ScJdspfUIServer** class.*

Otherwise, **processMessage** is called. If the message is something that doesn't require user interaction—which is just about anything other than an EXFMT operation—**processMessage** returns false, which causes the class to loop back to call the **receive** method. If an EXFMT is received, though, the **processMessage** method returns true and triggers a break, which in turn causes **run** to return false. The calling program (either the Swing program or the servlet) then performs the appropriate user interface. In the case of Swing, the data is loaded into the **JbuiDisplay** object and an EXFMT is performed, while the servlet issues a **callPage** to the appropriate JSP. Once the UI server receives a response (either by the EXFMT returning or by the **doPost** method being called), it copies the data into the current buffer and then restarts the application logic with another call to the **run** method.

There is one additional twist here. Remember the concept of a **JdspfDisplayFileListener** discussed in chapter 8? Well, if one is defined, the **processMessage** will call it when a user interaction is needed. Properly coded, this function can take the data from the **JdspfDisplayFile** object, present it to the user, retrieve the response, and put it back into the **JdspfDisplayFile**. At that point, it can simply return, and **processMessage** will not trigger a break.

As it turns out, the **ScJdspfJbuiDisplay** is set up so that it can indeed support this sort of interaction, and can even use a generic adapter object to move the data from the **JdspfDisplayFile** to the **ScJdspfJbuiDisplay** and back. Using this technique, the entire logic for the Swing interface boils down to a single call to the **run** method of the **ScJdspfUIServer**. That is the power of encapsulation—an entire user interface is created in one line of code. You'll see exactly how this works in chapter 10.

10

DESIGNING A SWING INTERFACE

In this chapter, you see how to subclass the ScJdspfUIServer to create a Swing interface. This is done by creating some classes specific to the Swing interface, and putting them into a package. (This package is sort of a subpackage underneath com.pbd.pub.sc400, so its package name is com.pbd.pub.sc400.jbui.) You use those classes to create an actual application object for the user interface. Since the ITMMNT1D_DisplayFile and the ITMMNT1_Client classes have already been created in earlier chapters, once you create the ITMMNT1_JbuiDisplay object, you have an entire server/client Swing UI implementation of the original monolithic green-screen program.

This is actually a very simple chapter; almost all the work has been done in the preceding chapters. Because this is a very, very simple interface, all of the logic for an entire program has been encapsulated in these four classes, to the point where the entire logic of the actual application program is in the constructor and a two-line main procedure. This shows exactly how powerful object-oriented programming techniques really are.

The chapter is divided into three sections:

- "Finishing the Application: ITMMNT1_JbuiDisplay" is almost identical to the first part of chapter 11, creating the specific UI server objects for the ITMMNT1 application client. They could be implemented with virtually the same code, but I decided to use two slightly different techniques. In this case, inner classes are used to show how that technique can be performed.

✦ "The SC400 JBUI Classes: Specialization through Subclassing" is an object lesson (no pun intended) about how solid generic classes can be extended to support your applications with little or no additional code. The four classes used to finally implement the Swing interface total well under 200 lines of code—not a bad return on investment.

✦ "The Future of SC400 JBUI: Bigger and Better JBUI Extensions" gives you a sneak preview into where JBUI, and by extension (again, no pun intended) the SC400 JBUI can go in the future.

✦ FINISHING THE APPLICATION: ITMMNT1_JBUIDISPLAY

From previous chapters, you have a display file object, **ITMMNT1D_DisplayFile**, and an application client object, **ITMMNT1_Client**. All you need to create a working application is the UI server object. This chapter shows how to create **ITMMNT1_JbuiDisplay**, the Swing interface. To do so, let's take a look at the **ScJdspfJbuiServer** class. It's covered in more detail later in this chapter; for now, it's enough to see the methods.

The documentation for the constructors for **ScJdspfJbuiServer** is shown in Listing 10.1. You can see that **ScJdspfJbuiServer** subclasses **ScJdspfUIServer**. Interestingly, the constructors are the only methods specific to **ScJdspfJbuiServer**. The only other method needed is the **run** method, which is inherited from **ScJdspfUIServer**.

Class com.pbd.pub.sc400.jbui.ScJdspfJbuiServer
 public class ScJdspfJbuiServer
 extends ScJdspfUIServer

Constructors

ScJdspfJbuiServer
 public ScJdspfJbuiServer() throws Sc400Exception

ScJdspfJbuiServer
 public ScJdspfJbuiServer(Sc400Client client,
     JdspfDisplayFile jdspf,
     ScJdspfJbuiRecordUI recordUIs[])
 throws Sc400Exception

---

*Listing 10.1: The constructors for the **ScJdspfJbuiServer** class (part 1 of 2).*

```
ScJdspfJbuiServer
    public ScJdspfJbuiServer(Sc400Client client,
                JdspfDisplayFile jdspf,
                JdspfDisplayFileListener listener,
                ScJdspfJbuiRecordUI recordUIs[])
    throws Sc400Exception
```

*Listing 10.1: The constructors for the **ScJdspfJbuiServer** class (part 2 of 2).*

The empty constructor isn't much use, but I always like to have an empty constructor because it allows me to create an object before I know exactly how it is going to be used. This is important when creating objects dynamically based on changing application requirements. In this case, though, you already know what the requirements are, so you can ignore the empty constructor for now.

The other constructors are basically identical, except that the third one allows you to specify a **JdspfDisplayFileListener** object. This would be for more advanced UI servers; our example can use the default listener (discussed later in this chapter), so we'll concentrate on the second constructor. For the purposes of the fast-path implementation, the parameters can be broken into two groups: the application-client-interface definition and the UI server definition.

Application Client Interface Definition

Only two objects need to be identified to describe the application client interface: the application client and the display file. You can use the **Sc400Client** class introduced in chapter 8 to identify the application client, and the **JdspfDisplayFile** class from chapter 7 to emulate the display file.

UI Server Definition

Although a **JdspfDisplayFileListener** could be identified, you can just use the default listener instead. So all you need to define is an array of **JdspfRecordUI** objects. In this case, since you know that this is a JBUI interface, you can use the specialized **ScJdspfJbuiRecordUI** class. **ScJdspfJbuiRecordUI** extends the **ScJdspfRecordUI** class by requiring that the UI object be of type **ScJdspfJbuiDisplay**, and **ScJdspfJbuiDisplay** extends **JbuiDisplay** by implementing the **JdspfUIAdapter** interface. (Refer to "Record UI Objects" in chapter 8 for more information.)

Now that you've seen the basic procedure, let's actually create the **ITMMNT1_JbuiDisplay** and find out how it's done.

Making ITMMNT1_JbuiDisplay

The **ITMMNT1_JbuiDisplay** class is shown in its entirety in Listing 10.2 because two supporting classes, **ScJdspfJbuiRecordUI** and **ScJdspfJbuiDisplay**, depend pretty heavily on the concepts of JBUI. While I don't have room in this book (and certainly not in this chapter!) to go over the JBUI architecture in detail, I can at least explain the basics so that if you decide to create your own Swing UI server, you can do so. JBUI is covered in more detail in chapters 11 and 12, but analyzing this simple example will give you the basic idea.

```
import com.pbd.pub.jbui.*;
import com.pbd.pub.sc400.*;
import com.pbd.pub.sc400.jbui.*;

public class ITMMNT1_JbuiDisplay extends ScJdspfJbuiServer
{
    class prompt extends ScJdspfJbuiDisplay {
        prompt() {
            super(

                // Title
                "Item Maintenance",

                // Two fields
                new JbuiFieldPanel(
                    new JbuiEntryField[] {
                        new JbuiEntryField("X1ITEM", "Item Number:", 100),
                        new JbuiOutputField("X1ERR", "Message:", 300),
                    }
                ),

                // Two buttons, Enter and F3
                new JbuiButtonPanel(
                    new JbuiButton[] {
                        new JbuiButton(0, "Edit"),
                        new JbuiButton(3, "Exit")
                    }
                )
            );
        }
    }

    class maint extends ScJdspfJbuiDisplay {
        maint() {
            super(

                // Title
                "Item Maintenance",

                // Seven fields
                new JbuiFieldPanel(
```

Listing 10.2: The complete listing of the **ITMMNT1_JbuiDisplay** class (part 1 of 2).

```
                        new JbuiEntryField[] {
                            new JbuiOutputField("X2MODE", "Mode:", 80),
                            new JbuiOutputField("X2ITEM", "Item Number:", 150),
                            new JbuiEntryField("X2DESC", "Description:", 300),
                            new JbuiEntryField("X2QTYO", "Qty Onhand:", 90),
                            new JbuiEntryField("X2UOMI", "Stocking UOM:", 20),
                            new JbuiEntryField("X2UOMS", "Selling UOM:", 20),
                            new JbuiOutputField("X2ERR",  "Message:", 300),
                        }
                    ),

                    // Enter, F3, F6 and F12
                    new JbuiButtonPanel(
                        new JbuiButton[] {
                            new JbuiButton(0, "Edit"),
                            new JbuiButton(3, "Exit"),
                            new JbuiButton(6, "Accept"),
                            new JbuiButton(12, "Cancel")
                        }
                    )
                );
            }
        }
/**
 * ITMMNT1_JbuiDisplay constructor.
 */
public ITMMNT1_JbuiDisplay() throws Sc400Exception {
    super(
        new ITMMNT1_Client(true),
        new ITMMNT1_DisplayFile(),
        new ScJdspfJbuiRecordUI[] {
            new ScJdspfJbuiRecordUI("PROMPT   ", new prompt()),
            new ScJdspfJbuiRecordUI("MAINT    ", new maint())
        }
    );
}
/**
 * ITMMNT1_JbuiDisplay main method - create a new display and run it.
 */
public static void main(String args[])
    throws Sc400Exception
{
    new ITMMNT1_JbuiDisplay().run();
    System.exit(0);
}
}
```

Listing 10.2: The complete listing of the **ITMMNT1_JbuiDisplay** class (part 2 of 2).

Running the first panel through from green screen to here should give you a decent understanding. First, review the original green screen and the DDS that creates it in Figure 10.1 and Listing 10.3.

153

PART 2: IMPLEMENTING REVITALIZATION

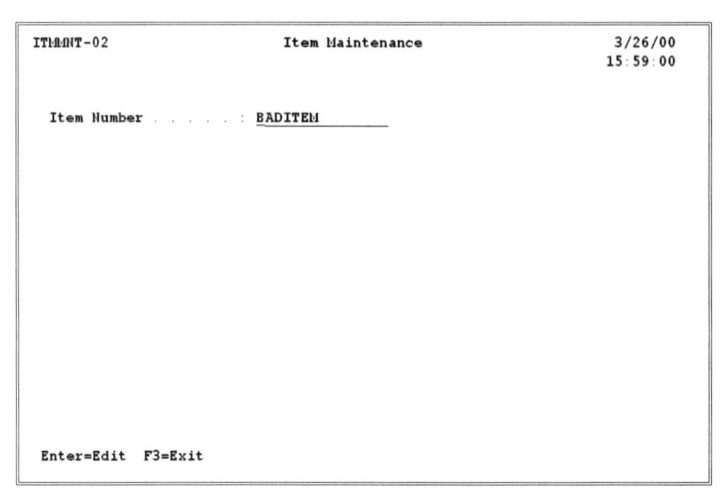

```
ITMMNT-02                  Item Maintenance                    3/26/00
                                                              15:59:00


       Item Number  . . . . . :  BADITEM_____










       Enter=Edit  F3=Exit
```

Figure 10.1: The PROMPT panel from the original item maintenance screen, ITMMNT1.

```
A            R PROMPT
A                                        CA03
A                                    1  3'ITMMNT1-01'
A                                       COLOR(BLU)
A                                    1 32'Item Maintenance'
A                                       COLOR(WHT)
A                                    1 69DATE
A                                       EDTCDE(Y)
A                                       COLOR(BLU)
A                                    2 69TIME
A                                       COLOR(BLU)
A                                    5  5'Item Number . . . . . :'
A              X1ITEM      15A  B   5 29
A              X1ERR       70   O  16  5COLOR(RED)
A                                   23  4'Enter=Edit   F3=Exit'
A                                       COLOR(BLU)
```

Listing 10.3: The DDS for the PROMPT panel.

As you can see in Listing 10.3, there are two non-constant fields, the item-number prompt field, X1ITEM, and the error-message output field, X1ERR. There is also a command key, F3.

Let's look at the corresponding JBUI version and the source for it. Figure 10.2 shows how to define an inner class. The new class **prompt** is visible only to the **ITMMNT1_JbuiDisplay** class. It extends the **ScJdspfJbuiDisplay** class, shown in Listing 10.4. **ScJdspfJbuiDisplay** is a

154

CHAPTER 10: DESIGNING A SWING INTERFACE

direct descendant of **JbuiDisplay**, and requires a string to define the title, a **JbuiFieldPanel** to define the fields, and a **JbuiButtonPanel** to define the buttons.

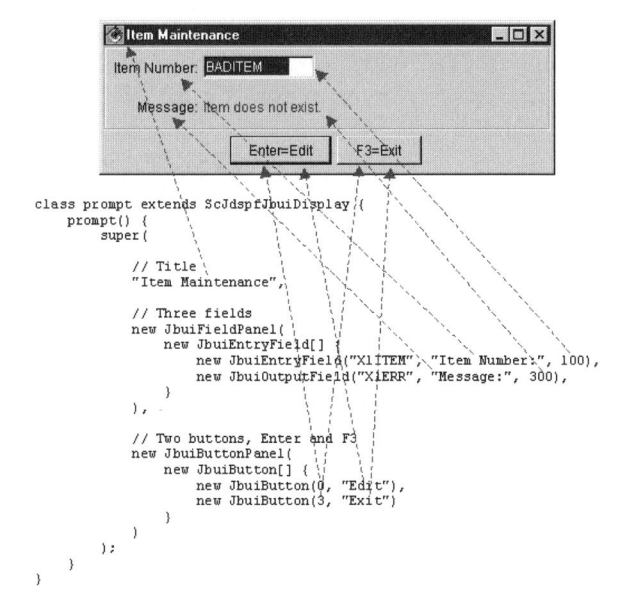

```
class prompt extends ScJdspfJbuiDisplay {
    prompt() {
        super(

        // Title
        "Item Maintenance",

        // Three fields
        new JbuiFieldPanel(
            new JbuiEntryField[] {
                new JbuiEntryField("X1ITEM", "Item Number:", 100),
                new JbuiOutputField("X1ERR", "Message:", 300),
            }
        ),

        // Two buttons, Enter and F3
        new JbuiButtonPanel(
            new JbuiButton[] {
                new JbuiButton(0, "Edit"),
                new JbuiButton(3, "Exit")
            }
        )
        );
    }
}
```

Figure 10.2: The relationship between the JBUI version of the PROMPT panel and its Java source code.

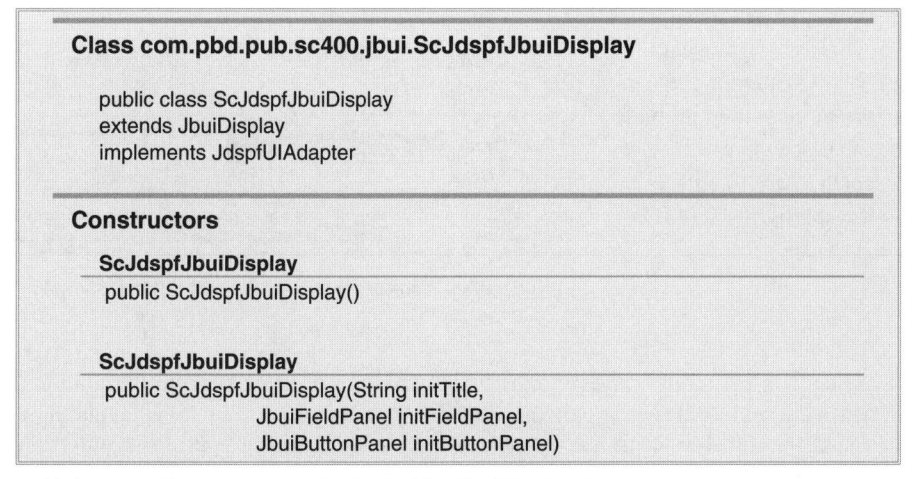

Class com.pbd.pub.sc400.jbui.ScJdspfJbuiDisplay

public class ScJdspfJbuiDisplay
extends JbuiDisplay
implements JdspfUIAdapter

Constructors

ScJdspfJbuiDisplay
public ScJdspfJbuiDisplay()

ScJdspfJbuiDisplay
public ScJdspfJbuiDisplay(String initTitle,
        JbuiFieldPanel initFieldPanel,
        JbuiButtonPanel initButtonPanel)

*Listing 10.4: The constructors for the **ScJdspfJbuiDisplay** class.*

155

PART 2: IMPLEMENTING REVITALIZATION

The **JbuiFieldPanel** class makes it very easy to create a panel of fields. You simply define the name, label, and size of the field. (The size is in pixels; depending on the data in the field, there should be about five to ten pixels per character.) The **JbuiFieldPanel** class aligns the fields properly and allows the panel to be resized without losing the relationships of the fields. If more fields are defined than will fit in the panel, **JbuiPanel** automatically generates a scrollbar. The panel in this example has the same two fields defined as the green screen, X1ITEM and X1ERR. Note that the message field X1ITEM is defined as a **JbuiEntryField**, while X1ERR is defined as a **JbuiOutputField**. This determines whether the field is input-capable or not.

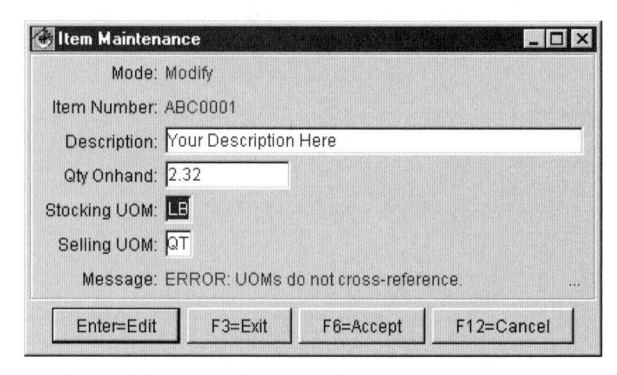

Figure 10.3: The JBUI version of the MAINT panel.

The **JbuiButtonPanel** class allows you to create a set of buttons. The buttons can optionally allow the function keys to act as accelerators. Since you are emulating the green-screen interface, you should take advantage of that fact by defining each **JbuiButton** with its accelerator-key ID and the text. The accelerator-key ID is a number from zero to 24, with zero being the Enter key, and one to 24 corresponding to the function keys F1 to F24. In this example, Enter is defined as the Edit button, and F3 is defined as the Exit button. You can define as many buttons as you need; the EXFMT method in the **JbuiDisplay** class (and in this case, its descendant **ScJdspfJbuiDisplay**) will return the appropriate key ID when the user presses a button.

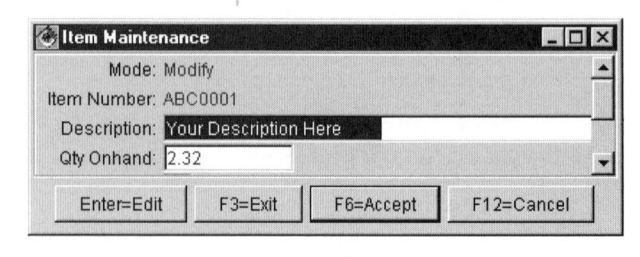

Figure 10.4: A smaller version of the MAINT panel, showing the automatic scrollbar.

The relationship between the JBUI version of the MAINT panel and the individual lines of its class is similar to the PROMPT panel and its class. Figure 10.3 shows the MAINT panel at full size, while Figure 10.4 shows that if you make the panel smaller, you'll automatically get a scrollbar. This is nice when you have a lot of fields on a panel.

Having discussed the classes, it's time to finish the rest of the class definition (which is actually only a few lines). First, let's examine the constructor, shown in Listing 10.5. As mentioned earlier in this chapter, the first two parameters for the constructor are the application-client-interface definition. Each of these has been defined in previous chapters— the display-file emulation object **ITMMNT1D_DisplayFile** in chapter 8 and the application-client proxy **ITMMNT1_Client** in chapter 9. Note that the value true is passed in the client constructor. This tells the client that the user will have to log on. The AS400 class from IBM's Java Toolbox for the AS/400 automatically prompts the user for the system name, user ID, and password when the program starts.

```
/**
 * ITMMNT1_JbuiDisplay constructor.
 */
public ITMMNT1_JbuiDisplay() throws Sc400Exception {
    super(
        new ITMMNT1_Client(true),
        new ITMMNT1_DisplayFile(),
        new ScJdspfJbuiRecordUI[] {
            new ScJdspfJbuiRecordUI("PROMPT  ", new prompt()),
            new ScJdspfJbuiRecordUI("MAINT   ", new maint())
        }
    );
}
```

Listing 10.5: The constructor for the **ITMMNT1_JbuiDisplay** class.

The third parameter is the one that ties the application client—and more importantly, the display file—to the appropriate UI objects, the **prompt** and **maint** inner classes. This is done through an array of **ScJdspfJbuiRecordUI** objects, whose constructor is shown in Listing 10.6. Each record UI object relates a record format from the original display file (which had two record formats, PROMPT and MAINT) to a UI object that is specific to this UI server. In this example, there are two inner classes based on **ScJdspfJbuiDisplay**: **prompt** and **maint**. In the constructor, you instantiate a new **prompt** object and a new **maint** object, and pass each one to a **ScJdspfJbuiRecordUI** class constructor along with the corresponding record format name. These two new record UI objects are then passed as an array into the **ITMMNT1_DisplayFile** constructor, and the object is created and ready to run.

Class com.pbd.pub.sc400.jbui.ScJdspfJbuiRecordUI

public class ScJdspfJbuiRecordUI
extends JdspfRecordUI

Constructor
ScJdspfJbuiRecordUI(String, ScJdspfJbuiDisplay)

Listing 10.6: The constructor for the **ScJdspfJbuiRecordUI** class.

How do you run the class? It's very easy. All that's required is to instantiate a new object and call its run method, as shown in Listing 10.7. Since you're using the default listener, the run method will not return until the application client sends a shutdown request. Therefore, you only call run once, and then end the program.

```
/**
 * ITMMNT1_JbuiDisplay main method - create a new display and run it.
 */
public static void main(String args[])
    throws Sc400Exception
{
    new ITMMNT1_JbuiDisplay().run();
    System.exit(0);
}
```

Listing 10.7: The main method for the *ScJdspfJbuiRecordUI* class.

Whew! It was a lot of work to get here, especially if you detoured off the fast path and read the in-depth technical stuff, but now you can do this for any program by simply changing the constructors for the client, the display file, and the JBUI display. And that is what I consider to be seriously productive programming.

✦ THE SC400 JBUI CLASSES: SPECIALIZATION THROUGH SUBCLASSING

The SC400 JBUI classes in package com.pbd.pub.sc400.jbui were designed to provide an easy way to create a JBUI interface for an application client. There is not room in this book to get into the JBUI interface in great detail—it has 18 classes and about 2,500 lines of code, which is enough for a book by itself. The example discussed in the following pages only uses a fraction of the JBUI features, however, so you don't have to know the package in detail to get it to work.

Making a JbuiDisplay Object

Let's start by dissecting a simple **JbuiDisplay** object. **JbuiDisplay** is only one of the various types of panels available from the JBUI package, but it's the one that most closely resembles a simple (non-subfile) 5250 screen. A JBUI display has two basic types of components: fields and buttons. These correspond to the fields and command keys (function keys) of a simple 5250 record format. The primary difference between the 5250 format and the JBUI display is that there are no constants on a JBUI display; any constants are integral parts of the field definitions. An example may help explain this concept.

Figure 10.5 shows the relationships between the 5250 screen components and the Swing components of the JBUI panel. There are some significant differences. The 5250 display allows you to position fields and constants anywhere on the screen, while the **JbuiDisplay** interface is designed to present a title, a list of fields, and a set of

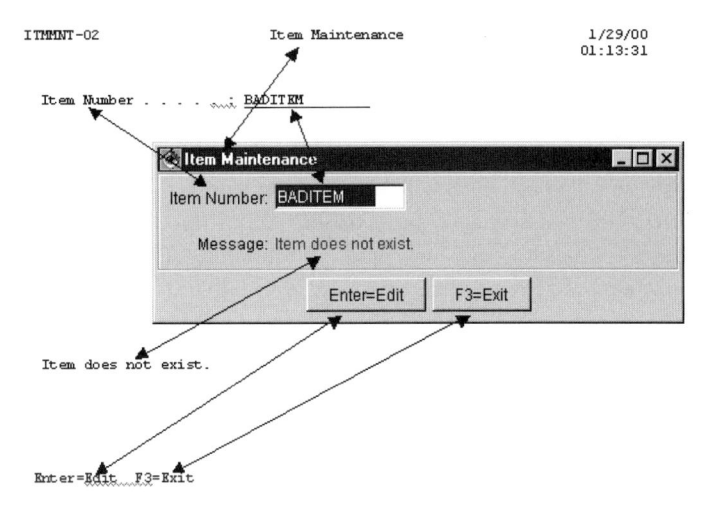

Figure 10.5: Relating the components of a 5250 display with those of a JBUI panel.

buttons, with no other extraneous data. (In chapter 11, you'll see how to mimic the 5250's flexibility in the browser interface.)

For example, the title of the 5250 display is a simple constant, but in the JBUI panel it's one of the parameters to the constructor:

```
                // Title
                "Item Maintenance",
```

The next relationship is for fields. The JBUI display has a very simple concept: each field is composed of a prompt and the field itself. The prompt information is actually a component of the field definition, not a separate entity. On a 5250 display, you have to define the field and its prompt text separately, and position them next to each other explicitly:

```
     A                                  5  5'Item Number . . . . . :'
     A           X1ITEM        15A  B   5 29
```

In the **JbuiDisplay** object, you simply create a **JbuiEntryField**, which includes both the field definition and the prompt text (for output only fields, use the **JbuiOutputField** class):

```
                new JbuiEntryField("X1ITEM", "Item Number:", 100),
```

The JbuiDisplay object is responsible for displaying the components of the field properly in relation to one another, and in relation to the other components of the panel. If the user resizes the panel, JbuiDisplay automatically repositions the components appropriately.

The last relationship is for function (command) keys. In the 5250 display, there's really no relationship between a function key and its visual representation on the screen. In fact, you don't have to have any visual indication that a key exists. If you do, there's often quite a bit of programming involved, especially if there are a lot of keys and they don't all fit on one line. Even for a simple screen, if you want to let the user know which keys are available, you have to define a text constant somewhere on the screen (usually near the bottom) that identifies the available keys. The source lines defining the keys and displaying the key definitions are often separated, as in this example:

```
A                                     CA03
(...)
A                              23  4'Enter=Edit  F3=Exit'
A                                     COLOR(BLU)
```

For the JbuiDisplay object, however, a simple object allows you to define the function-key ID and the text at the same time, and takes care of all the interface and positioning issues. These "key buttons" are grouped together and centered at the bottom of the screen. The corresponding function keys on the keyboard are enabled, so that they act the same as they would on the 5250 display. Here's the definition for the Edit and Exit buttons:

```
new JbuiButton(0, "Edit"),
new JbuiButton(3, "Exit")
```

This not only defines the buttons easily and in one place, but also helps to document the code. Now that we've covered the JbuiDisplay class in a little detail, let's continue on to SC400 JBUI classes.

SC400 JBUI

There are only four classes in the com.pbd.pub.sc400.jbui package, and one of them is an internal class you don't normally use (but which you should understand if you decide to either extend the classes or make your own UI server). Figure 10.6 shows the relationships among the classes. We're going to take the classes in reverse order, from right to left and from bottom to top. This allows us to build each class on the classes it contains.

ScJdspfJbuiDisplay

The **ScJdspfJbuiDisplay** class, shown in Listing 10.8, is one of those classes that extends its superclass by adding some new methods. Specifically, it implements the **JdspfUIAdapter** interface, which requires the methods **copyDataFromJdspf** and **copyDataToJdspf**. If you decide that you want to create your own record UI objects, it's probably a good idea to

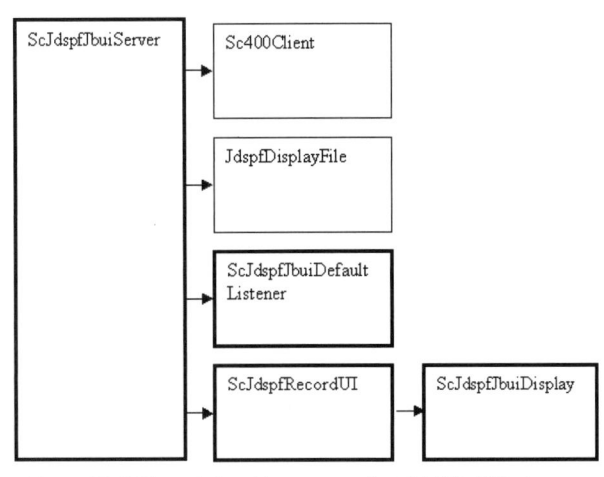

Figure 10.6: The relationships among the SC400 JBUI classes.

use this architecture. That way, you can use the **ScJdspfDefaultListener** (which you'll see a little later), and basically you have no other code to write.

```
package com.pbd.pub.sc400.jbui;

import com.pbd.pub.jbui.*;
import com.pbd.pub.jdspf.*;

/**
 * ScJdspfJbuiDisplay is the UI server adaptation of the JbuiDisplay object. It
 * implements the copyDataFromJdspf and copyDataToJdspf methods, so that the
 * ScJdspfJbuiDefaultListener can be used.
 */
public class ScJdspfJbuiDisplay extends JbuiDisplay implements JdspfUIAdapter {

/**
 * Normally unused empty constructor.
 */
public ScJdspfJbuiDisplay() {
        super();
}

/**
 * ScJbuiDisplay constructor, inherited from JbuiDisplay.
 * @param initTitle the title of the panel
 * @param initFieldPanel a JBUI field panel defining the fields for the display.
 * @param initButtonPanel a JBUI button panel defining the buttons for the
 *        display.
 */
```

*Listing 10.8: The **ScJdspfJbuiDisplay** class (part 1 of 2).*

```
public ScJdspfJbuiDisplay(String initTitle, JbuiFieldPanel initFieldPanel,
                          JbuiButtonPanel initButtonPanel)
{
        super(initTitle, initFieldPanel, initButtonPanel);
}

/**
 * This method copies fields from the current record of the JdspfDisplayFile
 * object to this display's field panel. It is assumed that every field in the
 * field panel will be defined in the JdspfRecord.
 *
 * @param jdspf the display file to copy data from.
 */
public void copyDataFromJdspf(JdspfDisplayFile jdspf) {
        JdspfAbstractRecord record = jdspf.getCurrentRecord();
        JbuiEntryField[] fields = getFieldPanel().getFields();
        for (int i = 0; i < fields.length; i++)
                fields[i].setData(record.getString(fields[i].getName()));
}

/**
 * This method copies fields from this display's field panel to the current record
 * of the JdspfDisplayFile object. It is assumed that every field in the field
 * panel will be defined in the JdspfRecord. Further, only input-capable fields
 * are copied back to the display file. Finally, the key pressed is indicated by
 * calling the setKeyPressed method of the display file.
 *
 * @param jdspf the display file to copy data to.
 */
public void copyDataToJdspf(JdspfDisplayFile jdspf) {
        JdspfAbstractRecord record = jdspf.getCurrentRecord();
        JbuiEntryField[] fields = getFieldPanel().getFields();
        for (int i = 0; i < fields.length; i++)
                if (fields[i].getProtect() == false)
                        record.setObject(fields[i].getName(),
fields[i].getData());
        jdspf.setKeyPressed(getPressedButton());
}
}
```

Listing 10.8: The **ScJdspfJbuiDisplay** class (part 2 of 2).

The constructor is copied directly from the **JbuiDisplay** superclass, and the two methods are inherited from the **JdspfUIAdapter** interface. The idea is very straightforward: **copyDataFromJdspf** is designed to be called prior to the user interaction, and **copyDataToJdspf** is called afterwards. In this example, **copyDataFromJdspf** gets a list of the fields in the **ScJdspfJbuiDisplay** object, and sets each one according to the value of the corresponding field in the current buffer of the **JdspfDisplayFile**. After calling the EXFMT method, this version of **copyDataToJdspf** reverses the operation, copying the fields from the **ScJdspfJbuiDisplay** back to the **ScJdspfDisplayFile**. Of course, that means that the field names must match, but that's done in the **ScJdspfJbuiDisplay** constructor.

If you wanted to change the names, you could do so by writing more sophisticated **copyData** routines. The only other line of note is the **setKeyPressed** line at the end of **copyDataToJdspf**. This line indicates which button the user pressed (which is eventually transformed to the appropriate command-key indicator in the application client).

ScJdspfJbuiRecordUI

One of the simplest classes in this book, the **ScJdspfJbuiRecordUI** class, shown in Listing 10.9, is a simple extension of the **JdspfRecordUI** class from chapter 8. While **JdspfRecordUI** accepts any sort of object as the record UI object, this class is defined to force the use of an **ScJdspfJbuiDisplay**. This technique is a powerful way to customize a generic interface for a particular role. This way, you can make assumptions later in the other classes (for example, in **ScJdspfJbuiDefaultListener**) about the type of object contained in the record UI object field.

```
package com.pbd.pub.sc400.jbui;

import com.pbd.pub.jbui.*;
import com.pbd.pub.jdspf.*;

/**
 * The specialized version of the JdspfRecordUI for the JBUI UI Server.
 */
public class ScJdspfJbuiRecordUI extends JdspfRecordUI {

/**
 * Creates an ScJdspfJbuiRecordUI for the specified record name and
 * ScJdspfJbuiDisplay.
 */
public ScJdspfJbuiRecordUI(String recordName, ScJdspfJbuiDisplay jbuiDisplay) {
    super(recordName, jbuiDisplay);
}

/**
 * Return the UI object as an ScJbuiDisplay
 * @return ScJbuiDisplay
 */
public ScJdspfJbuiDisplay getJbuiDisplay() {
    return (ScJdspfJbuiDisplay) getRecordUIObject();
}
}
```

Listing 10.9: The **ScJdspfJbuiRecordUI** class.

ScJdspfJbuiDefaultListener

The **ScJdspfJbuiDefaultListener**, shown in Listing 10.10, is a typical listener class. It is defined simply to contain the action method, which is called when a user interaction is required by the **JdspfDisplayFile** object. While this class is usually not seen by application programmers, you might want to make sure you understand it in case you decide build your own interfaces. If, for example, you decided to create an interface that sent an XML message out to another server and received the response back, this would be the place where you would format that message, send it, receive the response, and then put the response data into the display file to return to the application client.

```java
package com.pbd.pub.sc400.jbui;

import com.pbd.pub.jbui.*;
import com.pbd.pub.jdspf.*;

/**
 * ScJdspfJbuiDefaultListener is the default listener class for JBUI UI servers.
 * It will retrieve the ScJdspfJbuiDisplay object from the JdspfDisplayFile object
 * passed as the source of the action. Then it will copy the data from the display
 * file to the JBUI display using copyDataFromJdspf, call the EXFMT method, then
 * copy the results back to the display file using copyDataToJdspf.
 */
public class ScJdspfJbuiDefaultListener implements JdspfDisplayFileListener {

/**
 * This method is called when user interaction is required. The method retrieves
 * the JdspfDisplayFile and ScJdspfJbuiDisplay objects from the action, then copies
 * the data from display file to JBUI display, calls EXFMT, and copies the data
 * back from the JBUI display to the display file.
 *
 * @param action the JdspfDisplayFileAction object from the application client.
 * @return boolean always false to indicate no further intervention required.
 */
public boolean actionPerformed(JdspfDisplayFileAction action) {

        JdspfDisplayFile jdspf = (JdspfDisplayFile) action.getSource();
        ScJdspfJbuiDisplay display =
                (ScJdspfJbuiDisplay) jdspf.getCurrentRecord().getUIObject();

        display.copyDataFromJdspf(jdspf);
        display.EXFMT();
        display.copyDataToJdspf(jdspf);

        return false;
}
}
```

Listing 10.10: The **ScJdspfJbuiDefaultListener** class.

ScJdspfJbuiServer

Finally, the **ScJdspfJbuiServer** class is shown in Listing 10.11. Because of the way this package is designed, all of the work is actually done in the contained classes, so there is no code to speak of in the server, only a few constructors that identify the classes to contain. You'll see in chapter 11 that this is not the case in the browser version, since that interface must take into account the very different interface cycle of browser. For the Swing interface, though, you're done.

```java
package com.pbd.pub.sc400.jbui;

import com.pbd.pub.jdspf.*;
import com.pbd.pub.sc400.*;

/**
 * The ScJdspfJbuiServer is the prototype for all other JBUI UI servers,  It
 * defines a generic application client interface using Sc400Client
 * and JdspfDisplayFile, but forces the user to specify ScJdspfJbuiRecordUI
 * objects as the UI server interface.
 */
public class ScJdspfJbuiServer extends ScJdspfUIServer
{

/**
 * Normally unused empty constructor.
 */
public ScJdspfJbuiServer()
        throws Sc400Exception
{
}

/**
 * Standard constructor, takes advantage of the ScJdspfJbuiDefaultListener class.
 */
public ScJdspfJbuiServer(Sc400Client client, JdspfDisplayFile jdspf,
            ScJdspfJbuiRecordUI[] recordUIs)
        throws Sc400Exception
{
        this(client, jdspf, new ScJdspfJbuiDefaultListener(), recordUIs);
}

/**
 * Advanced constructor for use when the user interface requires more
 * sophisticated processing than simply copying fields from one object
 * to another and back.
 */
public ScJdspfJbuiServer(Sc400Client client, JdspfDisplayFile jdspf,
            JdspfDisplayFileListener listener,
            ScJdspfJbuiRecordUI[] recordUIs)
```

Listing 10.11: The **ScJdspfJbuiServer** class (part 1 of 2).

```
            throws Sc400Exception
{
        super(client, jdspf, listener, recordUIs);
}
}
```

Listing 10.11: The *ScJdspfJbuiServer* class (part 2 of 2).

THE FUTURE OF SC400 JBUI: BIGGER AND BETTER JBUI EXTENSIONS

This Swing-interface package was made possible entirely by the existence of the JBUI package. That in itself shows how object-oriented programming is a fantastic way to leverage work from one project to another. However, it stretches the limits of what JBUI can do today. While SC400 JBUI is not really the focus of this book, I'd like to take a brief look at the future of the Swing interface.

The Swing interface is much more sophisticated than the browser's HTML interface. Swing components offer a range of features far beyond that of the simple input fields and buttons of the browser. This includes the ability to support advanced GUI capabilities, such as drag-and-drop and programmable look and feel. The panel can be sized as the user sees fit, with the components in the panel rearranging themselves accordingly. The Swing table, in particular, is very powerful; columns can be resized or rearranged easily. The Swing interface is a very comfortable one, especially for users who are familiar with Windows-based products. Therefore, I plan to continue expanding the JBUI package and using it as a base for the SC400 JBUI package. Let's take a peek at what the Swing interface might look like for a subfile.

Subfiles

Figures 10.7 and 10.8 show the "before" and "after" versions of what a subfile program might look like. This is a fairly literal interpretation of how the translation from the 5250 model to the Swing interface might be accomplished. The user enters options for one or more lines in the input field under the option column, and then presses the Process button. The specified options are performed sequentially. A slight modification would allow the option field to be a drop-down list showing only the available options.

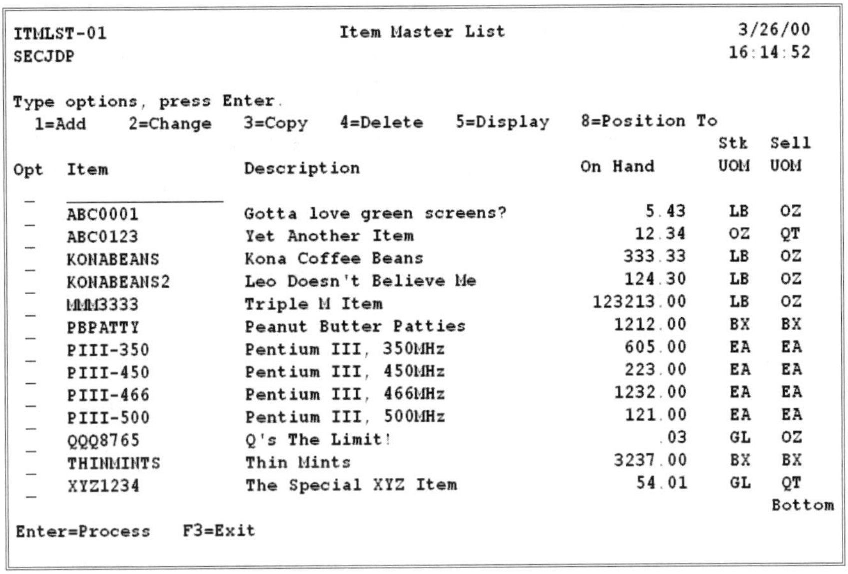

CHAPTER 10: DESIGNING A SWING INTERFACE

```
ITMLST-01                  Item Master List                    3/26/00
SECJDP                                                         16:14:52

Type options, press Enter.
   1=Add     2=Change   3=Copy    4=Delete    5=Display   8=Position To
                                                             Stk    Sell
Opt   Item               Description                  On Hand UOM    UOM

  _   ABC0001            Gotta love green screens?       5.43 LB     OZ
  _   ABC0123            Yet Another Item               12.34 OZ     QT
  _   KONABEANS          Kona Coffee Beans             333.33 LB     OZ
  _   KONABEANS2         Leo Doesn't Believe Me        124.30 LB     OZ
  _   MMM3333            Triple M Item              123213.00 LB     OZ
  _   PBPATTY            Peanut Butter Patties        1212.00 BX     BX
  _   PIII-350           Pentium III, 350MHz           605.00 EA     EA
  _   PIII-450           Pentium III, 450MHz           223.00 EA     EA
  _   PIII-466           Pentium III, 466MHz          1232.00 EA     EA
  _   PIII-500           Pentium III, 500MHz           121.00 EA     EA
  _   QQQ8765            Q's The Limit!                   .03 GL     OZ
  _   THINMINTS          Thin Mints                   3237.00 BX     BX
  _   XYZ1234            The Special XYZ Item           54.01 GL     QT
                                                                   Bottom
Enter=Process     F3=Exit
```

Figure 10.7: A typical 5250 subfile screen.

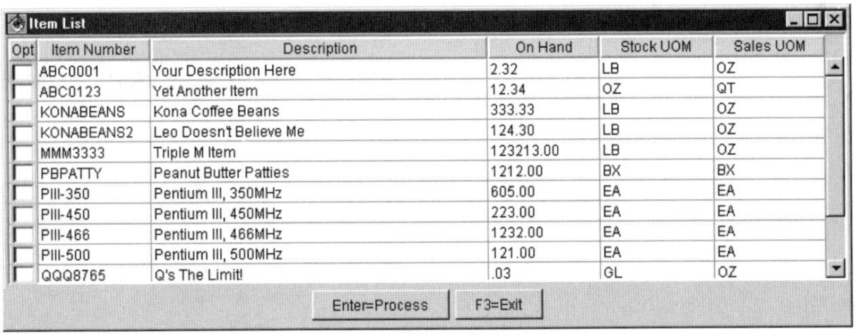

Opt	Item Number	Description	On Hand	Stock UOM	Sales UOM
☐	ABC0001	Your Description Here	2.32	LB	OZ
☐	ABC0123	Yet Another Item	12.34	OZ	QT
☐	KONABEANS	Kona Coffee Beans	333.33	LB	OZ
☐	KONABEANS2	Leo Doesn't Believe Me	124.30	LB	OZ
☐	MMM3333	Triple M Item	123213.00	LB	OZ
☐	PBPATTY	Peanut Butter Patties	1212.00	BX	BX
☐	PIII-350	Pentium III, 350MHz	605.00	EA	EA
☐	PIII-450	Pentium III, 450MHz	223.00	EA	EA
☐	PIII-466	Pentium III, 466MHz	1232.00	EA	EA
☐	PIII-500	Pentium III, 500MHz	121.00	EA	EA
☐	QQQ8765	Q's The Limit!	.03	GL	OZ

[Enter=Process] [F3=Exit]

Figure 10.8: The screen from Figure 10.7, using a Swing approach.

While Figure 10.8 is a good example of a strict GUI interpretation of the 5250 model, there are more creative ways to handle this sort of screen. Figure 10.9 shows one evolutionary path, in which the option column is replaced with a row of action buttons at the bottom of the screen. The user selects a line, and then presses an action button. While this allows the user to select only one action at a time, this sort of interface might be a better fit for Windows users.

Finally, Figure 10.10 shows the most radical departure from the original design, at least in appearance. A right click on a selected line brings up a popup menu that allows the user to select an action. If you were to combine this approach with a table allowing multiple rows to be selected, most Windows users would probably be quite comfortable.

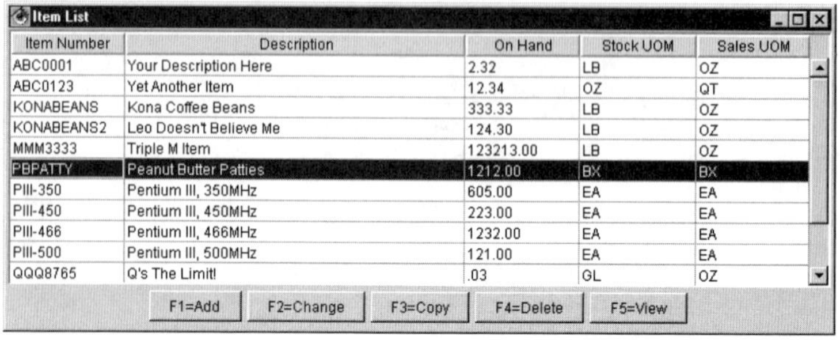

This would require some additional code in the JBUI package and in the SC400 JBUI package.

Figure 10.9: The same screen as Figure 10.8, using a slightly different Swing method.

There would have to be a way to define to the JBUI package which options were available, and then a way to translate the more sophisticated GUI approaches, such as the popup menu, to 5250 actions. For example, if the user selected three lines and then brought up the popup menu and selected Change, the interface would need to act as if the user typed option 2 into each of the selected lines. Those lines would then be returned on subsequent READC operations. That would all be part of the SC400 JBUI infrastructure, however, and transparent to the application programmer.

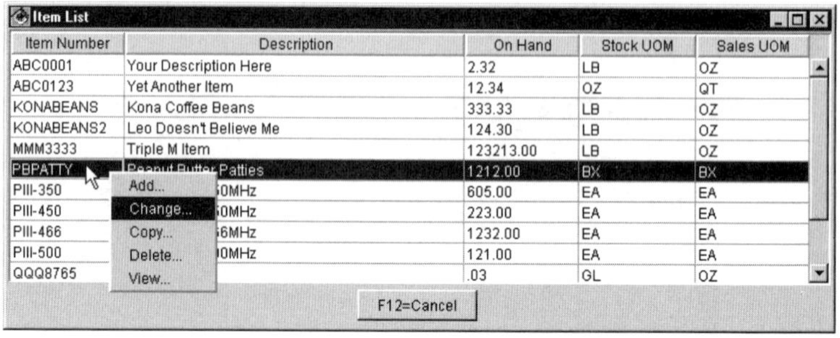

Figure 10.10: A very graphical point-and-click type of interface.

The Future Looks Bright

The way I've programmed **JdspfDisplayFile**, it could be used relatively easily as an intermediary to add more powerful features to the JBUI SC400 package. The JBUI package is already a long way towards allowing this to happen; it would simply be a matter of adding the attributes and subfiles to the underlying architecture. That's what I love about object-oriented programming: it keeps getting better.

11

DESIGNING THE BROWSER INTERFACE

This is the *pièce de résistance*, the reason you're here: to put a browser interface on an existing green-screen application. There is one more package to explore, **com.pbd.pub.sc400.jsp**, the SC400 JSP interface package. In order to do that, you also have to understand **com.pbd.pub.jsp**, the small but necessary JSP support package.

This chapter is not quite as simple as the previous chapter. Although the first section is similar to the first section of chapter 10, that's because the architecture was designed that way. In fact, creating the servlet is actually a little simpler than creating a Swing interface because there is no **main** method to implement in a servlet. However, unlike the self-contained entities of the Swing interface, there is more to the browser interface than just the Java programming. In addition to the servlet, you have to create the JavaServer Pages that actually provide the user interface (sort of like the display file on the AS/400), as well as install everything in the correct directories on the AS/400. All of that means beginning your journey into the land of the WebSphere Application Server, which is probably uncharted territory for you.

PART 2: IMPLEMENTING REVITALIZATION

This chapter contains the following sections:

- In "Finishing the Application: ITMMNT1_Servlet and Its JSPs," you create the servlet and the three JavaServer Pages used to run the program. This section touches on many areas, and if you don't follow the directions exactly, you can expect some difficult-to-diagnose problems. WebSphere is a notoriously finicky piece of software, more like its UNIX cousins than the comfortable, rock-solid systems software we've come to know and love with OS/400. But if you "follow the bouncing ball," you should be able to get an application up and running.

- "Running the Application: ITMMNT1_Servlet" explains the basics of the WebSphere architecture. Unfortunately, this is V4R3 OS/400, which means version 1.1 of WebSphere, so things will change with subsequent releases. (That's why I've pulled this information out into its own section.) Part 3 of this book goes into specific detail about the installation of all the pieces and gives you a few hints about debugging, but this section should be enough to get this specific example running.

- "Modeling an Object: The JSP Package" discusses one of the smallest packages in the PBD stable. Made up of two classes in about 250 lines, mostly comments, **com.pbd.pub.jsp** identifies the essential elements required to define a JavaServer Page to the rest of the world.

- In "More Extensions: The SC400 JSP Package," you learn that the SC400 JSP package is a bit bigger than the SC400 JBUI package, but there are some significant similarities. You define a UI server, a record UI interface, and the corresponding record UI object, in this case descended from the **Jsp** object in the **com.pbd.pub.jsp** package. However, a few additional classes are necessary to try to make HTML behave like a 5250 display. All in all, there are five classes and a little more than 400 lines of Java code to deal with.

- "The Future of SC400 JSP: Bigger and Better Extensions" takes a look at how the SC400 JSP package could be extended to support attributes, subfiles, and message subfiles. Unlike the SC400 JBUI package, which is built to interface to a package that was designed from the start to emulate an AS/400 green-screen interface, SC400 JSP must work with HTML, which is a rather inflexible interface. However, with the advent of JavaServer Pages, you can use a combination of HTML and just a little bit of Java code to create a pretty flexible UI definition.

FINISHING THE APPLICATION: ITMMNT1_SERVLET AND ITS JSPS

It's time to create the browser interface, but in order to do that, you need to understand all the pieces that are required. This section reviews the required components and shows how they were created for this example. First, take a look at an overview of the architecture in Figure 11.1.

As you can see, the servlet is started with a call to its **doGet** method. This is done by a button with the method GET rather than POST defined (you'll see more about that a little later in this chapter). This triggers a call to the **run** routine of the UI server. In Figure 11.1, the UI server is labeled **ITMMNT1_Client**, but that's a little bit of a misnomer; the **ITMMNT1_Client** class is contained within the UI server. The **run** method calls the **init** method of the application-client proxy (**ITMMNT1_Client**), which calls DQMUNITC to start the application client (ITMMNT1AC) on the host. From that point, the application client sends requests for each EXFMT operation it encounters. Each is received by the UI server through the application-client proxy and passed to the servlet by returning false from the **run** method. The servlet then performs a **callPage** to send the appropriate JavaServer Page to the user.

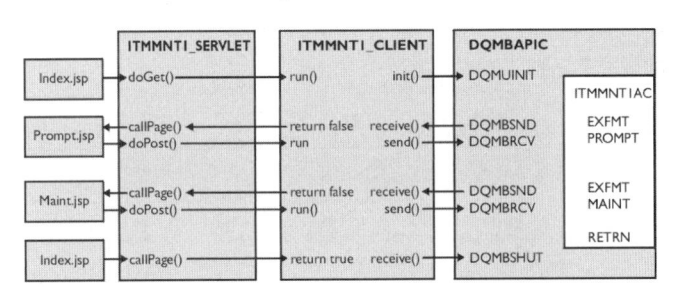

Figure 11.1: The overall data flow of the browser interface.

In this architecture, the JavaServer Page then POSTs the user's response back to the same servlet, which returns the data with another call to the **run** method of the UI server. The returned data is sent back via the **send** method of the application-client proxy to the application client. That completes the emulation of the EXFMT. Finally, when the application client is finished and ready to exit, the wrapper sends a shutdown request, which eventually gets back to the servlet, which then calls the exit JSP—in this case, the original index.jsp that started the whole thing.

In previous chapters, you've already created the application-client proxy **ITMMNT1_Client**, its display-file emulation object **ITMMNT1_DisplayFile**, and the AS/400 application client ITMMNT1AC. In addition, the browser interface requires the servlet **ITMMNT1_Servlet** and three JavaServer Pages, **index.jsp**, **ITMMNT1_PROMPT.jsp**, and **ITMMNT1_MAINT.jsp**. (In

Figure 11.1, these last two are called **prompt.jsp** and **maint.jsp**, respectively, just to conserve a little space.) First, let's create the class **ITMMNT1_Servlet**. To do that, start by examining Listing 11.1.

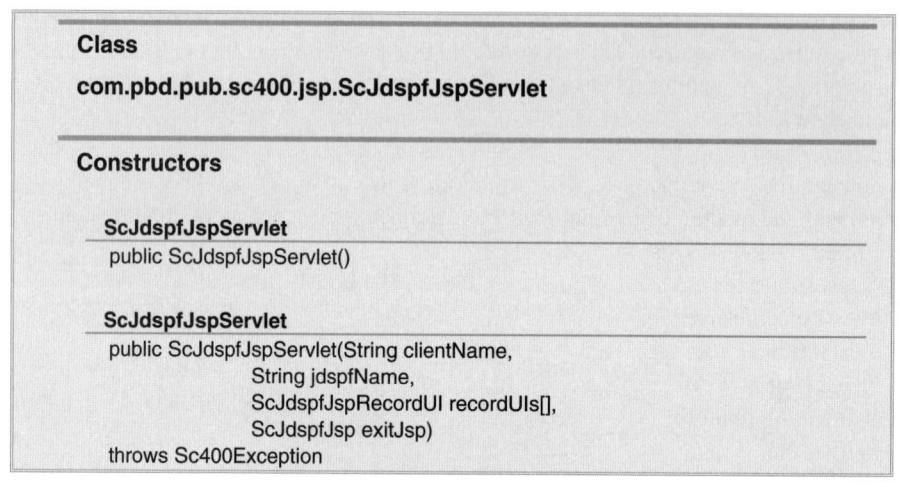

Class

com.pbd.pub.sc400.jsp.ScJdspfJspServlet

Constructors

ScJdspfJspServlet
  public ScJdspfJspServlet()

ScJdspfJspServlet
  public ScJdspfJspServlet(String clientName,
              String jdspfName,
              ScJdspfJspRecordUI recordUIs[],
              ScJdspfJsp exitJsp)
      throws Sc400Exception

---

*Listing 11.1: The constructors for the **ScJdspfJspServlet** class.*

Listing 11.1 shows the constructors for the **ScJdspJspServlet** class. As in chapter 10, you can ignore the empty constructor. Unlike the **ScJdspfJbuiServer**, which has two different concrete constructors, **ScJdspfJspServlet** has only one. On the other hand, like the constructors for the SC400 JBUI version, the parameters for the constructor are broken into two distinct groups: the application-client-interface definition and the UI server definition.

The Application-Client-Interface Definition

Only two objects need to be identified to describe the application-client interface: the application client and the display file. However, you don't pass in objects (another slight divergence from the SC400 JBUI version). Instead, you pass only the class names for the objects. This is because the servlet must use the **Beans.instantiate** method for classes it intends to use, rather than using the new keyword to create instances of them. Otherwise, the servlet gets an "invalid access" error.

The UI Server Definition

The UI server definition is very simple. You pass an array of record UI objects, which in this example uses **ScJdspfJsp** objects as the UI object, as well as a final **ScJdspfJsp** object, which is used as the exit JSP. The exit JSP is called when a shutdown request is received from the application client.

Making the JavaServer Pages

You can create the JavaServer Pages either before or after the servlet. In this book, the JSPs are created first. Without debating the finer points of HTML design, take a look at the 5250 version of the prompt panel in Figure 11.2 and its DDS source in Listing 11.2, for comparison with the browser version and its JSP source.

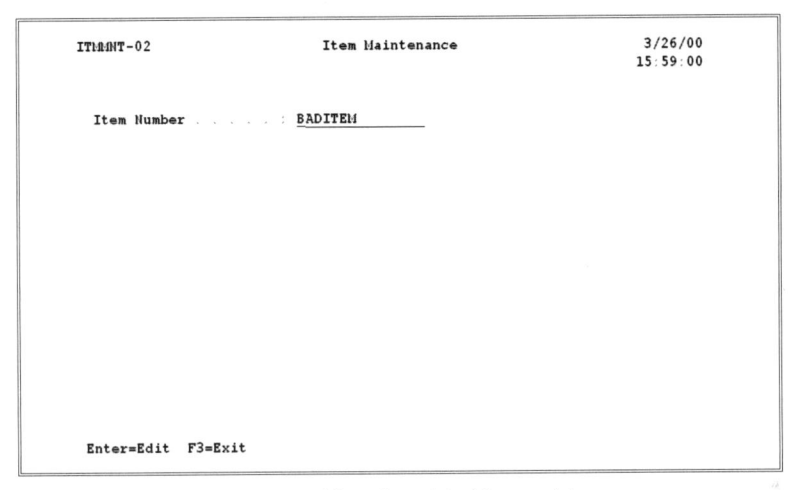

```
ITMMNT-02                   Item Maintenance                        3/26/00
                                                                   15:59:00

          Item Number . . . . . : BADITEM














          Enter=Edit   F3=Exit
```

Figure 11.2: The PROMPT panel from the original item maintenance screen, ITMMNT1.

```
     A              R PROMPT
     A                                        CA03
     A                                    1  3'ITMMNT1-01'
     A                                        COLOR(BLU)
     A                                    1 32'Item Maintenance'
     A                                        COLOR(WHT)
     A                                    1 69DATE
     A                                        EDTCDE(Y)
     A                                        COLOR(BLU)
     A                                    2 69TIME
     A                                        COLOR(BLU)
     A                                    5  5'Item Number . . . . . :'
     A              X1ITEM       15A  B   5 29
     A              X1ERR        70   O  16  5COLOR(RED)
     A                                   23  4'Enter=Edit   F3=Exit'
     A                                        COLOR(BLU)
```

Listing 11.2: The DDS for the PROMPT panel.

As you can see in Listing 11.2, there are two non-constant fields: the item number prompt field, X1ITEM, and the error message output field, X1ERR. There is also a command key, F3. Now, let's turn to the corresponding browser version and its source, **ITMMNT1_PROMPT.jsp**.

Figure 11.3 shows a very simple (and not particularly attractive) example of a browser interface for the PROMPT panel, along with the JavaServer Page that generated the HTML. As mentioned earlier, this book is not intended to be a primer on HTML or JSP. Figure 11.3 is a relatively simple example of a JavaServer Page. If it doesn't make sense to you, it's probably a good idea to do some additional research on JavaServer Pages. An excellent place to begin is at the Javasoft JSP page, http://web2.java.sun.com/products/jsp, where you'll find wonderful information on the JSP technology, along with tutorials and developer's materials.

Without going into a lot of detail, there are a few things to point out. First, there is the matter of "The Bean." I capitalize the phrase a little tongue-in-cheek because the term is so unassuming, yet very powerful. The term "The Bean" in this book identifies the data bean that is passed from the servlet to the JavaServer Page. Don Denoncourt refers to The Bean as a "smart parameter," which is a very apt term. The Bean carries with

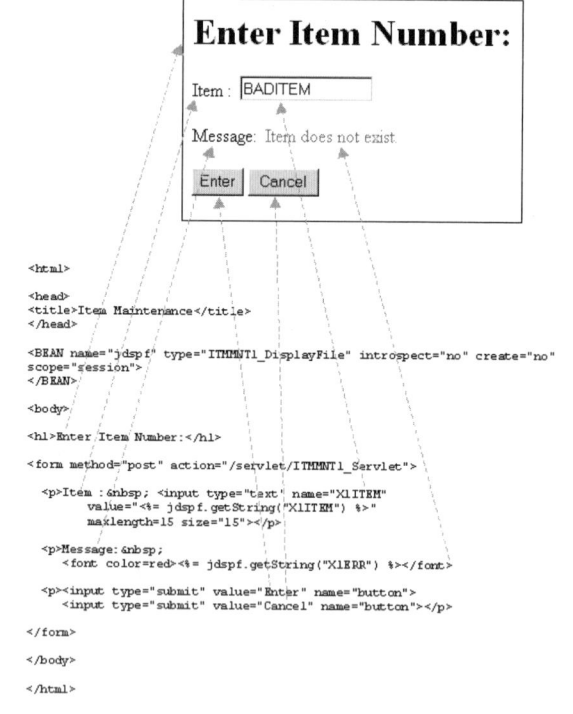

Figure 11.3: The relationship between the browser version of the PROMPT panel and its JSP source code.

it not only data, but methods that can be used to extract the data. In the revitalization architecture, The Bean is actually an object of type **JdspfDisplayFile**, which makes sense, since the **JdspfDisplayFile** object is the one that holds all the data to emulate the 5250 display file on the AS/400. The following lines in the source code give the JSP access to The Bean:

```
<BEAN name="jdspf" type="ITMMNT1_DisplayFile" introspect="no" create="no"
scope="session">
</BEAN>
```

There are lots of other options and option settings that can be used when defining a bean in a JSP, but this is the particular one used here. In short, it means The Bean already exists with the name **jdspf**, and is of class **ITMMNT1_DisplayFile**. This is sufficient to tell the JSP all it needs to know about accessing The Bean.

Another thing to note is the **<form>** command. This is the binding point between the JSP and the servlet. Look at the following line:

```
<form method="post" action="/servlet/ITMMNT1_Servlet">
```

The **action** keyword directs the Web server to send the results of this form to the servlet named **ITMMNT1_Servlet** when the user presses one of the submit buttons. It is absolutely crucial in your architecture that this is the same servlet that sent the data to the JSP in the first place. The **post** method keyword tells the Web server to call the **doPost** method (as well as telling it to include the user data).

That leaves field and button definitions. There are two types of fields, input and output. The output field is a little easier, so let's review that first. To display the results of the X1ERR output field, The Bean's **getString** method is called, which is designed to return the string representation of a field. This JSP should display "Message:" followed by the actual error text. One little twist is that an error message should appear in red. The following lines do this:

```
<p>Message: 
    <font color=red><%= jdspf.getString("X1ERR") %></font>
```

The first line outputs the label "Message:," while the second line (with the **<%=** and **%>** tags) outputs the contents of the X1ERR field. The **<font>** tags set the color for the error message.

The input field is slightly more complex. Again, you have to output a label, but then you have to define a form field. In addition to creating the form field, you need to give it an initial value of the current contents of the field. That's accomplished by these lines:

```
<p>Item :  <input type="text" name="X1ITEM"
   value="<%= jdspf.getString("X1ITEM") %>"
   maxlength=15 size="15"></p>
```

PART 2: IMPLEMENTING REVITALIZATION

The label "Item:" is output just the same as an output field, then an input field of type text is created, with the name corresponding to the field name. While it's not obvious here, it is very important that the name of the input field be the same as the name of the field in The Bean. This is the binding point; when you retrieve the user data, it will be by field name, and the Web server only knows the data by the name associated with it in the form field. The next line sets the default value of the field to be the current contents of the field in The Bean. The last line sets the length and size of the field.

Finally, let's review the buttons, the simplest part of the JSP. The only caveat has to do with the field name. Here's the source:

```
<p><input type="submit" value="Enter" name="button">
   <input type="submit" value="Cancel" name="button"></p>
```

In this case, there are two buttons, Enter and Cancel, both of type submit. Notice that they have the same name, "button." This is important; the name is used in the Java definition of the JSP to tell the UI server how to determine which button the user pressed.

That's about it for creating the **ITMMNT1_PROMPT** JavaServer Page. You'll probably want to reread this part of the chapter when you look at the source for the **ITMMNT1_MAINT.jsp** JavaServer Page. It's very similar, with just a few more fields and buttons.

The other JavaServer Page is the exit page, which is called when the application client ends. In this case, it's also the page that starts the application by sending a GET request to the servlet. The source, shown in Listing 11.3, is very simple.

```
<HTML>

<HEAD>
<TITLE>Revitalization Index</TITLE>
</HEAD>

<h2>Revitalization - The New Millennium!</h2>
<p><br>
<p>

<form method="get" action="/servlet/ITMMNT1_Servlet">
<h3>ITMMNT1 EXFMT JSP: </h3><input type="submit" value="Launch ITMMNT1!"
name="button">
</form>
```

Listing 11.3: The source for the *index.jsp* JavaServer Page (part 1 of 2).

176

```
<form method="get" action="/servlet/ITMMNT1A_Servlet">
<h3>Green Screen JSP: </h3><input type="submit" value="Launch ITMMNT1A!"
name="button">
</form>

<form method="get" action="/servlet/ITMMNT1B_Servlet">
<h3>Nice Format JSP: </h3><input type="submit" value="Launch ITMMNT1B!"
name="button">
</form>

</BODY>
</HTML>
```

*Listing 11.3: The source for the **index.jsp** JavaServer Page (part 2 of 2).*

The index.jsp page is set up to launch one of three servlets: **ITMMNT1_Servlet**, **ITMMNT1A_Servlet**, or **ITMMNT1B_Servlet**. You'll see them in a little more detail later in this chapter, but for now, you simply need to know that the form is a single button with the method set to **get** and the action set to the servlet. This tells the Web server to call the **doGet** method of the servlet, rather than **doPost**. That, in turn, directs the servlet to start a new application client.

Defining the Servlet

There's not a lot to the servlet in Listing 11.4. It simply needs to define the application-client-interface definitions and the UI server definitions, which in this case are simply an array of **ScJdspfJspRecordUI** objects and a single **ScJdspfJsp** object to define the exit JSP.

```
import com.pbd.pub.jsp.*;
import com.pbd.pub.sc400.*;
import com.pbd.pub.sc400.jsp.*;

public class ITMMNT1_Servlet extends ScJdspfJspServlet
{
    private static final String PATH = "/IBMWebAS/samples/revitalization";
/**
 * This is the servlet used to communicate with the application client
 * ITMMNT1AC on the host.
 */
public ITMMNT1_Servlet()
    throws Sc400Exception
{
```

*Listing 11.4: The **ITMMNT1_Servlet** class in its entirety (part 1 of 3).*

```
super(

// Application Client Interface Definition

    // Application Client Proxy
    "ITMMNT1_Client",

    // Display File Proxy
    "ITMMNT1_DisplayFile",

// UI Server Definition

    // Record UI Definitions
    new ScJdspfJspRecordUI[] {

        // PROMPT panel - ITMMNT1_PROMPT.jsp
        new ScJdspfJspRecordUI(
            "PROMPT   ",
            new ScJdspfJsp(
                PATH,
                "ITMMNT1_PROMPT.jsp",
                new JspField[] {
                    new JspField("X1ITEM"),
                    new ScJdspfJspButtonField("button",
                        new ScJdspfJspButtonDefinition[] {
                            new ScJdspfJspButtonDefinition("Enter", 0),
                            new ScJdspfJspButtonDefinition("Cancel", 3)
                        }
                    )
                }
            )
        ),

        // MAINT panel - ITMMNT1_MAINT.jsp
        new ScJdspfJspRecordUI(
            "MAINT    ",
            new ScJdspfJsp(
                PATH,
                "ITMMNT1_MAINT.jsp",
                new JspField[] {
                    new JspField("X2DESC"),
                    new JspField("X2QTYO"),
                    new JspField("X2UOMI"),
                    new JspField("X2UOMS"),
                    new ScJdspfJspButtonField("button",
                        new ScJdspfJspButtonDefinition[] {
                            new ScJdspfJspButtonDefinition("Edit", 0),
                            new ScJdspfJspButtonDefinition("Exit", 3),
                            new ScJdspfJspButtonDefinition("Accept", 6),
                            new ScJdspfJspButtonDefinition("Cancel", 12)
                        }
                    )
                }
            )
```

Listing 11.4: The **ITMMNT1_Servlet** class in its entirety (part 2 of 3).

```
                    }
                )
            )
        },
        // Exit Panel - index.jsp
        new ScJdspfJsp(PATH, "index.jsp")
    );
// Remove comment to enable logging
//     setLogTrace(true);
}
}
```

Listing 11.4: The **ITMMNT1_Servlet** class in its entirety (part 3 of 3).

Let's take a look in detail at the ScJdspfJspRecordUI definition for the PROMPT record. The ScJdspfJspRecordUI, shown in Listing 11.5, is a very simple class that relates an ScJdspfJsp to a record format name. An array of these is used to relate the record formats of a display file to their corresponding JavaServer Pages. The definition of a JavaServer Page is a bit more complex.

Class com.pbd.pub.sc400.jsp.ScJdspfJspRecordUI

public class ScJdspfJspRecordUI
extends JdspfRecordUI

Constructor
ScJdspfJspRecordUI(String, ScJdspfJsp)

Listing 11.5: The constructor for the **ScJdspfJspRecordUI** class.

There are two sections to the ScJdspfJsp definition shown in Listing 11.6: the location of the JSP, and the fields within the JSP. Only the location is required; a JSP with no input fields or buttons, such as the exit JSP, is defined by simply identifying its location.

The location has two parts, the path and the name. The path is used to define a common directory for all the JSPs. In an advanced environment, you might want to be able to call a system method to determine the appropriate path for a given application. The name is the specific name of the actual JavaServer Page source file. The second part of the

ScJdspfJsp is the field definition. This is an array of JspFields, but in the case of this example, a special class is designed to help the interface between the HTML and the 5250.

Class com.pbd.pub.sc400.jbui.ScJdspfJsp

public class ScJdspfJsp
extends Jsp
implements JdspfUIAdapter

Constructors

ScJdspfJsp
public ScJdspfJsp()

ScJdspfJsp
public ScJdspfJsp(String name)

ScJdspfJsp
public ScJdspfJsp(String name,
　　JspField fields[])

ScJdspfJsp
public ScJdspfJsp(String path,
　　String name)

ScJdspfJsp
public ScJdspfJsp(String path,
　　String name,
　　JspField fields[])

---

*Listing 11.6: The constructors for the **ScJdspJsp** class.*

To identify a button field, you first have to know its name. The discussion about the source for the ITMMNT1_PROMPT.jsp JavaServer Page pointed out that all the submit buttons were named "button." That name is used here to indicate which field the interface needs to check to determine which button was pressed.

The other thing you need to know is the names of the buttons and the corresponding function-key ID for each one. On the PROMPT panel, buttons called "Enter" and "Cancel" correspond to the Enter key and the F3 key. Listing 11.7 shows the entries that identify those values in the PROMPT panel definition.

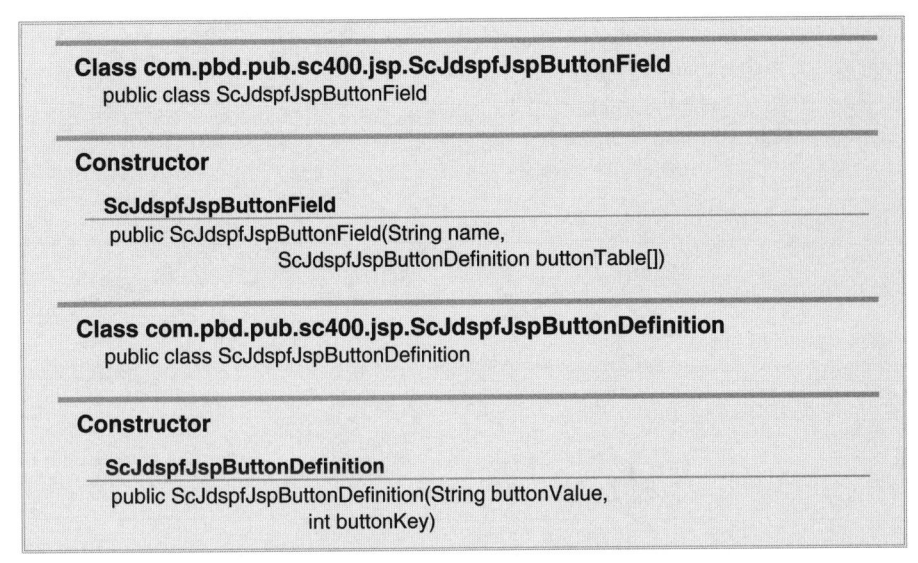

> **Class com.pbd.pub.sc400.jsp.ScJdspfJspButtonField**
> public class ScJdspfJspButtonField
>
> **Constructor**
>
> **ScJdspfJspButtonField**
> public ScJdspfJspButtonField(String name,
>   ScJdspfJspButtonDefinition buttonTable[])
>
> **Class com.pbd.pub.sc400.jsp.ScJdspfJspButtonDefinition**
> public class ScJdspfJspButtonDefinition
>
> **Constructor**
>
> **ScJdspfJspButtonDefinition**
> public ScJdspfJspButtonDefinition(String buttonValue,
>   int buttonKey)

*Listing 11.7: The **ScJdspfButtonField** and **ScJdspfButtonDefinition** constructors.*

Listing 11.8 shows that the ITMMNT1_PROMPT panel has one field and two buttons. Note that in defining a JSP, only the input-capable fields are defined because those are the only ones returned to the servlet by the Web server. Output-only fields are not returned. For the PROMPT panel JSP, there is only one input-capable field, X1ITEM. However, you also need to define a button field, which in this case happens to be named "button." It supports two different buttons, Enter and Cancel. The Enter button is interpreted as the Enter key, and Cancel is interpreted as F3.

```
// PROMPT panel - ITMMNT1_PROMPT.jsp
    new ScJdspfJspRecordUI(
        "PROMPT   ",
        new ScJdspfJsp(
            PATH,
            "ITMMNT1_PROMPT.jsp",
            new JspField[] {
                new JspField("X1ITEM"),
                new ScJdspfJspButtonField("button",
                    new ScJdspfJspButtonDefinition[] {
                        new ScJdspfJspButtonDefinition("Enter", 0),
                        new ScJdspfJspButtonDefinition("Cancel", 3)
                    }
                )
            }
        )
    ),
```

*Listing 11.8: The construction of an **ScJdspfJsp**, and the **ScJdspfJspRecordUI** that contains it.*

PART 2: IMPLEMENTING REVITALIZATION

The same exercise holds when analyzing the MAINT panel. Rather than bore you with the details, I'll just show the panel in Figure 11.4 and its associated source code in Listing 11.9.

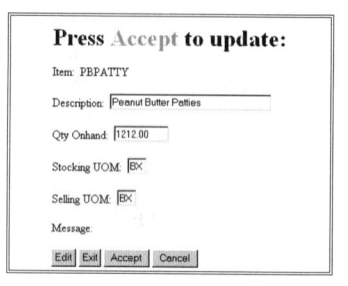

Figure 11.4: The browser version of the MAINT panel.

```html
<html>

<head>
<title>Item Maintenance</title>
</head>

<BEAN name="jdspf" type="ITMMNT1_DisplayFile" introspect="no" create="no"
scope="session">
</BEAN>

<body>

<h1>Press <font color=gray>Accept</font> to update:</h1>

<form method="post" action="/servlet/ITMMNT1_Servlet">

  <p>Item:  <%= jdspf.getString("X2ITEM") %>

  <p>Description:  <input type="text" name="X2DESC"
          value="<%= jdspf.getString("X2DESC") %>"
          maxlength=30 size="30"></p>

  <p>Qty Onhand:  <input type="text" name="X2QTYO"
          value="<%= jdspf.getString("X2QTYO") %>"
          maxlength=9 size="9"></p>

  <p>Stocking UOM:  <input type="text" name="X2UOMI"
          value="<%= jdspf.getString("X2UOMI") %>"
          maxlength=2 size="2"></p>

  <p>Selling UOM:  <input type="text" name="X2UOMS"
          value="<%= jdspf.getString("X2UOMS") %>"
          maxlength=2 size="2"></p>

  <p>Message:  <font color=red><%= jdspf.getString("X2ERR") %></font>
```

*Listing 11.9: The source code for the **ITMMNT1_MAINT.jsp** JavaServer Page (part 1 of 2).*

```
    <p><input type="submit" value="Edit" name="button">
       <input type="submit" value="Exit" name="button">
       <input type="submit" value="Accept" name="button">
       <input type="submit" value="Cancel" name="button"></p>

</form>

</body>

</html>
```

Listing 11.9: The source code for the **ITMMNT1_MAINT.jsp** JavaServer Page (part 2 of 2).

RUNNING THE APPLICATION: ITMMNT1_SERVLET

Note: At press time, the supported releases are V4R3 of OS/400 running version 1.1 of WebSphere and V4R4 of OS/400 running version 2.0 of WebSphere. Information on later releases can be found in appendix A.

This section is a little different than the rest of this chapter because it involves looking at some nonprogramming issues to get the application on its feet. There are really three pieces to the puzzle: the JavaServer Pages, the servlet, and the support classes. Each can reside in a different location (and in fact in this case they do), and you need to tell the Web server about each one of them. In order to do that, you have to modify a few pieces of the AS/400. Let's take a look at them.

The HTTP Configuration File, QUSRSYS/QATMHTTPC

The HTTP configuration file is a physical file on the AS/400, QUSRSYS/QATMHTTPC. If you have multiple HTTP configurations, there is a member for each configuration. The example in this chapter uses the default configuration, which is stored in member CONFIG. Unlike most configuration pieces on the AS/400, this is essentially a text file containing commands that are used to configure WebSphere at startup. Note that it is very easy to make mistakes in this file that can cause your Web applications to run incorrectly or not at all.

The Properties Files

If you thought the configuration file was bad, then you haven't looked at the properties files. The 18 different properties files obviously originated in UNIX. Most of them are probably best left untouched (at least by mere mortals), but you have to go into one, the **jvm.properties** file. This file, like all the properties files, is located in the IFS, specifically at the following location:

```
/QIBM/ProdData/IBMWebAS/properties/servers/servlets/servletservice/jvm.properties
```

There are other directories with properties files, but I have never touched them, and have no real desire to. I believe that within another release or two, IBM will get many of these properties back into the fold. I simply don't think that IBM is going to want the success or failure of their application servers to hinge on whether or not someone types a forward slash or a backward slash.

Now that you've seen where these configuration objects reside, it's time to modify them. To start, take a look at the requirements for each of the three components of the example application.

The JavaServer Pages

JavaServer Pages are roughly equivalent to HTML files, so they use the **Pass** directive in the HTTP configuration file to run. They also require a special **Service** directive in that same HTTP configuration. Here are the lines as they appear in my file:

```
Service /*.jsp /QSYS.LIB/QHTTPSVR.LIB/QZHJSVLT.SRVPGM:AdapterService
Pass    /IBMWebAS/samples/* /QIBM/ProdData/IBMWebAS/samples/*
```

The first line identifies that pages ending in ***.jsp** should be treated as JavaServer Pages and serviced by the **QZHJSVLT** service program. You should not have to add this line; it should have been added to your configuration automatically when you enabled servlets. The second line allows you to put things in your **samples** directory and access them. The JavaServer Pages will reside in the following directory:

```
/QIBM/ProdData/IBMWebAS/samples/revitalization
```

If you have the **Pass** line exactly as it is shown here, the examples in this book will work. If you have other **Pass** directives before this line, the examples might not work. Such are the wonders of the **Pass** directive. You'll see this in a little more detail later in this chapter.

The Servlet

Next, you need the servlet. The following specific **Service** line should exist in your HTTP configuration file to make the example work:

```
Service /servlet/* /QSYS.LIB/QHTTPSVR.LIB/QZHJSVLT.SRVPGM:AdapterService
```

This line identifies that any request made to the virtual directory **/servlet** should be treated as a servlet. The truth is that servlets do not reside in a directory named **/servlet**. Instead, they reside in a default directory named **/servlets** (note the *s* on the end). The full path to the servlets directory is:

```
/QIBM/ProdData/IBMWebAS/servlets
```

I have no idea who decided that the name **/servlets** was a magic directory name, but trust me, it is. You can specify other directories by messing with one of the properties files, but I haven't tried it, so won't suggest it here. Sticking with the defaults, *all* servlets are expected to end up in this directory. (If you look, you will indeed see that all of the IBM servlets, such as **XtremeTravel.class**, are in this directory.)

The Support Classes

Support classes are something a little closer to home, at least if you've been doing any Java programming (and I hope you have). There are two primary types of support classes: the .jar file with all the PBD packages, and the specific ITMMNT1* classes created throughout this book. In addition, you need to access IBM's Java Toolbox for the AS/400. All of these together reside in a **classpath** variable, and that variable is defined in the **jvm.properties** file discussed earlier. If you look in there, you should see a few lines like the following:

```
# NCF - Admin Service Properties for BasicNCFConfig Applet
# java.zip and sun.zip equals to classes.zip for other platforms
ncf.jvm.classpath=/QIBM/ProdData/Java400/lib/jdkptf.zip:/QIBM/ProdData/Java400/
lib/rawt_classes.zip:/QIBM/ProdData/Java400/lib/java.zip:/QIBM/ProdData/Java400/
lib/sun.zip:/QIBM/ProdData/Java400/com/ibm/db2/jdbc/app/db2_classes.zip:/QIBM/
ProdData/Java400:/QIBM/ProdData/IBMWebAS/lib/ibmwebas.jar:/QIBM/ProdData/IBMWebAS/
lib/jst.jar:/QIBM/ProdData/IBMWebAS/lib/jsdk.jar:/QIBM/ProdData/IBMWebAS/lib/
databeans.jar:/QIBM/ProdData/IBMWebAS/lib/xml4j.jar:/QIBM/ProdData/IBMWebAS/lib/
x509v1.jar:/QIBM/ProdData/IBMWebAS/lib:/QIBM/ProdData/IBMWebAS/web/admin/classes/
seadmin.jar:/QIBM/ProdData/IBMWebAS/web/classes:
ncf.jvm.path=/QIBM/ProdData/Java400/lib
ncf.jvm.use.system.classpath=false
```

A hashmark (#) at the beginning of a line indicates a comment, and then each line is of the form "property=value." Three properties are defined in this section of the code: **ncf.jvm.classpath, ncf.jvm.path,** and **ncf.jvm.use.system.classpath.** The first one is a very long line, and looks like multiple lines in most editors, but it is indeed only a single line and should stay that way. The latter two properties don't need to be changed here, just the first one, **ncf.jvm.classpath.**

You need to know where to put your ITMMNT* classes. Just put them where all the other classes go: in the directory **/QIBM/ProdData/IBMWebAS/web/classes**. This is where IBM puts its classes, so it's good enough for us. However, you have to point to the two .jar files, IBM's **jt400.jar** and your own **pbd400.jar.** The following will allow you to do that:

```
# NCF - Admin Service Properties for BasicNCFConfig Applet
# java.zip and sun.zip equals to classes.zip for other platforms
ncf.jvm.classpath=/QIBM/ProdData/Java400/lib/jdkptf.zip:/QIBM/ProdData/Java400/
lib/rawt_classes.zip:/QIBM/ProdData/Java400/lib/java.zip:/QIBM/ProdData/Java400/
lib/sun.zip:/QIBM/ProdData/Java400/com/ibm/db2/jdbc/app/db2_classes.zip:/QIBM/
ProdData/Java400:/QIBM/ProdData/IBMWebAS/lib/ibmwebas.jar:/QIBM/ProdData/IBMWebAS/
lib/jst.jar:/QIBM/ProdData/IBMWebAS/lib/jsdk.jar:/QIBM/ProdData/IBMWebAS/lib/
databeans.jar:/QIBM/ProdData/IBMWebAS/lib/xml4j.jar:/QIBM/ProdData/IBMWebAS/lib/
x509v1.jar:/QIBM/ProdData/IBMWebAS/lib:/QIBM/ProdData/IBMWebAS/web/admin/classes/
seadmin.jar:/QIBM/ProdData/IBMWebAS/web/classes:/QIBM/ProdData/HTTP/Public/jt400/
lib/jt400.jar:/java/pbd/pbd400.jar:
ncf.jvm.path=/QIBM/ProdData/Java400/lib
ncf.jvm.use.system.classpath=false
```

Notice that the following two entries have been added:

```
/QIBM/ProdData/HTTP/Public/jt400/lib/jt400.jar
/java/pbd/pbd400.jar
```

The first is IBM's Java Toolbox for the AS/400, and this is the place where it is normally located. If you've moved it, you will have to change that entry accordingly. The second entry is your own PBD .jar. It points to a directory that is not normally part of the AS/400; you'll add it in a moment.

Okay, you've modified the two files as they needed to be modified. Now you need to copy your files into the appropriate places. The following commands on the AS/400 will create the directories you need:

```
MKDIR '/java'
MKDIR '/java/pbd'
MKDIR '/QIBM/ProdData/IBMWebAS/samples/revitalization'
```

It's up to you how you want to work with your directories, but if you are planning any serious development, I strongly suggest that you get Client Access and map a network drive to allow you to access these directories. I have one drive mapped to **/QIBM/ProdData** and one mapped to **/java**.

Having created the directories, copy **pbdjsp400.jar** to **/java/pbd**, and copy all of the **ITMMNT1_Xxxxxx** classes to **/QIBM/ProdData/IBMWebAS/web/classes**. Copy all of the JavaServer Pages (the .jsp files) to **/QIBM/ProdData/IBMWebAS/samples/revitalization**. I also suggest that you run the following commands at this time:

```
CRTJVAPGM '/java/pbd/pbd400.jar' OPTIMIZE(40)
CRTJVAPGM '/QIBM/ProdData/HTTP/Public/jt400/lib/jt400.jar' OPTIMIZE(40)
```

These two commands can take a while to run, especially the second one (which took about 35 minutes on my little model 150 at home). By doing this, though, you will definitely reduce your initial run time for the servlets.

Okay, you've done everything as detailed in this chapter. What's next? Well, it's time to run the programs! If you've started your HTTP server, you should be able to enter the following URL into your browser:

```
http://yoursystem/IBMWebAS/samples/revitalization/index.jsp
```

You will see the screen in Figure 11.5 (after a bit of a delay).

Click the top button ("Launch ITMMNT1!") to get the screen in Figure 11.6 (after a rather lengthy delay, unfortunately).

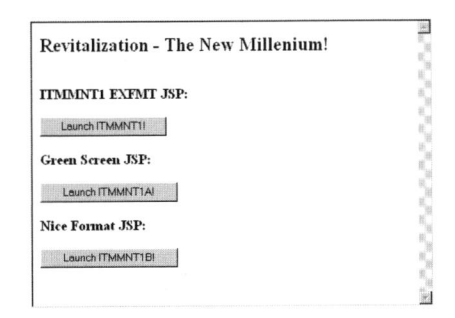

Figure 11.5: The index JavaServer Page, **index.jsp**.

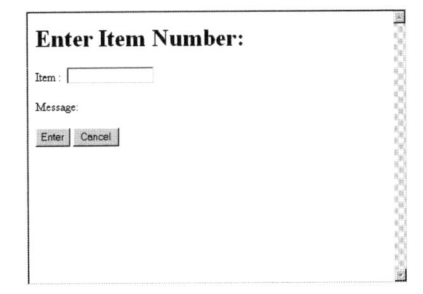

Figure 11.6: The browser version of the item-prompt panel.

Enter **PBPATTY** as the item number, and you'll get Figure 11.7 (after another seemingly interminable delay).[1]

Click the Exit button to return to the first page, and you can start all over again. This time, things will go much more quickly. In fact, the screen-to-screen time within the application is less than a second, at least on my little machine. If this doesn't work, you have some other issues to deal with, which should be solved by reviewing the chapters in part 3.

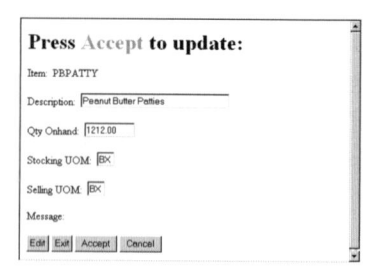

Figure 11.7: The item-maintenance panel in the browser.

MODELING AN OBJECT: THE JSP PACKAGE

The JSP package is made up of two simple classes combined to define the basic characteristics of a JavaServer Page. There are two primary features that define a JavaServer Page: its location and its fields. Let's take a look at the field first, as shown in Listing 11.10.

Class com.pbd.pub.jsp.JspField
public class JspField

JspField is used to define a field passed from a JavaServer Page back to a servlet via the POST method. These values are stored in the HttpRequest by name, and so by defining a named field, you can programmatically access that information. There are two primary types of fields: SINGLE and MULTIPLE. There's really not a lot of support for the MULTIPLE field type yet; I'll expand that in a later release. The other variation is to define a field as a button field. This is especially important to the 5250 interface emulation.

Fields

SINGLE
public static final int SINGLE

---

*Listing 11.10: The definition of the **JspField** class (part 1 of 2).*

---

[1] The first pass is so dreadfully slow because the system is compiling everything for the first time. This horrendous load time is only present the first time the servlet and JSPs are accessed after the server is brought up. IBM insists the load times are getting better with each release. Until then, there are some tricks you can play with preloading the servlets, but those are beyond the scope of this book.

MULTIPLE
public static final int MULTIPLE

Constructors
JspField
public JspField(String name)

JspField
public JspField(String name,
        int type)

JspField
public JspField(String name,
        int type,
        boolean isButtonField)

JspField
public JspField(String name,
        boolean isButtonField)

Methods

getName
public String getName()

getType
public int getType()

getValue
public String getValue()

getValues
public Enumeration getValues()

isButtonField
public boolean isButtonField()

setValue
public void setValue(String newValue)

Listing 11.10: The definition of the *JspField* class (part 2 of 2).

As the description of the **JspField** says, this class defines a field whose data is returned to the servlet during a POST operation. Therefore, by definition, it does not include fields that are only output, even if they come from The Bean, because by the time such fields make it to the HTML, they are simply strings of characters, indistinguishable from any of the other HTML in the JavaServer Page. The important thing to notice is the ability to define a button field. Button fields are very important; they are required in order to support the function-key feature during 5250 emulation. At this writing, there is only support for a single button field on a JSP because that's the nature of the 5250 emulation. This part of the architecture might need to be revisited at a later date.

To define a normal field in a JSP, you'd do something like the code shown in Listing 11.11, while a button field is defined as shown in Listing 11.12.

JSP Definition
```
<p>Item :  <input type="text" name="X1ITEM"
        value="<%= jdspf.getString("X1ITEM") %>"
        maxlength=15 size="15"></p>
```
Java Definition
```
JspField("X1ITEM");
```

*Listing 11.11: A simple input field in a JSP and its corresponding **JspField** definition.*

JSP Definition
```
<p><input type="submit" value="Enter" name="button">
    <input type="submit" value="Cancel" name="button"></p>
```
Java Definition
```
JspField("button", true);
```

*Listing 11.12: A button field in a JSP and its corresponding **JspField** definition.*

Notice that to define a button field, all of the form fields with **type="submit"** on the JSP must have the same name. In this case, that name is "button." This way, no matter which button is pressed, the corresponding value (Enter or Cancel, in this case) will be put into the field **button** and returned to the servlet in the POST data. It is crucial that you follow this format to make your JavaServer Pages function correctly.

The **ScJdspfJspButtonFieldDefinition** class extends the characteristics of the button field a little more; you'll see that in the next section. For now, let's go on to the **Jsp** class, shown in Listing 11.13.

Class com.pbd.pub.jsp.Jsp
   public class Jsp

Constructors

Jsp
   public Jsp()

Jsp
   public Jsp(String name)

Jsp
   public Jsp(String name,
              JspField fields[])

Jsp
   public Jsp(String path,
              String name)

Jsp
   public Jsp(String path,
              String name,
              JspField fields[])

Methods

copyDataFromRequest
   public void copyDataFromRequest(HttpServletRequest request)

getButtonField
   public JspField getButtonField()

getButtonValue
   public String getButtonValue()

Listing 11.13: The *Jsp* class (part 1 of 2).

getFields
public JspField[] getFields()

getName
public String getName()

getPath
public String getPath()

getURL
public String getURL()

setFields
public void setFields(JspField newValue[])

setName
public void setName(String newValue)

setPath
public void setPath(String newValue)

*Listing 11.13: The **Jsp** class (part 2 of 2).*

The **Jsp** class defines the location of the JavaServer Page and, optionally, a list of fields. While most JSPs in the revitalization architecture have a field array, exit JSPs are an exception. An exit JSP, you might recall, is the JavaServer Page that is called when an application ends. Usually, this would be an index of some kind. Index panels are used to make the initial call to a servlet, and so their buttons use a GET method rather than a POST method. By their nature, then, index panels don't return data, and therefore don't need to have fields defined. On the other hand, most other **Jsp** objects have an array of **JspFields**, even if the array is only a single button field to return the button pressed.

The **path** parameter usually defines the directory that the JavaServer Page resides in. Be careful to use the virtual directory recognized by the Web server, not the physical IFS directory. In the example, a **Pass** directive maps requests as follows:

```
/IBMWebAS/samples/*   map to /QIBM/ProdData/IBMWebAS/samples/*
```

The JavaServer Pages reside in **/QIBM/ProdData/IBMWebAS/samples/revitalization**, but the virtual location is simply **/IBMWebAS/samples/revitalization**. The virtual location is the one to use as the path when defining the **Jsp** class.

The name should just be the simple file name of the JavaServer Page. That way, if you decide to move files around a little bit, it will be easier to just change the path variable.[2]

The final parameter, that of the field array, is pretty straightforward. For every form field of type input in your JavaServer Page, create a corresponding **JspField** definition.[3] Put all the **JspField** definitions in an array, and pass them as the last parameter to the constructor.

Most of the setter and getter methods are self-explanatory, with the exception perhaps of **getButtonField** and **getButtonValue**. The **getButtonField** method returns the single button field specified in the **JspField** array. In fact, if no button fields are specified, the method returns null. If more than one is specified, the last one in the array is returned. The **getButtonValue** method is a convenience method that returns the value contained in the button returned by **getButtonField**. This is equivalent to asking the JavaServer Page which button the user pressed.

Finally, there's the matter of the **copyDataFromRequest** method. This method pulls the data from an **HttpRequest** and stores it in the individual fields in the JSP. It should be executed immediately after a POST (in the **doPost** method of the servlet). This method creates a sort of "demilitarized zone" between the application and the specifics of the Web server. If the mechanics of retrieving data from a POST method changes, only the **copyDataFromRequest** method needs to change. All other access to the data should be through the **JspFields**.

And that's about it for the JSP package.

---

2 I've been doing a little work with an application framework package that allows you to specify the base path as part of the application definition. That way, if you decide to move a whole group of pages to another directory, you can just change the path in the application definition. However, that's another story for another book.

3 Currently, the package only supports two fields types: regular text and button fields. More will be coming, but not in this release.

✦ MORE EXTENSIONS: THE SC400 JSP PACKAGE

Having seen the JSP package **com.pbd.pub.jsp**, let's see how the SC400 JSP package **com.pbd.pub.sc400.jsp** builds on it to create the 5250 emulation interface.

SC400 JSP

There are three primary "objects" at the highest level: the client, the display file, and the JavaServer Pages. The client is represented by an **Sc400Client** object. The display file is represented by a **JdspfDisplayFile** object. Each JavaServer Page has its own **ScJdspfJsp** object. Figure 11.8 shows the relationships among these objects.

The additional **ScJdspfJspRecordUI** objects are the glue that binds the JavaServer pages to the display-file record formats. There is one JavaServer Page per record format, and the record UI binds them together. Let's take a more in-depth look at the **ScJdspfJsp** object itself, since it is actually made up of several components.

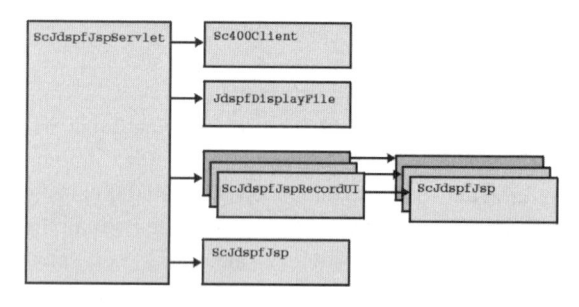

Figure 11.8: The relationships among ScJdspfJspServlet and its client, display file, and JSPs.

When you examined the JSP package, you saw that the definition for a JavaServer Page consists of its location and its fields, as shown in Figure 11.9. The JSP package is designed to allow all fields to be defined with a single class, because as far as a JavaServer Page is concerned, all fields really are the same—they return a value or a set of values to the servlet via the POST method. However, the SC400 JSP package needs a little more definition: each page will support a single button field, and not only do you need to know which field that is, but you must somehow map the possible values of that field back to a function key so that you can pass the function-key ID back up to the application client.

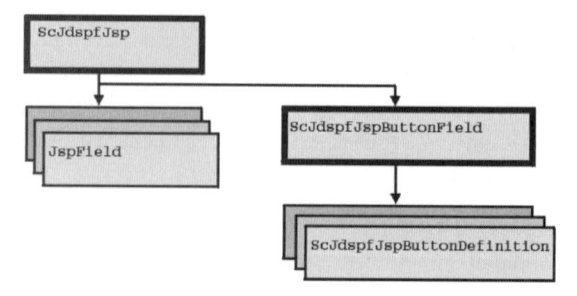

Figure 11.9: The way JSP and SC400 JSP classes define a JavaServer Page.

Defining a JavaServer Page

Let's start defining the JavaServer Page by working on the buttons. As you can see in Figure 11.10, there are two buttons in the **ITMMNT1_PROMPT** JavaServer Page, with the text literals *Enter* and *Cancel*. One of those text literals will be returned as the contents of the button field. If you check the original green-screen display file, you'll see that those two buttons correspond to the Enter key and the F3 key, respectively. Somehow, you need a way to tell the system to translate the string *Enter* to an Enter key and *Cancel* to an F3 key. This is accomplished by the special SC400 JSP classes **ScJdspfJspButtonField** and **ScJdspfJspButtonDefinition**.

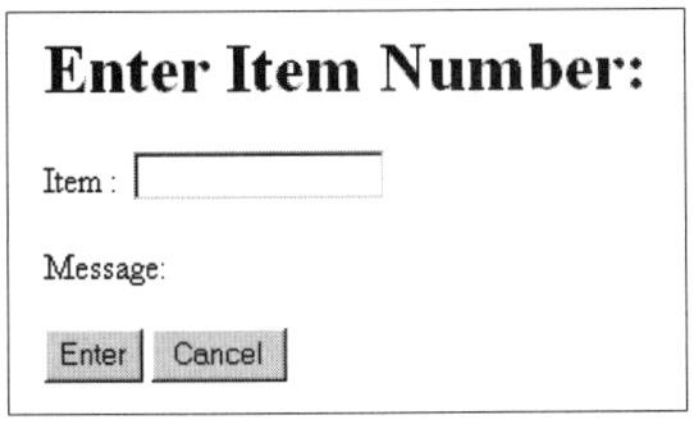

*Figure 11.10: The components output by the **ITMMNT1_PROMPT** JavaServer Page.*

Listing 11.14 shows how to define just such a field. The first line identifies the name of the field, **button**, which corresponds to the name attribute of the submit buttons. The second line indicates that an array is to follow; the next two lines are the entries in that array. The first of those two lines maps the string *Enter* to the function key ID 0, while the second line maps *Cancel* to 3. The 0 and 3 represent Enter and F3, respectively, and it is one of these values that is actually passed back to the application client, based on which button the user actually clicks.

```
JavaServer Page
    <p><input type="submit" value="Enter" name="button">
    <input type="submit" value="Cancel" name="button"></p>

SC400 JSP Button Field Definition
    new ScJdspfJspButtonField("bu tton",
        new ScJdspfJspButtonDefinition[] {
            new ScJdspfJspButtonDefinition("Enter", 0),
            new ScJdspfJspButtonDefinition("Cancel", 3)
        }
    )
```

Listing 11.14: The two SC400 JSP fields used to define a button field on a JavaServer Page.

ScJdspfJspButtonDefinition

Listing 11.15 is almost certainly the simplest class in the entire book. It doesn't subclass any other classes; it's nothing more than a placeholder that relates a string to an integer. It's used so that an array of these value pairs can be created in the constructor.

```
package com.pbd.pub.sc400.jbui;
package com.pbd.pub.sc400.jsp;

/**
 * ScJdspfJspButtonDefinition relates defines the function ID associated
 * with a particular button literal. An array of these is used to
 * define a button field in a JSP.
 */
public class ScJdspfJspButtonDefinition {
        private String buttonValue;
        private int buttonKey;

/**
 * Relate button string "buttonValue" to function key ID "buttonKey".
 */
public ScJdspfJspButtonDefinition(String buttonValue, int buttonKey) {
        setButtonValue(buttonValue);
        setButtonKey(buttonKey);
}

/**
 * Returns the function key ID.
 * @return the function key ID.
 */
int getButtonKey() {
        return buttonKey;
}

/**
 * Returns the string literal.
 * @return the string literal.
 */
String getButtonValue() {
        return buttonValue;
}

/**
 * Sets the function key ID.
 * @param newValue the new function key ID.
 */
private void setButtonKey(int newValue) {
        this.buttonKey = newValue;
}

/**
 * Sets the string literal.
 * @param newValue the new string literal.
 */
private void setButtonValue(String newValue) {
        this.buttonValue = newValue;
}
}
```

*Listing 11.15: The **ScJdspJspButtonDefinition** class.*

I could have created an array of strings and an array of integers, but experience has shown me that the entries in the two arrays can get out of sync, causing subtle debugging problems later. Instead, I create a single entry for each button, like so:

```
new ScJdspfJspButtonDefinition("Enter", 0)
```

The line above defines the button with the value of *Enter* as the Enter key. As shown in Listing 11.14, you can create a whole set of them in an array, and pass that to the constructor for the **ScJdspfJspButtonField** class, which follows.

ScJdspfJspButtonField

At this point, creating a button field is quite easy. All you have to do is specify the name, which matches the name on the submit form field on the JavaServer Page, and an array of button definitions, which will be used to translate the literals to the correct function key ID. **ScJdspfJspButtonField**, shown in Listing 11.16, extends **JspField** by adding an array of button definitions in the constructor and adding the methods **getKey** and **valueOf**.

The **getKey** method returns the function ID corresponding to the current value of the button. In the **ITMMNT1_PROMPT** panel, for example, if the button field contains the literal string *Enter*, **getKey** returns 0; if the field contains *Cancel*, **getKey** returns 3. An invalid value triggers an exception. The **valueOf** method translates in the other direction, except that it doesn't translate the value currently in the field. The function-key ID to be translated is passed in to the **valueOf** method. A function-key ID of 0 would translate to *Enter* and a function-key ID of 3 would translate to *Cancel*. (This method is primarily used by the WebSphere Application Server Emulator, WASE.)

```
package com.pbd.pub.sc400.jsp;

import com.pbd.pub.jsp.*;
import java.util.*;

/**
 * ScJdspfJspButtonField extends the standard JspField to allow conversion
 * of the literal returned from the button to a function key ID.
 */
public class ScJdspfJspButtonField extends JspField {
        private Hashtable buttonTable;
        private ScJdspfJspButtonDefinition[] definitions;

/**
 * Creates a button field with the specified button translation table.
 *
```

Listing 11.16: The **ScJdspJspButtonField** class (part 1 of 2).

```
 * @param name button field name.
 * @param buttonTable array used to translate the button to a function key.
 */
public ScJdspfJspButtonField(String name, ScJdspfJspButtonDefinition[]
buttonTable) {
        super(name, true);
        setButtonTable(buttonTable);
}

/**
 * Returns the translation of this button's value to a function key ID.
 *
 * @return the literal button value translated to a function key ID.
 */
public int getKey() {
        Integer keyObject = (Integer) buttonTable.get(getValue());
        return keyObject.intValue();
}

/**
 * Fill the buttonTable hashtable with the entries from the button definition
 * array.
 *
 * @param ScJdspfJspButtonDefinition[] array of button definitions.
 */
private void setButtonTable(ScJdspfJspButtonDefinition[] newValue) {
        this.definitions = newValue;
        buttonTable = new Hashtable();
        for (int i = 0; i < definitions.length; i++)
                buttonTable.put(definitions[i].getButtonValue(),
                        new Integer(definitions[i].getButtonKey()));
}

/**
 * Save the button definitions.
 *
 * @param newValue ScJspButtonDefinition[]
 */
private void setDefinitions(ScJdspfJspButtonDefinition[] newValue) {
        this.definitions = newValue;
}

/**
 * Returns the string literal associated with the specified function key ID.
 *
 * @param key the specified function key ID.
 * @return the button literal associated with the function key ID.
 */
public String valueOf(int key) {
        String button = "*NONE";
        for (int i = 0; i < definitions.length; i++)
                if (definitions[i].getButtonKey() == key) {
                        button = definitions[i].getButtonValue();
                        break;
                }
        return button;
}
}
```

Listing 11.16: The **ScJdspJspButtonField** class (part 2 of 2).

Finish the definition of the JavaServer Page for **ITMMNT1_PROMPT.jsp** as shown in Listing 11.17.

```
new ScJdspfJsp(
    PATH,
    "ITMMNT1_PROMPT.jsp",
    new JspField[] {
        new JspField("X1ITEM"),
        new ScJdspfJspButtonField("button",
            new ScJdspfJspButtonDefinition[] {
                new ScJdspfJspButtonDefinition("Enter", 0),
                new ScJdspfJspButtonDefinition("Cancel", 3)
            }
        )
    }
)
```

*Listing 11.17: The entire definition of the **ScJdspfJsp** for **ITMMNT1_PROMPT.jsp**.*

The three parameters are as follows:

- The path, which is defined as a string literal (in this case, of **/IBMWebAS/samples/revitalization**).
- The JavaServer Page name, **ITMMNT1_PROMPT.jsp**.
- The field array.

The field array contains the single input field X1ITEM, as well as the definition of the button field **button**. A more complex panel, such as **ITMMNT1_MAINT**, simply has more **JspField** entries in the field array. For more information on defining the non-button fields in a JavaServer Page, refer to **JspField** earlier in this chapter; otherwise, continue on to defining the servlet.

Defining an SC400 JSP Servlet

Now that you can define a JavaServer Page, it's time to actually define the servlet. You need to define the name of the application-client proxy class, the name of the display-file proxy class, an array of record UI objects, and an exit JSP. The record UI objects are the last supporting class for the **ScJdspfJsp**, so you should learn how to create one.

Listing 11.18 indicates that user interaction requests for the record format PROMPT should trigger the **ITMMNT1_PROMPT** JavaServer Page. (The details of Listing 11.4, which defines the **ScJdspfJsp** object as the **ITMMNT1_PROMPT.jsp** JavaServer Page, would go where the ellipsis is in Listing 11.18.)

PART 2: IMPLEMENTING REVITALIZATION

```
// PROMPT panel - ITMMNT1_PROMPT.jsp
new ScJdspfJspRecordUI(
    "PROMPT  ",
    new ScJdspfJsp(
        (...)
    )
),
```

Listing 11.18: *The additional lines added to Listing 11.14 to define the **ScJdspfJspRecordUI** for the* prompt *panel.*

ScJdspfJspRecordUI

ScJdspfJspRecordUI, shown in Listing 11.19, extends the **ScJdspfRecordUI** class from chapter 8, adding a constructor that requires an **ScJdspfJspRecordUI** object, and adding a **getScJdspfJsp** convenience method to return the record UI as an **ScJdspfJsp**.

```
package com.pbd.pub.sc400.jsp;

import com.pbd.pub.jsp.*;
import com.pbd.pub.jdspf.*;

/**
 * The specialized version of the JdspfRecordUI for the JSP UI Server.
 */
public class ScJdspfJspRecordUI extends JdspfRecordUI {

/**
 * Creates an ScJdspfJspRecordUI for the specified record name and
 * ScJdspfJsp.
 */
public ScJdspfJspRecordUI(String recordName, ScJdspfJsp jsp) {
    super(recordName, jsp);
}

/**
 * Return the UI object as an ScJdspfJsp
 * @return ScJdspfJsp
 */
public ScJdspfJsp getScJdspfJsp() {
    return (ScJdspfJsp) getRecordUIObject();
}
}
```

Listing 11.19: *The **ScJdspfJspRecordUI** class.*

At this point, you've seen every supporting class required to create an **ScJdspfJspServlet**. Now it's time to actually build the servlet, as shown in Listing 11.20.

```
import com.pbd.pub.jsp.*;
import com.pbd.pub.sc400.*;
import com.pbd.pub.sc400.jsp.*;

public class ITMMNT1_Servlet extends ScJdspfJspServlet
{
    private static final String PATH = "/IBMWebAS/samples/revitalization";
/**
 * This is the servlet used to communicate with the application client
 * ITMMNT1AC on the host.
 */
public ITMMNT1_Servlet()
    throws Sc400Exception
{
    super(

    // Application Client Interface Definition

        // Application Client Proxy
        "ITMMNT1_Client",

        // Display File Proxy
        "ITMMNT1_DisplayFile",

    // UI Server Definition

        // Record UI Definitions
        new ScJdspfJspRecordUI[] {

            // PROMPT panel - ITMMNT1_PROMPT.jsp
            new ScJdspfJspRecordUI(
                (...)
            ),

            // MAINT panel - ITMMNT1_MAINT.jsp
            new ScJdspfJspRecordUI(
                (...)
            )
        },

        // Exit Panel - index.jsp
        new ScJdspfJsp(PATH, "index.jsp")
    );

// Remove comment to enable logging
//    setLogTrace(true);
}
}
```

*Listing 11.20: The critical lines that define the **ITMMNT1_Servlet** class.*

Now that you've worked your way up the hierarchy, you can finally define the servlet itself. The first two parameters in Listing 11.20 are the two strings for the application-client-proxy class name and the display-file-proxy class name. The next parameter is an array of record UI objects (of type **ScJdspfJspRecordUI**), one for each record format. This leaves out the details of the two **ScJdspfJspRecordUIs**, but you can review those by viewing the source or going back to the full listing in of **ITMMNT1_Servlet** at the beginning of this chapter. The final parameter is a simple JavaServer Page definition of the exit JavaServer Page, **index.jsp**.

ScJdspfJspServlet

The **ScJdspfJspServlet** class, shown in Listing 11.21, provides the connection between the browser interface cycle and the 5250 emulation cycle. The 5250 interface is set up to send a panel to a user and receive the results; it's more of a *pull* interface, with the panel being used to pull data from the user. The browser interface, on the other hand, is a *push* interface: the user clicks a button, and the data entered into the form is pushed to a receiver, which could be either a servlet or a CGI (Common Gateway Interface) program.

```
package com.pbd.pub.sc400.jsp;

import java.io.*;

import javax.servlet.*;
import javax.servlet.http.*;
import java.beans.Beans;
import java.util.*;

import com.pbd.pub.dc400.*;
import com.pbd.pub.sc400.*;
import com.pbd.pub.jdspf.*;

/**
 * The ScJdspfJspServlet is the prototype for all other JSP UI servers.
 * It defines a generic application client interface using Sc400Client
 * and JdspfDisplayFile, but forces the user to specify ScJdspfJspRecordUI
 * objects as the UI server interface. It also requires an ScJdspfJsp
 * as the exit point to execute when the application ends.
 */
public class ScJdspfJspServlet extends HttpServlet
{
        // Attributes
        private String clientName = null;
        private String jdspfName = null;
        private ScJdspfJspRecordUI[] recordUIs = null;
        private boolean logTrace = false;
```

Listing 11.21: The *ScJdspfJspServlet* class (part 1 of 6).

```java
          // Bean definitions
          private Sc400Client client;
          private JdspfDisplayFile jdspf;
          private ScJdspfUIServer uiServer;

          // Session variables
          private ScJdspfJsp currentJsp;
          private ScJdspfJsp exitJsp;
          private boolean isExiting = false;
/**
 * Normally unused contructor.
 */
public ScJdspfJspServlet() {
}

/**
 * Standard constructor, identifying the names of the client class and the
 * display file class, an array of record UI objects and an exit JSP.
 */
public ScJdspfJspServlet(String clientName, String jdspfName,
                                              ScJdspfJspRecordUI[]
recordUIs, ScJdspfJsp exitJsp)
      throws Sc400Exception
{
      setClientName(clientName);
      setJdspfName(jdspfName);
      setRecordUIs(recordUIs);
      setExitJsp(exitJsp);
}

/**
 * Call the JSP for the current record of the display file.
 *
 * @param req HttpServletRequest from WAS
 * @param res HttpServletResponse from WAS
 * @param jdspf display file
 */
private void callJsp(HttpServletRequest req, HttpServletResponse res,
                                          JdspfDisplayFile jdspf)
      throws ServletException, IOException
{
      callJsp(req, res, (ScJdspfJsp) jdspf.getCurrentRecord().getUIObject());
}

/**
 * Call the specified JSP.
 *
 * @param req HttpServletRequest from WAS
 * @param res HttpServletResponse from WAS
 * @param jsp JSP to call
 */
```

Listing 11.21: The **ScJdspfJspServlet** class (part 2 of 6).

```
private void callJsp(HttpServletRequest req, HttpServletResponse res, ScJdspfJsp
jsp)
        throws ServletException, IOException
{
        currentJsp = jsp;
        logMessage("callPage: " + currentJsp.getURL());
        ((com.sun.server.http.HttpServiceResponse)
res).callPage(currentJsp.getURL(), req);
}

/**
 * Standard doGet method called for an HTTP GET request. Initialize the
 * servlet, then run the UI server.
 */
public void doGet(HttpServletRequest req, HttpServletResponse res)
        throws ServletException, IOException
{
        logMessage("doGet");
        try {
                init(req);
                runServer(req, res);
        } catch (Sc400Exception e) {
                throw new ServletException(e.getMessage());
        }
}

/**
 * Standard doPost method called for an HTTP POST request. Retrieve the
 * post data from the user, stuff it into the display file, and continue
 * running the UI server.
 */
public void doPost(HttpServletRequest req, HttpServletResponse res)
        throws ServletException, IOException
{
        logMessage("doPut");
        try {
                getPostData(req);
                runServer(req, res);
        } catch (Sc400Exception e) {
                throw new ServletException(e.getMessage());
        }
}

/**
 * Returns the current JSP.
 * @return the current JSP.
 */
public ScJdspfJsp getCurrentJsp() {
        return currentJsp;
}

/**
 * Returns the exit JSP.
```

Listing 11.21: The *ScJdspfJspServlet* class (part 3 of 6).

```
    * @return the exit JSP.
    */
   private ScJdspfJsp getExitJsp() {
           return exitJsp;
   }

   /**
    * Returns the display file object for this servlet.
    * @return the display file object for this servlet.
    */
   public JdspfDisplayFile getJdspf() {
           return jdspf;
   }

   /**
    * Copy the POST data from the user into the JSP, then copy it from
    * the JSP into the display file.
    */
   private void getPostData(HttpServletRequest req)
           throws Sc400Exception, ServletException
   {
           currentJsp.copyDataFromRequest(req);
           currentJsp.copyDataToJdspf(jdspf);
   }

   /**
    * Instantiate the client bean, instantiate the display file bean,
    * create a new UI server, initialize the UI server, and finally
    * create a new session.
    *
    * If logTrace is set to true, this section fires several timing
    * messages.
    */
    private void init(HttpServletRequest req)
           throws Sc400Exception, ServletException
   {
           logTimed("init start");
           logTimed("Making client...");
           client = (Sc400Client) makeBean(clientName);
           logTimed("Making display file...");
           jdspf = (JdspfDisplayFile) makeBean(jdspfName);
           logTimed("Making server...");
           uiServer = new ScJdspfUIServer(client, jdspf, null, recordUIs);
           logTimed("Initializing server...");
           uiServer.init();
           logTimed("init done");
           req.getSession(true);
   }

   /**
    * Returns true if the application is exiting, false if not.
    * @return true if the application is exiting, false if not.
    */
```

Listing 11.21: The *ScJdspfJspServlet* class (part 4 of 6).

```
public boolean isExiting() {
        return isExiting;
}

/**
 * If logging is enabled, send a log message.
 */
private void logMessage(String message) {
        if (logTrace) System.out.println(message);
}

/**
 * If logging is enabled, send a timed log message.
 */
private void logTimed(String message) {
        logMessage("" + System.currentTimeMillis() + ": " + message);
}

/**
 * Instantiate a bean of the specified class type, and throw a
 * ServletException if an error occurs.
 *
 * @param className name of the class to instantiate.
 * @return an object of the class specified.
 */
private Object makeBean(String className)
        throws ServletException
{
        Object bean = null;
        try {
                bean = Beans.instantiate(null, className);
        } catch (Exception e) {
                System.out.println(e.getClass().getName());
                String error = "Can't create " + className + ": " + e + ": " +
                                e.getMessage();
                System.out.println(error);
                throw new ServletException(error);
        }
        return bean;
}

/**
 * runServer is the meat of the servlet class. It calls the run method
 * of the UI server and waits for a return. If the server returns true,
 * that indicates a shutdown was received from the application client,
 * so we call the exit JSP. Otherwise, we put the display file proxy
 * into the session and call the appropriate JSP from the record UI object
 * of the current record of the display file.
 */
private void runServer(HttpServletRequest req, HttpServletResponse res)
        throws Sc400Exception, ServletException, IOException
{
        if (uiServer.run()) {
```

Listing 11.21: The *ScJdspfJspServlet* class (part 5 of 6).

```
                        isExiting = true;
                        callJsp(req, res, getExitJsp());
            } else {
                        req.getSession(false).putValue("jdspf", jdspf);
                        callJsp(req, res, jdspf);
            }
}

/**
 * Set new application client proxy class name.
 * @param newValue new application client proxy class name.
 */
protected void setClientName(String newValue) {
            this.clientName = newValue;
}

/**
 * Set the exit JSP for this application. Changing to value of this
 * JSP can cause the application to CHAIN to a different application
 * if necessary.
 *
 * @param newValue the ScJdspfJsp to execute when this application ends.
 */
public void setExitJsp(ScJdspfJsp newValue) {
            this.exitJsp = newValue;
}

/**
 * Set new display file proxy class name.
 * @param newValue new display file proxy class name.
 */
protected void setJdspfName(String newValue) {
            this.jdspfName = newValue;
}

/**
 * Set true to log messages.
 * @param traceOn true = log messages.
 */
protected void setLogTrace(boolean traceOn) {
            this.logTrace = traceOn;
}

/**
 * Set new array of record UI objects.
 * @param newValue new array of record UI objects.
 */
protected void setRecordUIs(ScJdspfJspRecordUI[] newValue) {
            this.recordUIs = newValue;
}
}
```

Listing 11.21: The **ScJdspfJspServlet** class (part 6 of 6).

The revitalization architecture reconciles these two approaches by having a single servlet both send the data to the JavaServer Page and receive the data back. Right now, that's done manually by making sure the submit buttons on the JavaServer Page are coded correctly, but you'll see in the next section that one possible enhancement to this interface would be to allow the automatic generation of buttons from the record UI object definitions. If you did that, you could automatically generate the right parameters, and the JSP designer wouldn't have to worry about it.

Let's examine the class in detail. The constructor has already been discussed; it expects the names of the two classes for the application-client proxy and the display-file proxy, the array of record UI objects, and the exit JSP. At that point, the servlet is quiescent, waiting for a call to the **doGet** method. It's important to enter with a **doGet**. This initializes the servlet via the **init** method, which does the following:

- Instantiates the application-client proxy.
- Instantiates the display-file proxy.
- Creates a new UI server object.
- Initializes the UI server object (which starts the application client).
- Creates a new session.

It then calls the **runServer** method, which provides the bulk of the processing. The **runServer** method is the point at which the two cycles, 5250 and browser, are connected. Whenever the 5250 cycle requires user interaction, the UI server returns to the servlet. The servlet then sends the appropriate JavaServer Page to the user via the **callJsp** method. The JavaServer Page to be called is specified in the record UI object for the current record format of the display-file proxy.

Let's look at this cycle from the AS/400 point of view. When the application client on the AS/400 requests an EXFMT for the PROMPT record, this request is transmitted down to the application-client proxy and is received by the UI server. The UI server, in turn, sends it to the display-file proxy. This causes the display-file proxy to set its current record format to the PROMPT record. The display-file proxy also recognizes that user interaction is required, and indicates this to the UI server. The UI server returns to the servlet. The servlet queries the display-file proxy to determine which JavaServer Page should be displayed (this information is retrieved from the record UI object for that record format), and sends that JSP to the user.

At this point, the servlet is again quiescent, but this time it is waiting for a call to its **doPost** method. It is crucial that the JavaServer Page does a POST back to this servlet; sending data anywhere else would throw the protocol out of sync, hanging the application client on the AS/400 and causing some sort of Web server error for the user. If the JavaServer Page is configured correctly, the data is POSTed back to the servlet, and the **doPost** method is executed.

All of the user data is in fields in the **HttpServletRequest** object, which is passed to the servlet as one of the parameters of the **doPost** method. (This is standard HTTP protocol.) Then, the servlet calls the **getPostData** method, which first calls **copyDataFromRequest** to copy the data from the **HttpServletRequest** to the JSP object. This is done because the mechanics of retrieving data from the HTTP request depend on the Web server software and can change from server to server—and indeed, from release to release of the same server. Therefore, if this syntax changes, you only need to rewrite the **copyDataFromRequest** method; the rest of the logic stays intact.

Once the data is in the JSP, **copyDataToJdspf** is called, which loads the data back into the current record of the display-file proxy. That done, the cycle continues by calling the **runServer** method again. This cycle repeats until the application client on the AS/400 requests a shutdown, at which point the **runServer** method returns true, and the servlet sends the exit JSP to the user. And that is the SC400 JSP servlet architecture in its entirety!

THE FUTURE OF SC400 JSP: BIGGER AND BETTER EXTENSIONS

If you have read chapter 10, you might have gotten the idea that I consider the HTML interface primitive. However, while it's certainly not as graphically oriented as the Swing interface, HTML can quite capably support most of the features of the AS/400's 5250 interface. The very simple exercise in this book is not intended to show the range of what the HTML interface can do, but instead show how properly designed support classes can make the conversion to the HTML interface cost-effective.

This section gives you a glimpse into where the HTML interface could go. It shows some "artist's depictions" of the types of browser panels you might expect to see as the HTML interface is expanded, at the same time giving some examples of how the support classes could be enhanced to make the JavaServer Page designer's life easier. That way, the designer can concentrate on integrating your legacy applications into a cohesive, productive, innovative Web site, rather than worry about the details of communicating with those legacy applications.

PART 2: IMPLEMENTING REVITALIZATION

Subfiles

Figure 11.11 shows the "standard" subfile interface again, while Figure 11.12 shows a simple, no-frills browser version of the same subfile. By "simple," I don't mean unsophisticated; there's still a bit of HTML required.

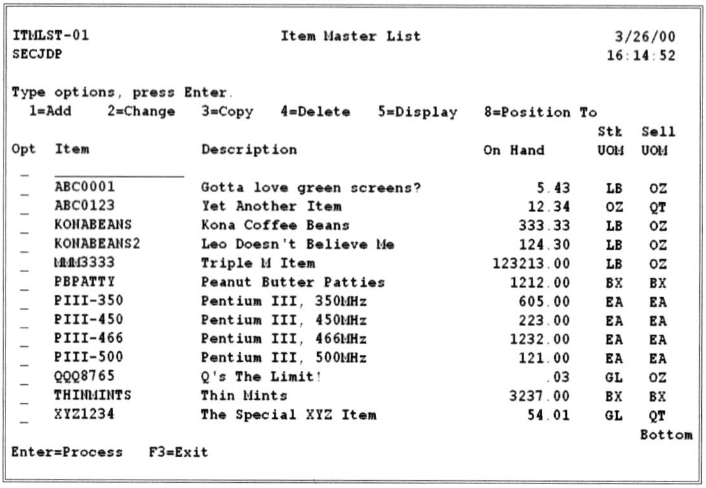

```
ITMLST-01                      Item Master List                   3/26/00
SECJDP                                                           16:14:52

Type options, press Enter.
   1=Add     2=Change    3=Copy    4=Delete    5=Display    8=Position To
                                                       Stk      Sell
Opt  Item             Description                 On Hand  UOM      UOM

_    ABC0001          Gotta love green screens?       5.43  LB       OZ
_    ABC0123          Yet Another Item               12.34  OZ       QT
_    KONABEANS        Kona Coffee Beans             333.33  LB       OZ
_    KONABEANS2       Leo Doesn't Believe Me        124.30  LB       OZ
_    MMM3333          Triple M Item              123213.00  LB       OZ
_    PBPATTY          Peanut Butter Patties        1212.00  BX       BX
_    PIII-350         Pentium III, 350MHz           605.00  EA       EA
_    PIII-450         Pentium III, 450MHz           223.00  EA       EA
_    PIII-466         Pentium III, 466MHz          1232.00  EA       EA
_    PIII-500         Pentium III, 500MHz           121.00  EA       EA
_    QQQ8765          Q's The Limit!                   .03  GL       OZ
_    THINMINTS        Thin Mints                   3237.00  BX       BX
_    XYZ1234          The Special XYZ Item           54.01  GL       QT
                                                                  Bottom
Enter=Process    F3=Exit
```

Figure 11.11: A typical 5250 subfile screen.

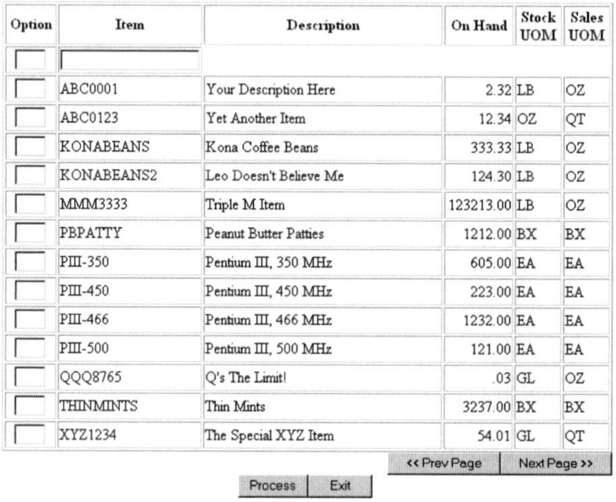

Option	Item	Description	On Hand	Stock UOM	Sales UOM
☐					
☐	ABC0001	Your Description Here	2.32	LB	OZ
☐	ABC0123	Yet Another Item	12.34	OZ	QT
☐	KONABEANS	Kona Coffee Beans	333.33	LB	OZ
☐	KONABEANS2	Leo Doesn't Believe Me	124.30	LB	OZ
☐	MMM3333	Triple M Item	123213.00	LB	OZ
☐	PBPATTY	Peanut Butter Patties	1212.00	BX	BX
☐	PIII-350	Pentium III, 350 MHz	605.00	EA	EA
☐	PIII-450	Pentium III, 450 MHz	223.00	EA	EA
☐	PIII-466	Pentium III, 466 MHz	1232.00	EA	EA
☐	PIII-500	Pentium III, 500 MHz	121.00	EA	EA
☐	QQQ8765	Q's The Limit!	.03	GL	OZ
☐	THINMINTS	Thin Mints	3237.00	BX	BX
☐	XYZ1234	The Special XYZ Item	54.01	GL	QT

[<< Prev Page]   [Next Page >>]
[Process] [Exit]

Figure 11.12: The same screen as Figure 11.11, on a browser.

Having seen some of the HTML, ASP, or JSP code currently required to provide this kind of interface, I think the code required from the SC400 JSP architecture would be considerably less. In fact, Listing 11.22 shows what it might look like.

```
<html>

<head>
<title>Item List Subfile</title>
</head>

<BEAN name="jdspf" type="ITMLST1_DisplayFile" introspect="no" create="no"
scope="session">
</BEAN>

<body>
<form method="POST" action="/servlet/ITMLST1_Servlet">
<table border="1" width="100%" height="394">
  <tr>
    <th width="10%" height="38">Option</th>
    <th width="18%" height="38"><b>Item</b></th>
    <th width="41%" height="38">Description</th>
    <th width="13%" height="38">On Hand</th>
    <th width="9%" height="38">Stock<br>
      UOM</th>
    <th width="9%" height="38">Sales<br>
      UOM</th>
  </tr>

<% jdspf.setCurrentRecord("CTL01"); %>

  <tr>
    <td width="10%" height="19" align="center"><%= jdspf.getField("X1OPT") %></td>
    <td width="18%" height="19"><%= jdspf.getField("X1ITEM") %></td>
  </tr>

<% jdspf.setCurrentRecord("SFL01"); %>

<% while (jdspf.nextRow()) { %>

  <tr>
    <td width="10%" height="19" align="center"><%= jdspf.getField("X2OPT") %></td>
    <td width="18%" height="19"><%= jdspf.getField("X2ITEM") %></td>
    <td width="41%" height="19"><%= jdspf.getField("X2DESC") %></td>
    <td width="13%" height="19" align="right"><%= jdspf.getField("X2QTYO") %></td>
    <td width="9%" height="19"><%= jdspf.getField("X2UOMI") %></td>
    <td width="9%" height="19"><%= jdspf.getField("X2UOMS") %></td>
  </tr>

<% } %>

</table>
```

Listing 11.22: The possible source for a subfile JavaServer Page (part 1 of 2).

```
<% jdspf.setCurrentRecord("CTL01"); %>
  <p align="right" style="margin-top: 0; margin-bottom: 0">
    <%= jdspf.getRollButtons() %>
  </p>
  <p align="center" style="margin-left: 0; margin-top: 0">
    <%= jdspf.getCommandButtons() %>
  </p>
</form>

</body>

</html>
```

Listing 11.22: The possible source for a subfile JavaServer Page (part 2 of 2).

While we're not there yet, Listing 11.22 shows the direction to head with the SC400 JSP interface. As you can see, there are a number of calls to the **jdspf** bean throughout the HTML, but for the most part, I think they're reasonably self-explanatory. The single biggest change from today's architecture is that the **getField** method returns *all* of the HTML necessary to display the field on the screen, including form-field keywords and font attributes.

An interesting enhancement to the **ScJdspfJsp** class would be to support the **getRollButtons** and **getCommandButtons** methods. These would require a little bit of work in the support classes, but they're certainly not outside the realm of the architecture. The nice thing about this idea is that the buttons would automatically post back to the correct servlet because the definition would come *from* the servlet. This would be one less issue for the JavaServer Page designer to worry about.

Figure 11.13 shows one possible further evolution of the subfile HTML. I've changed the option field to a dropdown list, and most of the column headings have been replaced with buttons. The values for the option field would only need to be coded in the **ScJdspfJsp** object; they would automatically be queried by the **getField** method. It would require an extension of the **JspField** object to automatically generate the appropriate HTML code.

The buttons on the top would require an actual change to the AS/400 code. They would be returned as function keys, so that the program could, say, sort the subfile based on column. Because the same functionality would then be available to the green screen via a function key, you'd be enhancing all of your interfaces at the same time.

Option	Item	Description	On Hand	Stock	Sales
Add...	NEWITEM				
(none)	ABC0001	Your Description Here	2.32	LB	OZ
Change...	ABC0123	Yet Another Item	12.34	OZ	QT
(none)	KONABEANS	Kona Coffee Beans	333.33	LB	OZ
(none)	KONABEANS2	Leo Doesn't Believe Me	124.30	LB	OZ
Copy...	MMM3333	Triple M Item	123213.00	LB	OZ
(none)	PBPATTY	Peanut Butter Patties	1212.00	BX	BX
(none)	PIII-350	Pentium III, 350 MHz	605.00	EA	EA
Delete...	PIII-450	Pentium III, 450 MHz	223.00	EA	EA
(none)	PIII-466	Pentium III, 466 MHz	1232.00	EA	EA
(none)	PIII-500	Pentium III, 500 MHz	121.00	EA	EA
View...	QQQ8765	Q's The Limit!	.03	GL	OZ
(none)	THINMINTS	Thin Mints	3237.00	BX	BX
(none)	XYZ1234	The Special XYZ Item	54.01	GL	QT

<< Prev Page | Next Page >>

Process | Exit

Figure 11.13: The screen from Figure 11.11 again, but with an enhanced browser interface.

SC400 JSP—It Just Keeps Getting Better

This sort of programming is what keeps me on the Java bandwagon. If the class hierarchies are created correctly, and the various pieces of the logic are separated from one another, you can continue to enhance the infrastructure without affecting the current interfaces. This means that you can quickly put together simple but functional interfaces for all the legacy applications that need them today, and then add additional features as your needs change, without having to retrofit the existing programs. That, to me, is the most important goal of any legacy redeployment strategy: having a quick time-to-market without being locked into an inflexible interface.

If all this seems beyond your current Java skills, I recommend that you spend some time at this book's Web site, *http://www.java400.net/edeployment*, where you can read more about these topics.

Part 3
RUNNING THE APPLICATION

Part 3 is designed to answer some of the practical questions you'll have while running your application. You'll find the actual details of the target application and the supporting software as well. Taking nothing for granted, this section of the book walks you through the process of using FTP to transfer software to your AS/400, helps you install the Java Development Kit, and even guides you through the configuration of IBM's WebSphere application server.

Chapter 12 explains how to download software, if necessary, and then upload the AS/400 portion to your AS/400. Once that's done, you'll restore the libraries and test the green-screen interface.

In chapter 13, you'll install and run the JBUI user interface. This chapter also describes how to install the JDK on your workstation, if you haven't already done so.

Chapter 14 deals with installing the servlet code and running the browser interface, using version 1.1 or 2.0 of IBM's WebSphere Application Server. OS/400 V4R3 supports version 1.1 of WAS, while V4R4 supports versions 2.0 and 3.0. There are significant differences between version 3.0 and earlier versions; updates for this version were not available as this book went to press. Please refer to appendix A for information on code updates.

12

THE GREEN SCREEN

Because the AS/400 application client is the driving force behind interface techniques, this chapter is required for any of them. In this chapter, you'll discover how to install and run the basic green-screen application. This chapter is broken down as follows:

- "Downloading the Software" explains how to get the latest version of the software online, although I suggest that you stick to the version on the CD that came with the book.

- "Installing the Green-Screen Software" includes everything you need to know about uploading a save file to the AS/400 and installing software from it.

- "Testing the Green-Screen" discusses to tests of the application and reviews some of the most common errors that can occur.

DOWNLOADING THE SOFTWARE

If for some reason your CD is damaged or you need to download a new copy of the software, you can go to the following link:

```
http://www.java400.net/edeployment/pbd_download.htm
```

You'll see a screen like that shown in Figure 12.1. Select the file marked **edeployment.zip**, and download it. A panel like the one in Figure 12.2 will appear. Save the file to disk.

PART 3: RUNNING THE APPLICATION

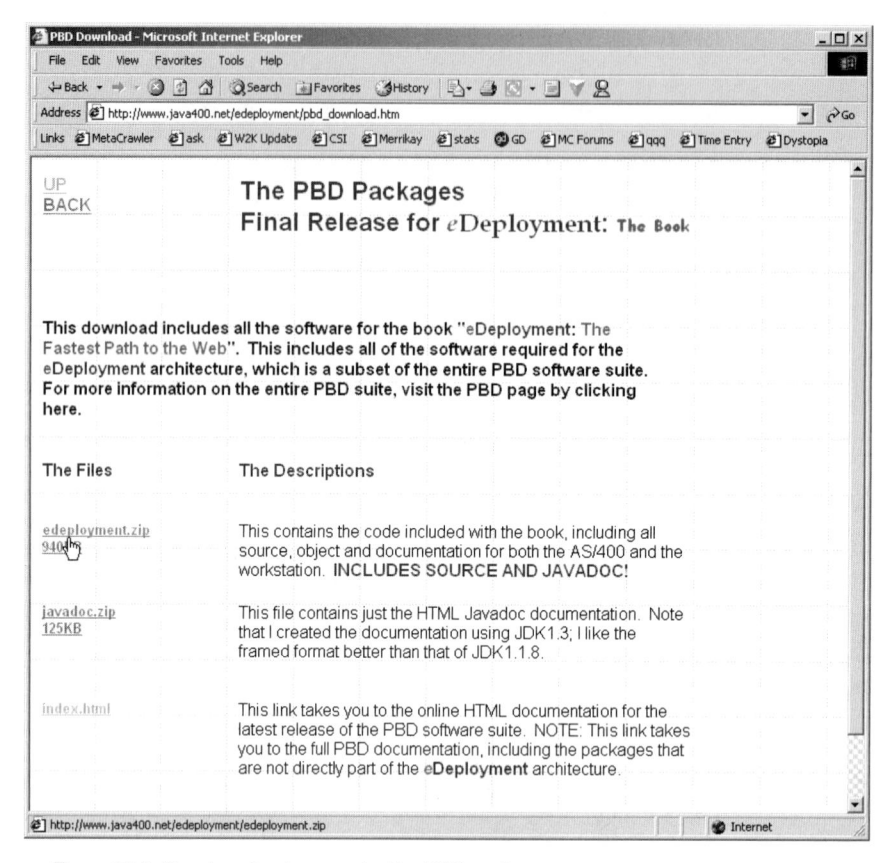

Figure 12.1: The download screen for the PBD packages.

Once you've done that, or if you're running from your CD, you need to extract the program. Double-click the .zip file, either where you've saved it or on your CD-ROM drive, as shown in Figure 12.3. You'll probably see a screen similar to the WinZip screen in Figure 12.4. Type in the directory name as shown, and click the Extract button.

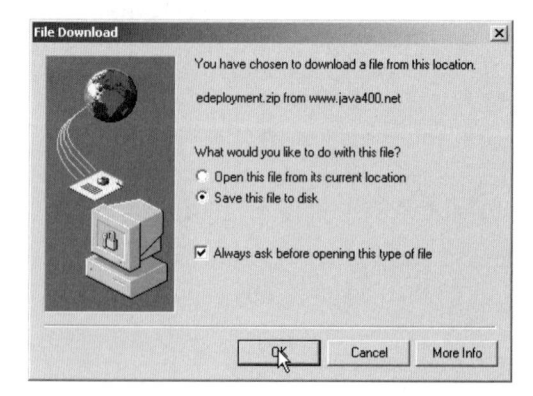

Figure 12.2: The download screen from Internet Explorer.

> **Note:** If you store your program information on a different drive, or your Java software is in a different location, feel free to change the directory name from the one in Figure 12.4, but remember that the rest of the document will expect the naming convention shown here.

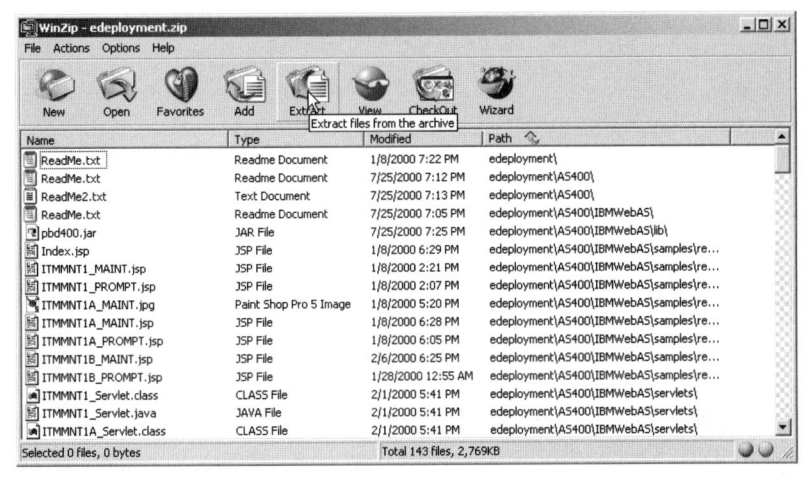

Figure 12.3: The WinZip screen for the edeployment.zip file.

INSTALLING THE GREEN-SCREEN SOFTWARE

This section covers the steps necessary to install the green-screen portion of the software. This includes not only the original maintenance program, but the green-screen revitalized version and the APIs that make revitalization happen. This step is crucial, because the green-screen APIs are used by the application client, and the application client is the component that is shared by all the user-interface techniques.

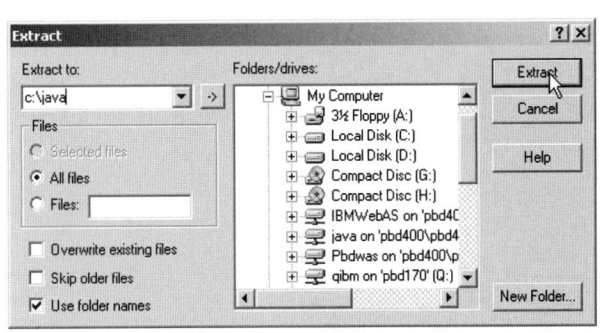

Figure 12.4: Entering the directory name for the Extract panel.

Create the Transfer Library and Save Files

First, you need to create a transfer library and some save files on the system. Follow the steps in Figures 12.5 through 12.7. At the end, you should see the display in Figure 12.8.

```
                        Create Library (CRTLIB)

 Type choices, press Enter.

 Library  . . . . . . . . . . . .   PBDXFER       Name
 Library type . . . . . . . . . .   *PROD         *PROD, *TEST
 Text 'description' . . . . . . .   PBD Transfer Library




                                                                       Bottom
 F3=Exit   F4=Prompt   F5=Refresh   F10=Additional parameters  F12=Cancel
 F13=How to use this display        F24=More keys
```

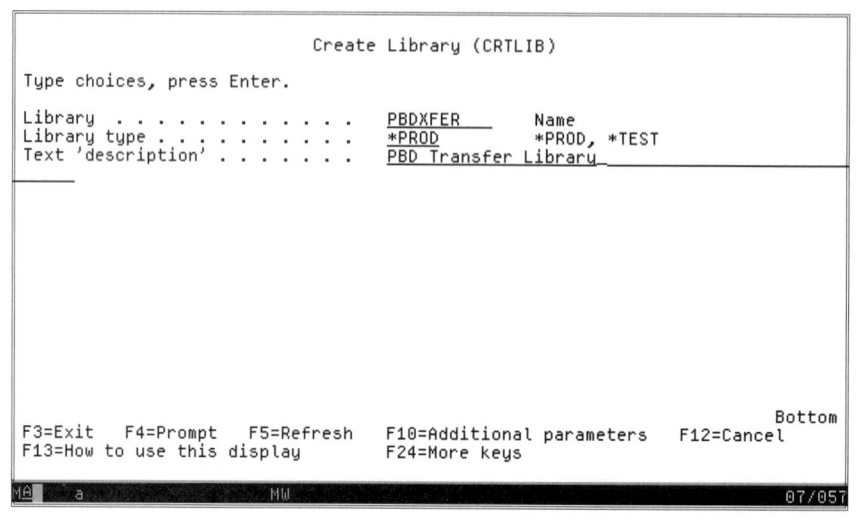

Figure 12.5: Use the CRTLIB command to create the transfer library.

```
                        Create Save File (CRTSAVF)

 Type choices, press Enter.

 Save file  . . . . . . . . . . .   JSPAPI        Name
   Library  . . . . . . . . . . .     PBDXFER     Name, *CURLIB
 Text 'description' . . . . . . .   *BLANK




                                                                       Bottom
 F3=Exit   F4=Prompt   F5=Refresh   F10=Additional parameters  F12=Cancel
 F13=How to use this display        F24=More keys
```

Figure 12.6: Use the CRTSAVF command to create the JSPAPI save file.

CHAPTER 12: THE GREEN SCREEN

```
                       Create Save File (CRTSAVF)

 Type choices, press Enter.

 Save file  . . . . . . . . . . .   JSPPROTO      Name
   Library  . . . . . . . . . . .     PBDXFER     Name, *CURLIB
 Text 'description' . . . . . . .   *BLANK




                                                                    Bottom
 F3=Exit    F4=Prompt    F5=Refresh    F10=Additional parameters   F12=Cancel
 F13=How to use this display           F24=More keys
```

Figure 12.7: Use the CRTSAVF command to create the JSPPROTO save file.

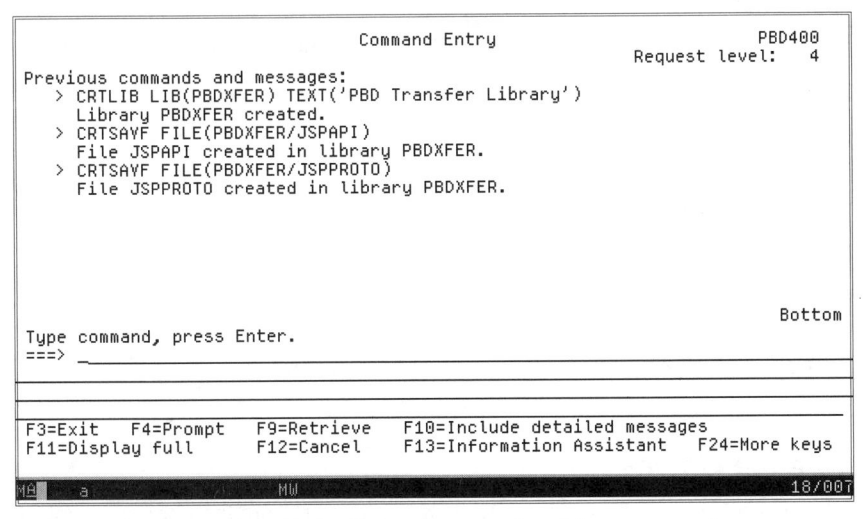

```
                         Command Entry                         PBD400
                                                   Request level:   4
 Previous commands and messages:
    > CRTLIB LIB(PBDXFER) TEXT('PBD Transfer Library')
      Library PBDXFER created.
    > CRTSAVF FILE(PBDXFER/JSPAPI)
      File JSPAPI created in library PBDXFER.
    > CRTSAVF FILE(PBDXFER/JSPPROTO)
      File JSPPROTO created in library PBDXFER.




                                                                    Bottom
 Type command, press Enter.
 ===> _____


 F3=Exit     F4=Prompt      F9=Retrieve    F10=Include detailed messages
 F11=Display full            F12=Cancel    F13=Information Assistant    F24=More keys
```

Figure 12.8: The command-entry display after executing all three commands.

FTP the Save Files to the AS/400

Now you need to start a DOS session on your workstation, as shown in Listing 12.1. This assumes that you followed the steps exactly as outlined earlier in this chapter to extract

221

PART 3: RUNNING THE APPLICATION

your files into the folder **c:\java\pbd20p**. If you've used a different folder, you'll need to position yourself there before executing the commands in Listing 12.1.

```
C:\>cd java\edeployment

C:\java\edeployment>cd as400

C:\java\edeployment\AS400>cd "save files"

C:\java\edeployment\AS400\Save files>ftp your400
Connected to YOUR400.
220-QTCP at YOUR400.YOURDOMAIN.COM.
220 Connection will close if idle more than 5 minutes.
User (YOUR400:(none)): youruserid
331 Enter password.
Password: (enter your password here)
230 YOURUSERID logged on.
ftp> cd pbdxfer
250 "PBDXFER" is current library.
ftp> bin
200 Representation type is binary IMAGE.
ftp> send jspapi
200 PORT subcommand request successful.
150 Sending file to member JSPAPI in file JSPAPI in library PBDXFER.
250 File transfer completed successfully.
734976 bytes sent in 2.63 seconds (279.99 Kbytes/sec)
ftp> send jspproto
200 PORT subcommand request successful.
150 Sending file to member JSPPROTO in file JSPPROTO in library PBDXFER.
250 File transfer completed successfully.
470448 bytes sent in 1.41 seconds (334.60 Kbytes/sec)
ftp> bye
221 QUIT subcommand received.

C:\java\edeployment\AS400\Save files>
```

Listing 12.1: Use this FTP session to send the save files to the AS/400.

Restore the Libraries

Issue the commands shown in Figures 12.9 and 12.10 to restore the libraries, resulting in Figure 12.11. At this point, all the AS/400 software, both source and object, is on your machine. After testing, you can continue with chapter 13 or 14, depending on the type of user interface you want to use first.

CHAPTER 12: THE GREEN SCREEN

```
                    Restore Library (RSTLIB)

Type choices, press Enter.

Saved library  . . . . . . . . . >  JSPAPI      Name, *NONSYS, *ALLUSR, *IBM
Device . . . . . . . . . . . . . >  *SAVF       Name, *SAVF
            + for more values        _____
Save file  . . . . . . . . . . .    jspapi      Name
  Library  . . . . . . . . . . .      pbdxfer   Name, *LIBL, *CURLIB




                                                                     Bottom
F3=Exit    F4=Prompt   F5=Refresh   F10=Additional parameters   F12=Cancel
F13=How to use this display         F24=More keys
```

Figure 12.9: Use the RSTLIB command to restore the JSPAPI library.

```
                    Restore Library (RSTLIB)

Type choices, press Enter.

Saved library  . . . . . . . . . >  JSPPROTO    Name, *NONSYS, *ALLUSR, *IBM
Device . . . . . . . . . . . . . >  *SAVF       Name, *SAVF
            + for more values        _____
Save file  . . . . . . . . . . . >  jspproto    Name
  Library  . . . . . . . . . . . >    pbdxfer   Name, *LIBL, *CURLIB




                                                                     Bottom
F3=Exit    F4=Prompt   F5=Refresh   F10=Additional parameters   F12=Cancel
F13=How to use this display         F24=More keys
```

Figure 12.10: Use the RSTLIB command to restore the JSPPROTO library.

223

```
                              Command Entry                        PBD400
                                                   Request level:      4
 Previous commands and messages:
   > RSTLIB SAVLIB(JSPAPI) DEV(*SAVF) SAVF(PBDXFER/JSPAPI)
     26 objects restored from JSPAPI to JSPAPI.
   > RSTLIB SAVLIB(JSPPROTO) DEV(*SAVF) SAVF(PBDXFER/JSPPROTO)
     21 objects restored from JSPPROTO to JSPPROTO.




                                                                   Bottom
 Type command, press Enter.
 ===> _____


 F3=Exit     F4=Prompt     F9=Retrieve    F10=Include detailed messages
 F11=Display full          F12=Cancel     F13=Information Assistant    F24=More keys
```

Figure 12.11: The command entry display after executing the two restore commands.

TESTING THE GREEN-SCREEN SOFTWARE

Finally, you can test the AS/400 software, as shown in the figures in the rest of this chapter.

Run ITMMNT1

Follow the directions in Figures 12.12 through 12.20. You should see screens identical to these. If not, your installation was incomplete or incorrect, and you should try installing again.

```
                             Edit Library List

 Type new/changed information, press Enter.
   To add a library, type name and desired sequence number.
   To remove a library, space over library name.
   To change position of a library, type new sequence number.

 Sequence                 Sequence                 Sequence
 Number   Library         Number   Library         Number   Library
   010                     120                      230
   020    QGPL             130                      240
   030    QTEMP            140                      250
   040    jspapi           150
   050    jspproto         160
   060                     170
   070                     180
   080                     190
   090                     200
   100                     210
   110                     220

 F3=Exit          F5=Refresh           F12=Cancel
```

Figure 12.12: The EDTLIBL command display. Change your library list as shown.

```
                         Command Entry                         PBD400
                                                   Request level:   4
Previous commands and messages:
  > edtlibl




                                                                Bottom
Type command, press Enter.
===> dsppfm item


F3=Exit     F4=Prompt    F9=Retrieve    F10=Include detailed messages
F11=Display full         F12=Cancel     F13=Information Assistant   F24=More keys
```

Figure 12.13: The DSPPFM command used to check the data. Press Enter.

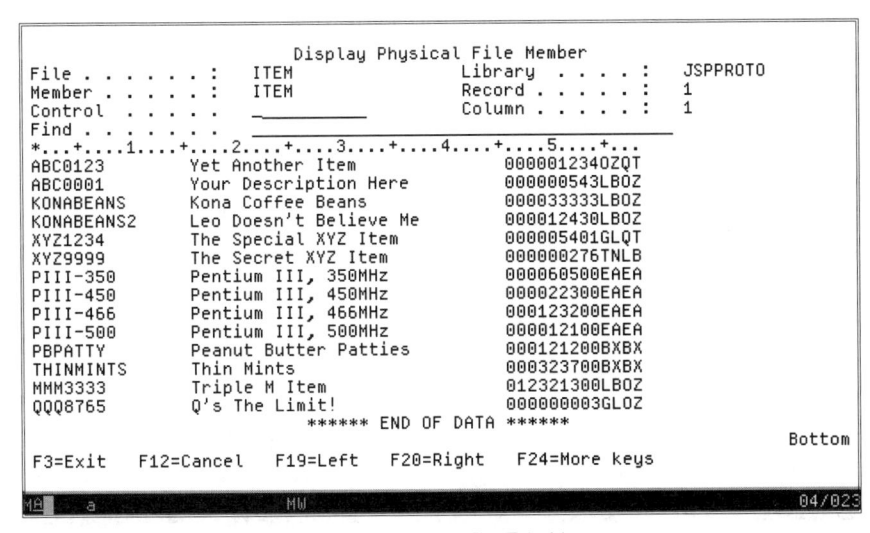

```
                     Display Physical File Member
File . . . . . . :   ITEM            Library . . . . :   JSPPROTO
Member . . . . . :   ITEM            Record . . . . . :   1
Control  . . . . .   _____        Column . . . . . :   1
Find . . . . . .     _____
*...+....1....+....2....+....3....+....4....+....5....+...
ABC0123         Yet Another Item           000001234OZQT
ABC0001         Your Description Here      000000543LBOZ
KONABEANS       Kona Coffee Beans          000033333LBOZ
KONABEANS2      Leo Doesn't Believe Me     000012430LBOZ
XYZ1234         The Special XYZ Item       000005401GLQT
XYZ9999         The Secret XYZ Item        000000276TNLB
PIII-350        Pentium III, 350MHz        000060500EAEA
PIII-450        Pentium III, 450MHz        000022300EAEA
PIII-466        Pentium III, 466MHz        000123200EAEA
PIII-500        Pentium III, 500MHz        000012100EAEA
PBPATTY         Peanut Butter Patties      000121200BXBX
THINMINTS       Thin Mints                 000323700BXBX
MMM3333         Triple M Item              012321300LBOZ
QQQ8765         Q's The Limit!             000000003GLOZ
                      ****** END OF DATA ******
                                                                Bottom
F3=Exit    F12=Cancel   F19=Left    F20=Right    F24=More keys
```

Figure 12.14: The correct contents of the ITEM file. Exit this program.

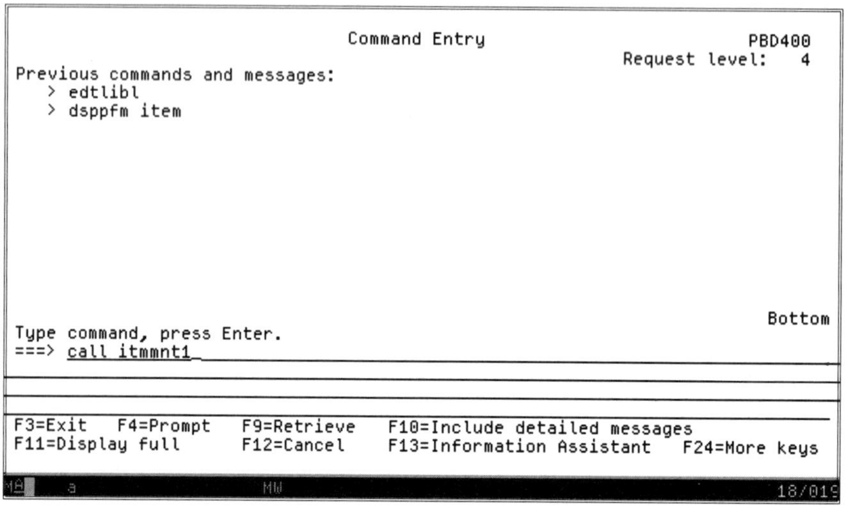

PART 3: RUNNING THE APPLICATION

```
                         Command Entry                        PBD400
                                                  Request level:    4
 Previous commands and messages:
   > edtlibl
   > dsppfm item




                                                                Bottom
 Type command, press Enter.
 ===> call itmmnt1_



 F3=Exit    F4=Prompt    F9=Retrieve   F10=Include detailed messages
 F11=Display full        F12=Cancel    F13=Information Assistant    F24=More keys
```

Figure 12.15: The call to the original, monolithic program, ITMMNT1.

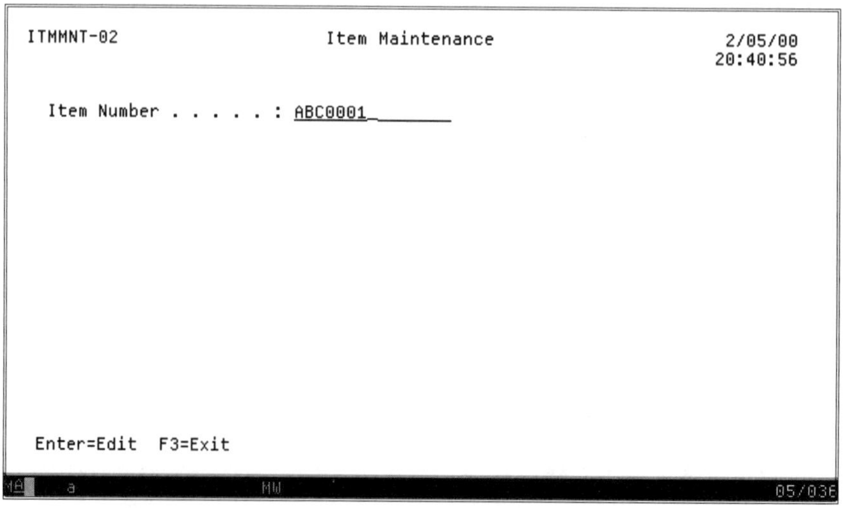

```
 ITMMNT-02                  Item Maintenance                  2/05/00
                                                             20:40:56

    Item Number . . . . . : ABC0001_








    Enter=Edit   F3=Exit
```

*Figure 12.16: The normal ITMMNT1 prompt. Type **ABC0001** and press Enter.*

```
ITMMNT-02                Item Maintenance              2/05/00
Modify                                                 20:41:03

   Item Number . . . . . : ABC0001
   Item Description  . . : Your Description Here
   Quantity On Hand  . . :       5.43
   Inventory UOM . . . . : LB
   Selling UOM . . . . . : OZ




   Enter=Edit   F3=Exit   F6=Accept   F12=Cancel
```

Figure 12.17: The detail screen for item ABC0001.

```
ITMMNT-02                Item Maintenance              2/05/00
Modify                                                 20:41:03

   Item Number . . . . . : ABC0001
   Item Description  . . : MY Description Here
   Quantity On Hand  . . :       5.43
   Inventory UOM . . . . : LB
   Selling UOM . . . . . : OZ




   Enter=Edit   F3=Exit   F6=Accept   F12=Cancel
```

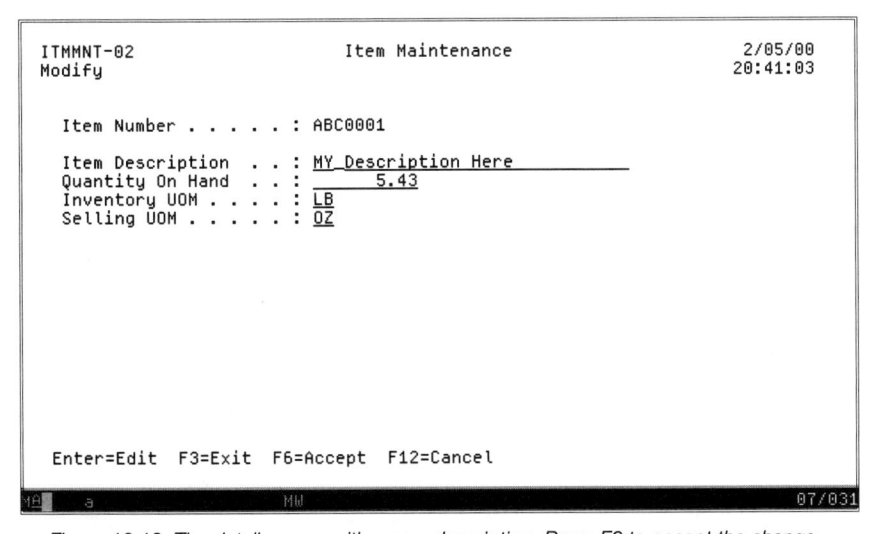

Figure 12.18: The detail screen with a new description. Press F6 to accept the change.

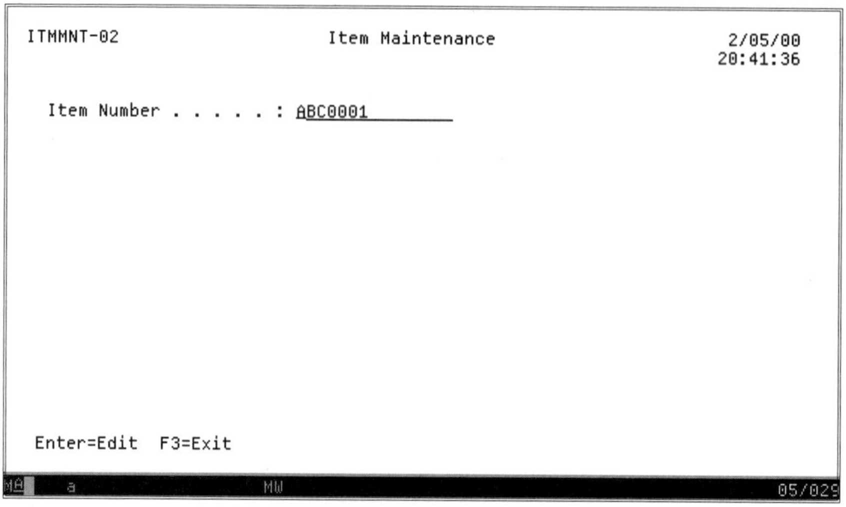
ITMMNT-02
Item Maintenance
2/05/00
20:41:36
Item Number . . . . . : ABC0001
Enter=Edit F3=Exit
MW
05/029

Figure 12.19: The first panel again after pressing F6. Press Enter again.

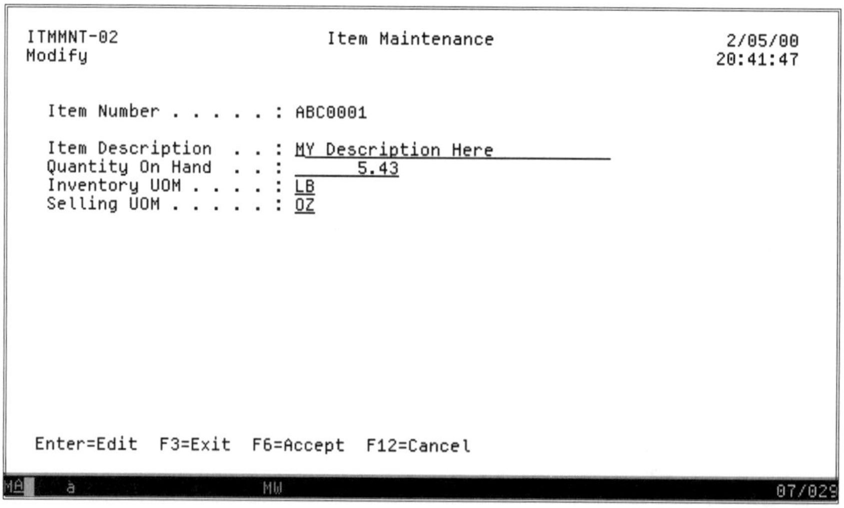
ITMMNT-02
Modify
Item Maintenance
2/05/00
20:41:47
Item Number . . . . . : ABC0001
Item Description . . : MY Description Here
Quantity On Hand . . : 5.43
Inventory UOM . . . . : LB
Selling UOM . . . . . : OZ
Enter=Edit F3=Exit F6=Accept F12=Cancel
MW
07/029

Figure 12.20: The detail screen confirming the change. Press F3 to exit the program.

Run ITMMNT1UI

Run the green-screen UI server ITMMNT1UI by calling it as shown in Figure 12.21. You'll see the prompt screen shown in Figure 12.22, which is identical to the one you get when you call ITMMNT1, as well is should be, since both programs use the same display file. There's a little twist, though: do a WRKACTJOB at this time, and you'll get the display shown in Figure 12.23, which shows a job named ITMMNT1AC running in QBATCH. You might guess that ITMMNT1AC is the application client for ITMMNT1UI, and you would be correct. This batch job ends when you exit ITMMNT1UI.

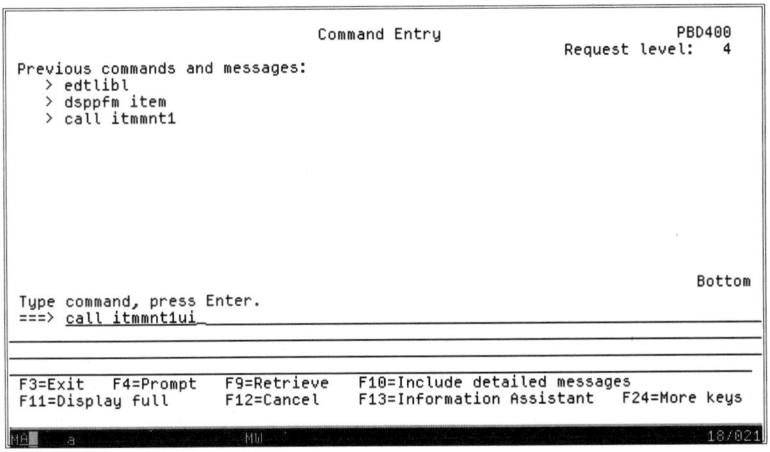

```
                        Command Entry                        PBD400
                                              Request level:   4
Previous commands and messages:
  > edtlibl
  > dsppfm item
  > call itmmnt1




                                                              Bottom
Type command, press Enter.
===> call itmmnt1ui_


F3=Exit    F4=Prompt    F9=Retrieve   F10=Include detailed messages
F11=Display full        F12=Cancel    F13=Information Assistant    F24=More keys
```

Figure 12.21: The command to launch the green-screen UI server, ITMMNT1UI.

```
ITMMNT-02                 Item Maintenance               2/05/00
                                                        20:50:09

  Item Number . . . . . :  _____








  Enter=Edit  F3=Exit
```

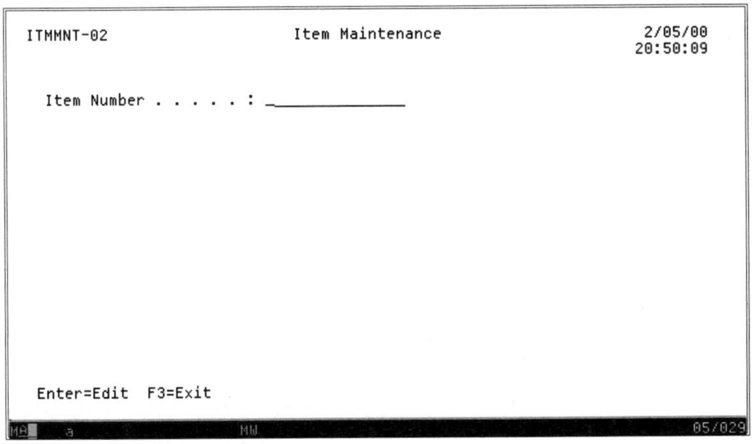

Figure 12.22: The screen is identical to ITMMNT1.

PART 3: RUNNING THE APPLICATION

```
                        Work with Active Jobs                    PBD400
                                                      02/05/00  23:52:52
 CPU %:    2.1      Elapsed time:   00:02:30    Active jobs:  107

 Type options, press Enter.
   2=Change    3=Hold    4=End     5=Work with   6=Release   7=Display message
   8=Work with spooled files    13=Disconnect ...

 Opt   Subsystem/Job   User        Type  CPU %  Function        Status
  _     QBATCH         QSYS        SBS    .0                    DEQW
  _       ITMMNT1AC    SPUD        BCH    .1    PGM-DQMBAPIC    DEQW
  _     QCMN           QSYS        SBS    .0                    DEQW
  _     QCTL           QSYS        SBS    .0                    DEQW
  _     QINTER         QSYS        SBS    .0                    DEQW
  _       QPADEV0003   SPUD        INT    .2    PGM-ITMMNT1UI   DSPW
  _       QPADEV0004   SPUD        INT    .3    CMD-WRKACTJOB   RUN
  _     QPGMR          QSYS        SBS    .0                    DEQW
  _     QSERVER        QSYS        SBS    .0                    DEQW
                                                                    More...
 Parameters or command
 ===>
 F3=Exit    F5=Refresh      F7=Find     F10=Restart statistics
 F11=Display elapsed data   F12=Cancel  F23=More options   F24=More keys
```

Figure 12.23: A WRKACTJOB display showing ITMMNT1AC running in QBATCH.

Continue on with Figures 12.24 through 12.28 to verify that the APIs have been installed and are running correctly. If you reach Figure 12.28, it's time to continue on to either chapter 13 or 14, depending on which client you plan to use. I recommend, however, that you at least install and run the shipped JBUI client to work out any TCP/IP connection issues; it is much easier to debug the JBUI client than the servlet.

```
 ITMMNT-02                    Item Maintenance                   2/05/00
                                                                 20:50:09

      Item Number . . . . . :  ABC0001_____








      Enter=Edit   F3=Exit
```

*Figure 12.24: Enter the item number **ABC0001** and press Enter.*

230

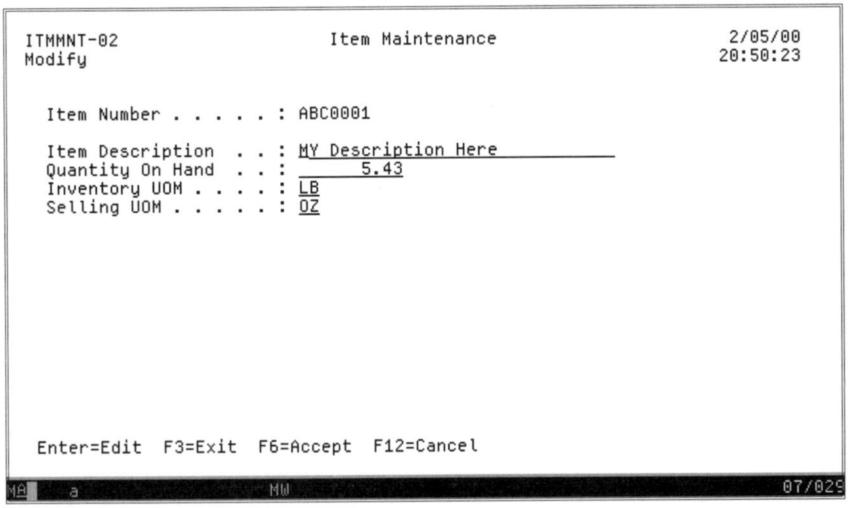
ITMMNT-02
Item Maintenance
2/05/00
Modify
20:50:23
Item Number . . . . . : ABC0001
Item Description . . : MY Description Here
Quantity On Hand . . : 5.43
Inventory UOM . . . . : LB
Selling UOM . . . . . : OZ
Enter=Edit F3=Exit F6=Accept F12=Cancel
MA a MW 07/029

Figure 12.25: The description changed with ITMMNT1.

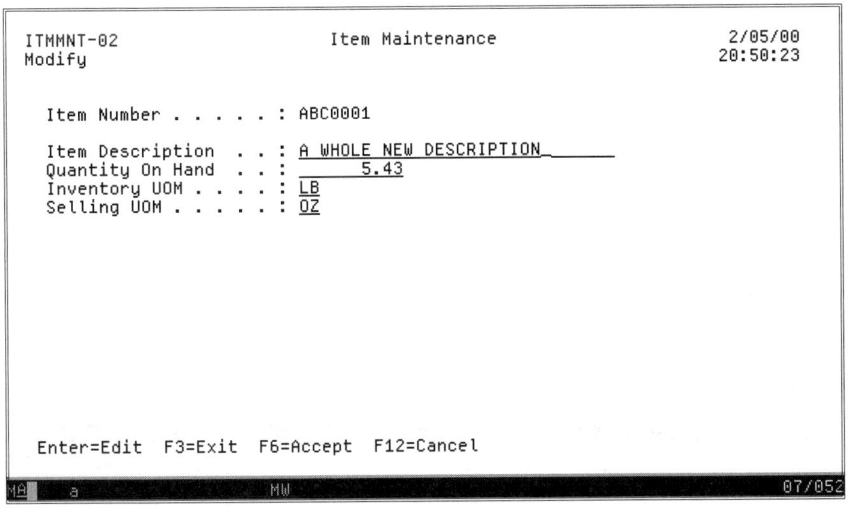
ITMMNT-02
Item Maintenance
2/05/00
Modify
20:50:23
Item Number . . . . . : ABC0001
Item Description . . : A WHOLE NEW DESCRIPTION
Quantity On Hand . . : 5.43
Inventory UOM . . . . : LB
Selling UOM . . . . . : OZ
Enter=Edit F3=Exit F6=Accept F12=Cancel
MA a MW 07/052

Figure 12.26: A new description keyed in. Press F6 to update the record.

PART 3: RUNNING THE APPLICATION

```
 ITMMNT-02                  Item Maintenance                 2/05/00
                                                            20:50:44

    Item Number . . . . . : ABC0001




    Enter=Edit   F3=Exit
```

Figure 12.27: The prompt screen again. Press Enter to verify the change.

```
 ITMMNT-02                  Item Maintenance                 2/04/00
 Modify                                                     20:51:07

    Item Number . . . . . : ABC0001

    Item Description  . . : A WHOLE NEW DESCRIPTION
    Quantity On Hand  . . :         5.43
    Inventory UOM . . . . : LB
    Selling UOM . . . . . : OZ




    Enter=Edit   F3=Exit   F6=Accept   F12=Cancel
```

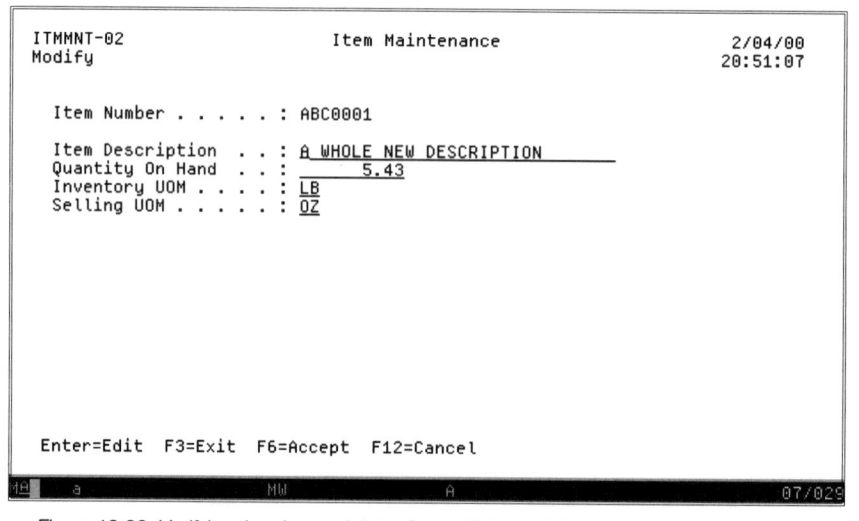

Figure 12.28: Verifying the changed data. Press F3 to end the program.

Error Conditions

A typical error occurs when you don't have JSPAPI in your library list. Figure 12.29 shows the error.

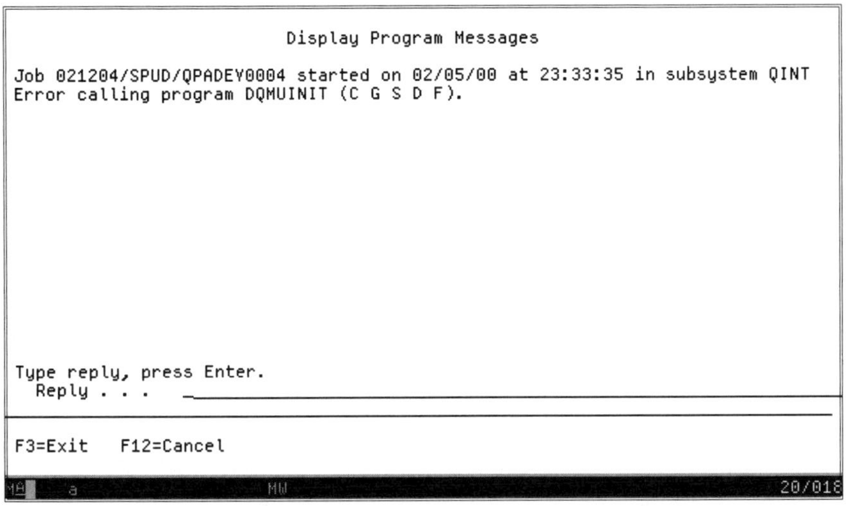
Display Program Messages
Job 021204/SPUD/QPADEV0004 started on 02/05/00 at 23:33:35 in subsystem QINT
Error calling program DQMUINIT (C G S D F).
Type reply, press Enter.
Reply . . .
F3=Exit F12=Cancel
MA a MW 20/018

Figure 12.29: The CPF0001 error that occurs if JSPAPI is not in your library list.

Another error occurs when you don't have authority to one or more objects. You'll see a CPF0001 error like the user SPUD got in Figure 12.30.

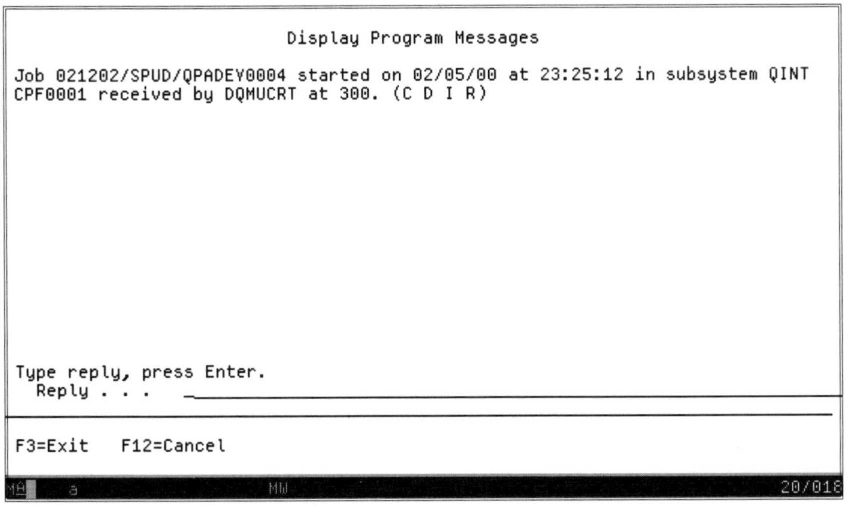
Display Program Messages
Job 021202/SPUD/QPADEV0004 started on 02/05/00 at 23:25:12 in subsystem QINT
CPF0001 received by DQMUCRT at 300. (C D I R)
Type reply, press Enter.
Reply . . .
F3=Exit F12=Cancel
MA a MW 20/018

Figure 12.30: User SPUD getting an authority violation.

On my system, the default subsystem for the SBMJOB command is QBATCH. If QBATCH is not started, I get an error such as the one shown in Figure 12.31. This error occurs after a

60-second wait, because that's the timeout value on the receive. The error shows up in the subsequent send.

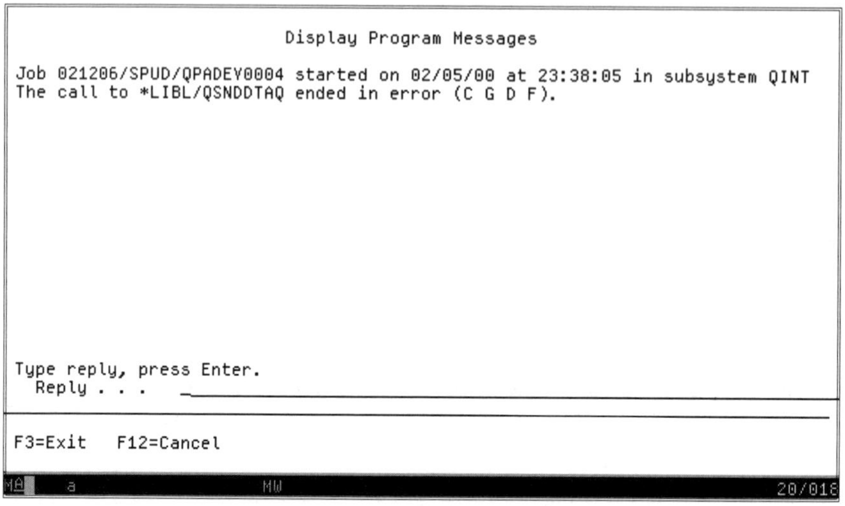

```
                        Display Program Messages
Job 021206/SPUD/QPADEV0004 started on 02/05/00 at 23:38:05 in subsystem QINT
The call to *LIBL/QSNDDTAQ ended in error (C G D F).




Type reply, press Enter.
  Reply . . .    _

F3=Exit    F12=Cancel
```

Figure 12.31: The problem when the batch subsystem isn't started.

13

THE JBUI
(THICK CLIENT) UI SERVER

This chapter describes how to install and test the "vanilla" version of the JBUI user interface (ITMMNT1_JbuiDisplay). "Vanilla," in this sense, means that you're not going to configure the application-client proxy for your particular machine; that's not necessary. Instead, the application-client proxy will prompt for the machine, user ID, and password whenever ITMMNT1_JbuiDisplay is run. You can, however, change the application-client proxy to automatically log into your machine with a specified user ID and password; see chapter 7 for details about this. This chapter is divided into two sections:

- "Check Your Java Environment" details the installation of Java that I use to run the JBUI user interface.

- "Test the JBUI UI Server" explains how to test the application, and reviews some of the most common errors that can occur.

CHECK YOUR JAVA ENVIRONMENT

In order to run client-side Java programs such as the JBUI UI server, you must have a Java environment on your workstation. This environment must support JDK1.1 and Swing1.1.1, or JDK1.2 or later. All the software required is free, but you do have to download it and install it.

My Environment

If you've used my Java installation page, you'll have an environment similar to the one shown in Figure 13.1.

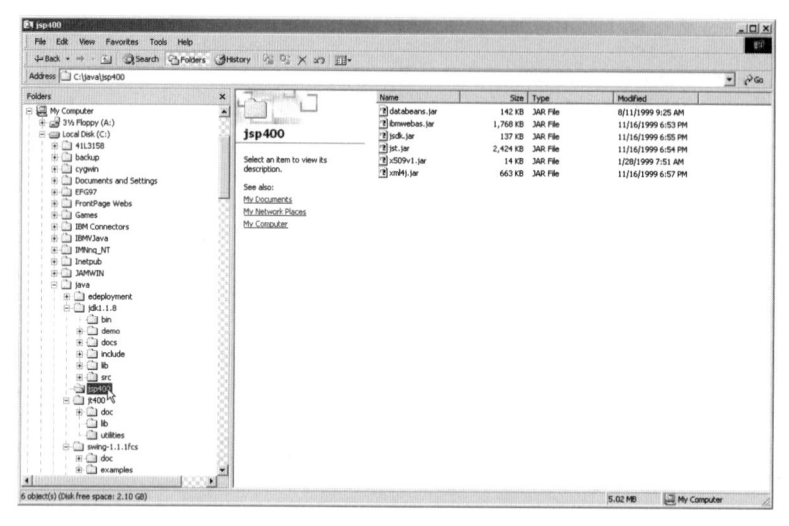

Figure 13.1: My Java environment.

You might not have the highlighted directory **jsp400**, since that is added during chapter 7. However, you should have the rest of the directories:

```
C:\java\jdk1.1.8
C:\java\jt400
C:\java\edeployment
C:\java\swing-1.1.1fcs
```

This book assumes that environment.

If you don't have Java installed yet, go to the page http://www.zappie.net/Java/Javatorium/installi.htm, shown in Figure 13.2, for step-by-step directions on downloading and installing the JDK (Java Development Kit).

My environment uses the final releases of JDK1.1.8 and Swing 1.1.1 because this is compatible with the JDK on the AS/400 as of V4R3. The AS/400 JDK is at release 1.1.7, and so is binary-compatible with release 1.1.8.

TEST THE JBUI UI SERVER

It's actually quite easy to run the JBUI user interface once your normal Java environment is set up. If you've followed the instructions up to this point in this chapter, you'll have a folder named c:\java\edeployment\Workstation, which contains the itmmnt.bat command. This command assumes that your CLASSPATH already includes Swing and IBM's Java Toolbox for the AS/400; it calls java.exe with the -classpath parameter to add the pbd.jar and windowsx.jar to the CLASSPATH and execute the class ITMMNT1_JbuiDisplay.

Run the JBUI UI Server

If you execute the commands in Listing 13.1, after a moment or two you'll see the prompt screen in Figure 13.3. There might be a bit of a delay the first time, since this will load the Java Virtual Machine. Subsequent calls will be much faster.

```
C:\>cd java\edeployment

C:\java\edeployment>cd workstation

C:\java\edeployment\Workstation>itmmnt
launching ITMMNT1_JbuiDisplay...
```

Listing 13.1: The commands required to start the JBUI UI Server.

After entering the name of your AS/400, your user ID, and your password, you'll see the screen in Figure 13.4.

> **Note:** The Item Number field is filled with 15 blanks to start. Press the Tab key to highlight the whole field before entering your item number. The item number must be the left-most characters of the entry field, or you'll get an "item not found" message. You might even crash the program.

Once you've entered the item number, you can press the Enter=Edit button to bring up the screen in Figure 13.5. Change the description and press the F6=Accept button, and you'll be returned to the screen in Figure 13.6. You can press Enter=Edit again to check your work, or F3=Exit to end the program.

237

PART 3: RUNNING THE APPLICATION

Errors

Environmental errors will stop the program. Listings 13.2 and 13.3 show two of the most common.

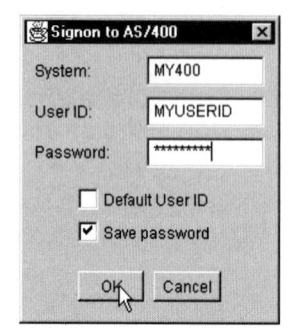

Figure 13.3 shows the AS/400 signon display.

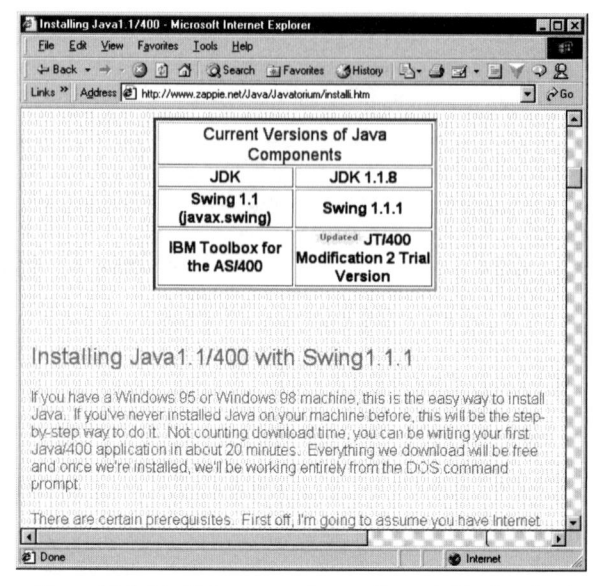

Figure 13.2: My Web page walks you through the download and installation of Java.

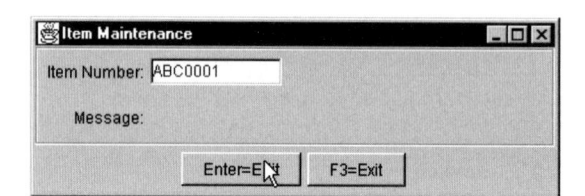

Figure 13.4: The JBUI version of the prompt panel. Enter the item number and press the Enter=Edit button.

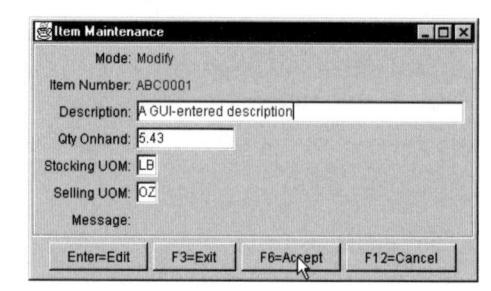

Figure 13.5: The JBUI maintenance panel. Change the description and press F6=Accept.

```
C:\java\edeployment\Workstation>itmmnt
launching ITMMNT1_JbuiDisplay...
The name specified is not recognized as an
internal or external command, operable program or batch file.
```

Listing 13.2: The error that occurs when the JDK is not installed.

```
C:\java\edeployment\Workstation>itmmnt
launching ITMMNT1_JbuiDisplay...
java.lang.NoClassDefFoundError: javax/swing/SwingConstants
        at ITMMNT1_JbuiDisplay.<init>(ITMMNT1_JbuiDisplay.java:66)
        at ITMMNT1_JbuiDisplay.main(ITMMNT1_JbuiDisplay.java:80)
```

Listing 13.3: The error that occurs when Swing is not installed.

Another area for errors is data entry. This interface does not have a lot of error handling, so it's not very robust. Simple keying errors can bring the interface down. Most of these errors will show up on the command entry display.

In Listing 13.4, you see the error you'll receive if the item number entered is too long. This usually happens when you don't delete the blanks that originally fill the field, as shown in Figure 13.7.

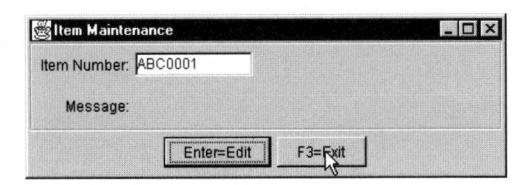

Figure 13.6: After making a change, you return to the prompt panel. Press F3=Exit to end the program.

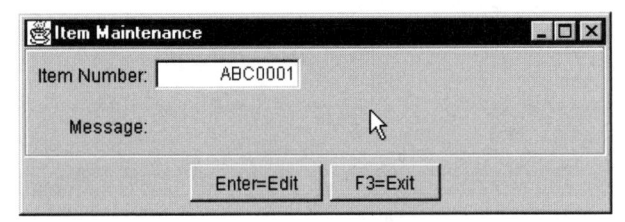

Figure 13.7: The area to the left of "ABC001" is filled with blanks, making the item number too long.

```
C:\java\edeployment\Workstation>itmmnt
launching ITMMNT1_JbuiDisplay...
com.pbd.pub.sc400.Sc400Exception: Error processing message: com.ibm.as400.access
.ExtendedIllegalArgumentException: javaValue (            abc0001): Length is
 not valid.
        at com.pbd.pub.sc400.ScJdspfUIServer.processMessage(ScJdspfUIServer.java
:73)
        at com.pbd.pub.sc400.ScJdspfUIServer.run(Compiled Code)
        at ITMMNT1_JbuiDisplay.main(ITMMNT1_JbuiDisplay.java:80)
```

Listing 13.4: The problem if the item number is too long.

In Listing 13.5 you see what happens when you enter nonnumeric data, such as that shown in Figure 13.8.

```
C:\java\edeployment\Workstation>itmmnt
launching ITMMNT1_JbuiDisplay...
com.pbd.pub.sc400.Sc400Exception: Error processing message: java.lang.NumberForm
atException: notnumeric
        at com.pbd.pub.sc400.ScJdspfUIServer.processMessage(ScJdspfUIServer.java
:73)
        at com.pbd.pub.sc400.ScJdspfUIServer.run(Compiled Code)
        at ITMMNT1_JbuiDisplay.main(ITMMNT1_JbuiDisplay.java:80)
^CTerminate batch job (Y/N)? y
```

Listing 13.5: A numeric data error.

In either of the data entry errors, you'll need to cancel the application client, which is now an orphan job running in your batch subsystem. Do a WRKACTJOB command to see the orphan, as shown in Figure 13.9, then cancel it.

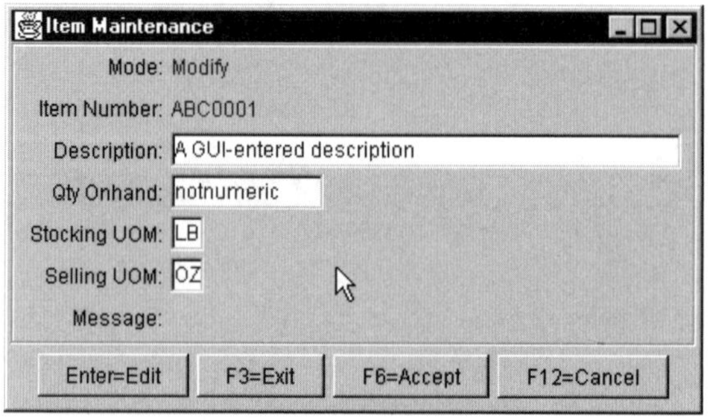

Figure 13.8: Nonnumeric data in the quantity field.

CHAPTER 13: THE JBUI (THICK CLIENT) UI SERVER

```
                          Work with Active Jobs                   PBD400
                                                    02/06/00    12:08:04
         CPU %:    4.3     Elapsed time:   00:31:21    Active jobs:   136

         Type options, press Enter.
           2=Change    3=Hold    4=End    5=Work with   6=Release   7=Display message
           8=Work with spooled files     13=Disconnect ...

         Opt  Subsystem/Job  User        Type   CPU %  Function      Status
         __    QBATCH        QSYS        SBS     .0                  DEQW
         __      ITMMNT1AC   SPUD        BCH     .0    PGM-DQMBAPIC  DEQW
         __    QCMN          QSYS        SBS     .0                  DEQW
         __    QCTL          QSYS        SBS     .0                  DEQW
         __    QHTTPSVR      QSYS        SBS     .0                  DEQW
         __      ADMIN       QTMHHTTP    BCH     .4    PGM-QZHBHTTP  TIMW
         __      ADMIN       QTMHHTTP    BCI     .0                  TIMW
         __      ADMIN       QTMHHTTP    BCI     .0                  TIMW
         __      ADMIN       QTMHHTTP    BCI     .0                  TIMW
                                                                       More...
         Parameters or command
         ===>
         F3=Exit    F5=Refresh      F7=Find       F10=Restart statistics
         F11=Display elapsed data   F12=Cancel    F23=More options   F24=More keys
```

Figure 13.9: The orphan ITMMNT1AC job after the client is cancelled due to error.

14

THE SERVLET

The servlet is the most difficult topic in this part of the book because it includes a lot of different technologies, many of which aren't all that well defined. For example, WebSphere is a rapidly changing product; this book deals with version 1.1 and 2.0 because that's what's most stable with V4R3 and V4R4. (If you're currently using WebSphere 3.0 or above, please refer to appendix A for more information.)

There's quite a bit of manual work involved here, and the execution depends largely on your directory setup. I can only tell you how I've set my machine up, so that you can follow along. This chapter is broken down as follows:

- In "Install the Servlet Software," you'll copy the files from the installation .zip file into their respective folders on the AS/400 IFS and create the Java programs necessary to help performance. You'll review the HTTP configuration file, and modify the **jvm.properties** file to set the CLASSPATH for WebSphere.

- "Customize ITMMNT1_Client" walks you through the steps required to customize the **ITMMNT1_Client** class for your environment. Since WebSphere requires a user ID and password to sign on, I put that information in this class. "Test the Servlet" shows you how to run the servlet. This requires several steps as well, and is prone to subtle errors. I'll show you some of the more common ones.

243

INSTALL THE SERVLET SOFTWARE

This is where things begin to get a little tricky. Since the servlet environment is truly a distributed development environment, you have to load pieces of software in different places. This chapter is *very* specific to versions 1.1 and 2.0 of IBM's WebSphere Application Server, and some things will be different if you're using a later version. I'll try to point those differences out, and I'll have updates on my Web site (discussed in appendix A) as they become available.

WebSphere

As you progress, you're going to see that the servlet environment is different from any other AS/400 development you've ever done, unless you've done UNIX work. WebSphere uses the IFS extensively, storing runtime characteristics in ASCII "properties" files, a very UNIX-like behavior. For example, the **CLASSPATH** variable is stored in a file called **jvm.properties**.[1]

These properties files aren't like anything you're accustomed to on the AS/400; they're much more like .ini files on a PC. There's also a file on the AS/400 that needs to be changed, but this is a physical file. Evidently, IBM expects you to edit the file with a database utility. Many of the design issues seem almost arbitrary, but this chapter will help to demystify the process a little bit.

Copy the Files

This chapter assumes two things: that you've extracted the PBD installation files to your disk the way I advised in the previous chapters, and that you are running a vanilla version of WebSphere, version 1.1, with servlets enabled.

If you've followed the installation instructions correctly, you'll have a **c:\java\edeployment** folder on your workstation that looks like Figure 14.1. If you have a vanilla version of WebSphere 1.1 or 2.0, you should have a **/QIBM/ProdData/IBMWebAS** folder on your AS/400 that looks exactly like Figure 14.2. If it doesn't, your installations are incomplete or incorrect; go back to chapters 12 and 13 to reinstall.

---

1 In later versions, that CLASSPATH moves to a file called **admin.properties** in a different folder entirely. It can get very confusing.

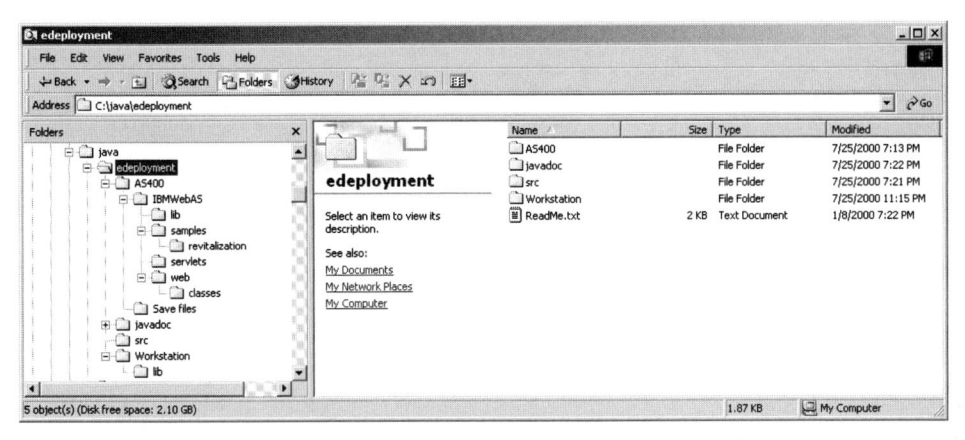

*Figure 14.1: The structure of the folder **C:\java\edeployment** on my workstation.*

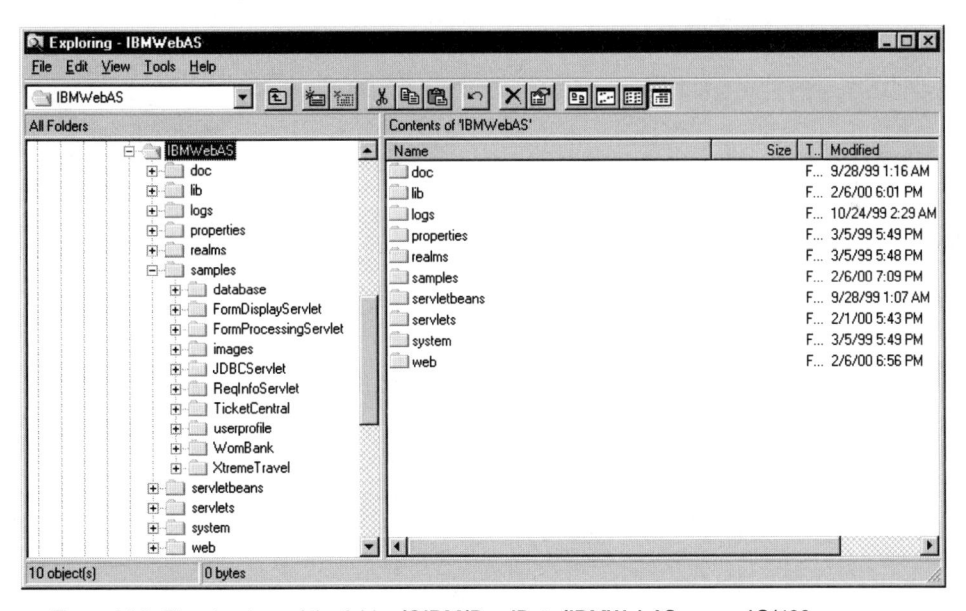

*Figure 14.2: The structure of the folder **/QIBM/ProdData/IBMWebAS** on my AS/400.*

Assuming your installations are correct, you need to copy information from the folders in Figure 14.1 to the folders in Figure 14.2. I created the listing in Figure 14.2 by mapping a drive to the folder **/QIBM/ProdData** on the AS/400, it makes life much easier. Figures 14.3 and 14.4 show just how easy.

PART 3: RUNNING THE APPLICATION

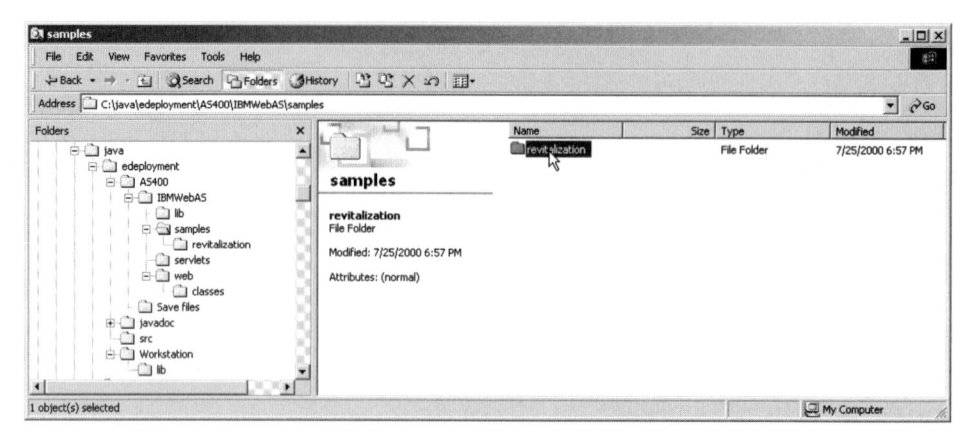

*Figure 14.3: Selecting **C:\java\edeployment\IBMWebAS\samples\AS400\revitalization** from the hard drive.*

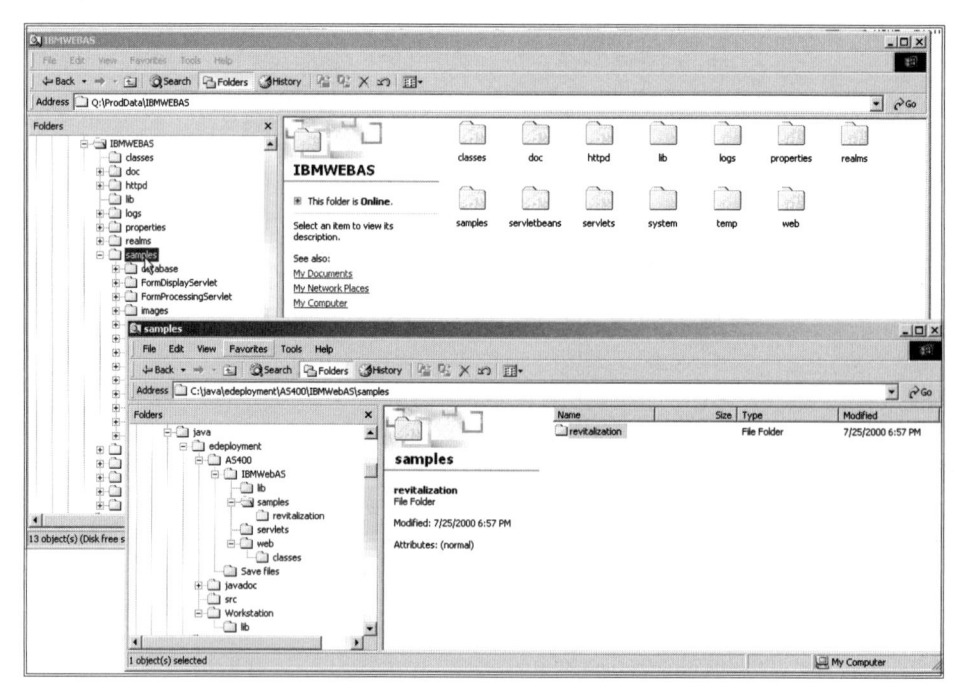

*Figure 14.4: Dragging and dropping the folder from Figure 14.3 into the folder **/QIBM/ProdData/BMWebAS/samples** on the AS/400.*

246

To drag and drop, start two Explorer windows, one on your workstation drive and the other on your AS/400 IFS. Select the **samples** directory in your local Explorer window, then drag the **revitalization** folder onto the **samples** folder of the AS/400 Explorer window. The folder is automatically copied. The capabilities of Windows and Client Access together make it quite easy to move data between the workstation and the AS/400.

You might not want to do that, however. Instead, you might want to use FTP. If so, you'll need to open an FTP session and send the file, much like you did in chapter 12 to copy the save files to the AS/400. However, be very careful not to convert the files from ASCII to EBCDIC during the copy; that would make them useless.

Regardless of your approach, the files in Table 14.1 must be copied. This copies the **pbd400.jar** file, the **revitalization** folder, and the **servlets** folder. The **pbd400.jar** file contains all the support classes, **revitalization** contains the application classes, and **servlets** contains the servlets.

Table 14.1: Files That Need to Be Copied

From Workstation (c:\java\edeployment\IBMWebAS)	To AS/400 (/QIBM/ProdData/IBMWebAS)	From file or folder	To file or folder
Lib	lib	pbd400.jar	pbd400.jar
Samples	samples	revitalization	revitalization
Servlets	servlets	*all	*all

Modify the CLASSPATH

Next, you need to go into the strange world of the properties files. Figure 14.5 shows the folder to go into to change the CLASSPATH for the JVM in WebSphere 1.1. Note that you don't have to change the CLASSPATH for version 2.0 of WebSphere; the CLASSPATH is automatically generated. You now need to edit the **jvm.properties** file with your favorite text editor. I use NoteTab Pro, which has been a favorite utility of mine for some time. If you open your file and it starts with the lines shown in Figure 14.6, you've got the right one.

PART 3: RUNNING THE APPLICATION

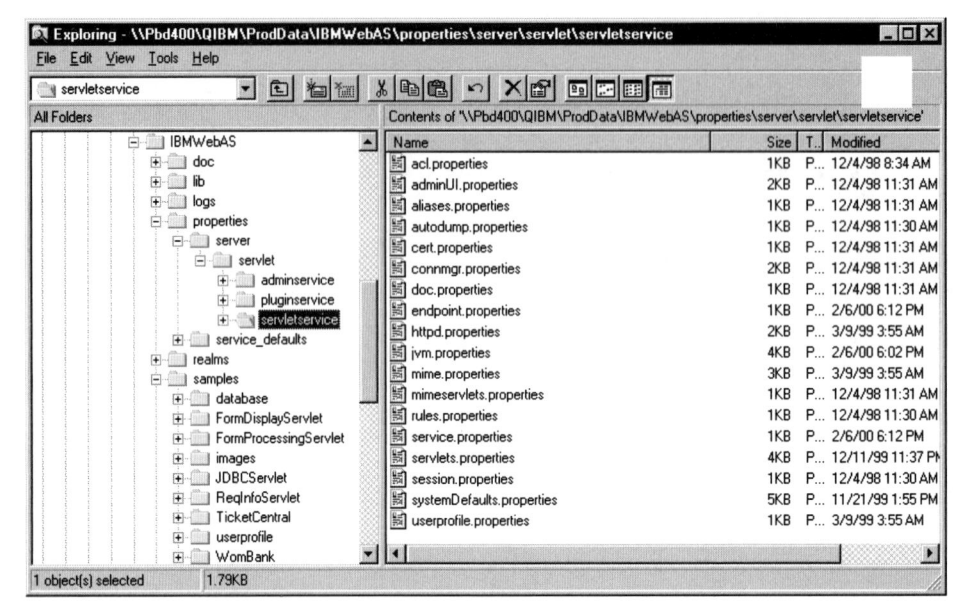

*Figure 14.5: The **servletservice** folder, which contains the **jvm.properties** file.*

```
# @(#)jvm.properties      1.81 97/12/02
#
# Configuration properties for JVM and plugin dll start-up
#

# System Properties
IBMWebASVersion=1.1.0
```

*Figure 14.6: The first few lines of a WebSphere 1.1 **jvm.properties** file.*

The areas to change are shown in Figure 14.7. The bold lines starting with ncf.jvn.stdoutlog define logging capabilities, and are good things to have for debugging. The system will run fine with no logging, but it will *not* run fine if you haven't set your CLASSPATH correctly, which is the line ncf.jvm.classpath. You must add the location of IBM's Java Toolkit for the AS/400 (jt400.jar). The default location is as shown. You must also add the PBD support jar (pbd400.jar) and the folder containing the application classes (revitalization). That done, you can save the file.

248

```
#
# Enable JVM logging by setting 'ncf.jvm.stdoutlog.enabled'
# to true. Change 'ncf.jvm.stdoutlog.file' to 'false' to write
# to a Java debugging console or 'true' for output to a log file.
# Uncomment the line for 'ncf.jvm.stdoutlog.popup', thus setting it
# to '2' to display the combined ResourceUsage/EnableTrace/Console
# popup. Otherwise, just the console popup is displayed.
# Change 'ncf.jvm.stdoutlog.filename' to the <fully-qualified >
# path of an alternate file location if desired.
#
ncf.jvm.stdoutlog.enabled=true
#ncf.jvm.stdoutlog.popup=2
ncf.jvm.stdoutlog.file=true
#ncf.jvm.stdoutlog.filename=c:\IBMWebAS\logs\ncf.log
ncf.jvm.stdoutlog.filename=/QIBM/ProdData/IBMWebAS/logs/ncf.log

# NCF - Admin Service Properties for BasicNCFConfig Applet
# java.zip and sun.zip equals to classes.zip for other platforms
ncf.jvm.classpath=/QIBM/ProdData/Java400/lib/jdkptf.zip:/QIBM/ProdData/Java400/
lib/rawt_classes.zip:/QIBM/ProdData/Java400/lib/java.zip:/QIBM/ProdData/Java400/
lib/sun.zip:/QIBM/ProdData/Java400/com/ibm/db2/jdbc/app/db2_classes.zip:/QIBM/
ProdData/Java400:/QIBM/ProdData/IBMWebAS/lib/ibmwebas.jar:/QIBM/ProdData/IBMWebAS/
lib/jst.jar:/QIBM/ProdData/IBMWebAS/lib/jsdk.jar:/QIBM/ProdData/IBMWebAS/lib/
databeans.jar:/QIBM/ProdData/IBMWebAS/lib/xml4j.jar:/QIBM/ProdData/IBMWebAS/lib/
x509v1.jar:/QIBM/ProdData/IBMWebAS/lib:/QIBM/ProdData/IBMWebAS/web/admin/classes/
seadmin.jar:/QIBM/ProdData/IBMWebAS/web/classes:**/QIBM/ProdData/HTTP/Public/jt400/
lib/jt400.jar:/QIBM/ProdData/IBMWebAS/lib/pbd400.jar:/QIBM/ProdData/IBMWebAS/
samples/revitalization:**
ncf.jvm.path=/QIBM/ProdData/Java400/lib
ncf.jvm.use.system.classpath=false
```

Figure 14.7: The changes that need to be made are in bold.

Modify the Configuration File

Modifying the HTTP server configuration file is a strange situation because it is sort of a cross between a UNIX file and an AS/400 file. It's an AS/400 file that contains a bunch of UNIX-like "directives." The file, called QATMHTPPC, is in QUSRSYS.

From your AS/400, execute the following command to get Figure 14.8:

```
WRKMBRPDM QUSRSYS/QATMHTTPC
```

PART 3: RUNNING THE APPLICATION

```
                        Work with Members Using PDM              PBD400
     File . . . . . .   QATMHTTPC
       Library . . . .    QUSRSYS           Position to  . . . . .  _____

     Type options, press Enter.
        3=Copy      4=Delete        5=Display    7=Rename      8=Display description
        9=Save      13=Change text  18=Change using DFU        25=Find string ...

     Opt  Member      Date       Text
          CONFIG      12/11/99   _____
          PBD001      09/18/99   _____




                                                                        Bottom
     Parameters or command
     ===> _____
     F3=Exit          F4=Prompt           F5=Refresh            F6=Create
     F9=Retrieve      F10=Command entry   F23=More options      F24=More keys
```

Figure 14.8: The member list for the QATMHTTPC file.

If you have a vanilla installation, you'll only see the first member. I suggest you immediately copy it and save it, which is what I did when I copied it to PBD001. You're going to modify the CONFIG member, but take a look at it first. Select option 5 on the CONFIG member to get Figure 14.9.

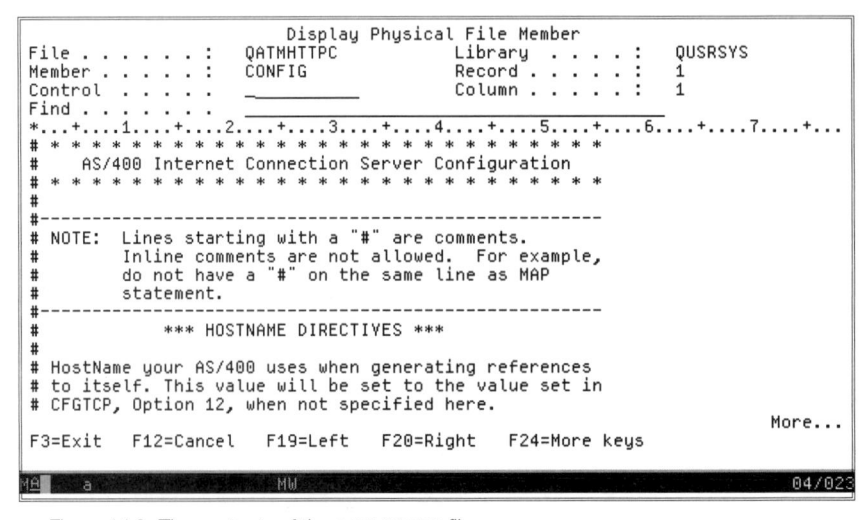

```
                        Display Physical File Member
     File . . . . . . :  QATMHTTPC          Library . . . . :  QUSRSYS
     Member . . . . . :  CONFIG             Record . . . . :  1
     Control  . . . . .  _____          Column . . . . :  1
     Find . . . . . . .
     *...+....1....+....2....+....3....+....4....+....5....+....6....+....7....+...
     # * * * * * * * * * * * * * * * * * * * * * * * * * * * *
     #    AS/400 Internet Connection Server Configuration
     # * * * * * * * * * * * * * * * * * * * * * * * * * * * *
     #
     #---------------------------------------------------------------
     # NOTE:  Lines starting with a "#" are comments.
     #        Inline comments are not allowed.  For example,
     #        do not have a "#" on the same line as MAP
     #        statement.
     #---------------------------------------------------------------
     #
     #          *** HOSTNAME DIRECTIVES ***
     #
     # HostName your AS/400 uses when generating references
     # to itself. This value will be set to the value set in
     # CFGTCP, Option 12, when not specified here.
                                                                     More...
     F3=Exit     F12=Cancel    F19=Left    F20=Right    F24=More keys
```

Figure 14.9: The contents of the QATMHTTPC file.

One way or another, you're going to have to edit this file. Actually, you might not have to edit it too much; you might be able to only add a line or two. There is a WRKHTTPCFG command which is almost an editor, but it's very cumbersome. There is a more efficient method.

First, create a source file with the following command:

```
CRTSRCPF FILE(PBDSYS/HTTPSRC) RCDLEN(240) MBR(CONFIG)
```

Note that PBDSYS is the system library; change this to suit your environment. Next, go in with PDM:

```
WRKMBRPDM PBDSYS/HTTPSRC
```

At this point, you'll have a single member, CONFIG, but it's currently empty. You need a way to get data from that QATMHTTPC file into the CONFIG member and back. You can do this by creating two PDM commands, **HttpGet (HG)** and **HttpPut (HP)**. **HG** copies data from QATMHTTPC into the member, and **HP** copies it back.

Add the **HG** and **HP** commands as shown in Figure 14.10, using F16 on the WRKMBRPDM display to do it. Now, you can copy the data into the member using the **HG** command, as shown in Figure 14.11.

```
   Option  . . . . . . . . :  HG

   Command . . . . . . . . :  CPYF FROMFILE(QUSRSYS/QATMHTTPC) TOFILE(&l/&f)
FR
OMMBR(&n) TOMBR(&n) MBROPT(*REPLACE) FMTOPT(*CVTSRC)


   Option  . . . . . . . . :  HP

   Command . . . . . . . . :  CPYF TOFILE(QUSRSYS/QATMHTTPC) FROMFILE(&l/&f)
FR
OMMBR(&n) TOMBR(&n) MBROPT(*REPLACE) FMTOPT(*CVTSRC)
```

Figure 14.10: The two user-defined PDM commands used to copy data to and from the QATMHTTPC file.

PART 3: RUNNING THE APPLICATION

```
                    Work with Members Using PDM              PBD400
 File . . . . . .  HTTPSRC
    Library . . . .   PBDSYS         Position to  . . . . .

 Type options, press Enter.
   2=Edit          3=Copy    4=Delete 5=Display     6=Print       7=Rename
   8=Display description  9=Save  13=Change text  14=Compile  15=Create module...

 Opt  Member       Type         Text
 HG   CONFIG
  _   PBD001       TXT




                                                                  Bottom
 Parameters or command
 ===>
 F3=Exit         F4=Prompt          F5=Refresh         F6=Create
 F9=Retrieve     F10=Command entry  F23=More options   F24=More keys
```

Figure 14.11: The command to get the data from the QATMHTTPC file into the source member.

The data will get truncated as shown in Figure 14.12, but that's all right for our purposes. I haven't yet found a record with data over 228 characters.

```
                    Work with Members Using PDM              PBD400
 File . . . . . .  HTTPSRC
    Library . . . .   PBDSYS         Position to  . . . . .

 Type options, press Enter.
   2=Edit          3=Copy    4=Delete 5=Display     6=Print       7=Rename
   8=Display description  9=Save  13=Change text  14=Compile  15=Create module...

 Opt  Member       Type         Text
  _   CONFIG
  _   PBD001       TXT




                                                                  Bottom
 Parameters or command
 ===>
 F3=Exit         F4=Prompt          F5=Refresh         F6=Create
 F9=Retrieve     F10=Command entry  F23=More options   F24=More keys
 Data from file QATMHTTPC in QUSRSYS truncated to 228 characters.         +
```

Figure 14.12: The command completing successfully. You can ignore the truncation message.

Let's now move on and change the data as needed, as shown in Figure 14.13.

```
Columns . . . :    1  71         Edit              PBDSYS/HTTPSRC
SEU==>                                                      CONFIG
FMT **   ...+... 1 ...+... 2 ...+... 3 ...+... 4 ...+... 5 ...+... 6 ...+... 7
0045.00 #
0046.00 #  The next two Pass directives are shipped in the IBM
0047.00 #  AS/400 Internet Connection server configuration in
0048.00 #  V4R1.  The first Pass directive serves a file called
0049.00 #  Welcome.html for a request of the form
0050.00 #  http://hostname. The second Pass directive allows
0051.00 #  image files referenced in the Welcome.html file to
0052.00 #  be served.
0053.00 #
0054.00 Service /*.jsp      /QSYS.LIB/QHTTPSVR.LIB/QZHJSVLT.SRVPGM:AdapterServic
0055.00 Service /servlet/*  /QSYS.LIB/QHTTPSVR.LIB/QZHJSVLT.SRVPGM:AdapterServic
0056.00 #
0057.00 Pass /IBMWebAS/samples/*       /QIBM/ProdData/IBMWebAS/samples/*
0058.00 Pass /IBMWebAS/doc/*           /QIBM/ProdData/IBMWebAS/doc/*
0059.00 Pass /IBMWebAS/system/admin/*  /QIBM/ProdData/IBMWebAS/system/admin/*
0060.00 Pass /IBMWebAS/*               /QIBM/ProdData/IBMWebAS/web/*
0061.00 #

 F3=Exit    F4=Prompt    F5=Refresh   F9=Retrieve   F10=Cursor   F11=Toggle
 F16=Repeat find         F17=Repeat change          F24=More keys
```

*Figure 14.13: The **Service** and **Pass** directives needed.*

As much as I'd like to go into detail about **Service** and **Pass** directives, there's only room here to say that these will do it. (Note: For V2.0 of WebSphere use library name QAPPSVR rather than QHTTPSVR.) The first **Service** directive supports JavaServer Pages, and the second supports servlets. Note that there's another e on the end of those two lines that you would see if you windowed right. To edit long lines, use the **P** line command as shown in Figure 14.14 rather than trying to do it in the full screen.

```
Columns . . . :    1  71         Edit              PBDSYS/HTTPSRC
SEU==>                                                      CONFIG
FMT **   ...+... 1 ...+... 2 ...+... 3 ...+... 4 ...+... 5 ...+... 6 ...+... 7
0045.00 #
0046.00 #  The next two Pass directives are shipped in the IBM
0047.00 #  AS/400 Internet Connection server configuration in
0048.00 #  V4R1.  The first Pass directive serves a file called
0049.00 #  Welcome.html for a request of the form
0050.00 #  http://hostname. The second Pass directive allows
0051.00 #  image files referenced in the Welcome.html file to
0052.00 #  be served.
0053.00 #
0054.00 Service /*.jsp      /QSYS.LIB/QHTTPSVR.LIB/QZHJSVLT.SRVPGM:AdapterServic
 Prompt type . . .     **       Sequence number . . .   0054.00

 Data area
 ....+... 1 ...+... 2 ...+... 3 ...+... 4 ...+... 5 ...+... 6 ...+... 7 ...+...
 Service /*.jsp     /QSYS.LIB/QHTTPSVR.LIB/QZHJSVLT.SRVPGM:AdapterService


 F3=Exit    F4=Prompt    F5=Refresh        F11=Previous record
 F12=Cancel              F23=Select prompt F24=More keys
```

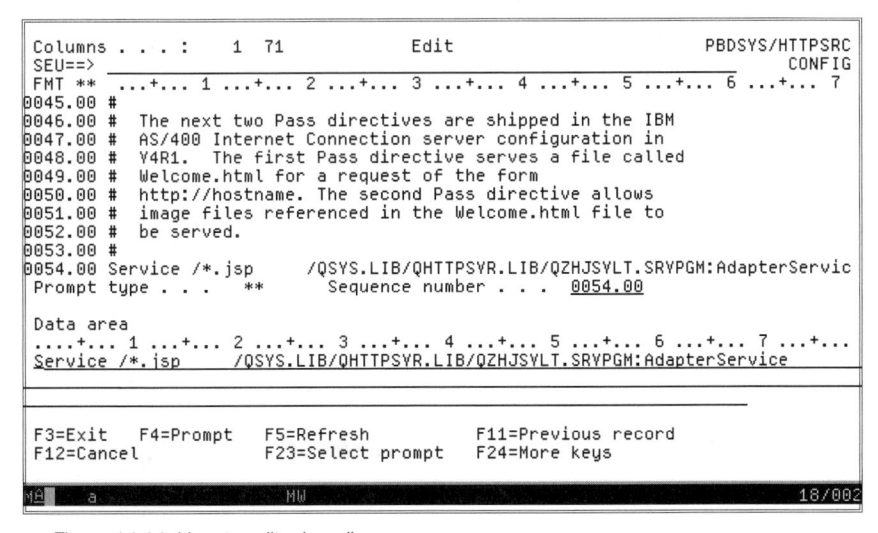

Figure 14.14: How to edit a long line.

The various **Pass** directives allow data to get through. More specifically, they point requests to specific directories. The one you're most interested in, the first one, points all requests to *http://your400/IBMWebAS/samples* to the folder **/QIBM/ProdData/IBMWebAS/samples** on your AS/400's IFS. If this line is not first, or if you change it, it's likely that your servlets and JSPs won't work.

Once you're done, save the member and execute the **HP** command from PDM to copy the data back to the QATMHTTPC file.

Create *JVAPGM for the Support Jar

To try to keep performance reasonable, you need to create objects of type *JVAPGM (Java Program) on the AS/400. These are precompiled versions of the Java bytecode. If you don't have these in place, subsequent accesses will force recompiles, which really destroys performance. Later versions of the AS/400 JVM do a better job of this, but still you should do the compile command shown in Figure 14.15. In a couple of minutes, you should see the screen in Figure 14.16, and you're finally done installing the servlet software. (Well, except for the part that needs to be customized, which is discussed in the next section.)

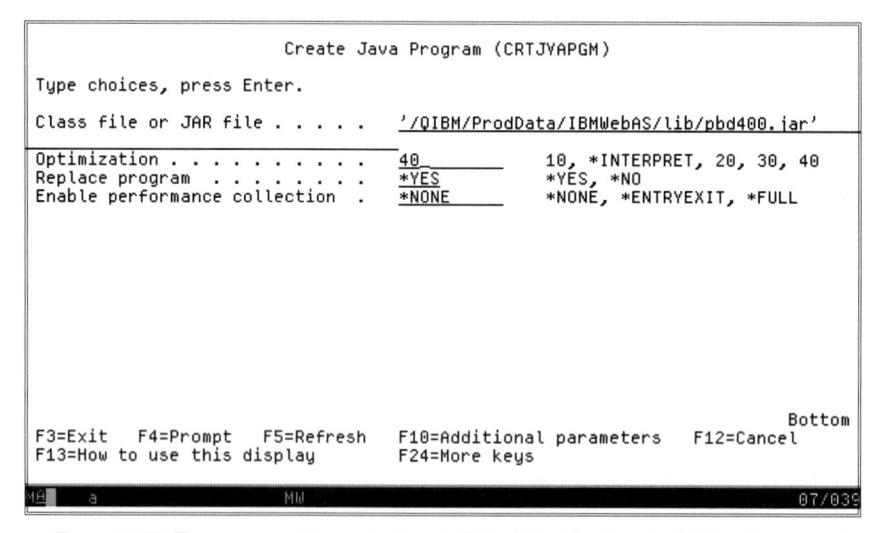

```
                        Create Java Program (CRTJVAPGM)

 Type choices, press Enter.

 Class file or JAR file . . . . .   '/QIBM/ProdData/IBMWebAS/lib/pbd400.jar'

 Optimization . . . . . . . . . .   40            10, *INTERPRET, 20, 30, 40
 Replace program  . . . . . . . .   *YES          *YES, *NO
 Enable performance collection  .   *NONE         *NONE, *ENTRYEXIT, *FULL










                                                                       Bottom
 F3=Exit   F4=Prompt   F5=Refresh   F10=Additional parameters   F12=Cancel
 F13=How to use this display        F24=More keys
```

*Figure 14.15: The command to create the *JVAPGM object for the **pbd400.jar** file.*

CHAPTER 14: THE SERVLET

```
                        Command Entry                         PBD400
                                               Request level:    4
 Previous commands and messages:
  > CRTJVAPGM CLSF('/QIBM/ProdData/IBMWebAS/lib/pbd400.jar') OPTIMIZE(40)
    Java program created for "< bAS/lib/pbd400.jar".




                                                             Bottom
 Type command, press Enter.
 ===> _

 F3=Exit    F4=Prompt   F9=Retrieve   F10=Include detailed messages
 F11=Display full       F12=Cancel    F13=Information Assistant   F24=More keys
```

Figure 14.16: The CRTJVAPGM successfully completed.

CUSTOMIZE ITMMNT1_CLIENT

In order to get the system to run properly, you have to customize the **ITMMNT1_Client** class with the appropriate logon information. To do that, you need some jar files from the AS/400. Then you can change the source, recompile the class, and copy it back to the AS/400.

Copy the Jar Files

To accomplish this step, you simply need to create a directory in your development folder on the workstation. From a command line, enter the following command:

```
md c:\java\edeployment\jsp400
```

This creates an empty folder named **jsp400**. Next, using the drag and drop technique discussed in chapter 13, copy all of the jar files from the folder **/QIBM/ProdData/IBMWeb AS/lib** into the newly created folder, as shown in Figure 14.17.

255

PART 3: RUNNING THE APPLICATION

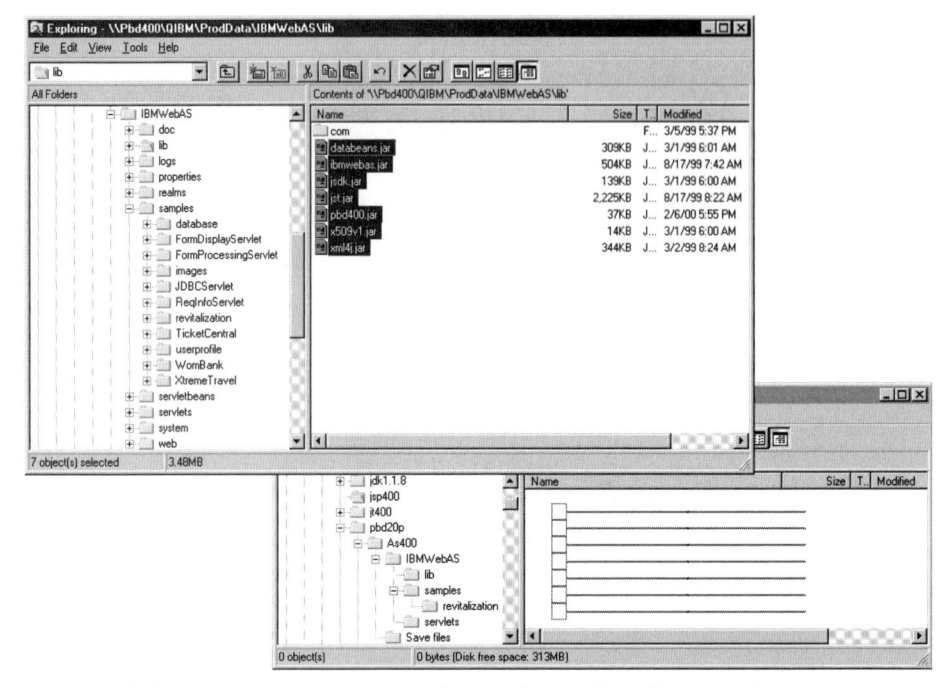

Figure 14.17: How to drag the required jar files from the AS/400 to the workstation.

Customize ITMMNT1_Client.java

There's very little work in changing the client. Simply edit the Java source in c:\java\edeployment\Workstation\ITMMNT1_Client.java, and change the lines that are shaded in Listing 14.1 to reflect your AS/400 name, your user ID, and your password. Then, compile it using the command shown in Listing 14.2.

```
import com.pbd.pub.sc400.*;
import java.beans.Beans;
import javax.servlet.*;

/**
 * This type was created in VisualAge.
 */
public class ITMMNT1_Client extends Sc400Client {
/**
 * ITMMNT1_Client constructor comment.
```

*Listing 14.1: The source for the **ITMMNT1_Client** class. Change the shaded lines (part 1 of 2).*

256

```
    */
    public ITMMNT1_Client()
            throws Sc400Exception
    {
            this(false);
    }
    /**
     * ITMMNT1_Client constructor comment.
     */
    public ITMMNT1_Client(boolean mustLogon)
            throws Sc400Exception
    {
            super();

            setClientName("ITMMNT1AC");
            setProductionLibrary("JSPPROTO");

            if (mustLogon)
                    setSystemName(Sc400Client.LOGON);
            else {
                    setSystemName("MY400");       // CHANGE THIS!
                    setUserID("MYUSERID");        // CHANGE THIS!
                    setPassword("MYPASSWORD");    // CHANGE THIS!
            }

    }
}
```

Listing 14.1: The source for the **ITMMNT1_Client** class. Change the shaded lines (part 2 of 2).

```
C:\>cd java\edeployment

C:\java\edeployment>cd workstation

C:\java\edeployment\Workstation>CompileClient
compiling ITMMNT1_Client...

C:\java\edeployment\Workstation>
```

Listing 14.2: Compiling the client.

Copy the resulting source and class back to the AS/400, into the folder **/QIBM/ProdData/IBMWebAS/samples/revitalization**, and you're almost ready to start testing.

Create *JVAPGM Objects for the Client and Display File

Remember how you created the *JVAPGM object for the **pbd400.jar** file in the previous chapter? You need to do the same thing for the two application objects, the application-client proxy **ITMMNT1_Client** and the display-file proxy **ITMMNT1_DisplayFile**. Figures 14.18 through 14.20 show the commands and the results.

```
                     Create Java Program (CRTJVAPGM)

 Type choices, press Enter.

 Class file or JAR file . . . . . > '/QIBM/ProdData/IBMWebAS/samples/revitalizat
 ion/ITMMNT1 Client.class'




                                                                           ...
 Optimization . . . . . . . . . . >   40             10, *INTERPRET, 20, 30, 40
 Replace program  . . . . . . . .     *YES           *YES, *NO
 Enable performance collection  .     *NONE          *NONE, *ENTRYEXIT, *FULL




                                                                        Bottom
 F3=Exit   F4=Prompt   F5=Refresh   F10=Additional parameters   F12=Cancel
 F13=How to use this display        F24=More keys
```

Figure 14.18: The command to create the *JVAPGM for the application-client proxy.

```
                     Create Java Program (CRTJVAPGM)

 Type choices, press Enter.

 Class file or JAR file . . . . . > '/QIBM/ProdData/IBMWebAS/samples/revitalizat
 ion/ITMMNT1 DisplayFile.class'




                                                                           ...
 Optimization . . . . . . . . . . >   40             10, *INTERPRET, 20, 30, 40
 Replace program  . . . . . . . .     *YES           *YES, *NO
 Enable performance collection  .     *NONE          *NONE, *ENTRYEXIT, *FULL




                                                                        Bottom
 F3=Exit   F4=Prompt   F5=Refresh   F10=Additional parameters   F12=Cancel
 F13=How to use this display        F24=More keys
```

Figure 14.19: The command to create the *JVAPGM for the display-file proxy.

```
                           Command Entry                          PBD400
                                                  Request level:    4
Previous commands and messages:
  > CRTJVAPGM CLSF('/QIBM/ProdData/IBMWebAS/samples/revitalization/ITMMNT1_Cl
    ient.class') OPTIMIZE(40)
    Java program created for "< MMNT1_Client.class".
  > CRTJVAPGM CLSF('/QIBM/ProdData/IBMWebAS/samples/revitalization/ITMMNT1_Di
    splayFile.class') OPTIMIZE(40)
    Java program created for "< _DisplayFile.class".




                                                                  Bottom
Type command, press Enter.
===> _


F3=Exit    F4=Prompt    F9=Retrieve    F10=Include detailed messages
F11=Display full         F12=Cancel    F13=Information Assistant    F24=More keys
```

Figure 14.20: The screen after successful completion of the commands.

TEST THE SERVLET

Testing the servlet is actually the easiest part of the battle, if you've gotten everything else done correctly. That's because you just use your browser.

Restart the HTTP Server

First, if your HTTP server is running, you have to restart it because you've made changes to the configuration file. I suggest using the following command:

```
ENDTCPSVR SERVER(*HTTP) HTTPSVR(*ALL)
```

Let that run until the subsystem QHTTPSVR ends. Figures 14.21 through 14.23 show the sequence of events as the subsystem shuts down.

PART 3: RUNNING THE APPLICATION

```
                        Work with Active Jobs                PBD400
                                                   02/06/00  21:39:04
CPU %:     8.0      Elapsed time:    03:49:29    Active jobs:   139

Type options, press Enter.
  2=Change    3=Hold    4=End    5=Work with   6=Release   7=Display message
  8=Work with spooled files    13=Disconnect ...

Opt  Subsystem/Job  User        Type   CPU %  Function        Status
 _     QBATCH       QSYS        SBS     .0                    DEQW
 _     QCMN         QSYS        SBS     .0                    DEQW
 _     QCTL         QSYS        SBS     .0                    DEQW
 _     QHTTPSVR     QSYS        SBS     .0                    DEQW
 _       ADMIN      QTMHHTTP    BCH     .4    PGM-QZHBHTTP    TIMW
 _       ADMIN      QTMHHTTP    BCI     .0                    TIMW
 _       ADMIN      QTMHHTTP    BCI     .0                    TIMW
 _       ADMIN      QTMHHTTP    BCI     .0                    TIMW
 _       ADMIN      QTMHHTTP    BCI     .0                    TIMW
                                                                More...
Parameters or command
===>
F3=Exit    F5=Refresh       F7=Find      F10=Restart statistics
F11=Display elapsed data    F12=Cancel   F23=More options   F24=More keys
```

Figure 14.21: The normal quiescent state of the QHTTPSVR subsystem.

```
                        Work with Active Jobs                PBD400
                                                   02/06/00  21:41:20
CPU %:     8.1      Elapsed time:    03:51:45    Active jobs:   139

Type options, press Enter.
  2=Change    3=Hold    4=End    5=Work with   6=Release   7=Display message
  8=Work with spooled files    13=Disconnect ...

Opt  Subsystem/Job  User        Type   CPU %  Function        Status
 _     QBATCH       QSYS        SBS     .0                    DEQW
 _     QCMN         QSYS        SBS     .0                    DEQW
 _     QCTL         QSYS        SBS     .0                    DEQW
 _     QHTTPSVR     QSYS        SBS     .0                    DEQW
 _       ADMIN      QTMHHTTP    BCH     .4    PGM-QZHBHTTP    EOJ
 _       ADMIN      QTMHHTTP    BCI     .0                    EOJ
 _       ADMIN      QTMHHTTP    BCI     .0                    EOJ
 _       ADMIN      QTMHHTTP    BCI     .0                    RUN
 _       ADMIN      QTMHHTTP    BCI     .0                    RUN
                                                                More...
Parameters or command
===>
F3=Exit    F5=Refresh       F7=Find      F10=Restart statistics
F11=Display elapsed data    F12=Cancel   F23=More options   F24=More keys
```

Figure 14.22: The QHTTPSVR subsystem is shutting down.

```
                        Work with Active Jobs                     PBD400
                                                        02/06/00  21:42:24
 CPU %:       .0      Elapsed time:   00:00:00    Active jobs:  118

 Type options, press Enter.
   2=Change   3=Hold    4=End     5=Work with    6=Release    7=Display message
   8=Work with spooled files      13=Disconnect ...

 Opt  Subsystem/Job    User         Type    CPU %   Function       Status
  _     QBATCH         QSYS         SBS       .0                   DEQW
  _     QCMN           QSYS         SBS       .0                   DEQW
  _     QCTL           QSYS         SBS       .0                   DEQW
  _     QINTER         QSYS         SBS       .0                   DEQW
  _       QPADEV0004   PLUTA        INT       .0    CMD-WRKACTJOB  RUN
  _     QPGMR          QSYS         SBS       .0                   DEQW
  _     QSERVER        QSYS         SBS       .0                   DEQW
  _       QPWFSERVSD   QUSER        BCH       .0                   SELW
  _       QPWFSERVSO   QUSER        PJ        .0                   DEQW
                                                                         More...
 Parameters or command
 ===>
 F3=Exit    F5=Refresh         F7=Find      F10=Restart statistics
 F11=Display elapsed data      F12=Cancel   F23=More options    F24=More keys
```

Figure 14.23: The QHTTPSVR subsystem has ended.

At this point, restart the server with the following command:

```
STRTCPSVR SERVER(*HTTP) HTTPSVR(*ALL)
```

Watch until the DEFAULT server gets back to a quiescent state. It takes a few minutes for the server to come back up. It has to completely load the JVM, and that's not a minor procedure. You'll see the server stay in JVAW state for a while, but with a relatively high amount of CPU usage, as in Figure 14.24. Until that first DEFAULT job goes to TIMW and a CPU usage under a couple of percent, it's still loading. When it gets down to something along the lines of Figure 14.25, you're done.

PART 3: RUNNING THE APPLICATION

```
                         Work with Active Jobs                PBD400
                                                    02/06/00  21:50:01
 CPU %:    69.9      Elapsed time:   00:00:05    Active jobs:    132

 Type options, press Enter.
   2=Change    3=Hold    4=End    5=Work with   6=Release   7=Display message
   8=Work with spooled files    13=Disconnect ...

 Opt  Subsystem/Job    User         Type   CPU %   Function      Status
  _      DEFAULT       QTMHHTTP     BCH    57.8    PGM-QZHBHTTP  JVAW
  _      DEFAULT       QTMHHTTP     BCI      .0                  TIMW
  _      DEFAULT       QTMHHTTP     BCI      .0                  TIMW
  _      DEFAULT       QTMHHTTP     BCI      .0                  TIMW
  _      DEFAULT       QTMHHTTP     BCI      .0                  TIMW
  _      DEFAULT       QTMHHTTP     BCI      .0                  TIMW
  _      DEFAULT       QTMHHTTP     BCI      .0                  TIMW
  _      DEFAULT       QTMHHTTP     BCI      .0                  TIMW
  _      QINTER        QSYS         SBS      .0                  DEQW
                                                                      More...
 Parameters or command
 ===>
 F3=Exit    F5=Refresh       F7=Find       F10=Restart statistics
 F11=Display elapsed data    F12=Cancel    F23=More options    F24=More keys
```

Figure 14.24: The server still coming up. Note the JVAW state.

```
                         Work with Active Jobs                PBD400
                                                    02/06/00  21:55:20
 CPU %:     5.9      Elapsed time:   00:00:05    Active jobs:    132

 Type options, press Enter.
   2=Change    3=Hold    4=End    5=Work with   6=Release   7=Display message
   8=Work with spooled files    13=Disconnect ...

 Opt  Subsystem/Job    User         Type   CPU %   Function      Status
  _      DEFAULT       QTMHHTTP     BCH       .4   PGM-QZHBHTTP  TIMW
  _      DEFAULT       QTMHHTTP     BCI      .0                  TIMW
  _      DEFAULT       QTMHHTTP     BCI      .0                  TIMW
  _      DEFAULT       QTMHHTTP     BCI      .0                  TIMW
  _      DEFAULT       QTMHHTTP     BCI      .0                  TIMW
  _      DEFAULT       QTMHHTTP     BCI      .0                  TIMW
  _      DEFAULT       QTMHHTTP     BCI      .0                  TIMW
  _      QINTER        QSYS         SBS      .0                  DEQW
                                                                      More...
 Parameters or command
 ===>
 F3=Exit    F5=Refresh       F7=Find       F10=Restart statistics
 F11=Display elapsed data    F12=Cancel    F23=More options    F24=More keys
```

Figure 14.25: The server back up and running.

Run the Servlet

And now, finally, you can run the application! Go to *http://my400/IBMWebAS/ samples/revitalization/index.jsp*, and then follow Figures 14.26 through 14.30. The screen in Figure 14.26 might take a while to load because it's loading for the first time. In fact, each of the screens will take some time. Be prepared. Once the index does appear, you have three options. For now, select the first one, ITMMNT1.

Again, it can take some time before Figure 14.27 appears. Enter the item number, making sure that you clear out all the blanks already in the field, then press the Edit button.

Enter new data, such as the description shown in Figure 14.28, and press Accept. That's it! You'll return to the PROMPT panel, where you can hit Edit again to check your work, but you now have a fully functional browser version of your original monolithic application.

Each of the other two buttons runs a slightly different servlet, in which the look and feel of the MAINT panel is changed. This is just to show how easy it is to have several different looks without changing your host programs at all. You only have to change the JSPs and then the servlet. Nothing to it!

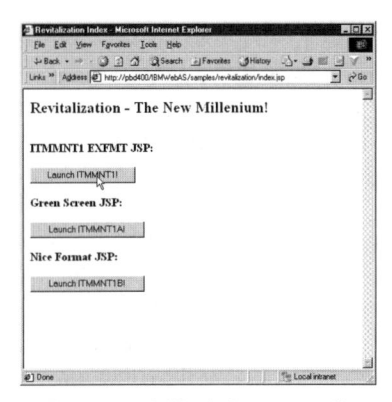

Figure 14.26: The index screen. Select "Launch ITMMNT1!"

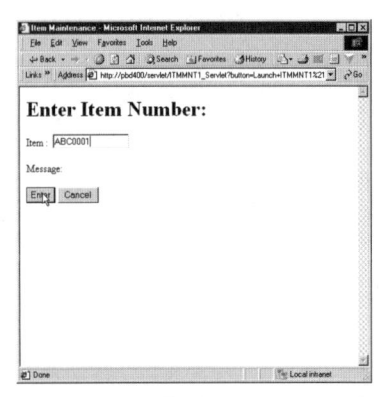

Figure 14.27: The browser version of the PROMPT panel.

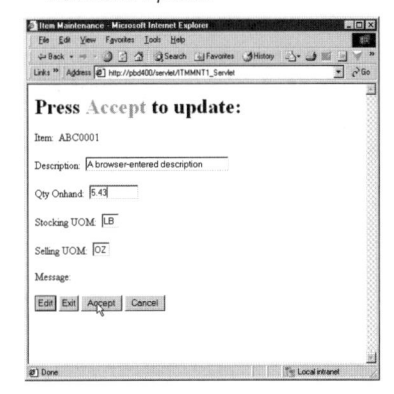

Figure 14.28: The browser version of the MAINT panel.

PART 3: RUNNING THE APPLICATION

Figure 14.29 has a much nicer layout because it uses a table. You can see the source for this one in the **ITMMNT1B_MAINT.jsp** JavaServer Page.

The image in Figure 14.30 is "reversed-out" so that it wouldn't look horrible in print: big blotches of black screen don't publish well. You'll have to run it yourself to see just how homely it is. It serves to prove a point, however: you can do *any* type of interface now, without changing your host programs at all. The source for this poor panel is in **ITMMNT1A_MAINT.jsp**.

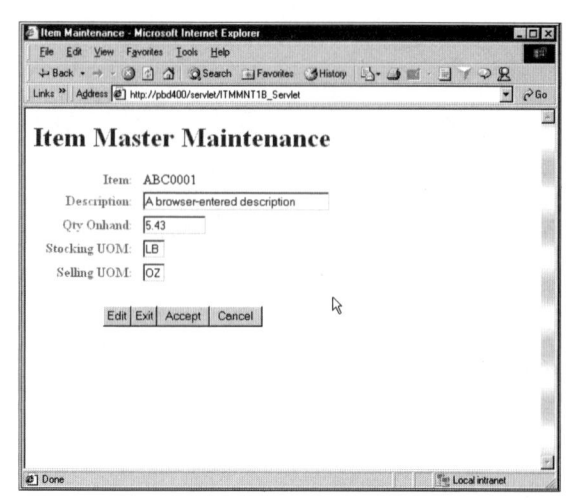

Figure 14.29: A prettier version of the MAINT panel.

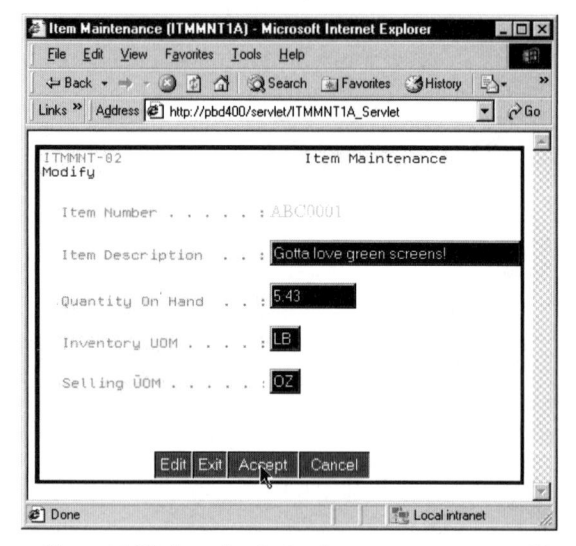

Figure 14.30: A version that only a green-screener could love.

264

Errors

Errors in the servlet are rather difficult to find, but it can be done. Many errors appear in your browser window. Consider the data entered in Figure 14.31. Since there is nonnumeric data in fields that expect only numbers, there will be an error.

WebSphere actually does a good job of trapping the error, formatting it into HTML, and then sending it to the browser, as you can see in Figure 14.32. In this case, it's fairly obvious that the nonnumeric data caused an exception.

Figure 14.31: Causing a numeric formatting error.

Figure 14.32: WebSphere's response in the browser window.

Even when the error is unknown, as in Figure 14.33, the error-trace information is often enough to determine the error. In this case, the null pointer on the **get** suggests that a field was not found. As it turns out, the error was caused by the JavaServer Page being incorrectly designed, and not returning the correct field names.

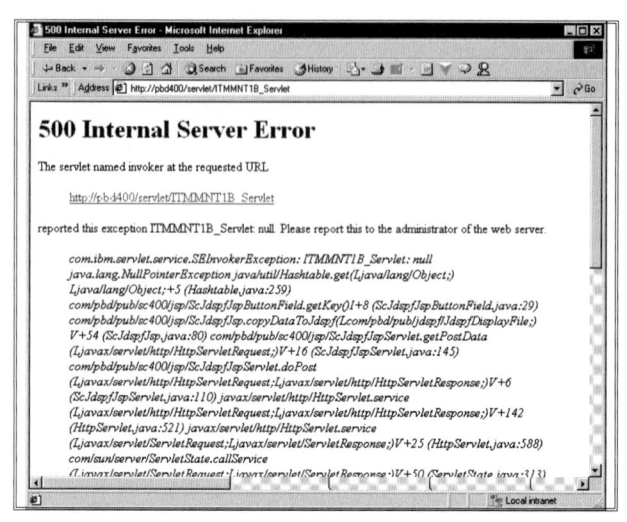

Figure 14.33: This error is unknown, but it happened somewhere in the **ScJdspfJsp** classes.

We've come to the end of the book. I hope you've learned as much reading it as I learned writing it, and I hope it continues to be a source of information for you in the future.

Thanks for reading!

APPENDIX A
WEB UPDATES

As mentioned elsewhere, the examples in this book are geared toward V4R3 of OS/400 and version 1.1 of WebSphere. Also, the example program is written in RPG III, rather than RPG IV or COBOL. I chose this particular combination of releases and features because they are the ones most applicable to the owners of existing legacy applications.

Few legacy systems today were written using RPG IV or the ILE compiler, and there are very few active installations of version 3.0 of WebSphere. Add to that the fact that version 3.0 of WebSphere is totally different from version 1.1 and 2.0, and you have the reasons that dictated the choices made in this book.

However, that's sure to change in the near future, and the last thing I want is for this technology to become out of date shortly after (or before?) you buy this book. For that reason, a Website is available specifically for the readers of this book:

http://www.java400.net/edeployment

APPENDIX A: WEB UPDATES

It will have updates to the example program as they become available: from a V4R4/WAS3.02 version to an RPG IV implementation. Hey, I might even be able to coerce someone into creating a COBOL version—you never know!

You can also use this Website to keep track of the newest features of the program. For example, I've already put together a prototype of a subfile protocol. I wrote about it in the July, 2000 issue of *Midrange Computing*, which you can preview at this address:

http://www.java400.net/mc/mc200007

When the subfile protocol is ready for release, you'll see it first on the revitalization Website, along with a link to a discussion group and whatever else makes sense. So please, stop by, and continue on the path you've started.

APPENDIX B
ABOUT THE CD-ROM

The CD-ROM that accompanies this book contains a considerable amount of software. Chapters 12, 13, and 14 give you step-by-step instructions on how to install the various pieces, depending on what you want to do. If you'd like to double-check the contents of the CD-ROM, open up the included .zip file, **edeployment.zip**. It contains the files listed in Figures B.1 to B.3. If any are missing, or if the file is damaged, you can download another copy from the Web page mentioned in chapter 12.

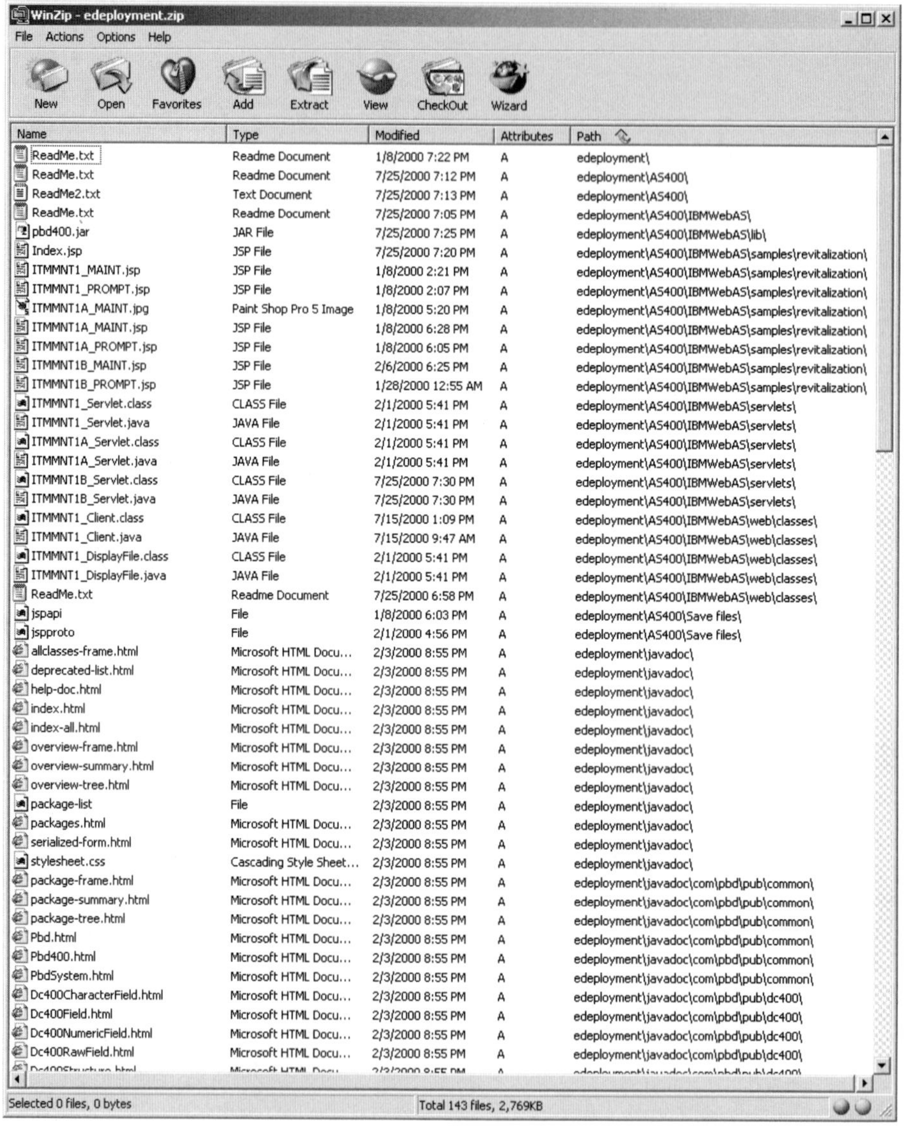

APPENDIX B: ABOUT THE CD-ROM

Figure B.1: The contents of the .zip file.

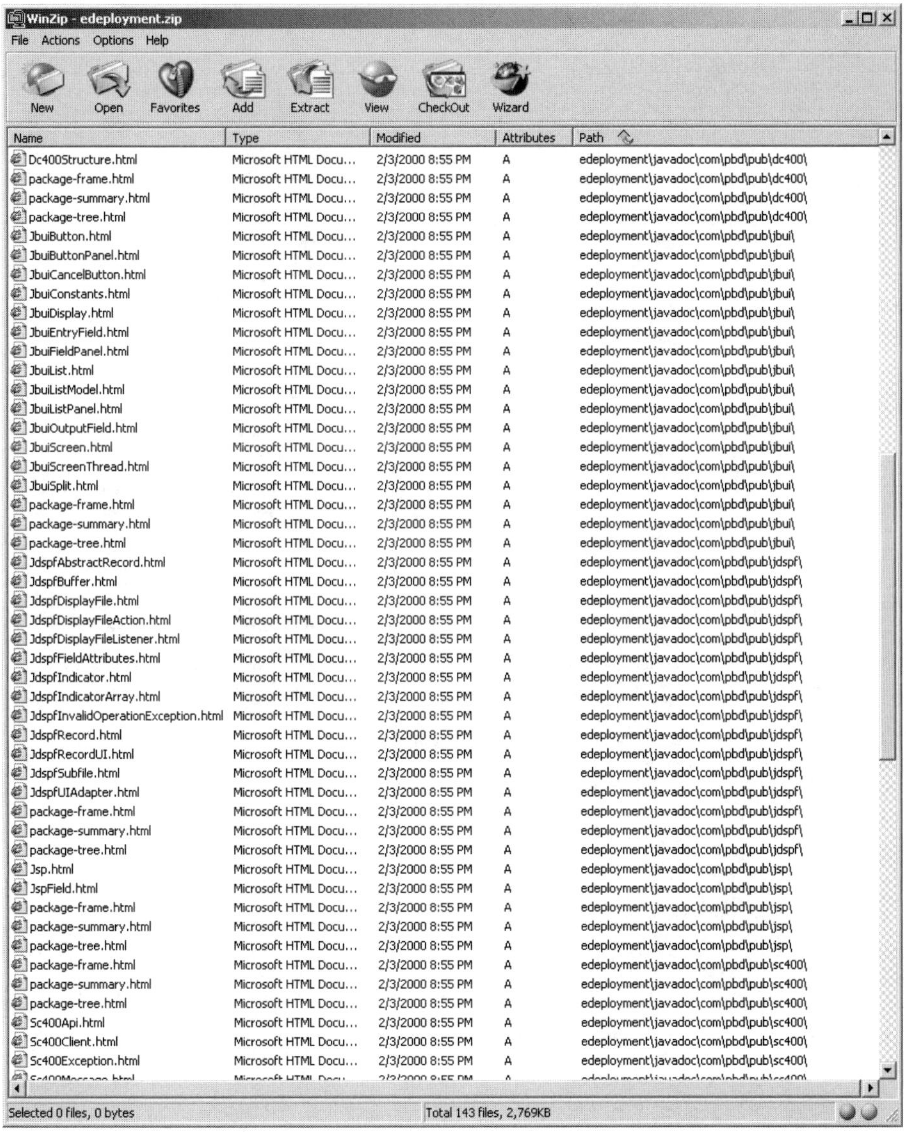
WinZip - edeployment.zip

File Actions Options Help

New Open Favorites Add Extract View CheckOut Wizard

Name	Type	Modified	Attributes	Path
Dc400Structure.html	Microsoft HTML Docu...	2/3/2000 8:55 PM	A	edeployment\javadoc\com\pbd\pub\dc400\
package-frame.html	Microsoft HTML Docu...	2/3/2000 8:55 PM	A	edeployment\javadoc\com\pbd\pub\dc400\
package-summary.html	Microsoft HTML Docu...	2/3/2000 8:55 PM	A	edeployment\javadoc\com\pbd\pub\dc400\
package-tree.html	Microsoft HTML Docu...	2/3/2000 8:55 PM	A	edeployment\javadoc\com\pbd\pub\dc400\
JbuiButton.html	Microsoft HTML Docu...	2/3/2000 8:55 PM	A	edeployment\javadoc\com\pbd\pub\jbui\
JbuiButtonPanel.html	Microsoft HTML Docu...	2/3/2000 8:55 PM	A	edeployment\javadoc\com\pbd\pub\jbui\
JbuiCancelButton.html	Microsoft HTML Docu...	2/3/2000 8:55 PM	A	edeployment\javadoc\com\pbd\pub\jbui\
JbuiConstants.html	Microsoft HTML Docu...	2/3/2000 8:55 PM	A	edeployment\javadoc\com\pbd\pub\jbui\
JbuiDisplay.html	Microsoft HTML Docu...	2/3/2000 8:55 PM	A	edeployment\javadoc\com\pbd\pub\jbui\
JbuiEntryField.html	Microsoft HTML Docu...	2/3/2000 8:55 PM	A	edeployment\javadoc\com\pbd\pub\jbui\
JbuiFieldPanel.html	Microsoft HTML Docu...	2/3/2000 8:55 PM	A	edeployment\javadoc\com\pbd\pub\jbui\
JbuiList.html	Microsoft HTML Docu...	2/3/2000 8:55 PM	A	edeployment\javadoc\com\pbd\pub\jbui\
JbuiListModel.html	Microsoft HTML Docu...	2/3/2000 8:55 PM	A	edeployment\javadoc\com\pbd\pub\jbui\
JbuiListPanel.html	Microsoft HTML Docu...	2/3/2000 8:55 PM	A	edeployment\javadoc\com\pbd\pub\jbui\
JbuiOutputField.html	Microsoft HTML Docu...	2/3/2000 8:55 PM	A	edeployment\javadoc\com\pbd\pub\jbui\
JbuiScreen.html	Microsoft HTML Docu...	2/3/2000 8:55 PM	A	edeployment\javadoc\com\pbd\pub\jbui\
JbuiScreenThread.html	Microsoft HTML Docu...	2/3/2000 8:55 PM	A	edeployment\javadoc\com\pbd\pub\jbui\
JbuiSplit.html	Microsoft HTML Docu...	2/3/2000 8:55 PM	A	edeployment\javadoc\com\pbd\pub\jbui\
package-frame.html	Microsoft HTML Docu...	2/3/2000 8:55 PM	A	edeployment\javadoc\com\pbd\pub\jbui\
package-summary.html	Microsoft HTML Docu...	2/3/2000 8:55 PM	A	edeployment\javadoc\com\pbd\pub\jbui\
package-tree.html	Microsoft HTML Docu...	2/3/2000 8:55 PM	A	edeployment\javadoc\com\pbd\pub\jbui\
JdspfAbstractRecord.html	Microsoft HTML Docu...	2/3/2000 8:55 PM	A	edeployment\javadoc\com\pbd\pub\jdspf\
JdspfBuffer.html	Microsoft HTML Docu...	2/3/2000 8:55 PM	A	edeployment\javadoc\com\pbd\pub\jdspf\
JdspfDisplayFile.html	Microsoft HTML Docu...	2/3/2000 8:55 PM	A	edeployment\javadoc\com\pbd\pub\jdspf\
JdspfDisplayFileAction.html	Microsoft HTML Docu...	2/3/2000 8:55 PM	A	edeployment\javadoc\com\pbd\pub\jdspf\
JdspfDisplayFileListener.html	Microsoft HTML Docu...	2/3/2000 8:55 PM	A	edeployment\javadoc\com\pbd\pub\jdspf\
JdspfFieldAttributes.html	Microsoft HTML Docu...	2/3/2000 8:55 PM	A	edeployment\javadoc\com\pbd\pub\jdspf\
JdspfIndicator.html	Microsoft HTML Docu...	2/3/2000 8:55 PM	A	edeployment\javadoc\com\pbd\pub\jdspf\
JdspfIndicatorArray.html	Microsoft HTML Docu...	2/3/2000 8:55 PM	A	edeployment\javadoc\com\pbd\pub\jdspf\
JdspfInvalidOperationException.html	Microsoft HTML Docu...	2/3/2000 8:55 PM	A	edeployment\javadoc\com\pbd\pub\jdspf\
JdspfRecord.html	Microsoft HTML Docu...	2/3/2000 8:55 PM	A	edeployment\javadoc\com\pbd\pub\jdspf\
JdspfRecordUI.html	Microsoft HTML Docu...	2/3/2000 8:55 PM	A	edeployment\javadoc\com\pbd\pub\jdspf\
JdspfSubfile.html	Microsoft HTML Docu...	2/3/2000 8:55 PM	A	edeployment\javadoc\com\pbd\pub\jdspf\
JdspfUIAdapter.html	Microsoft HTML Docu...	2/3/2000 8:55 PM	A	edeployment\javadoc\com\pbd\pub\jdspf\
package-frame.html	Microsoft HTML Docu...	2/3/2000 8:55 PM	A	edeployment\javadoc\com\pbd\pub\jdspf\
package-summary.html	Microsoft HTML Docu...	2/3/2000 8:55 PM	A	edeployment\javadoc\com\pbd\pub\jdspf\
package-tree.html	Microsoft HTML Docu...	2/3/2000 8:55 PM	A	edeployment\javadoc\com\pbd\pub\jdspf\
Jsp.html	Microsoft HTML Docu...	2/3/2000 8:55 PM	A	edeployment\javadoc\com\pbd\pub\jsp\
JspField.html	Microsoft HTML Docu...	2/3/2000 8:55 PM	A	edeployment\javadoc\com\pbd\pub\jsp\
package-frame.html	Microsoft HTML Docu...	2/3/2000 8:55 PM	A	edeployment\javadoc\com\pbd\pub\jsp\
package-summary.html	Microsoft HTML Docu...	2/3/2000 8:55 PM	A	edeployment\javadoc\com\pbd\pub\jsp\
package-tree.html	Microsoft HTML Docu...	2/3/2000 8:55 PM	A	edeployment\javadoc\com\pbd\pub\jsp\
package-frame.html	Microsoft HTML Docu...	2/3/2000 8:55 PM	A	edeployment\javadoc\com\pbd\pub\sc400\
package-summary.html	Microsoft HTML Docu...	2/3/2000 8:55 PM	A	edeployment\javadoc\com\pbd\pub\sc400\
package-tree.html	Microsoft HTML Docu...	2/3/2000 8:55 PM	A	edeployment\javadoc\com\pbd\pub\sc400\
Sc400Api.html	Microsoft HTML Docu...	2/3/2000 8:55 PM	A	edeployment\javadoc\com\pbd\pub\sc400\
Sc400Client.html	Microsoft HTML Docu...	2/3/2000 8:55 PM	A	edeployment\javadoc\com\pbd\pub\sc400\
Sc400Exception.html	Microsoft HTML Docu...	2/3/2000 8:55 PM	A	edeployment\javadoc\com\pbd\pub\sc400\

Selected 0 files, 0 bytes   Total 143 files, 2,769KB

*Figure B.2: The contents of the **.zip** file, continued.*

APPENDIX B: ABOUT THE CD-ROM

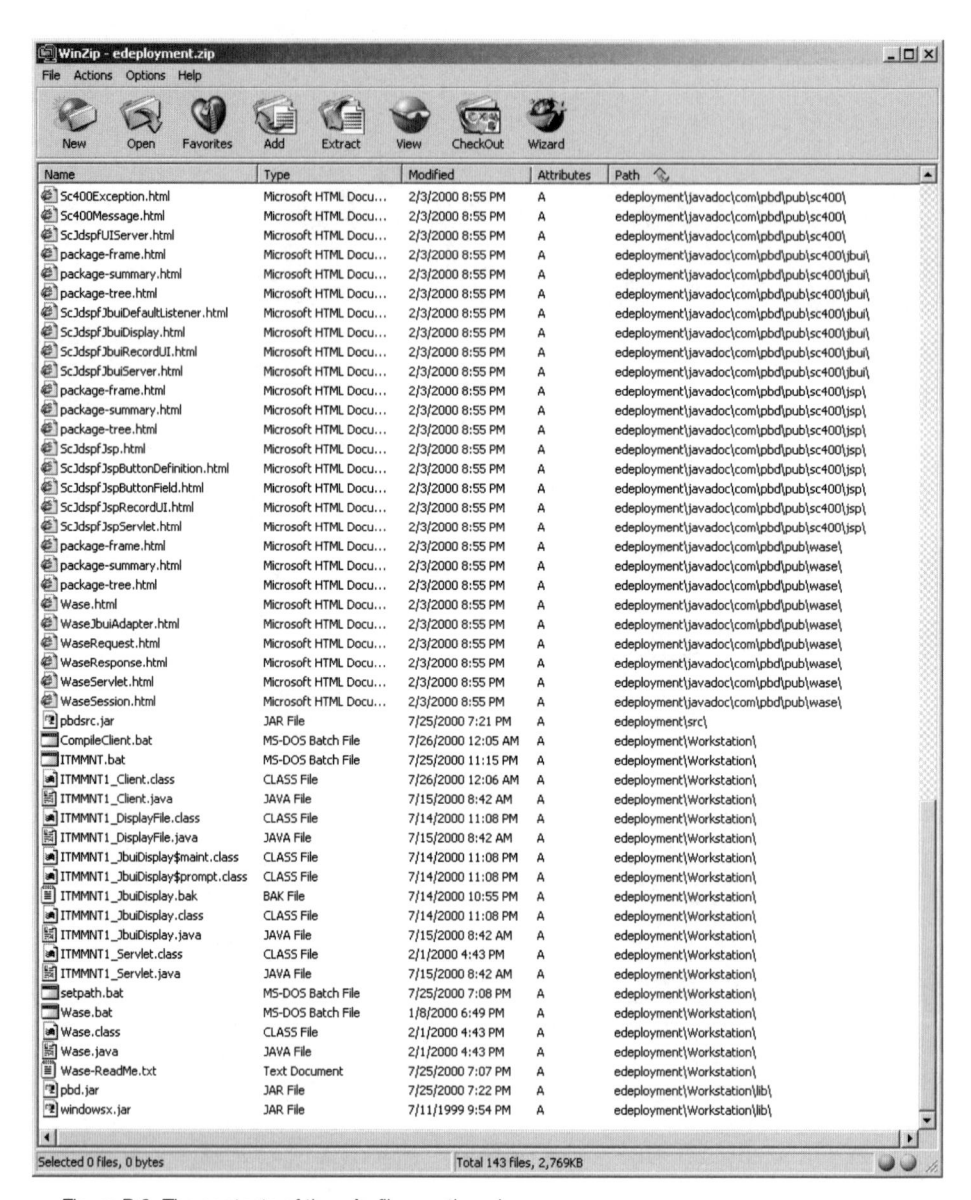

*Figure B.3: The contents of the **.zip** file, continued.*

Appendix C

Javadoc

Appendix C: JavaDoc

Overview Package Class **Tree** **Deprecated** **Index** **Help**
PREV NEXT   FRAMES NO FRAMES

Hierarchy For All Packages

Package Hierarchies:
    com.pbd.pub.common, com.pbd.pub.dc400, com.pbd.pub.jao400, com.pbd.pub.jbui, com.pbd.pub.jdb400, com.pbd.pub.jdqm400, com.pbd.pub.jdspf, com.pbd.pub.jsp, com.pbd.pub.sc400, com.pbd.pub.sc400.jbui, com.pbd.pub.sc400.jsp

Class Hierarchy

- class java.lang.Object
  - class javax.swing.table.AbstractTableModel (implements java.io.Serializable, javax.swing.table.TableModel)
    - class com.pbd.pub.jbui.**JbuiListModel**
  - class java.awt.Component (implements java.awt.image.ImageObserver, java.awt.MenuContainer, java.io.Serializable)
    - class java.awt.Container
      - class javax.swing.JComponent (implements java.io.Serializable)
        - class javax.swing.AbstractButton (implements java.awt.ItemSelectable, javax.swing.SwingConstants)
          - class javax.swing.JButton (implements javax.accessibility.Accessible)
            - class com.pbd.pub.jbui.**JbuiButton**
        - class javax.swing.JPanel (implements javax.accessibility.Accessible)
          - class com.pbd.pub.jbui.**JbuiButtonPanel**
            - class com.pbd.pub.jbui.**JbuiCancelButton**
          - class com.pbd.pub.jbui.**JbuiEntryField**
            - class com.pbd.pub.jbui.**JbuiOutputField**
          - class com.pbd.pub.jbui.**JbuiFieldPanel**
  - class com.pbd.pub.dc400.**Dc400Field**
    - class com.pbd.pub.dc400.**Dc400CharacterField**
    - class com.pbd.pub.dc400.**Dc400NumericField**
    - class com.pbd.pub.dc400.**Dc400RawField**
  - class com.pbd.pub.dc400.**Dc400Structure** (implements java.lang.Cloneable)
    - class com.pbd.pub.jdspf.**JdspfBuffer**
    - class com.pbd.pub.sc400.**Sc400Message**
  - class java.util.EventObject (implements java.io.Serializable)
    - class java.awt.AWTEvent
      - class java.awt.event.ActionEvent
        - class com.pbd.pub.jdspf.**JdspfDisplayFileAction**
  - class com.pbd.pub.jao400.**Jao400**
  - class com.pbd.pub.jao400.**Jao400Field**
  - class com.pbd.pub.jbui.**JbuiListPanel**
  - class com.pbd.pub.jbui.**JbuiScreen** (implements com.pbd.pub.jbui.JbuiConstants)
    - class com.pbd.pub.jbui.**JbuiDisplay**

Appendix C: Javadoc

- class com.pbd.pub.jao400.**Jao400Display**
- class com.pbd.pub.sc400.jbui.**ScJdspfJbuiDisplay** (implements com.pbd.pub.jdspf.JdspfUIAdapter)
    - class com.pbd.pub.jbui.**JbuiList**
        - class com.pbd.pub.jao400.**Jao400List**
    - class com.pbd.pub.jbui.**JbuiSplit**
        - class com.pbd.pub.jao400.**Jao400Split**
- class com.pbd.pub.jdb400.**Jdb400**
- class com.pbd.pub.jdb400.**Jdb400Constant** (implements com.pbd.pub.jdb400.Jdb400Constants)
- class com.pbd.pub.jdb400.**Jdb400Field**
- class com.pbd.pub.jdb400.**Jdb400File** (implements com.pbd.pub.jdb400.Jdb400Constants)
    - class com.pbd.pub.jdb400.**Jdb400KeyedFile**
        - class com.pbd.pub.jdb400.**Jdb400KeyedUpdateFile**
    - class com.pbd.pub.jdb400.**Jdb400SequentialFile**
        - class com.pbd.pub.jdb400.**Jdb400SequentialUpdateFile**
- class com.pbd.pub.jdqm400.**Jdqm400**
- class com.pbd.pub.jdqm400.**JdqmServer** (implements com.pbd.pub.jdqm400.JdqmConstants)
- class com.pbd.pub.jdqm400.**JdqmSession** (implements com.pbd.pub.jdqm400.JdqmConstants)
- class com.pbd.pub.jdspf.**JdspfAbstractRecord**
    - class com.pbd.pub.jdspf.**JdspfRecord**
    - class com.pbd.pub.jdspf.**JdspfSubfile**
- class com.pbd.pub.jdspf.**JdspfDisplayFile**
- class com.pbd.pub.jdspf.**JdspfFieldAttributes**
- class com.pbd.pub.jdspf.**JdspfIndicator**
- class com.pbd.pub.jdspf.**JdspfIndicatorArray**
- class com.pbd.pub.jdspf.**JdspfRecordUI**
    - class com.pbd.pub.sc400.jbui.**ScJdspfJbuiRecordUI**
    - class com.pbd.pub.sc400.jsp.**ScJdspfJspRecordUI**
- class com.pbd.pub.jsp.**Jsp**
    - class com.pbd.pub.sc400.jsp.**ScJdspfJsp** (implements com.pbd.pub.jdspf.JdspfUIAdapter)
- class com.pbd.pub.jsp.**JspField**
    - class com.pbd.pub.sc400.jsp.**ScJdspfJspButtonField**
- class com.pbd.pub.common.**Pbd**
- class com.pbd.pub.common.**Pbd400**
- class com.pbd.pub.common.**PbdSystem**
- class com.pbd.pub.sc400.**Sc400Client**
- class com.pbd.pub.sc400.jbui.**ScJdspfJbuiDefaultListener** (implements com.pbd.pub.jdspf.JdspfDisplayFileListener)
- class com.pbd.pub.sc400.jsp.**ScJdspfJspButtonDefinition**
- class com.pbd.pub.sc400.**ScJdspfUIServer**
    - class com.pbd.pub.sc400.jbui.**ScJdspfJbuiServer**
- class java.lang.Thread (implements java.lang.Runnable)
    - class com.pbd.pub.jbui.**JbuiScreenThread**
- class java.lang.Throwable (implements java.io.Serializable)
    - class java.lang.Exception
        - class com.pbd.pub.jdspf.**JdspfInvalidOperationException**
        - class com.pbd.pub.sc400.**Sc400Exception**
- class com.pbd.pub.sc400.**Sc400Api**
- class com.pbd.pub.sc400.jsp.**ScJdspfJspServlet**

Appendix C: JavaDoc

Interface Hierarchy

- interface com.pbd.pub.jdb400.**Jdb400Constants**
- interface com.pbd.pub.jdqm400.**JdqmConstants**
- interface com.pbd.pub.jdspf.**JdspfDisplayFileListener**
- interface com.pbd.pub.jdspf.**JdspfUIAdapter**
- interface javax.swing.SwingConstants
    - interface com.pbd.pub.jbui.**JbuiConstants**

Overview Package Class **Tree** **Deprecated** **Index** **Help**

PREV NEXT   FRAMES NO FRAMES

Overview Package Class **Tree** **Deprecated** **Index** **Help**
PREV NEXT   FRAMES   NO FRAMES

Packages	
com.pbd.pub.common	
com.pbd.pub.dc400	
com.pbd.pub.jao400	
com.pbd.pub.jbui	
com.pbd.pub.jdb400	
com.pbd.pub.jdqm400	
com.pbd.pub.jdspf	
com.pbd.pub.jsp	
com.pbd.pub.sc400	
com.pbd.pub.sc400.jbui	
com.pbd.pub.sc400.jsp	

Overview **Package** Class **Tree** **Deprecated** **Index** **Help**
PREV PACKAGE   NEXT PACKAGE   FRAMES   NO FRAMES

Package com.pbd.pub.common

Class Summary	
Pbd	PBD is the system class used to support all the static utility methods of the PBD package.
Pbd400	Pbd400 is the singleton class used to control PBD system parameters dealing with the AS/400.
PbdSystem	PbdSystem is the singleton class used to control PBD system parameters.

Appendix C: Javadoc

Overview **Package** **Class** **Tree** **Deprecated** **Index** **Help**
PREV CLASS   **NEXT CLASS**   **FRAMES**   **NO FRAMES**
SUMMARY: INNER | FIELD | CONSTR | METHOD   DETAIL: FIELD | CONSTR | METHOD

com.pbd.pub.common

Class Pbd

```
java.lang.Object
  |
  +-com.pbd.pub.common.Pbd
```

public class **Pbd**
extends java.lang.Object

PBD is the system class used to support all the static utility methods of the PBD package.

Since:
>   2.0P

Constructor Summary

Pbd()

Method Summary

static void	**appendToVector**(java.util.Vector v1, java.util.Vector v2) Appends vector v1 to vector v2.
static void	**copyToArray**(java.util.Vector vector, java.lang.Object[] objects) Copies a vector to an array.
static java.lang.Object[]	**makeArray**(java.lang.Object object) Create an Object array from a single Object.
static java.lang.Object[]	**makeArray**(java.util.Vector vector) Create an Object array from a Vector.
static java.util.Vector	**makeVector**(int[] ints) Creates a vector of Integers from an array of primitive ints.
static java.util.Vector	**makeVector**(java.lang.Object[] objects) Creates a vector of Objects from an array of Objects.
static java.util.Vector	**makeVector**(java.lang.Object[][] data) Creates a two-dimensional vector from a two-dimensional array of objects.

Methods inherited from class java.lang.Object

equals, getClass, hashCode, notify, notifyAll, toString, wait, wait, wait

Constructor Detail

Pbd

```
public Pbd()
```

Method Detail

appendToVector

```
public static void appendToVector(java.util.Vector v1,
                                  java.util.Vector v2)
```
Appends vector v1 to vector v2.
Parameters:
v1 - the target array.
v2 - the array to append.

copyToArray

```
public static void copyToArray(java.util.Vector vector,
                               java.lang.Object[] objects)
```
Copies a vector to an array. The array must be large enough to hold all the elements of the vector.
Parameters:
vector - the original Vector.
objects - the array to populate.
Returns:
the newly populated array.

makeArray

```
public static java.lang.Object[] makeArray(java.lang.Object object)
```
Create an Object array from a single Object.
Parameters:
object - single Object.
Returns:
one-element array of Objects containing the original Object.

makeArray

```
public static java.lang.Object[] makeArray(java.util.Vector vector)
```
Create an Object array from a Vector.
Parameters:
vector - the original Vector.
Returns:
the new array.

Appendix C: Javadoc

makeVector

```
public static java.util.Vector makeVector(java.lang.Object[][] data)
```
    Creates a two-dimensional vector from a two-dimensional array of objects.
    Parameters:
    data - the original two-dimensional array.
    Returns:
    the new two-dimensional vector.

makeVector

```
public static java.util.Vector makeVector(int[] ints)
```
    Creates a vector of Integers from an array of primitive ints.
    Parameters:
    ints - the original array of ints.
    Returns:
    the new vector.

makeVector

```
public static java.util.Vector makeVector(java.lang.Object[] objects)
```
    Creates a vector of Objects from an array of Objects.
    Parameters:
    objects - the original array of ints.
    Returns:
    the new vector.

Overview Package **Class** Tree Deprecated Index Help
PREV CLASS NEXT CLASS   FRAMES NO FRAMES
SUMMARY: INNER | FIELD | CONSTR | METHOD   DETAIL: FIELD | CONSTR | METHOD

---

com.pbd.pub.common

Class Pbd400

```
java.lang.Object
  |
  +-com.pbd.pub.common.Pbd400
```

public class **Pbd400**
extends java.lang.Object

Pbd400 is the singleton class used to control PBD system parameters dealing with the AS/400. Currently, the system supports only one AS/400 connection.

Since:
> 2.0P

See Also:
> `PbdSystem`

Constructor Summary

Pbd400()	

Method Summary

`static com.pbd.pub.common.AS400`	**getAS400**() Returns the AS/400 connection class.

Methods inherited from class java.lang.Object

`equals, getClass, hashCode, notify, notifyAll, toString, wait, wait, wait`

Constructor Detail

Pbd400

`public` **`Pbd400`**`()`

Method Detail

getAS400

`public static com.pbd.pub.common.AS400` **`getAS400`**`()`
> Returns the AS/400 connection class. If there is none, the method attempts to create one and establish record-level access.
>
> **Returns:**
> AS400 the AS400 connection class.

Appendix C: Javadoc

Overview	Package	**Class**	Tree	Deprecated	Index	Help
PREV CLASS NEXT CLASS				**FRAMES** NO FRAMES		
SUMMARY: INNER | FIELD | CONSTR | METHOD				DETAIL: FIELD | CONSTR | METHOD		

com.pbd.pub.common

Class PbdSystem

```
java.lang.Object
  |
  +-com.pbd.pub.common.PbdSystem
```

public class **PbdSystem**
extends java.lang.Object

PbdSystem is the singleton class used to control PBD system parameters. Currently, the system supports only one AS/400 connection, the default library is %LIBL% and the default look and feel is Windows. An initialization file, pbd.ini, is supported to default these parameters.

Since:
    1.2P

Method Summary

`static void`	**applyLookAndFeel**() PBD (c) 1999
`static java.lang.String`	**getAS400Name**() Gets the current AS/400 system name.
`static java.lang.String`	**getAS400Password**() Gets the current AS/400 password.
`static java.lang.String`	**getAS400UserID**() Gets the current AS/400 user ID.
`static java.lang.String`	**getLibrary**() Gets the current library for JDB/400 file objects.
`static java.lang.String`	**getLookAndFeel**() Gets the look-and-feel class name for the system.
`static java.lang.String`	**getSystemLibrary**() Gets the library name for system APIs.
`static void`	**setAS400**(`java.lang.String initName`) Sets the default value for the system name.
`static void`	**setAS400**(`java.lang.String initName, java.lang.String initUser`) Sets default values for user ID and password.
`static void`	**setAS400**(`java.lang.String initName,`

		`java.lang.String initUser, java.lang.String initPassword)` Sets default values for system name, user ID and password, bypassing the logon panel entirely.
	`static void`	**setLibrary**`(java.lang.String newLibrary)` Sets the current library for JDB/400 file objects.
	`static void`	**setLookAndFeel**`(java.lang.String newLookAndFeel)` Sets the current look and feel for JBUI screens.
	`static void`	**setSystemLibrary**`(java.lang.String newSystemLibrary)` PBD (c) 1999

Methods inherited from class java.lang.Object

`equals, getClass, hashCode, notify, notifyAll, toString, wait, wait, wait`

Method Detail

applyLookAndFeel

`public static void` **applyLookAndFeel**`()`
   PBD (c) 1999

getAS400Name

`public static java.lang.String` **getAS400Name**`()`
   Gets the current AS/400 system name.
   Returns:
   the current AS/400 system name.
   See Also:
   `setAS400`

getAS400Password

`public static java.lang.String` **getAS400Password**`()`
   Gets the current AS/400 password.
   Returns:
   the current AS/400 password.
   See Also:
   `setAS400`

getAS400UserID

`public static java.lang.String` **getAS400UserID**`()`
   Gets the current AS/400 user ID.
   Returns:
   the current AS/400 user ID.
   See Also:
   `setAS400`

Appendix C: Javadoc

getLibrary

```
public static java.lang.String getLibrary()
```
    Gets the current library for JDB/400 file objects. The current library defaults to "%LIBL%", which corresponds to *LIBL on the AS/400.
    Returns:
    the current library for JDB/400 file objects.
    See Also:
    `setLibrary`

---

getLookAndFeel

```
public static java.lang.String getLookAndFeel()
```
    Gets the look-and-feel class name for the system. Defaults to "javax.swing.plaf.windows.WindowsLookAndFeel".
    Returns:
    the current look-and-feel class name for PBD objects.
    See Also:
    `setLookAndFeel`

---

getSystemLibrary

```
public static java.lang.String getSystemLibrary()
```
    Gets the library name for system APIs. Defaults to "PBD400".
    Returns:
    the current system library name.
    See Also:
    `setSystemLibrary`

---

setAS400

```
public static void setAS400(java.lang.String initName)
```
    Sets the default value for the system name. This will cause the logon panel to be displayed with the system name protected. The user must enter user ID and password. The logon panel is displayed the first time a JDB/400 file object is created.

    Example use:

```
PbdSystem.setAS400("myas400.mydomain.com");
```
    Parameters:
    initName - is the AS/400 system name in domain format

---

setAS400

```
public static void setAS400(java.lang.String initName,
                            java.lang.String initUser)
```
    Sets default values for user ID and password. This will cause the logon panel to be displayed with the system name protected and the user ID filled in. The user must enter the password. The logon panel is displayed the first time a JDB/400 file object is created.

    Example use:

```
PbdSystem.setAS400("myas400.mydomain.com", "myuserid");
```
Parameters:
`initName` - is the AS/400 system name in domain format
`initUser` - is the AS/400 user ID

setAS400

```
public static void setAS400(java.lang.String initName,
                            java.lang.String initUser,
                            java.lang.String initPassword)
```
Sets default values for system name, user ID and password, bypassing the logon panel entirely. **The problem is that the password is in your program as clear text, so it is not secure.**

Example use:

```
PbdSystem.setAS400("myas400.mydomain.com", "myuserid", "mypassword");
```
Parameters:
`initName` - is the AS/400 system name in domain format
`initUser` - is the AS/400 user ID
`initPassword` - is the password for the user ID

setLibrary

```
public static void setLibrary(java.lang.String newLibrary)
```
Sets the current library for JDB/400 file objects. The current library defaults to "%LIBL%", which corresponds to *LIBL on the AS/400.

Example use:

PbdSystem.setLibrary("MYLIB");
Parameters:
`newLibrary` - is the AS/400 library name

setLookAndFeel

```
public static void setLookAndFeel(java.lang.String newLookAndFeel)
```
Sets the current look and feel for JBUI screens. The look and feel defaults to Windows.

Example use:

PbdSystem.setLookAndFeel("javax.swing.plaf.motif.MotifLookAndFeel");
Parameters:
`newLibrary` - is the AS/400 library name

setSystemLibrary

```
public static void setSystemLibrary(java.lang.String newSystemLibrary)
```
PBD (c) 1999
Parameters:
`newSystemLibrary` - String

Appendix C: Javadoc

Overview	**Package**	Class	**Tree**	**Deprecated**	**Index**	**Help**
PREV PACKAGE	**NEXT PACKAGE**				**FRAMES**	**NO FRAMES**

Package com.pbd.pub.dc400

Class Summary

Dc400CharacterField	Dc400CharacterField defines a character field.
Dc400Field	Dc400Field defines a field in a Dc400Structure.
Dc400NumericField	Dc400NumericField defines a numeric field.
Dc400RawField	Dc400RawField defines a raw (untranslated EBCDIC) field.
Dc400Structure	Dc400Structure defines a data structure.

Overview	Package	**Class**	**Tree**	**Deprecated**	**Index**	**Help**
PREV CLASS	**NEXT CLASS**				**FRAMES**	**NO FRAMES**
SUMMARY: INNER | FIELD | CONSTR | METHOD					DETAIL: FIELD | CONSTR | METHOD	

com.pbd.pub.dc400

Class Dc400CharacterField

```
java.lang.Object
  |
  +-com.pbd.pub.dc400.Dc400Field
        |
        +-com.pbd.pub.dc400.Dc400CharacterField
```

public class **Dc400CharacterField**
extends Dc400Field

Dc400CharacterField defines a character field. Its Java equivalent is a String.

Since:
    2.0P

Fields inherited from class com.pbd.pub.dc400.Dc400Field

CHARACTER, NUMERIC, RAW

286

Appendix C: Javadoc

Constructor Summary

Dc400CharacterField(java.lang.String name, int length)
  Creates an Sc400RawField with the specified name and length.

Method Summary

com.pbd.pub.dc400.AS400DataType	**getAS400DataType**() Returns the AS400 data type associated with this field, which in this case is AS400Text.

Methods inherited from class com.pbd.pub.dc400.Dc400Field

getAttributes, getDecimals, getLength, getName, getOffset, getStructure, getType, setAttributes

Methods inherited from class java.lang.Object

equals, getClass, hashCode, notify, notifyAll, toString, wait, wait, wait

Constructor Detail

Dc400CharacterField

```
public Dc400CharacterField(java.lang.String name,
                          int length)
```
  Creates an Sc400RawField with the specified name and length.
  Parameters:
  name - the field name
  length - the length of the field

Method Detail

getAS400DataType

```
public com.pbd.pub.dc400.AS400DataType getAS400DataType()
```
  Returns the AS400 data type associated with this field, which in this case is AS400Text.
  Overrides:
  getAS400DataType in class Dc400Field
  Returns:
  AS400DataType the AS400DataType for this field.

287

Appendix C: Javadoc

Overview	Package	**Class**	Tree	Deprecated	Index	Help
PREV CLASS NEXT CLASS				FRAMES NO FRAMES
SUMMARY: INNER	FIELD	CONSTR	METHOD		DETAIL: FIELD	CONSTR	METHOD

com.pbd.pub.dc400

Class Dc400Field

```
java.lang.Object
  |
  +-com.pbd.pub.dc400.Dc400Field
```
Direct Known Subclasses:
Dc400CharacterField, Dc400NumericField, Dc400RawField

public abstract class **Dc400Field**
extends java.lang.Object

Dc400Field defines a field in a Dc400Structure. Its primary characteristics are type and length (and decimals for numeric fields). Currently, I'm only supporting CHARACTER and NUMERIC fields, I expect to have some more sophisticated field types in later versions. There is also a type RAW, which converts to a byte array. These are used for filler fields. Dc400Field can be attached to an Dc400Structure; in fact, that's the idea. Once fields are attached to an Dc400Structure, they can be used to automatically generate the objects required to convert data between the EBCDIC buffer and Java objects. Finally, a Dc400FieldAttributes structure can be attached to a field. This will allow the definition of attributes such as color and field protect, and optionally to associate those attributes with an indicator.

Since:
> 2.0P

Field Summary

static int	**CHARACTER**
static int	**NUMERIC**
static int	**RAW**

Constructor Summary

Dc400Field()
> Empty constructor.

Dc400Field(java.lang.String name, int type, int length, int decimals)
> Creates a field of the specified name, type, length, and decimals.

Method Summary

abstract com.pbd.pub.dc400.AS400DataType	**getAS400DataType**() Abstract method which must be redefined for each subclass to return the correct AS400 data type object to convert this field.
JdspfFieldAttributes	**getAttributes**() Returns the attributes of this field.
int	**getDecimals**() Returns the decimal positions for this field.
int	**getLength**() Returns the length of the field.
java.lang.String	**getName**() Returns the name of the field.
int	**getOffset**() Returns the offset of the field within the EBCDIC buffer.
Dc400Structure	**getStructure**() Returns the Dc400Structure that this field is attached to.
int	**getType**() Returns the field type.
void	**setAttributes**(JdspfFieldAttributes newValue) Sets the attributes for this field.

Methods inherited from class java.lang.Object

equals, getClass, hashCode, notify, notifyAll, toString, wait, wait, wait

Field Detail

RAW

```
public static final int RAW
```

CHARACTER

```
public static final int CHARACTER
```

NUMERIC

```
public static final int NUMERIC
```

Appendix C: Javadoc

Constructor Detail

Dc400Field

```
public Dc400Field()
```
    Empty constructor.

Dc400Field

```
public Dc400Field(java.lang.String name,
                  int type,
                  int length,
                  int decimals)
```
    Creates a field of the specified name, type, length, and decimals. Dc400Field objects are used to convert data to and from flat EBCDIC structures without all the overhead of an actual Record object.
    Parameters:
    name - field name.
    type - field type.
    length - field length.
    decimals - number of decimals.

Method Detail

getAS400DataType

```
public abstract com.pbd.pub.dc400.AS400DataType getAS400DataType()
```
    Abstract method which must be redefined for each subclass to return the correct AS400 data type object to convert this field.
    Returns:
    the type used to convert this field.

getAttributes

```
public JdspfFieldAttributes getAttributes()
```
    Returns the attributes of this field.
    Returns:
    the attributes of this field.

getDecimals

```
public int getDecimals()
```
    Returns the decimal positions for this field.
    Returns:
    the decimal positions for this field.

getLength

```
public int getLength()
```
　　　　Returns the length of the field.
　　　　Returns:
　　　　　　the length of the field.

getName

```
public java.lang.String getName()
```
　　　　Returns the name of the field.
　　　　Returns:
　　　　　　the name of the field.

getOffset

```
public int getOffset()
```
　　　　Returns the offset of the field within the EBCDIC buffer.
　　　　Returns:
　　　　　　the offset of the field.

getStructure

```
public Dc400Structure getStructure()
```
　　　　Returns the Dc400Structure that this field is attached to.
　　　　Returns:
　　　　　　the Dc400Structure that this field is attached to.

getType

```
public int getType()
```
　　　　Returns the field type.
　　　　Returns:
　　　　　　the field type.

setAttributes

```
public void setAttributes(JdspfFieldAttributes newValue)
```
　　　　Sets the attributes for this field.
　　　　Parameters:
　　　　　　newValue - new attributes for this field.

Appendix C: Javadoc

Overview	Package	**Class**	Tree	Deprecated	Index	Help
PREV CLASS	**NEXT CLASS**			**FRAMES**	**NO FRAMES**	
SUMMARY: INNER | FIELD | CONSTR | METHOD				DETAIL: FIELD | CONSTR | METHOD		

com.pbd.pub.dc400

Class Dc400NumericField

```
java.lang.Object
  |
  +-com.pbd.pub.dc400.Dc400Field
        |
        +-com.pbd.pub.dc400.Dc400NumericField
```

public class **Dc400NumericField**
extends Dc400Field

Dc400NumericField defines a numeric field. Its Java equivalent is a BigDecimal.

Since:
    2.0P

Fields inherited from class com.pbd.pub.dc400.Dc400Field

CHARACTER, NUMERIC, RAW

Constructor Summary

Dc400NumericField(java.lang.String name, int length, int decimals)
    Creates an Sc400NumericField with the specified name, length, and decimals.

Method Summary

com.pbd.pub.dc400.AS400DataType	**getAS400DataType**() Returns the AS400 data type associated with this field, which in this case is AS400ZonedDecimal.

Methods inherited from class com.pbd.pub.dc400.Dc400Field

getAttributes, getDecimals, getLength, getName, getOffset, getStructure, getType, setAttributes

Methods inherited from class java.lang.Object

equals, getClass, hashCode, notify, notifyAll, toString, wait, wait, wait

Appendix C: Javadoc

Constructor Detail

Dc400NumericField

```
public Dc400NumericField(java.lang.String name,
                         int length,
                         int decimals)
```
Creates an Sc400NumericField with the specified name, length, and decimals.
Parameters:
name - the field name
length - the length of the field
decimals - the number of decimals

Method Detail

getAS400DataType

`public com.pbd.pub.dc400.AS400DataType getAS400DataType()`

Returns the AS400 data type associated with this field, which in this case is AS400ZonedDecimal.
Overrides:
getAS400DataType in class Dc400Field
Returns:
AS400DataType the AS400DataType for this field.

Overview Package **Class** Tree Deprecated Index Help
PREV CLASS NEXT CLASS   FRAMES NO FRAMES
SUMMARY: INNER | FIELD | CONSTR | METHOD   DETAIL: FIELD | CONSTR | METHOD

---

com.pbd.pub.dc400

Class Dc400RawField

```
java.lang.Object
   |
   +-com.pbd.pub.dc400.Dc400Field
         |
         +-com.pbd.pub.dc400.Dc400RawField
```

public class **Dc400RawField**
extends Dc400Field

Dc400RawField defines a raw (untranslated EBDIC) field. Its Java equivalent is a byte array.

Since:
2.0P

293

Appendix C: Javadoc

Fields inherited from class com.pbd.pub.dc400.Dc400Field
CHARACTER, NUMERIC, RAW

Constructor Summary
Dc400RawField(java.lang.String name, int length)
    Creates an Sc400RawField with the specified name and length.

Method Summary
com.pbd.pub.dc400.AS400DataType	**getAS400DataType**() Returns the AS400 data type associated with this field, which in this case is AS400ByteArray.

Methods inherited from class com.pbd.pub.dc400.Dc400Field
getAttributes, getDecimals, getLength, getName, getOffset, getStructure, getType, setAttributes

Methods inherited from class java.lang.Object
equals, getClass, hashCode, notify, notifyAll, toString, wait, wait, wait

Constructor Detail

Dc400RawField

```
public Dc400RawField(java.lang.String name,
                     int length)
```
Creates an Sc400RawField with the specified name and length.
Parameters:
name - the field name
length - the length of the field

Method Detail

getAS400DataType

```
public com.pbd.pub.dc400.AS400DataType getAS400DataType()
```
Returns the AS400 data type associated with this field, which in this case is AS400ByteArray.
Overrides:
getAS400DataType in class Dc400Field
Returns:
AS400DataType the AS400DataType for this field.

| Overview | Package | **Class** | Tree | Deprecated | Index | Help |

PREV CLASS   NEXT CLASS   **FRAMES**   **NO FRAMES**
SUMMARY: INNER | FIELD | CONSTR | METHOD   DETAIL: FIELD | CONSTR | METHOD

---

com.pbd.pub.dc400
Class Dc400Structure

```
java.lang.Object
  |
  +-com.pbd.pub.dc400.Dc400Structure
```
All Implemented Interfaces:
    java.lang.Cloneable
Direct Known Subclasses:
    JdspfBuffer, Sc400Message

---

public class **Dc400Structure**
extends java.lang.Object
implements java.lang.Cloneable

Dc400Structure defines a data structure. Its AS/400 form is as a contiguous set of data fields represented by an array of bytes. In its Java form, it is a Vector of objects.

The Dc400Structure is primarily used to pass messages to and from HLL programs. In the HLL, they would typically be defined as an externally described data structure. To make the transition from one form to another as smooth as possible, the objects in the Vector can be accessed by a "field name." At the same time, in order to speed up processing a little, it is possible to access the fields directly by index as well. Care should obviously be taken when using this latter technique, since the indices can easily get out of sync.

In its primary form, the Dc400Structure contains both the structure of the data and the data itself. The data is meant to be accessed in either direction -- that is, you can set the EBCDIC buffer, then retrieve the Java objects, or vice versa. The Dc400Structure is self-synchronizing; if either the EBCDIC or the Java side changes, subsequent gets to the other side will force a conversion.

The Dc400Structure can also be used strictly as a conversion device. You can create a Dc400Structure, then dynamically convert an array of EBCDIC bytes to a Vector of object, or vice versa, by calling the toObjects() or toBuffer() method, respectively.

Since:
    2.0P

Constructor Summary

Dc400Structure()
    Empty Dc400Structure constructor.

Dc400Structure(Dc400Field[] fields)
    Creates an empty Dc400Structure with the layout as specified by the array of Dc400Field objects.

Dc400Structure(Dc400Structure initStructure)
    Creates an empty Dc400Structure with the same layout as the specified Dc400Structure.

Appendix C: Javadoc

	Method Summary	
java.lang.Object	**clone**() Returns a copy of the structure and its EBCDIC data.	
java.math.BigDecimal	**getBigDecimal**(int index) Returns the BigDecimal for the field specified by the index.	
java.math.BigDecimal	**getBigDecimal**(java.lang.String name) Returns the BigDecimal for the field specified by the field name.	
byte[]	**getBuffer**() Returns the Dc400Structure as an array of EBCDIC bytes.	
int	**getBufferLength**() Returns the length of the EBCDIC representation of this structure.	
byte[]	**getByteArray**(int index) Returns the byte array for the field specified by the index.	
byte[]	**getByteArray**(java.lang.String name) Returns the byte array for the field specified by the field name.	
java.lang.Object	**getObject**(int index) Returns the Java object for the field specified by the index.	
java.lang.Object	**getObject**(java.lang.String name) Returns the Java object for the field specified by the field name.	
java.util.Vector	**getObjects**() Returns the Dc400Structure as an array of Java objects.	
java.lang.String	**getString**(int index) Returns the String for the field specified by the index.	
java.lang.String	**getString**(java.lang.String name) Returns the String for the field specified by the field name.	
void	**setBuffer**(byte[] newValue) Set the data of the Dc400Structure from an array of EBCDIC bytes.	
void	**setFields**(Dc400Field[] newValue) Set the field definitions for this structure.	
void	**setFields**(java.util.Vector newValue) Set the field definitions for this structure.	
void	**setObject**(int index, java.lang.Object newValue) This method was created in VisualAge.	
void	**setObject**(java.lang.String name, java.lang.Object newValue) This method was created in VisualAge.	
void	**setObjects**(java.util.Vector newValue) Set the data of the Dc400Structure from a Vector of Java objects.	
byte[]	**toBuffer**(java.util.Vector objects) Convert a Vector of Java objects to an EBCDIC buffer according to the fields of this structure.	
java.util.Vector	**toObjects**(byte[] buffer) Convert an EBCDIC buffer to a Vector of Java objects according to the fields of this structure.	

Methods inherited from class java.lang.Object

```
equals, getClass, hashCode, notify, notifyAll, toString, wait, wait, wait
```

Constructor Detail

Dc400Structure

public **Dc400Structure**()

>Empty Dc400Structure constructor.

Dc400Structure

public **Dc400Structure**(Dc400Field[] fields)

>Creates an empty Dc400Structure with the layout as specified by the array of Dc400Field objects.
>**Parameters:**
>fields - an array of Dc400Field objects.

Dc400Structure

public **Dc400Structure**(Dc400Structure initStructure)

>Creates an empty Dc400Structure with the same layout as the specified Dc400Structure. This is used to create multiple Dc400Structure objects with the same format without having to initialize all the structure definitions.
>**Parameters:**
>initStructure - structure whose layout to copy.

Method Detail

clone

public java.lang.Object **clone**()

>Returns a copy of the structure and its EBCDIC data.
>**Returns:**
>a copy of the structure and its EBCDIC data.

getBigDecimal

public java.math.BigDecimal **getBigDecimal**(int index)

>Returns the BigDecimal for the field specified by the index.
>**Parameters:**
>index - the index of the field to return.
>**Returns:**
>the BigDecimal for the field specified by the index.

getBigDecimal

public java.math.BigDecimal **getBigDecimal**(java.lang.String name)

> Returns the BigDecimal for the field specified by the field name.
> **Parameters:**
> name - the name of the field to return.
> **Returns:**
> the BigDecimal for the field specified by the field name.

getBuffer

public byte[] **getBuffer**()

> Returns the Dc400Structure as an array of EBCDIC bytes.
> **Returns:**
> the Dc400Structure as an array of EBCDIC bytes.

getBufferLength

public int **getBufferLength**()

> Returns the length of the EBCDIC representation of this structure.
> **Returns:**
> the length of the EBCDIC representation of this structure.

getByteArray

public byte[] **getByteArray**(int index)

> Returns the byte array for the field specified by the index.
> **Parameters:**
> index - the index of the field to return.
> **Returns:**
> the byte array for the field specified by the index.

getByteArray

public byte[] **getByteArray**(java.lang.String name)

> Returns the byte array for the field specified by the field name.
> **Parameters:**
> name - the name of the field to return.
> **Returns:**
> the byte array for the field specified by the field name.

getObject

public java.lang.Object **getObject**(int index)

> Returns the Java object for the field specified by the index.
> **Parameters:**
> index - the index of the field to return.
> **Returns:**
> the Java object for the field specified by the index.

getObject

```
public java.lang.Object getObject(java.lang.String name)
```
    Returns the Java object for the field specified by the field name.
    Parameters:
    name - the name of the field to return.
    Returns:
    the Java object for the field specified by the field name.

---

getObjects

```
public java.util.Vector getObjects()
```
    Returns the Dc400Structure as an array of Java objects.
    Returns:
    the Dc400Structure as an array of Java objects.

---

getString

```
public java.lang.String getString(int index)
```
    Returns the String for the field specified by the index.
    Parameters:
    index - the index of the field to return.
    Returns:
    the String for the field specified by the index.

---

getString

```
public java.lang.String getString(java.lang.String name)
```
    Returns the String for the field specified by the field name.
    Parameters:
    name - the name of the field to return.
    Returns:
    the String for the field specified by the field name.

---

setBuffer

```
public void setBuffer(byte[] newValue)
```
    Set the data of the Dc400Structure from an array of EBCDIC bytes.
    Parameters:
    newValue - the array of EBCDIC bytes.

---

setFields

```
public void setFields(Dc400Field[] newValue)
```
    Set the field definitions for this structure.
    Parameters:
    newValue - new field definitions.

setFields

```
public void setFields(java.util.Vector newValue)
```
    Set the field definitions for this structure.
    Parameters:
    newValue - new field definitions.

setObject

```
public void setObject(int index,
                      java.lang.Object newValue)
```
    This method was created in VisualAge.
    Parameters:
    newValue - java.lang.Object
    index - int

setObject

```
public void setObject(java.lang.String name,
                      java.lang.Object newValue)
```
    This method was created in VisualAge.
    Parameters:
    newValue - java.lang.Object
    index - int

setObjects

```
public void setObjects(java.util.Vector newValue)
```
    Set the data of the Dc400Structure from a Vector of Java objects.
    Parameters:
    newValue - the Vector of Java objects.

toBuffer

```
public byte[] toBuffer(java.util.Vector objects)
```
    Convert a Vector of Java objects to an EBCDIC buffer according to the fields of this structure.
    Parameters:
    objects - the Vector of Java objects.
    Returns:
    the buffer of EBCDIC bytes.

toObjects

```
public java.util.Vector toObjects(byte[] buffer)
```
    Convert an EBCDIC buffer to a Vector of Java objects according to the fields of this structure.
    Parameters:
    buffer - the buffer of EBCDIC bytes.

Overview **Package** Class **Tree** **Deprecated** **Index** **Help**
PREV PACKAGE NEXT PACKAGE   FRAMES NO FRAMES

Package com.pbd.pub.jao400

Class Summary

Jao400	
Jao400Display	Jao400Display is a standard display panel.
Jao400Field	This type was created in VisualAge.
Jao400List	Create a Jao400List for the specified file, list fields, and view fields.
Jao400Split	Create a Jao400Split for the specified file, list fields, and view fields.

Overview Package **Class** **Tree** **Deprecated** **Index** **Help**
PREV CLASS **NEXT CLASS**   **FRAMES** **NO FRAMES**
SUMMARY: INNER | FIELD | CONSTR | METHOD   DETAIL: FIELD | CONSTR | METHOD

com.pbd.pub.jao400

Class Jao400

```
java.lang.Object
   |
   +-com.pbd.pub.jao400.Jao400
```

public class **Jao400**
extends java.lang.Object
Since:
   1.2P

Constructor Summary

Jao400()

Appendix C: Javadoc

Method Summary

`static void`	**setAS400**`(java.lang.String initName)` Sets the default value for the system name.
`static void`	**setAS400**`(java.lang.String initName, java.lang.String initUser)` Sets default values for user ID and password.
`static void`	**setAS400**`(java.lang.String initName, java.lang.String initUser, java.lang.String initPassword)` Sets default values for system name, user ID, and password, bypassing the logon panel entirely.
`static void`	**setLibrary**`(java.lang.String newLibrary)` PBD (c) 1999
`static void`	**setLookAndFeel**`(java.lang.String newLookAndFeel)` PBD (c) 1999

Methods inherited from class java.lang.Object

`equals, getClass, hashCode, notify, notifyAll, toString, wait, wait, wait`

Constructor Detail

Jao400

`public Jao400()`

Method Detail

setAS400

`public static void setAS400(java.lang.String initName)`

Sets the default value for the system name. This will cause the logon panel to be displayed with the system name protected. The user must enter user ID and password. The logon panel is displayed the first time a JDB/400 file object is created.

Example use:

`Jao400.setAS400("myas400.mydomain.com");`
Parameters:
initName - is the AS/400 system name in domain format

setAS400

```
public static void setAS400(java.lang.String initName,
                            java.lang.String initUser)
```
Sets default values for user ID and password. This will cause the logon panel to be displayed with the system name protected and the user ID filled in. The user must enter the password. The logon panel is displayed the first time a JDB/400 file object is created.

Example use:

```
Jao400.setAS400("myas400.mydomain.com", "myuserid");
```
Parameters:
initName - is the AS/400 system name in domain format
initUser - is the AS/400 user ID

setAS400

```
public static void setAS400(java.lang.String initName,
                            java.lang.String initUser,
                            java.lang.String initPassword)
```
Sets default values for system name, user ID, and password, bypassing the logon panel entirely. **The problem is that the password is in your program as clear text, so it is not secure.**

Example use:

```
Jao400.setAS400("myas400.mydomain.com", "myuserid", "mypassword");
```
Parameters:
initName - is the AS/400 system name in domain format
initUser - is the AS/400 user ID
initPassword - is the password for the user ID

setLibrary

```
public static void setLibrary(java.lang.String newLibrary)
```
PBD (c) 1999
Parameters:
newLibrary - java.lang.String

setLookAndFeel

```
public static void setLookAndFeel(java.lang.String newLookAndFeel)
```
PBD (c) 1999
Parameters:
newLookAndFeel - java.lang.String

Appendix C: Javadoc

| Overview | Package | **Class** | Tree | Deprecated | Index | Help |

PREV CLASS NEXT CLASS   FRAMES   NO FRAMES
SUMMARY: INNER | FIELD | CONSTR | METHOD   DETAIL: FIELD | CONSTR | METHOD

---

com.pbd.pub.jao400

Class Jao400Display

```
java.lang.Object
  |
  +-com.pbd.pub.jbui.JbuiScreen
       |
       +-com.pbd.pub.jbui.JbuiDisplay
            |
            +-com.pbd.pub.jao400.Jao400Display
```

All Implemented Interfaces:
JbuiConstants, javax.swing.SwingConstants

---

public class **Jao400Display**
extends JbuiDisplay

Jao400Display is a standard display panel. It is used to display data from a single record from a Jdb400File. While useful in its own right, Jao400Display is meant to be a template for other, more complex classes.

Jao400Display requires a Jdb400File object and an array of field names. It will then build a display for the specified fields, with a single cancel button. Information about the fields is obtained from the Jdb400File object. When EXFMT() is executed, the panel is displayed and when Cancel (or F12) is hit, the panel is hidden.

Data for the panel is specified using the setHandle() method. setHandle expects an Object that can be downcast to a Record from the associated Jdb400File. An invalid object will cause an uncaught exception.

Of special note is the buildScreen() method. This is inherited from the highest level class in JBUI, the JbuiScreen. buildScreen() is executed automatically during the first call to EXFMT(). By subclassing this method, Jao400Display can dynamically create a JbuiFieldPanel and a JbuiButtonPanel based on the file and field names specified. The superclass version of buildScreen() is then called to create the appropriate Swing components.

This technique of subclassing buildScreen is used throughout JBUI and JAO/400.

Since:
    1.1P

Appendix C: Javadoc

Constructor Summary

Jao400Display ()
  Builds an empty Jao400Display.

Jao400Display (Jdb400File initFile)
  Builds a Jao400Display for the specified file.

Jao400Display (Jdb400File initFile, java.lang.String[] initFieldNames)
  Builds a Jao400Display for the specified file and the specified field names.

Jao400Display (java.lang.String initFileName)
  Builds a Jao400Display for the specified file name.

Jao400Display (java.lang.String initFileName, java.lang.String[] initFieldNames)
  Builds a Jao400Display for the specified file name and fields names.

Method Summary

java.lang.String[]	**getFieldNames** ()	Returns the field names to display for this record.
java.lang.String	**getFileName** ()	Returns the AS/400 file name.
void	**setFieldNames** (java.lang.String[] newFieldNames)	Sets the field names to display for a record.
void	**setFile** (Jdb400File newFile)	Sets the Jdb400File object to use for this display.
void	**setFileName** (java.lang.String newFileName)	Sets the name of the AS/400 file to use.
void	**setHandle** (java.lang.Object newHandle)	Process a change in handle.

Methods inherited from class com.pbd.pub.jbui.JbuiDisplay

clearData, clearErrors, getData, getData, getFieldPanel, setData, setData, setError, setError, setError, setFieldPanel, setProtect, setProtect, setProtect

Methods inherited from class com.pbd.pub.jbui.JbuiScreen

EXFMT, getFrame, getPosition, getPressedButton, isSomeoneWaiting, jbuiNotify, jbuiNotify, READ, setButtonPanel, setOwner, setPosition, setTitle, WRITE

Methods inherited from class java.lang.Object

equals, getClass, hashCode, notify, notifyAll, toString, wait, wait, wait

Appendix C: Javadoc

Constructor Detail

Jao400Display

```
public Jao400Display()
```
    Builds an empty Jao400Display.

Jao400Display

```
public Jao400Display(Jdb400File initFile)
```
    Builds a Jao400Display for the specified file.

Jao400Display

```
public Jao400Display(Jdb400File initFile,
                    java.lang.String[] initFieldNames)
```
    Builds a Jao400Display for the specified file and the specified field names.

Jao400Display

```
public Jao400Display(java.lang.String initFileName)
```
    Builds a Jao400Display for the specified file name.

Jao400Display

```
public Jao400Display(java.lang.String initFileName,
                    java.lang.String[] initFieldNames)
```
    Builds a Jao400Display for the specified file name and fields names.

Method Detail

getFieldNames

```
public java.lang.String[] getFieldNames()
```
    Returns the field names to display for this record.
    Returns:
        the field names to display for this record.

getFileName

```
public java.lang.String getFileName()
```
    Returns the AS/400 file name.
    Returns:
        the AS/400 file name.

setFieldNames

```
public void setFieldNames(java.lang.String[] newFieldNames)
```
    Sets the field names to display for a record.
    Parameters:
    newFieldNames - - the names of the fields to display.

setFile

```
public void setFile(Jdb400File newFile)
```
    Sets the Jdb400File object to use for this display.
    Parameters:
    newFile - - the Jdb400File to use.

setFileName

```
public void setFileName(java.lang.String newFileName)
```
    Sets the name of the AS/400 file to use.
    Parameters:
    newFileName - - the AS/400 file name to use.

setHandle

```
public void setHandle(java.lang.Object newHandle)
```
    Process a change in handle. The setHandle method copies the data from a record to the display using the field names in the fieldName array.
    Overrides:
    setHandle in class JbuiDisplay
    Parameters:
    handle - - JBUI passes a type Object, which is then downcast to Record.

Appendix C: Javadoc

Overview Package **Class** Tree Deprecated Index Help
PREV CLASS **NEXT CLASS**   **FRAMES** **NO FRAMES**
SUMMARY: INNER | FIELD | CONSTR | METHOD   DETAIL: FIELD | CONSTR | METHOD

com.pbd.pub.jao400

Class Jao400Field

```
java.lang.Object
  |
  +-com.pbd.pub.jao400.Jao400Field
```

public class **Jao400Field**
extends java.lang.Object

This type was created in VisualAge. Jao400Field is used to map database data to screen fields. This class will be greatly extended in future releases to include editing information, prompt information, and so on.

Since:
    1.1P

Constructor Summary

Jao400Field()   Creates a default Jao400Field.
Jao400Field(Jdb400Field `jdbField`)   Builds a Jao400Field for the specified Jdb400Field.
Jao400Field(`java.lang.String initName, java.lang.String initDescription, int initLength`)   Build a Jao400Field of the specified name, description, and length.
Jao400Field(`java.lang.String initName, java.lang.String initColumnHeading, java.lang.String initDescription, int initLength`)   Build a Jao400Field of the specified name, column heading, description, and length.

Method Summary

`java.lang.String`	**getColumnHeading**() Gets the column heading for this field.
`java.lang.String`	**getDescription**() Gets the description for this field.
`int`	**getLength**() Gets the length for this field.
`java.lang.String`	**getName**() Gets the name for this field.

Appendix C: Javadoc

static Jao400Field[]	**makeFields**(Jdb400File file, java.lang.String[] fieldNames) Build an array of Jao400Fields for a given Jdb400File.	
static java.util.Vector	**recordToVector**(com.pbd.pub.jao400.Record record, Jao400Field[] jaoFields) Builds a vector of objects based on the data in a record.	
void	**setColumnHeading**(java.lang.String newColumnHeading) Sets the column heading for this field.	
void	**setDescription**(java.lang.String newDescription) Sets the description for this field.	
void	**setLength**(int newLength) Sets the length (in pixels) for this field.	
void	**setName**(java.lang.String newName) Sets the name for this field.	

Methods inherited from class java.lang.Object

equals, getClass, hashCode, notify, notifyAll, toString, wait, wait, wait

Constructor Detail

Jao400Field

public **Jao400Field**()
    Creates a default Jao400Field.

Jao400Field

public **Jao400Field**(Jdb400Field jdbField)
    Builds a Jao400Field for the specified Jdb400Field. This is used to convert a database field directly to a display field.
    Parameters:
    jdbField - - the Jdb400Field to use as a template.

Jao400Field

public **Jao400Field**(java.lang.String initName,
                      java.lang.String initDescription,
                      int initLength)
    Build a Jao400Field of the specified name, description, and length.
    Parameters:
    initName - - the field name.
    initDescription - - the field description.
    initLength - - the field length in characters.

Appendix C: Javadoc

Jao400Field

```
public Jao400Field(java.lang.String initName,
                   java.lang.String initColumnHeading,
                   java.lang.String initDescription,
                   int initLength)
```
Build a Jao400Field of the specified name, column heading, description, and length.
Parameters:
initName - - the field name.
initColumnHeading - - the column heading.
initDescription - - the field description.
initLength - - the field length in characters.

Method Detail

getColumnHeading

```
public java.lang.String getColumnHeading()
```
Gets the column heading for this field.
Returns:
the column heading for this field.

getDescription

```
public java.lang.String getDescription()
```
Gets the description for this field.
Returns:
the description for this field.

getLength

```
public int getLength()
```
Gets the length for this field.
Returns:
the length for this field.

getName

```
public java.lang.String getName()
```
Gets the name for this field.
Returns:
the name for this field.

makeFields

```
public static Jao400Field[] makeFields(Jdb400File file,
                                       java.lang.String[] fieldNames)
```
Build an array of Jao400Fields for a given Jdb400File.

Parameters:
file - - the Jdb400File to process.
fieldNames - - the array of field names to process.
Returns:
an array of Jao400Fields (or errors if the name wasn't found).

recordToVector

public static java.util.Vector **recordToVector**(com.pbd.pub.jao400.Record record,
                                                 Jao400Field[] jaoFields)

Builds a vector of objects based on the data in a record. The Jao400Field array defines the names and order of fields to add to the vector.
Parameters:
record - - the record to extract data from.
jaoFields - - the array of Jao400Fields that determine the data to extract.
Returns:
a vector of objects containing the data from the record.

setColumnHeading

public void **setColumnHeading**(java.lang.String newColumnHeading)
Sets the column heading for this field.
Parameters:
newColumnHeading - - the new column heading for this field.

setDescription

public void **setDescription**(java.lang.String newDescription)
Sets the description for this field.
Parameters:
newDescription - - the new description for this field.

setLength

public void **setLength**(int newLength)
Sets the length (in pixels) for this field.
Parameters:
newLength - - the new length for this field.

setName

public void **setName**(java.lang.String newName)
Sets the name for this field.
Parameters:
newName - - the new name for this field.

Appendix C: Javadoc

| Overview | Package | **Class** | Tree | Deprecated | Index | Help |

PREV CLASS NEXT CLASS
SUMMARY: INNER | FIELD | CONSTR | METHOD

FRAMES NO FRAMES
DETAIL: FIELD | CONSTR | METHOD

com.pbd.pub.jao400

Class Jao400List

```
java.lang.Object
  |
  +-com.pbd.pub.jbui.JbuiScreen
        |
        +-com.pbd.pub.jbui.JbuiList
              |
              +-com.pbd.pub.jao400.Jao400List
```

All Implemented Interfaces:
 JbuiConstants, javax.swing.SwingConstants

---

public class **Jao400List**
extends JbuiList

Create a Jao400List for the specified file, list fields, and view fields.

Since:
 1.1P

Constructor Summary

Jao400List()
  Build a default Jao400List.

Jao400List(java.lang.String initFileName)
  Build a Jao400List for the specified AS/400 file name.

Jao400List(java.lang.String initFileName, java.lang.String[] initListFieldNames)
  Build a Jao400List for the specified AS/400 file name and field names.

Jao400List(java.lang.String initFileName, java.lang.String[] initListFieldNames, java.lang.String[] initViewFieldNames)
  Build a Jao400List for the specified AS/400 file name and field names.

Method Summary

Jdb400File	**getFile**() Returns the Jdb400File object.
java.lang.String	**getFileName**() Returns the AS/400 file name.
java.lang.String[]	**getListFieldNames**() Returns the list field names.

312

Appendix C: Javadoc

java.lang.String[]	**getViewFieldNames**() Returns the view field names.	
void	**setFileName**(java.lang.String newFileName) Sets the AS/400 file name.	
void	**setListFieldNames**(java.lang.String[] newListFieldNames) Sets the new list field names.	
void	**setViewFieldNames**(java.lang.String[] newViewFieldNames) Sets the new view field names.	

Methods inherited from class com.pbd.pub.jbui.JbuiList

getModel, getSelectedHandle, getViewClass, getViewer, setModel, setViewClass, setViewClass, setViewer, setViewer, setViewerPosition

Methods inherited from class com.pbd.pub.jbui.JbuiScreen

EXFMT, getFrame, getPosition, getPressedButton, isSomeoneWaiting, jbuiNotify, jbuiNotify, READ, setButtonPanel, setHandle, setOwner, setPosition, setTitle, WRITE

Methods inherited from class java.lang.Object

equals, getClass, hashCode, notify, notifyAll, toString, wait, wait, wait

Constructor Detail

Jao400List

```
public Jao400List()
```
Build a default Jao400List.

Jao400List

```
public Jao400List(java.lang.String initFileName)
```
Build a Jao400List for the specified AS/400 file name.

Jao400List

```
public Jao400List(java.lang.String initFileName,
                  java.lang.String[] initListFieldNames)
```
Build a Jao400List for the specified AS/400 file name and field names.

313

Appendix C: Javadoc

Jao400List

```
public Jao400List(java.lang.String initFileName,
                  java.lang.String[] initListFieldNames,
                  java.lang.String[] initViewFieldNames)
```
    Build a Jao400List for the specified AS/400 file name and field names. (Note: the view field names parameter doesn't work yet.)

Method Detail

getFile

```
public Jdb400File getFile()
```
    Returns the Jdb400File object.
    Returns:
    the Jdb400File object.

getFileName

```
public java.lang.String getFileName()
```
    Returns the AS/400 file name.
    Returns:
    the AS/400 file name.

getListFieldNames

```
public java.lang.String[] getListFieldNames()
```
    Returns the list field names.
    Returns:
    the list field names.

getViewFieldNames

```
public java.lang.String[] getViewFieldNames()
```
    Returns the view field names.
    Returns:
    the view field names.

setFileName

```
public void setFileName(java.lang.String newFileName)
```
    Sets the AS/400 file name.
    Parameters:
    newFileName - - the new AS/400 file name.

setListFieldNames

public void **setListFieldNames**(java.lang.String[] newListFieldNames)
>Sets the new list field names.
>**Parameters:**
>newListFieldNames - - the new list field names.

setViewFieldNames

public void **setViewFieldNames**(java.lang.String[] newViewFieldNames)
>Sets the new view field names. (Note: the view field names are not enabled in this release.)
>**Parameters:**
>newListFieldNames - - the new view field names.

Overview Package **Class** Tree Deprecated Index Help
PREV CLASS   NEXT CLASS   FRAMES   NO FRAMES
SUMMARY: INNER | FIELD | CONSTR | METHOD   DETAIL: FIELD | CONSTR | METHOD

---

com.pbd.pub.jao400

Class Jao400Split

```
java.lang.Object
   |
   +-com.pbd.pub.jbui.JbuiScreen
          |
          +-com.pbd.pub.jbui.JbuiSplit
                 |
                 +-com.pbd.pub.jao400.Jao400Split
```

All Implemented Interfaces:
>JbuiConstants, javax.swing.SwingConstants

---

public class **Jao400Split**
extends JbuiSplit

Create a Jao400Split for the specified file, list fields, and view fields.

Since:
>1.2P

315

Constructor Summary

Jao400Split()
  Build a default Jao400List.

Jao400Split(java.lang.String initFileName)
  Build a Jao400List for the specified AS/400 file name.

Jao400Split(java.lang.String initFileName, java.lang.String[] initListFieldNames)
  Build a Jao400List for the specified AS/400 file name and field names.

Jao400Split(java.lang.String initFileName, java.lang.String[] initListFieldNames, java.lang.String[] initViewFieldNames)
  Build a Jao400List for the specified AS/400 file name and field names.

Method Summary

Jdb400File	**getFile**()	Returns the Jdb400File object.
java.lang.String	**getFileName**()	Returns the AS/400 file name.
java.lang.String[]	**getListFieldNames**()	Returns the list field names.
java.lang.String[]	**getViewFieldNames**()	Returns the view field names.
void	**setFileName**(java.lang.String newFileName)	Sets the AS/400 file name.
void	**setHandle**(java.lang.Object newHandle)	Process a change in handle.
void	**setListFieldNames**(java.lang.String[] newListFieldNames)	Sets the new list field names.
void	**setViewFieldNames**(java.lang.String[] newViewFieldNames)	Sets the new view field names.

Methods inherited from class com.pbd.pub.jbui.JbuiSplit

getFieldPanel, getSelectedHandle, getSelectMode, setFieldPanel, setModel, setOrientation, setSelectMode

Methods inherited from class com.pbd.pub.jbui.JbuiScreen

EXFMT, getFrame, getPosition, getPressedButton, isSomeoneWaiting, jbuiNotify, jbuiNotify, READ, setButtonPanel, setOwner, setPosition, setTitle, WRITE

Methods inherited from class java.lang.Object

equals, getClass, hashCode, notify, notifyAll, toString, wait, wait, wait

Appendix C: Javadoc

Constructor Detail

Jao400Split

```
public Jao400Split()
```
        Build a default Jao400List.

Jao400Split

```
public Jao400Split(java.lang.String initFileName)
```
        Build a Jao400List for the specified AS/400 file name.

Jao400Split

```
public Jao400Split(java.lang.String initFileName,
                   java.lang.String[] initListFieldNames)
```
        Build a Jao400List for the specified AS/400 file name and field names.

Jao400Split

```
public Jao400Split(java.lang.String initFileName,
                   java.lang.String[] initListFieldNames,
                   java.lang.String[] initViewFieldNames)
```
        Build a Jao400List for the specified AS/400 file name and field names. (Note: the view field names parameter doesn't work yet).

Method Detail

getFile

```
public Jdb400File getFile()
```
        Returns the Jdb400File object.
        Returns:
        the Jdb400File object.

getFileName

```
public java.lang.String getFileName()
```
        Returns the AS/400 file name.
        Returns:
        the AS/400 file name.

getListFieldNames

```
public java.lang.String[] getListFieldNames()
```
        Returns the list field names.
        Returns:
        the list field names.

Appendix C: Javadoc

getViewFieldNames

```
public java.lang.String[] getViewFieldNames()
```
    Returns the view field names.
    Returns:
    the view field names.

setFileName

```
public void setFileName(java.lang.String newFileName)
```
    Sets the AS/400 file name.
    Parameters:
    `newFileName` - - the new AS/400 file name.

setHandle

```
public void setHandle(java.lang.Object newHandle)
```
    Process a change in handle. The setHandle method copies the data from a record to the display using the field names in the fieldName array.
    Overrides:
    setHandle in class JbuiScreen
    Parameters:
    `handle` - - JBUI passes a type Object, which is then downcast to Record.

setListFieldNames

```
public void setListFieldNames(java.lang.String[] newListFieldNames)
```
    Sets the new list field names.
    Parameters:
    `newListFieldNames` - - the new list field names.

setViewFieldNames

```
public void setViewFieldNames(java.lang.String[] newViewFieldNames)
```
    Sets the new view field names. (Note: the view field names are not enabled in this release.)
    Parameters:
    `newListFieldNames` - - the new view field names.

Appendix C: Javadoc

Overview **Package** Class Tree Deprecated Index Help
PREV PACKAGE   NEXT PACKAGE   FRAMES   NO FRAMES

Package com.pbd.pub.jbui

Interface Summary

JbuiConstants	These constants provide positional information.

Class Summary

JbuiButton	This type was created in VisualAge.
JbuiButtonPanel	JbuiButtonPanel is a one of the main components of a JbuiDisplay.
JbuiCancelButton	This is a convenience class.
JbuiDisplay	JbuiDisplay is the class used to emulate a 5250 display panel.
JbuiEntryField	JbuiEntryField is the main input/output component for a JbuiDisplay.
JbuiFieldPanel	JbuiFieldPanel is a UI component that presents an array of JbuiEntryFields vertically.
JbuiList	JbuiList is the class used to emulate a subfile select panel.
JbuiListModel	JbuiListModel is the table model used by JbuiList objects.
JbuiListPanel	JbuiList is the class used to emulate a subfile select panel.
JbuiOutputField	This is a convenience type.
JbuiScreen	JbuiScreen is the superclass for the other JBUI windows, such as JbuiDisplay and JbuiList.
JbuiScreenThread	JbuiScreenThread is a specialized thread designed specifically to display a JbuiScreen.
JbuiSplit	JbuiSplit is not directly analogous to any specific AS/400 screen type.

Appendix C: Javadoc

| Overview | Package | **Class** | Tree | Deprecated | Index | Help |

PREV CLASS NEXT CLASS   **FRAMES   NO FRAMES**
SUMMARY: INNER | FIELD | CONSTR | METHOD   DETAIL: FIELD | CONSTR | METHOD

---

com.pbd.pub.jbui

Interface JbuiConstants

All Superinterfaces:
   javax.swing.SwingConstants
All Known Implementing Classes:
   JbuiScreen

---

public interface **JbuiConstants**
extends javax.swing.SwingConstants

These constants provide positional information. They extend the normal Swing positional notation of compass points, such as NORTH_EAST and SOUTH. Note that this version does a very dangerous thing: it assumes that the Swing constants will range from zero to a positive number less than 256. We do this so that we can easily add some additional attributes, such as RELATIVE_TO_OWNER by specifying:

NORTH_EAST+RELATIVE_TO_OWNER

which indicates the window should be to the immediate right of the owner and at the same height. The concept of an owner window seems to be missing from JFC; it specifies the window that created this window and in more complex applications allows specific interactions. Today, the owner window is simply used for positioning.

Since:
   1.0P

Field Summary

static int	DOUBLECLICK_DISPLAY
static int	OVER
static int	RELATIVE_TO_OWNER
static int	SELECT_DISPLAY
static int	SELECT_DISPLAY_AND_DOUBLECLICK_DRILL
static int	UNDER

Fields inherited from interface javax.swing.SwingConstants

BOTTOM, CENTER, EAST, HORIZONTAL, LEADING, LEFT, NORTH, NORTH_EAST, NORTH_WEST, RIGHT, SOUTH, SOUTH_EAST, SOUTH_WEST, TOP, TRAILING, VERTICAL, WEST

Field Detail

RELATIVE_TO_OWNER

public static final int **RELATIVE_TO_OWNER**

UNDER

public static final int **UNDER**

OVER

public static final int **OVER**

SELECT_DISPLAY

public static final int **SELECT_DISPLAY**

DOUBLECLICK_DISPLAY

public static final int **DOUBLECLICK_DISPLAY**

SELECT_DISPLAY_AND_DOUBLECLICK_DRILL

public static final int **SELECT_DISPLAY_AND_DOUBLECLICK_DRILL**

Appendix C: Javadoc

Overview Package **Class** Tree Deprecated Index Help
PREV CLASS   NEXT CLASS   FRAMES   NO FRAMES
SUMMARY: INNER | FIELD | CONSTR | METHOD   DETAIL: FIELD | CONSTR | METHOD

com.pbd.pub.jbui

Class JbuiButton

```
java.lang.Object
  |
  +-java.awt.Component
      |
      +-java.awt.Container
          |
          +-javax.swing.JComponent
              |
              +-javax.swing.AbstractButton
                  |
                  +-javax.swing.JButton
                      |
                      +-com.pbd.pub.jbui.JbuiButton
```

All Implemented Interfaces:
    javax.accessibility.Accessible, java.awt.image.ImageObserver, java.awt.ItemSelectable, java.awt.MenuContainer, java.io.Serializable, javax.swing.SwingConstants

---

public class **JbuiButton**
extends javax.swing.JButton

This type was created in VisualAge.

See Also:
    Serialized Form

Inner classes inherited from class javax.swing.JComponent

`javax.swing.JComponent.AccessibleJComponent`

Fields inherited from class javax.swing.AbstractButton

`BORDER_PAINTED_CHANGED_PROPERTY, CONTENT_AREA_FILLED_CHANGED_PROPERTY, DISABLED_ICON_CHANGED_PROPERTY, DISABLED_SELECTED_ICON_CHANGED_PROPERTY, FOCUS_PAINTED_CHANGED_PROPERTY, HORIZONTAL_ALIGNMENT_CHANGED_PROPERTY, HORIZONTAL_TEXT_POSITION_CHANGED_PROPERTY, ICON_CHANGED_PROPERTY, MARGIN_CHANGED_PROPERTY, MNEMONIC_CHANGED_PROPERTY, MODEL_CHANGED_PROPERTY, PRESSED_ICON_CHANGED_PROPERTY, ROLLOVER_ENABLED_CHANGED_PROPERTY, ROLLOVER_ICON_CHANGED_PROPERTY, ROLLOVER_SELECTED_ICON_CHANGED_PROPERTY, SELECTED_ICON_CHANGED_PROPERTY, TEXT_CHANGED_PROPERTY, VERTICAL_ALIGNMENT_CHANGED_PROPERTY, VERTICAL_TEXT_POSITION_CHANGED_PROPERTY`

Fields inherited from class javax.swing.JComponent

TOOL_TIP_TEXT_KEY, UNDEFINED_CONDITION, WHEN_ANCESTOR_OF_FOCUSED_COMPONENT, WHEN_FOCUSED, WHEN_IN_FOCUSED_WINDOW

Fields inherited from class java.awt.Component

BOTTOM_ALIGNMENT, CENTER_ALIGNMENT, LEFT_ALIGNMENT, RIGHT_ALIGNMENT, TOP_ALIGNMENT

Constructor Summary

JbuiButton(int id, java.lang.String text)
   JbuiButton constructor comment.

JbuiButton(int id, java.lang.String text, java.awt.event.ActionListener listener)
   JbuiButton constructor comment.

JbuiButton(int id, java.lang.String text, java.awt.event.ActionListener listener, boolean fkey)
   JbuiButton constructor comment.

JbuiButton(int id, java.lang.String text, boolean fkey)
   JbuiButton constructor comment.

Method Summary

java.lang.String	**createButtonText**(java.lang.String text, int fkey) This method was created in VisualAge.
int	**getId**() This method was created in VisualAge.
java.awt.event.ActionListener	**getListener**() This method was created in VisualAge.
java.lang.String	**getText**() This method was created in VisualAge.
boolean	**getUsesFkey**() This method was created in VisualAge.

Methods inherited from class javax.swing.JButton

getAccessibleContext, getUIClassID, isDefaultButton, isDefaultCapable, removeNotify, setDefaultCapable, updateUI

Appendix C: Javadoc

Methods inherited from class javax.swing.AbstractButton

addActionListener, addChangeListener, addItemListener, doClick, doClick, getAction, getActionCommand, getDisabledIcon, getDisabledSelectedIcon, getHorizontalAlignment, getHorizontalTextPosition, getIcon, getLabel, getMargin, getMnemonic, getModel, getPressedIcon, getRolloverIcon, getRolloverSelectedIcon, getSelectedIcon, getSelectedObjects, getUI, getVerticalAlignment, getVerticalTextPosition, isBorderPainted, isContentAreaFilled, isFocusPainted, isRolloverEnabled, isSelected, removeActionListener, removeChangeListener, removeItemListener, setAction, setActionCommand, setBorderPainted, setContentAreaFilled, setDisabledIcon, setDisabledSelectedIcon, setEnabled, setFocusPainted, setHorizontalAlignment, setHorizontalTextPosition, setIcon, setLabel, setMargin, setMnemonic, setMnemonic, setModel, setPressedIcon, setRolloverEnabled, setRolloverIcon, setRolloverSelectedIcon, setSelected, setSelectedIcon, setText, setUI, setVerticalAlignment, setVerticalTextPosition

Methods inherited from class javax.swing.JComponent

addAncestorListener, addNotify, addPropertyChangeListener, addPropertyChangeListener, addVetoableChangeListener, computeVisibleRect, contains, createToolTip, firePropertyChange, firePropertyChange, firePropertyChange, firePropertyChange, firePropertyChange, firePropertyChange, firePropertyChange, firePropertyChange, getActionForKeyStroke, getActionMap, getAlignmentX, getAlignmentY, getAutoscrolls, getBorder, getBounds, getClientProperty, getConditionForKeyStroke, getDebugGraphicsOptions, getGraphics, getHeight, getInputMap, getInputMap, getInputVerifier, getInsets, getInsets, getListeners, getLocation, getMaximumSize, getMinimumSize, getNextFocusableComponent, getPreferredSize, getRegisteredKeyStrokes, getRootPane, getSize, getToolTipLocation, getToolTipText, getToolTipText, getTopLevelAncestor, getVerifyInputWhenFocusTarget, getVisibleRect, getWidth, getX, getY, grabFocus, hasFocus, hide, isDoubleBuffered, isFocusCycleRoot, isFocusTraversable, isLightweightComponent, isManagingFocus, isOpaque, isOptimizedDrawingEnabled, isPaintingTile, isRequestFocusEnabled, isValidateRoot, paint, paintImmediately, paintImmediately, print, printAll, putClientProperty, registerKeyboardAction, registerKeyboardAction, removeAncestorListener, removePropertyChangeListener, removePropertyChangeListener, removeVetoableChangeListener, repaint, repaint, requestDefaultFocus, requestFocus, resetKeyboardActions, reshape, revalidate, scrollRectToVisible, setActionMap, setAlignmentX, setAlignmentY, setAutoscrolls, setBackground, setBorder, setDebugGraphicsOptions, setDoubleBuffered, setFont, setForeground, setInputMap, setInputVerifier, setMaximumSize, setMinimumSize, setNextFocusableComponent, setOpaque, setPreferredSize, setRequestFocusEnabled, setToolTipText, setVerifyInputWhenFocusTarget, setVisible, unregisterKeyboardAction, update

Methods inherited from class java.awt.Container

add, add, add, add, add, addContainerListener, countComponents, deliverEvent, doLayout, findComponentAt, findComponentAt, getComponent, getComponentAt, getComponentAt, getComponentCount, getComponents, getLayout, insets, invalidate, isAncestorOf, layout, list, list, locate, minimumSize, paintComponents, preferredSize, printComponents, remove, remove, removeAll, removeContainerListener, setCursor, setLayout, validate

Appendix C: Javadoc

Methods inherited from class java.awt.Component

action, add, addComponentListener, addFocusListener, addHierarchyBoundsListener, addHierarchyListener, addInputMethodListener, addKeyListener, addMouseListener, addMouseMotionListener, bounds, checkImage, checkImage, contains, createImage, createImage, disable, dispatchEvent, enable, enable, enableInputMethods, getBackground, getBounds, getColorModel, getComponentOrientation, getCursor, getDropTarget, getFont, getFontMetrics, getForeground, getGraphicsConfiguration, getInputContext, getInputMethodRequests, getLocale, getLocation, getLocationOnScreen, getName, getParent, getPeer, getSize, getToolkit, getTreeLock, gotFocus, handleEvent, imageUpdate, inside, isDisplayable, isEnabled, isLightweight, isShowing, isValid, isVisible, keyDown, keyUp, list, list, list, location, lostFocus, mouseDown, mouseDrag, mouseEnter, mouseExit, mouseMove, mouseUp, move, nextFocus, paintAll, postEvent, prepareImage, prepareImage, remove, removeComponentListener, removeFocusListener, removeHierarchyBoundsListener, removeHierarchyListener, removeInputMethodListener, removeKeyListener, removeMouseListener, removeMouseMotionListener, repaint, repaint, repaint, resize, resize, setBounds, setBounds, setComponentOrientation, setDropTarget, setLocale, setLocation, setLocation, setName, setSize, setSize, show, show, size, toString, transferFocus

Methods inherited from class java.lang.Object

equals, getClass, hashCode, notify, notifyAll, wait, wait, wait

Constructor Detail

JbuiButton

public **JbuiButton**(int id,
                java.lang.String text)

JbuiButton constructor comment.
Parameters:
arg1 - java.lang.String

JbuiButton

public **JbuiButton**(int id,
                java.lang.String text,
                java.awt.event.ActionListener listener)

JbuiButton constructor comment.
Parameters:
arg1 - java.lang.String

JbuiButton

public **JbuiButton**(int id,
                java.lang.String text,
                java.awt.event.ActionListener listener,
                boolean fkey)

JbuiButton constructor comment.
Parameters:
arg1 - java.lang.String

JbuiButton

```
public JbuiButton(int id,
                  java.lang.String text,
                  boolean fkey)
```
JbuiButton constructor comment.
Parameters:
arg1 - java.lang.String

Method Detail

createButtonText

```
public java.lang.String createButtonText(java.lang.String text,
                                         int fkey)
```
This method was created in VisualAge.
Parameters:
text - java.lang.String
fkey - int
Returns:
java.lang.String

getId

```
public int getId()
```
This method was created in VisualAge.
Returns:
int

getListener

```
public java.awt.event.ActionListener getListener()
```
This method was created in VisualAge.
Returns:
java.awt.event.ActionListener

getText

```
public java.lang.String getText()
```
This method was created in VisualAge.
Overrides:
getText in class javax.swing.AbstractButton
Returns:
java.lang.String

getUsesFkey

```
public boolean getUsesFkey()
```
This method was created in VisualAge.
Returns:
boolean

Appendix C: Javadoc

| Overview | Package | **Class** | Tree | Deprecated | Index | Help |

PREV CLASS NEXT CLASS   FRAMES   NO FRAMES
SUMMARY: INNER | FIELD | CONSTR | METHOD   DETAIL: FIELD | CONSTR | METHOD

---

com.pbd.pub.jbui

Class JbuiButtonPanel

```
java.lang.Object
  |
  +-java.awt.Component
        |
        +-java.awt.Container
              |
              +-javax.swing.JComponent
                    |
                    +-javax.swing.JPanel
                          |
                          +-com.pbd.pub.jbui.JbuiButtonPanel
```

All Implemented Interfaces:
   javax.accessibility.Accessible, java.awt.image.ImageObserver, java.awt.MenuContainer, java.io.Serializable

Direct Known Subclasses:
   JbuiCancelButton

---

public class **JbuiButtonPanel**
extends javax.swing.JPanel

JbuiButtonPanel is a one of the main components of a JbuiDisplay. A JbuiButtonPanel defines the actions that can be performed by the user. There are several varieties of JbuiButtonPanel; in general, they all are used to support the EXFMT() method of the JbuiDisplay.

The constructors take arrays of parameters, each array containing one element for each button defined. The minimum parameter list is an array of strings for the button texts. The buttons are assigned sequential numbers from zero; when a button is pushed, the corresponding value is returned from the EXFMT() method (via the getPressedButton() method). A null value in the string array creates a gap.

The second form takes an array of texts like the first, as well as an array of integers, each representing a function key accelerator: 0 is Enter, 1-24 are F1-F24 respectively. The corresponding function key can be used in place of pressing the button, and is also added to the text of the button (for example, "F3="). Each button will return the corresponding function key value.

At this time, there are still some quirks with using the Enter key as an accelerator. This is most certainly because I've misunderstood some part of the event processing cycle. I hope to get it cleared up soon, but until then, please try to stick with using the function keys.

NOTE: Each form can also supply its own list of action listeners. This can be done if a key is intended to perform a discrete function without actually returning control to the user. This is one of the ways that JbuiButtonPanel begins to extend the block mode paradigm. Any key with a null listener will act as an EXFMT button, returning its position. Eventually, the user can design panels with no "EXFMT" buttons at all, moving to a true object architecture. Look for extended examples using this technique in the next release.

Appendix C: Javadoc

Since:
    1.0P
See Also:
    Serialized Form

Inner classes inherited from class javax.swing.JComponent

`javax.swing.JComponent.AccessibleJComponent`

Fields inherited from class javax.swing.JComponent

`TOOL_TIP_TEXT_KEY, UNDEFINED_CONDITION, WHEN_ANCESTOR_OF_FOCUSED_COMPONENT, WHEN_FOCUSED, WHEN_IN_FOCUSED_WINDOW`

Fields inherited from class java.awt.Component

`BOTTOM_ALIGNMENT, CENTER_ALIGNMENT, LEFT_ALIGNMENT, RIGHT_ALIGNMENT, TOP_ALIGNMENT`

Constructor Summary

JbuiButtonPanel(`JbuiButton[] buttons`)
    This method was created in VisualAge.

JbuiButtonPanel(`java.lang.String[] texts`)
    Creates a JbuiButtonPanel from an array of strings for the button texts.

JbuiButtonPanel(`java.lang.String[] texts, java.awt.event.ActionListener[] listeners`)
    Currently an unsupported internal variation

JbuiButtonPanel(`java.lang.String[] texts, java.awt.event.ActionListener[] listeners, int[] fkeys`)
    This is the internal constructor the other constructors use.

JbuiButtonPanel(`java.lang.String[] texts, int[] fkeys`)
    Creates a JbuiButtonPanel from an array of strings for the button texts and an array of function key identifiers each representing a function key accelerator: 0 is Enter, 1-24 are F1-F4 respectively.

Method Summary

void	**checkKey**(`java.awt.event.KeyEvent keyEvent`) This method was created in VisualAge.
int	**getPressedButton**() Return the button pressed.
void	**setButtons**(`JbuiButton[] newValue`) This method was created in VisualAge.
void	**setPressedButton**(`int button`) This method was created in VisualAge.
void	**setWaiter**(`JbuiScreen newWaiter`) This is an internal Jbui method used to communicate between a JbuiDisplay and the default button listener.

Appendix C: Javadoc

Methods inherited from class javax.swing.JPanel

getAccessibleContext, getUIClassID, updateUI

Methods inherited from class javax.swing.JComponent

addAncestorListener, addNotify, addPropertyChangeListener, addPropertyChangeListener, addVetoableChangeListener, computeVisibleRect, contains, createToolTip, firePropertyChange, firePropertyChange, firePropertyChange, firePropertyChange, firePropertyChange, firePropertyChange, firePropertyChange, firePropertyChange, getActionForKeyStroke, getActionMap, getAlignmentX, getAlignmentY, getAutoscrolls, getBorder, getBounds, getClientProperty, getConditionForKeyStroke, getDebugGraphicsOptions, getGraphics, getHeight, getInputMap, getInputMap, getInputVerifier, getInsets, getInsets, getListeners, getLocation, getMaximumSize, getMinimumSize, getNextFocusableComponent, getPreferredSize, getRegisteredKeyStrokes, getRootPane, getSize, getToolTipLocation, getToolTipText, getToolTipText, getTopLevelAncestor, getVerifyInputWhenFocusTarget, getVisibleRect, getWidth, getX, getY, grabFocus, hasFocus, hide, isDoubleBuffered, isFocusCycleRoot, isFocusTraversable, isLightweightComponent, isManagingFocus, isOpaque, isOptimizedDrawingEnabled, isPaintingTile, isRequestFocusEnabled, isValidateRoot, paint, paintImmediately, paintImmediately, print, printAll, putClientProperty, registerKeyboardAction, registerKeyboardAction, removeAncestorListener, removeNotify, removePropertyChangeListener, removePropertyChangeListener, removeVetoableChangeListener, repaint, repaint, requestDefaultFocus, requestFocus, resetKeyboardActions, reshape, revalidate, scrollRectToVisible, setActionMap, setAlignmentX, setAlignmentY, setAutoscrolls, setBackground, setBorder, setDebugGraphicsOptions, setDoubleBuffered, setEnabled, setFont, setForeground, setInputMap, setInputVerifier, setMaximumSize, setMinimumSize, setNextFocusableComponent, setOpaque, setPreferredSize, setRequestFocusEnabled, setToolTipText, setVerifyInputWhenFocusTarget, setVisible, unregisterKeyboardAction, update

Methods inherited from class java.awt.Container

add, add, add, add, add, addContainerListener, countComponents, deliverEvent, doLayout, findComponentAt, findComponentAt, getComponent, getComponentAt, getComponentAt, getComponentCount, getComponents, getLayout, insets, invalidate, isAncestorOf, layout, list, list, locate, minimumSize, paintComponents, preferredSize, printComponents, remove, remove, removeAll, removeContainerListener, setCursor, setLayout, validate

329

Appendix C: Javadoc

Methods inherited from class java.awt.Component

action, add, addComponentListener, addFocusListener, addHierarchyBoundsListener, addHierarchyListener, addInputMethodListener, addKeyListener, addMouseListener, addMouseMotionListener, bounds, checkImage, checkImage, contains, createImage, createImage, disable, dispatchEvent, enable, enable, enableInputMethods, getBackground, getBounds, getColorModel, getComponentOrientation, getCursor, getDropTarget, getFont, getFontMetrics, getForeground, getGraphicsConfiguration, getInputContext, getInputMethodRequests, getLocale, getLocation, getLocationOnScreen, getName, getParent, getPeer, getSize, getToolkit, getTreeLock, gotFocus, handleEvent, imageUpdate, inside, isDisplayable, isEnabled, isLightweight, isShowing, isValid, isVisible, keyDown, keyUp, list, list, list, location, lostFocus, mouseDown, mouseDrag, mouseEnter, mouseExit, mouseMove, mouseUp, move, nextFocus, paintAll, postEvent, prepareImage, prepareImage, remove, removeComponentListener, removeFocusListener, removeHierarchyBoundsListener, removeHierarchyListener, removeInputMethodListener, removeKeyListener, removeMouseListener, removeMouseMotionListener, repaint, repaint, repaint, resize, resize, setBounds, setBounds, setComponentOrientation, setDropTarget, setLocale, setLocation, setLocation, setName, setSize, setSize, show, show, size, toString, transferFocus

Methods inherited from class java.lang.Object

equals, getClass, hashCode, notify, notifyAll, wait, wait, wait

Constructor Detail

JbuiButtonPanel

public **JbuiButtonPanel**(JbuiButton[] buttons)

    This method was created in VisualAge.
    Parameters:
    buttons - com.pbd.pub.jbui.JbuiButton[]

JbuiButtonPanel

public **JbuiButtonPanel**(java.lang.String[] texts)

    Creates a JbuiButtonPanel from an array of strings for the button texts. The buttons are assigned sequential numbers from zero; when a button is pushed, the corresponding value is returned from the EXFMT() method (via the getPressedButton() method). A null value in the string array creates a gap.
    Parameters:
    texts - array of button texts.

JbuiButtonPanel

public **JbuiButtonPanel**(java.lang.String[] texts,
                         int[] fkeys)

    Creates a JbuiButtonPanel from an array of strings for the button texts and an array of function key identifiers each representing a function key accelerator: 0 is Enter, 1-24 are F1-F4 respectively. The corresponding function key can be used in place of pressing the button, and is also added to the text of the button (for example, "F3="). Each button will return the corresponding function key value.

Appendix C: Javadoc

Parameters:
texts - array of button texts.
fkeys - array of function key identifiers.

JbuiButtonPanel

```
public JbuiButtonPanel(java.lang.String[] texts,
                       java.awt.event.ActionListener[] listeners)
```
Currently an unsupported internal variation.

JbuiButtonPanel

```
public JbuiButtonPanel(java.lang.String[] texts,
                       java.awt.event.ActionListener[] listeners,
                       int[] fkeys)
```
This is the internal constructor the other constructors use. Currently, this variation is unsupported.

Method Detail

checkKey

```
public void checkKey(java.awt.event.KeyEvent keyEvent)
```
This method was created in VisualAge.
Parameters:
key - java.awt.event.KeyEvent

getPressedButton

```
public int getPressedButton()
```
Return the button pressed. This returns either the 0-based button index for non-accelerated JbuiButtonPanels, or the funtion key identifier for panels using function keys.
Returns:
the button identifier.

setButtons

```
public void setButtons(JbuiButton[] newValue)
```
This method was created in VisualAge.
Parameters:
buttons - JbuiButtons[]

setPressedButton

```
public void setPressedButton(int button)
```
This method was created in VisualAge.
Parameters:
button - int

331

Appendix C: Javadoc

setWaiter

```
public void setWaiter(JbuiScreen newWaiter)
```
    This is an internal Jbui method used to communicate between a JbuiDisplay and the default button listener.
    Parameters:
    newWaiter - the screen to notify when a button is pressed.

Overview Package **Class** Tree Deprecated Index Help
PREV CLASS   NEXT CLASS   FRAMES   NO FRAMES
SUMMARY: INNER | FIELD | CONSTR | METHOD   DETAIL: FIELD | CONSTR | METHOD

---

com.pbd.pub.jbui

Class JbuiCancelButton

```
java.lang.Object
  |
  +-java.awt.Component
        |
        +-java.awt.Container
              |
              +-javax.swing.JComponent
                    |
                    +-javax.swing.JPanel
                          |
                          +-com.pbd.pub.jbui.JbuiButtonPanel
                                |
                                +-com.pbd.pub.jbui.JbuiCancelButton
```

All Implemented Interfaces:
    javax.accessibility.Accessible, java.awt.image.ImageObserver, java.awt.MenuContainer, java.io.Serializable

---

public class **JbuiCancelButton**
extends JbuiButtonPanel

This is a convenience class. It provides a standard single-button panel with only F12=Cancel.

Since:
    1.0P
See Also:
    Serialized Form

Inner classes inherited from class javax.swing.JComponent

`javax.swing.JComponent.AccessibleJComponent`

Appendix C: Javadoc

Fields inherited from class javax.swing.Jcomponent

TOOL_TIP_TEXT_KEY, UNDEFINED_CONDITION, WHEN_ANCESTOR_OF_FOCUSED_COMPONENT, WHEN_FOCUSED, WHEN_IN_FOCUSED_WINDOW

Fields inherited from class java.awt.Component

BOTTOM_ALIGNMENT, CENTER_ALIGNMENT, LEFT_ALIGNMENT, RIGHT_ALIGNMENT, TOP_ALIGNMENT

Constructor Summary

JbuiCancelButton()
    This method was created in VisualAge.

Methods inherited from class com.pbd.pub.jbui.JbuiButtonPanel

checkKey, getPressedButton, setButtons, setPressedButton, setWaiter

Methods inherited from class javax.swing.Jpanel

getAccessibleContext, getUIClassID, updateUI

Methods inherited from class javax.swing.JComponent

addAncestorListener, addNotify, addPropertyChangeListener, addPropertyChangeListener, addVetoableChangeListener, computeVisibleRect, contains, createToolTip, firePropertyChange, firePropertyChange, firePropertyChange, firePropertyChange, firePropertyChange, firePropertyChange, firePropertyChange, firePropertyChange, getActionForKeyStroke, getActionMap, getAlignmentX, getAlignmentY, getAutoscrolls, getBorder, getBounds, getClientProperty, getConditionForKeyStroke, getDebugGraphicsOptions, getGraphics, getHeight, getInputMap, getInputMap, getInputVerifier, getInsets, getInsets, getListeners, getLocation, getMaximumSize, getMinimumSize, getNextFocusableComponent, getPreferredSize, getRegisteredKeyStrokes, getRootPane, getSize, getToolTipLocation, getToolTipText, getToolTipText, getTopLevelAncestor, getVerifyInputWhenFocusTarget, getVisibleRect, getWidth, getX, getY, grabFocus, hasFocus, hide, isDoubleBuffered, isFocusCycleRoot, isFocusTraversable, isLightweightComponent, isManagingFocus, isOpaque, isOptimizedDrawingEnabled, isPaintingTile, isRequestFocusEnabled, isValidateRoot, paint, paintImmediately, paintImmediately, print, printAll, putClientProperty, registerKeyboardAction, registerKeyboardAction, removeAncestorListener, removeNotify, removePropertyChangeListener, removePropertyChangeListener, removeVetoableChangeListener, repaint, repaint, requestDefaultFocus, requestFocus, resetKeyboardActions, reshape, revalidate, scrollRectToVisible, setActionMap, setAlignmentX, setAlignmentY, setAutoscrolls, setBackground, setBorder, setDebugGraphicsOptions, setDoubleBuffered, setEnabled, setFont, setForeground, setInputMap, setInputVerifier, setMaximumSize, setMinimumSize, setNextFocusableComponent, setOpaque, setPreferredSize, setRequestFocusEnabled, setToolTipText, setVerifyInputWhenFocusTarget, setVisible, unregisterKeyboardAction, update

333

Appendix C: Javadoc

Methods inherited from class java.awt.Container

add, add, add, add, add, addContainerListener, countComponents, deliverEvent, doLayout, findComponentAt, findComponentAt, getComponent, getComponentAt, getComponentAt, getComponentCount, getComponents, getLayout, insets, invalidate, isAncestorOf, layout, list, list, locate, minimumSize, paintComponents, preferredSize, printComponents, remove, remove, removeAll, removeContainerListener, setCursor, setLayout, validate

Methods inherited from class java.awt.Component

action, add, addComponentListener, addFocusListener, addHierarchyBoundsListener, addHierarchyListener, addInputMethodListener, addKeyListener, addMouseListener, addMouseMotionListener, bounds, checkImage, checkImage, contains, createImage, createImage, disable, dispatchEvent, enable, enable, enableInputMethods, getBackground, getBounds, getColorModel, getComponentOrientation, getCursor, getDropTarget, getFont, getFontMetrics, getForeground, getGraphicsConfiguration, getInputContext, getInputMethodRequests, getLocale, getLocation, getLocationOnScreen, getName, getParent, getPeer, getSize, getToolkit, getTreeLock, gotFocus, handleEvent, imageUpdate, inside, isDisplayable, isEnabled, isLightweight, isShowing, isValid, isVisible, keyDown, keyUp, list, list, list, location, lostFocus, mouseDown, mouseDrag, mouseEnter, mouseExit, mouseMove, mouseUp, move, nextFocus, paintAll, postEvent, prepareImage, prepareImage, remove, removeComponentListener, removeFocusListener, removeHierarchyBoundsListener, removeHierarchyListener, removeInputMethodListener, removeKeyListener, removeMouseListener, removeMouseMotionListener, repaint, repaint, repaint, resize, resize, setBounds, setBounds, setComponentOrientation, setDropTarget, setLocale, setLocation, setLocation, setName, setSize, setSize, show, show, size, toString, transferFocus

Methods inherited from class java.lang.Object

equals, getClass, hashCode, notify, notifyAll, wait, wait, wait

Constructor Detail

JbuiCancelButton

public **JbuiCancelButton**()
    This method was created in VisualAge.

Appendix C: Javadoc

Overview	Package	**Class**	Tree	Deprecated	Index	Help

PREV CLASS   NEXT CLASS   FRAMES   NO FRAMES
SUMMARY: INNER | FIELD | CONSTR | METHOD   DETAIL: FIELD | CONSTR | METHOD

com.pbd.pub.jbui

Class JbuiDisplay

```
java.lang.Object
  |
  +-com.pbd.pub.jbui.JbuiScreen
       |
       +-com.pbd.pub.jbui.JbuiDisplay
```
All Implemented Interfaces:
    JbuiConstants, javax.swing.SwingConstants
Direct Known Subclasses:
    Jao400Display, ScJdspfJbuiDisplay

public class **JbuiDisplay**
extends JbuiScreen

JbuiDisplay is the class used to emulate a 5250 display panel. The characteristics depend upon the constructor, and especially on the JbuiFieldPanel used.

Since:
    1.0P

Constructor Summary

JbuiDisplay()   Default Constructor
JbuiDisplay(java.lang.String initTitle, JbuiFieldPanel initFieldPanel, JbuiButtonPanel initButtonPanel)   Creates a JbuiDisplay.

Method Summary

void	**clearData**() Clears all data fields to blanks.
void	**clearErrors**() Clears all error indicators to false and clears the error message list.
java.lang.Object	**getData**(int fieldIndex) Sets the error indicator for the specified field to true.
java.lang.Object	**getData**(java.lang.String fieldName) Sets the error indicator for the specified field to true.

Appendix C: Javadoc

JbuiFieldPanel	**getFieldPanel**()	
	This method was created in VisualAge.	
void	**setData**(int fieldIndex, java.lang.String newData)	
	Sets the data of the specified field.	
void	**setData**(java.lang.String fieldName, java.lang.String newData)	
	Sets the data of the specified field.	
void	**setError**(int fieldIndex)	
	Sets the error indicator for the specified field to true.	
void	**setError**(int fieldIndex, boolean error)	
	Sets or clears the error indicator for the specified field.	
void	**setError**(int fieldIndex, java.lang.String errorMessage)	
	Sets the error indicator for the specified field to true and adds a message to the error list.	
void	**setFieldPanel**(JbuiFieldPanel newFieldPanel)	
	This method was created in VisualAge.	
void	**setHandle**(java.lang.Object newHandle)	
	This method was created in VisualAge.	
void	**setProtect**(boolean protect)	
	Sets the protected flag of the all fields in the panel.	
void	**setProtect**(int fieldIndex)	
	Sets the specified field to protected (output only).	
void	**setProtect**(int fieldIndex, boolean protect)	
	Sets the protected flag of the specified field.	

Methods inherited from class com.pbd.pub.jbui.JbuiScreen

EXFMT, getFrame, getPosition, getPressedButton, isSomeoneWaiting, jbuiNotify, jbuiNotify, READ, setButtonPanel, setOwner, setPosition, setTitle, WRITE

Methods inherited from class java.lang.Object

equals, getClass, hashCode, notify, notifyAll, toString, wait, wait, wait

Constructor Detail

JbuiDisplay

public **JbuiDisplay**()
    Default Constructor

JbuiDisplay

public **JbuiDisplay**(java.lang.String initTitle,
                  JbuiFieldPanel initFieldPanel,
                  JbuiButtonPanel initButtonPanel)

Appendix C: Javadoc

Creates a JbuiDisplay. This version takes a String for the title (like all versions do) and a predefined field panel and button panel. This simple constructor will therefore only display a single column of data. Later versions will allow multiple panels, creation using only primitive types and even a simple scripting language.

Parameters:
`initTitle` - the title of the window, displayed in the frame's title bar.
`initFieldPanel` - the entry fields for this panel.
`initButtonPanel` - the buttons for this panel.

Method Detail

clearData

`public void clearData()`
Clears all data fields to blanks.

clearErrors

`public void clearErrors()`
Clears all error indicators to false and clears the error message list.

getData

`public java.lang.Object getData(int fieldIndex)`
Sets the error indicator for the specified field to true.
Parameters:
`fieldIndex` - is the zero-based index of the field.

getData

`public java.lang.Object getData(java.lang.String fieldName)`
Sets the error indicator for the specified field to true.
Parameters:
`fieldIndex` - is the zero-based index of the field.

getFieldPanel

`public JbuiFieldPanel getFieldPanel()`
This method was created in VisualAge.
Returns:
com.pbd.pub.jbui.JbuiFieldPanel

setData

```
public void setData(int fieldIndex,
                    java.lang.String newData)
```
Sets the data of the specified field.
Parameters:
`fieldIndex` - is the zero-based index of the field.
`newData` - is the new data

337

Appendix C: Javadoc

setData

```
public void setData(java.lang.String fieldName,
                    java.lang.String newData)
```
Sets the data of the specified field.
Parameters:
fieldName - the name of the field.
newData - the new data.

---

setError

```
public void setError(int fieldIndex)
```
Sets the error indicator for the specified field to true.
Parameters:
fieldIndex - is the zero-based index of the field.

---

setError

```
public void setError(int fieldIndex,
                     java.lang.String errorMessage)
```
Sets the error indicator for the specified field to true and adds a message to the error list. If not already visible, this call will make the error list visible.
Parameters:
fieldIndex - is the zero-based index of the field.
errorMessage - is the associated error message.

---

setError

```
public void setError(int fieldIndex,
                     boolean error)
```
Sets or clears the error indicator for the specified field.
Parameters:
fieldIndex - is the zero-based index of the field.
error - is the error flag (true is an error).

---

setFieldPanel

```
public void setFieldPanel(JbuiFieldPanel newFieldPanel)
```
This method was created in VisualAge.
Parameters:
newFieldPanel - com.pbd.pub.jbui.JbuiFieldPanel

---

setHandle

```
public void setHandle(java.lang.Object newHandle)
```
This method was created in VisualAge.
Overrides:
setHandle in class JbuiScreen
Parameters:
newVector - java.util.Vector

setProtect

public void **setProtect**(int fieldIndex)
> Sets the specified field to protected (output only).
> **Parameters:**
> fieldIndex - is the zero-based index of the field.

setProtect

public void **setProtect**(int fieldIndex,
                           boolean protect)
> Sets the protected flag of the specified field.
> **Parameters:**
> fieldIndex - is the zero-based index of the field.
> protect - is the protect flag (true is protected).

setProtect

public void **setProtect**(boolean protect)
> Sets the protected flag of the all fields in the panel. This is primarily a convenience routine.
> **Parameters:**
> protect - is the protect flag (true is protected).

Overview Package **Class** Tree Deprecated Index Help
PREV CLASS   NEXT CLASS   **FRAMES   NO FRAMES**
SUMMARY: INNER | FIELD | CONSTR | METHOD   DETAIL: FIELD | CONSTR | METHOD

---

com.pbd.pub.jbui

Class JbuiEntryField

```
java.lang.Object
  |
  +-java.awt.Component
        |
        +-java.awt.Container
              |
              +-javax.swing.JComponent
                    |
                    +-javax.swing.JPanel
                          |
                          +-com.pbd.pub.jbui.JbuiEntryField
```

All Implemented Interfaces:
> javax.accessibility.Accessible, java.awt.image.ImageObserver, java.awt.MenuContainer, java.io.Serializable

Direct Known Subclasses:
> JbuiOutputField

Appendix C: Javadoc

public class **JbuiEntryField**
extends javax.swing.JPanel

JbuiEntryField is the main input/output component for a JbuiDisplay. A program defines a set of JbuiEntryFields, groups them into a JbuiEntryFieldPanel, then creates a JbuiDisplay. Each JbuiEntryField consists of a label and an entry field. The entry field can be either protected (a JTextField) or unprotected (a JLabel). The JbuiEntryField can also be set to error condition, where the colors will change.

The minimum constructor is a string for the label and a width for the entry field. Optionally, the constructors can accept field height and spacing as well as initial text for the entry field.

Since:
    1.0P
See Also:
    Serialized Form

Inner classes inherited from class javax.swing.JComponent

`javax.swing.JComponent.AccessibleJComponent`

Fields inherited from class javax.swing.JComponent

`TOOL_TIP_TEXT_KEY, UNDEFINED_CONDITION, WHEN_ANCESTOR_OF_FOCUSED_COMPONENT, WHEN_FOCUSED, WHEN_IN_FOCUSED_WINDOW`

Fields inherited from class java.awt.Component

`BOTTOM_ALIGNMENT, CENTER_ALIGNMENT, LEFT_ALIGNMENT, RIGHT_ALIGNMENT, TOP_ALIGNMENT`

Constructor Summary

`JbuiEntryField(java.lang.String labelText, int fieldWidth)`
    Creates a JbuiEntryField with a label and a blank entry field, with default height and spacing.

`JbuiEntryField(java.lang.String labelText, int fieldWidth, int height, int spacing)`
    Creates a JbuiEntryField with a label and a blank entry field, with the specified height and spacing.

`JbuiEntryField(java.lang.String labelText, int fieldWidth, java.lang.String fieldText)`
    Creates a JbuiEntryField with a label and a pre-filled entry field, with default height and spacing.

`JbuiEntryField(java.lang.String labelText, int fieldWidth, java.lang.String fieldText, int height, int spacing)`
    Creates a JbuiEntryField with a label and a pre-filled entry field, with the specified height and spacing.

`JbuiEntryField(java.lang.String name, java.lang.String labelText, int fieldWidth)`
    Creates a named JbuiEntryField with a label and a blank entry field, with default height and spacing.

`JbuiEntryField(java.lang.String name, java.lang.String labelText, int fieldWidth, int height, int spacing)`
    Creates a named buiEntryField with a label and a blank entry field, with the specified height and spacing.

Appendix C: Javadoc

JbuiEntryField(java.lang.String name, java.lang.String labelText, int fieldWidth, java.lang.String fieldText)
    Creates a named JbuiEntryField with a label and a pre-filled entry field, with default height and spacing.

JbuiEntryField(java.lang.String name, java.lang.String labelText, int fieldWidth, java.lang.String fieldText, int height, int spacing)
    Creates a named JbuiEntryField with a label and a pre-filled entry field, with the specified height and spacing.

Method Summary

java.lang.String	**getData**()	Returns the contents of the entry field.
java.lang.String	**getGroupName**()	PBD (c) 1999
java.lang.String	**getName**()	PBD (c) 1999
boolean	**getProtect**()	This method was created in VisualAge.
void	**init**(java.lang.String name, java.lang.String labelText, int fieldWidth, java.lang.String fieldText, int height, int spacing)	This method was created in VisualAge.
void	**setData**(java.lang.String data)	Sets the contents of the entry field.
void	**setError**(boolean error)	Sets the error condition of the field.
void	**setGroupName**(java.lang.String newValue)	PBD (c) 1999
void	**setName**(java.lang.String newValue)	PBD (c) 1999
void	**setProtect**(boolean protect)	Sets the protect condition of the field.

Methods inherited from class javax.swing.JPanel

getAccessibleContext, getUIClassID, updateUI

Methods inherited from class javax.swing.JComponent

addAncestorListener, addNotify, addPropertyChangeListener, addPropertyChangeListener, addVetoableChangeListener, computeVisibleRect, contains, createToolTip, firePropertyChange, firePropertyChange, firePropertyChange, firePropertyChange, firePropertyChange, firePropertyChange, firePropertyChange, getActionForKeyStroke, getActionMap, getAlignmentX, getAlignmentY, getAutoscrolls, getBorder, getBounds, getClientProperty, getConditionForKeyStroke, getDebugGraphicsOptions, getGraphics, getHeight, getInputMap, getInputMap, getInputVerifier, getInsets, getInsets, getListeners, getLocation, getMaximumSize, getMinimumSize, getNextFocusableComponent, getPreferredSize, getRegisteredKeyStrokes, getRootPane,

Appendix C: Javadoc

getSize, getToolTipLocation, getToolTipText, getToolTipText, getTopLevelAncestor, getVerifyInputWhenFocusTarget, getVisibleRect, getWidth, getX, getY, grabFocus, hasFocus, hide, isDoubleBuffered, isFocusCycleRoot, isFocusTraversable, isLightweightComponent, isManagingFocus, isOpaque, isOptimizedDrawingEnabled, isPaintingTile, isRequestFocusEnabled, isValidateRoot, paint, paintImmediately, paintImmediately, print, printAll, putClientProperty, registerKeyboardAction, registerKeyboardAction, removeAncestorListener, removeNotify, removePropertyChangeListener, removePropertyChangeListener, removeVetoableChangeListener, repaint, repaint, requestDefaultFocus, requestFocus, resetKeyboardActions, reshape, revalidate, scrollRectToVisible, setActionMap, setAlignmentX, setAlignmentY, setAutoscrolls, setBackground, setBorder, setDebugGraphicsOptions, setDoubleBuffered, setEnabled, setFont, setForeground, setInputMap, setInputVerifier, setMaximumSize, setMinimumSize, setNextFocusableComponent, setOpaque, setPreferredSize, setRequestFocusEnabled, setToolTipText, setVerifyInputWhenFocusTarget, setVisible, unregisterKeyboardAction, update

Methods inherited from class java.awt.Container

add, add, add, add, add, addContainerListener, countComponents, deliverEvent, doLayout, findComponentAt, findComponentAt, getComponent, getComponentAt, getComponentAt, getComponentCount, getComponents, getLayout, insets, invalidate, isAncestorOf, layout, list, list, locate, minimumSize, paintComponents, preferredSize, printComponents, remove, remove, removeAll, removeContainerListener, setCursor, setLayout, validate

Methods inherited from class java.awt.Component

action, add, addComponentListener, addFocusListener, addHierarchyBoundsListener, addHierarchyListener, addInputMethodListener, addKeyListener, addMouseListener, addMouseMotionListener, bounds, checkImage, checkImage, contains, createImage, createImage, disable, dispatchEvent, enable, enable, enableInputMethods, getBackground, getBounds, getColorModel, getComponentOrientation, getCursor, getDropTarget, getFont, getFontMetrics, getForeground, getGraphicsConfiguration, getInputContext, getInputMethodRequests, getLocale, getLocation, getLocationOnScreen, getParent, getPeer, getSize, getToolkit, getTreeLock, gotFocus, handleEvent, imageUpdate, inside, isDisplayable, isEnabled, isLightweight, isShowing, isValid, isVisible, keyDown, keyUp, list, list, list, location, lostFocus, mouseDown, mouseDrag, mouseEnter, mouseExit, mouseMove, mouseUp, move, nextFocus, paintAll, postEvent, prepareImage, prepareImage, remove, removeComponentListener, removeFocusListener, removeHierarchyBoundsListener, removeHierarchyListener, removeInputMethodListener, removeKeyListener, removeMouseListener, removeMouseMotionListener, repaint, repaint, repaint, resize, resize, setBounds, setBounds, setComponentOrientation, setDropTarget, setLocale, setLocation, setLocation, setSize, setSize, show, show, size, toString, transferFocus

Methods inherited from class java.lang.Object

equals, getClass, hashCode, notify, notifyAll, wait, wait, wait

Appendix C: Javadoc

Constructor Detail

JbuiEntryField

```
public JbuiEntryField(java.lang.String labelText,
                      int fieldWidth)
```
Creates a JbuiEntryField with a label and a blank entry field, with default height and spacing.

Parameters:
`labelText` - the text for the label.
`fieldWidth` - the width of the entry field.

JbuiEntryField

```
public JbuiEntryField(java.lang.String labelText,
                      int fieldWidth,
                      int height,
                      int spacing)
```
Creates a JbuiEntryField with a label and a blank entry field, with the specified height and spacing.

Parameters:
`labelText` - the text for the label.
`fieldWidth` - the width of the entry field.
`height` - the height of both the label and entry field.
`spacing` - the width of the gap between the label and the entry field.

JbuiEntryField

```
public JbuiEntryField(java.lang.String labelText,
                      int fieldWidth,
                      java.lang.String fieldText)
```
Creates a JbuiEntryField with a label and a pre-filled entry field, with default height and spacing.

Parameters:
`labelText` - the text for the label.
`fieldWidth` - the width of the entry field.
`fieldText` - the initial text for the field.

JbuiEntryField

```
public JbuiEntryField(java.lang.String labelText,
                      int fieldWidth,
                      java.lang.String fieldText,
                      int height,
                      int spacing)
```
Creates a JbuiEntryField with a label and a pre-filled entry field, with the specified height and spacing.

Parameters:
`labelText` - the text for the label.
`fieldWidth` - the width of the entry field.
`fieldText` - the initial text for the field.
`height` - the height of both the label and entry field.
`spacing` - the width of the gap between the label and the entry field.

Appendix C: Javadoc

JbuiEntryField

```
public JbuiEntryField(java.lang.String name,
                      java.lang.String labelText,
                      int fieldWidth)
```
Creates a named JbuiEntryField with a label and a blank entry field, with default height and spacing.

Parameters:
name - the name of this field.
labelText - the text for the label.
fieldWidth - the width of the entry field.

JbuiEntryField

```
public JbuiEntryField(java.lang.String name,
                      java.lang.String labelText,
                      int fieldWidth,
                      int height,
                      int spacing)
```
Creates a named buiEntryField with a label and a blank entry field, with the specified height and spacing.

Parameters:
name - the name of this field.
labelText - the text for the label.
fieldWidth - the width of the entry field.
height - the height of both the label and entry field.
spacing - the width of the gap between the label and the entry field.

JbuiEntryField

```
public JbuiEntryField(java.lang.String name,
                      java.lang.String labelText,
                      int fieldWidth,
                      java.lang.String fieldText)
```
Creates a named JbuiEntryField with a label and a pre-filled entry field, with default height and spacing.

Parameters:
name - the name of this field.
labelText - the text for the label.
fieldWidth - the width of the entry field.
fieldText - the initial text for the field.

JbuiEntryField

```
public JbuiEntryField(java.lang.String name,
                      java.lang.String labelText,
                      int fieldWidth,
                      java.lang.String fieldText,
                      int height,
                      int spacing)
```
Creates a named JbuiEntryField with a label and a pre-filled entry field, with the specified height and spacing.

Parameters:
name - the name of this field.
labelText - the text for the label.
fieldWidth - the width of the entry field.
fieldText - the initial text for the field.
height - the height of both the label and entry field.
spacing - the width of the gap between the label and the entry field.

Appendix C: Javadoc

Method Detail

getData

```
public java.lang.String getData()
```
        Returns the contents of the entry field.
        Returns:
        the contents of the entry field.

getGroupName

```
public java.lang.String getGroupName()
```
        PBD (c) 1999
        Returns:
        java.lang.String

getName

```
public java.lang.String getName()
```
        PBD (c) 1999
        Overrides:
        getName in class java.awt.Component.
        Returns:
        java.lang.String

getProtect

```
public boolean getProtect()
```
        This method was created in VisualAge.
        Returns:
        boolean

init

```
public void init(java.lang.String name,
                 java.lang.String labelText,
                 int fieldWidth,
                 java.lang.String fieldText,
                 int height,
                 int spacing)
```
        This method was created in VisualAge.

setData

```
public void setData(java.lang.String data)
```
        Sets the contents of the entry field.
        Parameters:
        data - the new data for the entry field.

setError

```
public void setError(boolean error)
```
        Sets the error condition of the field. If true, changes the colors to error colors, otherwise changes the fields to normal.
        Parameters:
        `error` - the error indicator (true is error).

setGroupName

```
public void setGroupName(java.lang.String newValue)
```
        PBD (c) 1999
        Parameters:
        `newValue` - java.lang.String

setName

```
public void setName(java.lang.String newValue)
```
        PBD (c) 1999
        Overrides:
        setName in class java.awt.Component.
        Parameters:
        `newValue` - java.lang.String

setProtect

```
public void setProtect(boolean protect)
```
        Sets the protect condition of the field. If true, displays the entry field data as a JLabel (making it output-only), otherwise displays a JTextField.
        Parameters:
        `protect` - the protect indicator (true is protect).

Appendix C: Javadoc

Overview Package **Class** Tree Deprecated Index Help
PREV CLASS **NEXT CLASS**   **FRAMES** **NO FRAMES**
SUMMARY: INNER | FIELD | CONSTR | METHOD   DETAIL: FIELD | CONSTR | METHOD

---

com.pbd.pub.jbui

Class JbuiFieldPanel

```
java.lang.Object
  |
  +-java.awt.Component
        |
        +-java.awt.Container
              |
              +-javax.swing.JComponent
                    |
                    +-javax.swing.JPanel
                          |
                          +-com.pbd.pub.jbui.JbuiFieldPanel
```

All Implemented Interfaces:
    javax.accessibility.Accessible, java.awt.image.ImageObserver, java.awt.MenuContainer, java.io.Serializable

---

public class **JbuiFieldPanel**
extends javax.swing.JPanel

JbuiFieldPanel is a UI component that presents an array of JbuiEntryFields vertically. All fields are aligned properly and the maximum width is chosen as the width of the panel. If there are too many fields to fit on the screen, the field panel will automatically scroll. While JbuiFieldPanel currently extends JPanel, there's really no need for it; it's a holdover from a previous version. Now it could just as easily extend Object; I'd just have to write my own get* and setPreferredSize methods.

Since:
    1.0P
See Also:
    Serialized Form

Inner classes inherited from class javax.swing.JComponent

`javax.swing.JComponent.AccessibleJComponent`

Fields inherited from class javax.swing.JComponent

`TOOL_TIP_TEXT_KEY, UNDEFINED_CONDITION, WHEN_ANCESTOR_OF_FOCUSED_COMPONENT, WHEN_FOCUSED, WHEN_IN_FOCUSED_WINDOW`

347

Appendix C: Javadoc

Fields inherited from class java.awt.Component

BOTTOM_ALIGNMENT, CENTER_ALIGNMENT, LEFT_ALIGNMENT, RIGHT_ALIGNMENT, TOP_ALIGNMENT

Constructor Summary

JbuiFieldPanel(JbuiEntryField[] initFields)
    Create a new JbuiFieldPanel from an array of JbuiEntryFields.

Method Summary

void	**clearData**() Clears all data fields to blanks.
void	**clearErrors**() Clears all error indicators to false.
java.lang.String	**getData**(int fieldIndex) Returns the data for the specified field.
java.lang.String	**getData**(java.lang.String fieldName) Returns the data for the specified field.
int	**getFieldIndex**(java.lang.String fieldName) PBD (c) 1999
JbuiEntryField[]	**getFields**() PBD (c) 1999
void	**setData**(int fieldIndex, java.lang.String data) Sets the data for the specified field.
void	**setData**(java.lang.String fieldName, java.lang.String newData) Sets the data for the specified field.
void	**setError**(int fieldIndex, boolean error) Sets the error indicator for the specified field.
void	**setError**(java.lang.String fieldName, boolean error) Sets the error flag for the specified field.
void	**setProtect**(boolean protect) Set the protect indicator for all fields in the panel.
void	**setProtect**(int fieldIndex, boolean protect) Sets the protect (output-only) indicator for the specified field.
void	**setProtect**(java.lang.String fieldName, boolean protect) Sets the protect (output-only) indicator for the specified field.

Methods inherited from class javax.swing.JPanel

getAccessibleContext, getUIClassID, updateUI

Appendix C: Javadoc

Methods inherited from class javax.swing.JComponent

addAncestorListener, addNotify, addPropertyChangeListener, addPropertyChangeListener, addVetoableChangeListener, computeVisibleRect, contains, createToolTip, firePropertyChange, firePropertyChange, firePropertyChange, firePropertyChange, firePropertyChange, firePropertyChange, firePropertyChange, firePropertyChange, getActionForKeyStroke, getActionMap, getAlignmentX, getAlignmentY, getAutoscrolls, getBorder, getBounds, getClientProperty, getConditionForKeyStroke, getDebugGraphicsOptions, getGraphics, getHeight, getInputMap, getInputMap, getInputVerifier, getInsets, getInsets, getListeners, getLocation, getMaximumSize, getMinimumSize, getNextFocusableComponent, getPreferredSize, getRegisteredKeyStrokes, getRootPane, getSize, getToolTipLocation, getToolTipText, getToolTipText, getTopLevelAncestor, getVerifyInputWhenFocusTarget, getVisibleRect, getWidth, getX, getY, grabFocus, hasFocus, hide, isDoubleBuffered, isFocusCycleRoot, isFocusTraversable, isLightweightComponent, isManagingFocus, isOpaque, isOptimizedDrawingEnabled, isPaintingTile, isRequestFocusEnabled, isValidateRoot, paint, paintImmediately, paintImmediately, print, printAll, putClientProperty, registerKeyboardAction, registerKeyboardAction, removeAncestorListener, removeNotify, removePropertyChangeListener, removePropertyChangeListener, removeVetoableChangeListener, repaint, repaint, requestDefaultFocus, requestFocus, resetKeyboardActions, reshape, revalidate, scrollRectToVisible, setActionMap, setAlignmentX, setAlignmentY, setAutoscrolls, setBackground, setBorder, setDebugGraphicsOptions, setDoubleBuffered, setEnabled, setFont, setForeground, setInputMap, setInputVerifier, setMaximumSize, setMinimumSize, setNextFocusableComponent, setOpaque, setPreferredSize, setRequestFocusEnabled, setToolTipText, setVerifyInputWhenFocusTarget, setVisible, unregisterKeyboardAction, update

Methods inherited from class java.awt.Container

add, add, add, add, add, addContainerListener, countComponents, deliverEvent, doLayout, findComponentAt, findComponentAt, getComponent, getComponentAt, getComponentAt, getComponentCount, getComponents, getLayout, insets, invalidate, isAncestorOf, layout, list, list, locate, minimumSize, paintComponents, preferredSize, printComponents, remove, remove, removeAll, removeContainerListener, setCursor, setLayout, validate

Methods inherited from class java.awt.Component

action, add, addComponentListener, addFocusListener, addHierarchyBoundsListener, addHierarchyListener, addInputMethodListener, addKeyListener, addMouseListener, addMouseMotionListener, bounds, checkImage, checkImage, contains, createImage, createImage, disable, dispatchEvent, enable, enable, enableInputMethods, getBackground, getBounds, getColorModel, getComponentOrientation, getCursor, getDropTarget, getFont, getFontMetrics, getForeground, getGraphicsConfiguration, getInputContext, getInputMethodRequests, getLocale, getLocation, getLocationOnScreen, getName, getParent, getPeer, getSize, getToolkit, getTreeLock, gotFocus, handleEvent, imageUpdate, inside, isDisplayable, isEnabled, isLightweight, isShowing, isValid, isVisible, keyDown, keyUp, list, list, list, location, lostFocus, mouseDown, mouseDrag, mouseEnter, mouseExit, mouseMove, mouseUp, move, nextFocus, paintAll, postEvent, prepareImage, prepareImage, remove, removeComponentListener, removeFocusListener, removeHierarchyBoundsListener, removeHierarchyListener, removeInputMethodListener, removeKeyListener, removeMouseListener, removeMouseMotionListener, repaint, repaint, repaint, resize, resize, setBounds, setBounds, setComponentOrientation, setDropTarget, setLocale, setLocation, setLocation, setName, setSize, setSize, show, show, size, toString, transferFocus

349

Appendix C: Javadoc

Methods inherited from class java.lang.Object
`equals, getClass, hashCode, notify, notifyAll, wait, wait, wait`

Constructor Detail

JbuiFieldPanel
```
public JbuiFieldPanel(JbuiEntryField[] initFields)
```
Create a new JbuiFieldPanel from an array of JbuiEntryFields.

Method Detail

clearData
```
public void clearData()
```
Clears all data fields to blanks.

clearErrors
```
public void clearErrors()
```
Clears all error indicators to false.

getData
```
public java.lang.String getData(int fieldIndex)
```
Returns the data for the specified field.

Parameters:
fieldIndex - the zero-based index of the field.

Returns:
contents of specified field.

getData
```
public java.lang.String getData(java.lang.String fieldName)
```
Returns the data for the specified field.

Parameters:
fieldName - the name of the field to retrieve.

Returns:
contents of specified field.

getFieldIndex
```
public int getFieldIndex(java.lang.String fieldName)
```
PBD (c) 1999

Parameters:
fieldName - java.lang.String

getFields

```
public JbuiEntryField[] getFields()
```
PBD (c) 1999
Returns:
JbuiEntryField[]

---

setData

```
public void setData(int fieldIndex,
                    java.lang.String data)
```
Sets the data for the specified field.
Parameters:
fieldIndex - the zero-based index of the field.
data - is the new data for the field.

---

setData

```
public void setData(java.lang.String fieldName,
                    java.lang.String newData)
```
Sets the data for the specified field.
Parameters:
fieldName - the name of the field to set.
newData - the new value for specified field.

---

setError

```
public void setError(int fieldIndex,
                     boolean error)
```
Sets the error indicator for the specified field.
Parameters:
fieldIndex - the zero-based index of the field.
error - the error indicator (true is error).

---

setError

```
public void setError(java.lang.String fieldName,
                     boolean error)
              throws java.lang.NoSuchFieldException
```
Sets the error flag for the specified field.
Parameters:
fieldName - the name of the field to set.
error - the error flag (true is error).

---

setProtect

```
public void setProtect(int fieldIndex,
                       boolean protect)
```
Sets the protect (output-only) indicator for the specified field.
Parameters:
fieldIndex - the zero-based index of the field.
protect - the protect indicator (true is protect).

Appendix C: Javadoc

setProtect

```
public void setProtect(java.lang.String fieldName,
                       boolean protect)
                throws java.lang.NoSuchFieldException
```
Sets the protect (output-only) indicator for the specified field.
Parameters:
fieldName - the name of the field to set.
protect - the protect flag (protect is error).

---

setProtect

```
public void setProtect(boolean protect)
```
Set the protect indicator for all fields in the panel. This is a convenience method and is rarely used.
Parameters:
protect - the protect indicator (true is protect).

Overview Package **Class** Tree Deprecated Index Help
PREV CLASS   NEXT CLASS   FRAMES   NO FRAMES
SUMMARY: INNER | FIELD | CONSTR | METHOD   DETAIL: FIELD | CONSTR | METHOD

---

com.pbd.pub.jbui

Class JbuiList

```
java.lang.Object
  |
  +-com.pbd.pub.jbui.JbuiScreen
        |
        +-com.pbd.pub.jbui.JbuiList
```
All Implemented Interfaces:
JbuiConstants, javax.swing.SwingConstants
Direct Known Subclasses:
Jao400List

---

public class **JbuiList**
extends JbuiScreen

JbuiList is the class used to emulate a subfile select panel. This is a very simplified panel, and its charcteristics are very dependent upon the JbuiListModel specified.

There are two primary variations of the JbuiListPanel: with or without viewer. If no viewer is specified, double clicking on a row simply returns zero as the result of the EXFMT() method (the Cancel button returns 12). It is then the caller's responsibility to determine which row was selected and to perform the appropriate action.

Appendix C: Javadoc

A JbuiList handles double-clicks itself if a viewer is defined. A viewer must either be an object or a Class of a type that subclasses JbuiDisplay. If a Class is specified, a new instance is created each time the user double-clicks (an invalid Class causes the JbuiList to execute as if no viewer were specified), otherwise the specified object acts as the viewer. In either case, a double click will fire off a thread that will pass the data to the viewer via setHandle() and then display the panel with EXFMT().

Note that this means that if a Class is specified, a new window is created for each double-click, but if an object is specified, that object is updated via setHandle() for each double-click.

The data passed to the viewer is either the associated handle from the JbuiListModel, or if no handles are specified a Vector containing the data in the selected row is passed.

Since:
    1.1P

Constructor Summary

JbuiList()
    Creates a default JbuiList.

JbuiList(java.lang.String initTitle, JbuiListModel initModel)
    Creates a JbuiList with the specified title and data model.

Method Summary

JbuiListModel	**getModel**() PBD (c) 1999
java.lang.Object	**getSelectedHandle**() Returns either the handle for the selected row, or if handles were not specified, returns the Vector containing the row data.
java.lang.Class	**getViewClass**() Returns the Class specified for the viewer, or null if none specified.
JbuiScreen	**getViewer**() Returns either the viewer object if specified, or a new instance of the viewer class.
void	**setModel**(JbuiListModel newModel) Sets the model for this JbuiList.
void	**setViewClass**(java.lang.Class newViewClass) Sets the viewer Class for this JbuiList.
void	**setViewClass**(java.lang.String newViewClassName) Sets the viewer Class for this JbuiList.
void	**setViewer**(JbuiDisplay newViewer) Sets the viewer for this JbuiList.
void	**setViewer**(JbuiScreen newViewer) Sets the viewer for this JbuiList.
void	**setViewerPosition**(int newViewerPosition) Sets the position of the viewer window.

Appendix C: Javadoc

Methods inherited from class com.pbd.pub.jbui.JbuiScreen

EXFMT, getFrame, getPosition, getPressedButton, isSomeoneWaiting, jbuiNotify, jbuiNotify, READ, setButtonPanel, setHandle, setOwner, setPosition, setTitle, WRITE

Methods inherited from class java.lang.Object

equals, getClass, hashCode, notify, notifyAll, toString, wait, wait, wait

Constructor Detail

JbuiList
public **JbuiList**()
    Creates a default JbuiList.

JbuiList
public **JbuiList**(java.lang.String initTitle,
           JbuiListModel initModel)
    Creates a JbuiList with the specified title and data model.
    Parameters:
    initTitle - - the title for the JbuiList.
    initModel - - the JbuiListModel containing the data for the JbuiList.

Method Detail

getModel
public JbuiListModel **getModel**()
    PBD (c) 1999
    Returns:
    com.pbd.pub.jbui.JbuiListModel

getSelectedHandle
public java.lang.Object **getSelectedHandle**()
    Returns either the handle for the selected row, or if handles were not specified, returns the Vector containing the row data. If no rows are selected, the method returns null.
    Returns:
    either the handle or the row data for the selected row (or null if no row is selected).

getViewClass
public java.lang.Class **getViewClass**()
    Returns the Class specified for the viewer, or null if none specified.
    Returns:
    the Class specified for the viewer.

getViewer

public JbuiScreen **getViewer**()
> Returns either the viewer object if specified, or a new instance of the viewer class.
> **Returns:**
> the viewer object if specified or a new instance of the viewer class.

setModel

public void **setModel**(JbuiListModel newModel)
> Sets the model for this JbuiList.
> **Parameters:**
> newModel - - the new model for this JbuiList.

setViewClass

public void **setViewClass**(java.lang.Class newViewClass)
> Sets the viewer Class for this JbuiList. A new instance of this class is created every time the user double-clicks on a row in this JbuiList.
> **Parameters:**
> newViewClass - - the new viewer Class for this JbuiList.

setViewClass

public void **setViewClass**(java.lang.String newViewClassName)
> Sets the viewer Class for this JbuiList. A new instance of this class is created every time the user double-clicks on a row in this JbuiList.
> **Parameters:**
> newViewClassName - - the name of the new viewer Class for this JbuiList.

setViewer

public void **setViewer**(JbuiDisplay newViewer)
> Sets the viewer for this JbuiList. The same viewer object is used every time the user double-clicks on this JbuiList.
> **Parameters:**
> newViewer - - the new viewer for this JbuiList.

setViewer

public void **setViewer**(JbuiScreen newViewer)
> Sets the viewer for this JbuiList. The same viewer object is used every time the user double-clicks on this JbuiList.
> **Parameters:**
> newViewer - - the new viewer for this JbuiList.

setViewerPosition

public void **setViewerPosition**(int newViewerPosition)
> Sets the position of the viewer window.
> **Parameters:**
> newViewerPosition - - the new viewer position.

Appendix C: Javadoc

Overview **Package** **Class** **Tree** **Deprecated** **Index** **Help**

PREV CLASS NEXT CLASS   FRAMES   NO FRAMES
SUMMARY: INNER | FIELD | CONSTR | METHOD   DETAIL: FIELD | CONSTR | METHOD

com.pbd.pub.jbui

Class JbuiListModel

```
java.lang.Object
  |
  +-javax.swing.table.AbstractTableModel
      |
      +-com.pbd.pub.jbui.JbuiListModel
```
All Implemented Interfaces:
    java.io.Serializable, javax.swing.table.TableModel

---

public class **JbuiListModel**
extends javax.swing.table.AbstractTableModel

JbuiListModel is the table model used by JbuiList objects. It provides one-dimensional vectors of information for headings and column widths, a two dimensional vector (columns and rows) for the actual data, and a one-dimensional (by row) vector for handles.

Since:
    1.1P
See Also:
    Serialized Form

Constructor Summary

JbuiListModel(java.lang.String[] initHeadings, int[] initColumnWidths, java.lang.Object[][] initData)
JbuiListModel(java.lang.String[] initHeadings, int[] initColumnWidths, java.util.Vector initData)
JbuiListModel(java.lang.String[] initHeadings, int[] initColumnWidths, java.util.Vector initData, java.util.Vector initHandles)
JbuiListModel(java.lang.String[] initHeadings, java.lang.Object[][] initData)
JbuiListModel(java.lang.String[] initHeadings, java.util.Vector initData)
JbuiListModel(java.util.Vector initHeadings, java.util.Vector initData)   JbuiListModel constructor comment.

Appendix C: Javadoc

JbuiListModel(java.util.Vector initHeadings, java.util.Vector initColumnWidths, java.util.Vector initData)
    JbuiListModel constructor comment.

JbuiListModel(java.util.Vector initHeadings, java.util.Vector initColumnWidths, java.util.Vector initData, java.util.Vector initHandles)
    JbuiListModel constructor comment.

Method Summary

void	**appendData**(java.lang.Object[][] newData) PBD (c) 1999
void	**appendData**(java.util.Vector newData) PBD (c) 1999
java.lang.Class	**getColumnClass**(int column)
int	**getColumnCount**() getColumnCount method comment.
java.lang.String	**getColumnName**(int column)
java.util.Vector	**getColumnWidths**() This method was created in VisualAge.
java.util.Vector	**getHandles**() This method was created in VisualAge.
java.util.Vector	**getRow**(int row) This method was created in VisualAge.
int	**getRowCount**() getRowCount method comment.
java.lang.Object	**getValueAt**(int row, int col) getValueAt method comment.

Methods inherited from class javax.swing.table.AbstractTableModel

addTableModelListener, findColumn, fireTableCellUpdated, fireTableChanged, fireTableDataChanged, fireTableRowsDeleted, fireTableRowsInserted, fireTableRowsUpdated, fireTableStructureChanged, getListeners, isCellEditable, removeTableModelListener, setValueAt

Methods inherited from class java.lang.Object

equals, getClass, hashCode, notify, notifyAll, toString, wait, wait, wait

Constructor Detail

JbuiListModel
```
public JbuiListModel(java.lang.String[] initHeadings,
                     java.lang.Object[][] initData)
```

JbuiListModel
```
public JbuiListModel(java.lang.String[] initHeadings,
                     int[] initColumnWidths,
                     java.lang.Object[][] initData)
```

JbuiListModel
```
public JbuiListModel(java.lang.String[] initHeadings,
                     int[] initColumnWidths,
                     java.util.Vector initData)
```

JbuiListModel
```
public JbuiListModel(java.lang.String[] initHeadings,
                     int[] initColumnWidths,
                     java.util.Vector initData,
                     java.util.Vector initHandles)
```

JbuiListModel
```
public JbuiListModel(java.lang.String[] initHeadings,
                     java.util.Vector initData)
```

JbuiListModel
```
public JbuiListModel(java.util.Vector initHeadings,
                     java.util.Vector initData)
```
JbuiListModel constructor comment.

JbuiListModel
```
public JbuiListModel(java.util.Vector initHeadings,
                     java.util.Vector initColumnWidths,
                     java.util.Vector initData)
```
JbuiListModel constructor comment.

JbuiListModel
```
public JbuiListModel(java.util.Vector initHeadings,
                     java.util.Vector initColumnWidths,
                     java.util.Vector initData,
                     java.util.Vector initHandles)
```
JbuiListModel constructor comment.

Method Detail

appendData
```
public void appendData(java.lang.Object[][] newData)
```
PBD (c) 1999
Parameters:
newData - java.lang.Object[][]

---

appendData
```
public void appendData(java.util.Vector newData)
```
PBD (c) 1999
Parameters:
newData - java.lang.Object[][]

---

getColumnClass
```
public java.lang.Class getColumnClass(int column)
```
Overrides:
getColumnClass in class javax.swing.table.AbstractTableModel

---

getColumnCount
```
public int getColumnCount()
```
getColumnCount method comment.
Overrides:
getColumnCount in class javax.swing.table.AbstractTableModel

---

getColumnName
```
public java.lang.String getColumnName(int column)
```
Overrides:
getColumnName in class javax.swing.table.AbstractTableModel

---

getColumnWidths
```
public java.util.Vector getColumnWidths()
```
This method was created in VisualAge.
Returns:
java.util.Vector

---

getHandles
```
public java.util.Vector getHandles()
```
This method was created in VisualAge.
Returns:
java.util.Vector

Appendix C: Javadoc

getRow

```
public java.util.Vector getRow(int row)
```
    This method was created in VisualAge.
    Parameters:
    row - int
    Returns:
    Vector

---

getRowCount

```
public int getRowCount()
```
    getRowCount method comment.
    Overrides:
    getRowCount in class javax.swing.table.AbstractTableModel

---

getValueAt

```
public java.lang.Object getValueAt(int row,
                                   int col)
```
    getValueAt method comment.
    Overrides:
    getValueAt in class javax.swing.table.AbstractTableModel

Overview Package **Class** Tree Deprecated Index Help
PREV CLASS **NEXT CLASS**   **FRAMES** **NO FRAMES**
SUMMARY: INNER | FIELD | CONSTR | METHOD   DETAIL: FIELD | CONSTR | METHOD

---

com.pbd.pub.jbui

Class JbuiListPanel

```
java.lang.Object
  |
  +-com.pbd.pub.jbui.JbuiListPanel
```

public class **JbuiListPanel**
extends java.lang.Object

JbuiList is the class used to emulate a subfile select panel. This is a very simplified panel, and its characteristics are very dependent upon the JbuiListModel specified.

There are two primary variations of the JbuiListPanel: with or without viewer. If no viewer is specified, double clicking on a row simply returns zero as the result of the EXFMT() method (the Cancel button returns 12). It is then the caller's responsibility to determine which row was selected and to perform the appropriate action.

A JbuiList handles double-clicks itself if a viewer is defined. A viewer must either be an object or a Class of a type that subclasses JbuiDisplay. If a Class is specified, a new instance is created each time the user double-clicks (an invalid Class causes the JbuiList to execute as if no viewer were specified), otherwise the specified object acts as the viewer. In either case, a double click will fire off a thread that will pass the data to the viewer via setHandle() and then display the panel with EXFMT().

Note that this means that if a Class is specified, a new window is created for each double-click, but if an object is specified, that object is updated via setHandle() for each double-click.

The data passed to the viewer is either the associated handle from the JbuiListModel, or if no handles are specified a Vector containing the data in the selected row is passed.

Since:
    1.2P

Constructor Summary

JbuiListPanel(JbuiListModel initModel)
    Creates a JbuiListPanel for the specified data model.

Method Summary

java.util.Vector	**getRow**(int row) Returns the Vector of data for the specified row.
java.lang.Object	**getSelectedHandle**() Returns either the handle for the selected row, or if handles were not specified, returns the Vector containing the row data.
java.awt.Dimension	**getStartSize**() This method was created in VisualAge.
javax.swing.JTable	**getTable**() This method was created in VisualAge.

Methods inherited from class java.lang.Object

equals, getClass, hashCode, notify, notifyAll, toString, wait, wait, wait

Constructor Detail

JbuiListPanel

public **JbuiListPanel**(JbuiListModel initModel)
    Creates a JbuiListPanel for the specified data model.
    Parameters:
    initModel - - the JbuiListModel containing the data for the JbuiList.

Appendix C: Javadoc

Method Detail

getRow

```
public java.util.Vector getRow(int row)
```
Returns the Vector of data for the specified row.
Parameters:
row - - row to retrieve.
Returns:
a Vector containing the data for the specified row.

getSelectedHandle

```
public java.lang.Object getSelectedHandle()
```
Returns either the handle for the selected row, or if handles were not specified, returns the Vector containing the row data. If no rows are selected, the method returns `null`.
Returns:
either the handle or the row data for the selected row (or null if no row is selected).

getStartSize

```
public java.awt.Dimension getStartSize()
```
This method was created in VisualAge.
Returns:
java.awt.Dimension

getTable

```
public javax.swing.JTable getTable()
```
This method was created in VisualAge.
Returns:
javax.swing.JTable

Appendix C: Javadoc

Overview	Package	**Class**	Tree	Deprecated	Index	Help

PREV CLASS NEXT CLASS   FRAMES NO FRAMES
SUMMARY: INNER | FIELD | CONSTR | METHOD   DETAIL: FIELD | CONSTR | METHOD

---

com.pbd.pub.jbui

Class JbuiOutputField

```
java.lang.Object
  |
  +-java.awt.Component
        |
        +-java.awt.Container
              |
              +-javax.swing.JComponent
                    |
                    +-javax.swing.JPanel
                          |
                          +-com.pbd.pub.jbui.JbuiEntryField
                                |
                                +-com.pbd.pub.jbui.JbuiOutputField
```

All Implemented Interfaces:
javax.accessibility.Accessible, java.awt.image.ImageObserver, java.awt.MenuContainer, java.io.Serializable

---

public class **JbuiOutputField**
extends JbuiEntryField

This is a convenience type. It is in effect a JbuiEntryField with protect set to true.

Since:
1.1P

See Also:
JbuiEntryField, Serialized Form

Inner classes inherited from class javax.swing.JComponent

`javax.swing.JComponent.AccessibleJComponent`

Fields inherited from class javax.swing.JComponent

`TOOL_TIP_TEXT_KEY, UNDEFINED_CONDITION, WHEN_ANCESTOR_OF_FOCUSED_COMPONENT, WHEN_FOCUSED, WHEN_IN_FOCUSED_WINDOW`

Fields inherited from class java.awt.Component

`BOTTOM_ALIGNMENT, CENTER_ALIGNMENT, LEFT_ALIGNMENT, RIGHT_ALIGNMENT, TOP_ALIGNMENT`

Constructor Summary

JbuiOutputField(java.lang.String labelText, int fieldWidth)
  Creates a JbuiOutputField with a label and a blank entry field, with default height and spacing.

JbuiOutputField(java.lang.String labelText, int fieldWidth, int height, int spacing)
  Creates a JbuiOutputField with a label and a blank entry field, with the specified height and spacing.

JbuiOutputField(java.lang.String labelText, int fieldWidth, java.lang.String fieldText)
  Creates a JbuiOutputField with a label and a pre-filled entry field, with default height and spacing.

JbuiOutputField(java.lang.String labelText, int fieldWidth, java.lang.String fieldText, int height, int spacing)
  Creates a JbuiOutputField with a label and a pre-filled entry field, with the specified height and spacing.

JbuiOutputField(java.lang.String name, java.lang.String labelText, int fieldWidth)
  Creates a named JbuiOutputField with a label and a blank entry field, with default height and spacing.

JbuiOutputField(java.lang.String name, java.lang.String labelText, int fieldWidth, int height, int spacing)
  Creates a named JbuiOutputField with a label and a blank entry field, with the specified height and spacing.

JbuiOutputField(java.lang.String name, java.lang.String labelText, int fieldWidth, java.lang.String fieldText)
  Creates a named JbuiOutputField with a label and a pre-filled entry field, with default height and spacing.

JbuiOutputField(java.lang.String name, java.lang.String labelText, int fieldWidth, java.lang.String fieldText, int height, int spacing)
  Creates a named JbuiOutputField with a label and a pre-filled entry field, with the specified height and spacing.

Methods inherited from class com.pbd.pub.jbui.JbuiEntryField

getData, getGroupName, getName, getProtect, init, setData, setError, setGroupName, setName, setProtect

Methods inherited from class javax.swing.JPanel

getAccessibleContext, getUIClassID, updateUI

Methods inherited from class javax.swing.JComponent

addAncestorListener, addNotify, addPropertyChangeListener, addPropertyChangeListener, addVetoableChangeListener, computeVisibleRect, contains, createToolTip, firePropertyChange, firePropertyChange, firePropertyChange, firePropertyChange, firePropertyChange, firePropertyChange, firePropertyChange, firePropertyChange, getActionForKeyStroke, getActionMap, getAlignmentX, getAlignmentY, getAutoscrolls, getBorder, getBounds, getClientProperty, getConditionForKeyStroke, getDebugGraphicsOptions, getGraphics, getHeight, getInputMap, getInputMap, getInputVerifier, getInsets, getInsets, getListeners, getLocation, getMaximumSize, getMinimumSize, getNextFocusableComponent, getPreferredSize, getRegisteredKeyStrokes, getRootPane, getSize, getToolTipLocation, getToolTipText, getToolTipText, getTopLevelAncestor, getVerifyInputWhenFocusTarget, getVisibleRect, getWidth, getX, getY, grabFocus, hasFocus, hide, isDoubleBuffered, isFocusCycleRoot, isFocusTraversable, isLightweightComponent, isManagingFocus, isOpaque, isOptimizedDrawingEnabled,

Appendix C: Javadoc

isPaintingTile, isRequestFocusEnabled, isValidateRoot, paint, paintImmediately, paintImmediately, print, printAll, putClientProperty, registerKeyboardAction, registerKeyboardAction, removeAncestorListener, removeNotify, removePropertyChangeListener, removePropertyChangeListener, removeVetoableChangeListener, repaint, repaint, requestDefaultFocus, requestFocus, resetKeyboardActions, reshape, revalidate, scrollRectToVisible, setActionMap, setAlignmentX, setAlignmentY, setAutoscrolls, setBackground, setBorder, setDebugGraphicsOptions, setDoubleBuffered, setEnabled, setFont, setForeground, setInputMap, setInputVerifier, setMaximumSize, setMinimumSize, setNextFocusableComponent, setOpaque, setPreferredSize, setRequestFocusEnabled, setToolTipText, setVerifyInputWhenFocusTarget, setVisible, unregisterKeyboardAction, update

Methods inherited from class java.awt.Container

add, add, add, add, add, addContainerListener, countComponents, deliverEvent, doLayout, findComponentAt, findComponentAt, getComponent, getComponentAt, getComponentAt, getComponentCount, getComponents, getLayout, insets, invalidate, isAncestorOf, layout, list, list, locate, minimumSize, paintComponents, preferredSize, printComponents, remove, remove, removeAll, removeContainerListener, setCursor, setLayout, validate

Methods inherited from class java.awt.Component

action, add, addComponentListener, addFocusListener, addHierarchyBoundsListener, addHierarchyListener, addInputMethodListener, addKeyListener, addMouseListener, addMouseMotionListener, bounds, checkImage, checkImage, contains, createImage, createImage, disable, dispatchEvent, enable, enable, enableInputMethods, getBackground, getBounds, getColorModel, getComponentOrientation, getCursor, getDropTarget, getFont, getFontMetrics, getForeground, getGraphicsConfiguration, getInputContext, getInputMethodRequests, getLocale, getLocation, getLocationOnScreen, getParent, getPeer, getSize, getToolkit, getTreeLock, gotFocus, handleEvent, imageUpdate, inside, isDisplayable, isEnabled, isLightweight, isShowing, isValid, isVisible, keyDown, keyUp, list, list, list, location, lostFocus, mouseDown, mouseDrag, mouseEnter, mouseExit, mouseMove, mouseUp, move, nextFocus, paintAll, postEvent, prepareImage, prepareImage, remove, removeComponentListener, removeFocusListener, removeHierarchyBoundsListener, removeHierarchyListener, removeInputMethodListener, removeKeyListener, removeMouseListener, removeMouseMotionListener, repaint, repaint, repaint, resize, resize, setBounds, setBounds, setComponentOrientation, setDropTarget, setLocale, setLocation, setLocation, setSize, setSize, show, show, size, toString, transferFocus

Methods inherited from class java.lang.Object

equals, getClass, hashCode, notify, notifyAll, wait, wait, wait

365

Appendix C: Javadoc

Constructor Detail

JbuiOutputField

```
public JbuiOutputField(java.lang.String labelText,
                       int fieldWidth)
```
Creates a JbuiOutputField with a label and a blank entry field, with default height and spacing.
Parameters:
labelText - the text for the label.
fieldWidth - the width of the entry field.
fieldText - the initial text for the field.

JbuiOutputField

```
public JbuiOutputField(java.lang.String labelText,
                       int fieldWidth,
                       int height,
                       int spacing)
```
Creates a JbuiOutputField with a label and a blank entry field, with the specified height and spacing.
Parameters:
labelText - the text for the label.
fieldWidth - the width of the entry field.
height - the height of both the label and entry field.
spacing - the width of the gap between the label and the entry field.

JbuiOutputField

```
public JbuiOutputField(java.lang.String labelText,
                       int fieldWidth,
                       java.lang.String fieldText)
```
Creates a JbuiOutputField with a label and a pre-filled entry field, with default height and spacing.
Parameters:
labelText - the text for the label.
fieldWidth - the width of the entry field.
fieldText - the initial text for the field.

JbuiOutputField

```
public JbuiOutputField(java.lang.String labelText,
                       int fieldWidth,
                       java.lang.String fieldText,
                       int height,
                       int spacing)
```
Creates a JbuiOutputField with a label and a pre-filled entry field, with the specified height and spacing.
Parameters:
labelText - the text for the label.
fieldWidth - the width of the entry field.
fieldText - the initial text for the field.
height - the height of both the label and entry field.
spacing - the width of the gap between the label and the entry field.

JbuiOutputField

```
public JbuiOutputField(java.lang.String name,
                       java.lang.String labelText,
                       int fieldWidth)
```
Creates a named JbuiOutputField with a label and a blank entry field, with default height and spacing.
Parameters:
name - the name of this field.
labelText - the text for the label.
fieldWidth - the width of the entry field.
fieldText - the initial text for the field.

JbuiOutputField

```
public JbuiOutputField(java.lang.String name,
                       java.lang.String labelText,
                       int fieldWidth,
                       int height,
                       int spacing)
```
Creates a named JbuiOutputField with a label and a blank entry field, with the specified height and spacing.
Parameters:
name - the name of this field.
labelText - the text for the label.
fieldWidth - the width of the entry field.
height - the height of both the label and entry field.
spacing - the width of the gap between the label and the entry field.

JbuiOutputField

```
public JbuiOutputField(java.lang.String name,
                       java.lang.String labelText,
                       int fieldWidth,
                       java.lang.String fieldText)
```
Creates a named JbuiOutputField with a label and a pre-filled entry field, with default height and spacing.
Parameters:
name - the name of this field.
labelText - the text for the label.
fieldWidth - the width of the entry field.
fieldText - the initial text for the field.

JbuiOutputField

```
public JbuiOutputField(java.lang.String name,
                       java.lang.String labelText,
                       int fieldWidth,
                       java.lang.String fieldText,
                       int height,
                       int spacing)
```
Creates a named JbuiOutputField with a label and a pre-filled entry field, with the specified height and spacing.
Parameters:
name - the name of this field.
labelText - the text for the label.
fieldWidth - the width of the entry field.

`fieldText` - the initial text for the field.
`height` - the height of both the label and entry field.
`spacing` - the width of the gap between the label and the entry field.

Overview Package **Class** Tree Deprecated Index Help	
PREV CLASS NEXT CLASS	FRAMES NO FRAMES
SUMMARY: INNER | FIELD | CONSTR | METHOD	DETAIL: FIELD | CONSTR | METHOD

com.pbd.pub.jbui

Class JbuiScreen

```
java.lang.Object
  |
  +-com.pbd.pub.jbui.JbuiScreen
```

All Implemented Interfaces:
    JbuiConstants, javax.swing.SwingConstants

Direct Known Subclasses:
    JbuiDisplay, JbuiList, JbuiSplit

---

public class **JbuiScreen**
extends java.lang.Object
implements JbuiConstants

JbuiScreen is the superclass for the other JBUI windows, such as JbuiDisplay and JbuiList. JbuiScreen provides all the basic support, including the EXFMT() support and the button handling. It does not, however, add components to the frame. It is the responsibility of the subclass to add things to the frame. This way the subclass has more control over the layout of the panel (for example, JbuiDisplay adds the error message line below the button panel).

In order to circumvent the event-driven nature of the Swing GUI, JbuiScreen() needed to force a wait when the screen was displayed. This "block mode" interface was created by having the EXFMT() method perform a wait() on the JbuiScreen object. The JbuiButtonPanel is smart enough to then notify its owner's screen when appropriate.

Since:
    1.1P

Fields inherited from interface com.pbd.pub.jbui.JbuiConstants

DOUBLECLICK_DISPLAY, OVER, RELATIVE_TO_OWNER, SELECT_DISPLAY, SELECT_DISPLAY_AND_DOUBLECLICK_DRILL, UNDER

Fields inherited from interface javax.swing.SwingConstants

BOTTOM, CENTER, EAST, HORIZONTAL, LEADING, LEFT, NORTH, NORTH_EAST, NORTH_WEST, RIGHT, SOUTH, SOUTH_EAST, SOUTH_WEST, TOP, TRAILING, VERTICAL, WEST

Constructor Summary

JbuiScreen()
  Default constructor.

JbuiScreen(java.lang.String initTitle)
  This constructor supplies a title.

JbuiScreen(java.lang.String initTitle, JbuiButtonPanel initButtonPanel)
  This constructor supplies a title and a button panel.

Method Summary

int	**EXFMT**() EXFMT displays the JbuiPanel and waits for the user to press one of the buttons in the associated JbuiButtonPanel.
javax.swing.JFrame	**getFrame**() Returns the frame for this screen.
int	**getPosition**() This method was created in VisualAge.
int	**getPressedButton**() This method was created in VisualAge.
boolean	**isSomeoneWaiting**() Returns true if another thread is currently waiting on this screen.
void	**jbuiNotify**() This is an internal method that should only be used by the JbuiButtonPanel, although it can be used to prematurely end a dialog.
void	**jbuiNotify**(int button) This is an internal method that simulates a button press.
int	**READ**() READ waits for the user to press one of the buttons in the associated JbuiButtonPanel.
void	**setButtonPanel**(JbuiButtonPanel newButtonPanel) Sets the button panel for this screen.
void	**setHandle**(java.lang.Object newHandle) This method was created in VisualAge.
void	**setOwner**(JbuiScreen newOwner) Sets the owner screen for this screen.
void	**setPosition**(int newValue) This method was created in VisualAge.
void	**setTitle**(java.lang.String newTitle) Sets the title for this screen.
void	**WRITE**() WRITE displays the JbuiPanel.

Methods inherited from class java.lang.Object

equals, getClass, hashCode, notify, notifyAll, toString, wait, wait, wait

Appendix C: Javadoc

Constructor Detail

JbuiScreen

`public JbuiScreen()`
   Default constructor.

JbuiScreen

`public JbuiScreen(java.lang.String initTitle)`
   This constructor supplies a title.
   Parameters:
   initTitle - - title of the screen.

JbuiScreen

`public JbuiScreen(java.lang.String initTitle,`
                `JbuiButtonPanel initButtonPanel)`
   This constructor supplies a title and a button panel.
   Parameters:
   initTitle - - title of the screen.
   initButtonPanel - - button panel to use for this screen.

Method Detail

EXFMT

`public int EXFMT()`
   EXFMT displays the JbuiPanel and waits for the user to press one of the buttons in the associated JbuiButtonPanel. If function keys are enabled in the JbuiButtonPanel, then the associated function keys can be used as accelerators.
   Returns:
   button index or function key identifier used to exit panel.

getFrame

`public javax.swing.JFrame getFrame()`
   Returns the frame for this screen.
   Returns:
   the frame for this screen.

getPosition

`public int getPosition()`
   This method was created in VisualAge.
   Returns:
   int

getPressedButton

`public int getPressedButton()`
> This method was created in VisualAge.
> **Returns:**
> int

isSomeoneWaiting

`public boolean isSomeoneWaiting()`
> Returns `true` if another thread is currently waiting on this screen.
> **Returns:**
> `true` if another thread is currently waiting on this screen.

jbuiNotify

`public void jbuiNotify()`
> This is an internal method that should only be used by the JbuiButtonPanel, although it can be used to prematurely end a dialog.

jbuiNotify

`public void jbuiNotify(int button)`
> This is an internal method that simulates a button press.
> **Parameters:**
> `button` - - the index of the button to simulate.

READ

`public int READ()`
> READ waits for the user to press one of the buttons in the associated JbuiButtonPanel. If function keys are enabled in the JbuiButtonPanel, then the associated function keys can be used as accelerators.
> **Returns:**
> button index or function key identifier used to exit panel.

setButtonPanel

`public void setButtonPanel(JbuiButtonPanel newButtonPanel)`
> Sets the button panel for this screen.
> **Parameters:**
> `newButtonPanel` - - the new button panel.

setHandle

`public void setHandle(java.lang.Object newHandle)`
> This method was created in VisualAge.
> **Parameters:**
> `newHandle` - java.lang.Object

Appendix C: Javadoc

setOwner

```
public void setOwner(JbuiScreen newOwner)
```
   Sets the owner screen for this screen.
   Parameters:
   newOwner - - the new owner for this screen.

setPosition

```
public void setPosition(int newValue)
```
   This method was created in VisualAge.
   Parameters:
   newValue - int

setTitle

```
public void setTitle(java.lang.String newTitle)
```
   Sets the title for this screen.
   Parameters:
   newTitle - - the new title for this screen.

WRITE

```
public void WRITE()
```
   WRITE displays the JbuiPanel.

Overview	Package	**Class**	Tree	Deprecated	Index	Help
PREV CLASS	**NEXT CLASS**			**FRAMES**	**NO FRAMES**	
SUMMARY: INNER | FIELD | CONSTR | METHOD				DETAIL: FIELD | CONSTR | METHOD		

---

com.pbd.pub.jbui

Class JbuiScreenThread

```
java.lang.Object
   |
   +-java.lang.Thread
         |
         +-com.pbd.pub.jbui.JbuiScreenThread
```
All Implemented Interfaces:
   java.lang.Runnable

---

public class **JbuiScreenThread**
extends java.lang.Thread

372

Appendix C: Javadoc

JbuiScreenThread is a specialized thread designed specifically to display a JbuiScreen. This threads lives only long enough to display the screen and wait for a button to be pressed. Normally, screens displayed via this method should only have a single cancel button.

Since:
> 1.1P

Fields inherited from class java.lang.Thread

`MAX_PRIORITY, MIN_PRIORITY, NORM_PRIORITY`

Constructor Summary

`JbuiScreenThread(JbuiScreen initScreen)`
> JbuiScreenThread constructor.

Method Summary

void	`run()`
	Display the specified screen and exit.

Methods inherited from class java.lang.Thread

`activeCount, checkAccess, countStackFrames, currentThread, destroy, dumpStack, enumerate, getContextClassLoader, getName, getPriority, getThreadGroup, interrupt, interrupted, isAlive, isDaemon, isInterrupted, join, join, join, resume, setContextClassLoader, setDaemon, setName, setPriority, sleep, sleep, start, stop, stop, suspend, toString, yield`

Methods inherited from class java.lang.Object

`equals, getClass, hashCode, notify, notifyAll, wait, wait, wait`

Constructor Detail

JbuiScreenThread

`public JbuiScreenThread(JbuiScreen initScreen)`
> JbuiScreenThread constructor.
> **Parameters:**
> initScreen - - the screen to display.

373

Appendix C: Javadoc

Method Detail

run

```
public void run()
```
    Display the specified screen and exit.
    Overrides:
        run in class java.lang.Thread

Overview   Package   **Class**   Tree   Deprecated   Index   Help
PREV CLASS   NEXT CLASS   FRAMES   NO FRAMES
SUMMARY: INNER | FIELD | CONSTR | METHOD   DETAIL: FIELD | CONSTR | METHOD

---

com.pbd.pub.jbui

Class JbuiSplit

```
java.lang.Object
  |
  +-com.pbd.pub.jbui.JbuiScreen
       |
       +-com.pbd.pub.jbui.JbuiSplit
```
All Implemented Interfaces:
    JbuiConstants, javax.swing.SwingConstants
Direct Known Subclasses:
    Jao400Split

---

public class **JbuiSplit**
extends JbuiScreen

JbuiSplit is not directly analogous to any specific AS/400 screen type. Instead, the JbuiSplit is a combination of a subfile select panel and a display panel. The window is divided into two panels, either horizontally or vertically. The top or left panel is the select panel and contains a table with rows of data from the selected file, while the other panel displays the details of a row which has been double-clicked.

Since:
    1.2P

Constructor Summary

JbuiSplit()
    Creates a default JbuiSplit.

JbuiSplit(java.lang.String initTitle, JbuiListModel initModel, JbuiFieldPanel initFieldPanel)

374

Appendix C: Javadoc

	Creates a JbuiList with the specified title and data model.
JbuiSplit(java.lang.String initTitle, JbuiListModel initModel, JbuiFieldPanel initFieldPanel, int initOrientation) Creates a JbuiList with the specified title and data model.	
JbuiSplit(java.lang.String initTitle, JbuiListModel initModel, JbuiFieldPanel initFieldPanel, int initOrientation, int initSelectMode) Creates a JbuiList with the specified title and data model.	

Method Summary

JbuiFieldPanel	**getFieldPanel**() This method was created in VisualAge.
java.lang.Object	**getSelectedHandle**() Returns either the handle for the selected row, or if handles were not specified, returns the Vector containing the row data.
int	**getSelectMode**() PBD (c) 1999
void	**setFieldPanel**(JbuiFieldPanel newFieldPanel) Sets the field panel.
void	**setModel**(JbuiListModel newModel) Sets the model for this JbuiList.
void	**setOrientation**(int newOrientation) This method was created in VisualAge.
void	**setSelectMode**(int newValue) PBD (c) 1999

Methods inherited from class com.pbd.pub.jbui.JbuiScreen

EXFMT, getFrame, getPosition, getPressedButton, isSomeoneWaiting, jbuiNotify, jbuiNotify, READ, setButtonPanel, setHandle, setOwner, setPosition, setTitle, WRITE

Methods inherited from class java.lang.Object

equals, getClass, hashCode, notify, notifyAll, toString, wait, wait, wait

Constructor Detail

JbuiSplit

public **JbuiSplit**()
   Creates a default JbuiSplit.

375

JbuiSplit

```
public JbuiSplit(java.lang.String initTitle,
                 JbuiListModel initModel,
                 JbuiFieldPanel initFieldPanel)
```
Creates a JbuiList with the specified title and data model.
Parameters:
initTitle - - the title for the JbuiList.
initModel - - the JbuiListModel containing the data for the JbuiList.

JbuiSplit

```
public JbuiSplit(java.lang.String initTitle,
                 JbuiListModel initModel,
                 JbuiFieldPanel initFieldPanel,
                 int initOrientation)
```
Creates a JbuiList with the specified title and data model.
Parameters:
initTitle - - the title for the JbuiList.
initModel - - the JbuiListModel containing the data for the JbuiList.

JbuiSplit

```
public JbuiSplit(java.lang.String initTitle,
                 JbuiListModel initModel,
                 JbuiFieldPanel initFieldPanel,
                 int initOrientation,
                 int initSelectMode)
```
Creates a JbuiList with the specified title and data model.
Parameters:
initTitle - - the title for the JbuiList.
initModel - - the JbuiListModel containing the data for the JbuiList.

Method Detail

getFieldPanel

```
public JbuiFieldPanel getFieldPanel()
```
This method was created in VisualAge.
Returns:
com.pbd.pub.jbui.JbuiFieldPanel

getSelectedHandle

```
public java.lang.Object getSelectedHandle()
```
Returns either the handle for the selected row, or if handles were not specified, returns the Vector containing the row data. If no rows are selected, the method returns null.
Returns:
either the handle or the row data for the selected row (or null if no row is selected).

getSelectMode

public int **getSelectMode**()
    PBD (c) 1999
    Returns:
    int

setFieldPanel

public void **setFieldPanel**(JbuiFieldPanel newFieldPanel)
    Sets the field panel.
    Parameters:
    newFieldPanel - - the new field panel.

setModel

public void **setModel**(JbuiListModel newModel)
    Sets the model for this JbuiList.
    Parameters:
    newModel - - the new model for this JbuiList.

setOrientation

public void **setOrientation**(int newOrientation)
    This method was created in VisualAge.
    Parameters:
    newOrientation - int

setSelectMode

public void **setSelectMode**(int newValue)
    PBD (c) 1999
    Parameters:
    newValue - int

Appendix C: Javadoc

Overview **Package** Class Tree Deprecated Index Help
PREV PACKAGE NEXT PACKAGE   FRAMES NO FRAMES

Package com.pbd.pub.jdb400

Interface Summary

Jdb400Constants	Jdb400Constants defines all the constants used by the various JDB/400 internal routines.

Class Summary

Jdb400	
Jdb400Constant	Jdb400Constant provides the toString() method to convert a JDB/400 constant to its string format.
Jdb400Field	Jdb400Field is the Java representation of an AS/400 field.
Jdb400File	Jdb400File is the superclass underlying the Jdb400 file types.
Jdb400KeyedFile	Jdb400KeyedFile provides standard keyed I/O routines:
Jdb400KeyedUpdateFile	Jdb400KeyedUpdateFile provides standard keyed I/O routines:
Jdb400SequentialFile	Jdb400SequentialFile provides standard sequential I/O routines:
Jdb400SequentialUpdateFile	Jdb400SequentialOutputFile provides standard sequential I/O routines:

Overview Package **Class** Tree Deprecated Index Help
PREV CLASS NEXT CLASS   FRAMES NO FRAMES
SUMMARY: INNER | FIELD | CONSTR | METHOD   DETAIL: FIELD | CONSTR | METHOD

com.pbd.pub.jdb400

Interface Jdb400Constants

All Known Implementing Classes:
> Jdb400File, Jdb400Constant

public interface **Jdb400Constants**

Jdb400Constants defines all the constants used by the various JDB/400 internal routines.

Since:
> 1.0P

Field Summary

static int	**JDB_CHAIN**
static int	**JDB_CLOSE**
static int	**JDB_DELET**
static int	**JDB_DUMPRECORD**
static int	**JDB_GETFIELD**
static int	**JDB_KEYED**
static int	**JDB_OPEN**
static int	**JDB_READ**
static int	**JDB_READALL**
static int	**JDB_READE**
static int	**JDB_READP**
static int	**JDB_REDPE**
static int	**JDB_REWIND**
static int	**JDB_SEQUENTIAL**
static int	**JDB_SETCONTENTS**
static int	**JDB_SETFIELD**
static int	**JDB_SETLL**
static int	**JDB_UPDAT**
static int	**JDB_WRITE**

Appendix C: Javadoc

Field Detail

JDB_KEYED

public static final int **JDB_KEYED**

JDB_SEQUENTIAL

public static final int **JDB_SEQUENTIAL**

JDB_OPEN

public static final int **JDB_OPEN**

JDB_CLOSE

public static final int **JDB_CLOSE**

JDB_READ

public static final int **JDB_READ**

JDB_READP

public static final int **JDB_READP**

JDB_CHAIN

public static final int **JDB_CHAIN**

JDB_SETLL

public static final int **JDB_SETLL**

JDB_READE

public static final int **JDB_READE**

JDB_REDPE

public static final int **JDB_REDPE**

JDB_UPDAT

public static final int **JDB_UPDAT**

JDB_WRITE

public static final int **JDB_WRITE**

JDB_DELET

public static final int **JDB_DELET**

JDB_READALL

public static final int **JDB_READALL**

JDB_REWIND

public static final int **JDB_REWIND**

JDB_GETFIELD

public static final int **JDB_GETFIELD**

JDB_SETFIELD

public static final int **JDB_SETFIELD**

JDB_SETCONTENTS

public static final int **JDB_SETCONTENTS**

JDB_DUMPRECORD

public static final int **JDB_DUMPRECORD**

Appendix C: Javadoc

Overview **Package** **Class** **Tree** **Deprecated** **Index** **Help**

PREV CLASS NEXT CLASS   **FRAMES** **NO FRAMES**
SUMMARY: INNER | FIELD | CONSTR | METHOD   DETAIL: FIELD | CONSTR | METHOD

com.pbd.pub.jdb400

Class Jdb400

```
java.lang.Object
  |
  +-com.pbd.pub.jdb400.Jdb400
```

public class **Jdb400**
extends java.lang.Object
Since:
    1.0P

Constructor Summary

Jdb400()	

Method Summary

static void	**setAS400**(java.lang.String initName) Sets the default value for the system name.
static void	**setAS400**(java.lang.String initName, java.lang.String initUser) Sets default values for user ID and password.
static void	**setAS400**(java.lang.String initName, java.lang.String initUser, java.lang.String initPassword) Sets default values for system name, user ID, and password, bypassing the logon panel entirely.
static void	**setLibrary**(java.lang.String newLibrary) PBD (c) 1999

Methods inherited from class java.lang.Object

equals, getClass, hashCode, notify, notifyAll, toString, wait, wait, wait

Constructor Detail

Jdb400

public **Jdb400**()

Method Detail

setAS400

public static void **setAS400**(java.lang.String initName)

Sets the default value for the system name. This will cause the logon panel to be displayed with the system name protected. The user must enter user ID and password. The logon panel is displayed the first time a JDB/400 file object is created.

Example use:
Jdb400.setAS400("myas400.mydomain.com");
Parameters:
initName - is the AS/400 system name in domain format.

setAS400

public static void **setAS400**(java.lang.String initName,
                               java.lang.String initUser)

Sets default values for user ID and password. This will cause the logon panel to be displayed with the system name protected and the user ID filled in. The user must enter the password. The logon panel is displayed the first time a JDB/400 file object is created.

Example use:
Jdb400.setAS400("myas400.mydomain.com", "myuserid");
Parameters:
initName - is the AS/400 system name in domain format.
initUser - is the AS/400 user ID.

setAS400

public static void **setAS400**(java.lang.String initName,
                               java.lang.String initUser,
                               java.lang.String initPassword)

Sets default values for system name, user ID, and password, bypassing the logon panel entirely. **The problem is that the password is in your program as clear text, so it is not secure.**

Example use:
Jdb400.setAS400("myas400.mydomain.com", "myuserid", "mypassword");
Parameters:
initName - is the AS/400 system name in domain format.
initUser - is the AS/400 user ID.
initPassword - is the password for the user ID.

Appendix C: Javadoc

setLibrary

```
public static void setLibrary(java.lang.String newLibrary)
```
PBD (c) 1999
Parameters:
newLibrary - java.lang.String

Overview **Package** **Class** **Tree** **Deprecated** **Index** **Help**
PREV CLASS NEXT CLASS
SUMMARY: INNER | FIELD | CONSTR | METHOD

FRAMES NO FRAMES
DETAIL: FIELD | CONSTR | METHOD

---

com.pbd.pub.jdb400

Class Jdb400Constant

```
java.lang.Object
  |
  +-com.pbd.pub.jdb400.Jdb400Constant
```
All Implemented Interfaces:
Jdb400Constants

---

public class **Jdb400Constant**
extends java.lang.Object
implements Jdb400Constants

Jdb400Constant provides the toString() method to convert a JDB/400 constant to its string format.

Since:
1.0P

Fields inherited from interface com.pbd.pub.jdb400.Jdb400Constants

JDB_CHAIN, JDB_CLOSE, JDB_DELET, JDB_DUMPRECORD, JDB_GETFIELD, JDB_KEYED, JDB_OPEN, JDB_READ, JDB_READALL, JDB_READE, JDB_READP, JDB_REDPE, JDB_REWIND, JDB_SEQUENTIAL, JDB_SETCONTENTS, JDB_SETFIELD, JDB_SETLL, JDB_UPDAT, JDB_WRITE

Constructor Summary

Jdb400Constant()

Method Summary

static java.lang.String	toString(int constant)

Methods inherited from class java.lang.Object

equals, getClass, hashCode, notify, notifyAll, toString, wait, wait, wait

Constructor Detail

Jdb400Constant

public **Jdb400Constant**()

Method Detail

toString

public static java.lang.String **toString**(int constant)

Overview Package **Class** Tree Deprecated Index Help
PREV CLASS NEXT CLASS   FRAMES NO FRAMES
SUMMARY: INNER | FIELD | CONSTR | METHOD   DETAIL: FIELD | CONSTR | METHOD

---

com.pbd.pub.jdb400

Class Jdb400Field

```
java.lang.Object
  |
  +-com.pbd.pub.jdb400.Jdb400Field
```

public class **Jdb400Field**
extends java.lang.Object

Jdb400Field is the Java representation of an AS/400 field. In this version, it contains little more than name, length, and description information. It may be expanded to include business rule processing.

Since:
    1.1P

Appendix C: Javadoc

Constructor Summary

Jdb400Field()
    Jdb400Field constructor comment.

Jdb400Field(java.lang.String initName, java.lang.String initColumnHeading, java.lang.String initDescription, int initLength)
    This method was created in VisualAge.

Method Summary

java.lang.String	**getColumnHeading**() Gets the column heading for this field.
java.lang.String	**getDescription**() Gets the description for this field.
int	**getLength**() Gets the length for this field.
java.lang.String	**getName**() Gets the name for this field.
void	**setColumnHeading**(java.lang.String newColumnHeading) Sets the column heading for this field.
void	**setDescription**(java.lang.String newDescription) Sets the description for this field.
void	**setLength**(int newLength) Sets the length (in pixels) for this field.
void	**setName**(java.lang.String newName) Sets the name for this field.

Methods inherited from class java.lang.Object

equals, getClass, hashCode, notify, notifyAll, toString, wait, wait, wait

Constructor Detail

Jdb400Field

```
public Jdb400Field()
```
    Jdb400Field constructor comment.

Jdb400Field

```
public Jdb400Field(java.lang.String initName,
                   java.lang.String initColumnHeading,
                   java.lang.String initDescription,
                   int initLength)
```
    This method was created in VisualAge.

Parameters:
initName - - the name of the field on the AS/400.
initColumnHeading - - the field's column heading.
initDescription - - the field's description.
initLength - - the field's length.

Method Detail

getColumnHeading

```
public java.lang.String getColumnHeading()
```
Gets the column heading for this field.
Returns:
the column heading for this field.

---

getDescription

```
public java.lang.String getDescription()
```
Gets the description for this field.
Returns:
the description for this field.

---

getLength

```
public int getLength()
```
Gets the length for this field.
Returns:
the length for this field.

---

getName

```
public java.lang.String getName()
```
Gets the name for this field.
Returns:
the name for this field.

---

setColumnHeading

```
public void setColumnHeading(java.lang.String newColumnHeading)
```
Sets the column heading for this field.
Parameters:
newColumnHeading - - the new column heading for this field.

---

setDescription

```
public void setDescription(java.lang.String newDescription)
```
Sets the description for this field.
Parameters:
newDescription - - the new description for this field.

setLength

public void **setLength**(int newLength)
    Sets the length (in pixels) for this field.
    Parameters:
        newLength - - the new length for this field.

setName

public void **setName**(java.lang.String newName)
    Sets the name for this field.
    Parameters:
        newName - - the new name for this field.

Overview Package **Class** Tree Deprecated Index Help
PREV CLASS **NEXT CLASS**   **FRAMES** **NO FRAMES**
SUMMARY: INNER | FIELD | CONSTR | METHOD   DETAIL: FIELD | CONSTR | METHOD

---

com.pbd.pub.jdb400

Class Jdb400File

```
java.lang.Object
  |
  +-com.pbd.pub.jdb400.Jdb400File
```

All Implemented Interfaces:
    Jdb400Constants

Direct Known Subclasses:
    Jdb400KeyedFile, Jdb400SequentialFile

---

public class **Jdb400File**
extends java.lang.Object
implements Jdb400Constants

Jdb400File is the superclass underlying the Jdb400 file types. It will create either a com.ibm.as400.access.KeyedFile or com.ibm.as400.access.SequentialFile and return it via the getFile method as an AS400File; the subclass must downcast the returned object appropriately.

Jdb400File provides implicit open support, along with READ and READP methods for all file types. It also provides all the field level support.

In the public version, all error processing is provided by Jdb400File, which prints an error message and exits the program. The professional version provides exception processing.

Since:
    1.0P
See Also:
    Jdb400KeyedFile, Jdb400SequentialFile

Fields inherited from interface com.pbd.pub.jdb400.Jdb400Constants

JDB_CHAIN, JDB_CLOSE, JDB_DELET, JDB_DUMPRECORD, JDB_GETFIELD, JDB_KEYED, JDB_OPEN, JDB_READ, JDB_READALL, JDB_READE, JDB_READP, JDB_REDPE, JDB_REWIND, JDB_SEQUENTIAL, JDB_SETCONTENTS, JDB_SETFIELD, JDB_SETLL, JDB_UPDAT, JDB_WRITE

Method Summary

void	**CLOSE**() Closes the file.
void	**dumpRecord**() Internal routine used for error processing.
java.lang.String	**getAlpha**(java.lang.String fieldName) Returns the contents of a specific field in the current record as a String.
java.lang.Object	**getField**(java.lang.String fieldName) Returns the contents of a specific field in the current record as an Object.
java.lang.String[]	**getFieldNames**() Returns the names of all the fields in this file's record format.
Jdb400Field	**getJdbField**(java.lang.String fieldName) Returns the Jdb400Field for the specified field.
java.math.BigDecimal	**getNumeric**(java.lang.String fieldName) Returns the contents of a specific field in the current record as a BigDecimal.
com.pbd.pub.jdb400.Record	**getRecord**() Returns the current record for this file.
boolean	**READ**() Gets the next record in the file.
com.pbd.pub.jdb400.Record[]	**READALL**() Gets all records in the file.
boolean	**READP**() Gets the previous record in the file.
void	**REWIND**() Positions the cursor to the beginning of the file (before the first record).
void	**setField**(java.lang.String fieldName, java.lang.Object newValue) Updates the contents of a specific field in the current record.

Methods inherited from class java.lang.Object

equals, getClass, hashCode, notify, notifyAll, toString, wait, wait, wait

Method Detail

CLOSE

public void **CLOSE**()
    Closes the file.

dumpRecord

public void **dumpRecord**()
    Internal routine used for error processing. Primarily a diagnostic routine, dumpRecord will print a list of all fields in the current record and their contents.

getAlpha

public java.lang.String **getAlpha**(java.lang.String fieldName)
    Returns the contents of a specific field in the current record as a String.

    This example gets the first source line from the source member MYPROGRAM in MYLIB/QRPGSRC.

```
Jdb400SequentialFile MYPROGRAM = new
Jdb400SequentialFile("MYLIB/QRPGSRC.MYPROGRAM");
MYPROGRAM.CHAIN(1);
String srcLine = MYPROGRAM.getAlpha("SRCDTA");
```
    Parameters:
    fieldName - is the AS/400 field name.
    Returns:
    an object of the corresponding type for the AS/400 field type.

getField

public java.lang.Object **getField**(java.lang.String fieldName)
    Returns the contents of a specific field in the current record as an Object.
    This example gets the first sequence number and first source line from the source member MYPROGRAM in MYLIB/QRPGSRC. Note the explicit downcasting required.

```
Jdb400SequentialFile MYPROGRAM = new
Jdb400SequentialFile("MYLIB/QRPGSRC.MYPROGRAM");
MYPROGRAM.CHAIN(1);
BigDecimal sequenceNumber = (BigDecimal) MYPROGRAM.getField("SRCSEQ");
String srcLine = (String) MYPROGRAM.getField("SRCDTA");
```
    Parameters:
    fieldName - is the AS/400 field name.
    Returns:
    an object of the corresponding type for the AS/400 field type.
    See Also:
    getAlpha, getNumeric

getFieldNames

public java.lang.String[] **getFieldNames**()
>Returns the names of all the fields in this file's record format.
>**Returns:**
>an array of Strings containing all the field names of the record format.

getJdbField

public Jdb400Field **getJdbField**(java.lang.String fieldName)
>Returns the Jdb400Field for the specified field.
>**Returns:**
>the Jdb400Field for the specified field.

getNumeric

public java.math.BigDecimal **getNumeric**(java.lang.String fieldName)
>Returns the contents of a specific field in the current record as a BigDecimal.
>This example gets the first sequence number from the source member MYPROGRAM in MYLIB/QRPGSRC.
>
>```
>Jdb400SequentialFile MYPROGRAM = new
>Jdb400SequentialFile("MYLIB/QRPGSRC.MYPROGRAM");
>MYPROGRAM.CHAIN(1);
>BigDecimal sequenceNumber = MYPROGRAM.getNumeric("SRCSEQ");
>```
>**Parameters:**
>fieldName - is the AS/400 field name.
>**Returns:**
>an object of the corresponding type for the AS/400 field type.

getRecord

public com.pbd.pub.jdb400.Record **getRecord**()
>Returns the current record for this file. In the public domain version, this is the result of the last successful READ operation or null if the last operation set on EOF.
>
>**Returns:**
>the current record for this file (or null for EOF).

READ

public boolean **READ**()
>Gets the next record in the file.
>**Returns:**
>true if a record is read, false for EOF.

READALL

public com.pbd.pub.jdb400.Record[] **READALL**()
>Gets all records in the file.
>**Returns:**
>array of all records in file.

READP

```
public boolean READP()
```
        Gets the previous record in the file.
        Returns:
        true if a record is read, false for EOF.

REWIND

```
public void REWIND()
```
        Positions the cursor to the beginning of the file (before the first record).

setField

```
public void setField(java.lang.String fieldName,
                     java.lang.Object newValue)
```
        Updates the contents of a specific field in the current record.
        Parameters:
        fieldName - is the AS/400 field name.
        newValue - is the Java object containing the new value.

Overview Package **Class** Tree Deprecated Index Help
PREV CLASS NEXT CLASS   FRAMES NO FRAMES
SUMMARY: INNER | FIELD | CONSTR | METHOD   DETAIL: FIELD | CONSTR | METHOD

---

com.pbd.pub.jdb400

Class Jdb400KeyedFile

```
java.lang.Object
  |
  +-com.pbd.pub.jdb400.Jdb400File
       |
       +-com.pbd.pub.jdb400.Jdb400KeyedFile
```
All Implemented Interfaces:
    Jdb400Constants
Direct Known Subclasses:
    Jdb400KeyedUpdateFile

---

public class **Jdb400KeyedFile**
extends Jdb400File

Jdb400KeyedFile provides standard keyed I/O routines:

Appendix C: Javadoc

- READ
- READP
- CHAIN
- SETLL
- READE

READ and READP are inherited from the Jdb400File class. All field access is inherited from Jdb400File as well. Keyed file operations use objects as the key fields. The object types depend on the AS/400 field type. In general, alpha fields are represented as String objects and packed and zoned decimal fields are represented as BigDecimal objects. Each keyed I/O method allows either a single object (for a one-field key) or an array of objects (this works like a key list).

This version does not support SETGT or REDPE. I hope to include those in a later release.

Since:
    1.0P

Constructor Summary

Jdb400KeyedFile(`java.lang.String qsysFileName`)
    Constructs a Jdb400KeyedFile for the specified qsysFileName.

Method Summary

boolean	**CHAIN**(`java.lang.Object key`) Gets the record with the specified key.
boolean	**CHAIN**(`java.lang.Object[] keys`) Gets the record with the specified key.
boolean	**READE**(`java.lang.Object key`) Reads the next record with a key equal to the specified key.
boolean	**READE**(`java.lang.Object[] keys`) Reads the next record with a key equal to the specified key.
void	**SETLL**(`java.lang.Object key`) Positions the file to the first record with a key less than the specified key.
void	**SETLL**(`java.lang.Object[] keys`) Positions the file to the first record with a key less than the specified key.

Methods inherited from class com.pbd.pub.jdb400.Jdb400File

CLOSE, dumpRecord, getAlpha, getField, getFieldNames, getJdbField, getNumeric, getRecord, READ, READALL, READP, REWIND, setField

Methods inherited from class java.lang.Object

`equals, getClass, hashCode, notify, notifyAll, toString, wait, wait, wait`

393

Appendix C: Javadoc

Constructor Detail

Jdb400KeyedFile

```
public Jdb400KeyedFile(java.lang.String qsysFileName)
```
Constructs a Jdb400KeyedFile for the specified qsysFileName.

The file name is in standard AS/400 QSYS format, "MYLIB/MYFILE.MYMEMBER", or "MYLIB/MYFILE(MYMEMBER)". If member is not specified, it defaults to %FIRST%, which is the IBM Toolbox equivalent of *FIRST. If library is not specified, it uses the default library from the Jdb400 class, which is initially %LIBL%, the equivalent of *LIBL. The default library can be changed with the setDefaultLibrary method of Jdb400.

Examples:
```
Jdb400KeyedFile ORDHDRL1 = new Jdb400KeyedFile("ORDHDRL1");
Jdb400KeyedFile ORDHDRL1 = new Jdb400KeyedFile("MYLIB/ORDHDRL1");
Jdb400KeyedFile QUOTESL1 = new Jdb400KeyedFile("MYLIB/ORDHDRL1.QUOTES");
Jdb400KeyedFile QUOTESL1 = new Jdb400KeyedFile("MYLIB/ORDHDRL1(QUOTES)");
```
Parameters:
qsysFileName - is the name of the file to be opened, in QSYS format.
See Also:
Jdb400

Method Detail

CHAIN

```
public boolean CHAIN(java.lang.Object[] keys)
```
Gets the record with the specified key.
Parameters:
keys - is an array of objects containing the key.
Returns:
true if the record is found, false for not found.

CHAIN

```
public boolean CHAIN(java.lang.Object key)
```
Gets the record with the specified key.
Parameters:
key - is the single object containing the key.
Returns:
true if the record is found, false for not found.

READE

```
public boolean READE(java.lang.Object[] keys)
```
Reads the next record with a key equal to the specified key.
Parameters:
keys - is an array of objects containing the key.
Returns:
true if the record is found, false for not found.

READE

public boolean **READE**(java.lang.Object key)
>Reads the next record with a key equal to the specified key.
>**Parameters:**
>key - is the single object containing the key.
>**Returns:**
>true if the record is found, false for not found.

SETLL

public void **SETLL**(java.lang.Object[] keys)
>Positions the file to the first record with a key less than the specified key.
>**Parameters:**
>keys - is an array of objects containing the key.

SETLL

public void **SETLL**(java.lang.Object key)
>Positions the file to the first record with a key less than the specified key.
>**Parameters:**
>key - is the single object containing the key.

Overview Package **Class** Tree Deprecated Index Help
PREV CLASS NEXT CLASS   FRAMES NO FRAMES
SUMMARY: INNER | FIELD | CONSTR | METHOD   DETAIL: FIELD | CONSTR | METHOD

---

com.pbd.pub.jdb400

Class Jdb400KeyedUpdateFile

```
java.lang.Object
  |
  +-com.pbd.pub.jdb400.Jdb400File
       |
       +-com.pbd.pub.jdb400.Jdb400KeyedFile
            |
            +-com.pbd.pub.jdb400.Jdb400KeyedUpdateFile
```

All Implemented Interfaces:
>Jdb400Constants

---

public class **Jdb400KeyedUpdateFile**
extends Jdb400KeyedFile

Jdb400KeyedUpdateFile provides standard keyed I/O routines:

395

Appendix C: Javadoc

- READ
- READP
- CHAIN
- SETLL
- READE
- DELET
- UPDAT
- WRITE

READ, READP, DELET, UPDAT, and WRITE are inherited from the Jdb400File class. All field access is inherited from Jdb400File as well. Keyed file operations use objects as the key fields. The object types depend on the AS/400 field type. In general, alpha fields are represented as String objects and packed and zoned decimal fields are represented as BigDecimal objects. Each keyed I/O method allows either a single object (for a one-field key) or an array of objects (this works like a key list).

This version does not support SETGT or REDPE. I hope to include those in a later release. I also plan on adding delete by key.

Since:
1.2P

Constructor Summary

Jdb400KeyedUpdateFile(java.lang.String qsysFileName)
    Constructs a Jdb400KeyedUpdateFile for the specified qsysFileName.

Method Summary

void	**DELET**()	
	Deletes the current record.	
void	**setContents**(byte[] newContents)	
	This method was created in VisualAge.	
void	**UPDAT**()	
	Updates the current record with the contents of the record buffer.	
void	**WRITE**()	
	Writes a new record with the contents of the record buffer.	

Methods inherited from class com.pbd.pub.jdb400.Jdb400KeyedFile

CHAIN, CHAIN, READE, READE, SETLL, SETLL

Methods inherited from class com.pbd.pub.jdb400.Jdb400File

CLOSE, dumpRecord, getAlpha, getField, getFieldNames, getJdbField, getNumeric, getRecord, READ, READALL, READP, REWIND, setField

Appendix C: Javadoc

Methods inherited from class java.lang.Object
`equals, getClass, hashCode, notify, notifyAll, toString, wait, wait, wait`

Constructor Detail

Jdb400KeyedUpdateFile

`public` **`Jdb400KeyedUpdateFile`**`(java.lang.String qsysFileName)`
   Constructs a Jdb400KeyedUpdateFile for the specified qsysFileName.

   The file name is in standard AS/400 QSYS format, "MYLIB/MYFILE.MYMEMBER", or "MYLIB/MYFILE(MYMEMBER)". If member is not specified, it defaults to %FIRST%, which is the IBM Toolbox equivalent of *FIRST. If library is not specified, it uses the default library from the Jdb400 class, which is initially %LIBL%, the equivalent of *LIBL. The default library can be changed with the setDefaultLibrary method of Jdb400.

   Examples:
   ```
   Jdb400KeyedFile ORDHDRL1 = new Jdb400KeyedFile("ORDHDRL1");
   Jdb400KeyedFile ORDHDRL1 = new Jdb400KeyedFile("MYLIB/ORDHDRL1");
   Jdb400KeyedFile QUOTESL1 = new Jdb400KeyedFile("MYLIB/ORDHDRL1.QUOTES");
   Jdb400KeyedFile QUOTESL1 = new Jdb400KeyedFile("MYLIB/ORDHDRL1(QUOTES)");
   ```
   Parameters:
   qsysFileName - is the name of the file to be opened, in QSYS format.
   See Also:
   Jdb400

Method Detail

DELET

`public void` **`DELET`**`()`
   Deletes the current record.

---

setContents

`public void` **`setContents`**`(byte[] newContents)`
   This method was created in VisualAge.
   Parameters:
   newContents - byte[]

UPDAT

`public void` **`UPDAT`**`()`
   Updates the current record with the contents of the record buffer.

Appendix C: Javadoc

WRITE

public void **WRITE**()
    Writes a new record with the contents of the record buffer.

Overview | Package | **Class** | Tree | Deprecated | Index | Help
PREV CLASS   NEXT CLASS   FRAMES   NO FRAMES
SUMMARY: INNER | FIELD | CONSTR | METHOD   DETAIL: FIELD | CONSTR | METHOD

---

com.pbd.pub.jdb400

Class Jdb400SequentialFile

```
java.lang.Object
  |
  +-com.pbd.pub.jdb400.Jdb400File
        |
        +-com.pbd.pub.jdb400.Jdb400SequentialFile
```

All Implemented Interfaces:
    Jdb400Constants

Direct Known Subclasses:
    Jdb400SequentialUpdateFile

---

public class **Jdb400SequentialFile**
extends Jdb400File

Jdb400SequentialFile provides standard sequential I/O routines:

- READ
- READP
- CHAIN

READ and READP are inherited from the Jdb400File class. All field access is inherited from Jdb400File as well.

Since:
    1.0P

Constructor Summary

Jdb400SequentialFile(java.lang.String qsysFileName)
    Constructs a Jdb400SequentialFile for the specified qsysFileName.

Appendix C: Javadoc

Method Summary

boolean	<u>CHAIN</u>(int recordNumber) Reads the record at the specified record number.

Methods inherited from class com.pbd.pub.jdb400.<u>Jdb400File</u>

<u>CLOSE</u>, <u>dumpRecord</u>, <u>getAlpha</u>, <u>getField</u>, <u>getFieldNames</u>, <u>getJdbField</u>, <u>getNumeric</u>, <u>getRecord</u>, <u>READ</u>, <u>READALL</u>, <u>READP</u>, <u>REWIND</u>, <u>setField</u>

Methods inherited from class java.lang.Object

equals, getClass, hashCode, notify, notifyAll, toString, wait, wait, wait

Constructor Detail

Jdb400SequentialFile

public **Jdb400SequentialFile**(java.lang.String qsysFileName)

Constructs a Jdb400SequentialFile for the specified qsysFileName.

The file name is in standard AS/400 QSYS format, "MYLIB/MYFILE.MYMEMBER", or "MYLIB/MYFILE(MYMEMBER)". If member is not specified, it defaults to %FIRST%, which is the IBM Toolbox equivalent of *FIRST. If library is not specified, it uses the default library from the Jdb400 class, which is initially %LIBL%, the equivalent of *LIBL. The default library can be changed with the setDefaultLibrary method of Jdb400.

Examples:
```
Jdb400SequentialFile QRPGSRC = new Jdb400SequentialFile("QRPGSRC");
Jdb400SequentialFile QRPGSRC = new Jdb400SequentialFile("MYLIB/QRPGSRC");
Jdb400SequentialFile MYPROGRAM = new Jdb400SequentialFile("MYLIB/QRPGSRC.MYPROGRAM");
Jdb400SequentialFile MYPROGRAM = new Jdb400SequentialFile("MYLIB/QRPGSRC(MYPROGRAM)");
```
Parameters:
qsysFileName - is the name of the file to be opened, in QSYS format.

See Also:
<u>Jdb400</u>

Method Detail

CHAIN

public boolean **CHAIN**(int recordNumber)

Reads the record at the specified record number.
Parameters:
recordNumber - is the record number.
Returns:
true if the record is found, false for not found.

Appendix C: Javadoc

| Overview | Package | **Class** | Tree | Deprecated | Index | Help |

PREV CLASS NEXT CLASS   **FRAMES** **NO FRAMES**
SUMMARY: INNER | FIELD | CONSTR | METHOD   DETAIL: FIELD | CONSTR | METHOD

---

com.pbd.pub.jdb400

Class Jdb400SequentialUpdateFile

```
java.lang.Object
  |
  +-com.pbd.pub.jdb400.Jdb400File
        |
        +-com.pbd.pub.jdb400.Jdb400SequentialFile
              |
              +-com.pbd.pub.jdb400.Jdb400SequentialUpdateFile
```

All Implemented Interfaces:
> Jdb400Constants

---

public class **Jdb400SequentialUpdateFile**
extends Jdb400SequentialFile

Jdb400SequentialOutputFile provides standard sequential I/O routines:

- READ
- READP
- CHAIN
- DELET
- UPDAT
- WRITE

READ, READP, DELET, UPDAT, and WRITE are inherited from the Jdb400File class. All field access is inherited from Jdb400File as well.

Since:
> 1.2P

Constructor Summary

Jdb400SequentialUpdateFile(java.lang.String qsysFileName)
> Constructs a Jdb400SequentialUpdateFile for the specified qsysFileName.

Method Summary

void	**DELET**() Deletes the current record.
void	**setContents**(byte[] newContents) This method was created in VisualAge.
void	**UPDAT**() Updates the current record with the contents of the record buffer.
void	**WRITE**() Writes a new record with the contents of the record buffer.

Methods inherited from class com.pbd.pub.jdb400.Jdb400SequentialFile

CHAIN

Methods inherited from class com.pbd.pub.jdb400.Jdb400File

CLOSE, dumpRecord, getAlpha, getField, getFieldNames, getJdbField, getNumeric, getRecord, READ, READALL, READP, REWIND, setField

Methods inherited from class java.lang.Object

equals, getClass, hashCode, notify, notifyAll, toString, wait, wait, wait

Constructor Detail

Jdb400SequentialUpdateFile

public **Jdb400SequentialUpdateFile**(java.lang.String qsysFileName)
    Constructs a Jdb400SequentialUpdateFile for the specified qsysFileName.

    The file name is in standard AS/400 QSYS format, "MYLIB/MYFILE.MYMEMBER", or "MYLIB/MYFILE(MYMEMBER)". If member is not specified, it defaults to %FIRST%, which is the IBM Toolbox equivalent of *FIRST. If library is not specified, it uses the default library from the Jdb400 class, which is initially %LIBL%, the equivalent of *LIBL. The default library can be changed with the setDefaultLibrary method of Jdb400.

    Examples:
    Jdb400SequentialFile QRPGSRC = new Jdb400SequentialFile("QRPGSRC");
    Jdb400SequentialFile QRPGSRC = new Jdb400SequentialFile("MYLIB/QRPGSRC");
    Jdb400SequentialFile MYPROGRAM = new Jdb400SequentialFile("MYLIB/QRPGSRC.MYPROGRAM");
    Jdb400SequentialFile MYPROGRAM = new Jdb400SequentialFile("MYLIB/QRPGSRC(MYPROGRAM)");
    Parameters:
    qsysFileName - is the name of the file to be opened, in QSYS format.
    See Also:
    Jdb400

Appendix C: Javadoc

Method Detail

DELET

```
public void DELET()
```
    Deletes the current record.

setContents

```
public void setContents(byte[] newContents)
```
    This method was created in VisualAge.
    Parameters:
    newContents - byte[]

UPDAT

```
public void UPDAT()
```
    Updates the current record with the contents of the record buffer.

WRITE

```
public void WRITE()
```
    Writes a new record with the contents of the record buffer.

Overview **Package** Class Tree Deprecated Index Help
PREV PACKAGE   NEXT PACKAGE   FRAMES   NO FRAMES

Package com.pbd.pub.jdqm400

Interface Summary

JdqmConstants	

Class Summary

Jdqm400	
JdqmServer	
JdqmSession	

402

Appendix C: Javadoc

Overview Package **Class** Tree Deprecated Index Help
PREV CLASS   NEXT CLASS   FRAMES   NO FRAMES
SUMMARY: INNER | FIELD | CONSTR | METHOD   DETAIL: FIELD | CONSTR | METHOD

com.pbd.pub.jdqm400

Interface JdqmConstants

All Known Implementing Classes:
   JdqmServer, JdqmSession

public interface **JdqmConstants**
Since:
   1.2P

Field Summary

static int	**MESSAGE_DATA**
static int	**OPER_CODE**
static int	**OPER_SUBCODE**
static int	**RETURN_CODE**
static int	**RETURN_SUBCODE**
static int	**SEGMENT_ID**
static int	**SERVER_NAME**
static int	**SESSION_ID**

Field Detail

SESSION_ID

public static final int **SESSION_ID**

403

SERVER_NAME
public static final int **SERVER_NAME**

SEGMENT_ID
public static final int **SEGMENT_ID**

OPER_CODE
public static final int **OPER_CODE**

OPER_SUBCODE
public static final int **OPER_SUBCODE**

RETURN_CODE
public static final int **RETURN_CODE**

RETURN_SUBCODE
public static final int **RETURN_SUBCODE**

MESSAGE_DATA
public static final int **MESSAGE_DATA**

Overview Package **Class** Tree Deprecated Index Help
PREV CLASS   NEXT CLASS   FRAMES   NO FRAMES
SUMMARY: INNER | FIELD | CONSTR | METHOD   DETAIL: FIELD | CONSTR | METHOD

---

com.pbd.pub.jdqm400

Class Jdqm400

```
java.lang.Object
  |
  +-com.pbd.pub.jdqm400.Jdqm400
```

public class **Jdqm400**
extends java.lang.Object
Since:
    1.0P

Appendix C: Javadoc

Constructor Summary

Jdqm400()

Method Summary

static void	**setAS400**(java.lang.String initName) Sets the default value for the system name.
static void	**setAS400**(java.lang.String initName, java.lang.String initUser) Sets default values for user ID and password.
static void	**setAS400**(java.lang.String initName, java.lang.String initUser, java.lang.String initPassword) Sets default values for system name, user ID, and password, bypassing the logon panel entirely.
static void	**setSystemLibrary**(java.lang.String newSystemLibrary) PBD (c) 1999

Methods inherited from class java.lang.Object

`equals, getClass, hashCode, notify, notifyAll, toString, wait, wait, wait`

Constructor Detail

Jdqm400

```
public Jdqm400()
```

Method Detail

setAS400

```
public static void setAS400(java.lang.String initName)
```
Sets the default value for the system name. This will cause the logon panel to be displayed with the system name protected. The user must enter user ID and password. The logon panel is displayed the first time a JDQM/400 object is created.

Example use:

```
Jdqm400.setAS400("myas400.mydomain.com");
```
Parameters:
initName - is the AS/400 system name in domain format.

405

setAS400

```
public static void setAS400(java.lang.String initName,
                            java.lang.String initUser)
```
Sets default values for user ID and password. This will cause the logon panel to be displayed with the system name protected and the user ID filled in. The user must enter the password. The logon panel is displayed the first time a JDQM/400 object is created.

Example use:

```
Jdqm400.setAS400("myas400.mydomain.com", "myuserid");
```
Parameters:
initName - is the AS/400 system name in domain format.
initUser - is the AS/400 user ID.

setAS400

```
public static void setAS400(java.lang.String initName,
                            java.lang.String initUser,
                            java.lang.String initPassword)
```
Sets default values for system name, user ID, and password, bypassing the logon panel entirely. **The problem is that the password is in your program as clear text, so it is not secure.**

Example use:

```
Jdqm400.setAS400("myas400.mydomain.com", "myuserid", "mypassword");
```
Parameters:
initName - is the AS/400 system name in domain format.
initUser - is the AS/400 user ID.
initPassword - is the password for the user ID.

setSystemLibrary

```
public static void setSystemLibrary(java.lang.String newSystemLibrary)
```
PBD (c) 1999
Parameters:
newSystemLibrary - String

Appendix C: Javadoc

Overview	Package	**Class**	Tree	Deprecated	Index	Help

PREV CLASS **NEXT CLASS**   **FRAMES** **NO FRAMES**
SUMMARY: INNER | FIELD | CONSTR | METHOD   DETAIL: FIELD | CONSTR | METHOD

com.pbd.pub.jdqm400

Class JdqmServer

```
java.lang.Object
  |
  +-com.pbd.pub.jdqm400.JdqmServer
```
All Implemented Interfaces:
    JdqmConstants

---

public class **JdqmServer**
extends java.lang.Object
implements JdqmConstants
Since:
    1.2P

Fields inherited from interface com.pbd.pub.jdqm400.JdqmConstants

MESSAGE_DATA, OPER_CODE, OPER_SUBCODE, RETURN_CODE, RETURN_SUBCODE, SEGMENT_ID, SERVER_NAME, SESSION_ID

Constructor Summary

JdqmServer(java.lang.String serverName)

Method Summary

java.lang.Object[]	convertError(byte[] error400)
byte[]	createError(int fieldID, java.lang.String messageData) This method was created in VisualAge.
byte[]	createError(int fieldID, java.lang.String messageID, java.lang.String messageData) This method was created in VisualAge.
void	exit()
java.lang.Object[]	receive()

407

Appendix C: Javadoc

void	**send**(java.lang.String returncode, java.lang.String returnsubcode, byte[] message400)
void	**send**(java.lang.String segmentID, java.lang.String returncode, java.lang.String returnsubcode, byte[] message400)
void	**sendError**(int fieldID, java.lang.String messageData) This method was created in VisualAge.

Methods inherited from class java.lang.Object

```
equals, getClass, hashCode, notify, notifyAll, toString, wait, wait, wait
```

Constructor Detail

JdqmServer

```
public JdqmServer(java.lang.String serverName)
```

Method Detail

convertError

```
public java.lang.Object[] convertError(byte[] error400)
```

createError

```
public byte[] createError(int fieldID,
                          java.lang.String messageData)
```
This method was created in VisualAge.

Parameters:
fieldID - int
messageData - java.lang.String

Returns:
byte[]

createError

```
public byte[] createError(int fieldID,
                          java.lang.String messageID,
                          java.lang.String messageData)
```
This method was created in VisualAge.

Parameters:
fieldID - int
messageID - java.lang.String
messageData - java.lang.String

Returns:
byte[]

408

exit

```
public void exit()
```

receive

```
public java.lang.Object[] receive()
```

send

```
public void send(java.lang.String returncode,
                 java.lang.String returnsubcode,
                 byte[] message400)
```

send

```
public void send(java.lang.String segmentID,
                 java.lang.String returncode,
                 java.lang.String returnsubcode,
                 byte[] message400)
```

sendError

```
public void sendError(int fieldID,
                      java.lang.String messageData)
```
This method was created in VisualAge.
Parameters:
fieldID - int
messageData - java.lang.String
Returns:
byte[]

Appendix C: Javadoc

| Overview | Package | **Class** | Tree | Deprecated | Index | Help |

PREV CLASS NEXT CLASS   **FRAMES**   **NO FRAMES**
SUMMARY: INNER | FIELD | CONSTR | METHOD   DETAIL: FIELD | CONSTR | METHOD

---

com.pbd.pub.jdqm400

Class JdqmSession

```
java.lang.Object
  |
  +-com.pbd.pub.jdqm400.JdqmSession
```
All Implemented Interfaces:
    JdqmConstants

---

public class **JdqmSession**
extends java.lang.Object
implements JdqmConstants

Since:
    1.2P

Fields inherited from interface com.pbd.pub.jdqm400.JdqmConstants

MESSAGE_DATA, OPER_CODE, OPER_SUBCODE, RETURN_CODE, RETURN_SUBCODE, SEGMENT_ID, SERVER_NAME, SESSION_ID

Constructor Summary

JdqmSession()
JdqmSession(boolean initQueued)

Method Summary

java.lang.Object[]	convertError(byte[] error400)
void	exit()
java.lang.Object[]	receive()
void	send(java.lang.String server, java.lang.String opcode, java.lang.String opsubcode, byte[] message400)

Methods inherited from class java.lang.Object

equals, getClass, hashCode, notify, notifyAll, toString, wait, wait, wait

Constructor Detail

JdqmSession

public **JdqmSession**()

JdqmSession

public **JdqmSession**(boolean initQueued)

Method Detail

convertError

public java.lang.Object[] **convertError**(byte[] error400)

exit

public void **exit**()

receive

public java.lang.Object[] **receive**()

send

```
public void send(java.lang.String server,
                 java.lang.String opcode,
                 java.lang.String opsubcode,
                 byte[] message400)
```

Appendix C: Javadoc

Overview | **Package** | Class | **Tree** | **Deprecated** | **Index** | **Help**
PREV PACKAGE **NEXT PACKAGE** | **FRAMES** **NO FRAMES**

Package com.pbd.pub.jdspf

Interface Summary

JdspfDisplayFileListener	This type was created in VisualAge.
JdspfUIAdapter	This interface was designed to provide the ability to copy data from a display file to a record UI object and back.

Class Summary

JdspfAbstractRecord	The JdspfAbstractRecord class is designed as the base class for any record found in a display file.
JdspfBuffer	The JdspfBuffer class is an extension of the Dc400Structure class.
JdspfDisplayFile	The JdspfDisplayFile is the central object in the entire revitalization architecture.
JdspfDisplayFileAction	While the JdspfDisplayFileAction is designed to eventually expand to support other uses, its primary designed purpose was to serve as the message sent to display file listeners when an EXFMT has been requested.
JdspfFieldAttributes	NOT YET IMPLEMENTED.
JdspfIndicator	NOT YET IMPLEMENTED.
JdspfIndicatorArray	NOT YET IMPLEMENTED.
JdspfRecord	JdspfRecord represents a "regular" record in a display file, and supports the READ and WRITE operations.
JdspfRecordUI	This object associates a record UI object with a record name.
JdspfSubfile	NOT YET IMPLEMENTED.

Exception Summary

JdspfInvalidOperationException	This exception is thrown for invalid operations, such as attempting to perform an EXFMT on a subfile record, or a READC on a regular record.

412

Appendix C: Javadoc

| Overview | Package | **Class** | Tree | Deprecated | Index | Help |

PREV CLASS NEXT CLASS   FRAMES NO FRAMES
SUMMARY: INNER | FIELD | CONSTR | METHOD   DETAIL: FIELD | CONSTR | METHOD

com.pbd.pub.jdspf

Interface JdspfDisplayFileListener

All Known Implementing Classes:
   ScJdspfJbuiDefaultListener

---

public interface **JdspfDisplayFileListener**

This type was created in VisualAge.

Since:
   2.0P
See Also:
   JdspfDisplayFile, JdspfDisplayFileListener

Method Summary

boolean	**actionPerformed**(JdspfDisplayFileAction action) This method was created in VisualAge.

Method Detail

actionPerformed

public boolean **actionPerformed**(JdspfDisplayFileAction action)
   This method was created in VisualAge.
   Parameters:
   action - com.pbd.pub.jdspf.JdspfDisplayFileAction
   Returns:
   boolean

Appendix C: Javadoc

| Overview | Package | **Class** | Tree | Deprecated | Index | Help |

PREV CLASS   NEXT CLASS   **FRAMES**   **NO FRAMES**
SUMMARY: INNER | FIELD | CONSTR | METHOD   DETAIL: FIELD | CONSTR | METHOD

com.pbd.pub.jdspf

Interface JdspfUIAdapter

All Known Implementing Classes:
>   ScJdspfJsp, ScJdspfJbuiDisplay

public interface **JdspfUIAdapter**

This interface was designed to provide the ability to copy data from a display file to a record UI object and back. It is used when extending a concrete user interface object to support display file emulation.

Since:
> 2.0P

Method Summary

void	**copyDataFromJdspf**(JdspfDisplayFile jdspf) This method was created in VisualAge.
void	**copyDataToJdspf**(JdspfDisplayFile jdspf) This method was created in VisualAge.

Method Detail

copyDataFromJdspf

```
public void copyDataFromJdspf(JdspfDisplayFile jdspf)
```
> This method was created in VisualAge.
> **Parameters:**
> jdspf - com.pbd.pub.jdspf.JdspfDisplayFile

copyDataToJdspf

```
public void copyDataToJdspf(JdspfDisplayFile jdspf)
```
> This method was created in VisualAge.
> **Parameters:**
> jdspf - com.pbd.pub.jdspf.JdspfDisplayFile

Appendix C: Javadoc

| Overview | Package | **Class** | Tree | Deprecated | Index | Help |

PREV CLASS NEXT CLASS FRAMES NO FRAMES
SUMMARY: INNER | FIELD | CONSTR | METHOD   DETAIL: FIELD | CONSTR | METHOD

---

com.pbd.pub.jdspf

Class JdspfAbstractRecord

```
java.lang.Object
  |
  +-com.pbd.pub.jdspf.JdspfAbstractRecord
```
Direct Known Subclasses:
JdspfRecord, JdspfSubfile

---

public abstract class **JdspfAbstractRecord**
extends java.lang.Object

The JdspfAbstractRecord class is designed as the base class for any record found in a display file. At this point, I only support regular records, but you can see fledgling support for subfiles and subfile control records. From there, it's just a short step to message subfile support. I'm not sure what I'll do for windowed records; they'll probably have slightly different characteristics in the thick client interface as opposed to the browser UI, but at this level, it'll just be a flag.

The primary goal of the JdspfAbstractRecord is to provide a simple, consistent interface for getting data out of the display file object, whether you're dealing with a subfile or a single record. To that end, the JdspSubfile class will support a "current record" concept, which will be affected by the READ, WRITE, and CHAIN methods. But that won't be until the subfile class is available.

The idea of the abstract record is to make available all common attributes of a display file record: its name, its structure and the display file it belongs to. These values stay fairly constant and are really based on the original display file. The fourth attribute is the key to the flexibility of the architecture: the UI object. The user interface object is the object which responds to I/O requests that require user interaction. Depending on the UI object, such interaction may be through a thick client or a browser in this release, or some completely new interface -- say, a wireless protocol -- in future releases.

Since the entire com.pbd.pub.jdspf package is designed to emulate the display file, and particularly the display file as used in an RPG program, you'll see several methods that mirror the RPG opcodes from the AS/400: READ, WRITE, CHAIN and the ubiquitous EXFMT. These methods provide a link between the display file and the application client on the host. On the other side of the interface are the Java access methods such as getString, which allow access to the data in the record.

The data is stored in a Dc400Structure, which will eventually support the definition of display attributes, but for now simply defines the field's name, type and length. However, since there is also a need to pass the indicators from the application client to the UI object, the Dc400Structure is actually wrapped in an enclosing class, the JdspfBuffer class. Objects of type JdspfBuffer are the primary means of communication with the HLL emulation methods of the abstract record.

Since:
  2.0P
See Also:
  Dc400Structure, JdspfDisplayFile

415

Appendix C: Javadoc

Method Summary

java.lang.String	**getName**() Returns the name of this record.
java.lang.String	**getString**(int index) Returns the value of the specified field as a String.
java.lang.String	**getString**(java.lang.String name) Returns the value of the specified field as a String.
java.lang.Object	**getUIObject**() Returns the UI object for this record.
void	**setObject**(int index, java.lang.Object newValue) Sets the value of the specified field.
void	**setObject**(java.lang.String name, java.lang.Object newValue) Sets the value of the specified field.

Methods inherited from class java.lang.Object

`equals, getClass, hashCode, notify, notifyAll, toString, wait, wait, wait`

Method Detail

getName

`public java.lang.String getName()`

Returns the name of this record.

Returns:
the name of this record.

---

getString

`public java.lang.String getString(int index)`

Returns the value of the specified field as a String.

Parameters:
`index` - the index of the field.

Returns:
the value of the specified field as a String.

---

getString

`public java.lang.String getString(java.lang.String name)`

Returns the value of the specified field as a String.

Parameters:
`name` - the name of the field.

Returns:
the value of the specified field as a String.

Appendix C: Javadoc

getUIObject

```
public java.lang.Object getUIObject()
```
   Returns the UI object for this record.
   Returns:
   the UI object for this record.

setObject

```
public void setObject(int index,
                      java.lang.Object newValue)
```
   Sets the value of the specified field.
   Parameters:
   newValue - the new value of the field.
   index - the index of the field.

setObject

```
public void setObject(java.lang.String name,
                      java.lang.Object newValue)
```
   Sets the value of the specified field.
   Parameters:
   newValue - the new value of the field.
   name - the name of the field.

Overview Package **Class** Tree Deprecated Index Help
PREV CLASS   NEXT CLASS   FRAMES   NO FRAMES
SUMMARY: INNER | FIELD | CONSTR | METHOD   DETAIL: FIELD | CONSTR | METHOD

---

com.pbd.pub.jdspf

Class JdspfBuffer

```
java.lang.Object
  |
  +-com.pbd.pub.dc400.Dc400Structure
        |
        +-com.pbd.pub.jdspf.JdspfBuffer
```
All Implemented Interfaces:
   java.lang.Cloneable

---

public class **JdspfBuffer**
extends Dc400Structure

The JdspfBuffer class is an extension of the Dc400Structure class. The only difference is that the JdspfBuffer also contains an object of type JdspfIndicatorArray, which will eventually be used to communicate the settings of the HLL program indicators to the user interface object.

417

Appendix C: Javadoc

Since a JdspfBuffer is normally created in response to a message sent from the host, the constructors are designed to accept byte arrays of EBCDIC data, both for the actually fields and for the indicators.

Since:
    2.0P

See Also:
    `Dc400Structure`, `JdspfDisplayFile`

Constructor Summary

JdspfBuffer`()`
    Empty JdspfBuffer constructor.

JdspfBuffer`(Dc400Structure structure)`
    Create a JdspfBuffer of the specified structure with no data.

JdspfBuffer`(Dc400Structure structure, byte[] buffer, byte[] indicators)`
    Create a JdspfBuffer of the specified structure, using the specified buffer and indicators.

JdspfBuffer`(JdspfAbstractRecord record, byte[] buffer, byte[] indicators)`
    Create a JdspfBuffer with the same layout as the specified abstract record structure, using the specified buffer and indicators.

Method Summary

JdspfIndicatorArray	**getIndicators**`()` Returns the indicators associated with this buffer.
`boolean`	**isChanged**`()` NOT YET IMPLEMENTED
`void`	**setIndicators**`(byte[] indicators)` Sets the indicators from the specified EBCDIC byte array.
`void`	**setIndicators**`(JdspfIndicatorArray newValue)` Sets the indicators from the specified JdspfIndicatorArray.

Methods inherited from class com.pbd.pub.dc400.Dc400Structure

clone, getBigDecimal, getBigDecimal, getBuffer, getBufferLength, getByteArray, getByteArray, getObject, getObject, getObjects, getString, getString, setBuffer, setFields, setFields, setObject, setObject, setObjects, toBuffer, toObjects

Methods inherited from class java.lang.Object

`equals, getClass, hashCode, notify, notifyAll, toString, wait, wait, wait`

Appendix C: Javadoc

Constructor Detail

JdspfBuffer

public **JdspfBuffer**()

    Empty JdspfBuffer constructor.

JdspfBuffer

public **JdspfBuffer**(Dc400Structure structure)

    Create a JdspfBuffer of the specified structure with no data.
    Parameters:
    structure - a Dc400Structure representing the layout of the buffer.

JdspfBuffer

public **JdspfBuffer**(Dc400Structure structure,
                   byte[] buffer,
                   byte[] indicators)

    Create a JdspfBuffer of the specified structure, using the specified buffer and indicators.
    Parameters:
    structure - a Dc400Structure representing the layout of the buffer.
    buffer - the EBCDIC data for this buffer.
    indicators - the EBCDIC indicators for this structure.

JdspfBuffer

public **JdspfBuffer**(JdspfAbstractRecord record,
                   byte[] buffer,
                   byte[] indicators)

    Create a JdspfBuffer with the same layout as the specified abstract record structure, using the specified buffer and indicators.
    Parameters:
    structure - a JdspfAbstractRecord representing the layout of the buffer.
    buffer - the EBCDIC data for this buffer.
    indicators - the EBCDIC indicators for this structure.

Method Detail

getIndicators

public JdspfIndicatorArray **getIndicators**()

    Returns the indicators associated with this buffer.
    Returns:
    the indicators associated with this buffer.

Appendix C: Javadoc

isChanged

```
public boolean isChanged()
```
    NOT YET IMPLEMENTED
    Returns:
        true

---

setIndicators

```
public void setIndicators(byte[] indicators)
```
    Sets the indicators from the specified EBCDIC byte array.
    Parameters:
        newValue - byte array containing the EBCDIC indicators.

---

setIndicators

```
public void setIndicators(JdspfIndicatorArray newValue)
```
    Sets the indicators from the specified JdspfIndicatorArray.
    Parameters:
        newValue - the new JdspfIndicatorArray.

Overview	Package	**Class**	Tree	Deprecated	Index	Help
PREV CLASS NEXT CLASS				FRAMES NO FRAMES		
SUMMARY: INNER | FIELD | CONSTR | METHOD				DETAIL: FIELD | CONSTR | METHOD		

com.pbd.pub.jdspf

Class JdspfDisplayFile

```
java.lang.Object
  |
  +-com.pbd.pub.jdspf.JdspfDisplayFile
```

public class **JdspfDisplayFile**
extends java.lang.Object

The JdspfDisplayFile is the central object in the entire revitalization architecture. JdspfDisplayFile is designed to emulate a display file. It performs all the standard I/O operations via the `execute` method, which accepts a record name, an operation code, and a buffer. The `execute` method is meant to replace the typical RPG I/O opcode, such as:

```
EXFMTRECORD1
```

Instead, the `execute` method is called:

```
displayFile.execute("RECORD1", "EXFMT", record1Buffer);
```

Appendix C: Javadoc

Where `record1Buffer` is a JdspfBuffer with the layout of RECORD1 in the original display file, containing the current contents of the fields of the RECORD1 format.

The JdspfDisplayFile object will store data from all output operations, and then when an operation requiring user interaction is executed (such as EXFMT), it will invoke the listener object. If there is no listener, or if the listener returns `true`, the execute method returns to the caller. This allows special processing during I/O, such as that required by the browser interface (where the input operation actually occurs asynchronously to the output operation).

Since:
 2.0P
See Also:
 JdspfAbstractRecord, JdspfBuffer, JdspfDisplayFileListener, JdspfRecordUI

Constructor Summary

JdspfDisplayFile(java.lang.String name, JdspfAbstractRecord[] records)
 Create a JdspfDisplayFile with the specified record types.

JdspfDisplayFile(java.lang.String name, JdspfRecord record)
 Create a JdspfDisplayFile with a single record type.

Method Summary

boolean	**execute**(java.lang.String recordName, java.lang.String operation, JdspfBuffer buffer) Executes an I/O operation of the specified type on the specified record using the data in the buffer.	
JdspfAbstractRecord	**findRecord**(java.lang.String recordName) Returns the record with the specified name.	
JdspfAbstractRecord	**getCurrentRecord**() Returns the current record.	
java.lang.String	**getKeyPressed**() Returns the last command key pressed.	
void	**setKeyPressed**(int keyPressed) Sets the value of the last key pressed for this display file.	
void	**setKeyPressed**(java.lang.String keyPressed) Sets the value of the last key pressed for this display file.	
void	**setListener**(JdspfDisplayFileListener newValue) Sets the listener object for this display file.	
void	**setRecordUIObject**(java.lang.String recordName, java.lang.Object UIObject) Assigns a record UI object to the specified record.	
void	**setRecordUIObjects**(JdspfRecordUI[] uis) Assigns a set of UI objects to records.	

421

Methods inherited from class java.lang.Object

`equals, getClass, hashCode, notify, notifyAll, toString, wait, wait, wait`

Constructor Detail

JdspfDisplayFile

```
public JdspfDisplayFile(java.lang.String name,
                        JdspfAbstractRecord[] records)
```
Create a JdspfDisplayFile with the specified record types.
Parameters:
`name` - the name of the display file.
`records` - array of JdspfAbstractRecord objects.

JdspfDisplayFile

```
public JdspfDisplayFile(java.lang.String name,
                        JdspfRecord record)
```
Create a JdspfDisplayFile with a single record type. Note that there is only one valid way to create a single-record display file, and that is when the only record is a simple JdspfRecord type. That's why the constructor accepts only a JdspfRecord rather than a JdspfAbstractRecord.
Parameters:
`name` - the name of the display file.
`record` - JdspfRecord defining the record format.

Method Detail

execute

```
public boolean execute(java.lang.String recordName,
                       java.lang.String operation,
                       JdspfBuffer buffer)
                throws JdspfInvalidOperationException
```
Executes an I/O operation of the specified type on the specified record using the data in the buffer.
Parameters:
`recordName` - name of the record to access.
`operation` - the operation to perform.
`buffer` - the JdspfBuffer containing the data.

findRecord

```
public JdspfAbstractRecord findRecord(java.lang.String recordName)
```
Returns the record with the specified name.
Parameters:
`recordName` - the name of the record to find.
Returns:
the record with the specified name.

getCurrentRecord

public JdspfAbstractRecord **getCurrentRecord**()
> Returns the current record.
> **Returns:**
> the current record.

getKeyPressed

public java.lang.String **getKeyPressed**()
> Returns the last command key pressed.
> **Returns:**
> the last command key pressed.

setKeyPressed

public void **setKeyPressed**(int keyPressed)
> Sets the value of the last key pressed for this display file. This identifies which button the user pressed, either on the thick client or on the browser screen.
> **Parameters:**
> keyPressed - the integer value representing the pressed key.

setKeyPressed

public void **setKeyPressed**(java.lang.String keyPressed)
> Sets the value of the last key pressed for this display file. This identifies which button the user pressed, either on the thick client or on the browser screen.
> **Parameters:**
> keyPressed - the String value representing the pressed key.

setListener

public void **setListener**(JdspfDisplayFileListener newValue)
> Sets the listener object for this display file. This is primarily used when some sort of special processing is required by the user interface.
> **Parameters:**
> newValue - the new listener.

setRecordUIObject

public void **setRecordUIObject**(java.lang.String recordName,
                                  java.lang.Object UIObject)
> Assigns a record UI object to the specified record.
> **Parameters:**
> recordName - the name of the record.
> UIObject - the UI object to associate with the record.

setRecordUIObjects

public void **setRecordUIObjects**(JdspfRecordUI[] uis)
> Assigns a set of UI objects to records.
> **Parameters:**
> uis - the record UIs to assign.

Appendix C: Javadoc

Overview Package **Class** Tree Deprecated Index Help
PREV CLASS   NEXT CLASS   **FRAMES   NO FRAMES**
SUMMARY: INNER | FIELD | CONSTR | METHOD   DETAIL: FIELD | CONSTR | METHOD

com.pbd.pub.jdspf
Class JdspfDisplayFileAction

```
java.lang.Object
  |
  +-java.util.EventObject
        |
        +-java.awt.AWTEvent
              |
              +-java.awt.event.ActionEvent
                    |
                    +-com.pbd.pub.jdspf.JdspfDisplayFileAction
```

All Implemented Interfaces:
   java.io.Serializable

---

public class **JdspfDisplayFileAction**
extends java.awt.event.ActionEvent

While the JdspfDisplayFileAction is designed to eventually expand to support other uses, its primary designed purpose was to serve as the message sent to display file listeners when an EXFMT has been requested.

Since:
   2.0P
See Also:
   JdspfDisplayFile, JdspfDisplayFileListener, Serialized Form

---

Field Summary

static int	**JDSPF_EXFMT**

Fields inherited from class java.awt.event.ActionEvent

ACTION_FIRST, ACTION_LAST, ACTION_PERFORMED, ALT_MASK, CTRL_MASK, META_MASK, SHIFT_MASK

Fields inherited from class java.awt.AWTEvent

ACTION_EVENT_MASK, ADJUSTMENT_EVENT_MASK, COMPONENT_EVENT_MASK, CONTAINER_EVENT_MASK, FOCUS_EVENT_MASK, HIERARCHY_BOUNDS_EVENT_MASK, HIERARCHY_EVENT_MASK, INPUT_METHOD_EVENT_MASK, INVOCATION_EVENT_MASK, ITEM_EVENT_MASK, KEY_EVENT_MASK, MOUSE_EVENT_MASK, MOUSE_MOTION_EVENT_MASK, PAINT_EVENT_MASK, RESERVED_ID_MAX, TEXT_EVENT_MASK, WINDOW_EVENT_MASK

Appendix C: Javadoc

Constructor Summary

JdspfDisplayFileAction(java.lang.Object source, int id, JdspfAbstractRecord record)
    Creates a JdspfDisplayFileAction with the specified display file, id, and record.

JdspfDisplayFileAction(java.lang.Object source, int id, java.lang.String recordName)
    Creates a JdspfDisplayFileAction with the specified source, id, and record name.

Method Summary

JdspfAbstractRecord	**getRecord**()
	Returns the record associated with this action.

Methods inherited from class java.awt.event.ActionEvent
getActionCommand, getModifiers, paramString

Methods inherited from class java.awt.AWTEvent
getID, toString

Methods inherited from class java.util.EventObject
getSource

Methods inherited from class java.lang.Object
equals, getClass, hashCode, notify, notifyAll, wait, wait, wait

Field Detail

JDSPF_EXFMT
```
public static final int JDSPF_EXFMT
```

Constructor Detail

JdspfDisplayFileAction
```
public JdspfDisplayFileAction(java.lang.Object source,
                              int id,
                              JdspfAbstractRecord record)
```
Creates a JdspfDisplayFileAction with the specified display file, id and record.
Parameters:
    source - the display file.
    id - the action code.
    record - the record.

Appendix C: Javadoc

JdspfDisplayFileAction

```
public JdspfDisplayFileAction(java.lang.Object source,
                              int id,
                              java.lang.String recordName)
```
Creates a JdspfDisplayFileAction with the specified source, id, and record name.

Parameters:
source - the display file.
id - the action code.
recordName - the record name.

Method Detail

getRecord

```
public JdspfAbstractRecord getRecord()
```
Returns the record associated with this action.

Returns:
the record associated with this action.

Overview Package **Class** Tree Deprecated Index Help
PREV CLASS NEXT CLASS   FRAMES NO FRAMES
SUMMARY: INNER | FIELD | CONSTR | METHOD   DETAIL: FIELD | CONSTR | METHOD

---

com.pbd.pub.jdspf

Class JdspfFieldAttributes

```
java.lang.Object
   |
   +-com.pbd.pub.jdspf.JdspfFieldAttributes
```

public class **JdspfFieldAttributes**
extends java.lang.Object

NOT YET IMPLEMENTED.

Should eventually have function-specific methods:
getColor(), getProtect(), getDisplay()
Also, may test a global variable to determine HTML flavor.

Appendix C: Javadoc

Constructor Summary

JdspfFieldAttributes()
    NOT YET IMPLEMENTED.

Methods inherited from class java.lang.Object

`equals, getClass, hashCode, notify, notifyAll, toString, wait, wait, wait`

Constructor Detail

JdspfFieldAttributes

`public JdspfFieldAttributes()`
    NOT YET IMPLEMENTED.

Overview Package **Class** Tree Deprecated Index Help
PREV CLASS **NEXT CLASS**   **FRAMES** **NO FRAMES**
SUMMARY: INNER | FIELD | CONSTR | METHOD   DETAIL: FIELD | CONSTR | METHOD

---

com.pbd.pub.jdspf

Class JdspfIndicator

```
java.lang.Object
  |
  +-com.pbd.pub.jdspf.JdspfIndicator
```

public class **JdspfIndicator**
extends java.lang.Object

NOT YET IMPLEMENTED.

Constructor Summary

JdspfIndicator(int indicator)
    NOT YET IMPLEMENTED.
JdspfIndicator(int indicator, boolean state)
    NOT YET IMPLEMENTED.

Appendix C: Javadoc

Method Summary

boolean	**test** (JdspfIndicatorArray array) NOT YET IMPLEMENTED.

Methods inherited from class java.lang.Object

equals, getClass, hashCode, notify, notifyAll, toString, wait, wait, wait

Constructor Detail

JdspfIndicator

public **JdspfIndicator**(int indicator)
   NOT YET IMPLEMENTED.

JdspfIndicator

public **JdspfIndicator**(int indicator,
                       boolean state)
   NOT YET IMPLEMENTED.

Method Detail

test

public boolean **test**(JdspfIndicatorArray array)
   NOT YET IMPLEMENTED.

428

Appendix C: Javadoc

Overview Package **Class** Tree Deprecated Index Help
PREV CLASS **NEXT CLASS**   **FRAMES** **NO FRAMES**
SUMMARY: INNER | FIELD | CONSTR | METHOD   DETAIL: FIELD | CONSTR | METHOD

com.pbd.pub.jdspf

Class JdspfIndicatorArray

```
java.lang.Object
  |
  +-com.pbd.pub.jdspf.JdspfIndicatorArray
```

public class **JdspfIndicatorArray**
extends java.lang.Object
NOT YET IMPLEMENTED.

Constructor Summary

JdspfIndicatorArray(byte[] indicators) NOT YET IMPLEMENTED.	

Method Summary

byte[]	**getIndicators**() NOT YET IMPLEMENTED.
boolean	**isIndicatorOn**(int index) NOT YET IMPLEMENTED.
boolean	**test**(JdspfIndicator indicator) NOT YET IMPLEMENTED.

Methods inherited from class java.lang.Object

equals, getClass, hashCode, notify, notifyAll, toString, wait, wait, wait

Constructor Detail

JdspfIndicatorArray

public **JdspfIndicatorArray**(byte[] indicators)
    NOT YET IMPLEMENTED.

Appendix C: Javadoc

Method Detail

getIndicators
`public byte[] getIndicators()`
> NOT YET IMPLEMENTED.

isIndicatorOn
`public boolean isIndicatorOn(int index)`
> NOT YET IMPLEMENTED.

test
`public boolean test(JdspfIndicator indicator)`
> NOT YET IMPLEMENTED.

Overview Package **Class** Tree Deprecated Index Help
PREV CLASS   NEXT CLASS   FRAMES   NO FRAMES
SUMMARY: INNER | FIELD | CONSTR | METHOD   DETAIL: FIELD | CONSTR | METHOD

---

com.pbd.pub.jdspf

Class JdspfRecord

```
java.lang.Object
   |
   +-com.pbd.pub.jdspf.JdspfAbstractRecord
         |
         +-com.pbd.pub.jdspf.JdspfRecord
```

public class **JdspfRecord**
extends JdspfAbstractRecord

JdspfRecord represents a "regular" record in a display file, and supports the READ and WRITE operations. There is only a single buffer associated with this record, so the getCurrentBuffer method always returns that record.

Since:
>   2.0P

See Also:
>   JdspfDisplayFile, JdspfDisplayFileListener

Appendix C: Javadoc

Constructor Summary

JdspfRecord(java.lang.String name, Dc400Structure structure)
    Creates a JdspfRecord with the specified name and layout.

Method Summary

boolean	**READ**(JdspfBuffer ioBuffer) Stores the contents of the record into the buffer.
boolean	**WRITE**(JdspfBuffer buffer) Updates the record with the data from the specified buffer.

Methods inherited from class com.pbd.pub.jdspf.JdspfAbstractRecord

getName, getString, getString, getUIObject, setObject, setObject

Methods inherited from class java.lang.Object

equals, getClass, hashCode, notify, notifyAll, toString, wait, wait, wait

Constructor Detail

JdspfRecord

public **JdspfRecord**(java.lang.String name,
                  Dc400Structure structure)

Creates a JdspfRecord with the specified name and layout.

Parameters:
name - the name of the record.
structure - a Dc400Structure representing the layout of the record.

Method Detail

READ

public boolean **READ**(JdspfBuffer ioBuffer)

Stores the contents of the record into the buffer.

Parameters:
the - buffer to receive the data.
Returns:
false

WRITE

public boolean **WRITE**(JdspfBuffer buffer)

Updates the record with the data from the specified buffer.

Parameters:
buffer - the buffer containing the new data.
Returns:
false

Appendix C: Javadoc

| Overview | Package | **Class** | Tree | Deprecated | Index | Help |

PREV CLASS NEXT CLASS 　　　　　　　　　FRAMES NO FRAMES
SUMMARY: INNER | FIELD | CONSTR | METHOD 　　DETAIL: FIELD | CONSTR | METHOD

com.pbd.pub.jdspf

Class JdspfRecordUI

```
java.lang.Object
  |
  +-com.pbd.pub.jdspf.JdspfRecordUI
```
Direct Known Subclasses:
　　ScJdspfJbuiRecordUI, ScJdspfJspRecordUI

---

public class **JdspfRecordUI**
extends java.lang.Object

This object associates a record UI object with a record name.

Since:
　　2.0P
See Also:
　　JdspfDisplayFile, JdspfDisplayFileListener

Constructor Summary

JdspfRecordUI(java.lang.String recordName, java.lang.Object recordUIObject)
　　Creates a JdspfRecordUI with the specified record name and UI object.

Methods inherited from class java.lang.Object

`equals, getClass, hashCode, notify, notifyAll, toString, wait, wait, wait`

Constructor Detail

JdspfRecordUI

```
public JdspfRecordUI(java.lang.String recordName,
                     java.lang.Object recordUIObject)
```
　　Creates a JdspfRecordUI with the specified record name and UI object.

Appendix C: Javadoc

Overview Package **Class** Tree Deprecated Index Help
PREV CLASS NEXT CLASS   **FRAMES** **NO FRAMES**
SUMMARY: INNER | FIELD | CONSTR | METHOD   DETAIL: FIELD | CONSTR | METHOD

com.pbd.pub.jdspf

Class JdspfSubfile

```
java.lang.Object
  |
  +-com.pbd.pub.jdspf.JdspfAbstractRecord
        |
        +-com.pbd.pub.jdspf.JdspfSubfile
```

public class **JdspfSubfile**
extends JdspfAbstractRecord
NOT YET IMPLEMENTED.

Constructor Summary

JdspfSubfile(java.lang.String name, Dc400Structure structure)
    NOT YET IMPLEMENTED.

Method Summary

JdspfBuffer	**CHAIN**(int row) NOT YET IMPLEMENTED.
void	**clear**() NOT YET IMPLEMENTED.
boolean	**getNextRow**() NOT YET IMPLEMENTED.
JdspfBuffer	**READC**() NOT YET IMPLEMENTED.
void	**UPDAT**(byte[] buffer, byte[] indicators) NOT YET IMPLEMENTED.
void	**WRITE**(byte[] buffer, byte[] indicators) NOT YET IMPLEMENTED.

Methods inherited from class com.pbd.pub.jdspf.JdspfAbstractRecord

getName, getString, getString, getUIObject, setObject, setObject

Appendix C: Javadoc

Methods inherited from class java.lang.Object
equals, getClass, hashCode, notify, notifyAll, toString, wait, wait, wait

Constructor Detail

JdspfSubfile

public **JdspfSubfile**(java.lang.String name,
            Dc400Structure structure)
    NOT YET IMPLEMENTED.

Method Detail

CHAIN

public JdspfBuffer **CHAIN**(int row)
    NOT YET IMPLEMENTED.

clear

public void **clear**()
    NOT YET IMPLEMENTED.

getNextRow

public boolean **getNextRow**()
    NOT YET IMPLEMENTED.

READC

public JdspfBuffer **READC**()
    NOT YET IMPLEMENTED.

UPDAT

public void **UPDAT**(byte[] buffer,
            byte[] indicators)
    NOT YET IMPLEMENTED.

WRITE

public void **WRITE**(byte[] buffer,
            byte[] indicators)
    NOT YET IMPLEMENTED.

Appendix C: Javadoc

| Overview | Package | **Class** | Tree | Deprecated | Index | Help |

PREV CLASS NEXT CLASS   FRAMES NO FRAMES
SUMMARY: INNER | FIELD | CONSTR | METHOD   DETAIL: FIELD | CONSTR | METHOD

---

com.pbd.pub.jdspf

Class JdspfInvalidOperationException

```
java.lang.Object
  |
  +-java.lang.Throwable
        |
        +-java.lang.Exception
              |
              +-com.pbd.pub.jdspf.JdspfInvalidOperationException
```
All Implemented Interfaces:
    java.io.Serializable

---

public class **JdspfInvalidOperationException**
extends java.lang.Exception

This exception is thrown for invalid operations, such as attempting to perform an EXFMT on a subfile record, or a READC on a regular record.

Since:
    2.0P
See Also:
    Serialized Form

Constructor Summary

JdspfInvalidOperationException(java.lang.String displayFile, java.lang.String record, java.lang.String operation)
    Creates a JdspfInvalidOperationException.

Methods inherited from class java.lang.Throwable

fillInStackTrace, getLocalizedMessage, getMessage, printStackTrace, printStackTrace, printStackTrace, toString

Methods inherited from class java.lang.Object

equals, getClass, hashCode, notify, notifyAll, wait, wait, wait

435

Constructor Detail

JdspfInvalidOperationException

```
public JdspfInvalidOperationException(java.lang.String displayFile,
                                      java.lang.String record,
                                      java.lang.String operation)
```
Creates a JdspfInvalidOperationException.
Parameters:
displayFile - the name of the display file.
record - the name of the record.
operation - the (invalid) operation requested.

Overview **Package** Class **Tree** **Deprecated** **Index** **Help**
PREV PACKAGE NEXT PACKAGE   FRAMES NO FRAMES

Package com.pbd.pub.jsp

Class Summary	
Jsp	The Jsp class is designed to represent a real JavaServer Page on the web server.
JspField	The JspField defines a single form field on a JavaServer page.

Appendix C: Javadoc

Overview **Package** **Class** **Tree** **Deprecated** **Index** **Help**
PREV CLASS   NEXT CLASS   FRAMES   NO FRAMES
SUMMARY: INNER | FIELD | CONSTR | METHOD   DETAIL: FIELD | CONSTR | METHOD

com.pbd.pub.jsp

Class Jsp

```
java.lang.Object
  |
  +-com.pbd.pub.jsp.Jsp
```
Direct Known Subclasses:
   ScJdspfJsp

public class **Jsp**
extends java.lang.Object

The Jsp class is designed to represent a real JavaServer Page on the web server. The Jsp class has two attributes: the file name and the fields.

The file name can either be specified in two parts, a path name and a file name, or a fully qualified file name. The first type is preferred because that makes it easier to move JavaServer Pages from directory to directory as needed. Note that the path name when specified must not have a trailing '/'.

The fields identify the form fields on the JavaServer Page. Currently, the architecture supports only a single form on a JavaServer Page. In addition, only one SUBMIT field is supported: that is, all buttons of type SUBMIT must have the same name (but different values). This may be a bit restrictive, but it is all that is necessary to support the revitalization architecture today.

Since:
   2.0P

Field Summary

JspField	buttonField

Constructor Summary

Jsp()
   Empty Jsp constructor.

Jsp(java.lang.String name)
   Creates a JSP with the specified fully qualified name and no fields.

437

Appendix C: Javadoc

Jsp(java.lang.String name, JspField[] fields) Creates a JSP with the specified fully qualified name, and fields.	
Jsp(java.lang.String path, java.lang.String name) Creates a JSP with the specified path, name, and no fields.	
Jsp(java.lang.String path, java.lang.String name, JspField[] fields) Creates a JSP with the specified path, name, and fields.	

Method Summary

JspField	**getButtonField**() Returns the button field for this Jsp.
java.lang.String	**getButtonValue**() Returns the value of the button field for this Jsp.
JspField[]	**getFields**() Returns the fields associated with this Jsp.
java.lang.String	**getName**() Returns the file name associated with this Jsp.
java.lang.String	**getPath**() Returns the path associated with this Jsp.
java.lang.String	**getURL**() Returns the fully qualified file name for this Jsp by concatenating the path (if any) with the file name.
void	**setFields**(JspField[] newValue) Sets the fields for this Jsp.
void	**setName**(java.lang.String newValue) Sets the file name for this Jsp.
void	**setPath**(java.lang.String newValue) Sets the path for this Jsp.

Methods inherited from class java.lang.Object

equals, getClass, hashCode, notify, notifyAll, toString, wait, wait, wait

Field Detail

buttonField

public JspField **buttonField**

Constructor Detail

Jsp

```
public Jsp()
```
        Empty Jsp constructor.

Jsp

```
public Jsp(java.lang.String name)
```
        Creates a JSP with the specified fully qualified name and no fields.
        Parameters:
        `name` - the fully qualified name of the JSP.

Jsp

```
public Jsp(java.lang.String name,
           JspField[] fields)
```
        Creates a JSP with the specified fully qualified name and fields.
        Parameters:
        `name` - the fully qualified name of the JSP.
        `fields` - the array of fields for the JSP.

Jsp

```
public Jsp(java.lang.String path,
           java.lang.String name)
```
        Creates a JSP with the specified path, name, and no fields.
        Parameters:
        `path` - the path name of the JSP, with no trailing '/'.
        `name` - the file name of the JSP.

Jsp

```
public Jsp(java.lang.String path,
           java.lang.String name,
           JspField[] fields)
```
        Creates a JSP with the specified path, name and fields.
        Parameters:
        `path` - the path name of the JSP, with no trailing '/'.
        `name` - the file name of the JSP.
        `fields` - the array of fields for the JSP.

Appendix C: Javadoc

Method Detail

getButtonField

```
public JspField getButtonField()
```
    Returns the button field for this Jsp.
    Returns:
    the button field for this Jsp.

getButtonValue

```
public java.lang.String getButtonValue()
```
    Returns the value of the button field for this Jsp.
    Returns:
    the value of the button field for this Jsp.

getFields

```
public JspField[] getFields()
```
    Returns the fields associated with this Jsp.
    Returns:
    the fields associated with this Jsp.

getName

```
public java.lang.String getName()
```
    Returns the file name associated with this Jsp.
    Returns:
    the file name associated with this Jsp.

getPath

```
public java.lang.String getPath()
```
    Returns the path associated with this Jsp.
    Returns:
    the path associated with this Jsp.

getURL

```
public java.lang.String getURL()
```
    Returns the fully qualified file name for this Jsp by concatenating the path (if any) with the file name.
    Returns:
    the fully qualified file name for this Jsp.

setFields

```
public void setFields(JspField[] newValue)
```
    Sets the fields for this Jsp.
    Parameters:
    newValue - the new fields for this Jsp.

setName

```
public void setName(java.lang.String newValue)
```
    Sets the file name for this Jsp.
    Parameters:
        newValue - the new file name for this Jsp.

setPath

```
public void setPath(java.lang.String newValue)
```
    Sets the path for this Jsp.
    Parameters:
        newValue - the new path for this Jsp.

Overview Package **Class** Tree Deprecated Index Help
PREV CLASS NEXT CLASS   **FRAMES** **NO FRAMES**
SUMMARY: INNER | FIELD | CONSTR | METHOD   DETAIL: FIELD | CONSTR | METHOD

---

com.pbd.pub.jsp

Class JspField

```
java.lang.Object
  |
  +-com.pbd.pub.jsp.JspField
```
Direct Known Subclasses:
    ScJdspfJspButtonField

---

public class **JspField**
extends java.lang.Object

The JspField defines a single form field on a JavaServer page. While there is some code to support multiple-value fields, this feature is not yet implemented. Therefore, all fields must be single-value fields. An array of JspField objects used to build a Jsp object should have one and only one button field (isButtonField = true). The last one so defined will be the only field recognized as a "command" button.

Since:
    2.0P

Field Summary

static int	**MULTIPLE**
static int	**SINGLE**

Constructor Summary

JspField(java.lang.String name)
  Creates a SINGLE, non-button JspField with the specified name.

JspField(java.lang.String name, boolean isButtonField)
  Creates a type SINGLE JspField with the specified name and button attributes.

JspField(java.lang.String name, int type)
  Creates a non-button JspField with the specified name and type.

JspField(java.lang.String name, int type, boolean isButtonField)
  Creates a JspField with the specified name, type, and button attributes.

Method Summary

Java.lang.String	**getName**() Returns the name of the JspField.
int	**getType**() Returns the type of the JspField.
Java.lang.String	**getValue**() Returns the value of the JspField.
java.util.Enumeration	**getValues**() NOT CURRENTLY SUPPORTED.
boolean	**isButtonField**() Returns true if this is a button field.
void	**setValue**(java.lang.String newValue) Sets the value of this JspField.

Methods inherited from class java.lang.Object

equals, getClass, hashCode, notify, notifyAll, toString, wait, wait, wait

Field Detail

SINGLE

```
public static final int SINGLE
```

MULTIPLE

```
public static final int MULTIPLE
```

Constructor Detail

JspField

```
public JspField(java.lang.String name)
```
Creates a SINGLE, non-button JspField with the specified name.
Parameters:
name - the field name.

JspField

```
public JspField(java.lang.String name,
                int type)
```
Creates a non-button JspField with the specified name and type..
Parameters:
name - the field name.
type - the field type.

JspField

```
public JspField(java.lang.String name,
                int type,
                boolean isButtonField)
```
Creates a JspField with the specified name, type, and button attributes.
Parameters:
name - the field name.
type - the field type.
isButtonField - true indicates this is a button field.

JspField

```
public JspField(java.lang.String name,
                boolean isButtonField)
```
Creates a type SINGLE JspField with the specified name and button attributes.
Parameters:
name - the field name.
isButtonField - true indicates this is a button field.

443

Method Detail

getName

```
public java.lang.String getName()
```
　　　　Returns the name of the JspField.
　　　　Returns:
　　　　the name of the JspField.

getType

```
public int getType()
```
　　　　Returns the type of the JspField.
　　　　Returns:
　　　　the type of the JspField.

getValue

```
public java.lang.String getValue()
```
　　　　Returns the value of the JspField.
　　　　Returns:
　　　　the value of the JspField.

getValues

```
public java.util.Enumeration getValues()
```
　　　　NOT CURRENTLY SUPPORTED.
　　　　Returns:
　　　　null

isButtonField

```
public boolean isButtonField()
```
　　　　Returns true if this is a button field.
　　　　Returns:
　　　　true if this is a button field.

setValue

```
public void setValue(java.lang.String newValue)
```
　　　　Sets the value of this JspField.
　　　　Parameters:
　　　　newValue - the new value.

Appendix C: Javadoc

Overview **Package** Class Tree Deprecated Index Help
PREV PACKAGE   NEXT PACKAGE   FRAMES   NO FRAMES

Package com.pbd.pub.sc400

Class Summary	
Sc400Api	The Sc400Api class encapsulates the ProgramCall class of the JT400 toolbox.
Sc400Client	The Sc400Client object is the application client proxy.
Sc400Message	The Sc400Message is the communication message between UI servers and application clients in the server/client architecture.
ScJdspfUIServer	The ScJdspfUIServer class encapsulates the conversation between a UI server and the application client.

Exception Summary	
Sc400Exception	The overall Sc400Exception, the root of the Exception hierarchy for the server/client packages.

Overview Package **Class** Tree Deprecated Index Help
PREV CLASS   NEXT CLASS   FRAMES   NO FRAMES
SUMMARY: INNER | FIELD | CONSTR | METHOD   DETAIL: FIELD | CONSTR | METHOD

com.pbd.pub.sc400

Class Sc400Api

```
com.pbd.pub.sc400.Sc400Api
```

public class **Sc400Api**

The Sc400Api class encapsulates the ProgramCall class of the JT400 toolbox. Since all APIs have the same parameter structure (a single parameter whose layout is defined by Sc400Message), most of the complexity of the call can be hidden from the programmer.

Since:
    2.0P

445

Appendix C: Javadoc

Constructor Summary

Sc400Api(com.pbd.pub.sc400.AS400 as400, java.lang.String apiLib, java.lang.String apiProgram)
    Creates an Sc400Api for the specified AS400, library, and program name.

Method Summary

void	**call**(Sc400Message message, boolean getData)
	Calls the API, and retrieves the returned data if specified.

Constructor Detail

Sc400Api

```
public Sc400Api(com.pbd.pub.sc400.AS400 as400,
                java.lang.String apiLib,
                java.lang.String apiProgram)
```
Creates an Sc400Api for the specified AS400, library, and program name.

Parameters:
as400 - the AS/400 where the API resides.
apiLib - the library where the API resides.
apiProgram - the name of the API program.

Method Detail

call

```
public void call(Sc400Message message,
                 boolean getData)
          throws Sc400Exception
```
Calls the API, and retrieves the returned data if specified.

Parameters:
Sc400Message - the message to send and optionally receive data.
getData - if true, the buffer is set to the data returned.

Appendix C: Javadoc

Overview **Package** **Class** **Tree** **Deprecated** **Index** **Help**
PREV CLASS **NEXT CLASS**   **FRAMES** **NO FRAMES**
SUMMARY: INNER | FIELD | CONSTR | METHOD   DETAIL: FIELD | CONSTR | METHOD

---

com.pbd.pub.sc400

Class Sc400Client

```
java.lang.Object
  |
  +-com.pbd.pub.sc400.Sc400Client
```

---

public class **Sc400Client**
extends java.lang.Object

The Sc400Client object is the application client proxy. It provides the wrapper around the UI Server APIs used by the UI server objects to communicate with the application client on the host. A client is defined primarily by its name. Other information includes the AS/400 where the application client resides, the library of the client, and the library for the UI Server APIs.

The libraries can be defaulted, and in the case of the thick client interface, we can simply leave the AS/400 information undefined; the JT400 toolbox will then prompt for the appropriate information when we attempt to connect. For servlets, we must define the AS/400 connection, which you can see by taking a look at the ScJdspfJspServlet class.

Since:
>   2.0P

Field Summary

static java.lang.String	**LOGON**

Constructor Summary

Sc400Client()
> Sc400Client constructor comment.

Sc400Client(java.lang.String clientName)
> Sc400Client constructor comment.

447

Method Summary

java.lang.String	**getApiLibrary**() Returns the API library for this client.
java.lang.String	**getClientName**() Returns the name for this client.
Sc400Message	**getMessage**() This method was created in VisualAge.
java.lang.String	**getProductionLibrary**() Returns the production library for this client.
java.lang.String	**getSystemName**() Returns the system name for this client.
java.lang.String	**getUserID**() Returns the user ID for this client.
Sc400Message	**init**() Performs all initialization for the client, attaching to the host and initializing the APIs.
boolean	**receive**() Receives a request from the application client.
void	**send**() Sends the current contents of the message back to the application client as a response.
void	**setApiLibrary**(java.lang.String newValue) Sets the value of the API library.
void	**setClientName**(java.lang.String newValue) Sets the value of the client name.
void	**setPassword**(java.lang.String newValue) Sets the value of the password.
void	**setProductionLibrary**(java.lang.String newValue) Sets the value of the production library.
void	**setSystemName**(java.lang.String newValue) Sets the value of the system name.
void	**setUserID**(java.lang.String newValue) Sets the value of the user ID.
void	**shutdown**() Shuts down the application client.

Methods inherited from class java.lang.Object

equals, getClass, hashCode, notify, notifyAll, toString, wait, wait, wait

Appendix C: Javadoc

Field Detail

LOGON
```
public static final java.lang.String LOGON
```

Constructor Detail

Sc400Client
```
public Sc400Client()
```
Sc400Client constructor comment.

Sc400Client
```
public Sc400Client(java.lang.String clientName)
```
Sc400Client constructor comment.

Method Detail

getApiLibrary
```
public java.lang.String getApiLibrary()
```
Returns the API library for this client.
Returns:
the API library for this client.

getClientName
```
public java.lang.String getClientName()
```
Returns the name for this client.
Returns:
the name for this client.

getMessage
```
public Sc400Message getMessage()
```
This method was created in VisualAge.
Returns:
com.pbd.pub.sc400.Sc400Message

getProductionLibrary
```
public java.lang.String getProductionLibrary()
```
Returns the production library for this client.
Returns:
the production library for this client.

getSystemName

```
public java.lang.String getSystemName()
```
        Returns the system name for this client.
        Returns:
        the system name for this client.

getUserID

```
public java.lang.String getUserID()
```
        Returns the user ID for this client.
        Returns:
        the user ID for this client.

init

```
public Sc400Message init()
                  throws Sc400Exception
```
        Performs all initialization for the client, attaching to the host and initializing the APIs.

receive

```
public boolean receive()
                throws Sc400Exception
```
        Receives a request from the application client.
        Returns:
        `true` is an EOF message is received.

send

```
public void send()
          throws Sc400Exception
```
        Sends the current contents of the message back to the application client as a response.

setApiLibrary

```
public void setApiLibrary(java.lang.String newValue)
```
        Sets the value of the API library.
        Parameters:
        `newValue` - the new API library.

setClientName

```
public void setClientName(java.lang.String newValue)
```
        Sets the value of the client name.
        Parameters:
        `newValue` - the new client name.

setPassword

```
public void setPassword(java.lang.String newValue)
```
    Sets the value of the password.
    Parameters:
    newValue - the new password.

setProductionLibrary

```
public void setProductionLibrary(java.lang.String newValue)
```
    Sets the value of the production library.
    Parameters:
    newValue - the new production library.

setSystemName

```
public void setSystemName(java.lang.String newValue)
```
    Sets the value of the system name.
    Parameters:
    newValue - the new system name.

setUserID

```
public void setUserID(java.lang.String newValue)
```
    Sets the value of the user ID.
    Parameters:
    newValue - the new user ID.

shutdown

```
public void shutdown()
            throws Sc400Exception
```
    Shuts down the application client.

Appendix C: Javadoc

Overview Package **Class** Tree Deprecated Index Help
PREV CLASS   NEXT CLASS   FRAMES   NO FRAMES
SUMMARY: INNER | FIELD | CONSTR | METHOD   DETAIL: FIELD | CONSTR | METHOD

com.pbd.pub.sc400

Class Sc400Message

```
java.lang.Object
  |
  +-com.pbd.pub.dc400.Dc400Structure
        |
        +-com.pbd.pub.sc400.Sc400Message
```

All Implemented Interfaces:
  java.lang.Cloneable

public class **Sc400Message**
extends Dc400Structure

The Sc400Message is the communication message between UI servers and application clients in the server/client architecture. All fields are defined in this type and correspond to the physical file DQMMSG on the host. The index for each field is defined as well, to provide better performance. This class would change if for any reason the DQMMSG file should change.

Since:
  2.0P

Constructor Summary

Sc400Message()
  Creates an Sc400Message with no client.

Sc400Message(java.lang.String applicationClientName)
  Creates an Sc400Message for the specified application client.

Method Summary

java.lang.String	**getApplicationClientID**() Returns the application client session ID.
java.lang.String	**getApplicationClientName**() Returns the application client name.
byte[]	**getDataBuffer**() Returns the EBCDIC data buffer.

Appendix C: Javadoc

`byte[]`	**getIndicators**() Returns the EBCDIC indicator array.	
`java.lang.String`	**getOperationCode**() Returns the operation code.	
`java.lang.String`	**getRecordName**() Returns the record name.	
`java.lang.String`	**getSessionID**() Returns the UI server sesion ID.	
`boolean`	**isEof**() Returns `true` if this is an end-of-file request.	
`boolean`	**requiresResponse**() Returns `true` if this operation requires a response.	
`void`	**setApplicationClientName**(`java.lang.String newValue`) Sets the application client name.	
`void`	**setDataBuffer**(`byte[] newValue`) Sets the EBCDIC data buffer.	
`void`	**setIndicators**(`byte[] newValue`) Sets the new indicator array.	
`void`	**setReturnCode**(`java.lang.String newValue`) Sets the return code.	

Methods inherited from class com.pbd.pub.dc400.Dc400Structure

clone, getBigDecimal, getBigDecimal, getBuffer, getBufferLength, getByteArray, getByteArray, getObject, getObject, getObjects, getString, getString, setBuffer, setFields, setFields, setObject, setObject, setObjects, toBuffer, toObjects

Methods inherited from class java.lang.Object

`equals, getClass, hashCode, notify, notifyAll, toString, wait, wait, wait`

Constructor Detail

Sc400Message

`public Sc400Message()`
  Creates an Sc400Message with no client.

Sc400Message

`public Sc400Message(java.lang.String applicationClientName)`
  Creates an Sc400Message for the specified application client.
  Parameters:
  `applicationClientName` - application client name.

Method Detail

getApplicationClientID

`public java.lang.String` **`getApplicationClientID()`**
Returns the application client session ID.
Returns:
the application client session ID.

getApplicationClientName

`public java.lang.String` **`getApplicationClientName()`**
Returns the application client name.
Returns:
the application client name.

getDataBuffer

`public byte[]` **`getDataBuffer()`**
Returns the EBCDIC data buffer.
Returns:
the EBCDIC data buffer.

getIndicators

`public byte[]` **`getIndicators()`**
Returns the EBCDIC indicator array.
Returns:
the EBCDIC indicator array.

getOperationCode

`public java.lang.String` **`getOperationCode()`**
Returns the operation code.
Returns:
the operation code.

getRecordName

`public java.lang.String` **`getRecordName()`**
Returns the record name.
Returns:
the record name.

getSessionID

`public java.lang.String` **`getSessionID()`**
Returns the UI server sesion ID.
Returns:
the UI server sesion ID.

isEof

public boolean **isEof**()
> Returns true if this is an end-of-file request.
> **Returns:**
> true if this is an end-of-file request.

---

requiresResponse

public boolean **requiresResponse**()
> Returns true if this operation requires a response.
> **Returns:**
> true if this operation requires a response.

---

setApplicationClientName

public void **setApplicationClientName**(java.lang.String newValue)
> Sets the application client name.
> **Parameters:**
> newValue - the new application client name.

---

setDataBuffer

public void **setDataBuffer**(byte[] newValue)
> Sets the EBCDIC data buffer.
> **Parameters:**
> newValue - the new EBCDIC data buffer.

---

setIndicators

public void **setIndicators**(byte[] newValue)
> Sets the new indicator array.
> **Parameters:**
> newValue - the new indicator array.

---

setReturnCode

public void **setReturnCode**(java.lang.String newValue)
> Sets the return code.
> **Parameters:**
> newValue - the new return code.

Appendix C: Javadoc

Overview **Package** **Class** **Tree** **Deprecated** **Index** **Help**
PREV CLASS NEXT CLASS   **FRAMES** **NO FRAMES**
SUMMARY: INNER | FIELD | CONSTR | METHOD   DETAIL: FIELD | CONSTR | METHOD

com.pbd.pub.sc400

Class ScJdspfUIServer

```
java.lang.Object
   |
   +-com.pbd.pub.sc400.ScJdspfUIServer
```
Direct Known Subclasses:
    ScJdspfJbuiServer

---

public class **ScJdspfUIServer**
extends java.lang.Object

The ScJdspfUIServer class encapsulates the conversation between a UI server and the application client. This is the class that reconciles the differences between the thick client interface and the browser interface.

The thick client interface simply executes the `run` method, which then loops processing the messages from the application client. Internally, the `processMessage` method invokes the listener object attached to the display file whenever user interaction is required. The ScJdspfJbuiDefaultListener class will then invoke the `EXFMT` method of the appropriate record UI object. SC400 JBUI record UI objects are decendants of the JBUI classes that implement the JdspfUIAdapter interface.

The servlet interface is a bit more complex. While servlets still call the `run` method, whenever a user interaction is required, the `run` method returns, and the servlet then invokes a ScJdspfJsp object to send the data to the browser. When the browser then returns the user input via a POST, the `doPost` method of the servlet then invokes the `send` method of the ScJdspfUIServer to send the response back to the application client before calling the `run` method again to continue the conversation.

Since:
    2.0P
See Also:
    ScJdspfJbuiDefaultListener, ScJdspfJspServlet

Constructor Summary

ScJdspfUIServer()
    Empty ScJdspUIServer constructor.

ScJdspfUIServer(Sc400Client `client`, JdspfDisplayFile `jdspf`, JdspfDisplayFileListener `listener`, JdspfRecordUI[] `recordUIs`)
    Creates an ScJdspfUIServer object with the specified client, display file, listener, and record UI objects.

Method Summary

JdspfDisplayFile	**getJdspf**() Returns the display file serviced by this UI server.
void	**init**() Initializes the application client.
boolean	**run**() Begins or continues the conversation with the application client.
void	**send**() Sends the current contents of the internal message to the application client.
void	**send**(JdspfBuffer buffer) Sets the contents of the internal message to those of the JdspfBuffer and then sends the message to the application client.

Methods inherited from class java.lang.Object

equals, getClass, hashCode, notify, notifyAll, toString, wait, wait, wait

Constructor Detail

ScJdspfUIServer

```
public ScJdspfUIServer()
```
Empty ScJdspUIServer constructor.

ScJdspfUIServer

```
public ScJdspfUIServer(Sc400Client client,
                       JdspfDisplayFile jdspf,
                       JdspfDisplayFileListener listener,
                       JdspfRecordUI[] recordUIs)
                throws Sc400Exception
```
Creates an ScJdspfUIServer object with the specified client, display file, listener, and record UI objects.

Parameters:
client - the application client.
jdspf - the display file.
listener - the display file listener (or null for none)
the - record UI objects.

Method Detail

getJdspf

```
public JdspfDisplayFile getJdspf()
```
Returns the display file serviced by this UI server.

Returns:
the display file serviced by this UI server.

457

Appendix C: Javadoc

init

```
public void init()
         throws Sc400Exception
```
Initializes the application client.

run

```
public boolean run()
            throws Sc400Exception
```
Begins or continues the conversation with the application client.

send

```
public void send()
         throws Sc400Exception
```
Sends the current contents of the internal message to the application client.

send

```
public void send(JdspfBuffer buffer)
         throws Sc400Exception
```
Sets the contents of the internal message to those of the JdspfBuffer and then sends the message to the application client.

Parameters:
buffer - the buffer containing the data to send.

Overview Package **Class** Tree Deprecated Index Help
PREV CLASS   NEXT CLASS   FRAMES   NO FRAMES
SUMMARY: INNER | FIELD | CONSTR | METHOD   DETAIL: FIELD | CONSTR | METHOD

---

com.pbd.pub.sc400

Class Sc400Exception

```
java.lang.Object
   |
   +-java.lang.Throwable
         |
         +-java.lang.Exception
               |
               +-com.pbd.pub.sc400.Sc400Exception
```

All Implemented Interfaces:
    java.io.Serializable

Appendix C: Javadoc

public class **Sc400Exception**
extends java.lang.Exception

The overall Sc400Exception, the root of the Exception hierarchy for the server/client packages.

Since:
    2.0P
See Also:
    Serialized Form

Constructor Summary

Sc400Exception()
    Empty Sc400Exception constructor.

Sc400Exception(java.lang.String s)
    Creates an Sc400Exception with the specified message.

Methods inherited from class java.lang.Throwable

`fillInStackTrace, getLocalizedMessage, getMessage, printStackTrace, printStackTrace, printStackTrace, toString`

Methods inherited from class java.lang.Object

`equals, getClass, hashCode, notify, notifyAll, wait, wait, wait`

Constructor Detail

Sc400Exception

`public Sc400Exception()`
    Empty Sc400Exception constructor.

Sc400Exception

`public Sc400Exception(java.lang.String s)`
    Creates an Sc400Exception with the specified message.
    Parameters:
    s - the exception message.

Appendix C: Javadoc

Overview **Package** Class Tree Deprecated Index Help
PREV PACKAGE　NEXT PACKAGE　　　　　　　　　FRAMES　NO FRAMES

Package com.pbd.pub.sc400.jbui

Class Summary	
ScJdspfJbuiDefaultListener	The ScJdspfJbuiDefaultListener can handle most normal thick client UI server requirements.
ScJdspfJbuiDisplay	The ScJdspfJbuiDisplay object is the UI object used to handle normal record I/O (that is, a single, non-subfile record format) for the thick client interface.
ScJdspfJbuiRecordUI	Associates an ScJdspfJbuiDisplay with a record name.
ScJdspfJbuiServer	The ScJdspfJbuiServer class simply extends the basic ScJdspfUIServer, but makes the record UI parameter specific to the SC400 JBUI package.

Overview　Package　**Class**　Tree　Deprecated　Index　Help
PREV CLASS　NEXT CLASS　　　　　　　　　　　FRAMES　NO FRAMES
SUMMARY: INNER | FIELD | CONSTR | METHOD　　DETAIL: FIELD | CONSTR | METHOD

com.pbd.pub.sc400.jbui

Class ScJdspfJbuiDefaultListener

```
java.lang.Object
  |
  +-com.pbd.pub.sc400.jbui.ScJdspfJbuiDefaultListener
```
All Implemented Interfaces:
　　　JdspfDisplayFileListener

---

public class **ScJdspfJbuiDefaultListener**
extends java.lang.Object
implements JdspfDisplayFileListener

The ScJdspfJbuiDefaultListener can handle most normal thick client UI server requirements. Its `actionPerformed` method is invoked whenever an EXFMT operation is processed.

Since:
　　　2.0P

Constructor Summary

ScJdspfJbuiDefaultListener()

Method Summary

Boolean	**actionPerformed**(JdspfDisplayFileAction action) Invoked whenever user interaction is required, this method will copy the data from the display file to the appropriate UI object, display the UI object, then copy the user input back to the display file.

Methods inherited from class java.lang.Object

equals, getClass, hashCode, notify, notifyAll, toString, wait, wait, wait

Constructor Detail

ScJdspfJbuiDefaultListener

public **ScJdspfJbuiDefaultListener**()

Method Detail

actionPerformed

public boolean **actionPerformed**(JdspfDisplayFileAction action)

Invoked whenever user interaction is required, this method will copy the data from the display file to the appropriate UI object, display the UI object, then copy the user input back to the display file.

Specified by:
actionPerformed in interface JdspfDisplayFileListener

Parameters:
action - the action event.

Appendix C: Javadoc

| Overview | Package | **Class** | Tree | Deprecated | Index | Help |

PREV CLASS NEXT CLASS   FRAMES NO FRAMES
SUMMARY: INNER | FIELD | CONSTR | METHOD   DETAIL: FIELD | CONSTR | METHOD

---

com.pbd.pub.sc400.jbui

Class ScJdspfJbuiDisplay

```
java.lang.Object
   |
   +-com.pbd.pub.jbui.JbuiScreen
        |
        +-com.pbd.pub.jbui.JbuiDisplay
             |
             +-com.pbd.pub.sc400.jbui.ScJdspfJbuiDisplay
```

All Implemented Interfaces:
JbuiConstants, JdspfUIAdapter, javax.swing.SwingConstants

---

public class **ScJdspfJbuiDisplay**
extends JbuiDisplay
implements JdspfUIAdapter

The ScJdspfJbuiDisplay object is the UI object used to handle normal record I/O (that is, a single, non-subfile record format) for the thick client interface. It simply extends a JbuiDisplay object and implements the JdspfUIAdapter interface.

It is important to note that this very simple form of UI object has some restrictions: all field names in the ScJdspfJbuiDisplay object **must** match the names of the fields in the JdspfDisplayFile, and there can be no other fields in the display (note that you *can* skip some of the fields in the display file, but you can't add extra fields).

To extend the interface, for example to perform more complex editing, the ScJdspfJbuiDefaultListener would be replaced with a correspondingly more sophisticated object.

Since:
    2.0P

Constructor Summary

ScJdspfJbuiDisplay()
    Empty ScJbuiDisplay constructor.

ScJdspfJbuiDisplay(java.lang.String initTitle, JbuiFieldPanel initFieldPanel, JbuiButtonPanel initButtonPanel)
    Creates an ScJdspJbuiDisplay with the specified title, fields, and buttons.

Method Summary

void	**copyDataFromJdspf**(JdspfDisplayFile jdspf) Copies data from the display file to the record UI object.
void	**copyDataToJdspf**(JdspfDisplayFile jdspf) Copies data from the record UI object to the display file.

Methods inherited from class com.pbd.pub.jbui.JbuiDisplay

clearData, clearErrors, getData, getData, getFieldPanel, setData, setData, setError, setError, setError, setFieldPanel, setHandle, setProtect, setProtect, setProtect

Methods inherited from class com.pbd.pub.jbui.JbuiScreen

EXFMT, getFrame, getPosition, getPressedButton, isSomeoneWaiting, jbuiNotify, jbuiNotify, READ, setButtonPanel, setOwner, setPosition, setTitle, WRITE

Methods inherited from class java.lang.Object

equals, getClass, hashCode, notify, notifyAll, toString, wait, wait, wait

Constructor Detail

ScJdspfJbuiDisplay

```
public ScJdspfJbuiDisplay()
```
Empty ScJbuiDisplay constructor.

ScJdspfJbuiDisplay

```
public ScJdspfJbuiDisplay(java.lang.String initTitle,
                          JbuiFieldPanel initFieldPanel,
                          JbuiButtonPanel initButtonPanel)
```
Creates an ScJdspJbuiDisplay with the specified title, fields, and buttons.

Parameters:
initTitle - the title of the window, displayed in the frame's title bar.
initFieldPanel - the entry fields for this panel.
initButtonPanel - the buttons for this panel.

Appendix C: Javadoc

Method Detail

copyDataFromJdspf

```
public void copyDataFromJdspf(JdspfDisplayFile jdspf)
```
    Copies data from the display file to the record UI object.
    Specified by:
    copyDataFromJdspf in interface JdspfUIAdapter
    Parameters:
    jdspf - the display file.

copyDataToJdspf

```
public void copyDataToJdspf(JdspfDisplayFile jdspf)
```
    Copies data from the record UI object to the display file.
    Specified by:
    copyDataToJdspf in interface JdspfUIAdapter
    Parameters:
    jdspf - the display file.

Overview Package **Class** Tree Deprecated Index Help
PREV CLASS   NEXT CLASS   FRAMES   NO FRAMES
SUMMARY: INNER | FIELD | CONSTR | METHOD   DETAIL: FIELD | CONSTR | METHOD

---

com.pbd.pub.sc400.jbui

Class ScJdspfJbuiRecordUI

```
java.lang.Object
  |
  +-com.pbd.pub.jdspf.JdspfRecordUI
         |
         +-com.pbd.pub.sc400.jbui.ScJdspfJbuiRecordUI
```

public class **ScJdspfJbuiRecordUI**
extends JdspfRecordUI

Associates an ScJdspfJbuiDisplay with a record name.

Since:
    2.0P

Constructor Summary

ScJdspfJbuiRecordUI(java.lang.String recordName, ScJdspfJbuiDisplay jbuiDisplay)
    Creates an ScJdspfJbuiRecordUI for the specified record name and UI object.

Method Summary

ScJdspfJbuiDisplay	**getJbuiDisplay**() Returns the record UI object as an ScJdspfJbuiDisplay.

Methods inherited from class java.lang.Object

equals, getClass, hashCode, notify, notifyAll, toString, wait, wait, wait

Constructor Detail

ScJdspfJbuiRecordUI

public **ScJdspfJbuiRecordUI**(java.lang.String recordName,
                              ScJdspfJbuiDisplay jbuiDisplay)

Creates an ScJdspfJbuiRecordUI for the specified record name and UI object.

Parameters:
recordName - the name of the record.
jbuiDisplay - the record UI object.

Method Detail

getJbuiDisplay

public ScJdspfJbuiDisplay **getJbuiDisplay**()

Returns the record UI object as an ScJdspfJbuiDisplay.

Returns:
the record UI object as an ScJdspfJbuiDisplay.

Appendix C: Javadoc

Overview	Package	**Class**	Tree	Deprecated	Index	Help

PREV CLASS   NEXT CLASS   FRAMES   NO FRAMES
SUMMARY: INNER | FIELD | CONSTR | METHOD   DETAIL: FIELD | CONSTR | METHOD

com.pbd.pub.sc400.jbui

Class ScJdspfJbuiServer

```
java.lang.Object
  |
  +-com.pbd.pub.sc400.ScJdspfUIServer
       |
       +-com.pbd.pub.sc400.jbui.ScJdspfJbuiServer
```

public class **ScJdspfJbuiServer**
extends ScJdspfUIServer

The ScJdspfJbuiServer class simply extends the basic ScJdspfUIServer, but makes the record UI parameter specific to the SC400 JBUI package.

Since:
  2.0P

Constructor Summary

ScJdspfJbuiServer()
   Empty ScJdspfJbuiServer constructor.

ScJdspfJbuiServer(Sc400Client client, JdspfDisplayFile jdspf, JdspfDisplayFileListener listener, ScJdspfJbuiRecordUI[] recordUIs)
   Creates an ScJdspfJbuiServer object with the specified client, display file, listener, and record UI objects.

ScJdspfJbuiServer(Sc400Client client, JdspfDisplayFile jdspf, ScJdspfJbuiRecordUI[] recordUIs)
   Creates an ScJdspfJbuiServer object with the specified client, display file, and record UI objects, and using an ScJdspfJbuiDefaultListener as the listener.

Methods inherited from class com.pbd.pub.sc400.ScJdspfUIServer

getJdspf, init, run, send, send

Methods inherited from class java.lang.Object

equals, getClass, hashCode, notify, notifyAll, toString, wait, wait, wait

Constructor Detail

ScJdspfJbuiServer

public **ScJdspfJbuiServer**()
                    throws Sc400Exception

Empty ScJdspfJbuiServer constructor.

ScJdspfJbuiServer

public **ScJdspfJbuiServer**(Sc400Client client,
                         JdspfDisplayFile jdspf,
                         ScJdspfJbuiRecordUI[] recordUIs)
                    throws Sc400Exception

Creates an ScJdspfJbuiServer object with the specified client, display file, and record UI objects, and using an ScJdspfJbuiDefaultListener as the listener.

Parameters:
client - the application client.
jdspf - the display file.
the - record UI objects.

ScJdspfJbuiServer

public **ScJdspfJbuiServer**(Sc400Client client,
                         JdspfDisplayFile jdspf,
                         JdspfDisplayFileListener listener,
                         ScJdspfJbuiRecordUI[] recordUIs)
                    throws Sc400Exception

Creates an ScJdspfJbuiServer object with the specified client, display file, listener, and record UI objects.

Parameters:
client - the application client.
jdspf - the display file.
listener - the display file listener (or null for none).
the - record UI objects.

Appendix C: Javadoc

Overview **Package** Class Tree Deprecated Index Help
PREV PACKAGE NEXT PACKAGE   FRAMES NO FRAMES

Package com.pbd.pub.sc400.jsp

Class Summary	
ScJdspfJsp	The ScJdspfJsp object is the UI object used to handle normal record I/O (that is, a single, non-subfile record format) in the browser interface.
ScJdspfJspButtonDefinition	This field associates a string value from a button field with a "command key ID" from 00 to 24, which can then be passed back up to the display file to simulate a command key.
ScJdspfJspButtonField	The ScJdspJspButtonField extends the normal JspField class by adding a table of values associating values with command keys.
ScJdspfJspRecordUI	Associates an ScJdspfJsp with a record name.
ScJdspfJspServlet	The ScJdspfJspServlet class is classic example of an Adapter design, which converts one protocol to another - in this case, adapting the HTTP protocol to work with the 5250 protocol.

Overview Package **Class** Tree Deprecated Index Help
PREV CLASS NEXT CLASS   FRAMES NO FRAMES
SUMMARY: INNER | FIELD | CONSTR | METHOD   DETAIL: FIELD | CONSTR | METHOD

---

com.pbd.pub.sc400.jsp

Class ScJdspfJsp

```
java.lang.Object
  |
  +-com.pbd.pub.jsp.Jsp
         |
         +-com.pbd.pub.sc400.jsp.ScJdspfJsp
```

All Implemented Interfaces:
  JdspfUIAdapter

---

public class **ScJdspfJsp**
extends Jsp
implements JdspfUIAdapter

The ScJdspfJsp object is the UI object used to handle normal record I/O (that is, a single, non-subfile record format) in the browser interface. It simply extends a Jsp object and implements the JdspfUIAdapter interface.

Appendix C: Javadoc

This is a very simple version, and requires that the field names in the JSP match the field names in the display file. This in turn means that the fields in the actual JavaServer Page must match the same way. In addition, the JSP (and JavaServer Page) must have a single button field defined in order to return a valid command key to the display file.

For more on this, please refer to the example programs that are included in the PBD distribution.

Since:
    2.0P

See Also:
    `ScJdspfJspButtonField`

Fields inherited from class com.pbd.pub.jsp.Jsp

buttonField

Constructor Summary

ScJdspfJsp()
    Empty ScJdspfJsp contructor.

ScJdspfJsp(`java.lang.String name`)
    Creates an ScJdspfJsp with the specified fully qualified name and no fields.

ScJdspfJsp(`java.lang.String name,` JspField`[] fields`)
    Creates an ScJdspfJsp with the specified fully qualified name and fields.

ScJdspfJsp(`java.lang.String path, java.lang.String name`)
    Creates an ScJdspfJsp with the specified path and name and no fields.

ScJdspfJsp(`java.lang.String path, java.lang.String name,` JspField`[] fields`)
    Creates an ScJdspfJsp with the specified path, name, and fields.

Method Summary

void	**copyDataFromJdspf**(JdspfDisplayFile `jdspf`)	
	Unused.	
void	**copyDataFromRequest**(`com.pbd.pub.sc400.jsp.HttpServletRequest request`)	
	Copies data from the HTTP servlet request to the record UI object.	
void	**copyDataToJdspf**(JdspfDisplayFile `jdspf`)	
	Copies data from the record UI object to the display file.	

Methods inherited from class com.pbd.pub.jsp.Jsp

getButtonField, getButtonValue, getFields, getName, getPath, getURL, setFields, setName, setPath

Methods inherited from class java.lang.Object

`equals, getClass, hashCode, notify, notifyAll, toString, wait, wait, wait`

Appendix C: Javadoc

Constructor Detail

ScJdspfJsp

public **ScJdspfJsp**()

　　　　Empty ScJdspfJsp contructor.

ScJdspfJsp

public **ScJdspfJsp**(java.lang.String name)

　　　　Creates an ScJdspfJsp with the specified fully qualified name and no fields.
　　　　Parameters:
　　　　name - the fully qualified name of the JSP.

ScJdspfJsp

public **ScJdspfJsp**(java.lang.String name,
　　　　　　　　　　JspField[] fields)

　　　　Creates an ScJdspfJsp with the specified fully qualified name and fields.
　　　　Parameters:
　　　　name - the fully qualified name of the JSP.
　　　　fields - the array of fields for the JSP.

ScJdspfJsp

public **ScJdspfJsp**(java.lang.String path,
　　　　　　　　　　java.lang.String name)

　　　　Creates an ScJdspfJsp with the specified path and name and no fields.
　　　　Parameters:
　　　　path - the path name of the JSP, with no trailing '/'.
　　　　name - the file name of the JSP.

ScJdspfJsp

public **ScJdspfJsp**(java.lang.String path,
　　　　　　　　　　java.lang.String name,
　　　　　　　　　　JspField[] fields)

　　　　Creates an ScJdspfJsp with the specified path, name and fields.
　　　　Parameters:
　　　　path - the path name of the JSP, with no trailing '/'.
　　　　name - the file name of the JSP.
　　　　fields - the array of fields for the JSP.

Method Detail

copyDataFromJdspf

```
public void copyDataFromJdspf(JdspfDisplayFile jdspf)
```
    Unused. Copies data from the display file to the record UI object.
    Specified by:
    copyDataFromJdspf in interface JdspfUIAdapter
    Parameters:
    jdspf - the display file.

copyDataFromRequest

```
public void copyDataFromRequest(com.pbd.pub.sc400.jsp.HttpServletRequest request)
```
    Copies data from the HTTP servlet request to the record UI object. This method is used to retrieve the information from a POST request.
    Parameters:
    jdspf - the display file.

copyDataToJdspf

```
public void copyDataToJdspf(JdspfDisplayFile jdspf)
```
    Copies data from the record UI object to the display file.
    Specified by:
    copyDataToJdspf in interface JdspfUIAdapter
    Parameters:
    jdspf - the display file.

Appendix C: Javadoc

Overview	Package	**Class**	Tree	Deprecated	Index	Help		
PREV CLASS	NEXT CLASS				FRAMES	NO FRAMES		
SUMMARY: INNER	FIELD	CONSTR	METHOD				DETAIL: FIELD	CONSTR	METHOD		

com.pbd.pub.sc400.jsp

Class ScJdspfJspButtonDefinition

```
java.lang.Object
  |
  +-com.pbd.pub.sc400.jsp.ScJdspfJspButtonDefinition
```

public class **ScJdspfJspButtonDefinition**
extends java.lang.Object

This field associates a string value from a button field with a "command key ID" from 00 to 24, which can then be passed back up to the display file to simulate a command key.

Since:
    2.0P

Constructor Summary

ScJdspfJspButtonDefinition(java.lang.String buttonValue, int buttonKey)
    Creates an ScJdspfJspButtonDefinition associating the specified value with the specified command key ID.

Methods inherited from class java.lang.Object

equals, getClass, hashCode, notify, notifyAll, toString, wait, wait, wait

Constructor Detail

ScJdspfJspButtonDefinition

public **ScJdspfJspButtonDefinition**(java.lang.String buttonValue,
                                     int buttonKey)

Creates an ScJdspfJspButtonDefinition associating the specified value with the specified command key ID.

Parameters:
buttonValue - the string value of the button.
buttonKey - the associated command key.

Overview	Package	**Class**	Tree	Deprecated	Index	Help

PREV CLASS NEXT CLASS   **FRAMES** **NO FRAMES**
SUMMARY: INNER | FIELD | CONSTR | METHOD   DETAIL: FIELD | CONSTR | METHOD

com.pbd.pub.sc400.jsp

Class ScJdspfJspButtonField

```
java.lang.Object
  |
  +-com.pbd.pub.jsp.JspField
        |
        +-com.pbd.pub.sc400.jsp.ScJdspfJspButtonField
```

public class **ScJdspfJspButtonField**
extends JspField

The ScJdspfJspButtonField extends the normal JspField class by adding a table of values associating values with command keys. This table is used to determine which "command key ID" to send to the display file when a specific button is pressed.

Since:
    2.0P

Fields inherited from class com.pbd.pub.jsp.JspField

MULTIPLE, SINGLE

Constructor Summary

ScJdspfJspButtonField(java.lang.String name, ScJdspfJspButtonDefinition[] buttonTable)
    Creates an ScJdspfJspButtonField with the specified field name and array of button definitions.

Method Summary

int	**getKey**() Returns the command key ID associated with the current value of the button field.
java.lang.String	**valueOf**(int key) Returns the button value associated with the specified command key ID.

Methods inherited from class com.pbd.pub.jsp.JspField

getName, getType, getValue, getValues, isButtonField, setValue

Methods inherited from class java.lang.Object

equals, getClass, hashCode, notify, notifyAll, toString, wait, wait, wait

Constructor Detail

ScJdspfJspButtonField

```
public ScJdspfJspButtonField(java.lang.String name,
                             ScJdspfJspButtonDefinition[] buttonTable)
```
Creates an ScJdspfJspButtonField with the specified field name and array of button definitions.
Parameters:
name - the name of the button field in the JSP.
buttonTable - the array of ScJdspfJspButtonDefinitions.

Method Detail

getKey

```
public int getKey()
```
Returns the command key ID associated with the current value of the button field.
Returns:
the command key ID associated with the current value of the button field.

valueOf

```
public java.lang.String valueOf(int key)
```
Returns the button value associated with the specified command key ID.
Returns:
the button value associated with the specified command key ID.

Appendix C: Javadoc

Overview	Package	**Class**	Tree	Deprecated	Index	Help

PREV CLASS NEXT CLASS
SUMMARY: INNER | FIELD | CONSTR | METHOD
FRAMES NO FRAMES
DETAIL: FIELD | CONSTR | METHOD

---

com.pbd.pub.sc400.jsp

Class ScJdspfJspRecordUI

```
java.lang.Object
  |
  +-com.pbd.pub.jdspf.JdspfRecordUI
        |
        +-com.pbd.pub.sc400.jsp.ScJdspfJspRecordUI
```

public class **ScJdspfJspRecordUI**
extends JdspfRecordUI

Associates an ScJdspfJsp with a record name.

Since:
> 2.0P

Constructor Summary

ScJdspfJspRecordUI(java.lang.String recordName, ScJdspfJsp jsp)
> Creates an ScJdspfJspRecordUI for the specified record name and UI object.

Method Summary

ScJdspfJsp	**getScJdspfJsp**() Returns the record UI object as an ScJdspfJsp.

Methods inherited from class java.lang.Object

equals, getClass, hashCode, notify, notifyAll, toString, wait, wait, wait

Constructor Detail

ScJdspfJspRecordUI

public **ScJdspfJspRecordUI**(java.lang.String recordName,
                             ScJdspfJsp jsp)

> Creates an ScJdspfJspRecordUI for the specified record name and UI object.
> **Parameters:**
> recordName - the name of the record.
> jsp - the record UI object.

Appendix C: Javadoc

Method Detail

getScJdspfJsp

```
public ScJdspfJsp getScJdspfJsp()
```
Returns the record UI object as an ScJdspfJsp.

Returns:
the record UI object as an ScJdspfJsp.

Overview Package **Class** Tree Deprecated Index Help
PREV CLASS   NEXT CLASS   FRAMES   NO FRAMES
SUMMARY: INNER | FIELD | CONSTR | METHOD   DETAIL: FIELD | CONSTR | METHOD

---

com.pbd.pub.sc400.jsp

Class ScJdspfJspServlet

`com.pbd.pub.sc400.jsp.ScJdspfJspServlet`

public class **ScJdspfJspServlet**

The ScJdspfJspServlet class is classic example of an Adapter design, which converts one protocol to another - in this case, adapting the HTTP protocol to work with the 5250 protocol. The browser interface requires an output operation and a completely separate input operation, while the typical 5250 server/client protocol tightly binds the write and read operations.

The two primary methods of the ScJdspfJspServlet class, `doGet` and `doPost` serve as the entry points to the cycle, but the class encapsulates calls to the ScJdspfUIServer cycle in such a way as to integrate the two cycles seamlessly. Internal routines such as `init`, `send`, and `receive` are called in response to the HTTP requests, and allow the two interfaces to cooperate.

One other concession to the HTTP protocol has to do with the concept of the "exit JSP." In order to make this as non-platform specific as possible, I decided that, rather than make use of the somewhat non-standard concept of a "referring URL," I would instead allow the programmer to designate a specific JSP to be executed when the current application ends.

Since:
2.0P

Constructor Summary

ScJdspfJspServlet ()
    Empty ScJdspfJspServlet constructor.

ScJdspfJspServlet (java.lang.String clientName, java.lang.String jdspfName, ScJdspfJspRecordUI[] recordUIs, ScJdspfJsp exitJsp)
    Creates an ScJdspfJspServlet for the specified client, display file, record Uis, and exit JSP.

Method Summary

void	**callJsp** (com.pbd.pub.sc400.jsp.HttpServletRequest req, com.pbd.pub.sc400.jsp.HttpServletResponse res, ScJdspfJsp jsp) Calls the JSP specified by the ScJdspfJsp.
void	**callJsp** (com.pbd.pub.sc400.jsp.HttpServletRequest req, com.pbd.pub.sc400.jsp.HttpServletResponse res, java.lang.String recordName) Calls the JSP associated with the specified record.
void	**doGet** (com.pbd.pub.sc400.jsp.HttpServletRequest req, com.pbd.pub.sc400.jsp.HttpServletResponse res) Standard HTTP GET request handler.
void	**doPost** (com.pbd.pub.sc400.jsp.HttpServletRequest req, com.pbd.pub.sc400.jsp.HttpServletResponse res) Standard HTTP POST request handler.
ScJdspfJsp	**getCurrentJsp** () Returns the current JSP.
ScJdspfJsp	**getExitJsp** () Returns the exit JSP.
JdspfDisplayFile	**getJdspf** () Returns the display file.
boolean	**isExiting** () Returns `true` if the application is exiting.
void	**setExitJsp** (ScJdspfJsp newValue) Sets the exit JSP for this servlet.

Constructor Detail

ScJdspfJspServlet

```
public ScJdspfJspServlet()
```
    Empty ScJdspfJspServlet constructor.

Appendix C: Javadoc

ScJdspfJspServlet

```
public ScJdspfJspServlet(java.lang.String clientName,
                         java.lang.String jdspfName,
                         ScJdspfJspRecordUI[] recordUIs,
                         ScJdspfJsp exitJsp)
                  throws Sc400Exception
```
Creates an ScJdspfJspServlet for the specified client, display file, record Uis, and exit JSP.

Parameters:
String - the name of the client.
String - the display file name.
ScJdspfJspRecordUI[] - the array of record UI objects.
ScJdspfJsp - the exit JSP.

Method Detail

callJsp

```
public void callJsp(com.pbd.pub.sc400.jsp.HttpServletRequest req,
                    com.pbd.pub.sc400.jsp.HttpServletResponse res,
                    ScJdspfJsp jsp)
             throws com.pbd.pub.sc400.jsp.ServletException,
                    java.io.IOException
```
Calls the JSP specified by the ScJdspfJsp.

Parameters:
req - from the HTTP request.
res - from the HTTP request.
jsp - the JSP to execute.

callJsp

```
public void callJsp(com.pbd.pub.sc400.jsp.HttpServletRequest req,
                    com.pbd.pub.sc400.jsp.HttpServletResponse res,
                    java.lang.String recordName)
             throws com.pbd.pub.sc400.jsp.ServletException,
                    java.io.IOException
```
Calls the JSP associated with the specified record.

Parameters:
req - from the HTTP request.
res - from the HTTP request.
recordName - the name of the record.

doGet

```
public void doGet(com.pbd.pub.sc400.jsp.HttpServletRequest req,
                  com.pbd.pub.sc400.jsp.HttpServletResponse res)
           throws com.pbd.pub.sc400.jsp.ServletException,
                  java.io.IOException
```
Standard HTTP GET request handler.

doPost

```
public void doPost(com.pbd.pub.sc400.jsp.HttpServletRequest req,
                   com.pbd.pub.sc400.jsp.HttpServletResponse res)
            throws com.pbd.pub.sc400.jsp.ServletException,
                   java.io.IOException
```
   Standard HTTP POST request handler.

getCurrentJsp

```
public ScJdspfJsp getCurrentJsp()
```
   Returns the current JSP.
   Returns:
   the current JSP.

getExitJsp

```
public ScJdspfJsp getExitJsp()
```
   Returns the exit JSP.
   Returns:
   the exit JSP.

getJdspf

```
public JdspfDisplayFile getJdspf()
```
   Returns the display file.
   Returns:
   the display file.

isExiting

```
public boolean isExiting()
```
   Returns `true` if the application is exiting.
   Returns:
   `true` if the application is exiting.

setExitJsp

```
public void setExitJsp(ScJdspfJsp newValue)
```
   Sets the exit JSP for this servlet.
   Parameters:
   newValue - the new exit JSP.

GLOSSARY

24x80 (or 24-by-80)

This term refers to the standard size of a 5250 screen, with 24 rows of 80 characters. While modern terminals allow 25 or even 43 lines, and up to 132 characters per line, *24x80* is still used to describe the 5250 interface.

5250

The term *5250* has a number of different meanings, from the physical 5250 terminal, to the 24x80 green-screen display of that terminal, to the protocol used to support it. The 5250 is a block-mode transfer protocol, where an entire screen of data is sent to the device. This data is presented to the user by the workstation, the user enters data in fields on the screen, and then the entire screen is sent back to the host. This block-mode communication reduces load on the host, and is completely different than the key-press or mouse-movement nature of most graphical interfaces.

API

See *Application Program Interface*.

APPC

APPC, Advanced Peer-to-Peer Communications, was (and in some areas still is) IBM's standard of communication between machines, and in particular was the primary means of communication between the AS/400 and its devices. APPC is typically run over SNA (System Network Architecture) networks as an alternative to TCP/IP networks, although you can run APPC over TCP/IP. For more information, visit IBM's networking site at `http://www.netoworking.ibm.com`, and search on the term *APPC*.

Application client

An application client is a monolithic legacy program that has been rewritten to use a UI server. The application client contains both application-control logic and business rules. The display file is removed and replaced by externally described data structures, which are then sent to and received from the client APIs as messages.

The second generation of the application client does not remove the display file, but instead uses it conditionally. If the program is run interactively, the display file is used, but if the program runs in batch, it uses the client APIs.

Application-control logic

Application control logic is primarily used to determine which panel should be displayed based on the results of the current operation. It may also include default value initialization and security checks based on the session information. This portion of the code is responsible for calling the business rules and, based on the outcome, deciding what to do next. This logic only exists in monolithic and server/client models; as the architecture moves to client/server, the end user decides the flow of control. This is the primary difference between client/server and server/client architectures.

Application controller

During the restructuring stage, the application-control logic and business rules are separated out of the application client. The application-control logic is moved into the application controller, while the business rules are encapsulated as business-rules servers. The application controller initializes data, then displays the first panel of the program. Based on the data entered by the user, the appropriate business-rules servers are called. The results of those calls are used to determine the next panel to display. At this point, the programs are still in the server/client architecture, since the application controller determines the sequence of displays. However, once this separation is accomplished, it becomes quite easy to move to a full client/server paradigm. The reason to use this intermediate step is to allow testing of the business rules servers under a controlled environment. Once they are fully tested, they can be released to the client/server developers.

Application modernization

The latest in industry terms (I hesitate to use the word *buzzword*, which is now a buzzword itself), application modernization can mean many things. It usually means updating some area of an application's programming, usually the area that the vendor is most familiar with. Beyond that somewhat cynical description, application modernization is actually the idea of transforming one or more of the four tiers of an application—user interface, application control, business logic or database access—into a newer, more flexible format. Examples include replacing a green-screen interface with a graphical user interface, or encapsulating business logic into servers.

Application Program Interface

An Application Program Interface, or API, is the contract between two layers of software. In most cases, an API is an interface between an application program (hence the term) and the operating system. An API is a standard contract between the application and the operating system, which, in the best environments, is stable from one release to another. OS/400 is usually very good about maintaining such release compatibility.

In another sense, the base classes that come with the Java Development Kit can be thought of as an API, since they too define a contract between the programmer and, in this case, the Java Virtual Machine. In this instance, Sun has done an outstanding job of maintaining compatibility from one release to another.

Application server

An application server is a software product that allows you to encapsulate your business logic on a server and let client programs access those servers via the Internet. Your servers then access the back-end database through APIs. There are varying levels of what an application server can do, and it depends greatly on the particular application server you choose. This book concentrates on application servers designed

GLOSSARY

to serve Java servlets and JavaServer Pages, and specifically on IBM's WebSphere product.

AS/400

The AS/400 is the most recent addition to the long and illustrious line of IBM midrange computers, which includes the System/3, System/34, System/36, and System/38. The AS/400 is arguably the most flexible, scalable, and reliable server of any midrange to date, with the lowest total cost of ownership. Interestingly, part of the short description of *AS/400* on the Internet at ask.com is as follows:

> The machine survives because its API layer allows the operating system and application programs to take advantage of advances in hardware without recompilation and which means that a complete system that costs $9000 runs the exact same operating system and software as a $2 million system.

Not a bad testimonial. If only we could explain to corporate executives what that means for their businesses!

ASCII

ASCII, which stands for *American Standard Code for Information Interchange*, is the standard character set used by most non-IBM computers prior to the mid-1990s. Most files on the AS/400 IFS are stored in ASCII. However, ASCII, especially the seven-bit variety known as US-ASCII, does not deal well with foreign languages. Also see *EBCDIC*.

Attribute

When discussing a Java class, an attribute is a field that can be stored and retrieved through setter and getter functions. However, throughout most of this book, an attribute is usually assumed to mean a display attribute.

Block mode

Block-mode user interfaces are designed to display a panel of data, allow the user to modify fields if needed, and press a function key or button to return the panel to the user. Most AS/400 green-screen applications use a block-mode interface. They were originally designed to reduce the load on the operating system, since they only send data in blocks, and don't have to handle every individual user keystroke. However, as business application programming matured, it became clear that the concept of heads-down keying of blocks of data was an inherently productive way of entering large amounts of information. Contrast this with *event-driven programming*.

Browser (or Web browser)

A browser is a program such as Microsoft Internet Explorer or Netscape Navigator that allows a user to read HTML. Modern browsers support JavaScript and applets, as well as standard HTML. The browser is a very thin client; the user needs no other software on their workstation in order to access applications that communicate via HTML. The first browser was Mosaic, released by the NCSA in 1993, while the first Java application released to the public was the HotJava Web browser.

Browser-based applications

Browser-based applications are applications designed to run entirely within a Web browser. All code either runs on the server or is downloaded (as an applet) to the browser on demand. I don't actually consider applets to be strictly browser-based because of the large amount of information, in the form of the applet program code, that is communicated to the browser. A true browser-based application communicates only in a simple, standard language such as HTML, thereby making it practical over slower-speed connections.

Business logic

See *business rules*.

Business rules (or business logic)

Business rules define the way an application processes data at the logical business-entity level. For example, business rules determine how prices are calculated or how general-ledger numbers are formatted. They tend to be higher level than simple database rules, although as databases become more sophisticated, many business rules can be integrated directly into the database (using techniques such as triggers and referential integrity).

Business-rules server

During the restructuring stage, the application-control logic and business rules are separated out of the application client. The application-control logic is moved into the application controller, while the business rules are encapsulated as business-rules servers. Business-rules servers receive and respond to messages. The messages normally have a standard format throughout the entire application. For example, most business entity servers support the basic CRUD requests.

CGI

See *Common Gateway Interface*.

Client APIs

The client APIs are a set of programs designed specifically to make it easy to convert a monolithic program into an application client. After replacing the display file with externally described data structures, the other step is to replace all display file I/O op codes with calls to the client APIs.

Client/server

One of the most widely overused terms in today's computing landscape, *client/server* is used to describe everything from workstation emulation to distributed object architecture. While an architectural discussion is outside the scope of this book, it's important to understand that revitalization is not a client/server architecture; it's a *server/client* architecture, and a waypoint to the full object approach of redeployment.

When discussing legacy systems redeployment, client/server is the point at which business logic becomes encapsulated in server programs, and is the first step toward object technology. In the redeployment strategy, the second phase, *restructuring*, converts the server/client approach of the application client to a true client/server environment. Finally, reengineering transforms those servers into objects to be used in a distributed object environment.

com.pbd.pub.common

This package contains the common routines shared throughout the PBD packages. It contains vector/array conversion methods as well as methods that manage the connection to the AS/400.

com.pbd.pub.dc400 (or DC400)

This package contains the data conversion routines used to convert data from EBCDIC to ASCII, and also from the AS/400's decimal format to Java's numeric classes. The DC400 classes can be used to create classes to represent complex AS/400 data types, such as data structures and records.

com.pbd.pub.jao400 (or JAO400)

Not used in this book, JAO400 is a set of client/server application frameworks.

com.pbd.pub.jbui (or JBUI)

JBUI is the Java Block Mode User Interface. This package allows the programmer to quickly and easily define graphical panels that support block-mode operations such as EXFMT (*execute format*, now known as *write then read format*). Fields support attributes such as PROTECT and ERROR, and there is support for an error list that is meant to emulate a message subfile.

com.pbd.pub.jdb400 (or JDB400)

Not used in this book, the JDB400 package is a set of AS/400 file access classes that support native AS/400 functions such as CHAIN and UPDAT.

com.pbd.pub.jdqm400 (or JDQM400)

Not used in this book, the JDQM400 package is a set of classes designed to support client/server communications.

com.pbd.pub.jdspf (or JDSPF)

The JDSPF package is used to define a display-file proxy. This design allows the display file to be treated as the data model in a traditional model-view-controller (MVC) architecture, in which the application client has no idea what the final user-interface representation will be. The application client simply writes data to the display-file proxy, knowing that the UI server will eventually display the data appropriately.

com.pbd.pub.jsp (or JSP)

This small package allows the programmer to define a JavaServer Page. It supports the definition of the fields in a form on that page.

com.pbd.pub.sc400 (or SC400)

The SC400 package is the heart of the server/client architecture. It encapsulates the server-side I/O proxy APIs into the ScJdspfUIServer class in such a way that the only method a UI server needs to call is run. The rest of the server/client protocol is handled internally.

GLOSSARY

com.pbd.pub.sc400.jbui (or SC400 JBUI)

The SC400 JBUI package is a subpackage of SC400 designed specifically to support a Swing user interface.

com.pbd.pub.sc400.jsp (or SC400 JSP)

The SC400 JSP package is a subpackage of SC400 designed specifically to support a browser user interface, and more specifically a JSP/servlet user interface.

com.pbd.pub.wase (or WASE)

WASE stands for *WebSphere Application Server Emulator*, a package designed to allow a servlet to be debugged directly on the workstation, without running in the Web server.

com.ibm.as400.access

This package is part of IBM's Java Toolbox for the AS/400, and contains all the non-graphical classes that provide access to the AS/400 data and programs. This includes classes to call programs, access objects such as data queues, and read and write files using native DB2 access.

com.ibm.as400.vaccess

Not used in this book, this package contains all the graphical classes of IBM's Java Toolbox for the AS/400.

Command keys

A command key is part of the 5250 interface. A user presses a command key (also known as a *function key*) to indicate to the workstation that he or she is done entering data. There are 24 different command keys, allowing the user to request a particular function from the host.

Common Gateway Interface

Common Gateway Interface, or *CGI*, defines a protocol by which HTTP requests can be redirected to a program. Rather than simply serving a static Web page from disk, the Web server calls a program. It is then the program's responsibility to format and output an HTML data stream. This is probably the simplest way to allow dynamic HTML generation. The primary disadvantage is that the HTML strings are actually hard-coded into the program, and the program performs string manipulation to output the data stream correctly.

Some languages, such as RPG, are unsuitable for string manipulation of this type. Even for those that are, you face the fundamental problem of modifying and recompiling the program whenever a simple change to the appearance of Web page is needed. Contrast this approach with *servlets* and *JavaServer Pages*.

Condition

A condition is a combination of an indicator and a state (true or false), which is used to "condition" whether a given event will occur or whether a display attribute will be activated.

CRUD

CRUD ("create, read, update, and delete") is an acronym for the basic functions of a business-entity maintenance server. CRUD supports all the lowest-level requirements for accessing a traditional relational database. Simple CRUD works at a single file, record level, while more sophisticated servers use a message-based approach that hides the underlying database structure from the application.

Data Description Specifications (or DDS)

The DDS for a display file is the source code that defines the file. DDS is also used to define physical files, logical files, and externally described data structures.

Data queue

A data queue is an AS/400 object that provides queuing between two programs. Data queues can be accessed sequentially, either in FIFO (first in, first out) or LIFO (last in, first out) sequence, or they can be keyed. The APIs in this book all use FIFO data queues.

Data structure

A data structure is a contiguous collection of data fields. In RPG, a data structure can be used to define fields, but in this book data structures associate a group of related fields into a message.

DC400

See *com.pbd.pub.dc400*.

DDS

See *Data Description Specifications*.

Display attribute

A display attribute is used to alter the presentation of a field of a 5250 screen. For example, the display attribute PROTECT prevents input, while the display attribute UNDERLINE causes the field to be underlined on the screen. Display attributes are often conditioned by indicators sent from the application program.

Display file

A display file is an AS/400 object that defines a 5250 screen or a set of related screens. The display file supports single-panel displays, subfiles, and other screen types. Each different screen is defined as a record format within the display file. Some record types, such as the subfile record and subfile control record, are explicitly related, while other records are implicitly related by their use within the RPG program. A fully implemented display-file proxy must support these relationships between different record formats in the display file.

Display-file proxy

A display-file proxy is a Java class used to store and forward I/O requests from the application client to the UI server and return responses back to the application client. The display-file proxy is the interface object between the application client and the various UI servers. Since the display-file proxy is independent of the type of UI server, it serves as the "model" in the model-view-controller design of the server/client architecture.

Distributed programming

Distributed programming is a generic term that covers any type of cooperative processing between two or more different computers (or even, in its broadest sense, between two processors on the same computer). It encompasses everything from batch upload and processing to true interactive client/server systems.

Dumb terminal

A dumb terminal is the common, and in many ways mistaken, term for the green-screen terminals hooked up to most midrange and mainframe systems. In IBM circles, these are typically 3270- or 5250-type terminals. I say the term is mistaken because the 5250, especially, is a very intelligent device, allowing the user to define fields and attributes on the screen, and then allowing the user to key data (with all sorts of different validations) before finally uploading the whole stream back to the host.

EBCDIC

EBCDIC stands for *Extended Binary-Coded-Decimal Interchange Code*, and is used almost exclusively by IBM to store data. It was adapted from punched-card code in the 1960s, and is still the primary means of data storage on IBM midrange and mainframe computers, including the AS/400.

EJB

See *Enterprise JavaBeans*.

Enterprise JavaBeans

Enterprise JavaBeans, or *EJB*, is a technology developed by Sun to allow developers to create reusable server-side components. Like redeployment, EJB is not just a technical solution, but more of an architectural strategy. EJB incorporates a wide range of technologies, from naming services to remote method invocation to transaction APIs. Together, they are meant to provide a platform- and vendor-neutral interface for access to any of the existing transaction services, such as X/Open DTP, OSF DCE, and OMG CORBA.

The idea is that an Enterprise JavaBean will replace the traditional message-based interface to a server in a client/server environment. Client programs will no longer rely on a vendor-specific interface, but instead will be coded to the EJB specification, thereby ensuring that they are platform independent. At the same time, the servers will be designed to operate within the EJB framework, thereby allowing a wider range of client access. EJB is one of the possible endpoints of the redeployment model—after splitting your code into clients and servers, you would replace the hard-coded messaging interface with an EJB interface.

Event-driven programming

Event-driven programming describes the model where small pieces of code are executed based on operator actions or system events (such as timers or error conditions). In the early days of computer programming, operating systems were called "interrupt driven" when they could respond asynchronously to a hardware signal—the opposite was a "polled" interface. The same sort of difference can be drawn between event-driven programs and traditional, imperative programs.

Event-driven programming is more easily implemented in an object-oriented programming language because the concept of calling the method of an object can be easily viewed instead as sending a message to a receiver. In fact, many of the concepts of event-driven programming are implemented in various Java packages, the most obvious being the concept of a "listener" class, whose methods are invoked when specific events occur.

Externally described data structure (or external data structure)

An externally described data structure is a uniquely AS/400 technique that allows a programmer to define a data structure as a physical file, and then have the compiler read in the definition. This way, multiple programs can be kept in sync if the data structure changes by simply recompiling them.

Framework

In object terms, a framework is a generic class that is meant to be extended to provide specific functions for a given requirement. The framework generally provides common routines shared by different variations of the requirement, but usually not enough for a full implementation. The SC400 package is a framework package, which is extended for specific use by the SC400 JBUI and SC400 JSP packages.

Function keys

See *command keys*.

Green screen

The term *green screen* refers to the original green coloring of the characters on a 5250 display terminal. Green-screen interfaces are fixed-format, usually 24 lines by 80 characters, with limited attribute capabilities. This is the normal interface method for an AS/400.

Green-screen UI server

The green-screen UI server is the specific UI server used to emulate the traditional monolithic program. The green-screen UI server uses the display file that is removed from the monolithic program when it is converted to an application client.

HTML

HTML (*HyperText Markup Language*) is a document format used on the World Wide Web. HTML provides standard tags to allow formatting of data independent of the graphic capabilities of the user's workstation. It is up to the browser to interpret the HTML and display the data appropriately.

HTTP

HTTP (*HyperText Transfer Protocol*) is the standard protocol used to exchange HTML between a Web server and a browser. HTTP is the protocol that performs the GET and POST operations passed to a servlet by the Web server.

I/O proxy APIs

The I/O proxy APIs are a set of very low-level programs that provide basic message support between an application client and a UI Server. They are specifically designed to allow the emulation of display-file I/O op codes.

IBM's Java Toolbox for the AS/400

This package is probably the single reason why Java and the AS/400 will be able to coexist in the future. It provides access to nearly every AS/400 feature necessary to build robust, powerful, distributed applications, and it's distributed free with the AS/400. IBM did an incredible job with this package.

Imperative languages

Imperative languages are the languages you've grown up with over the years: RPG, COBOL, BASIC, Pascal, and C. These languages are characterized by their basic features: assignment of values to variables and explicit control of the flow of the language. Contrast this with object-oriented languages, where the control of the program depends on the objects that make up the program.

GLOSSARY

Index panel

An index panel is used to select a program in an application. It serves the same purpose as a menu in a legacy system. The purpose of the index panel is to initiate a program.

Indicator

An indicator is a uniquely RPG feature. An indicator is a predefined Boolean value. There are 99 program indicators, 24 command-key indicators, and a few special indicators such as "last record" used to control program flow. The earliest versions of RPG allowed a programmer to compare two values and set the indicators based on the result of the comparison (high, low, or equal). These indicators were then used to condition subsequent lines of code, or to condition database or printer output. These indicators are still in the language, and are the primary vehicle by which display attributes are conditioned.

Java

Java is the language of the Internet. Developed by Sun Microsystems, Java is a truly portable object-oriented language that is currently growing in popularity every day. IBM has fully embraced Java as an important part of its server strategy and is integrating it with the AS/400 more and more completely with each release of OS/400.

Java Development Kit

The Java Development Kit, or *JDK*, is a software bundle that allows a programmer to develop Java programs. It includes not only the Java runtime environment, but also the compiler and debugger, as well as the source for the base Java classes themselves. If you are using an interactive development environment (IDE), you don't need the JDK, but the nice thing about the JDK is that it is always available for free, as long as you have an Internet connection.

Java/400

This is my own term for anything relating to the use of Java in conjunction with the AS/400. That's a wide spectrum of possibilities, and to be honest, I don't do much server-side Java programming, other than servlets. My business logic is primarily written in RPG today. That doesn't mean, however, that Java/400 isn't a vibrant field—the servlets are written in Java, as are the thick clients. As server-side Java is better integrated into the OS/400 programming environment (ILE Java?), I'll spend more time working with it as well.

JavaBeans

JavaBeans are a specific type of Java class with carefully defined characteristics. They include attributes, which are variables that can be accessed via getter and setter methods, and a default constructor. They are defined this way so that they can be manipulated via builder tools to construct applications. The term JavaBean, or just *bean*, has become slightly diluted, and is used to mean any class that stores data and is passed to another class. This usage is particularly prevalent when talking about JavaServer Pages and servlets.

JavaServer Page

A JavaServer Page is an HTML page with added tags that support embedded Java syntax in the HTML, as well as access to JavaBeans passed from the servlet. In this way, the JavaServer Page can act as the "view" portion of the model-view-controller design. The revitalization architecture takes advantage of this design by sending a display-file proxy as the bean to a specially designed JavaServer Page.

JBUI

See *com.pbd.pub.jbui*.

JDB400

See *com.pbd.pub.jdb400*.

JDBC

JDBC (*Java Database Connectivity*) is the Java package (java.sql) that supports SQL-like requests to a database, much like Microsoft's ODBC interface. The two primary differences are that JDBC supports a whole range of different connectivity schemes, with different levels of integration to the native database, and that JDBC is evolving support for objects directly. (That is, there is the ability to directly load and store objects using JDBC statements.)

JDK

See *Java Development Kit*.

GLOSSARY

JDQM400

See *com.pbd.pub.jdqm400*.

JDSPF

See *com.pbd.pub.jdspf*.

JSP

JSP can mean the **com.pbd.pub.jsp** package, but in common usage, it refers to a JavaServer Page. See *com.pbd.pub.jsp* and *JavaServer Page*.

JSPAPI

JSPAPI is the AS/400 library containing the I/O proxy APIs and the client APIs.

JSPPROTO

JSPPROTO is the AS/400 library containing the application programs used to demonstrate the revitalization architecture.

JT400

See *IBM's Java Toolbox for the AS/400*.

Legacy programs (or legacy applications)

Legacy programs are programs written in older imperative languages such as RPG or COBOL, usually using the traditional monolithic model. These programs often are many years old, and have undergone years of modification to match evolving business needs. Usually, these programs have become unique to the organization and, while not object-oriented, do encapsulate the business rules of the organization. The problem is that the business rules are too often intermingled with the application control and user interface logic, and can't be easily untangled. That's why revitalization is so important—it creates a buffer period that allows you to do the untangling while still providing new user interface features for the end users.

Legacy programmers

More important even than your legacy programs are your legacy programmers. Strangely enough, though, they're often the most overlooked assets in a company.

Forays into CASE tools in the 1980s may have had something to do with the idea that programmers are basically interchangeable pieces. In fact, however, your legacy programmers, the ones who have been around for a long time, are often the only ones who know how your system works and why.

The move to new technologies sometimes loses sight of the huge knowledge base represented by these programmers, and systems are implemented that make them obsolete, but the new programmers who must maintain and customize the new systems have no idea what the business requirements are. The fundamental goal of revitalization is to provide a buffer zone between old and new technologies, where the legacy programmers can still a provide useful service to the company for as long as is beneficial, both for them and the company.

Message

The term *message* has many meanings, especially in programming. For example, AS/400 errors and information are sent from program to program using messages. One view of Java programming is that, rather than one object calling the method of another object, the first object instead sends a message to the other object. In this book, however, the concept of a message is more like that of a data structure: a message is a set of data elements that both the sender and receiver agrees upon. The message is a self-contained entity that can request a specific action, and at the same time identifies both the sender and the receiver so that program-independent middleware can route the message and response correctly.

Message subfile

A message subfile is a specialized subfile on the AS/400 used primarily to present error information to the user. Typically, the user sends a message with first- and second-level text; the first-level text is kept under 80 characters and displayed on a single line, while the second-level text is much more extensive and is displayed by pressing a function key with the cursor on the first-level text.

Midrange

The term *midrange* was pretty much invented for the System $3x$ line of computers, to identify a computer that wasn't a PC, but wasn't a mainframe. At one point, there was a very specific niche for these computers, which were often used at individual sites of a corporation to consolidate local operations and then communicate with a corporate mainframe for big number-crunching. As the industry has evolved, however, PCs have gotten far more powerful, so that the low end of the midrange is fuzzy, while midranges have gotten larger, so that they can handle the workload of any but the largest mainframes. Still, there are certain characteristics that position the AS/400 as the premier midrange computer: a powerful, scalable platform and an integrated database that allows high-volume business processing for most small and medium-size companies, as well as the processing for individual sites of multinational corporations.

Monolithic

Monolithic programs combine user interface code, application code, and business rules all in the same program. This is the normal architecture for AS/400 green-screen applications.

Object-oriented programming

Object-oriented programming refers not only to the highly publicized concepts of inheritance, polymorphism, and encapsulation, but also to the idea of modeling a process as a series of objects that communicate with each other via messages. OOP is a very event-driven paradigm, where the actual bits of code that get executed cannot be accurately predicted, since their order depends entirely on user actions and system events. Because of this, the individual objects must be very robust, and at the same time have very focused functions.

Object technology

Interestingly enough, object technology is not limited to object-oriented programming environments. Imperative languages can take advantage of object technology to obtain services from servers. Lots of middleware exists to allow traditional programming languages to make calls to the object brokers. In fact, there are entire languages that are "object based" rather than object-oriented, in which the language predefines a set of objects that the programmer can use. These languages don't allow programmers to define their own classes, but they still provide some of the benefits of an object architecture. (LotusScript is a good example of this type of language.)

ODBC

ODBC (*Open Database Connectivity*) is a Microsoft standard that implements the call-level interface (CLI) of X/Open to access an SQL database. Since DB2 supports CLI, it can be accessed via ODBC, and since one form of JDBC makes use of an ODBC driver, JDBC can, by definition, access DB2 data. This is the most platform-independent way of accessing data, but it costs dearly in the form of a huge performance premium, especially in transaction processing.

Op code

Op code is short for *operation code*. In this book, it is used primarily to identify one of the RPG operation codes used to communicate with a display file, such as WRITE or EXFMT.

Panel

A panel interacts with the user. It defines a specific display format, but also incorporates dynamic data from the calling program. Panels can be green-screen, thick-client, or thin-client (HTML).

Platform independence

Platform independence is the Holy Grail of late 20th century programming, and has carried forward into the 21st century. The explosion of workstation operating systems has spawned this movement, which is actually ironic, since the end of the 20th century saw the mass standardization on the Wintel platform. Regardless, platform independence is an important trait, especially as we begin the move to vastly distributed programming environments.

There are several ways to achieve platform independence between platforms. Once is to "dumb down" the interface, which is precisely the reason that HTML has had such enormous success. The other is to write programs that will run anywhere. This requires some sort of virtual machine, and the Java Virtual Machine is the perfect answer to that.

The more important issue, however, is to decide where platform independence is necessary. At one extreme, the software required to back up an AS/400 device description is, of necessity, platform dependent, so it wouldn't make much sense to rewrite it in some platform-independent manner. At the other extreme, a piece of code that sends an urgent message to a user should be as platform-independent as possible. Consider a message originally intended to be displayed in text instead broadcasting an audio message in a house for someone who is blind. Platform independence can take on a wide variety of forms, and it's important to judge each one on its own merits.

Procedural programming

Procedural programming is the programming most of us have grown up with. I have programmed in procedural languages since the 1970s, and I thoroughly understand the concepts involved. It's nice to be able to predict with great precision the contents of every field and variable in your program, because you wrote the code. Similarly, you can tell which paths the program will take depending on the data.

Unfortunately, that paradigm falls apart in the event-driven world, because the code that executes is determined entire by real-world outside stimuli, which are notorious for not following any rigid set of assumptions. There is still a need for the basics of procedural programming, however, because while object technology is good for directing the control of flow based on outside occurrences, once that flow is directed, something has to tell the computer what to do. Today, that's still, at its lowest level, a procedural function.

Program

A program identifies a single host-based legacy program. This program may display and process zero or more panels before returning to the index panel for its application.

Record

The term *record* typically refers to a record in a database file. Occasionally, this book refers to the PROMPT record of a display file, which is actually shorthand for "the PROMPT record format."

Record format

A record format is the unique grouping of fields within a file that defines a specific record. Most business applications use files with a single record format, with the exception of display files, which often contain multiple record formats.

Redeployment

Redeployment is the process of transforming a legacy system into a distributed application. Redeployment has three stages: revitalization, restructuring, and reengineering. Revitalization quickly places a graphical interface on existing legacy systems while not disrupting the original code, leaving it maintainable by legacy programmers. Restructuring separates application control from business logic and moves the business logic into servers, thereby changing the fundamental architecture of the system from server/client to client/server. Reengineering completes the transformation by rewriting the server programs as reusable, server-side components, providing a completely platform-neutral interface for any type of clients or peers.

Reengineering

Phase 3 of redeployment, reengineering involves converting the remaining server code to platform-independent objects. Once you've actually rewritten your servers, this is the point when you can choose to go to a platform-independent object-oriented language for those processes that you foresee moving off of the AS/400. While there shouldn't be many such processes, there are likely candidates. For example, most simulations, such as those done for forecasting and material requirements planning, should be done on a separate processor, and not take away cycles from your primary line-of-business processor. This sort of program should be reviewed as a possible candidate for reengineering.

Regions of change

I devised the term *region of change* to denote an area where a contract exists that allows either side to change its implementation without affecting the other side. This contract is fulfilled either by an agreed-upon message structure in the case of a server program, or an interface, in the case of a Java object. In revitalization, the contract separates the application client from the user interface server. For the application client, it is enforced by the client APIs, while in the UI server, it is the interface to the display-file emulation object. Either side can change in any way necessary, provided that the responses to the contract stay constant.

Restructuring

Phase 2 of redeployment, restructuring means moving application control from the legacy system to the servlet. In this phase, the business logic is separated out of the legacy systems and written into servers, but still using the original host language. At this point, your programs will have reached a client/server architecture.

As more systems are restructured, you will find it increasingly easy to add features and functionality to your client programs. At the same time, you'll find it easier to add new features or change business-processing rules because your business logic will be centralized in the servers, not spread out, duplicated, and cloned across a wide range of monolithic applications. This is probably the hardest phase, but it can be done "off to the side," without affecting your day-to-day operations, because your end

GLOSSARY

users are now separated from the business logic by a region of change bounded by the user-interface objects and the display-file emulation objects.

Revitalization

Phase 1 of redeployment, revitalization moves a legacy system onto the Web with the minimum effort. Revitalization, in its simplest form, removes the display-file I/O codes and replaces them with calls to a UI server. Revitalization can be implemented with any combination of green-screen, thick, and thin clients. Even after fully revitalizing an application, the code remains basically in its original form, maintainable by your legacy programmers.

If a system simply needs a GUI facelift, revitalization provides it with almost no modification. However, when you decide you need to move to a more object-oriented architecture, revitalization allows you to go to the next step, restructuring, without disrupting your end users.

SC400

See *com.pbd.pub.sc400*.

SC400 JBUI

See *com.pbd.pub.sc400.jbui*.

SC400 JSP

See *com.pbd.pub.sc400.jsp*.

Server/client

Server/client, in its strictest sense, means an architecture in which a client program sends a message to a server either requesting information or requesting that a function be performed. The request and response are entirely self-contained, and the completion of the request is usually "all or nothing."

Servlet

A servlet is a Java program running under a Web server that processes HTTP requests, either outputting HTML or initiating a JavaServer Page.

Session

In the context of a distributed business application, a session is used to hold the information about the end user. In a green-screen AS/400 application, the job object is used to identify the user, but for distributed applications, that information is normally gotten through a sign-on panel, and is then associated with the requesting IP address via a session object.

SQL

SQL stands for *Structured Query Language* (although there is some discrepancy as to the origin of the name). The first implementation was at IBM in the mid-1970s in the form of the SEQUEL language. Oracle then presented it as a commercial database in 1979. The most recent version of ANSI-standard SQL was agreed upon in 1991, and another is in the works.

Today, almost any database can be accessed using SQL statements. It has become the *de facto* standard for database programming, despite some very serious performance problems. Also, SQL requires knowledge of the table and column names (that is, the file and field names) of the underlying database, which is in direct opposition to the concepts of encapsulation. Because of that, SQL in a client program is fundamentally not object-oriented.

Subfile

A subfile is a feature unique to the 5250 protocol, in which a single display line is defined to the application program, but multiple lines can be displayed on the screen at a time. The application program can write many lines to the display file, and then present them to the user with a single I/O operation.

Subfile control record

The subfile control record is the primary means of controlling the presentation of a subfile to the user. The subfile control record is used to initialize, clear, and display the subfile.

Subfile record

A subfile record is the definition of the repeating line within a subfile. The subfile record supports multiple write operations, as well as the ability to retrieve a specific record in the list, or retrieve only those records changed by the user.

Swing user interface (or Swing UI server)

In this book, the term *Swing user interface* refers specifically to the Swing version of a thick client used as a UI server. Swing UI servers use the Swing package (javax.swing) to provide the GUI capabilities. In my opinion, Swing is the best choice for a thick-client interface because it is 100% portable to nearly every workstation, from Linux to Windows.

TCP/IP

TCP/IP is actually the name of a family of protocols in which TCP (*Transmission Control Protocol*) and IP (*Internet Protocol*) are two of the members. UDP is another member. TCP runs on top of IP, providing a set of services such as file transfer and remote command execution between computers. With the explosive growth of the Internet, TCP/IP has become the *de facto* standard for computer communications, although APPC is still very much in use by IBM. (In fact, APPC is often used as an additional firewall from a secured computer to an Internet-attached computer.)

Thick client

A thick-client interface uses a program running on the workstation to display a sophisticated graphical interface. Unlike the less complex thin-client interface, a thick client can use all the features of the desktop, including multimedia, drag and drop, and interactive graphics. Note that the term *thick client* is used by convention, even though revitalization uses the workstation as a UI server, not a client.

Thin client

In its broadest sense, a thin client is any interface in which no programs need to be downloaded to the workstation (the client) in order to access a host application. By that standard, a 5250 emulator is a thin client. For the purposes of this book, the term *thin client* refers specifically to a browser interface. The browser interface communicates with users using HTML received from a Web server. Although thin clients are usually thought of in conjunction with the World Wide Web, they can be just as effective on a local intranet.

UI request

A user-interface request consists of a panel ID and initial data to display. For RPG legacy-application revitalization, the UI request contains the fields normally sent to the display file, as well as the state of the indicators.

UI server (or user interface server)

A user-interface server is a program that accepts UI requests and displays a specific form to the user, then returns the data to the calling program. Its interface can be green-screen, thick-client, or thin-client (HTML).

WASE

See *com.pbd.pub.wase*.

Web server

A Web server (or HTTP server) is a program that resides on a host and responds to HTTP requests. The simplest Web servers just read static HTML pages and send them to the requester. More advanced Web servers provide additional functions. For example, Microsoft's IIS provides a whole range of specialized Web services that make it easy to design sophisticated Web pages. Other services might include support for CGI, servlets, and JavaServer Pages. IBM has its own HTTP server software, although it might eventually allow the use of industry-standard software, such as Apache.

WebSphere

WebSphere is IBM's version of the application server. An application server provides additional features to its simple HTTP server. WebSphere is required to support servlets and JavaServer Pages. Since this book is solely concerned with running applications on the AS/400, it necessarily deals with WebSphere directly.

INDEX

A

actionPerformed, 123, 413, 461
Active Server Pages, 25
advanced peer to peer communications (APPC), 19, 482
AIX, 31
appendData, 359
appendToVector, 279
applets, 25, 29
application client (ITMMNT1AC), 42, 43, 482
    API naming conventions, 82, 84
    in browser-based interface, 171, 172, 194, 208
    calls in, 70, 71, 72, 75, 84, 86, 89
    client APIs in, 69-81, 70, **71**
    data flow in, 88
    data handling in, 86
    data queues in, 84, 87
    data structures in, 62, **63**, **65**, 67, 69, 87
    display files changed to data structures in, 63, 64-65, **63**, 69
    DQMBAPI in, 70, 72, 73, **73**, **74**
    DQMBAPI1 in, 71, 75, **75**
    DQMBAPI2 in, 63, 64, **63**, 71-72, 72, 75-76, **76**, **77-81**, 87, 89
    DQMBAPI3 in, 72, 81, **81**, 90

DQMBAPIC in, 70, 71, 72, **72**, 84, 90
DQMBCRT in, 86, **86**
DQMBDLT in, 90, **90**
DQMBINIT in, 71, 86, **86**
DQMBRCV in, 87, 89, **90**
DQMBSHUT in, 90, **90**
DQMBSND in, 72, 90
DQMDTA in, 84, 86
DQMIND in, 84
DQMMSG in, 67, 69, 71, 73, 83, **83**, 86, 87
DQMOPC in, 68, 84, 86, 90
DQMRTC in, 84, 87, 89
DQMRTS in, 84, 87
DQMSCR in, 68, 84, 86
DQMSID in, 84, 87
DQMSNO in, 84
DQMUDLT in, 91, **91**
DQMUINIT in, 71
DQMUINITC in, 84-85, **85**
DQMURCT, 85, **85**
DQMURCV in, 72, 87, **88**
DQMUSBN in, 84-85, **85**
DQMUSHUT in, 68, 91, **91**
DQMUSND in, 86, **89**, 87, **87**, 89
encapsulation of data in, 70, 71

Note: boldface numbers indicate illustrations.

application client, *continued*
   error handling in, 84, 87, 88, 89
   externally described data structures in, 69
   field definitions in, 69
   function key assignment in, 70, 75-76, **76**, 89
   goals of interface in, 69
   green screen application in, 65-68
   I/O processing in, 65-68, **66-67**
   I/O Proxy APIs in, 67, 68, 69, 81-91, **82**, **83**
   initialization routine in, **66**, 67, 68, 70, 84
   JSPAPI library in, 69-91
   message processing in, **66**, 68, 70
   naming convention for programs in, 62
   primary processing loop in, **66**, 67
   session IDs in, 71
   shudown routine in, **67**, 67, 68, 70, 72, 88, 90-91, **90**
   in Swing interface, 151
   timeout values in, 87-88
   wrappers in, 70
application client proxy (ITMMNT1_Client), in Swing interface, 157
application controller, 482-483
application modernization, 483
application program interface (API) (*See also* client APIs; JSPAPI library; proxy I/O APIs), 13, 24, 27-28, 43, 135, 483
   in client/server interface, 132, 133
   display files and, 39
   ITMMNI/in ITMMNI maintenance program, 45
   revitalizing legacy applications, 60, 61
application server, 483-484
application-control logic, 482
applyLookAndFeel, 283
arrays, 279
AS/400, 10, 25, 135, 484
AS400ByteArray, 100
AS400DataType, 105
AS400PackedDecimal object, 105
AS400Structure, 98
AS400Text, 100
AS400ZonedDecimal, 100
ASCII, 484
attributes, 484
attributes fields, 103, 104

B

batch processing, 9, 18
Bean (*See also* Enterprise JavaBean; Java Beans), in browser-based interface, 174-175, 190, 212

Beans.instantiate method, 172
BigDecimal object, 107
BLOB, 98
block mode, 484-485
BPCS, 26, 52
breaking apart the monolith (*See* separation of database/business logic)
"brochureware" type of sites, 22
browser, 485
brower-based applications/interfaces, xiv-xv, 9-10, 18, 20-21, **20**, 29, 30, 30, 41-43, **41**, 169-213, 485
   application client in, 171, 172, 194, 208
   Bean in, 174-175, 190, 212
   Beans.instantiate method in, 172
   "brochureware" type of sites in, 22
   buttons in, 175, 176, 180, **181**, 190, **190**, 192, 193, 195-199, 212
   callJsp method in, 208
   callPage method in, 171
   classpath variable in, 185, 186
   in client/server interface, 131, 144-148, **146**
   com.pbd.pub.jsp in, 170
   com.pbd.pub.sc400.jsp in, 169
   comments (hashmarked) in, 186
   common gateway interface (CGI) in, 21, 22, **22**
   copyDataFromRequest in, 191, 193, 209
   copyDataToJdspf in, 209
   data flow in, 171, **171**, 193
   DDS for, 173
   defining JavaServer Page for, 170, 195-199
   defining SC400 JSP servlet in, 199-209
   dex.jsp in, 171
   directory organization in, 186-187, 192, 193
   display file emulation in, 39, 169, 171, 194, 208
   doGet in, 171, 208
   doPost in, 175, 193, 208-209
   DQMUNITC in, 171
   error handling in, 174, 175
   EXFMT in, 171, 208
   existing technology vs., 21-23, **22**
   exit page in, 176-177, **176-177**, 192
   extensions for, SC400 JSP package, 170, 194-213
   field arrays in, 193
   form command in, 175
   forms for data entry in, 22
   function key assignment in, 190, 194, 212
   GET method in, 171, 177
   getButtonField in, 191, 193
   getButtonValue in, 191, 193
   getCommandButtons in, 212
   getField in, 212

B ❖ INDEX

getFields in, 192
getKey in, 197
getName in, 189, 192
getPath in, 192
getPostData in, 209
getRollButtons in, 212
getScJdspfJsc in, 200
getString method in, 175
getType in, 189
getURL in, 192
getValue in, 189
getValues in, 189
HTML in, 21-22, 23, 170, 173, 174, 184, 190, 209, 212
HTTP configuration file QUSRSY/QATMHTTPC, 183
HTTP server for, 187
HttpServletRequest in, 209
hyperlinks in, 22, 23
index.jsp in, 171-172, 176, **176-177**, 187, **187**
indexing in, 192
init interface in, 208
input field in, 175-176
isButtonField in, 189
ITMMNT1_Client in, 171
ITMMNT1_DisplayFile in, 171, 175
ITMMNT1_MAINT.jsp in, 171-172, 176, **182-183**, 199
ITMMNT1_PROMPT.jsp in, 171-172, 174, 176, 180, 181, 195, 199, **199**
ITMMNT1_Servlet in, 170, 171-183, 175, 177, **177-179**, **201**
ITMMNT1A_Servlet in, 177
ITMMNT1B_Servlet in, 177
jar files in, 187
Java programming in, 21, 169, 170, 213
Java Toolbox for, 186
JavaBeans in, 21-22, 23
JavaServer Pages (JSP) in, 21-23, **23**, 169, 170, 171, 173-177, 184, 187, 190, 192, 193, 194, 208
jdspf bean in, 212
JdspfDisplayFile in, 174
Jsp class in, 191-192, **191-192**
Jsp objects in, 170
JspField in, 188, **188-189**, 190, 193, 197, 212
MAINT panel in, 172, 182, **182**, 188, **188**
message handling in, 175
modeling objects in, JSP package for, 188-193
ncf.jvm.classpath in, 186
ncf.jvm.path in, 186
ncf.jvm.use.system.classpath in, 186

output field in, 176
Pass directive in, 184, 192
path in, 192
pbdjsp400.jar in, 187
POST in, 171, 175, 190, 193, 194, 208-209
PROMPT panel in, 172, 173, **173**, 174, 180, 181, **187**, 208
properties file in, 183-184
pull vs. push interfaces, 202
relationship among ScJdspfJspServlet, client, display file, JSP, 194, **194**
run method in, 171
running the application ITMMNT1_Servlet, 183-188
runServer in, 208, 209
SC400 JBUI in, 170
ScJdspfButtonDefinition in, **181**
ScJdspfButtonField in, **181**
ScJdspfJbuiServer in, 172
ScJdspfJsp in, 177, 179, **180**, **181**, 212
ScJdspfJspButtonDefinition in, 195-199, **196**
ScJdspfJspButtonField in, 195-199, **197-198**
ScJdspfJspButtonFieldDefinition in, 191
ScJdspfJspe in, 172
ScJdspfJspRecordUI in, 177, 179, 179, **181**, 200, **200**
ScJdspfJspServlet in, 172, **172**, 194, 202, **202-207**
send method in, 171
Service directive in, 184, 185
servlets in, 21-23, **22**, **23**, 169, 171, 175, 177-183, 185, 192, 199-209
setFields in, 192
setName in, 192
setPath in, 192
setValue in, 189
shutdown routine in, 171, 172
smart parameters of JSP in, 23
static Web pages in, 21-22, **22**
subfiles in, 210-212, **210**, **211-212**
support classes in, 185-188
UI server definitioin in, 172
uniform resource locators (URLs) in, 21
valueOf method in, 197
WebSphere in, 169, 170, 215
buffers, in display file building, 118, 125, 126
business logic (*See also* separation of database/business logic), 485
business rules, 485
business-rules server, 485-486
busy flags, 18

Note: boldface numbers indicate illustrations.

509

buttons
    in browser-based interface, 175, 176, 180, **181**, 190, **190**, 192, 195-199, 193, 212
    in Swing interface, 155, 156

C

call logs, 10
call method, 446
callJsp method, 208, 478
callPage, 171, 147
calls, 9
    in application client ITMMNT1AC, 70, 71, 72, 75, 84, 86, 89
    in client/server interface, 143-144
CCSID, 98
CD-ROM companion disc, xvi, 269-272
    downloading software for, 217-218, B
CHAIN, 118, 120, 122, 125, 394, 399, 434
CHARACTER, 289
Character field type, 94
checkKey, 331
class hierarchy, 93, 274-275
classes
    in client/server interface, 131
    in display file building, 112, 114
    in Swing interface, 149, 156-157, 160
classpath
    in browser-based interface, 185, 186
    JBUI/in JBUI thick client UI server, 237
    Web/in WebSphere and servlet, 243, 244, 247-248
clear, 434
clearData, 337, 350
clearErrors, 337, 350
client APIs, 60, 94, 486
    in application client ITMMNT1AC, 69-81, 70, **71**
    DQMBAPI, 73, **73**, **74**
    DQMBAPI1, 75, **75**
    DQMBAPI2, 75-76, **76**, **77-81**
    DQMBAPI3, 81, **81**
    DQMBAPIC, 72, **72**, 84
    I/O Proxy APIs, 69
    revitalizing legacy applications, 61
client/server applications (*See also* server/client interface), xiv-xv, 2, 18, 40, 41-43, **41**, 486
CLOB, 98
clone method, 297
CLOSE, 390
COBOL, xv, 2
code divergence vs., 12
collision detection, 18

com.ibm.as400.access, 488
com.ibm.as400.vaccess, 488
com.pbd.pub.common, 277, 486
com.pbd.pub.dc400, 97, 286, 486
com.pbd.pub.jao400, 301, 487
com.pbd.pub.jbui, 319, 487
com.pbd.pub.jdb400, 378-381, 487
com.pbd.pub.jdqm400, 402, 487
com.pbd.pub.jdspf, 111, 412
com.pbd.pub.jsp, 170, 436, 487
com.pbd.pub.sc400, 445, 487
com.pbd.pub.sc400.jbui, 149, 158, 160, 460, 488
com.pbd.pub.sc400.jsp, 169, 468, 488
com.pbd.pub.wase, 488
com.pbdpub.jdspf, 487
command keys, 488
comments (hashmarked), 186
common gateway interface (CGI), 21, 22, **22**, 25, 26, 202, 488-489
Common Object Request Broker Architecture (CORBA), 32
composition, 131, 132, 144-148
condition, 489
conditional code, 100
conflicts, xiv
conversion factors, ITMMNI/in ITMMNI maintenance program, 56
convertError, 408, 411
converting data, 93-109
    array passing in, 96
    AS400ByteArray in, 100
    AS400DataType in, 105
    AS400Field class in, 93
    AS400PackedDecimal object in, 105
    AS400Structure in, 98
    AS400Text in, 100
    AS400ZonedDecimal in, 100
    attributes fields in, 103, 104
    BigDecimal object in, 107
    Character field type in, 94
    class hierarchy in, 93, 100
    com.pbd.pub.dc400 in, 97
    constructors, Dc400Field class, **101-103**
    creating classes in, 99
    data structure in, 96, 106
    data types in, 98
    Dc400 classes in, 93, 97-107
    Dc400 package in, 93
    Dc400CharacterField in, 94, 96, 99, 104
    Dc400Exception class in, 108
    Dc400Field class in, 94, 95, 96, 97, 99, 105

C - D ❖ INDEX

Dc400NumericField in, 94, 96, 99, 104, 105
Dc400PackedField in, 105
Dc400RawField in, 94, 96, 104, 103, **103**, 106
Dc400Structure in, 93, 94-97, 99, 106-107, **106-107**
DDS for externally described data structure in, 96, 97
defining classes in, 99
display attributes of Dc400 classes, 108-109
EBCDIC to ASCII conversion, 93
editing Dc400 classes (edit words), 108
error handling in, 108
field attributes in, 93
field definition in, 96
field exit editing in, 108
field types in, 93, 94, 98, 100
formatting Dc400 classes, 108
getAS400DataType method in, 103-104, 103, 104, 105
Java methods in, 107
JdspfAttributes object in, 104
MAINT record and Dc400Structure, 104-105, **105**
methods, Dc400Field class, **101-103**
nested data structures in, 106
Numeric field type in, 94
object-oriented programming concepts in, 100
packed fields in, 94
Raw field type in, 94
String object in, 107
subclasses in, 94, 98, 100
superclasses in, 98
variables, Dc400Field class, 96, **101-103**
copyDataFromJdspf, 161, 162, 414, 464, 471
copyDataFromRequest, 191, 103, 209, 471
copyDataToJdspf, 161, 162, 163, 209, 414, 464, 471
copyToArray, 279
Create Library (CRTLIB) command, 220, **220**
Create Save File (CRTSAVF) command, 220, **220**, **221**
createButtonText, 326
createError, 408
CRUD, 489

D

data description specifications (DDS), 489
data entry, 10
data flow, in browser-based interface, 171, **171**, 193
data queues, 24, 27-28, 41-43, **41**, 489
 in application client ITMMNT1AC, 84, 87
 revitalizing legacy applications, 60
data structures, 94, 489
 in application client ITMMNT1AC, 69, 87
 converting data with Dc400, 96, 106
 Dc400Structure definition, 94-97
 in display file building, 126
 display files replaced by, 63, 64-65, **63**
 nested, 106
data types, in converting data, 98
database (*See also* separation of database/business logic)
 ITMMNI/in ITMMNI maintenance program, 45, 48-49, **48**
DataConversion 400, 42
Dc400 classes, 93, 97-107
Dc400CharacterField, 94, 96, 99, 104, 286-287
Dc400Exception class, 108
Dc400Field, 94, **95**, 96, 99, **101-103**, 105, 115, 141, 142, 288-291
Dc400NumericField, 94, 96, 99, 104, 105, 292-293
Dc400PackedField, 105
Dc400RawField, 94, 96, 103, **103**, 104, 106, 293-294
Dc400Structure, 295-300
 in client/server interface, 138, 141-142
 converting data with Dc400, 93, 99, 106-107, **106-107**
 in display file building, 113, 118, **118-119**, 119
debugging, 11, 26
DELET, 397, 402
designing applications, xv
desktop integration, 10
detached processing (*See* offline processing)
developing applications, xv
dex.jsp, 171
dirctories and directory organization
 in browser-based interface, 186-187, 192, 193
 green/in green screen interface, 219, **219**
display attributes, 490
 in display file building, 126
 ITMMNI/in ITMMNI maintenance program vs., 57
 converting data with Dc400, 108-109
display files/display file emulation, 24, 27, 35-37, **36**, **37**, 41-43, **41**, 1110-130, 490
 actionPerformed method in, 123
 APIs in, 39
 in application client ITMMNT1AC, 63, 64-65, **63**, 69
 in browser-based interface, 39, 169, 171, 194, 208
 buffers in, 118, 125, 126
 CHAIN method in, 118, 120, 122, 125
 class hieararchy in, 125, **125**

Note: boldface numbers indicate illustrations.

511

INDEX ❖ D

display files/display file emulation, *continued*
   classes in, 112, 114
   in client/server interface, 131
   com.pbd.pub.jdspf package, 111
   data structure replacement of, 63, 64-65, **63**, 126
   Dc400Fields in, 115
   Dc400Structure in, 113, 118, **118-119**, 119
   DDS for, 117, 128, **128-129**
   defining JdspfDisplayFile, 112
   display attributes in, 126
   doPost method in, 122
   DQMBAPI2 in, 126
   DQMMSG in, 126
   emulation package for, 37, 39, 40
   error handling in, 122
   EXFMT in, 35, 39, 115, 117, 120, 123, 130
   function keys in, 37
   getCurrentBuffer in, 121, 125
   getNextRow in, 124, 125
   getString in, 121, 124, 125
   getUIObject in, 123
   I/O operations in, 117
   indicators in, 36, 37, 118, 126
   inheritance in, 114
   input operation in, 37, 37, 37
   input/output fields in, 35
   ITMMNI/in ITMMNI maintenance program, 45, 49-51
   ITMMNT1D_DisplayFile in, 111, 112, 114
   Java emulation for, 39, 40
   Java Server Pages (JSP) application in, 39, 40
   JavaBean emulation for, 39
   JbuiDisplay in, 122, 123
   JdspaMessageSubfileControl in, 125
   JDSPF classes in, 111-112, 117-124
   JdspfAbstractRecord class in, 112-113, **112**, 114, 115, 119, **120-121**, 121, 122, 125, 129
   JdspfBuffer in, 118, **118-119**, 119, 126
   JdspfDisplayFile in, 48, 57, 58, 97, 111, 112, 114-115, **114**, 117, 122-126, 129, **129-130**
   JdspfDisplayFileAction in, 117
   JdspfIndicator in, 126
   JdspfInvalidOperationException in, 122
   JdspfMessageSubfile in, 125, 129
   JdspfOutputRecord in, 129
   JdspfRecord in, 112, 113, **113-114**, 115, 121, **121-122**
   JdspfRecordGroup in, 129
   JdspfRecordUI class in, 117
   JdspfSubfile in, 125
   JdspfSubfileControl in, 125
   listener objects in, 123
   meta-records in, 127
   output operation in, 36, **36**
   platform independence in, 39
   putGetUI in, 122-123, **123**
   READ in, 35, 37, **37**, 118, 120, 122, 125
   READC method in, 118, 120, 122, 125
   record creation in, 113-114
   record UI objects in, 117
   related record formats in, 127-130
   ScJdspfJbuiDisplay in, 122, 123
   separation of database/business logic in, 40
   servlets for, 39, 122
   setRecord method, 124
   setRecordUIObjects method in, 117
   SFLRCD01 code for, 124
   single-record display file, 115, **115**
   subclasses in, 112, 115, **115-116**
   subfiles in, 117-118, 124-125, **124**, **125**, 126, 127-130, **127**
   Swing for, 39, 40, 118
   UIObject in, 122, 123
   UPDAT in, 118, 121, 122, 125, 126
   Web-enabling for, 39
   WRITE, 35, 36, **36**, 39, 117, 121, 122, 123, 126
display-file emulation object (ITMMNT1D_DisplayFile) in Swing interface, 157
display-file proxy, 490
distributed applications, xvi, 2, 9-11, 490
   APPC in, 19
   AS/400-specific applications in, 10
   batch processing in, 18
   browser-based applications in, 9-10, 10, 18, 20-21, **20**
   call logs in, 10
   client/server applications in, 18, 19, **19**
   data entry in, 10
   desktop integration in, 10
   drag-and-drop capabilities in, 10
   dumb terminals in, 18
   end-user information tools in, 11
   existing technology vs., 18-21
   graphical interfaces in, 9-10, 20-21
   HTML interfaces for, 10
   hyperlinks in, 10
   inquiry applications in, 11
   Java clients as, 10
   object architecture for, 10-11
   object-oriented programming in, 11
   ODBC in, 18, 20

offline processing in, 18-19
online transaction processing (OTP) in, 18
platform independence in, 10, 21
queries in, 11
separation of database/business logic in, 11, 19
SQL in, 18, 19-20, **20**
TCP/IP in, 19
thick clients in, 10
doGet, 171, 145, 208, 478
doPost, 122, 145, 147, 175, 193, 208-209, 479
DOUBLECLICK_DISPLAY, 321
downloading software, 215, 217-218, **218**, **219**
DQMBAPI, 61, 70, 72, 73, **73**, **74**
DQMBAPI1, 61, 71, 75, **75**
DQMBAPI2, 61, 63, **63**, 64, 71-72, 75-76, **76-81**, 87, 89, 126
DQMBAPI3, 61, 72, 81, **81**, 90
DQMBAPIC, 61, 70, 71, 72, **72**, 84, 90
DQMBCRT, 86, **86**
DQMBDLT, 90, **90**
DQMBINIT, 61, 71, 86, **86**
DQMBRCV, 61, 87, 89, **90**
DQMBSHUT, 61, 90, **90**
DQMBSND, 61, 72, 90
DQMDTA, 84, 86
DQMIND, 84
DQMMSG, 67, 69, 71, 73, 83, **83**, 86, 87, 126, 137
DQMOPC, 68, 84, 86, 90
DQMRTC, 84, 87, 89
DQMRTS, 84, 87
DQMSCR, 68, 84, 86
DQMSID, 84, 87
DQMSNO, 84
DQMUDLT, 91, **91**
DQMUINIT, 60, 71, 133
DQMUINITC, 60, 84-85, **85**, 135, 137, 171
DQMURCT, 85, **85**
DQMURCV, 60, 72, 87, **88**, 133
DQMUSBN, 84-85, **85**
DQMUSHUT, 60, 68, 91, **91**, 133
DQMUSND, 60, 86, **89**, 87, **87**, **89**, 133
drag-and-drop capabilities, 10
Drake, Gary, 52
drill downs, 9
dumb terminals, 18, 491
dumpRecord, 390

E

EBCDIC, 491
e-commerce applications, 32
e-deployment objectives, 13
edit words/editing Dc400 classes, 108
emulation package (*See* display files/display file emulation)
encapsulation, 11, 42, 43
  in client/server interface, 132, 133, 137, 148
  in application client ITMMNT1AC, 70, 71
end-user information tools (*See also* help), 11
Enterprise JavaBeans (EJB), 2, 32, 491
enterprise resource planning (ERP), 26
ERROR attribute (JBUI), 57
error handling/error messaging
  in application client ITMMNT1AC, 84, 88, 89
  in browser-based interface, 174, 175
  converting data with Dc400, 108
  in display file building, 122
  green/in green screen interface, 232-234, **233**, **234**
  ITMMNI/in ITMMNI maintenance program, 46-47, **47**, 50, 52, 56, 57-58
  JBUI/in JBUI thick client UI server, 238-240, **238-241**
  in Swing interface, 154
  Web/in WebSphere and servlet, 265, **265**, **266**
error message subfile, 7
event-driven programming, 1, 31, 492
execute, 422
EXFMT, 370
  in browser-based interface, 171, 208
  in display file building, 115, 117, 120, 123, 130
  display files and, 35, 39
  server/client interface, 146, 147
  in Swing interface, 156, 162
existing technology/legacy applications, 15-24
  APIs in, 27-28
  applets in, 29
  browser-based applications vs., 21-23, **22**, 29, 30, **30**
  Common Object Request Broker Architecture (CORBA) in, 32
  data queues in, 27-28
  display files in, 27
  distributed applications vs., 18-21
  e-commerce applications in, 32
  Enterprise JavaBeans (EJB) in, 32
  event-driven interfaces in, 31
  graphical interfaces in, 29
  green-screen applications in, 28, 32, 33
  intranets and, 32
  Java in, 28, 31-32
  JavaBeans in, 32
  JavaServer Pages (JSP) in, 31

513

existing technology/legacy applications, *continued*
   maintenance programs in, 31
   object-oriented programming vs., 17-18, 28, 30, 33
   platform independence in, 28, 32, **32**, 33
   process of, 27-32
   re-engineering in, 28, 29, 31-32, **32**, 33
   refacing in, 16-17, **16**
   replacement, 15-16
   restructuring in, 28, 29-31, **30**, **31**, 33
   revitalization stage in, 27, 28, **28**, **29**
   rewriting of, 17-18
   screen scrapers and, 16-17, **17**, 19, 29
   separation of database/business logic in, 29, 30, **31**, 33
   server/client applications vs., 19, **19**, 24, **24**
   servers, 28, 30-33
   servlets in, 28
   terminal emulation for, 16-17, **16**
   thick clients in, 28, 29
   thin clients in, 28, 30, **30**
   wrappers in, 32
exit, 409, 411
exit page, in browser-based interface, 176, **176-177**, 192
extensibility, 12
extensions, JBUI, in Swing interface, 150, 166-168
extensions, SC400 JSP package, 170, 194-213
externally described data structure, 492
   in application client ITMMNT1AC, 69
   converting data with Dc400, 96, **97**

F

5250, 481
fast-path features of book, xv-xvi, 42
field arrays, in browser-based interface, 193
field attributes, converting data with Dc400, 93
field definition
   in application client ITMMNT1AC, 69
   converting data with Dc400, 96
   in Swing interface, 156
field exit editing, converting data with Dc400, 108
field names, ITMMNI/in ITMMNI maintenance program, 51
field types, converting data with Dc400, 93, 94, 98, 100
file-level definitions, ITMMNI/in ITMMNI maintenance program, 49, **49**, 51, **51**
filtering, 7, 9
findRecord, 422
form command, 175

formatting Dc400 classes, 108
forms for data entry, 22
framework, 492
FTP file transfer, xvi, 215, 221-222, **222**
full-procedural files, ITMMNI/in ITMMNI maintenance program, 51
full-screen data entry, 7, 8, **8**
function key assignment
   in application client ITMMNT1AC, 70, 75-76, 76, 89
   in browser-based interface, 190, 194, 212
   display files and, 37
   ITMMNI/in ITMMNI maintenance program, 46
   in Swing interface, 160

G

get, 171, 177
getAlpha, 390
getApiLibrary, 449
getApplicationClientID, 454
getApplicationClientName, 454
getAS400, 281
getAS400DataType, 103-105, **103**, **104**, 287, 290, 293, 294
getAs400Name, 283
getAS400Password, 283
getAS400UserID, 283
getAttributes, 290
getBigDecimal, 297, 298
getBuffer, 298
getBufferLength, 298
getButtonField, 191, 193, 440
getButtonValue, 191, 193, 440
getByteArray, 298
getClientName, 449
getColumnClass, 359
getColumnCount, 359
getColumnHeading, 310, 387
getColumnName, 359
getColumnWidths, 359
getCommandButtons, 212
getCurrentBuffer, 121, 125
getCurrentJsp, 479
getCurrentRecord, 423
getData, 337, 345, 350
getDataBuffer, 454
getDecimals, 290
getDescription, 310, 387
getExitJsp, 479
getField, 212, 390

getFieldIndex, 350
getFieldNames, 306, 391
getFieldPanel, 337, 376
getFields, 192, 351, 440
getFile, 314, 317
getFileName, 306, 314, 317
getFrame, 370
getGroupName, 345
getHandles, 359
getId, 326
getIndicators, 419, 430, 454
getJbuiDisplay, 465
getJdbField, 391
getJdspf, 457, 479
getKey, 197, 474
getKeyPressed, 423
getLength, 291, 310, 387
getLibrary, 284
getListener, 326
getListFieldNames, 314, 317
getLookAndFeel, 284
getMessage, 134, 449
getModel, 354
getName, 189, 192, 291, 310, 345, 387, 416, 440, 444
getNextRow, 124, 125, 434
getNumeric, 391
getObject, 298, 299
getObjects, 299
getOffset, 291
getOperationCode, 142, 454
getPath, 192, 440
getPosition, 370
getPostData, 209
getPressedButton, 331, 371
getProductionLibrary, 449
getProtect, 345
getRecord, 391, 426
getRecordName, 454
getRollButtons, 212
getRow, 362
getRowCount, 360
getRows, 360
getScJdspfJsp, 200, 476
getSelectedHandle, 354, 362, 376
getSelectMode, 377
getSessionID, 454
getStartSize, 362
getString, 121, 124, 125, 175, 299, 416
getStructure, 291
getSystemLibrary, 284
getSystemName, 450

getTable, 362
getText, 326
getType, 189, 291, 444
getUIObject, 123, 417
getURL, 192, 440
getUserID, 450
getUsesFkey, 326
getValue, 189, 444
getValueAt, 360
getValues, 189, 444
getViewClass, 354
getViewer, 355
getViewFieldNames, 314, 318
graphical interfaces, xiv, 9-10, 17, 20-21, 29, 43
graphics, 25
green screen applications, xv, 2, 5, 24, 27, 28, 32, 33, 41-43, **41**, 217-234, 492, 493
    directories in, 219, **219**
    downloading software for, 217-218, **218**, 219
    error handling, 232-234, **233**, **234**
    FTP file transfer to AS/400, 221-222, **222**
    installing software for, 219-223
    ITMMNT1 test run, 224, 225, **228**
    ITMMNT1UI test run, 229-234, **229-234**
    restoring libraries for, 222, **223**, 224
    revitalizing legacy applications, 59, **59**, 61
    saving files, 220, **220**, 221
    screen scrapers for, 16-17, **17**
    terminal emulation for, 16-17, **16**
    testing, 224-227
    transfer library creation, 220, **220**, 221
    UI server, 493

H

hardware obsolescence, 12
Hartman, Barry, 52
header screens, 8, **8**
help, 7
    ITMMNI/in ITMMNI maintenance program vs., 58
hidden fields, 7
hidden I/O operations, revitalizing legacy applications, 38
hotkeys, 16
HTTP configuration file, in WebSphere and servlet, 243, 249-254, **250-254**
    QUSRSY/QATMHTTPC, in browser-based interface, 183
HTTP server, 187, 259-261, 260, **261**, **262**
HttpGet, 251
HttpPut, 251

HttpServletRequest, 209
human element in revitalization/redeployment, 26-27
hyperlinks, 10, 22, 23
hypertext markup language (HTML), xvi, 10, 21-23, 40, 57, 124, 145, 493
    in browser-based interface, 170, 173, 174, 184, 190, 209, 212
    in client/server interface, 137
    converting data with Dc400, 108-109
    in Swing interface, 166
hypertext transfer protocol (HTTP), 493

I

I/O processing
    in browser-based interface, 175-176
    in client/server interface, 131
    in display file building, 117
I/O Proxy API, 43, 81-91, **82**, **83**, 94, 493
    API naming conventions, 82, 84
    in application client ITMMNT1AC, 67-69
    in client/server interface, 132, 137, 143, 144
    DQMDTA, 84
    DQMIND, 84
    DQMMSG, 83, **83**
    DQMOPC, 84
    DQMRTC, 84
    DQMRTS, 84
    DQMSCR, 84
    DQMSID, 84
    revitalizing legacy applications, 60, 61
icons used in book, xv-xvi, 42
If statements, 100
imperative languages, 493
implementation strategies, xiv
index screen, 262, 263, 494
index.jsp, in browser-based interface, 171-172, 176-177, **176-177**, 187, **187**, 192
indicators, 494
    in display file building, 36, 37, 118, 126
    ITMMNI/in ITMMNI maintenance program, 54
inheritance, 11, 100, 114, 131, 137-144
init, 132, 208, 345, 450, 458
initialization routine, in application client ITMMNT1AC, 70, 84
input/output fields, display files and, 35, 37, **37**
inquiry applications, 9, 11, 19-20
installing servlet software, Web/in WebSphere and servlet, 243
Integrated Language Environment (ILE), 267-268
interface hierarchy, 276

Internet (*See* Web-enabling your applications)
interoperability, 26
intranets, xiv, 27, 32
isButtonField, 189, 444
isChanged, 420
isEof, 142
isExiting, 479
isIndicatorOn, 430
isSomeoneWaiting, 371
ITEM master file, ITMMNI/in ITMMNI maintenance program, 46, 48, **48**, 51
ITMMN1_DisplayFile, 171
ITMMNT1 maintenance program, 43, 45-58
    APIs in, 45
    application client, changing to ITMMNT1AC (*See also* application client ITMMNT1AC) 62-65
    conversion factors in, 56
    database in, 45, 48-49, **48**
    display attributes in, 57
    display files in, 45, 49-51
    error messages in, 46-47, **47**, 50, 52, 56-58
    field names in, 51
    file-level definitions in, 49, **49**, 51, **51**
    full-procedural files in, 51
    function key assignment in, 46
    help support, 58
    indicators in, 54
    issues for, 45, 56-58
    ITEM master file in, 46, 48, **48**, 51
    JSPAPI interface vs., 57
    keying records in, 50
    Maintenance panel in, 50, **50**, 54, **54-55**
    message subfiles in, 57-58
    named constants vs. literals in, 52
    primary processing loop of, 52, **52**
    program flow control (XWSCR field) in, 52-53, 54
    Prompt screen in, 46, **46**, 50, **50**, 53, **53-54**
    RPG program for, 45, 51-56
    screens in, 45, 46-48
    subfiles in, 57
    test run, 224, **225-228**
    unit-of-measure (UOM) fields in, 46, 56
    unit-of-measure cross-ref (UXRF) in, 46, 48, **49**
    unit-of-measure master file (UNIT) in, 46, 48, 48
    validation files in, 51
ITMMNT1_Client
    in browser-based interface, 171
    in client/server interface, 132-137, **136**
    customization, 243, 255-258, **256-259**

I – J ❖ INDEX

ITMMNT1_Client.java customization in, 256-257, **257**
jar files for, 255, **256**
JVAPGM creation in, 257-258, **258**, **259**
in Swing interface, 149
ITMMNT1_Client.java customization, 256-257, **257**
ITMMNT1_DisplayFile, 175
ITMMNT1_JbuiDisplay, 149, 150-158, **152-153**, **157**, 235-241
ITMMNT1_MAIN.jsp, 171-172, 176, **182-183**, 199
ITMMNT1_PROMPT.jsp, 171-172, 174, 176, 180, 181, 195, 199, **199**
ITMMNT1_Servlet, 170, 171-183, **177-179**, 183-188, **201**
ITMMNT1A_MAINT.jsp, 264
ITMMNT1A_Servlet, 177
ITMMNT1AC application client, 62-65, 135
ITMMNT1B_MAINT.jsp, 264
ITMMNT1B_Servlet, 177
ITMMNT1D_DisplayFile, 111, 112
in display file building, 114
in Swing interface, 149
ITMMNT1UI, test run, 229-234, **229-234**

J

J.D. Edwards, 26
Jao400, 301-303
Jao400Display, 304-307
Jao400Field, 308-311
Jao400List, 312-315
Jao400Split, 315
JaoSplit, 317
jar files
in browser-based interface, 187
ITMMNT1_Client customization, 255, **256**
Web/in WebSphere and servlet, 248, 254, **254**, **255**
Java, xiii, xv, 1, 10, 21, 25, 28, 31-32, 40-43, **41**, 58, 97, 99-100, 213, 494
in browser-based interface, 169, 170
in client/server interface, 131
converting data with Dc400, 107
JBUI/in JBUI thick client UI server, environment for, 235-236, **236**
Java Database Connectivity (JDBC), 495
Java Development Kit, xvi, 215, 236, 494
Java emulation, display files and, 39
Java Toolbox (IBM), 42, 43, 93, 98, 131, 493
in browser-based interface, 186
in client/server interface, 132, 137, 143
in Swing interface, 157

Java/400, xv, 1, 494-495
JavaBean, 2, 12, 21-24, 32, 39, 495
Javadoc, xvi, 3
JavaHelp, 58
JavaScript, 57
JavaServer Page (JSP), 21-24, **23**, 31, 40, 43, 495, 496
in browser-based interface, 169, 170-177, 184, 187, 190, 192-194, 208
in client/server interface, 146
display files and, 39
JBUI package, 57, 58, 215
in Swing interface, 150, 156
in client/server interface, 146
JBUI thick client UI server, 235-241
classpath parameter in, 237
error handling in, 238-240, **238-241**
ITMMNT1_JbuiDisplay, 235-241
Java Development Kit for, 236
Java environment for, 235-236, **236**
testing the server, 237-240, **237-241**
JbuiButton, 322, 325, 326
JbuiButtonPanel, 155, 156, 327-331
JbuiCancelButton, 332-334
JbuiConstants, 320
JbuiDisplay, 335-339
in client/server interface, 147
in display file building, 122, 123
in Swing interface, 155, 156, 158-160, **159**
JbuiEntryField, 159, 339-346
JbuiFieldPanel, 156, 347-352
JbuiList, 57, 352-355
JbuiListModel, 356-360
JbuiListPanel, 360-362
JbuiNotify, 371
JbuiOutputField, 159, 363-367
JbuiScreen, 368-372
JbuiScreenThread, 372-373
JbuiSplit, 374-377
JDB_CHAIN, 380
JDB_CLOSE, 380
JDB_DELET, 381
JDB_DUMPRECORD, 381
JDB_GETFIELD, 381
JDB_KEYED, 380
JDB_OPEN, 380
JDB_READ, 380
JDB_READALL, 381
JDB_READE, 380
JDB_READP, 380
JDB_READPE, 380

Note: boldface numbers indicate illustrations.

JDB_REWIND, 381
JDB_SEQUENTIAL, 380
JDB_SETCONTENTS, 381
JDB_SETFIELD, 381
JDB_SETLL, 380
JDB_UPDAT, 381
JDB_WRITE, 381
Jdb400, 382-384
Jdb400Constants, 378-381, 384-385
Jdb400Field, 385-388
Jdb400File, 388-392
Jdb400KeyedFile, 392-395
Jdb400KeyedUpdateFile, 395-398
Jdb400SequentialFile, 398-399
Jdb400SequentialUpdateFile, 400-402
JDBC, xiv, 495
Jdqm400, 404-406
JdqmConstants, 403-404
JdqmServer, 407-409
JdqmSession, 410-411
JdspaMessageSubfileControl, 125
JdspfvalidOperationException, 122
JDSPF
   in browser-based interface, 212
   converting data with Dc400, 108, 109
   in display file building, 111-112, 117-124
   subfiles in, 124-125, **124**, **125**
JdspfAbstractRecord, 112-115, **112**, 119, 121-122, **120-121**, 125, 129, 415-417
JdspfAttributes object, 104
JdspfBuffer, 118-119, **118-119**, 126, 417-420
JdspfDisplayFile, 48, 57, 58, 97, 111, 126, 420-423
   in browser-based interface, 174
   in client/server interface, 132, 144, 147, 148
   in display file building, 112, 114-115, **114-116**, 117, 122-125, 129, **129-130**
   in Swing interface, 151, 164
JdspfDisplayFileAction, 117, 424-426
JdspfDisplayFileListener, 147, 151, 413
JdspfFieldAttributes, 426-427
JdspfIndicator, 126, 427-428
JdspfIndicatorArray, 429-430
JdspfInvalidOperationException, 435-436
JdspfMessageSubfile, 125, 129
JdspfOutputRecord, 129
JdspfRecord, 112-115, **113-114**, 121, **121-122**, 430-431
JdspfRecordGroup, 129
JdspfRecordUI, 117, 151, 163, 432
JdspfSubfile, 125, 433-434
JdspfSubfileControl, 125

JdspfUIAdapter, 151, 161, 414
Jsp class, 170, 191-192, **191-192**, 437-441
JSPAPI API library, xvi, 496
   API naming conventions, 82, 84
   in application client ITMMNT1AC, 69-91
   client APIs in, 69-81
   in client/server interface, 135
      DQMBAPI in, 73, **73**, **74**
      DQMBAPI1 in, 75, **75**
      DQMBAPI2 in, 75-76, **76**, **77-81**
      DQMBAPI3 in, 81, **81**
      DQMBAPIC in, 72, **72**, 84
   I/O Proxy APIs in, 81-91, **82**, **83**
      DQMDTA in, 84
      DQMIND in, 84
      DQMMSG in, 83, 83, 83
      DQMOPC in, 84
      DQMRTC in, 84
      DQMRTS in, 84
      DQMSCR in, 84
      DQMSID in, 84
   ITMMNI/in ITMMNI maintenance program vs., 57
   revitalizing legacy applications, 61, 69-91
JspField, 188, **188-189**, 190, 193, 197, 212, 441-444
JSPPROTO, xvi, 135, 137, 496
JVAPGM
   ITMMNT1_Client customization, 257-258, **258**, **259**
   Web/in WebSphere and servlet, 254, **254**, **255**
jvm.properties file, Web/in WebSphere and servlet, 243, 244, **248**

K

keying records, ITMMNI/in ITMMNI maintenance program, 50

L

legacy applications (*See also* existing technology/legacy applications), 12-13, 496
legacy programmers, 496-497
line-item screens, 8, **8**
Linux, 31
list boxes, 17
listener objects
   in client/server interface, 147
   in display file building, 123
   in Swing interface, 151, 161, 164

literals, 52
log on, 137, 157
LOGON, 449

M

macros, 16
maint class, in Swing interface, 157
Maintenance/MAINT panel
   in browser-based interface, 172, 182, **182**, 188, **188**
   ITMMNI/in ITMMNI maintenance program, 50, **50**, 54, **54-55**
   in Swing interface, 156, **156**, 157
   Web/in WebSphere and servlet, 262, **263**, **264**
MAINT record and Dc400Structure, converting data with Dc400, 104-105, **105**
maintenance program master file, 5, **6**, 7
maintenance programs, 31
makeArray, 279
makeFields, 310-311
makeVector, 280
MAPICS, 26
master files, 5, 6, 7, 17
message handling, 13, 497
   in application client ITMMNT1AC, 70
   in browser-based interface, 175
   in client/server interface, 137, 144, 147
message subfile, 39, 497
   ITMMNI/in ITMMNI maintenance program vs., 57-58
MESSAGE_DATA, 404
meta-records, in display file building, 127
midrange computers, 497-498
migrating applications/software, 13
mobile computing, 19
modeling, 19
model-view-controller (MVC), 144
monolithic applications, 498

N

named constants, 52
ncf.jvm.classpath, 186
ncf.jvm.path, 186
ncf.jvm.use.system.classpath, 186
nested data structures, 106
nested Web pages, in client/server interface, 137
Novell NetWare, 31
NUMERIC, 289
Numeric field type, 94

O

object architecture, 10-11
object brokers, 1
Object Query Language (OQL), 11
object technology, 498
object-oriented programming, 11, 12, 13, 17-18, 26, 28, 30, 33, 100, 498
   in client/server interface, 131
   debugging vs., 11
   encapsulation in, 11
   inheritance in, 11
   polymorphism in, 11
offline processing, 18-19
online transaction processing (OTP), 18
op code, 499
open database connectivity (ODBC), xiv, 18, 20, 498-499
open systems, 11-13, 26
   code divergence vs., 12
   extensibility in, 12
   goals of, 11
   hardware obsolescence vs., 12
   Java Beans in, 12
   legacy system integration in, 12-13
   object-oriented programming in, 11, 12
   persistence engines in, 12
   platform independence in, 11, 12
   portability of code in, 12
   reusable software in, 11, 12
   separation of database/business logic in, 11
   SQL in, 12
   standards in, 12
   tiered application structures in, 12
OPER_CODE, 404
OPER_SUBCODE, 404
output operation, display files and, 36, **36**
OVER, 321

P

packed fields, converting data with Dc400, 94
panels, 499
Pass directive, 184, 192, 253-254
passwords, 283
path, in browser-based interface, 192
Pbd class, 278-279
Pbd400 class, 280-281
pbdjsp400.jar, 187
PbdSystem class, 282
PDM interface, 5
persistence engines, 12

platform dependence, 28
platform independence, 10-13, 21, 26, 32, **32**, 33, 39, 499
Pluta Brothers Design (PBD), xv, 2
polymorphism, 11, 100, 131
portability of code, 12
POST, 145, 171, 175, 193, 194, 208-209
preservation of existing HLL code, in revitalizing legacy applications, 38
PRMS, 26
procedural programming, 500
processMessage, 147
program flow control (XWSCR field), in ITMMNI maintenance program, 52-53, 54
ProgramCall, 132, 143, 144
programs, 500
prompt class, in Swing interface, 154, 157
PROMPT panel/screen, 154, **154**, **155**
    in browser-based interface, 172, 173, **173**, **174**, 180, 181, **187**
    ITMMNI/in ITMMNI maintenance program, 46, **46**, 50, **50**, 53, **53-54**
    in Swing interface, 157
    Web/in WebSphere and servlet, 262, **263**
PROMPT record, in browser-based interface, 208
promptable fields, 7, 9, **9**
properties file, 183-184, 243, 244
PROTECT attribute (JBUI), 57
pull vs. push interfaces, 202
putGetUI, 122-123, **123**

Q

QATMHTPPC/QUSRSYS, 183, 249-252, **250**, **252**
QHTTPSVR subsystem, Web/in WebSphere and servlet, 259-261, **260**, **261**
queries, 11, 19-20

R

RAW, 289
Raw field type, 94
re-engineering, 2, 29
READ, 35, 37, **37**, 118, 120, 122, 125, 371, 391, 431
READALL, 391
READC, 118, 120, 122, 125, 434
READE, 394, 395
READP, 392
receive, 132-134, 147, 409, 411, 450
record creation
    in display file building, 113-114
    in Swing interface, 157

record formats, 500
record UI objects, in display file building, 117
records, 500
recordToVector, 311
redeploying legacy applications, xiii-xv, 1-3, 10, 25-33, 500-501
re-engineering, 28, 31-32, **32**, 33, 501
refacing existing technology/legacy applications, 16-17, **16**
regions of change, 133, 501
RELATIVE_TO_OWNER, 321
replacing existing technology/legacy applications, 15-16
requiresResponse, 455
Restore Library (RSTLIB), 222, **223**, **224**
restructuring legacy applications, 28, 29-31, **30**, **31**, 33, 501-502
RETURN_CODE, 404
RETURN_SUBCODE, 404
reusable software, 11, 12, 13, 26-27, **27**
revitalizing legacy applications, xiii-xv, 1-3, 27, 28, **28**, **29**, 35-43, 502
    APIs in, 39, 43, 60, 61
    application client in, 42, 43, 59, **59**, 61, 62-65
    browser-based interface in, 41-43, **41**, 169-213
    client API in, 60, 61, 69-81
    com.pub.pbd.dc400 conversion package for, 93
    common gateway interface (CGI) in, 202
    converting data (*See also* converting data), 93-109
    data queues in, 41-43, **41**, 60
    DataConversion 400 in, 42
    display files in, 35-39, **36**, **37**, 41-43, **41**, 111-130
    encapsulation in, 42, 43
    fast path for, 42
    goals of, 37-38
    graphical interfaces in, 43
    green screen applications in, 41-43, **41**, 59, **59**, 61, 65-68
    hidden I/O operations in, 38
    HTML in, 40
    I/O Proxy API in, 43, 60, 61, 67-69
    implementation of, 38-40, 41-43, **41**
    ITMMNI maintenance program in, 42, 43, 45-58
    ITMMNT1 changed to application client (*See* application client ITMMNT1AC), 62-65
    Java in, 40-43, **41**
    Java Toolbox (IBM) in, 42, 43
    JavaServer Pages (JSP) in, 40, 43
    JSPAPI library in, 61, 69-91
    message subfiles in, 39
    preservation of existing HLL code, 38

pull vs. push interfaces, 202
requirements of, 38
reusable software in, 37
RPG in, 41-43, **41**
RPG-to-application client conversion, steps in, 64-65
screen scrapers in, 38, 39
separation of database/business logic in, 40, 59-91, **59**
server/client appications in, 40-43, **41**, 131-148
servers in, 41-43, **41**
subfiles in, 39
Swing in, 40-43, **41**, 149-168
user interface (UI) servers in, 41-43, 41, 61
WebSphere in, 43
wrappers in, 60
REWIND, 392
rewriting legacy code, 17-18
RPG, 10, 26, 41-43, **41**
application client conversion of, 64-65
in client/server interface, 143
ITMMNI/in ITMMNI maintenance program, 45, 51-56
RPG III, 27
RPG IV, 27, 267-268
run, 146, 148, 158, 171, 458
runServer, 208, 209

S

SAP, 26
Sc400 JBUI
in browser-based interface, 170
in Swing interface, 150, 158-166, 166-168
Sc400Api, 132, 137-144, **142-143**, 445-446
Sc400Client, 131-133, 133-135, 151, 447-451
Sc400Client.LOGON, 135
Sc400Exception class, 131, 458-459
Sc400Message, 106, 132, 137-144, **138-141**, 106, 452-455
ScJdspfButtonDefinition, **181**
ScJdspfButtonField, **181**
ScJdspfDefaultListener, 161
ScJdspfDisplayFile, 163
ScJdspfJbuiDefaultListener, 163, 164, 164, 460-461
ScJdspfJbuiDisplay, 462-464
in client/server interface, 148
in display file building, 122, 123
in Swing interface, 151-152, 154-157, **155**, **157**, **158**, 161-163, **161-162**, 163
ScJdspfJbuiRecordUI, 464-465
ScJdspfJbuiServer, 466-467
in browser-based interface, 172
in Swing interface, 150, **150-151**, 165, **165-166**
ScJdspfJsp, 177, 179, **180**, **181**, 212, 468-471
ScJdspfJspButtonDefinition, 195-199, **196**, 472
ScJdspfJspButtonField, 195-199, **197-198**, 473-474
ScJdspfJspButtonFieldDefinition, 191
ScJdspfJspe, 172
ScJdspfJspRecordUI, 151, 177, 179, **179**, **181**, 200, **200**, 475-476
ScJdspfJspServlet, 172, **172**, 194, 202, **202-207**, 476-479
ScJdspfUIServer, 132, 136, 144-148, **147**, 149, 456-458
screen scrapers, 16-17, **17**, 19, 26, 29, 38, 39
scrollbars, in Swing interface, 156
SEGMENT_ID, 404
SELECT_DISPLAY, 321
SELECT_DISPLAY_AND_DOUBLECLICK_DRIL
L, 321
Semantic Message Gateways, 26
send, 132, 133, 134, 171, 409, 411, 450, 458
sendError, 409
separation of database/business logic, 11, 13, 19, 24, 27, 29, 30, **31**, 33, 40, 59-91, **59**
server/client interfaces, xiv-xv, 2, 18, 19, **19**, 24, **24**, 40-43, **41**, 131-148, 502
APIs in, 24, 132, 133, 135
AS/400 definitions in, 135
browser-based application support in, 131, 144-148, **146**
callPage in, 147
calls in, 143-144
classes in, 131
composition, 131, 132, 144-148
creating classes for, 131
data queues in, 24
Dc400Field in, 141, 142
Dc400Structure in, 138, 141-142
display-file emulation in, 24, 131
doGet in, 145
doPost in, 145, 147
DQMMSG in, 137
DQMUNIT in, 133
DQMUNITC in, 135, 137
DQMURCV in, 133
DQMUSHUT in, 133
DQMUSND in, 133
encapsulation in, 132, 133, 137, 148
EXFMT method in, 146, 147
existing technology vs., 24, **24**
getMessage in, 134

INDEX ❖ S

server/client interfaces, *continued*
  getOperationCode in, 142
  green screen applications in, 24
  HTML in, 137, 145
  I/O processing in, 131
  I/O Proxy APIs in, 132, 137, 143, 144
  indexing in, 141
  inheritance in, 131, 137-144
  init interface in, 132, 133, 134
  isEof in, 142
  ITMMNT1_Client in, 132-137, **136**
  ITMMNT1AC in, 135
  Java in, 131
  Java Toolbox in, 131, 132, 137, 143
  JavaBeans in, 24
  JavaServer Page (JSP) in, 24, 146
  JBUI classes in, 146
  JbuiDisplay in, 147
  JdspfDisplayFile in, 132, 144, 147, 148
  JdspfDisplayFileListener in, 147
  JSPAPI library in, 135
  JSPPROTO in, 135, 137
  listeners in, 147
  logon parameters in, 137
  message handling in, 137, 144, 147
  model-view-controller (MVC) in, 144
  nested Web pages in, 137
  object-oriented programming in, 131
  polymorphism in, 131
  POST data in, 145
  processMessage in, 147
  ProgramCall class in, 132, 143, 144
  receive interface in, 132, 133, 134, 147
  regions of change in, 133
  RPG in, 143
  run method in, 146, 148
  Sc400Api in, 132, 137-144, **142-143**
  Sc400Client class in, 131-133, **133-135**
  Sc400Client.LOGON in, 135
  Sc400Exception class in, 131
  Sc400Message in, 132, 137-144, **138-141**
  ScJdspfJbuiDisplay in, 148
  ScJdspfUIServer in, 132, 136, 144-148, **147**
  send interface in, 132, 133, 134
  separation of database/business logic in, 24
  server/client definitions in, 135
  server-side I/O proxy APIs in, 132
  servlets in, 24, 145-148
  setApiLibrary in, 134
  setClientName in, 134
  setPassword in, 134
  setProductionLibrary in, 134
  setReturnCode in, 142
  setSystemName in, 135
  setUserID in, 135
  shutdown interface in, 132, 133, 135
  subclasses in, 131, 132-137, 141-142, 144
  superclasses in, 144
  Swing support in, 131, 137, 144-148, **146**
  thick clients in, 24
SERVER_NAME, 404
servers, 10, 27-33, 41-43, **41**, 151
server-side I/O proxy APIs, 132
Service directive, 184, 185, 253
servlets, 21-25, **22**, **23**, 28, 43, 215, 243-266, 502-503
  in browser-based interface, 169, 171, 175, 177-183, 185, 192, 199-209
  classpath in, 243, 244, 247-248
  in client/server interface, 145-148
  copying files for, 244-247
  in display file building, 122
  display files and, 39
  error handling, 265, **265**, 266
  HTTP configuration file in, 243, 249-254, **250-254**
  HTTP server restart in, 259-261, **260**, **261**, **262**
  HttpGet in, 251
  HttpPut in, 251
  index screen in, 262, **263**
  installing servlet software, 243, 244-247, **245-247**
  ITMMNT1_Client customization in, 243, 255-258, **256-259**
  jar files in, 248, 254, **254**, **255**
  JVAPGM jar file in, 254, **254**, **255**
  jvm.properties file in, 243, 244, **248**
  MAINT panel in, 262, **263**, **264**
  Pass directive in, 253-254
  PROMPT panel in, 262, **263**
  properties file in, 243, 244
  QATMHTPPC/QUSRSYS in, 249-252, **250**, **252**
  QHTTPSVR subsystem in, 259-261, **260**, **261**
  running servlet in, 262-264, **263**, **264**
  Service directive in, 253
  testing servlet, 259-261, **260-262**
session IDs, 71
SESSION_ID, 403
sessions, 503
setApiLibrary, 134, 450
setApplicationClientName, 455
setAS400, 284, 285, 302, 303, 383, 405, 406
setAttributes, 291
setBuffer, 299
setButtonPanel, 371

522

setButtons, 331
setClientName, 134, 450
setColumnHeading, 311, 387
setContents, 397, 402
setData, 337, 338, 345, 351
setDataBuffer, 455
setDescription, 311, 387
setError, 338, 346, 351
setExitJsp, 479
setField, 392
setFieldNames, 307
setFieldPanel, 338, 377
setFields, 192, 299, 300, 440
setFile, 307
setFileName, 307, 314, 318
setGroupName, 346
setHandle, 307, 318, 338, 371
setIndicators, 420, 455
setKeyPressed, 163, 423
setLength, 311, 388
setLibrary, 285, 303, 384
setListener, 423
setListFieldNames, 315, 318
SETLL, 395
setLookAndFeel, 285, 303
setModel, 355, 377
setName, 192, 311, 346, 388, 441
setObject, 300, 417
setObjects, 300
setOrientation, 377
setOwner, 372
setPassword, 134, 451
setPath, 192, 441
setPosition, 372
setPressedButton, 331
setProductionLibrary, 134, 451
setProtect, 339, 346, 351, 352
setRecord, 124
setRecordUIObject, 117, 423
setReturnCode, 142, 455
setSelectMode, 377
setSystemLibrary, 285, 406
setSystemName, 135, 451
setTitle, 372
setUserID, 135, 451
setValue, 189, 444
setViewClass, 355
setViewer, 355
setViewerPosition, 355
setViewFieldNames, 315, 318
setWaiter, 332

SFLRCD01 code, 124
shutdown, 451
　in application client ITMMNT1AC, 70, 72, 88, 90-91, **90**
　in browser-based interface, 171, 172
　in client/server interface, 132, 133, 135
simulations, 19
single-record display file, 115, **115**
smart parameters of JSP, 23
sorting, 7, 9
SQL, xiv, 12, 18, 19-20, 26, 503
standards, 12
static Web pages, 21-22, **22**
String object, 107
subclasses
　in client/server interface, 131, 132-137, 141-142, 144
　converting data with Dc400, 94, 98, 100
　in display file building, 112, 115, **115-116**
　in Swing interface, 150, 158-166
subfile control records, 503
subfile records, 503
subfiles, 5, 17, 25, 503
　in browser-based interface, 210-212, **210**, **211-212**
　in display file building, 117-118, 124-125, **124**, **125**, 126-130, **127**
　error message subfile, 7
　ITMMNI/in ITMMNI maintenance program vs., 57
　revitalizing legacy applications, 39
　in Swing interface, 166-168, **167**, **168**
summary applications, 9
superclasses
　in client/server interface, 144
　converting data with Dc400, 98
support classes, in browser-based interface, 185-188
Swing interface, 40, 41-43, **41**, 57, 149-168, 236, 504
　application client definition in, 151
　application client proxy (ITMMNT1_Client) in, 157
　buttons in, 155, 156
　class relationships in, 160, **161**
　classes in, 149, 156-157, 160
　in client/server interface, 131, 137, 144-148, **146**
　com.pbd.pub.sc400.jbui, 149, 158, 160
　constructors in, 151, 157
　copyDataFromJdspf method in, 161, 162
　copyDataToJdspf in, 161-163
　DDS for, 153, 154, 153
　in display file building, 39, 118
　display-file emulation object (ITMMNT1D_DisplayFile) in, 157

Swing interface, *continued*
   empty constructor in, 151
   error handling in, 154
   EXFMT method in, 156, 162
   extensions, JBUI in, 150, 166-168
   field definition in, 156
   function key assignment in, 160
   HTML in, 166
   ITMMNT1_Client classes in, 149
   ITMMNT1_JBUIDisplay in, 150-158, 150
   ITMMNT1_JbuiDisplay in, 149, 152-158, **152-153**, **157**
   ITMMNT1D_DisplayFile in, 149
   Java Toolbox in, 157
   JBUI in, 150, 156
   JbuiButtonPanel in, 155, 156
   JbuiDisplay in, 155, 156, 158-160, **159**
   JbuiEntryField in, 159
   JbuiFieldPanel in, 156
   JbuiOutputField in, 159
   JdspfDisplayFile in, 151, 164
   JdspfDisplayFileListener in, 151
   JdspfRecordUI in, 151, 163
   JdspfUIAdapter in, 151, 161
   listeners in, 151, 161, 164
   log on routine for, 157
   maint class in, 157
   MAINT panel in, 156, **156**, 157
   packaging in, 149
   prompt class in, 154, 157
   PROMPT panel in 154, **154**, **155**, 157
   record creation in, 157
   run method in, 158
   SC400 JBUI classes in, 150, 158-166
   SC400 JBUI in, 160, 166-168
   Sc400Client in, 151
   ScJdspfDefaultListener in, 161
   ScJdspfDisplayFile in, 163
   ScJdspfJbuiDefaultListener in, 163, 164, **164**
   ScJdspfJbuiDisplay in, 152, 154-156, **155**, 157, 161-163, **161-162**
   ScJdspfJbuiRecordUI in, 151, 152, 157, **157**, **158**, 163, **163**
   ScJdspfJbuiServer in, 150, **150-151**, 165, **165-166**
   ScJdspfRecordUI in, 151
   ScJdspfUIServer in, 149
   scrollbars in, 156
   setKeyPressed method in, 163
   subclasses in, 150, 158-166
   subfiles in, 166-168, **167**, **168**
   UI server definition in, 151
System Software Associates (SSA), 52

T

24x80, 481
tables, 17
TCP/IP, 19, 504
terminal emulation, 16-17, **16**
test, 430
thick client (*See also* JBUI thick client UI server), 10, 24, 28-29, 235, 504
thin clients, 28, 30, **30**, 504
tiered application structures, 12
timeout values, in application client ITMMNT1AC, 87-88
toBuffer, 300
toObjects, 300
toString, 385
transaction data, 8
transaction files, 5, 17

U

UI request, 504
UIM, 5
UIObject, 122, 123
UNDER, 321
uniform resource locators (URLs), 21
unit-of-measure (UOM) fields, in ITMMNI maintenance program, 46, 56
unit-of-measure cross-ref (UXRF), ITMMNI/in ITMMNI maintenance program, 46, 48, **49**
unit-of-measure master file (UNIT), in ITMMNI maintenance program, 46, 48, **48**
UNIX, 26
UPDAT, 118, 121, 122, 125, 126, 397, 402, 434
uploading programs to AS/400, 215
user IDs, 283
user interface (UI) server, 41-43, **41**, 61, 172, 505

V

validation files, in ITMMNI maintenance program, 51
valueOf, 197, 474
variables
   converting data with Dc400, 96
   Dc400Field class, **101-103**
vectors, 279, 280

W

Web server, 505
Web updates, 267-268
Web-based applications, xiv, 2, 25, 27, 39

WebSphere and servlet, xvi, 31, 43, 215, 243-266, 505
  in browser-based interface, 169, 170, 215
  classpath in, 243, 244, 247-248
  copying files for, 244-247
  error handling, 265, **265**, **266**
  HTTP configuration file in, 243, 249-254, **250-254**
  HTTP server restart in, 259-261, **260**, **261**, **262**
  index screen in, 262, **263**
  installing servlet software, 243, 244-247, **245-247**
  ITMMNT1_Client customization in, 243, 255-258, **256-259**
  jar files in, 248, 254, **254**, **255**
  JVAPGM jar file in, 254, **254**, **255**
  jvm.properties file in, 243, 244, **248**
  MAINT panel in, 262, **263**, **264**
  PROMPT panel in, 262, **263**
  properties file in, 243, 244
  QATMHTPPC/QUSRSYS in, 249-252, **250**, **252**
  running servlet in, 262-264, **263**, **264**
  testing servlet, 259-261, **260-262**
WebSphere Application Server Emulator (WASE), 488
windows, 5
Windows NT, 31
Work with Active Job (WRKACTJOB), 229, **230**
wrappers, 13, 32, 60, 70
  in application client ITMMNT1AC, 70
  revitalizing legacy applications, 60
WRITE, 35, 36, **36**, 39, 117, 121-123, 126, 372, 398, 402, 431, 434

X

XWSCR field, 52-53, 54

Y

Y2K, xiv, 12, 16, 18